# THE PAPER OFFICE FOR THE DIGITAL AGE

## Also by Edward L. Zuckerman

Clinician's Electronic Thesaurus, Version 7.0:
Software to Streamline Psychological Report Writing

Clinician's Thesaurus, 7th Edition:
The Guide to Conducting Interviews and Writing Psychological Reports

# The Paper Office for the Digital Age

## FIFTH EDITION

Forms, Guidelines, and Resources to Make Your
Practice Work Ethically, Legally, and Profitably

**Edward L. Zuckerman, PhD**

**Keely Kolmes, PsyD**

THE GUILFORD PRESS
New York    London

Published by The Guilford Press
A Division of Guilford Publications, Inc.
370 Seventh Avenue, Suite 1200, New York, NY 10001
www.guilford.com

Printed in Canada

This book is printed on acid-free paper.

Last digit is print number:   9   8   7   6   5   4   3   2

The authors have checked with sources believed to be reliable in their efforts to
provide information that is complete and generally in accord with the standards of
practice that are accepted at the time of publication. However, in view of the possibility
of human error or changes in behavioral, mental health, or medical sciences, neither
the authors, nor the editor and publisher, nor any other party who has been involved
in the preparation or publication of this work warrants that the information contained
herein is in every respect accurate or complete, and they are not responsible for any
errors or omissions or the results obtained from the use of such information. Readers
are encouraged to confirm the information contained in this book with other sources.

**Library of Congress Cataloging-in-Publication Data**

Names: Zuckerman, Edward L., author. | Kolmes, Keely, author.
Title: The paper office for the digital age : forms, guidelines, and resources to make
    your practice work ethically, legally, and profitably / Edward L. Zuckerman and
    Keely Kolmes.
Other titles: Paper office
Description: Fifth edition. | New York, NY : The Guilford Press, [2017] |
    Originally published: Paper office / Edward L. Zuckerman. 4th ed. |
    Includes bibliographical references and index.
Identifiers: LCCN 2016023578 | ISBN 9781462528004 (paperback)
Subjects: LCSH: Psychiatric records—Forms. | Psychiatric records—Handbooks,
    manuals, etc. | BISAC: PSYCHOLOGY / Practice Management. |
    MEDICAL / Psychiatry / General. | SOCIAL SCIENCE / Social Work. |
    BUSINESS & ECONOMICS / Small Business. | LAW / Ethics & Professional
    Responsibility.
Classification: LCC RC455.2.M38 Z828 2017 | DDC 616.8900285—dc23
LC record available at https://lccn.loc.gov/2016023578

*Edward L. Zuckerman:*

*To my beloved daughter, Lilly Charlotte Lawrence Zuckerman.*
*This book is for the education you richly deserve.*


*Keely Kolmes:*

*Thanks to Dan Taube, Jeff Younggren, Jeffrey Barnett, Ofer Zur,*
*Michael Donner, and Stephen Behnke, significant ethics leaders,*
*colleagues, and friends, who helped me believe in myself. And, of course,*
*my deepest gratitude to Ed Zuckerman for the honor of inviting me to*
*collaborate with him on this new edition of his wonderful book.*

# About the Authors

**Edward L. Zuckerman, PhD,** found his life's passion while working as a psychiatric aide at New York's Bellevue Hospital in the 1960s. He earned his doctorate in clinical psychology at the University of Pittsburgh and worked in community mental health while gaining his license. He has worked with adults with developmental disabilities and those with severe alcohol addiction, acted as liaison with state hospitals, taught undergraduates, and maintained an independent practice in general clinical psychology for many years. He now lives with his family in rural western Pennsylvania, with some geese and lots of mud and trees. There, he consults and creates worthwhile practice tools for clinicians.

**Keely Kolmes, PsyD,** is in private practice in San Francisco. She has served on the Ethics Committee of the California Psychological Association and as California's Council Representative for the American Psychological Association (APA). Dr. Kolmes is a Fellow of APA Division 42 (Psychologists in Independent Practice) and received its award for Best Article of the Year in *Independent Practitioner* for her influential paper "Developing My Private Practice Social Media Policy." A graduate of the APA's Leadership Institute for Women in Psychology, she is founder and president of Bay Area Open Minds, a group of therapists affirming sexual and gender diversity. Dr. Kolmes teaches and consults nationally and internationally on digital ethics and technology issues for clinicians. Her website is http://drkkolmes.com.

# Acknowledgments

Many professional colleagues have generously taken the time to offer their advice, suggestions, and creations for this book (and we hope that you, the present reader, will do the same; see p. 501). In most cases their names appear next to their contributions throughout this book, and we restate here our gratitude for their assistance in making this book as useful to our professions as it has become. Thank you all.

Joan Anderson, PhD, Houston, TX
Dorothy Ashman, MA, Bloomsburg, PA
Bruce Barrett, MA, LMHC, Duxbury, MA
Sheila Carluccio, MA, Dickson City, PA
Beverly Celotta, PhD, Gaithersburg, MD
Sandra L. Ceren, PhD, Del Mar, CA
David Clovard, MD, Raleigh, NC
Allan J. Comeau, PhD, West Los Angeles, CA
Harry Corsover, PhD, Castle Rock, CO
Karen Davison, PsyD, San Francisco, CA
Estelle Disch, PhD, Cambridge, MA
Steve Eichel, PhD, Newark, DE
Constance Fischer, PhD, Pittsburgh, PA
J. Lamar Freed, PhD, Elkins Park, PA
Muriel L. Golub, PhD, Tustin, CA
Irvin P. R. Guyett, PhD, Pittsburgh, PA
Gordon I. Herz, PhD, Madison, WI
Glenn W. Humphrey, OFM, PhD, New York, NY
Richard E. Jensen, PhD, St. Charles, IL
Sam Knapp, EdD, Harrisburg, PA
Robert E. McCarthy, PhD, Myrtle Beach, SC
Kathleen Quinn, EdD, Cheyenne, WY
Jackson Rainer, PhD, Norcross, GA
John Roraback, PhD, Moline, IL (deceased)
Kathie Rudy, PsyD, Great Neck, NY
Valerie Shebroe, PhD, East Lansing, MI
John M. Smothers, PhD, ABPP, Bethesda, MD (deceased)
Charles H. Steinmeyer, PhD, Warren, PA
Pauline Wallin, PhD, Camp Hill, PA
Nora Fleming Young, Pocatello, ID

We also wish to express appreciation to Bob Matloff, Seymour Weingarten, and Jim Nageotte of The Guilford Press for their continuing support of and trust in the value of this project, as well as for their honesty and openness as friends and associates. The best thing they did for us was to provide us with an ideal editor, Barbara Watkins. She has been consistently smart, articulate, patient, enthusiastic, and a damn quick learner. We must also express our great appreciation for the tireless efforts of Editorial Project Manager Anna Brackett, Assistant Editor Jane Keislar, and copyeditor Marie Sprayberry, whose superb sense of style, proportion, and language have greatly increased this book's readability, clarity, and value.

# Contents

# List of Figures, Forms, Handouts, and Tables

Most of the forms and handouts listed below can be found on the accompanying CD in .pdf format so they can easily be printed out and look exactly as they do in the book. Nearly all forms are also available on the disk in .docx format, so they can be tailored to your needs in a word processor.

# THE PAPER OFFICE FOR THE DIGITAL AGE

# Introduction

*The Paper Office for the Digital Age* is about using *both* paper and digital means for planning and documenting your work, communicating with clients and colleagues, marketing your psychotherapy practice, maintaining legal records, dealing with finances, and handling many other aspects of running your business. This book offers digital as well as print versions of the essential forms and client education handouts you need for your practice. Whether you copy or print them out, you need *paper* versions of forms for a range of documents that require clients' legal signatures; there are also good reasons to stick with paper charts, including client confidentiality, your own comfort, and protection against loss of electronic data. Many of you will choose to have "hybrid" practices in which you use paper documentation but also use electronic technologies. Whether you are a novice or an experienced practitioner, this book is designed to help you.

## Ways This Book Can Help You

If you are a clinician just entering independent practice who wishes to start up a practice properly, this book will help you get organized and develop good professional habits. It will make your practice

- less vulnerable (and you therefore less anxious) when you are doing clinical work,

- more efficient because so many details are already taken care of, and

- more stable and profitable as a business.

All of this should make you more satisfied with your career as a therapist. This book cannot contain everything you should know to be in independent practice. However, it does contain what we believe you need to make the correct initial decisions about office practices and paperwork, and so it will help you start out right.

If you have been in private practice for a few years, this book can help you to update your practice to conform to current legal and ethical developments. We live in a world that has become far more litigious, and in which we are far more closely monitored, than in decades past. Standards of professional practice and conduct have evolved rapidly, becoming ever more complex and subtle. Licensing boards, government agencies, and third-party payers are watching more carefully. Private practice has become more difficult because of the anxieties raised by malpractice cases and board complaints. For all of us, the remedies for this anxiety lie in increasing our coping skills (such as by acquiring particular expertise), developing more accurate perceptions and more realistic understanding of the issues, and taking preventative actions against threats. As therapists, our best defenses against malpractice, complaints, and investigations are to offer high-quality and thoughtful care, use rational and effective procedures, and document our reasons and decisions thoroughly.

The resources in this book are carefully tailored to meet each of these needs. *The Paper Office for the Digital Age* provides the basic operational "tools" for private practice needed by psychotherapists of any orientation, training level, or discipline—social workers, marriage and family therapists, professional counselors, psychiatrists, or psychologists. The guidelines and principles are widely shared, and so the forms and client education materials can be adapted and applied to your practice, no matter what your discipline is.

It should be emphasized *that The Paper Office for the Digital Age* is designed for the solo practitioner and the small-group practice. It may not meet the needs of a large or diverse group, agency, criminal justice setting, school, or military practice. In addition, the book's forms and other materials are designed only for outpatient settings.

## What This Book Contains

This book provides both practical information and ready-to-use resources:

- Brief guidelines and checklists alert you to the most important legal and ethical issues, and direct you in developing solid working procedures.

- Sample documents and reproducible forms and handouts offer effective ways to meet specific challenges to your practice. Digital versions of the forms and handouts, included on the CD, allow you to adapt them to your specific needs.

- Discussions explain and contextualize the relevant issues and offer specifics and subtleties. This book is designed to function as "a malpractice risk reduction kit."

The forms and other materials offered are administrative and procedural, as well as clinical. They organize information to support the delivery of clinical services and to protect both you and your clients. These materials will help you to do the following:

- Understand and manage the financial side of practice, including fees and dealing with managed care organizations (MCOs).

- Efficiently collect such client information as demographic data and insurance coverage.

- Document each client's presenting problems, mental status, and risk factors.

- Organize the intake information into diagnoses, prognoses, and treatment plans.

- Make and keep all your records so that they meet current federal legal standards for privacy and security—especially those of the Health Insurance Portability and Accountability Act (HIPAA) of 1996. You are expected and assumed to know your local legal rules and standards.

- Comply with ethical and legal standards in getting fully informed consent to evaluate, treat, release records, and so on.

- Respond proactively to the need for boundary clarifications and maintenance, and so the prevention of many ethical violations.

- Relate to MCOs, supervisees, students, and trainees in legal and ethical ways.

- Reduce your risk of malpractice suits, licensing board complaints, and similar problems.

**This book assumes that you, the reader, are already a fully trained clinician.** It assumes that you know how to do evaluations and therapy, and that you deal with clients and their families. Therefore, the forms offered in this book are not forms for collecting data on symptoms or dynamics. For example, although you are offered a way of summarizing a client's mental status (Form 6.17), you are not given any tests or protocol of questions to collect the data the form summarizes. If you need questions to assess a client's presentation, history, symptoms, and mental status, and the words to describe these, you can find these in the *Clinician's Thesaurus* (Zuckerman, 2010), which contains the entire language of mental health.

## Unique Features

**We have made efforts to incorporate various professions' ethical standards, principles, and guidelines into each form, handout, and sample document.** This avoids the remoteness of reading about abstract principles, the narrowness of individual case studies, and the possibility of overlooking the necessary application of an important principle in your practice's procedures and paperwork. After the principles are learned through these applications, they can be more easily applied to new situations through your sensitized and enhanced ethical reasoning.

**The forms and other materials have been designed and updated to meet current legal and ethical standards for the practice of psychotherapy in the various disciplines.** As you know, there are significant differences in these standards by state, discipline, and population. To be comprehensive, this book tries to include points or issues raised in any jurisdiction. We believe it is very likely that concerns now raised in only a few places will eventually be applied in every location, and so these should be addressed now. The courts, the mass media, and the public have generally not paid attention to the differences among the professions, and so the book is inclusive in this respect as well. It will always be important, however, to monitor local developments and changes as an ongoing aspect of your practice.

Crucially, **you must know your local rules.** Although we have made sincere and extensive efforts to be complete, we cannot guarantee that these materials will meet *all* the ethical and legal rules of *all* professions and jurisdictions, particularly over time. Your best sources of current and localized information are your state's and discipline's organizations. Join them, contribute to them, and participate in them; doing so will make you more aware and sophisticated, and will keep your practice up to date. For example, psychologists who belong to the Pennsylvania Psychological Association (PPA) have had a much lower rate of licensing board complaints than nonmembers have (Sam Knapp, Professional Affairs Officer, PPA, personal communication, 2010).

In a similar vein, some readers have asked whether this book has been read and reviewed by lawyers. It has not, both because of the problem stated above of local and discipline differences, and because there would be some conflicting opinions that could not be resolved.

Instead, we have relied heavily on published articles that have had the benefit of peer review, and on books by authorities who represent the consensus or vanguard in the field.

# How to Use This Book in Your Practice

If you are a beginning practitioner, we recommend that you start with the materials offered in "Quick Start," below.

If you are an experienced clinician, read the table of contents for the forms and other materials you think are most important to the way you currently practice. There may be some you know you should implement to meet ethical and legal standards; others will make you more efficient and help you become better organized. Some will be new to your practice, and others will update materials you have been using.

The chapters of the book start with the administrative, financial, ethical, and legal foundations of practice (Chapters 1–5), and then follow the sequence of a case from intake to termination (Chapters 6–7). In-depth discussions of confidentiality and releasing records (Chapter 8) and of marketing (Chapter 9) round out the book. The sections within chapters are generally organized as follows:

- The **background** you need to make use of the forms or other materials is offered first. Much of this information is displayed for rapid learning in the form of guidelines and checklists.

- The **legal and ethical aspects** of the forms or sample documents are described next, along with options for modifying them for your own practice.

- The **model forms** or other materials are then presented.

# Quick Start: Recommended Core Materials

The materials below can be produced for your practice in just a few minutes for a few cents. The forms as printed in the book can be photocopied or can be downloaded from the CD and printed from your computer. They are designed to look professional. On these forms, a space at the top is provided for your own letterhead. If you anticipate using a small label on your paperwork to identify the client by name, ID number, barcode, or something similar, you can offset your "letterhead" information to the left and leave room for the label on the right side. If you want to modify the forms or tailor them to your practice, the CD contains the text of almost every form in a common word processor format.

The following are the basic forms for any client intake. First will be the Client Information Brochure (see Chapter 5), Handout 5.1, or one of the other methods for aiding a client in providing informed consent to treatment, as described in Chapter 5. Then come these forms:

| | |
|---|---|
| Form 6.1 | First-contact record |
| Form 6.3 | Notice of privacy practices (unabridged) |
| Form 6.4 | Notice of privacy practices (brief version) |
| Form 6.5 | Consent to privacy practices |
| Form 6.6 | Adult client information form 1 |

Form 6.7    Adult client information form 2
Form 6.8    Health information form
Form 6.10   Financial information form
Form 7.2    Case progress note, structured

Depending on what you learn about the client during the intake, any of the following could be appropriate:

Form 6.9    Chemical use survey
Form 6.12   Adult checklist of concerns
Form 6.13   Child checklist of characteristics
Form 6.17   Mental status evaluation checklist
Form 6.19   Suicide risk assessment summary and recommendations
Form 8.2    Form for requesting or releasing confidential records and information

If you expect the client to use health insurance that is managed, the managed care organization (MCO) is likely to want the information from this form:

Form 6.20   Intake summary and case formulation

We suggest that you use the forms for 3 months with every new (and some old) clients. When you start, mark the end of the 3-month period in your appointment book. Then relax and focus on doing a fine job as a therapist. After 3 months, review how well the forms are working for you. Decide which additional forms you want to incorporate into your practice, or what changes you need to make to fit them better into your practice. Make any modifications or additions, and write to us with your suggestions and criticisms. If you make changes, please see the section below on sharing your changes.

## Availability of Materials on CD

To save you time and effort, all the forms and handouts you might use in your practice are available on the CD inside the back cover. The materials are supplied in two formats, so virtually any computer can open and display them. Instructions for using the CD are on the last page of this book.

## A Cautionary Note and Disclaimer

Although we have made reasonable efforts to assure that the contents of this book are both accurate and up to date, neither we nor the publisher can be responsible for matters beyond its scope or level of detail, local variations, or future developments. For example, the laws and regulations that apply to your work as a clinician may be federal, state, or local; or they may pertain differently to clients with substance use problems, clients of mental health and intellectual or developmental disability programs, clients of specific government programs, or children or adolescents. In addition, special rules may govern practitioners working in schools, inpatient and residential facilities, the criminal justice system, or the like. Your local professional societies and colleague experts on the scene are the best sources for information about current and applicable rules, both ethical and legal. Your professional liability insurer may be able to provide helpful guidance.

The comments about HIPAA and its regulations reflect our own interpretations from reading the Act and other resources, and have not been reviewed by lawyers. We offer general guidance, as opposed to legal advice. The wording of the HIPAA forms is ours and is designed for small practices. HIPAA is discipline-blind and encourages practitioners to use language tailored to their settings, clients, and practices.

The listing of websites in this book does not constitute an endorsement by the publisher (The Guilford Press) or by us (Edward L. Zuckerman and Keely Kolmes) of those websites, or of the information, products, or services contained therein. Other than at those sites authorized and maintained by the publisher or by us, we do not exercise any editorial control over the information you may find at these other locations. Neither the publisher nor we assume responsibility for any loss incurred as a result of the application of any of the information contained in this book, or for any incidental or consequential damages in connection with or arising out of the furnishing of the materials in this book. No representation is made that they are the only or best ways to practice as a professional psychotherapist. **This book is intended to assist an informed intermediary in the treatment of clients and patients—that is, the professional psychotherapist. It is neither recommended nor appropriate for use by amateurs or for self-help.**

This book is sold with the understanding that the publisher, distributors, and we are not attorneys, accountants, or ethicists; nor are we engaged in rendering legal, financial, ethical, or other professional consulting services. If materials other than those presented here are needed to manage your (the purchaser's) professional practice or a specific clinical case in any respect, we advise you to engage the services of a competent professional. Any forms that create a contract between a practitioner and a client should be reviewed by your legal counsel and should be modified to conform to local law and practice.

No warranty is expressed or implied, and in no event shall the publisher, we the authors, or any reseller be liable for consequential or incidental damages.

## About Reproducing Materials in This Book

One of the main advantages of this book over other books on ethics or practice is the high quality of the materials—the forms, checklists, client education handouts, and so forth—and it was probably for these materials that you purchased it. However, before you begin using these materials to enhance your practice, we must remind you of the legal context of copyright in which they exist. **Except where noted, we retain all copyright to the content, including forms and handouts, in this book,** but we want you to be able to use forms and handouts in your practice. Therefore, please read and respect the following:

1. You, the individual professional who purchased this book, may copy any of the forms and handouts in the book for which copying permission is expressly granted in the form's or handout's caption. This permission to copy and print applies only for use in your individual clinical practice and with your own clients. Refer to the "Limited Duplication License" on the copyright page (p. iv) for full details.

   This means you cannot give copies to your associates, supervisees, friends, or other professionals for their use. Why? Because no one should use these forms without understanding fully their ethical and legal underpinnings, context, and implications. If others want to use these materials, as a matter of ethics, professionalism and law, they must purchase a copy of *The Paper Office for the Digital Age* for themselves.

2. You may modify the reproducible forms and handouts to suit your practice or your needs. In fact, **you should modify them** for the specific legal or other conditions that apply to your practice, and in any way that will further your clients' understanding. However, modification does not invalidate our copyrights. Again, the modified version can only be used in your individual clinical practice with your own clients, and you should take care to note that you are solely responsible for the content of any modifications, which should not be attributed to the authors or the publisher.

3. If you work in a group practice and want to use these materials in that setting, you must buy a copy of this book for each individual who will use the materials.

4. If you are leading a class, workshop, or other educational program and want to distribute copies of some of these materials, you should review the standards for "fair use" under copyright law, and you should both avoid charging for the materials and advise your students or participants that they are not for redistribution or reuse.

5. Some materials in this book are copyrighted by individuals who did not grant reproduction rights beyond their publication in *The Paper Office for the Digital Age*. Therefore, such materials may not be reproduced without the written permission of the copyright holder, as indicated on the materials themselves.

6. All materials that are not copyrighted by other individuals are copyrighted by the authors of this book. Except as provided in the limited photocopy license in this book (see the copyright page), to the extent permitted by law their reproduction is forbidden without prior written permission from The Guilford Press. See http://www.guilford.com/permissions for further details.

## We Invite Your Feedback

If you're disappointed with any part of this book, don't keep it a secret. Be a good customer, citizen, and therapist: Complain. Send in your criticisms and improvements. If you need forms or materials not offered here, let us know. See the Feedback Form on page 501 of the book.

Send your complaints and suggestions to this address:

Keely Kolmes, PsyD
220 Montgomery Street, Suite 400
San Francisco, CA 94104

Or send an email to Dr. Kolmes (drkkolmes@gmail.com).

As this field develops, this book will continue to be revised to meet the needs of practicing clinicians. It is our hope that by sharing the best efforts and ideas we have been able to borrow, modify, and devise—and by learning from you, our readers, in turn—this book will make your professional life easier and more productive, and will further the professional development of all practitioners of the craft of therapy.

# CHAPTER 1

# Essential Documents, Procedures, and Communication Tools

## 1.1 Basic Practice Management Documents and Communication Tools: An Overview

**Your psychotherapeutic skills and personal resources are the basis of your effectiveness as a therapist.** But independent practice also requires the effective operation of your professional office, and this is based on specialized forms and procedures. This book presents the essential tools to help you operate a solo or small-group psychotherapy practice ethically, legally, and profitably.

**Therapeutic practice has ethical dimensions.** Mental health clinicians have been at the forefront of the development of professional ethical guidelines. Concepts such as confidentiality, informed consent, and boundary issues have been articulated through careful deliberations. Professional ethics safeguard clients, enhance therapists' trustworthiness, and improve the climates of communities.

**Therapeutic practice has legal dimensions.** Therapists live and work in a complex and rapidly evolving legal context designed to protect the individual and reinforce socially approved behaviors. The United States is a nation under laws, and social policies are incorporated into laws.

Finally, **therapeutic practice has financial dimensions.** The delivery of health care services is inescapably intertwined with commerce, and mental health services are no exception. Therapists must be paid for services, and so financial functions such as income, expenses, fees, billing, and taxes must be attended to. Therapists operate in offices and meet for appointments, and so they use standard business procedures and office equipment.

Thus there are four aspects of a psychotherapy practice: the therapeutic, the ethical, the legal, and the financial. These four dimensions interact, intertwine, and may compete with one another. We, as professional therapists, need to take account of all four of them. We must also respond effectively to their continually evolving interactions. Sometimes the demands of doing so seem burdensome, but we cannot ignore them. This book is one carefully reasoned response to this burden and obligation.

Each tool in *The Paper Office for the Digital Age* has a primary function in one of these four areas, but each tool also has ramifications that extend into the other areas. For example, letterheads and business cards are important business tools. But the professions have legal and ethical rules about how therapists present themselves. Similarly, the making and keeping of financial and treatment records are basic administrative office tasks. But rules of confidentiality mean that treatment records cannot be handled and copied like documents in other kinds of business. Ensuring payment for services is essential, but the way this is done can affect treatment in many ways that are unique to the practice of psychotherapy. **This book's forms, patient education handouts, guidelines, checklists, and step-by-step procedures will help you integrate the relevant legal and ethical principles and current practices into your ordinary workflows, thus lightening both your worry and your administrative burdens.** The adoption of just those tools and procedures suitable to your practices will reduce your malpractice and ethics violation risks substantially. Review the materials described in the following chapters, and evaluate for yourself how much they will lower your anxiety over your practices.

This first chapter covers some office administration basics: What needs to go on a letterhead and in a resume, and what should not? What records do you need to keep? Where and how should you keep them, and for how long? Chapter 2 takes a detailed look at basic financial tools and procedures, from tracking income and expenses to procedures for billing clients and getting paid. Chapter 3 addresses billing third parties, which involves health insurance and managed care. Chapters 4 and 5 explore practical ways to meet the ethical and legal requirements of practice, including methods for reducing malpractice risk, and a range of specific tools for obtaining informed consent. Chapters 6 and 7 offer detailed forms and procedures for recording treatment from intake through termination. Chapter 8 offers methods for ensuring confidentiality, along with many forms and form letters for releasing and obtaining client records. Chapter 9 addresses an inseparable need of a private practice—marketing, or getting the word out about what you can offer. The Appendices are guides to further resources.

## 1.2  Presenting Yourself

### Ethical Aspects of Self-Presentation

In choosing the wording that presents you and your practice to the public, it is important to recognize that there are legal, ethical, and rational differences among competence, credentials, and titles. The American Psychological Association's (APA's) code of ethics (APA, 2010, Standard 5.01b) states that a psychologist must not misrepresent him- or herself in regard to training, skills, or credentials; other disciplines' codes assert the same expectations. Furthermore, it is solely the professional's responsibility to assure the absence of confusion, ambiguity, or falsity. **Be certain that your credentials are always stated accurately and cannot mislead anyone in any way.**

### Guidelines for Clear and Accurate Self-Presentations

- Almost always, use just your highest degree. Earlier ones are unnecessary, and their use suggests pomposity (always inappropriate in a therapist) rather than extra training. However, it *is* appropriate to use two degrees if the degrees are in different but relevant fields (e.g., a forensic psychologist's possession of a PhD and a JD). Use the exact degree's abbreviation rather than "Dr."; this lessens confusion. Do not use both, as in "Dr. Joe Rorschach, PhD." This is redundant; it also confounds the social title of "doctor" and the professional educational qualification "PhD," a rampant boundary crossing (see Section 4.5). "Ph.D." and "PhD" are both acceptable styles because they do not mislead. "PhD" (without periods) is a more modern style.

- The use of "Doctor" for nonphysicians is acceptable in casual conversations and nonmedical settings, where it will not mislead. Similarly, those having a doctorate from a nonpsychological program (such as biochemistry) should not use "Doctor" in psychological settings. Those with a possibly related doctorate, such as in theology, should add clarifying language—for example, "PhD (Theology), MA (Psychology), and licensed MFT" or " . . . MFT, license ###."

- A professional title is optional but often clarifying. However, depending on the state, some titles have legal definitions. Check your state's definition of the following to ensure legitimacy: "consultant," "evaluator," "clinical psychologist," "counselor," "therapist," "psychoanalyst," and "psychotherapist." Similarly, to prevent both misrepresentations and misunderstandings, clarify your status where relevant (in addition to giving your degree) as "Psychologist in training" or "Supervised by [Name and Degree of Supervisor]."

- No one can use the title "psychologist" in any state unless he or she is licensed or similarly credentialed. "Licensed psychologist" (or "certified psychologist") is now considered acceptable, but this was not always the case. Using both words together was seen as redundant. It was also seen as misleading, in that it seemed to suggest that a "*licensed* psychologist" was somehow better than just a "psychologist," or even that there were *unlicensed* psychologists. "Licensed psychologist" is currently permissible. Include your license number on all print and electronic materials, emails, websites, and announcements for groups and other services. This is required in many states for clarity, but we believe it is a good idea in general, so that people can verify your license and its good standing.

- Specialties of practice (e.g., "practice confined to children" or specialty in "forensic evaluations") are useful to introduce yourself to other professionals or possible referrers, and to emphasize your areas of competence. However, beware of creating false impressions, because you will have to deliver what you advertise. When clinicians present themselves to clients as having specific areas of competence, the courts have generally held them to the standards that professional organizations set, even if the clinician is not a member of such organizations or qualified for membership. For example, those who offer "marriage counseling" are likely to be held to the standards and codes of the American Association for Marriage and Family Therapy or of those possessing licenses as marriage and family therapists. Evidence of competence differs by specialty (e.g., certification by the Academy of Certified Social Workers [ACSW] or the American Board of Professional Psychology [ABPP]), so know and use only the ones appropriate for your profession, and be scrupulous about your qualifications. There are "boards" whose only requirement for membership is paying a fee. Other professionals know which are real credentials and which aren't. They will think less of you and your real credentials if you indicate membership in such "vanity boards" (Dattilio, 2002).

- "Member/Fellow [as appropriate] of the American Psychological Association" is now acceptable. For years it was frowned on because it suggested a credential where there was none; there is no special training or particular skill required for APA membership. However, it does represent conformance to the APA's ethical code and accomplishment recognized by one's colleagues, and so is worth indicating.

- Board certification or "diplomate" status can be evidence of competence, and so such designations are very appropriate inclusions. As noted above, however, you need to be aware of "vanity boards" whose qualifications do not include evidence of skill. The same applies to degrees from "diploma mills" and "universities" without regional accreditation.

## The Name of Your Practice

Your practice's name is up to you. The simplest option is to be yourself: "[First Name Last Name, Degree]," as in "John Doe, PhD." Using your name may become a liability if you take on other professionals or try to pass on your practice, though. Moreover, be aware that laypersons will not understand "clinical" or differentiate "PhD" from "PsyD," much less understand "doctor" as it applies to nonmedical professionals. Your licensing law may require you to use particular words or a format.

You may also create a name for your practice, such as the professional-sounding "Associated [Type of Professionals]" or [Name of Discipline] Associates," or the grandiose "The American Research Foundation for Interpersonal Therapeutics." This is called a "doing business as" (D/B/A or just dba) name. Descriptive terms such as "Psychotherapy" or "Counseling" may be useful pegs to keep you in others' memories and allow laypersons to understand what you do far better than using just your name and credentials may. However, some such terms have been used so often that they offer no individuality. Check directories for examples, and try for some uniqueness. Location names are assumed to stick in memory (e.g., Allegheny, Gateway, and Three Rivers are popular in the Pittsburgh area), and they may be helpful, as clients (or at least referrers) seem to prefer a nearby therapist.

If you are going to operate your practice under anything other than your real name, you need to register this D/B/A name with your state government for legal reasons. Usually the appropriate government office is called something like the Corporation Bureau of the Department of State. You can call your practice anything except a name someone else has already taken, or something a government official finds improper. You will need to fill out a simple form that identifies you as the person behind the facade, pay a fee, and publish the name in your local newspaper of legal record. The newspaper's classified ads department will help you with the procedure, and the fee for this is modest.

Don't forget to get a business license to open a business and practice. Your local government should have the application online. It is typically required that you display this in your office in a place where clients can readily see it.

If you share office space with other similar professionals, take care not to be perceived by members of the public (or their lawyers) as being part of a group practice. Having a general practice name, advertising or doing public education together, regularly referring clients to each other, sharing office personnel or software, and the like all create this impression, which you must vitiate with specific language in your practice brochure (see Section 5.2). The risk is that if one of these other professionals is sued, you are likely to be included, and the costs of defending yourself constitute a substantial risk and may not be covered by your insurance.

## Your Letterhead and Cards

### Checklist for Necessary Information for Letterheads

☐ Use your legal name without nicknames (unless you live a locality where nicknames are acceptable). If there is a similarly named professional in your area, add initials— or, better yet, a distinguishing subtitle or practice name.

☐ Include your highest *clinical* degree, specializations, and other credentials. Include your complete address with all nine digits of the ZIP code. (Remember, a referral or check lost in the mail is worse than worthless; it's a hassle.) Some states require listing your license number in any professional context, and we agree that this is good practice. If you have multiple addresses, indicate them, but make it clear to which address mail (especially payments to you) is to be sent. Do not use abbreviations (e.g., Bldg.), as they are inelegant and do not save space on a letterhead. In particular, avoid using erroneous or outdated abbreviations (e.g., Penna. and Penn are archaic for Pennsylvania).

☐ If you will be using email for business purposes (with encryption), but *only* if, add your business email address to your letterhead. If you have a website, indicate the URL for the site as well. There are good reasons both to use email in your practice and to opt out of using it. We discuss these in Chapter 9 on marketing your practice.

☐ Your telephone numbers should *always* include your area code.

☐ There are services that integrate faxes, multiple phones and phone lines, email and voicemail, and so forth, and secure all of these. Some clinicians are moving to consolidation services such as Google Voice to have a single number that rings to either professional or personal phones (or both), depending on who is calling. Thus you can use a single phone for personal and business lines, and you can manage business calls from a masked personal number. Nevertheless, there are privacy implications if voice messages are transcribed (by the consolidation service's computers) and these messages are then sent to a nonsecure email address or to Short Message Service (SMS, for text messaging) on your cellphone. The advantage of such transcriptions is that they constitute an automatic way to document the content of your calls in high-risk situations; the disadvantage is that receiving the transcriptions creates the risk of loss of privacy, depending upon where they are sent. New options are always being developed, so revisit your phone plans yearly.

☐ Email attachments and Internet fax services are rapidly replacing stand-alone faxes. Current alternatives include sending faxes from your computer or photographing the pages with a smartphone and attaching the pictures to an SMS text message or encrypted email.

☐ There is no consensus on making your home phone number available to your clients. Some therapists report that calls are rare, are almost always justified by a true emergency, and are grist for the therapy mill when they are not. Others do not want to involve their family members inside the boundaries of therapy and are concerned about the possibilities of violent or harassing clients. An unlisted number may be worth the added cost.

❑ If you ever make calls from your home to clients, you should consider arranging for blocking of caller ID, because without this a client will be able to discover the number from which you called. You can let clients know, "I'll be calling again at 3 P.M., and when I call, it may be from a blocked and private number," so that they will accept your call.

❑ You should also decide whether you want to be available on a 24-hour basis. Membership in insurance panels often requires you to agree to be "available 24 hours" (or similar language). Consider your philosophy: Is such availability part of your responsibility to your clients, or is your privacy part of maintaining boundaries? Decide how to handle this with an answering machine, answering service, or pager, and state your rules clearly in your practice brochure (see Section 5.2).

❑ Consider what to include in your voicemail's or answering machine's message:

  • Explain, "This is a confidential message" (if only you will pick it up). You can add, "If you don't hear from me in 24 hours, assume there is a mechanical failure and call back." Then continue: "If this is an emergency . . . " (describe how to reach you and what to do when you are not available—e.g., calling a covering colleague, a crisis center, or a personal physician). Other things you may wish to include: "Speak slowly and clearly," "Spell an unusual name," "You may send an email to me at [give your email address]," "For possible new clients, note that my practice is only fee-for-service, but most insurance plans will reimburse part of the fee."

  • Ask the caller to leave at least one return call number, to suggest the best times for calling back, and to indicate whether each number left is safe and private.

❑ List your Tax Identification Number (TIN) or National Provider Identifier (NPI) and license number (with type and state) on anything that will become a bill or accompany a bill, because insurers need these to pay you. Incidentally, when you bill anyone who is likely to pay you more than $600 in a single year, include a copy of your W-9. It saves a lot of work for the other party and will be appreciated.

❑ Check and recheck the accuracy of *every word and number* before you print any card or paper document. One of us (ELZ) once had to rewrite his area code on 1,000 cards.

### Logos

Logos are popular but not yet standardized. Orthopedists are using a braced-tree design, podiatrists a foot in a winged serpent (Aesculapius) design, and psychologists and psychotherapists the Greek letter "psi" (Ψ), but these devices have no meaning for the uninitiated. Most commercial printers offer at least one other logo you might consider, or you could use a simple letter monogram. You may want to design a logo suitable for the name of your practice (tree motifs are nonthreatening). You could have the printer do it for a small charge, or actually hire a professional who has done this before and have a really good job done. (Therapists are notorious for their resistance to using other professionals.) If you can't find an experienced artist, call the owners of a funeral home that has a nice text/logo and ask who did theirs. (This is a good tip—really!)

Phrases such as "We care for you" can seem insincere. You don't really care for the people who may see your card until they become clients, and we should presume that all therapists care for their clients (as noted by Constance Fischer, PhD, of Pittsburgh, PA).

## Type Style and Size

Use no more than two common typefaces; creativity gains no points with a loss of readability. Roman is preferable to *italic*. **Bold** in small sizes is not sharp and uses more space. Serif and **sans serif** fonts are equally acceptable these days for professionals. Larger type is easier to read for seniors (over 40 and also your likely referrers) and for anyone struggling with a seventh-generation photocopied form. This is 10 point, this is 12 point, this is 14 point.

## Paper and Envelopes

When ELZ receives it, he always notices heavy, linen-textured, laid, 100% cotton rag, watermarked, ivory-colored bond paper. He fiddles with it and admires it, but is not impressed by the professional behind it—only curious about how much extra they have to charge him or his clients for this affectation. Are there any documents created by therapists that deserve or need anything but ordinary 20-pound white paper? If the client's records are to be destroyed in a few years to prevent misinterpretation, why use archival paper that will last 200 years?

If you use a computer, you are not likely to need printed stationery at all. You can show the letterhead's information on each page by putting it in the header or footer, or both, of your templates. Similarly, you can print your return address on envelopes when you need them. No business occasion requires fancier stationery, so spend your money on your well-earned pleasures.

## Business Cards

**Business cards are essential.** Carry a few in your wallet and in your datebook, because they have many purposes. You can offer a card to introduce yourself tactfully; the recipient can easily make conversation by inquiring about your location or what you have listed as your specialties. When you make presentations, always bring lots of cards to give to audience members, so that they may call on you for professional services (sometimes years later). You can also use them for small notes to others, or can use others' cards to note your promises to send something to them.

Plain black ink and slightly raised roman lettering, on a firm (but not too stiff), very white card, are always acceptable. Online printing services offer dozens of designs, typefaces, and colors. Because they are so convenient, consider making several designs tailored to your different professional activities and even to the larger presentations you make.

After you have made some contacts in your practice area, you can discover the local standards of good taste by examining the cards for which you have traded, and you can then follow these examples. Even so, wait until you have been in practice a few years before ordering 5,000, baby blue, translucent smoky plastic, gold-foil-lettered cards with a logo of doughboy figures hugging each other. (Yes, ELZ received these from a therapist.) Remember the old rule about dressing for a party: You can always dress down from formal attire, but you can't dress up from jeans.

Some business cards incorporate an appointment card on the back. These can provide for single or multiple appointments and different formats; these features make the card even more useful and not much more expensive. If you cannot fill a cancelled appointment with "24 hours notice," change this to meet your needs. If you have two related positions (e.g., a clinic staff job and a private practice), you can have each printed on one side of a card. If you do business in another language or country, you can have cards printed with translations or addresses on each side.

Do-it-yourselfers can buy sheets of precut business cards for their office printer and download templates for layouts from many sources. Clip art can be added from hundreds of collections on the Web.

## Your Resume and Curriculum Vitae

A *resume* usually presents your current job functions or future goals, the strongest of your educational and vocational accomplishments, or other relevant experiences. Two pages is the maximum length, and one page is often all that others expect to read. A *curriculum vitae* (Latin for "course of life," usually abbreviated as CV) is more formal and professional in orientation. It is usually sequential and emphasizes any activities that bear on your career development (education, honors, scholarships, professional experiences, grants received, publications, memberships, licenses, etc.). The distinctions between a resume and a CV are often blurred these days.

It is helpful to have at least two versions of your resume or CV. The "maximum version" should have every heading and entry, name and date. New positions and accomplishments can be added as you acquire these, and selections from these can be tailored to specific audiences. You can easily add new information, reorganize existing information, and tailor your material to a particular recipient's needs. For example, you might emphasize your teaching experience for a school consulting job, your clinical work and training for a hospital, or your publications for a research position. Always date the resume or CV currently. A single-page "synoptic version" can be used for others less fascinated with *all* of your accomplishments. As an alternative that will get more attention when many people apply to the same job, you can write up your resume as a letter, describing your skills and history together.

Your CV should be available on your website in .pdf format (so that it cannot be modified by others) or through a link, such as Dropbox.com, that can be easily shared and emailed. This will be especially handy when you are arranging to do any public speaking or providing continuing education for organizations.

When you do public speaking, you will typically be asked to send your full CV and to provide a short biography of your relevant credentials and experiences. It can be smart to bring along a copy printed in larger text for the person introducing you. Remember, your peers (and an ethics committee) will hold you alone fully responsible for assuring that the media present you correctly.

Many situations require full documentation of your history and training: applying for jobs, joining certain professional organizations, applying for licensure, responding to legal matters (e.g., complaints) or testifying in court, and applying insurance panels. For psychologists, the Association of State and Provincial Psychology Boards (http://www.asppb.org) offers two excellent tools for these situations. Its Credentials Bank will hold transcripts, records of supervision, continuing education records, letters of recommendation, and similar materials that may be very hard to produce at a much later time. And becoming licensed in another state is greatly simplified by the Association's Certificate of Professional Qualification in Psychology (CPQ). Insurance panels require frequent "recertifications," and the

Council for Affordable Quality Healthcare (at http://www.caqh.org) has a templated form for your credentials that most insurers will accept.

Figure 1.1 shows a partially filled-in sample CV, to illustrate the headings and layout for a maximum version.

### Checklist for Your Resume or CV

❑ Plain white paper is sufficient unless you are applying for a job where your sense of style matters.

❑ More than two or three pages may seem like bragging, so unless you are applying for an academic position, are seeking a place on a professional committee or board, or want to teach courses—in short, unless your history of publications and presentations matters—consider keeping your resume or CV skimmably short.

❑ Use one or at most two typefaces, and only a few **boldfaced** words. Boldface is a tasteful emphasizer if used with discretion. Use italics instead of underlining and do not double space between sentences on any computer-created document. Using ALL CAPITALS is like shouting, so be judicious. Do not use fancy layout or display typefaces, and even headline fonts may be too fancy for a professional, noncommercial document.

❑ Your resume or CV must be scrupulously accurate—no omissions, distortions, exaggerations, or other misrepresentations. These are ethical violations and reportable as such, which might cut short your promising career. Careful readers who find inappropriate statements will lose faith in your competence. Ask your more scrupulous colleagues to review your work.

❑ Professional work can be presented as an employment history or by function, responsibilities, or titles (as in the example in Figure 1.1). Both are acceptable, so choose for maximum clarity for the reader. Omit minor publications such as letters to the editor, single articles in local newspapers, and inaccessible online publications.

❑ Both resumes and CVs are business forms, and so there is no room for your sex or gender identity, marital status, age, children, hobbies, musical interests, charitable or religious activities, or the like. If in doubt, leave it out. Many people offer both a work and home address and phone number, because professional contacts often overlap with social ones these days. However, be aware that your CV is likely to be publicly accessed, and thus that discretion is advisable. One of us (KK) believes that your full CV should be on your website, as clients these days may be interested in your training, and clinicians who value more transparency may want to make it accessible to these clients. For this reason, KK suggests keeping home and personal phone numbers off the CV. It is far easier simply to email a different contact number or address to a person when necessary, and train yourself to keep it off business materials.

## 1.3  **Your Appointment Book**

We all need a simple way to keep track of our obligations. Call it an "appointment book," "datebook," "calendar," "schedule," "little black book," or *vade mecum,*" but it is a necessity

# Curriculum Vitae

## SIGMUND J. THERAPIST
1001 Spectacular View Lane
Terrific City, Supreme State 12345-6789
(900) 555-1212

January 15, 2017

### EDUCATION

| | |
|---|---|
| 2005 | PhD in Clinical Psychology—Distinguished University, Sovereign State |
| 2001–2002 | Internship in Clinical Psychology (American Psychological Association-approved)—Psychology Department, Splendid Health Center, Altered State University, Altered State |

### ADDITIONAL EDUCATIONAL EXPERIENCES

### HONORS

### CREDENTIALS

| | |
|---|---|
| 2005 | Licensed as a Psychologist in Supreme State, Number 12345 |
| 2014 | Fellow, American Psychological Association, Number 1234-5678 |
| 2015 | Certified in Clinical Psychology by the American Board of Professional Psychology, Number 12345 |

### TEACHING EXPERIENCE

| | |
|---|---|
| 2007–2012 | Superb University, Department of Psychology, Terrific City, Supreme State 12345 Adjunct Associate Professor since 2008 |

### CLINICAL PRACTICE

| | |
|---|---|
| 2006–present | Independent Practice of General Clinical Psychology at Excellent Hospital, Terrific City, Supreme State 12345 |

### RESEARCH, GRANTS/CONTRACTS, CONSULTATION, EDITORIAL EXPERIENCE

| | |
|---|---|
| 2003–2005 | Research Assistant (half-time)—Project Champion, Psychology Department, Magnificent University, Marvelous City, Ecstatic State 54321 |

### PUBLICATIONS

### TRAINING PROGRAMS PRESENTED

### REFERENCES

Professional, business, and personal recommendations are available on request.

FIGURE 1.1. Sample curriculum vitae, partially filled in.

for every practitioner. A practical rule might be "If it is not in my book, it does not exist," and so we strongly recommend writing down all plans and appointments, both personal and professional.

Your appointment book is a record of your business. It not only documents your activities, but also records the services you rendered. It can be of value with the tax people or in court, and can be used to reconstruct your day even years later, so keep your old ones for many years, perhaps with your tax records.

## What an Appointment Book Should Include

Look for a book that covers an 8 A.M. to 9 P.M. schedule. For example, *The National Psychologist* (http://www.nationalpsychologist.com) sells an appointment calendar that has a 13-hour-per-day, 6-day-per-week schedule, with 15-minute intervals to meet the needs of even the busiest clinician. It also includes diagnostic codes, a listing of psychotropic medications, and other useful sections. It is 8½" × 11" and lies flat when open.

## A List of Current Clients

Keeping a list of your current or recently active clients in your datebook or on a cellphone may be very helpful if you need to cancel or reschedule appointments, or to reach clients in an emergency. Of course, such a roster could breach confidentiality if the people are identifiable as clients, and so you could use a simple letter substitution code if you are using a paper roster, or encryption if you are using a phone that is also password-protected and allows you to erase messages remotely if the phone is lost. If people are not identified as clients, but simply names on a general list, the risk seems small.

## Pros and Cons of Paper versus Electronic Appointment Books

Many people are now keeping track of appointments in online calendars and smartphones. Doing so has both risks and benefits. A smartphone is a much more likely target of theft than a hard-copy appointment book, which can be kept locked in your office. KK has also found that she makes fewer entry errors in a paper version, especially when managing cancellations and repeat entries. So she trusts her paper book over the electronic schedule, and she transfers events to the electronic calendar at the end of each week for the week ahead. It may be convenient to use an online calendar system as a backup for the smartphone's calendar. Whichever method you use, it's important to protect privacy. Clients' full names and contact information are not included in KK's paper book.

We also must acknowledge that many psychotherapists find value in using an online scheduling system for consultations, client appointments, or phone intakes with potential clients. Setting up your open blocks of time every couple of weeks and sending links to those who wish to speak with you can make conferencing appointments easier, especially if you do not have someone handling administrative matters for you. An online search will reveal a variety of such tools. Be aware that if your scheduling software includes protected health information (PHI), it is subject to the rules of the Health Insurance Portability and Accountability Act (HIPAA), and so you will need a HIPAA-compliant system. If your form simply says "book time to talk" or "consultations," and asks for only name and contact information as well as the hours scheduled, then HIPAA concerns will not be relevant. See Section 1.5 for more on HIPAA.

# 1.4   Basics of Record Keeping

One of the attractions of private practice is the freedom from agency-imposed requirements, and one of the requirements most eagerly dispensed with is elaborate record keeping. Although you cannot escape the need for records, you can adopt record-keeping methods that are simpler and more closely tailored to your needs.

You will need to keep both business or financial records and case or clinical records. Keeping them separate is necessary, so that there is never a hint that you made a clinical decision because of some financial benefit to you. Business records consist of your income and expense records, checkbook, bank statements, tax forms, business and professional licenses, billing forms, and so forth. Your accountant can help you set these up efficiently. (Get an accountant as soon as you consider entering practice, and you may also want to hire a bookkeeper; it's a good investment.) For a more detailed discussion of financial record keeping, see Chapter 2.

Clinical records (whose confidentiality must be protected because they contain PHI) include your appointment book or schedule; case records (including intake forms, treatment plans, progress notes, referral notes, periodic summaries, discharge plans, etc.); correspondence with clients and with others about clients (including email and/or SMS texting exchanges); and the like. It is also a good idea to keep telephone and office visit logs for years in the event that a complaint calls for a reconstruction of events.

For guidance in recording the intake and initial evaluation of a case, see the forms in Chapter 6. Chapter 7 covers treatment plans and ways to record the progress of treatment. For a full discussion of confidentiality concerns, see Chapter 8.

The remainder of this chapter provides an overview of clinical records, including the reasons to keep them, the nature of their contents, and their physical structure and organization. It also includes a discussion of how to maintain the security of your records, and how long to retain them.

### Why Keep Records?

**First, records must be kept to comply with your profession's ethical expectations.** For example, Standard 6.01 of the APA ethics code (APA, 2010) states: "(a) Psychologists create . . . records and data relating to their professional and scientific work in order to (1) facilitate provision of services later by them or by other professionals, . . . (3) meet institutional requirements, (4) ensure accuracy of billing and payments, and (5) ensure compliance with law." On the basis of these guidelines, **many states' licensing boards are *requiring* licensed mental health practitioners to keep specific kinds of records**. You cannot disregard these requirements on the basis of expediency, concern for confidentiality, or a feeling that "My notes are only about process or are illegible, so they would be of no use to anyone else."

**As a consequence, not keeping records is now grounds for a malpractice claim, because it falls below the standard of practice.** Having no records is illegal and unprofessional, thus demonstrating poor care. Reid (1999, p. 12) notes further that "Skimpy notes imply skimpy care."

**Adequate record keeping allows you to defend yourself.** Records will be your best defense in the event of a malpractice or ethics complaint or other litigation.

**In addition, your records document your provision of services.** This is a legal obligation and is necessary to receive payment from anyone. "Courts and external review bodies view the absence of documentation in the record about an event as evidence that it never occurred, no matter what the subsequent claims of the clinicians" (Weiner & Wettstein, 1993, p. 179).

**Records document the thoroughness of your assessments if the untoward should happen, and they have many additional uses.** Your records establish a baseline of current functioning for structuring treatment, or for evaluating progress and the impact of providing services. They can show whether and when a client met an eligibility requirement (e.g., disability). They are needed for supervisory review, consultation, peer review, quality control, and statistical reporting. They may be needed to maintain the client's continuity of care in future therapy or with other therapists. They provide clues as to which treatments have been successful and which are to be avoided. They offer crucial information for interdisciplinary communication. They allow you to review past successes at a future time. They replace memory, which is often inaccurate. Records are useful for self-education and student education, or for research. Lastly, you need to keep records because you are being paid to.

**To summarize, keeping records is not optional.** If you currently keep insufficient ones, you are playing with fire as well as doing your clients a disservice. Change now; revise your record-keeping practices before the sun goes down again.

This is also a good time to review whether and why your system isn't working for you. Perhaps electronic records will help make record keeping more routine for you. (Paper vs. electronic records are discussed a bit later in this chapter.) Or perhaps you are writing too much and need to review how to whittle down a session into a few brief points, including any treatment decisions, and the next time you plan to see the client.

Caution is in order, however: Making records risks exposing confidential information and subjecting yourself to "self-incrimination" in licensing board procedures when you have to proffer your notes, and so creating safeguards against these and other foreseeable threats needs to be part of your work.

## What Should Be in the Records?

You cannot record all you observe, say, or hear, and so you must select. You may have heard, "If if was not written down, it didn't happen." This is intimidating, illogical, and unrealistic. We are always editing what we choose to record, and so we do and say lots of things that we don't record because those were not relevant to our work at the time. With rare exceptions, you should focus on what is significant for the client's current treatment, and not write notes that are geared toward securing your payments, protecting yourself from malpractice claims, or with the intent to deceive (Dwyer & Shih, 1998).

Here are 10 categories of information we need to keep on each client. Each of these categories is described below.

### Intake and Assessment

1. *Intake forms.* The client's record should contain demographic information on the client and the client's chief concerns. Sections 6.2 and 6.4 offer three examples: the

first-contact record and two client information forms. In addition, HIPAA requires that the client see your Notice of Privacy Practices (NPP) at first contact. Section 1.5 explains this further. This notice can be included in the preappointment package mailed to the client if there is time, or it can be given to the client before the initial interview. Alternatively, you may want to place your intake forms on your website so that clients can view and complete them in time to have them available for the first session. If a client first contacted you via email and described the issues the client wanted to address in treatment, you should include this in the chart.

2. *Histories.* The record can include personal and family histories, history of the presenting complaint, and those of previous interventions or treatments. Section 6.4 includes an interview guide and history forms.

3. *Evaluations and assessments.* The client record needs to include clinical assessments, previous evaluations, and any testing. Section 6.4 offers two problem checklists (one for adults and one for children). Guides for the evaluation of chemical use, mental status, health information and medication can also be found in Section 6.4. A guide for suicide risk assessment can be found in Section 4.7.

4. *Diagnoses and case formulations.* Each client record should include complete diagnoses and a case formulation. An intake summary is offered in Section 6.6. It can help in case formulation and treatment planning.

## Treatment Planning, Progress, and Termination

5. *Treatment plan.* The plan should include the target problems, methods of intervention, review dates, and progress measures. Chapter 7 offers some guidance.

6. *Progress notes.* Besides or instead of the notes taken in session these might include coherent summaries of treatment sessions. See Section 7.2 for more possibilities for progress notes. Under the HIPAA Privacy Rule, you can create separate "psychotherapy notes" that receive special privacy protection. By definition, these are not part of the client's medical chart (see Section 7.2 for clarification).

7. *Termination summary.* This should summarize treatments provided, the progress made, any remaining problems, the client's prognosis, the reasons for termination, and any clinical recommendations. See Section 7.3.

## Other Important Client Record Contents

8. *Correspondence.* This might include records from past treaters, notes of nontrivial phone calls with the client, and correspondence with other professionals about the client. If you exchange or even receive emails with PHI, these should be preserved. Emails and text messages with very routine contents like appointment changes need not be preserved unless you expect clinical, legal, or ethical problems with the client.

9. *Financial records.* These might include a signed agreement to pay; the dates of services; bills showing the charges, payments, and collection phone calls; and letters to the client, insurance companies, and managed care organizations (MCOs) about bills and payments.

10. *Legal documents.* These would include any releases of information (ROIs) signed by the client and the HIPAA consent form (see Section 6.4), and documentation of informed consent through contracts or the client information brochure (see Chapter 5).

More generally, Knapp (1992a) states that records should be the following:

- **Comprehensive.** All the relevant data should be included: names and addresses, fee arrangements, dates and kinds of services rendered, results of consultations and testing, correspondence, releases, reports prepared, notes of phone calls and meetings, progress notes, and discharge summary.

- **Objective.** Facts need to be separated from opinion; observable behaviors need to be included.

- **Substantive.** The diagnosis, presenting problem, treatment plans, and your rationale for each of these should be contained in the records.

- **Consistent.** Your behavior should match your treatment plan and diagnosis, or you should document the reasons for any inconsistencies.

- **Retrievable.** Your records need to be accessible, your notes need to be readable, and your charts need to be organized. They also need to be protected against various threats to their loss as HIPAA requires.

- **Secure.** You must make certain that your records are inaccessible to unauthorized others.

- **Current.** You should make your notes in a timely fashion.

All of these characteristics are discussed below. We also wish to point out that notes should be signed on each page, with your appropriate credential (LMFT, LCSW, PsyD, PhD, etc.), and it is also wise to indicate when you plan to meet with the client next for documentation of continuity of care.

As indicated above, each client must have a range of specific information in his or her record. HIPAA considers these documents to be the "case record," and much of the law is concerned with whom it can be shared either with or without the client's consent. While all of HIPAA applies to all health care, only mental health professionals can create a more private kind of notes it calls "psychotherapy notes." To distinguish them from all other kinds of records that can be made during psychotherapy, we refer to them in this book as "HIPAA-protected psychotherapy notes." HIPAA has requirements for these notes, so see Section 7.2 on keeping "HIPAA-protected psychotherapy notes."

## Pros and Cons of Paper versus Electronic Records

Some clinicians are simply more comfortable with having paper charts. They prefer such a chart's way of organizing and accessing information. It can be locked in a file cabinet, and they do not have to worry about the loss or theft of a digital device, hackers into cloud-based records, or loss of access to charts if the computer or Internet connection fails. However, in some practices paper charts will eventually take up a lot of physical space, and it is handy to have access to client information without having to go physically to your office when you need to talk with a client or consult a colleague.

If you are keeping only paper records, you can print emails and other electronic documents to place in the chart. One of us (KK) does not store any client records on a computer, but she uses her machine to write summaries of sessions, and prints these summaries without saving electronic copies. She reuses the paper to fit about three sessions on each page, spacing down on a blank electronic document before typing and printing the new note. The only documents saved on her work laptop are generic patient education materials that may be printed or emailed to clients. The laptop is locked in a file cabinet at the end of the day. A similar protection for a desktop computer is to use a wireless mouse and keyboard and lock them away when not in use.

Electronic records are easier for clinicians who are willing to learn new workflows and who are more facile on the computer. However, such records will require taking measures to protect their security—both in how they are saved on the computer (it is usually simplest to encrypt your entire hard drive as well as the notes themselves, rather than encrypting just the clinical files or folders) and in how they are stored through your Internet connection (WPA2 Enterprise security is the current security standard). Records should be encrypted before being backed up (copied) to a remotely stored hard drive or in a secured cloud archive.

There are dozens of electronic health record (EHR) systems, which incorporate billing, scheduling capabilities, and secure messaging with clients, along with the ability to create and store records, and manage the functioning of a practice. Because these change so often, we cannot provide specifics here.

Clinicians who switch to electronic versions of paper records must decide on storing the older paper records or converting them to electronic copies with a scanner. Because the hardware and software for this process changes so rapidly, we do not make recommendations (but one source for such information is http://www.documentsnap.com, which can help you efficiently become "paper*less*").

### Client Records on Your Computer

The simplest way to keep progress notes on a computer without using a commercial record-keeping program is to create a folder or directory for each client, and to add a file or document for each visit. You can do this by creating a blank progress note (see Forms 7.2 and 7.3 for formats you can adopt), saved as a "template" or "stationery." Open it each time you want to make a record. Fill in the current information, title it with the client's initials and the day's date, and save it to the client's folder. If you don't want to write so much, you can just open a file in each client's folder or directory called "Progress Notes" and add to what you have written before. Of course, such notes will need to be encrypted. The Proskauer (2009) law firm recommends encrypting your entire computer; it observes that if you lose an encrypted machine, HIPAA's breach notification process is nullified.

Be aware that documents created in common word processors cannot be authenticated—that is, confidently connected to the real person who wrote or changed them and to when this happened. Even computers or programs that track changes do not have these functions, and so you have three options:

1. Print out, sign, and date all your notes right after creating them. Destroy the electronic version and make the paper one your record. Signatures can be authenticated.

2. Use a separate but inexpensive program that adds a "digital signature" to each document before it is saved.

3. Adopt an EHR program, which will include authentication in its record-keeping function. EHR programs will be widely, if not universally, used by private practitioners in the future because of legal pressures (such as HIPAA requirements and the Affordable Care Act), infatuation with all things computerized, and the benefits to the insurance community.

## The Physical Structure for Organizing Paper Records

Those keeping electronic records may wish to skip this discussion, but if you are keeping paper charts, the following methods may be useful.

### The Basic Manila Folder Method

An ordinary manila folder for each client is traditional. Although this format is simple and cheap, it has liabilities: Loose pages can get lost or misplaced; also, pages and entries are kept in the sequence in which they were created, and so information is not organized by topic or relevance. This traditional, even classic, approach to record keeping can be improved by developing a checklist of the contents (see Form 1.1), which can be printed on the outside of each manila folder. This is designed to ensure that everything important is obtained. The client's name should not appear on the outside, for privacy reasons. KK keeps all charts in a locked filing cabinet and only updates them between sessions, when alone. You should tailor Form 1.1 to your own office procedures and forms.

**FORM 1.1**

### Some Other Options for Folders

How much do you charge other people for your time? How much of it do *you* waste each month searching in your folders? Here are some time-saving options:

- Use different-colored folders for clients of different sexes, genders, or sexual identities and orientations; or for families, couples and individuals; or for any other meaningful distinctions. (Suggested by Beverly Celotta, PhD, of Gaithersburg, MD.)

- File your charts by day of the week, so that charts for all your Monday clients are in one section, and so on. (Suggested by Valerie Shebroe, PhD, of East Lansing, MI.)

- Use charts that have dividers preprinted with various headings ("Intake," "Treatment Plan," "Legal Stuff," etc.) in a standard hospital or medical office pasteboard folder.

### Checklist for the Contents of Each Client's Folder

The following are listed in sequential order, not in order of importance. These contents are discussed, and specific forms or sample documents are provided, later in *The Paper Office for the Digital Age* as indicated. These supplement Form 1.1.

# Checklist for Client Records

**Client #** _____  **Intake date** ____/____/_____

| | Date | By whom? |
|---|---|---|
| **1. Informed consent materials** | | |

- ❑ NPP given and consent signed*
- ❑ Information brochure for clients given and signed*
- ❑ Treatment options, benefits, and risks discussed and understanding noted
- ❑ Consent/contract to treatment given and signed*
- ❑ Duty to protect, danger to self/others discussed, and understanding noted
- ❑ Requests for information/records from others signed and sent*
- ❑ Payment policy discussed.
- ❑ Agreement to pay signed*
- ❑ Consent for posttreatment survey or other follow-up given and signed or declined*
- ❑ Consent to evaluate without commitment to treat discussed and noted
- ❑ Other consents discussed and noted (research, recordings, managed care issues*)

**2. Further evaluations or consultations needed—indicate questions to be addressed**

- ❑ Medical: _____  ❑ Psychiatric: _____
- ❑ Vocational/educational: _____  ❑ Other: _____

**3. Case management information**

- a. Referral received: ____/____/____  By whom? _____
- b. First contact: ____/____/____  By whom? _____
- c. Intake completed: ____/____/____  By whom? _____
- d. *Initial* treatment plan sent to MCO: ____/____/____  By whom? _____

  Consultation with MCO reviewer named: _____ on: ____/____/____

  Authorization #: _____  # sessions authorized: _____  Review on: ____/____/____

- e. *First reauthorization request*: ____/____/____  By whom? _____

  Consultation with MCO reviewer named: _____ on: ____/____/____

  Authorization #: _____  # sessions authorized: _____  Review on: ____/____/____

- f. *Second reauthorization request*: ____/____/____  By whom? _____

  Consultation with MCO reviewer named: _____ on: ____/____/____

  Authorization #: _____  # sessions authorized: _____  Review on: ____/____/____

**4. Forms and records requested and released***

| Form/record | Sought from/sent to | On date | By |
|---|---|---|---|
| | | | |
| | | | |

**FORM 1.1. Checklist for client records.** Asterisked (*) items can be found in this book. From *The Paper Office for the Digital Age, Fifth Edition.* Copyright © 2017 Edward L. Zuckerman and Keely Kolmes. Published by The Guilford Press. Permission to reproduce this material is granted to purchasers of this book for personal use or use with individual clients (see copyright page for details).

❑ A billing record (see Section 2.3), so that you can address unpaid balances if necessary.

❑ The first-contact record (Form 6.1) and similar records (see Section 6.4).

❑ Paper for notes. You can use blank paper, or print up the case progress note form (Form 7.2) or the HIPAA-protected psychotherapy note form (Form 7.1) if you decide to use either. See Section 7.2.

❑ Documentation of informed consent—for example, a signed copy of the client information brochure (see Section 5.2), and other forms and materials regarding treatment and consent to evaluation that appear in Chapter 5.

❑ Assessments and testing done by you.

❑ Previous treatment records that you obtain (see Section 8.4). These would include copies of release forms you have used to obtain those records.

❑ Correspondence from, to, and about the client.

❑ Any materials the client has brought related to diagnosis or treatment.

❑ Anything else you think is relevant at present or will be in the future.

### When a Case Is Closed

After termination, or if the records become too bulky, a client's pages can be transferred to a manila folder and filed for "permanent" storage in a different section of your locked cabinet. If you indicate the dates of service provision on the outside, it will make it easier to prune your records after 10 years (as suggested by Constance Fischer, PhD, of Pittsburgh, PA). See Section 1.6 on retention of records and their disposal.

## 1.5　Record Security

Privacy of information is the goal; the methods of achieving it are security. HIPAA—which was originally passed in 1996, took effect in 2003, and has been updated with the Health Information Technology for Economic and Clinical Health (HITECH) Act in 2009 and the HIPAA Omnibus Final Rule in 2013—set minimum standards for protecting the security of health and mental health records, as well as standards for the security of electronic and other health information. It also established a set of clients' rights regarding their health and mental health information. To function in health care, clinicians must understand HIPAA, and this means learning a new set of acronyms. Sorry, but we'll try to make it as smooth as we can.

HIPAA's rules apply to five kinds of "covered entities" (CEs)—individuals and organizations required to comply with HIPAA:

1. Recognized health care providers, which do not include some types of providers (e.g., acupuncturists).

2. Health plans, including health maintenance organizations (HMOs), managed care organizations (MCOs), and other insurers and payers.

3. Health care payment clearinghouses, which are companies that translate bills and claim forms for electronic claims submission (ECS) to payers.

4. Administrators of health savings accounts (HSAs) of different kinds, such as flexible spending accounts (FSAs).

5. Medicare discount drug card providers.

All of these CEs collect, store, and transmit PHI, and so are subject to HIPAA. Financial institutions that may process client payments (such as banks or credit card processors) are not included and so are not required to comply with HIPAA. They are also not business associates (BAs), since their actions are normal financial transactions and not carried out just for CEs (see below and HIPAA's Sections 164.504(e) and 164.532(d–e) for more).

The reason why financial institutions are not subject to HIPAA illustrates an important point about PHI. PHI is defined as information that "relates to the past, present, or future physical or mental health or condition of an individual; the provision of health care to an individual; or the past, present, or future payment for the provision of health care to an individual" (HIPAA Section 164.501). In the course of their businesses, financial institutions see only the client's identifiers; these are not linked to any clinical information. The large but often unclear point is that the health care information has to be "attached" to a person to become PHI and so be in need of protection. For example, even specific information like diagnoses and treatments is not in need of protection if it is not and cannot be linked to an individual's identity. HIPAA lists many kinds of information (names, addresses, phone numbers, medical record numbers, URLs, fingerprints, etc.) that, when removed, "deidentify" a record—making it no longer PHI.

## HIPAA and Privacy

HIPAA's privacy and security regulations concern how client information is safeguarded when it is collected, created, stored in your office, shared with other providers, used in teaching, training, consultation, or research, and sent to insurers. It is the *information* in the record that is protected by this law; the format or medium in which the information is kept is irrelevant. So the law applies not only to electronic records (e.g., computer documents, faxes, data entry), but also to paper records, faxes, even oral communications (e.g., conversations, telephone calls, and messages), or records in any medium. Most consultations and teaching are also covered. The full text of the most relevant parts of HIPAA can be found at a dedicated website (http://www.hhs.gov/ocr/privacy/hipaa/administrative/index.html).

HIPAA, though large and detailed, can be divided into three sections, each with a number of rules and standards.

1. The Privacy Standards concern the maintenance of confidentiality and the access to an individual's PHI. This is the part clinicians are most concerned about.

2. The Security and Electronic Signature Standards concern verification of identity and accuracy of *electronically* transferred data. Passwords and encryption are essential. Again of concern and application to clinicians.

3. The Electronic Health Transactions Standards concern information like membership in health insurance programs, eligibility for specific benefits, coordination of

benefits across different insurers, charges and payments, and so forth. These require the adoption of Standard Code Sets for each kind of transaction to describe persons, disorders (*International Classification of Diseases* [ICD] codes), services (*Current Procedural Terminology* [CPT] codes), and payments. This very complex set of computer programs is provided to you by your billing service, your billing program's developers, or the insurers you deal with. It is the support system for health care in the United States, and although it is much less visible to clinicians than to billers and insurers, it has a major and increasing impact on clinicians' work.

PHI is used for **treatment, payment, and health care operations (TPO).** Exact definitions can be found in HIPAA Section 164.501, but here are some simplified versions.

"Treatment" takes place when a provider offers or manages health care or related services, consults with other providers, or makes a referral. It includes communicating with family members.

"Payment" includes what a health care plan does to obtain premiums, determine eligibility and benefits (coverage), and provide payment to the provider or reimbursement to the patient. These activities can include coordinating benefits with other insurance providers, monitoring copayments and deductibles, assessing the client's health, determining the medical necessity of care, and reviewing utilization.

"Health care operations" is a very general term that includes at least the following activities: quality assessment and improvement activities; review of the performance, competence, or qualifications of health care or non-health-care professionals; training of students or practitioners; accrediting, licensing, or credentialing of health care professionals and organizations; medical reviews, legal services, and auditing functions, including fraud and abuse detection and compliance programs; and a variety of actions to support business administration, planning, sales/marketing, customer service, grievance resolution, due diligence, and so forth.

As you can see, almost every kind of activity is addressed by these regulations, which allow a great deal of freedom to share information about the individual.

HIPAA requires that at their first contact with you, clients must receive information about your ways of handling their PHI and assuring its privacy and security. This is done with an invitation to read your **NPP** and then to sign a separate **consent form**. But this is *not* a consent to release records, to treatment, or to anything else. It merely indicates that the client acknowledges that he or she has been exposed to the NPP—not that he or she understands or agrees with it. By HIPAA's rules, this is the only form of consent needed to allow you to share the client's PHI among all of HIPAA's CEs (see Section 164.506 of HIPAA).

No "accounting" (record, list) of these TPO uses (in your office) and disclosures (to other CEs or others) is required. However, if the PHI ever needs to be used for anything other than TPO or disclosed to most of those outside the organization, a written authorization (**release of information, or ROI**) is required. You must keep a record of these (rare) disclosures (but not of those common ones made for TPO), although if any disclosure is of electronic PHI you must keep such an accounting. We recommend keeping a record of all disclosures that involve using a ROI by keeping a copy of the ROI.

Your state's laws preempt HIPAA if they more stringently protect the client's privacy. In the regulations, there are so many exceptions and exclusions to these requirements for control over a client's PHI that the result is a very basic level of privacy protection. However, HIPAA will be improved over time.

## Steps for Becoming HIPAA-Compliant

1. Select someone in your practice to be the "HIPAA privacy officer" (or "security official" or "compliance official")—that is, the person responsible for implementing HIPAA. In a small practice, this is most likely to be you. Using your office manager in this role may not ensure that all clinical and legal considerations will be adequately integrated, and if this person should leave, continuity will be compromised.

   a. Your first task is to become informed about the Act (a good place to start is http://www.hhs.gov/ocr/privacy/hipaa/understanding/training).

   b. Second, you need to understand the flow of PHI in your practice. How is PHI currently accepted into, created, stored, accessed, used (in your practice), and disclosed (to those outside your office)? This is accomplished by conducting a **risk analysis**—that is, seeking to discover ways in which an "unauthorized release" of PHI might occur during these processes. The written version of this risk analysis becomes a crucial document in case of a HIPAA investigation. Roy Huggins has written a clarifying article (http://www.onlinetech.com/resources/references/what-s-in-a-hipaa-risk-analysis).

   c. Third, you must discover, from reading, consultation, and continuing education programs, how much of HIPAA you will actually have to implement, considering that your local laws are likely to be more stringent and that HIPAA allows you to tailor safeguards to your risks and setting. For example, HIPAA is "scalable," meaning that small practices do not have to manage security the ways a clinic has to.

2. Create a written set of policies for implementing the procedures of HIPAA (a **HIPAA Policies and Procedures Manual, or HP&PM**). Begin with a simple folder of your HIPAA-related documents and procedures and organize it over time. The rationale for creating an HP&PM offered by the APA Practice Organization's lawyers is that such a manual will become crucial if you are investigated. This manual and the documentation that its practices are being followed will be the way to show that the "unauthorized disclosure" of PHI could not have come from your office.

   **FORM 1.2**

   The checklist offered as Form 1.2 is not a substitute for an HP&PM, but it can guide your implementation of privacy/security practices and can provide some documentation of your efforts and their effectiveness, especially if it is completed every year or as necessary to address changes.

3. Any staff members who may see clients' PHI must be trained in HIPAA's rules on privacy. This is an opportunity to review ethical and local legal rules, as well as your office's practices with them. (See Section 8.2 for more on training staff members in privacy practices.)

4. Develop the following paperwork. Most chapters include the needed forms:

   a. An NPP. (See Section 6.4.)

   b. A HIPAA consent form. (See Section 6.4.)

   c. A HIPAA-informed, ethically aware, and locally legal authorization form for disclosures of PHI and ROI. (See Section 8.4.)

# A Checklist of Security Procedures for a Small Psychotherapy Practice

To the privacy/security compliance officer,

For each statement below, circle T (true), F (false), or ? (don't know), and take any immediate actions necessary to block potential threats to privacy. Write notes on the back. Repeat at least yearly.

Date completed: ____ / ____ / ____ by _____, who is the

privacy/security compliance officer of_____.

1. **Personnel**

   a. A privacy/security compliance officer has been appointed and made responsible for data security. This person keeps informed about legal developments (such as HIPAA and HITECH) and technical issues (such as hardware and software); trains all current staff members, new hires, and temporary workers; makes necessary changes when an employee leaves the practice; and similar continuing and developing functions.  T  F  ?

   b. We conduct background checks on all new hires, and comply with all laws and regulations about employees.  T  F  ?

   c. All employees have been trained in all our office rules and the consequences of breaking them.  T  F  ?

   d. All employees receive initial training in privacy and security, periodic security reminders, in-service training, and monitoring from the privacy/security compliance officer.  T  F  ?

   e. These training efforts and their outcomes are documented and evaluated.  T  F  ?

   f. All staff members have access to only the information and records they need to perform their job functions.  T  F  ?

2. **Physical controls over information**

   a. The staff areas are locked at the end of the workday and whenever no staff member is present.  T  F  ?

   b. Former employees do not have keys or access to the office, files, or computers.  T  F  ?

   c. Passwords and IDs are not written in any easily accessible locations or kept on the computers.  T  F  ?

   d. All office computers are in areas with no client access, or have covers, or are arranged so that no client can see the screens.  T  F  ?

   e. Staff members have been trained never to leave a monitor unattended. We use "sleep" programs, password-activated automatic screen savers, timed logoff programs, or other means as appropriate to make access to protected health information (PHI) unavailable when a computer is not being used.  T  F  ?

*(continued)*

f.  We do not call out clients' last names in the waiting room and do not have them sign in on a sheet that other clients might see, or use only first names or other acceptable methods.    T   F   ?

g.  All papers with PHI are placed in locked files or are shredded on the premises by the time the office is closed for the day.    T   F   ?

h.  Only bonded records destruction companies are employed, and records of all destruction are maintained.    T   F   ?

i.  The privacy/security/compliance officer keeps records of all PHI-containing equipment that we own, lease, or operate. The officer monitors this equipment at regular intervals and whenever it is sent for maintenance, repair, or replacement, to ensure against accidental unauthorized releases of PHI.    T   F   ?

j.  <u>We do not use Social Security numbers for record-keeping purposes or identification purposes.</u> When these need to be recorded, they are not easily visible or accessible.    T   F   ?

## 3. Security of electronic data and electronic PHI

a.  Each staff member needing access to records or documents has a different, unguessable, sufficiently complex, and regularly changed password.    T   F   ?

b.  All computers and mobile devices have malware protection, which is updated regularly.    T   F   ?

c.  When we access the Internet, we have a software firewall, private networks, and similar protections, which are updated and tested regularly.    T   F   ?

d.  Portable computers, cellphones, tablets, and other mobile devices are either prevented from using wireless connections or used only over secure wireless connections.    T   F   ?

e.  Passwords or other secure identification and access methods are used on all portable devices.    T   F   ?

f.  Encryption is used for all messages transmitted to and from employees' homes or outside the office to the office's computers, and from the office to any other sites.    T   F   ?

g.  All documents of any kind used in the office are safeguarded to current standards of security when stored in our office or other places for which we have responsibility.    T   F   ?

h.  Backups of all electronic client data are frequent, regularly scheduled, checked for accuracy and availability, encrypted, stored off-site, and destroyed at regular intervals.    T   F   ?

i.  The systems administrator or the compliance officer has prepared a written plan to handle emergencies and recover our PHI from disasters.    T   F   ?

j.  The computer's systems will not allow any new software to be added. Only the systems administrator can overcome this restriction.    T   F   ?

k.  All computer drives, magnetic tapes, DVDs or CD-ROMs, flash drives and other portable drives, and other devices that hold electronic PHI or other data are either physically destroyed or wiped with proven utility programs before they are junked, recycled, sold, donated, or otherwise disposed of or serviced (on the premises or off).    T   F   ?

l.  Lost or misplaced mobile devices have methods to erase their contents remotely.    T   F   ?

m. Emails requesting consultation or referrals on listservs to forums are double-checked before being sent, to be sure that they do not contain PHI. Specific ages, occupations, or other identifying details are removed. Rather than provide identifying information about the client the poster will describe the services needed.    T   F   ?

*(continued)*

**4. Telephones, answering machines, voicemail, and facsimile machines**

    a.  Staff members have been trained to keep their voices low, so that their phone conversations cannot be overheard by patients or uninvolved employees.    T  F  ?

    b.  All staff members have been trained about what questions to ask and what to tell or not to tell callers about our clients.    T  F  ?

    c.  The compliance officer regularly arranges calls to our staff to ask for client information, in order to test our telephone security measures.    T  F  ?

    d.  Employees are trained to leave only nonspecific messages on clients' answering machines/voicemail, unless a client has previously agreed to the leaving of messages with confidential information.    T  F  ?

    e.  The office voicemail's or answering machine's volume is turned low when incoming messages are recorded and when messages are played, so that no one else can hear.    T  F  ?

    f.  All fax transmissions have a cover sheet with the phone numbers, number of pages, and a note about contents' confidentiality, and what to do in case of mistakes.    T  F  ?

    g.  Users of the fax machine do not use numbers not stored in the fax (so as to prevent dialing errors).    T  F  ?

    h.  When there is any concern, the recipient is phoned to confirm reception of the fax.    T  F  ?

    i.  No confidential information is ever discussed on portable, cordless, wireless, or cellular telephones, unless these are encrypted.    T  F  ?

**5. Releasing records**

    a.  Records are reviewed by a single designated person before being released.    T  F  ?

    b.  Requests for records are examined for legal compliance, completeness, relevance, accuracy, and so forth.    T  F  ?

    c.  Nonessential information is deleted, obliterated, or masked in our records before transmission.    T  F  ?

    d.  Only the HIPAA-compliant "minimum necessary information" is sent out.    T  F  ?

    e.  The recipient is always verified.    T  F  ?

    f.  No records are released until all uncertainties are resolved.    T  F  ?

    g.  The original request is maintained in the client's chart.    T  F  ?

**6. Administration**

    a.  We have HIPAA-compliant business associate contracts with all appropriate entities.    T  F  ?

    b.  The compliance officer tests all safeguards at irregular, unpublicized, but frequent intervals and document the results.    T  F  ?

    c.  Changes and improvements to these safeguards are budgeted for and implemented in a timely fashion.    T  F  ?

**7. Other points unique to our office or practice:**

    d. Business associate (BA) contracts. BAs are nonemployees who are not CEs, but who perform services for a CE. They may send out your bills or answer your phone, and so have access to your clients' PHI. They must agree, by means of a BA contract, to safeguard the privacy of PHI with methods like the ones CEs must use. Many such contracts are available on the Internet (see, e.g., http://mbpros.com/pdfs/business_associate_agreement.pdf), but you should ask your BAs for these, rather than try to develop your own.

    e. Keep records of your HIPAA efforts and compliance, and monitor your practice's adherence to your "HIPAA Policy and Procedures Manual."

5. Develop policies and procedures concerning PHI, to allow clients to do the following:

    a. "Access" their records. Because access is deliberately not defined in HIPAA, it can mean clients' reading records; having the records read to them; reviewing the records, either alone or with you; or receiving a summary, a copy, or any alternative to which you and a client agree.

    b. "Amend" their PHI. Clients who disagree with anything in your records cannot force you to change ("alter") or delete information from your records, but you must offer them the opportunity to add to ("amend") your records with written statements, which you then include in any records you release after that date.

    c. Complain about privacy violations. (See Section 8.9.)

    d. Revoke and revise an authorization to disclose their records. (See Chapter 8.)

## Tips for Record Security

We must keep all our case records, including the identifying data in a billing system, in a secure place (APA, 2010, Standard 6). But we also need to remember that no place is totally secure. We are not required to use methods that are as secure as U.S. military regulations or European health care standards require; we are only required to use the methods considered typical of our peers–the standards of practice–and required by HIPAA.

- HIPAA requires you to secure your computerized records from disasters as well as prying eyes, so design a simple-to-use, practical-to-implement, regular backup program for your computer records. The classic backup method is to make a copy each week of your clinical files to an external hard disk and store it off-site in a secure place. This method has several steps that must be remembered and performed, and so it may actually be less effective for security, because the procedures are not often carried out. Online backup systems (see, e.g., Mozy.com, Carbonite.com, Crashplan.com, SugarSync.com, and SpiderOak.com) are automated, inexpensive, reliable, size-efficient, and speedy, and they are encrypted, off-site, stored in multiple locations, and professionally maintained., Because there are so many online backup systems and because they are continually adding features, do a search and visit some developers' sites when you are ready to implement such a system (and perhaps again at intervals of a few years). We believe that in order to maintain security, it is a necessity first to encrypt on your computer any data you want to back up before uploading it to any site.

- Some therapists quaintly insist on a paper "hard copy" backup of computerized records, without realizing that by printing out their records they have increased the risk of disclosure from almost zero to fairly high, because many more people can read paper than can access their computers.

- Another recommendation is to have a laptop just for work, which goes into a locked file cabinet at the end of the day. If it doesn't leave your office, there is a lower risk of its getting lost or stolen. Some use a laptop for client records that is never connected to the Internet ("air-gapped"), and thus is better protected.

- If your computer ever needs service or upgrading, anyone at the repair facility can read your clinical files if you have not encrypted them, so encryption is a must. The repair facility will need a BA contract as well.

- Operating systems include encryption (Apple computers come with FileVault, which will encrypt your entire machine, and Windows has BitLocker). However, if you want greater convenience, buy and *use* a file encryption program (such as those available from Symantec.com [PGP], Axantum.com, and gnupg.org). Some programs are free of charge, but they are not costless to produce, so consider making a donation. Programs may allow encryption of individual files, only of folders, or only of the whole hard disk. Encrypting the entire hard drive is recommended in case you lose your machine. It will not slow your work when you are doing word processing. Some programs encrypt email as well as documents, web connections, mobile devices, and so forth. Some may secure email, but there are specialized programs for this purpose (see, e.g., Zixsecurity.com, ciphersend.com, and Hushmail.com), or your current email program may have available add-ons to secure it.

- When you sell or give away your old computer, you should erase the files on your hard drive. Deleting the files or using the Trash/Recycle Bin application is not enough; when you do this, only their addresses are removed, and they can easily be recovered. You need to use an overwriting program like Eraser (a free program for PCs) to make them truly unrecoverable. For Macs use full disk encryption with File Vault 2 to achieve the same result.

- If you are sharing an office with another clinician, and if your two practices are independent of one another, you are should have separate, locked file cabinets.

### Breaches of Privacy

The HIPAA Omnibus Final Rule of late 2013 extended and clarified many issues, the major one being a redefinition of the loss of confidentiality of medical records. What was "an unauthorized disclosure" that might cause harm is now called "an impermissible use or disclosure" of PHI, which actually implies several new risks and procedures. It no longer requires the presumption or documentation of harm. For example, it can include just viewing of PHI by insiders who are not authorized to see such PHI.

CEs must now *presume* that any suspicion of loss of privacy when PHI is in their or their BAs' possession is a breach and carry out the burdensome procedures, including completing a full investigation, notifying all affected clients, starting mitigation procedures, and publishing public notices. The Omnibus Final Rule also created a hierarchy of financial penalties ranging from $100 to $50,000. The good news here is that small practices that have tried to comply with HIPAA are very unlikely to be fined more than the minimum.

The best news is that you can avoid all of this by showing that there is a "low probability" that the PHI has been compromised. This is achieved by a thorough and documented risk assessment of (1) the nature and extent of the PHI involved; (2) to whom the PHI may have been disclosed; (3) whether that PHI was actually acquired or viewed; and (4) the extent to which the risk to the PHI has been mitigated (e.g., promises from a medical office that received misdirected faxed PHI that the faxes have been destroyed). The risk assessment process should be specified in your office's HP&PM. After doing this risk assessment, a CE can decide whether it needs to go through the breach notification process or not. There is one more important protection: **If the PHI was encrypted** ("secured"), the notification process can be avoided, although the investigation described above is still necessary and the report of the investigation must be maintained for years.

# 1.6  Retention of Records

When therapy ends and a case is closed, the records need to be preserved so that you can do the following:

- Comply with laws and ethics. The ethics codes of all the mental health professions require us to preserve our records, as do state licensing laws.

- Assure continuity of care (e.g., when a client transfers to a new clinician).

- Defend ourselves from some belated accusation. Despite statutes of limitations, the laws are in flux, and court decisions have extended the client's time to sue (e.g., "2 years after the discovery of damage").

- Licensing boards rarely have such statutes of limitation.

- Qualify the client for some services in the future (e.g., Social Security Disability Insurance, or a special college program for a person with a learning disability).

- Restart a case if a client returns for treatment.

- Cope with some other situation that is presently unforeseeable.

## How Long Should Records Be Kept?

The rules for retention of records are complex, overlapping, and dependent on a host of variables—such as type of services, location, professional discipline, contractual obligations, and contents of the record. Partly to eliminate some confusion, HIPAA set a minimum of 6 years for retaining all PHI, and this is often the best simple rule. However, the Internal Revenue Service expects you to keep financial records for 7 years, as do the current APA guidelines (APA, Committee on Professional Practice and Standards, 2007). Medicare requires keeping records for 10 years (42 C.F.R. Section 422.504 (d)(2)(iii)). Social Security Disability Insurance can be awarded retroactively. Malpractice suits may have short time limits, but breach of contract may go back further, depending on state tort laws and even criminal laws. Suits alleging later discovery of harm done to a child in treatment can go back much further. Generally, complaints to licensing boards have no time limit, and your records will be your main (and probably your only) defense. We therefore recommend keeping all records for 10 years from last contact, and children's records for 10 years after they reach your state's age of majority. This second recommendation exceeds most rules, since the likelihood of a suit decreases greatly over time and is small after 10 years.

## Suggestions about Retaining Records

- If you have a secure space, keep the whole record forever for your own protection.

- Write the "discard date" on the outside of the folder when you close the case and store the record.

- At your established "discard date," destroy the records (see below).

- We do not recommend offering clients the choice of receiving the records directly or of destroying the records, because (1) they cannot anticipate the needs for the records; (2) they do not own the records, only the control of the contents; (3) they do not have the training to understand the records; and (4) you may need the records.

- Whatever retention procedures you choose, be sure to document it in sufficient detail in your HP&PM (see Section 1.5), and keep copies where your attorney, your family, or another therapist (see the discussion of professional wills and emergency plans in Section 1.7) can find it.

- An additional consideration is the constant changing of technology. Old electronic records will not be readable on newer computers. Storage media such as optical disks and even USB ports are disappearing from computers now, and so records maintained on them will soon be inaccessible. Storage in the "cloud" will be permanent (until you stop paying for the account), but the documents' format may not be readable in the future. You could save your records as ASCII code ("plain text" or "text only"), which will never be unrecognizable, but all formatting (highlighting, text size, boldface, etc.) will be lost. Alternatively, Adobe Acrobat has a version of .pdf suitable for archiving, called PDF/A. For convenience, devise a plan to remind yourself to transfer all old records for which the format may change when you update your computer.

## Disposing of Your Records

Papers may be shredded, as can CDs and DVDs. External drives can be securely erased for reuse or physically destroyed for recycling. Also, be absolutely consistent in using your procedures, because any exceptions would suggest to a malpractice attorney that you have something to hide. Lastly, you may consider developing some standard form for recording which records you disposed of, when, and how, for both documentation and defense.

Even when destroying records, you have to maintain their confidentiality. You can't just throw them in the trash. A simple shredder is inexpensive, but shredding takes time. You might organize a group of your peers with old records to take them all to a professional disposal firm that offers large-volume shredding services (do a Web search of "records management" for your locality) and get a "certificate of destruction." Or a mobile shredding truck may come to banks near you. Costs are usually $100–200 for a large weight of records.

## 1.7 When You Close Your Practice, Retire, or Die: Preserving Your Records with a Professional Will

You are ethically and legally responsible for protecting the confidentiality of and access to your records if you should become unable to care for them. The ethical codes of the professions require these preparations: See Standards 3.12, 6.02, and 10.09 of the APA code (APA, 2010); Sections 1.07, 1.15, and 3.04(d) of the National Association of Social Workers (NASW) code (NASW, 2008); and Sections B.6.g, B.6.h, and C.2.h of the American Counseling Association (ACA) code (ACA, 2005). McGee (2003) further describes the ethical points and other considerations in a highly recommended article.

The closing of your practice because of your relocation, disability, or incapacity; temporary or permanent retirement; loss of license to practice; or untimely demise requires assuring the well-being of your clients. Accordingly, there are significant ethical, legal, and practical matters to be addressed.

There do not appear to be any universal standards for a "professional will" to address these concerns, but at this writing at least three states and one Canadian province require psychologists to submit a will to their licensing board, and so writing such a will is likely to become a more general requirement in the future. Such a will is an informal document and requires only signatures. It is not related to your personal will and will not be probated.

The suggestions below have been gathered from many sources and the guidelines of other professions. (A list of additional resources, entitled "Resources for Closing a Practice and Making a Professional Will," is provided as Appendix A of this book.) We have organized the discussion below into two large sections. The first addresses closing your practice over a period of time, as would happen when you retire or move. The second section addresses what to do now to prepare for the possibility of unexpected death or sudden incapacity. Because you cannot foretell the future, we recommend that you negotiate all these arrangements with your colleagues, **this month.**

There are at least three professional roles for which you should leave instructions, so that these can be filled by one or more persons (the three roles do not have to be filled by three different individuals). First, the **administrator** of your professional will is the one responsible for carrying out its provisions. The best choice would be a member of your discipline, who will understand the issues. If your unavailability is sudden, a **successor professional** will provide at least emergency or brief services (as a "bridge therapist") to your clients and may take on their cases. It would be best to name several successors to work together, if one successor is unavailable when an emergency arises, or if one has a personal or other conflictual relationship with any of your clients. Last, the **custodian of your records** maintains their security and assures their legal release. This may be the same person who assumes one of the other roles, or it may be a different person for reasons of practical access or longevity. Do not simply ask a friend or friends to assume these obligations as a personal favor; too much work is involved, and the emotional burden is high. Select and negotiate these functions with trusted colleagues. Arrange remuneration for each role out of your collectibles or estate. Pay the custodian for the costs of storage and the burdens of maintaining the security and potential access as a necessary expense of your retirement or estate.

## Closing Your Practice

Despite what you may have heard, practices are rarely worth much, because they are so closely tied to an individual. It may be preferable simply to pay another professional to assume the duties of safeguarding your records and responding to calls and mail, and to explicitly allow a "bridge therapist" to refer or to accept as clients any who might call or show up after you become unavailable.

### Your Obligations to Clients: Continuity of Care

If you retire or otherwise close your practice, you have obligations to your current clients. With some, you will finish therapy or refer them to other professionals. All will need to be informed that you are leaving practice, when your office will close, and how they may obtain their records should they need them. They must be given sufficient time to make the best resolutions and least traumatic alternative arrangements. We recommend allowing clients not less than 60 days, depending on how often you are seeing them and how termination issues will be dealt with; the earlier they are notified, the better. You should make clear recommendations for those you believe require continued services. You simply cannot discontinue treatment with clients in need, because this can be seen as "abandonment"—which is both unethical and grounds for a malpractice suit. Of course, make sure that the practitioners to whom you refer clients are both available and offer appropriate and high-quality services, in order to avoid problems with "negligent referrals." It is entirely appropriate for you to make the initial calls to these successor therapists, once you have a signed ROI from the client(s) you wish to refer.

If you are retiring, set a hard date after which you will not take new clients, and then let your caseload wind down; this will be easier on you and others. But, because you may not have the time, **prepare, this week, a termination letter** to be sent to your current and recent clients (e.g., clients you have seen within the last 18 months) notifying them of why you are closing up shop; exactly when the office will close; who will keep your records and how to reach them; whom clients can call in an emergency; what other therapists and community resources (agencies, professional organizations) are available if they want more services; and so on. Make it clear that it is the clients' choice to pursue services, and that the confidentiality of their records will be preserved. A copy of this letter (and any returned mail) should be placed in each client's file. Post a copy of this letter in your office, on your website, in any online directories where you are listed, and in any other suitable places. Have your staff remind clients of the date of your closing your practice. Finally, place copies with your professional will, regular will, life insurance policies, transfer-on-death notices to your bank, and so forth. Instruct your administrator where to look for these.

### The Duties of the Custodian of Your Case Records

You must assure your records' confidentiality and security (against theft, prying eyes, accidental discarding, etc.), preservation (against fire, rodents, water damage, etc.), and access (for a successor therapist, defense against a complaint or suit, response to a subpoena, etc.).

These needs will be present even after your death or a client's. The following checklist will help you address them.

❑ Devise a letter of explanation for the custodian about your files. The letter should cover such items as how client records are filed and named (by last name, by date of last contact or discharge,[1] by a case number,[2] etc.) where they are kept,[3] the short-hand or abbreviations you have used in your notes, and destruction schedules and procedures. It may be appropriate to explain where to find the office keys and your appointment book (Spayd & Wiley, 2001).

❑ Provide the custodian with information about your professional online accounts; these should include your website, domain, and social media accounts. All login and password information should be provided. The custodian should update your website with an announcement about whom to contact for information related to your practice. All online directory accounts should be canceled, as well as memberships in professional organizations (which may also include your contact information in online directories). Social media accounts should also have a notice urging people to contact the custodian if they wish to contact you. In addition, provide the password to your smartphone, along with instructions for deleting clinical contacts. Explain how to transfer or delete records from computers or other digital devices. Lastly, all professional email account passwords should be given to the custodian, along with instructions for an auto-reply email to tell those who email that they should contact the administrator of your practice for any outstanding issues. Much of this can be facilitated with a password manager program such as Dashlane, Last Pass, or 1Password.

❑ Close out case records with summaries, and bring all case notes up to date. Respond to any unfinished correspondence.

❑ Destroy some out-of-date records, following your usual procedures, so there will be less to transfer.

❑ Scanning your paper records may make sense. Do a Web search of "document management" or "records management" in your area for local companies.

❑ Actually transfer the records physically to your records' custodian, or contract to have this done.

❑ Send copies of the termination letter described earlier (about closing your practice and who will have custody of your records) to the following:

  ❑ Your state licensing board. If you wish either to surrender your license or to become inactive, request this as well.

  ❑ Your referral resources, and those who refer clients to you.

  ❑ Your professional friends.

---

[1]So that the files can be pruned regularly by destroying files older than the number of years they legally must be kept.

[2]And, if so, where to find the cross-index of names and numbers.

[3]With the keys for your locked files and the locations and passwords for your computerized records, both clinical and financial.

❑ Your professional insurance carrier.

❑ Your billing service, if you use one.

❑ Your business and personal lawyers.

❑ All health plans with which you have done business. (Prepare a list of these organizations; note that the letter described earlier may not be sufficient for such organizations if you must also address the issues of unpaid bills.)

### Your Financial and Contractual Obligations

The following checklist will aid you in resolving any outstanding financial or contractual issues.

❑ Meet with your lawyer, banker, accountant, financial advisor, and others to review any unmet obligations you have. Draft any needed letters, notifications, forms, or agreements.

❑ Review the procedures for dissolution that are written into any partnership, professional corporation, or professional association agreements. Take the appropriate legal, financial, or other actions.

❑ Devise a plan for the formal dissolution of your business entity (i.e., distribution and liquidation of assets; notification of the appropriate authorities, such as your state government's Secretary of State). Your professional lawyer should handle this along with your accountant, so make sure they are notified of your circumstances.

❑ Deal with all your rental agreements and leases—office space, cars, equipment, utilities, telephone, Internet access, advertising contracts, cleaning contracts, and so on, as well as social media accounts.

❑ Arrange to dispose of your real assets. Used office equipment typically brings 10–50 cents on the dollar, depending on age and condition. Decide who is to receive it, or donate, sell, or otherwise dispose of your office equipment, supplies, and any other real property or real estate.

❑ Make arrangements for ethical disposal, sale, or transfer of your psychological tests, library, biofeedback equipment, or other professional materials.

❑ Arrange the authority and means to satisfy your accounts payable and accounts receivable. Make sure that your administrator can legally accept monies due you and pay your bills. Decide on an appropriate collection process and assign responsibility for it. Consider forgiving debts.

❑ Create a plan to make timely payments of federal, state, local, and other taxes; employee insurance; workers' compensation premiums; and the like.

❑ Make arrangements for your professional liability insurance. Receive or purchase a "tail" for your professional liability insurance if you have a "claims-made" policy (see Section 4.3). You (or your estate) can still be sued or complained against after you close up shop, and a "tail" protects against future complaints about your previous actions. Some insurance companies offer this at no cost if you have been a client for a while, but they must be notified. If you have the time and have had a number of high-risk cases, consider raising your coverage significantly for the last year of your practice, as your tail's limits will be based on the coverage limits in force during this time. Do not cancel your policy; let it expire some time after you stop practicing.

❑ Do not cancel premises insurance when you move out; wait until you are no longer the legal tenant.

❑ Notify your state, national, and other professional associations, and any other professional committees, groups, or organizations to which you belong or pay dues. Resign or choose an inactive status rather than letting your membership lapse for lack of dues.

❑ Consider canceling your journal subscriptions, depending on what professional roles (if any) you intend to maintain in retirement.

## If You Should Suddenly Become Incapacitated or Die

Devise now a contingency plan for your practice. Then discuss it with your family, some colleagues, and your staff, and perhaps your personal lawyer; again, however, this plan is not part of your personal will and will not be probated. Assure that your plan, which is called here a "letter of instructions," is very rapidly accessible to all those who must carry out your directions. It should address all the concerns and issues raised above, as well as some that arise because of the sudden loss. The checklist that follows can guide you in devising a contingency plan.

❑ Arrange for a staff member, specific friend, or family member to notify others of your disability or death. Besides those described above, rapid notification should be given to your professional and personal lawyers and your accountant. You should include all the ways of reaching each of these persons in your letter of instructions.

❑ Because a situation might arise suddenly in which you are unavailable, a list of all of the ways and places in which you could be contacted by those concerned about your well-being should be easily available to your staff and family. Your staff should have "all contact information for [your] spouse, life partner, adult children, or anyone else who would likely know of [your] whereabouts or sudden health problems" (Tracy, n.d.). Tracy suggests that staff members should be formally permitted to make such calls and be told how long to wait after your unexplained absence before making such calls. Train your staff in all these procedures.

❑ Since we have recommended that some records be maintained indefinitely, your custodian will have to make a similar "professional will" for the maintenance of your records in the event of his or her own retirement, disability, or death. (This could lead to an infinite regress; 15 years after treatment ends should cover all but infinitesimal risks, and CMS says that HIPAA does not apply to records more than 50 years old.)

❑ If you have not prepared a termination letter (see above), your administrator should be instructed to write a brief letter explaining your death or incapacity and the closing of your practice. It should address the issues of relevance to clients, such as access to records and referrals. This letter should explain the circumstances and suggest options. It can be sent to those who call and in reply to any professional mail or email you receive. You should provide a backup person, in the event that your administrator happens to have a conflicting dual role with any of the clients he or she will be contacting.

❑ The administrator should place a notice of your demise in the local newspaper of record and on your website. This can also be emailed or mailed to all recent clients, so that all are informed rapidly, explicitly, and simultaneously.

❑ You should also write an obituary for yourself, rather than burdening others with this responsibility. It should contain at least the facts of your life. See your current newspaper for guidelines. Keep it at your lawyer's office.

❑ Arrange a method to remind yourself regularly to review and update your letter of instructions. Your practice or that of your administrator may have changed.

❑ If you should die unexpectedly, a brief message should be placed on your voicemail or answering machine, or with your answering service, for future potential clients who call your office when referred by friends, colleagues, or advertisements. Try to arrange for these messages to be available for the next 12–18 months.

# CHAPTER 2

# Financial Tools and Procedures

## 2.1 Setting Financial Policies for Your Practice

The provision of psychotherapy in our society is both a business and a profession. As a business, it involves unavoidable dealings with money, and this is often problematic for therapists. They enter the field with a commitment to human service. Many have been trained at public expense or have been employed in a public service setting; they may worry that making a profit from the misery in others' lives is unjust. However, they may also be entering the field with student loan debt, and they certainly need to afford to survive. The simple truth is that a therapist who does not succeed as a businessperson will not be able to work independently. Private practice is not for every therapist, and this book can help you decide whether it suits you. You may discover that the effort is simply not worth the cost to your life.

As an independent practitioner, you *must* make decisions about many aspects of the business relationship with your clients. Choose options that seem fair, ethical, protective of both parties, and enforceable; then communicate them clearly, both orally and in writing. You will need policies and procedures to answer questions like these:

- When will you discuss money with the client, and how will you do it? On your website? During the phone intake? At the first meeting? Only when asked?

- How much will you charge (your "fee")?
  - Will you have different charges for different activities, or a per-hour charge for everything you do?
  - Will you do some free (*pro bono*) therapy, offer some discounts, use a sliding scale of charges based on a client's income and expenses, or charge everyone the same fee?
  - Will you charge for broken appointments (no-shows, late cancellations), and if so, how much?
  - Will you charge for everything you do like writing letters, longer phone calls, copying of records?

- How will you handle insurance coverage?
  - Will you join managed care organizations' (MCOs') "panels" of providers and "participate" (i.e., agree to provide services at the rates offered to you by these third-party payers)?

- If so, can you negotiate a higher fee from the MCO because of your specialties or on a case-by-case basis by being "out of network" (OON)? And will your clients then pay a larger part of your fee?
- Will you require "assignment of benefits" and be paid directly by the insurance company, or will you trust the client to pay you when the client is reimbursed?
- Will you prepare and submit insurance claims for clients, or simply supply bills they can submit?

- How will you handle delinquent accounts and when?
  - When will you discontinue seeing a client for not paying your fees?
  - Will you only send reminders, call the client, just rebill, or use collection letters?
  - At what point will you use collection agencies? Lawyers? Small-claims court?
  - When will you write off bad debts?

When you have made these decisions, incorporate them into your means of gaining informed consent (see the discussion of the client information brochure in Section 5.2).

This chapter does not fully address dealing with insurance. We discuss insurance and managed care issues in detail in Chapter 3.

## About Fees

Because few professional training programs teach about fees, the basics are covered here. Some other resources on marketing in independent practice can be found in Chapter 9.

One of the "professional pleasures" offered by private practice is the freedom to take on a case that interests you without regard to the client's ability to pay. Do not let greed or fear take away this freedom.

Our professional organizations recommend that we all do some unpaid work. The amount of such work is left to the conscience of the individual clinician. Many therapists dedicate a percentage (5–15%) of their practice to *pro bono* (unpaid or very-low-fee) services as part of their responsibility to society. Ethically, free therapy cannot be of a lesser quality or extent than paid therapy, so do not try to cut corners; either accept this rule or do no *pro bono* work. If a client has an unexpected and long-lasting loss of income, and neither termination, less frequent or shorter sessions, nor transfer is desirable, you might consider further work *pro bono* and bite the bullet. Many clinicians do *pro bono* work in nonclinical areas, such as consulting to civic organizations, mentoring or sponsoring students, and engaging in other charitable activities.

Finally, if you are terminating a client for lack of payment, be cautious and thorough, and try to get a payment plan agreed to. If it appears that it will be a sticky situation, consult with a colleague about issues of abandonment, client welfare, and the like, and note the consultation in your records. See also Section 7.3 on termination.

## Ethical Guidelines on Fees

Pope (1988c) has examined the laws and ethics pertaining to fee policies and procedures. The following discussion is based on his suggestions for avoiding common pitfalls.

**Ethically, you must make financial arrangements in advance of treatment,** so that consent to treatment is fully informed. Standard 6.04a of the American Psychological Association (APA) ethics code (APA, 2010) requires that "As early as feasible in a professional or scientific relationship, [the psychologist] and the client/patient . . . reach an agreement specifying the compensation and the billing arrangements." Tell the client your policies on charging for missed appointments, the maximum balance due you will tolerate, your policy on raising fees during the course of treatment, your use of a collection agency, and so forth. Make certain that the financial arrangements are fully understood by the client. For this, a written fee policy is a necessary part of your client information brochure (see Section 5.2).

It is best to have clients know your charges before you even meet for the first time, so that they are not seduced by your interview into forming a relationship that then imposes financial hardship or is even exploitative. You can place this information on your website and reiterate it during your phone or email intake, if you provide one.

You should know by the end of the first evaluation hour, from the social history information you have obtained, whether a client is able to pay you. For those who cannot, options include offering a referral elsewhere, *pro bono* work (for a limited number of client slots or hours per month), a sliding-scale fee policy, half-sessions at about half the full-session fee, less frequent sessions, and reduced fees for early afternoon or late morning hours (which are more difficult for employed clients and so are less often filled).

**Fee splitting** is taking a fee or paying a percentage of what is received from the client solely for making a referral. Although fee splitting is a common business practice, it can create conflicts of interest in human services: For instance, did you refer a client to Dr. F because she was the best clinician for that client, or because you were paid a fee or received compensation by other means from Dr. F? In an agreement with the Federal Trade Commission ("The FTC consent order text . . . ," 1992), the APA agreed not to prohibit paying for referrals. The rules in psychology (APA, 2010, Standard 6.07) allow payments that are based on the services provided (such as evaluation and recommendations before the referral) and not simply on making the referral. However, this may be too vague to enforce; state and discipline rules may differ; and arrangements are often complex. It is best to avoid even the appearance of fee splitting. Do not take payments of any kind for a referral, and be careful that you can justify the clinical appropriateness of a referral to a specific clinician—especially when you share an office, are friends, or have any kind of business connections. In each case, offer a client several options and let the client choose; treat all referrals similarly; and document your rationales in the client's file.

Accepting payment for your services in anything but money is **barter.** Barter is an ancient and flexible practice, and may give more people access to your services. The APA code of ethics (APA, 2010, Standard 6.05) allows barter and offers some guidelines. However, barter also presents great potential for exploitation, conflicts, and distortion of the professional relationship. Besides, you will have to declare the fair market value of your services as income. We recommend that you **do not barter** or exchange therapy for either goods (whose value can be questioned) or services (as this creates a dual relationship—i.e., that of employer–employee). Barter is a frequent source of ethics complaints. If a client has no money and you decide to help, offer your services *pro bono.*

## Setting Your Fees

Your "fee" is the amount you are willing to sell your services for. This should be the same as the amount you actually charge every client. If you decide to accept a lower payment from a client in financial distress or for any other reason, do so only occasionally, with good reasons, and document your rationale in detail in your notes to avoid any appearance of unfairness. And, for clarity, on your bill indicate your full fee, the fact of an "adjustment" (a credit to the client) but without giving a reason, and then your final "charge." Make sure you can justify the charge you set for each client; you may have to justify this to your board, an MCO, or a judge.

There is no standard method for setting fees, but here are several options to expand your horizons.

### Competitive Pricing

**Competitive pricing** is setting your prices to match, exceed, or underprice your competition, depending on whom you see as your competitors. Psychiatrists charge the most, with psychologists charging about 80% of that, and social workers charging 70% or less. Counselors and psychiatric nurses charge about 50%. By reading the online directory of clinicians at *Psychology Today* (http://therapists.psychologytoday.com/rms/prof_search.php) or other directories, you can see what those in your ZIP code are charging. Another source of information is http://www.fairhealthconsumer.org.

One more point about comparative fee setting deserves mention. Because of **antitrust laws**, professionals, who are supposed to be competitors, cannot conspire with each other in order to fix prices. We cannot say or even suggest to another practitioner, "I won't accept less than $75 an hour, and you shouldn't either," or "We should all refuse referrals from a company that pays less than $N per hour." The limitations do not apply to fees from government organizations, but be aware that this is all open to legal interpretation. For more on antitrust laws, see DeLeon et al. (2006). Also, professionals are free to exchange information about their rates (as above) in the context of providing information to the public on websites or online directories.

### Pricing by Negotiation

**Pricing by negotiation** is accepting a price that is arranged in the marketplace of buyers and sellers. With private-pay clients, be mindful that they are needy and therefore not your equals in negotiating a fee. The negotiation process requires self-confidence and autonomy (the freedom to look and go elsewhere), which stressed clients may lack. Most clients also lack an appreciation of your (quite high) costs in providing your services.

For many clients, the actual buyers of mental health services are their employers or their employers' human resources departments that deal with MCOs. If you join a panel, the MCO will offer you a fee, which is almost always not negotiable. Although there are alternatives to managed care (see especially Ackley, 1997, and Appendix C), marketing for independent practitioners is unavoidable: see Chapter 9 for a full discussion.

### Cost-Plus Pricing

**Cost-plus pricing** is determining your fee by adding together your fixed and variable costs plus a profit. This is the traditional pricing method in business, although not in private practice. If you take the time to compute your true costs (your "nut"), it can protect you from going out of business through excessive kindness or procrastination.

Knowing your nut is crucial for making all kinds of business decisions: "Should I hire an assistant or do this myself? Should I move my office? Can I afford this marketing plan?

Can I go on a vacation?" Look over your last year's expenses for everything related to your business (Schedule C of your 1040 will have most of these totals). Divide your total costs by the clinical hours you work to get your hourly cost of doing business—your hourly nut. You will be surprised at how high it is. Subtract your total costs from your gross income to discover your profit. Divide your profit by the *all* the hours you put into your practice to find out how little you really earn. Aim to reduce costs and increase income.

Do not try to add, say, 10% for "administrative expenses" when a client requires billing, or 20% for "extended contacts with MCOs for authorizations." First, your contract with an MCO will clearly state that you may not bill any of its clients separately for any other charges, and that the MCO will not pay such charges. Second, the MCO will see this as illegal because you will be charging insurance-covered clients a higher fee, not your agreed-to fee.

### Pricing by Time

**Pricing by time** is charging for each hour, regardless of the services provided (therapy, consulting, teaching, supervising, etc.). This is the most common practice, but disregards the stressors and subjective rewards of different activities, as well as preparation time for some activities.

### Pricing by Setting an Income Goal

**Pricing by setting an income goal** is choosing a desired yearly net income, adding your costs, dividing the sum by the number of hours you want to work, and calculating your hourly charge. This is worth considering for life or financial planning.

## Other Fee Arrangements

### Offering Discounts

Discounts can take several forms. First, MCOs demand a lower charge than your usual fee, with the rationale that it is a discount for a bulk order. They offer to send you many referrals, keep you busy, and fill your empty hours, and so they contend that they deserve a lower price than if you had to recruit and negotiate with one client at a time. See Chapter 3 for more on managed care.

You can offer discounts for various reasons, and most businesses do. However, you must make the rationale perfectly clear to the client and any insurance company, make it consistent with your state's insurance and business laws, and be entirely consistent in its application. It is altogether proper to offer clients who need less of your time a lower fee. A 15% discount for clients who pay by check, cash, or credit card at the time of service, and who do not need any paperwork or phone calls for insurance authorizations or billing or any other reason, is justified. The results are complete confidentiality, no nasty surprises if an MCO refuses to pay, and a predictable cash flow for both parties. This is the policy of the Boulder, CO, Psychotherapists' Guild (http://www.psychotherapistsguild.com), where the discount for no paperwork is 20% and requires payment at time of service. The only paperwork you might offer is a yearly statement with just the dates of service and payments made, to be used for the client's income taxes. For a medical savings account, a diagnosis and procedure code will be necessary, but providing these is still simple. If any other services are needed later, you could charge for them at the rates indicated originally. Note that you cannot do this with MCO clients, as you and the MCO have a contracted fee and the MCO prohibits you from charging more, but it is allowable when you are out of network for the client's insurance.

Another inventive, successful, and encouraging option has been developed by Volunteers in Psychotherapy of West Hartford, CT (http://www.ctvip.org), which describes itself as "a community nonprofit organization that provides truly private psychotherapy for no fee (or a low fee). Clients 'pay for' their therapy by doing independent volunteer work for the charity of their choice." Clients do not use insurance, and the more they volunteer, the less they pay. With this plan, all managed care intrusions are avoided—no reports, no confidentiality issues, no limits on treatment length or type (e.g., medications may be offered too). It may work for your setting.

### Sliding-Scale Fees

A sliding fee scale provides discounts based on a client's income, expenses, family size, etc. but can be problematic. It does not appear that any other business offers such discounts. Verification is awkward and may invite lying on the client's part and resentment on yours. Unless their use is made available to all clients and inclusive of other debts and income sources, they are discriminatory, and any rule will be unfair to some clients because everyone's circumstances are different. Also, since you are no longer charging everyone the same fee, insurers may see this as at least a violation of your contract. See below and Harris (2013).

While obviously relevant at intake and during treatment, sliding-scale fees can be offered when a client has had financial reversals and may be required by regulations to qualify for educational loan repayments, or in some publicly funded settings. As an example, Rachel Robbins, PsyD, has posted her sliding scales on a page of her website (http://www.drrachelrobbins.com/#!fees/c21vm).

**Caution:** Do not offer a payment plan of regularly spaced payments, because it may require your full participation in the rules of the federal and state laws on providing credit. Accepting credit cards is a much better alternative and is covered in Section 2.3.

### Pro-Rated Fees

By offering to charge essentially by the minute, you can often accommodate sessions that run over what was scheduled or shorten sessions, perhaps with follow-up appointments. This also works for phone consultation, simple check-ins, or sessions that fall toward the end of an episode of treatment.

### Self-Pay Arrangements for Confidentiality

If you can offer clients the option of not using their health insurance, the records you create (which you must keep both to be legal and to protect yourself) need never be released to a health insurer. The Health Insurance Portability and Accountability Act (HIPAA) Omnibus Final Rule clarified this option in September 2013. However, their release can still be required for other policies, such as disability and life insurance.

Someday the clients might be asked, "Have you ever been treated for a mental disorder?" or something similar. Should they say "no," knowing that your records will not then be requested? What about some future legal proceeding, such as a lawsuit that brings their current mental state into question and for which your records may help them (or not)? How can you maintain their privacy?

Here is one option. If a client wants to consult you about a "problem in living" and you work on that, doing no diagnostic work and with no mention of a "psychological condition," then the client could answer honestly that no such condition was diagnosed or treated. Similarly, Miller (2001) has indicated:

> I consider a diagnostic evaluation to be a separate service that I only conduct if the client requests it. Therefore, when I see a self-pay client, I do not record a diagnosis . . . for the vast majority of my clients, I am providing psychological consultation for personal and interpersonal issues. In other words, my clients are merely exercising their right to talk with or consult with a psychologist, and there is no reason that they need to carry a [DSM/ICD] diagnosis because they wanted to exercise that right. Therefore, if I have not diagnosed them, they can say that they have never been treated for a psychiatric condition. (p. 78)

### Pricing School Services

If you plan to do school consultation or training, develop a letter explaining your services (in nontechnical terms, if possible) and fee schedules. Give it to any school personnel who inquire about your services, and provide an estimate of the amount of your time required. Their response should be an authorizing note and signature on the estimate, a purchase order, or a letter agreeing to accept responsibility to pay for the services.

MCOs usually refuse to pay for educational testing, no matter how much pathology is involved. If a parent wants to use some insurance or agency resources to pay your fees, make it clear that you will bill the parents, and that *they* must talk to a case manager to arrange payment for your several hours of consulting. You may get the school to pay for your training the school's staff after you have done your work with the child (and thus make your fees a worthwhile cost to the parents), especially if the previously provided school services have been unproductive.

## Arranging and Discussing Fees with Clients

The resistance to setting up a fee arrangement in the first session comes almost completely from the therapist. There is a saying that if you tell a client, "We can worry about the money later," you are increasing your noncollectable fees by 20%. It is also unethical because it prevents informed consent. One of us (ELZ) has used phrasing like this:

> "There is one more issue we must talk about, and that is fees. My regular fee is $N per session. This is in line with the fees others with similar professional education and experience charge. I don't want finances to prevent your getting therapy. Take a minute and consider what I have said about how long your treatment is likely to take, and weigh your income and expenses, and tell me what you can manage."

ELZ finds that most clients agree to pay the regular fee. If they say they cannot or appear very reluctant, he has said, "Well, in light of your situation, tell me what you can afford, and I will accept that." ELZ has used this policy for years with few regrets. This is also a good time to introduce or reinforce paying for each session at its start. Note that this approach will not apply to managed care clients.

KK's approach is to mention the fee on her website and on the phone. KK has adopted a policy of not taking reduced-fee clients at intake, but reserving low-fee slots for current psychotherapy clients who are experiencing financial hardship. This allows KK to assess a person's commitment to therapy, and to have a sense of the treatment alliance by the time this circumstance may arise. Once her practice became well established, this approach worked well.

During the first session, KK will also review her policies and remind clients about her 48-hour cancellation policy and her late fees for clients who do not pay at the time of service. She frames these policies as "things that you already read in my forms, but that people sometimes forget about and don't like to be surprised by later." She also indicates that "if we are still working together next January, my fee will increase and I will begin letting you know several months before, so you can let me know if it will pose any problems for you and we will have time to discuss it."

Another therapist suggests that you consider making fee increases effective in April. Why? Selecting a time several months into the new year allows for people's deductibles to be applied to *other* medical providers. If clients start therapy after their insurance reimbursements apply, your services will feel more affordable to them. Announce your fee increase several months in advance. For people who are considering therapy, it's an incentive to get started right away, while the fee is lower. After your new fee goes into effect, give your current clients an extra month or two at the old rate. During this period, their bills and statements should show the new fee, but with a "courtesy discount" deducted. All these ideas are from Pauline Wallin, PhD, of Camp Hill, PA (personal communication, 2014).

If someone other than the client pays the fee, formal clarification may be needed (see Form 6.11) about fees, access to records and to the therapist, and other particulars. When the client is a child, however, parents do have the right to general information on progress and problems. This should be carefully spelled out in your client information brochure (see Section 5.2). Because divorce agreements and other settlements are binding only on those parties, not on their therapists, it is best to have the person who brings the child pay for services and collect reimbursement from the ex-spouse.

**Treating couples** may raise billing problems. MCOs have routinely not paid for treatment of couples by claiming that their policies do not cover marriage counseling because it is not medically necessary. Even when the focus is solely on the relationship, a relationship cannot be a client, cannot have medically necessary services, and so will not generally be covered by insurance. Medical necessity criteria ignore the relationships with partner, family, society and other contexts. (For more on the criteria, see Form 3.2.) Medical necessity requires that one person meets a diagnosis, that the treatment offered is appropriate and likely to lessen the symptoms, and that the documentation support alleviating this diagnosable condition. Because of these conditions, the chart will concern only the client (and not the couple), and the partner is included only as a collateral. Some therapists have alternated the identified client, and therefore the billing, from one partner to the other after, say, 10 sessions. The safest procedure would be to ask the insurers how they want this handled and to be extremely careful with documentation. If neither partner meets diagnostic criteria, do not pursue insurance, although the therapy may be very helpful. If the second partner is highly distressed, making him or her a second client, while clinically justified, creates confusion and risks for misusing insurance.

Clients with health maintenance organization (HMO), preferred provider organization (PPO), or other MCO contracts may expect their insurance to pay all your fees and will often ask about fees early in the first contact. If you do not participate in managed care, they may balk at your charges. Here is the way Beverly Celotta, PhD, of Gaithersburg, MD, handles this situation (personal communication, October 22, 2014). She tells clients something like this:

"First, I do not accept insurance and am not on any HMO [or PPO or other MCO] plans. However, I find that many clients can still afford treatment with me. Some are allowed to go out of their plan [network of providers] for slightly higher copays. Second, consider the costs of your deductible and coinsurance when you evaluate the total cost of treatment; using insurance may not be a bargain. Third, because I have lots of experience, I frequently can see clients for 12 sessions or fewer, and rarely over 20, and this will lower the total cost of treatment. When appropriate, some clients come every 2 weeks and some for a 30-minute session, either of which will lower the cost. By using these methods and not your insurance, treatment decisions will be entirely between us, no one else will have to know any details about your sessions, and I can use strategies (such as family therapy or parent consultations) that are often not covered by insurers. I can offer you a brief, free meeting so that we can further discuss these issues."

Be aware that if a client has managed care and you are on the client's insurance panel, you cannot charge the client more than what you have agreed to with the MCO and must charge him or her the contracted fee. For more on the financial problems and other risks of using insurance, see Handout 3.1.

## 2.2 The Income and Expense Records

An early and essential step in opening your business is to get an accountant[1]—first, to show you how to organize your business life, and then to provide ongoing guidance. Ask your colleagues for names, because familiarity with our kind of work is valuable. While many clinicians use computer tools such as Quicken and QuickBooks, an accountant can teach you how to think about income, expenses, taxes, and records. Even if you have been doing your own taxes for years, you may find it a comfort to have some additional support.

Every legitimate business expense (what you buy to make money) is really very valuable to you. Each reduces the income on which you must pay taxes. You are probably in the 50% tax bracket (federal income tax of 28%, state and local income taxes of about 5%, FICA of 15.7%, Medicare tax of about 4%, sales tax on non-business-related purchases of about 6%, etc.). Therefore, the true cost of purchases for your business is about 50% of what you pay or have to earn to buy it, because they are tax-deductible. This is the way the U.S. Congress, in its wisdom, has set up the country. Enjoy it. Buy whatever will make your business life easier and more efficient. Develop a business mindset; it can be fun and is essential for survival.

There are four components to recording your professional expenses. The first is a record

---

[1]If your accountant, your business lawyer, or any nonemployee will see clients' names, such a person should sign a business associate (BA) contract with you.

of all income; the second and third are a business checkbook and business credit card. The last is a summary record of outgo or expenses.

A record of your income can be as simple as a single page of paper for each month with appropriate column headings. One of us (ELZ) adds initials to names that are common. He receives income at two offices and so uses two columns because taxes are paid to two municipalities. Paychecks, from which taxes have already been deducted, go into a third column, with a fourth column reserved for other kinds of income. Checks are clustered in each deposit with a large bracket, with the total amount and date of deposit in the last column. If you are keeping electronic records, paper may be unnecessary, as long as you are checking your deposits and expenses each week and making sure there are no discrepancies in your online banking records. Some people do a hybrid method and keep mostly electronic records, with backup receipts in case of an audit or any other confusion.

## Your Checkbook

A checking account used exclusively for your practice is crucial in business record keeping, as well as for paying your business-related obligations and doing your taxes correctly. Try to avoid getting a business account, which is likely to cost more. Choose whether to compute a balance (double-entry bookkeeping) with each check, or to maintain a cushion of funds and just look at your balance when you need to write large checks. When you get a card to access your account (ATM card), try to get a credit card rather than a debit card, because of the possibility of greater financial loss if the debit card is stolen and misused.

## Choosing a Business Credit Card

It makes sense to get a separate credit card for your business and avoid using it for personal purchases. If you have more than one business, get a card for each; write a note on an adhesive slip on each card, to keep each card's use clear. Get bank cards (Visa or MasterCard) for all your accounts to save costs. Choose cards in terms of offered services you actually will use, such as rental car insurance coverage. Most of us do not use enough of the added services to make paying a yearly fee worthwhile. If you maintain a balance each month, look for the lowest interest rates; if you pay off your balance, look for cash-back rewards. Cards that give points or miles can lower the value of those by raising the number of miles to make a particular trip (inflation). Using the checks that are sent along with a credit card account and its statements should be avoided, due to huge interest rates.

## The Monthly/Quarterly Expense Summary

The last step in systematic recording of expenses is keeping a running summary of them. This helps you monitor expenses and is the basis for paying just the precise amount of quarterly estimated taxes. Getting a large refund after you file your yearly taxes means you've made an expensive (to you) loan to the government. We do not include a form for an expense summary, because each practice has different kinds of expenses. Look into your checkbook and credit card statements to develop your own list.

# 2.3    Methods of Billing for Payment

Be aware that billing and collecting are often stressful and complex. We suggest deciding either to invest the time needed to master and perform these tasks, or to delegate most of the functions (but not the responsibility) to a skilled biller.

Therapists rarely enjoy billing and often procrastinate (at considerable cost). Generating statements, sending bills, receiving and confirming payments, and following up on collections are all tasks that take time away from what you are trained to do, do well, and enjoy more. To save yourself grief, find a billing method that works for you in terms of your resources (time, secretarial help, computer access, size of your practice, and the use of your expensive time), and use it until something *markedly* better comes along. The common options are covered below.

**The simplest and cheapest method of billing is *not* having to bill: Have clients pay at the time of each session if at all possible**. Some clients will want a receipt, so use a simple paper form or a printer for credit card payments. But for any other arrangement, you need a way of tracking debt. You could make a note in your session notes, or in your appointment book, or keep a page listing sessions and payments in the front of the chart so that it can be settled quickly at the next session.

## Accepting Credit Cards or Smartphone Services

The second simplest method of collecting is to accept payments with debit, credit, and health savings account (HSA) cards. This is convenient for almost all clients, is rapid, avoids the delay of billing and later collecting, and makes being paid certain. Credit cards also make therapy more affordable by spreading its cost over more time, keep you from entering into a multiple relationship (in which you are creditor as well as therapist), and are often the preferred and may be the only method of payment for younger persons. Accepting cards does not make you invulnerable; some clients may still defraud you by canceling their cards or disputing your charges. However, some clinicians see accepting cards as encouraging poor financial responsibility and deepening debt.

With a smartphone and a service like Square's Register (https://squareup.com) or PayPal (https://www.paypal.com), accepting cards is simple. Typically, such services take 2.65% of what you charge and accept any card (including flexible spending account [FSA] and medical savings account [MSA] cards), but no other fees. For very small practices, it may make sense to have clients pay you with PayPal or a similar service, and perhaps invoice them this way as well. Google Wallet and other alternatives are available, so do your own evaluation. More traditional card processors use a swiper machine in your office and a phone line; these processors have multiple monthly and other expenses, but take lower percentages of what you charge.

Compute for yourself the costs of each type of service at different dollar amounts each month, such as $1,000, $2,500, and $5,000 of charges, over a year's time to make your choice. If you don't anticipate much credit card business, it's better to go with a higher percentage fee and lower monthly fees, rather than vice versa. The least expensive traditional arrangements may be from a warehouse club (Sam's Club, Costco, etc.) or https://www.professionalcharges.com. Although you may be able (depending on your state) to pass on the card's fees to clients, doing so is complex and often resented. Therefore, we do not recommend doing this, but instead suggest that you simply consider these fees a part of operating your business (for more suggestions, see https://smartpay.gsa.gov/content/about-gsa-smartpay#sa376). However, you can legally offer a discount for cash or check payments in every state.

We should note that the smartphone services such as PayPal do not store PHI and so are not subject to HIPAA. For the same reason, financial processors, like your bank, are not considered your BAs by HIPAA (see http://www.hhs.gov/hipaa/for-professionals/privacy/guidance/business-associates/index.html for more information).

You can charge clients who have forgotten their cards by having them sign a card payment consent form; you can then indicate that you have their "signatures on file" when you enter the charges using your smartphone or computer terminal. There are many examples of such a form, so just search online and download one of these. If you get a credit card's information at the start of treatment, you can keep it until the insurance claim is processed and you know the deductible and copayment. When the actual amount owed is clear, you can ask clients for payment by any means, and most will tell you to use the cards you have on record for them. If the clients are not available, their cards can simply be charged, since they have previously authorized you to do so.

## Accepting Checks

You can ask clients who seem hesitant to pay by check whether they expect a problem with their check; if they do, you can offer to hold the check until after their payday. Sometimes clients forget their checkbooks. By providing a stamped, self-addressed envelope at that time and asking them to send a check before you can schedule a next appointment with them, you can avoid problems or confront issues. Accepting checks can be simplified with the use of smartphone photographs for deposits. Ask at your bank.

## Statements

Although few clients will accumulate enough medical expenses to make them tax-deductible, offering a yearly statement of their payments is a courtesy. Some clients will ask to be billed on a monthly basis. Monthly statements can be printed and handed to clients at the start of their sessions, or they can be emailed as encrypted .pdf documents via a secure email site (e.g., https://www.Hushmail.com or http://www.ciphersend.com/Works.html). A few clients will have indemnity policies and submit your statements to their health insurers for reimbursement to them. Others may have FSAs and just need a receipt with no diagnosis. These receipts should say only "for professional services."

## Superbills

You may wish to provide clients with a receipt for each payment, or a statement when they pay at the end of each month in support of income tax deductibility or the client's submission of an insurance claim. A common way of doing this is the Superbill.

The Superbill is typically printed as a three-part "no-carbon-required" (NCR) form imprinted with common diagnostic codes,[2] client insurance submission instructions, service codes (*Current Procedural Terminology* or CPT), and your practice's tax identification. It only requires some checkoffs and your signature. Medical printers can supply these, and some computerized billing programs create these; to find these, search online for "Superbill."

Depending on its use, a Superbill may *not* include your Taxpayer Identification Number (TIN), Employer Identification Number (EIN),[3] National Provider Identifier (NPI),[4] diagnosis, CPT codes,[5] or the like for privacy and simplicity if those are unneeded. On KK's intake form, she asks clients whether they want a receipt and, if so, whether this will be for insurance ("diagnosis required and we will discuss this") or for FSAs and HSAs ("no diagnosis necessary"). Incidentally, although HIPAA allows it, and the MCO will say that the client signed a ROI when they signed up for insurance, getting a release of information (ROI) to discuss any aspects of your services with the client's insurance company is more protective of both you and the client when the discussion will be complicated or extensive.

## Completing the CMS-1500 Standard Billing Form

The standard way to bill insurance is to complete the current version of the CMS-1500[6] form to send to insurance companies to "claim benefits" for reimbursement to the client or to direct payment to the clinician. A main motivator for adopting an electronic health record (EHR) is to generate these forms (the paper CMS-1500 and its electronic equivalent, 837p) and then to send them electronically to the payers, which is called "electronic claims submission" (ECS). For more on health insurance billing, see Chapter 3.

It is crucial to distinguish your fees from your charges when dealing with insurers. You set a fee for each of the services you provide. Let's say that this is $100. If you then contract with an MCO for a payment of, say, $60, that is all you will receive. On your bill, however, always indicate your full fee and then add an "adjustment" of $40, which brings your charge to the insurance company down to the contracted $60. If your bill shows only what you expect to collect (the $60), then the payer will consider that your full fee and discount its payments from that. Clients without insurance will pay your full fee unless you arrange and indicate an "adjustment," and document in your notes a reason, such as "due to established poverty."

---

[2]As of October 2015, the codes required for psychotherapy are those of the *International Classification of Diseases*, 10th revision, Clinical Modification (ICD-10-CM).

[3]For both legal reasons and your privacy, obtain an EIN and use it instead of your Social Security number on most forms (see http://www.irs.gov/Businesses/Small-Businesses-&-Self-Employed/Employer-ID-Numbers-EINs).

[4]For more about the NPI, see this website (https://nppes.cms.hhs.gov/NPPES/Welcome.do).

[5]CPT codes describe all the medical services possible and are published by the American Medical Association. Mental health clinicians use only a small proportion of these codes.

[6]CMS stands for Centers for Medicare and Medicaid Services, part of the federal Department of Health and Human Services (DHHS).

## Billing Services and Clearinghouses

Billing services and clearinghouses can provide a variety of valuable services, as well as ECS. They can bill all kinds of insurers and third parties, using these parties' current forms, procedures, and policies, and with faster turnaround (payments to you) on your accounts receivable (unpaid bills). They offer help with audits by payers, verification of benefits, and toll-free assistance; they can also save you postage. They send nicely printed bills to the client, claims to third parties with all the needed information ("clean claims," which are less likely to be denied and delayed), and monthly reports on the status of your accounts receivable. The decision about when to hire one of these services is complex and is addressed in Chapter 3.

## Computerized Billing Programs

Mental health billing is the most complex area of medical billing. To meet the needs of practitioners, there are a few computer programs and Internet-based services (e.g., https://www.officeally.com) that will do just the billing. We recommend submitting insurance claims electronically. The billing function has been the basis for the dozens of EHR programs available for small practices. They construct a bill to give to clients, track MCOs' session limits, bill multiple payers separately, send out appointment reminders, help with treatment planning, and try to be HIPAA-compliant. These typically also include a clinical documentation (case notes) function, a scheduling program, and the ability to produce practice management information. See Section 3.7 for a fuller discussion of submitting claims.

## Tips on Collecting Fees

- **Make it your standard practice not to allow clients to run up large unpaid bills.** You should allow no more than one session without payment to elapse before you raise the issue with a client, because ultimately you cannot terminate a client (for nonpayment) who is in great psychological need (that would be "abandonment"). A protective and assertive policy is to refuse to schedule a new appointment if one has not been paid for (or if the agreed-to minimum or the copayment amount when the client uses health insurance has not been paid). KK's office policies state:

  > I do not permit clients to carry a balance of more than two sessions, and if you are unable to pay this balance, we will discuss whether it makes sense to pause your care or develop another strategy so that you can avoid incurring additional debt. Please let me know if any problem arises during the course of therapy regarding your ability to make timely payments.

  She would prefer to renegotiate and reduce the fee than to have clients owe her money.

- If you defer payment (avoid the phrase "extend credit"), you should set a dollar limit, such as $750, on a maximum balance. Do not try to charge interest on the balance, as you then have to complete state and federal legal agreements as a creditor (according to the Truth in Lending Act of 1968), which are quite burdensome. There is also an ethical aspect of extending credit just by allowing an unpaid bill. As Gordon I. Herz, PhD, of Madison, WI, notes (personal communication, August 27, 2000), you are in effect entering into a second (multiple) relationship with the client. You are the therapist trying to do what is best for the client, and also a creditor putting your personal financial profit ahead of the client's benefit. It is also possible that accruing debt, even for therapy, is not in some clients' best interest.

- Unpayable balances may tempt clients to pursue licensing board complaints to escape them. This is a common trigger for complaints.

- The longer the delay, the smaller the collection. The established wisdom among debt collectors is that if a debt payment is over 90 days late, you will collect about 15% of it.

- If you allow a client not to pay, you will both feel rotten. Failing to handle disagreeable and important issues with the client, or delaying their handling, sets a poor example. The client may come to believe that you are not a good therapist.

- You may need a simple book of two-part receipts for the few clients who pay cash. Don't waste your money on custom-printed receipts.

- If a client gives you a large check that makes you suspicious, cash it *immediately* at the client's bank. If the account does not have sufficient funds, don't try again until you know the check will clear; you can call the bank every day or two and ask if the funds are there. When the account has the funds, cash the check immediately.

- If you are charged bank fees for bounced checks ("insufficient funds"), do pass these fees on to your clients. Not doing so could lead them to think you tend to shy away from financial matters. Insurance will not cover these fees.

## 2.4   Collecting Overdue Fees from Clients

*Note.* Collecting from insurance companies is covered in Chapter 3.

Regular billing gives you a good grasp of your accounts, so that you will know when someone slips from 30 to 45 days behind. Do your part by billing often. You will collect more money in the long run and be happier. The later a client is in paying, the less likely it is that you will collect the full sum owed you.

Having a few clients owe you money is almost unavoidable, especially given the complexity of managed care. For example, you may have agreed to delay payment for perfectly good reasons and later get no payment; you may have forgotten to submit a bill before a filing deadline; perhaps the parents of a child you are seeing choose to fight over paying you; or many other things may happen.

If you are squeamish about dunning your clients for money or think that it negatively affects the intimate therapeutic relationship, find another way to assure that you will be paid, or you will have to leave private practice. You can work it through with your own therapist (more work and more costly), hire someone to dun clients (cheaper and easier), or use a paperwork solution such as those described below.

As mentioned earlier, large debt is a frequent cause of board complaints (see Section 4.1). Whichever method you choose, proceed with caution, treat all cases similarly, document the details, and put the client's needs first.

## Calling the Client

A face-to-face discussion with you is the best, but a phone call is a good way to assure payment. A second choice is a personal call from a secretary or office manager to slow payers. This has been shown to be many times more productive than using the mail. Be sure, though, that whoever makes the call understands the limitations on what he or she can do and say. Read up on the federal and state laws and practices in this area before starting, and educate your staff in these. In general, the caller must always be polite, show concern for the client's best interests, listen to explanations, offer to work out a payment schedule, and follow up methodically. Commonly, calls may be made only between 8 A.M. and 9 P.M. The caller should carefully note his or her efforts and the client's response, in whatever format works for your office.

## Sending a Note on the Bill

When there is an unpaid balance, a handwritten note can be attached to the statement, which then can still be submitted to an insurance company. Since such a client's case is usually closed, the note usually says something like "Is there some problem with this account?" or "Are you having a money problem?" or "Is there some trouble with your insurance company?" It then requests or informs the client of action: "Please call and talk to me if there is some difficulty with this," or "Can you pay me something on this account?" or "I will call you next week about this." Gentle nudges that indicate your concern for the client as well as for getting paid can be helpful to you here.

## Sending Collection Letters

Collection letters seem to work better than notes on clients' statements. For those of you who have never received them, collection letters come in increasing intensity of wording (and often of paper color as well). The "first-level" notes are increasingly demanding in tone, but all indicate a willingness to talk and work out a payment plan. The "second-level" letter informs the client that you will no longer provide services until payment is made. The "third-level" letter threatens legal action.

## Using Legal Methods

If a bill is several years old, and you don't want to sue now but might in the future, you may be able to extend the debt's payment time. Try to get an acknowledgment of the debt (by a dated signature on a letter), a small payment, or even a promise to pay. Sometimes people's financial situations change, and they will actually pay off their old debts. Ask; it's cheap to try.

As the third-level collection letter suggests, you can use small-claims court in your district. It is simple and cheap, and no lawyer is required. It is almost always successful, but you need to decide the following: (1) Have I tried all other methods first? (2) Is there anything to collect (i.e., does the client have the money)? (3) Do I want to make an enemy for this much money? An old saying is that if you make 20 customers happy, some of them will tell 1 other person, but if you make 1 customer angry, that person will tell 20 others. With the rise of Internet consumer review sites such as Yelp.com, many more than 20 are likely to hear complaints about you if you proceed.

The APA's ethics code allows the use of collection agencies, but you must inform the client first (in your practice brochure and ideally in person) and provide him or her with the opportunity to pay before proceeding (APA, 2010, Standard 6.04e). Indeed, never turn over a debt to a collection agency without first having spoken with the client. Surprising the client with a call from a collection agency may provoke a retaliatory board complaint. Alban (2010a) has good advice on collection agencies.

Investigate and carefully read your contract with a collection agency or attorney. Problems may include being locked into a single agency for collecting your money; being required to pay a fee if you discontinue having an agency collect for you; having collection activities dropped if you or the agency is sued or threatened with a suit by the client; receiving very limited (and often ineffective) investigation to find a client who has "skipped out"; and having to supply a lot of documents or client information to support your bill. Overall, some agencies are clearer and fairer than others, so be thorough and ask lots of questions.

As noted earlier, we recommend that you not add an interest charge on overdue bills. While it is possible to add a "processing fee" or "bookkeeping fee" to avoid conflicting therapist–client and creditor–debtor relationships, we recommend simply bundling the costs into your overhead in setting your regular fees. Some therapists, however, do tack on a late fee (such as $20 for payments made after the day the payment is due, and $30 if the payment delay extends into the next week). Such flat fees should be high enough to be a deterrent to late payments.

## Avoiding Illegal and Unethical Billing Procedures

The APA code of ethics (APA, 2010) states simply that "Psychologists' fee practices are consistent with law" (Standard 6.04b) and that "Psychologists do not misrepresent their fees" (Standard 6.04c). This makes accurate billing an ethical responsibility and subject to ethical censure, as well as the obvious and commonly enforced legal risks. To avoid such risks, we recommend the following:

❑ Bill only for services actually rendered, not for missed or shortened appointments at full fee. (You can collect for these from the client under some conditions, but read your MCO contract. See Chapter 3.)

❑ Bill only in the name of the client. Bill members of a therapy group for group therapy, not as if they were individual therapy clients. If you see a couple, do not "double-bill" (i.e., charge each person separately as an individual). As noted earlier, few insurers will pay for couple treatment; so, when you can justifiably do so, you may bill one's member's insurance for treating that person with the other member of the couple indicated as a collateral.

More discussion on the ethics of billing insurers is provided in Chapter 3.

## A Valuable Resource

Starting in about 2008, APA has developed a number of very fine documents about the business of practice, but these are only available to APA members who also pay to join the APA

Practice Organization. Start at the Business of Practice site (http://www.apapracticecentral. org/business/index.aspx). Some of the sections are Practice Management (which includes resources for creating a professional will), Practice Marketing, Financial Management, Technology and Electronic Health Records, Legal and Regulatory Compliance, HIPAA Compliance, and Collaborating with Other Providers. Members of the Practice Organization also receive the quarterly publication *Good Practice: Tools and Information for Professional Psychologists* (typically about 25 pages long) and have access to the APA Practice Directorate's Legal and Regulatory Affairs Department (phone: 202-336-5886; email: praclegal@apa.org).

# CHAPTER 3

# Health Insurance and Managed Mental Health Care

## BILLING THIRD PARTIES AND GETTING PAID

*Edward L. Zuckerman with Gordon I. Herz*

## 3.1    The Health Care Landscape

Health care constitutes some 18% of the U.S. gross national product and is being industrialized just as many other economic sectors have been (e.g., as family farms have been replaced by agribusinesses). Lots of money and technology, some science, and politics are shaping our unique way of industrializing health care. For example, the United States has "the uniquely American employer-based health insurance system" that evolved "so that companies could attract and maintain private-sector workers during the war [i.e., World War II] years" (Potter, 2010, p. 92). Health insurance is one of many interacting forces that include federal laws and policies (e.g., the Health Insurance Portability and Accountability Act of 1996 [HIPAA], the Health Information Technology for Economic and Clinical Health [HITECH] Act of 2009, and the Patient Protection and Affordable Care Act of 2010 [PPACA, aka "Obamacare"]); the increased efficiencies and profits of professional management (i.e. managed care); electronic health record (EHR) systems; treatment process and outcome research; public health policies; and still others

In the old days, a psychotherapist (a second party) had a professional relationship only

---

**Gordon I. Herz, PhD,** has been in full-time independent practice in Madison, Wisconsin, for more than 15 years, after serving 10 years as Director of Neuropsychology Services within the Meriter Hospital Department of Rehabilitation Medicine. His specialties include neuropsychology, health psychology, and rehabilitation psychology. He frequently consults with and provides services to residents in nursing homes, assisted living facilities, and senior residential campuses in Madison and surrounding communities. He has been an advocate in health insurance and financing reform. He also created and hosts a peer consultation group for psychologists working in Medicare. Dr. Herz was elected Distinguished Practitioner and Fellow, National Academies of Practice and the Psychology Academy in 2013, and served in 2014 as President of the American Psychological Association's Division 42, Psychologists in Independent Practice. He regularly provides training opportunities for doctoral students in his practice. He can be reached through his website (http://www.DrHerz.us).

with the client (first party) and not with any third party as payer such as an insurance company. These days we are more likely as providers to contract with third parties such as a managed care organization (MCO) or a preferred provider organization (PPO), or to take part in an independent practice association (IPA) or an accountable care organization (ACO). As professionals, we get to decide what each client needs, but the client's insurers decide what to pay for, to whom, and how much.

Managed health care is pervasive and ever-evolving. Mental health and substance abuse treatment constitute only about 2% of total health care expenditures, and the great majority of the expenditures in these areas are for medications and hospitalizations. Mental health care has suffered disproportionately from the failure to distinguish between inpatient services (high cost and lesser effectiveness) and outpatient services (lower immediate and long-term costs with more effectiveness for almost all conditions). Similarly, MCOs support very short-term treatments, despite minimal evidence for their benefits. But MCOs are not clinicians' sworn enemies; they are only businesses filling a need, expanding their markets, and directing their processes. Their contractual agreements are not aimed at destroying or depriving us of our livelihoods; they simply reflect the way any industrial, capitalist, legal process works.

The current effects of managed care on mental health services are varied, and many are addressed in detail in this chapter. The issues include conflicts of loyalty, the complexities of contracting with MCOs, threats to confidentiality, dealing with MCO reviewers and restrictions on treatment, maintaining continuity of care, and the administrative burdens of treating MCO clients.

## 3.2   To Take Insurance or Not?

As a professional, you can decide whether or not to take health insurance. In our view, this should largely be a business decision, and you should make it by taking into account all relevant factors—many of which will be individual to your practice. These factors also include some ethical considerations. To what extent will you provide services to people who do not have or cannot get insurance (e.g., the undocumented, those in legal limbo), or to those unable to afford your services even with insurance (i.e., those whose plans involve high deductibles and copayments)? Will you provide services not covered by a client's insurance or by any insurance, such as marriage counseling, personal growth, leadership and other business training, or coaching?

### Your Time

You have a finite number of hours available in a week or a year. For example, you may intend to work a 40-hour week, and you may decide that you can provide 30 hours of direct service during that week, reserving the rest of the time for documentation, case coordination, practice administration, marketing, and similar activities. If you plan 2 weeks of vacation per year, close your office for 7 national holidays, and need 30 hours per year for continuing education, you have 1,904 hours *at the most* during the year to provide services. (This tentative schedule also ignores cancellations, slow times of the year, time to build to a full practice, bad weather, illness, and many other likely factors.) If you determine that you will be able to provide direct, billable service for 75% of those hours, this leaves 1,428 hours.

Multiply this figure by your average fee, and that will provide an estimate of the *maximum gross* receipts you may anticipate. You might change these numbers if you want or need more vacation or family time away from the office, if your practice is not full, or if you can work more hours per week.

## What You Can Collect

The next step is to estimate the maximum amount you *actually will collect* per hour. This, of course, means taking into account the percentage of clients who may end up not paying their bills and the other discounts you may make available (perhaps by using a "sliding scale"). Understand that insurance reimbursement invariably will be much less than your full usual fee. You will not be able to collect from anyone the difference ("balance bill") between your full fee and the amount the insurance company will reimburse, due to your contract with an insurance company. You must make efforts to collect, and not routinely "write off" a balance because of an unpaid copayment. You should estimate what percentage of your clients will be charged full fees and what percentage will be charged various partial fees. This is your "case mix," and varying it by accepting and refusing some clients will alter your net income more than changing costs.

How much will insurance actually reimburse? Traditionally, this question has been difficult to answer unless you are reviewing specific insurance contracts. Fortunately, we are living in the era of big data, and the picture is becoming clearer. For example, FairHealth-Consumer.org (http://fairhealthconsumer.org/faq.php) allows professionals and consumers to look up fees typically charged, amounts usually reimbursed by insurance, and amounts consumers may expect to pay "out of pocket," by ZIP code for the locality where the coverage is purchased. Insurance companies used to determine reimbursement rates based on what they termed "usual, customary, and reasonable" (UCR) fees. It turned out that they were illegally complicit with each other and with the processors of their data in creating and using numbers that were below the actual UCR fees, which lowered their costs and providers' incomes. FairHealth is the result of a 2009 legal agreement and a huge fine. In April 2014, there was a similar release of data by Medicare, which "gives consumers unprecedented transparency on the medical services physicians provide and how much they are paid" (see http://www.cms.gov/Newsroom/MediaReleaseDatabase/Press-releases/2014-Press-releases-items/2014-04-09.html). Medicare covers about 50 million Americans, and 91% of all physicians are accepting new Medicare patients; the percentages vary among the specialties, from about 63% of psychiatrists up to 99% of surgeons (see http://kff.org/medicare/issue-brief/medicare-patients-access-to-physicians-a-synthesis-of-the-evidence). Your Medicare participation is discussed separately below.

## Your Costs

Now that you have some ideas about what you might collect per hour under insurance, you need to know the actual minimum costs of providing services (your "nut" to stay in business), so that you can determine profitability. See the discussion of cost-plus pricing in Section 2.1 for guidance in determining this number. Accepting insurance will cost you much more administrative time per hour of service than you will need for clients who pay you directly. Compute the lowest fee you can profitably accept from an insurer before signing any contract.

Your decision should not be based entirely on finances. Haas and Cummings (1991) offer thoughtful and realistic guidance for those considering joining panels, and this publication is highly recommended, despite its being well over 20 years old. Its second author, Nick Cummings, practically invented managed psychological care. Three short online articles by lawyers with checklists for evaluating managed care contracts are useful: those by Zeil (https://ispub.com/IJANP/1/2/5245), DeBlasio (http://corporate.findlaw.com/law-library/managed-care-contracts-key-provisions-for-providers.html), and Gibbs (http://www.managedcaremag.com/archives/9607/9607.dealkiller.html).

## 3.3   Getting NPI Number(s)

The National Provider Identifier (NPI), a 10-digit number, is required to bill insurers, costs nothing, and lasts a professional lifetime. It is public information, and those searching for it will also find your office and phone. You may get one for yourself and an additional one for your business (see below). Once you get your NPI, keep it handy, as you will enter it on each claim form and will probably share it with other covered entities (CEs)—those that must comply with HIPAA (see Section 1.5). You must furnish updates to its database within 30 days of making any changes such as moving.

Go to the National Plan and Provider Enumeration System (NPPES) website (https://nppes.cms.hhs.gov) or call the toll-free NPPES phone number (800-465-3203), to see what will be required to apply for an NPI, and then return with the information to submit your actual NPI application. The Internet application process takes 15–30 minutes, and you will get your number in a few days by email.

Individual clinicians ("rendering providers") need NPI numbers; also, their practices may bill under the practice or business names, and so use different NPIs. To help decide the need for more than one NPI, see a list of frequently asked questions (https://questions.cms.gov/faq.php?id=5005&faqId=2511). A potentially confusing portion of the application is selecting a "taxonomy" code that identifies your primary professional designation. Additional guidance has been issued, for example, by psychologist practice organizations (http://www.apapracticecentral.org/update/2006/11-16/choosing-taxonomy.aspx), and may be available for other mental health professionals through their associations.

You can use the NPPES website to look up any other health care entity's NPI. This can be very useful if you are referred a client by another health care professional, and you need to put the "referring provider's" NPI on the claim form and do not know that number.

## 3.4   Which Insurance Company Panels Should I Consider Joining?

From which insurance companies will you accept payments? There are a number of factors to consider. First, insurance companies are not required to work with you. Section 2706 of the PPACA (again, this is the acronym for what is commonly called "Obamacare") requires "nondiscrimination" toward health care providers, in the sense that insurance plans may not bar *classes* of health professionals who are functioning within their scope of practice under state law or certification. For example, an insurance company may not simply say, "We will not deal with psychologists." However, insurers are not required to contract with every provider who is willing to agree to their requirements for participation (including payment amounts). A number of states previously had enacted "any willing provider" laws, which "require managed care organizations to grant network participation to health care providers willing to join and meet network requirements" (http://definitions.uslegal.com/a/any-willing-provider-law). As of 2014, twenty-seven states had passed such laws, according to the National Conference of State Legislatures (http://www.ncsl.org/research/health/any-willing-or-authorized-providers.aspx), but these laws vary considerably by the number or classes of health care providers covered (http://scholarship.law.upenn.edu/faculty_scholarship/438). You may find out whether your state has such a law through your state's Office of the Commissioner of Insurance (http://www.naic.org/state_web_map.htm).

When insurers wish to enter a market (say, a new state), they need to create panels of providers before seeking contracts with employers. So it is not uncommon for mental health professionals to receive solicitations by mail or otherwise to join a panel. When you receive such solicitations, carefully read all the information you obtain from such companies in light of the recommendations below, especially contractual obligations and fee schedules. It is unlikely that you will receive many actual referrals from these new companies, because they will still have to win contracts from employers against the current insurers in the market.

Other considerations in deciding which insurance companies' panels (of providers) you might join include the following points.

## The National and Local Reach of a Company

Some companies provide coverage across the United States and may have tens of millions of policy holders ("covered lives"). The largest public plan, Medicare, has approximately 50 million beneficiaries. The largest private plan (Blue Cross/Blue Shield) reports in excess of 100 million subscribers. Some local and regional companies may cover from a few tens of thousands to hundreds of thousands of individuals.

What proportion of your client population is likely to have coverage with a particular company? The overall number of subscribers, and particularly the density of coverage in your local area ("market penetration"), are important factors to consider in deciding to enroll with a company.

## The Structure of the Company

An insurer's structure indicates how open the company is to accepting new professionals. Options include a point-of-service (POS) plan (basically fees for services rendered); a preferred provider organization (PPO), which has a small number of providers on panels; or a health maintenance organization (HMO), which usually consists only of employee providers. Two other structures, mentioned previously, are IPAs (with loose groups of independent providers together seeking contracts) and ACOs (which take responsibility for numbers of covered lives for a set fee per person per month (PPPM). Plans may offer "out-of-network" (OON) coverage, in which you can be paid without joining the panel, but these usually require a case-by-case negotiation. You will find most success if you are armed with the facts of plans' (usually low) ratios of providers to covered lives in your area, or can argue that you possess needed special skills.

Plan structures have implications for the flexibility in consumers' choice of health care professionals and the extent to which referrals to specialists like us may be self-generated. They also indicate the level of oversight and other expectations of mental health professionals. For example, referrals may be closely controlled by the insurers (i.e., preapproval is required) or by gatekeepers within the system (e.g., referral by a primary care provider is required).

## The Level of Independence versus Oversight

In an effort to contain costs, insurance companies delegate oversight and management responsibilities for mental health and substance abuse treatment to a second set of companies. Research has shown (see http://ivanjmiller.com/disparity_article.html and http://www.drherz.us/blog42/ReimbursementAccessSolutions.pdf) that insurers with such "managed care carve-out" arrangements typically reimburse mental health professionals at rates lower than those of other insurers, and that they also tend to micromanage care through requiring prior authorization of treatment visits, approval of treatment plans, frequent case review during the course of treatment, and written requests for reauthorization of ongoing coverage (see the later discussion of outpatient treatment reports or OTRs).

## Ethical Challenges

You should be aware that working in an MCO environment can raise ethical conflicts, particularly if the insurer micromanages care:

- Your loyalties can be divided between a client's needs and those of the MCO, which employs and pays you. Your client did not choose the MCO or design its coverage (the client's employer did), and yet you will be under contract to the MCO.

- Decisions the MCOs make about care are often based on cost "containment" (reduction), and not on the quality of services, long-term benefits to clients, the research on treatments' effectiveness, or your or your clients' informed preferences. Thus you may be pressured to provide care you know (or should know) to be inadequate or inappropriate.

- You may be invited to treat problems and diagnoses beyond your expertise, in order to prevent the loss of referrals and income.

- Your clients essentially have no real confidentiality. You must either omit information from your records (which you may later need to demonstrate your thoughtful decision making if you are complained against or sued), or force the clients to trust their privacy to the MCO (which does not operate by your professional standards).

## Public Health Plans

As discussed below, providing services to Medicare clients on public health plans (e.g., Medicare, Medicaid, Tricare) may be a viable option, although Medicaid plans typically pay too little to be worthwhile to private practitioners. See below for more on Medicare. Depending on your credentials, skills, interests, and location, you might explore providing services to veterans, the military, or participants in other publicly funded programs outside the above programs.

### The Reputation of the Company among Your Peers

The experiences of your professional peers are likely to predict your own experiences with an insurer.

## 3.5   Applying to Insurance Companies to Become a Provider

### Joining an MCO Panel

You will find that almost all MCOs have full panels of providers and are not interested in your applying to become one, unless you have a specialty they want or you are located in an underserved area (with enough of their "covered lives" living there). Be aware that the companies have almost complete freedom to decide how many and what kind of providers they wish to empanel, regardless of any computations of need completed by independent researchers. For instance, they can decide to empanel 5 psychiatrists per 10,000 of their clients, regardless of any other information available. MCOs generally will not accept newer professionals onto their panels, and will simply not make referrals to those who practice styles of therapy they do not understand or consider too long-term.

If you join a panel, you are agreeing to accept almost all clients the panel refers to you and to receive only what the contract allows—a payment from the MCO and a payment from the client (a "copayment"). You may not bill anyone for the rest of your usual charge (no "balance billing"). You will be accepting clients at a much lower fee than is customary in your setting; the hope is to come out ahead by filling empty hours. You should be aware that **MCOs' fees for therapy have rarely been raised in the last 20 years**, although inflation has doubled the cost of living. No one expects fees to be raised, because it is a buyer's market with too many providers.

Your state insurance office may have lists of insurance companies operating in your area, or you may ask your peers for ones they deal with. On an insurance company's website, look for the company's "provider enrollment" area. There will be a written (or online) application that will require information such as your licensure and certifications (including national identifiers such as your NPI); education and training; specialties; board certification; location and nature of practice (independent vs. member of a group); professional liability coverage; any adverse profession-related legal actions; and other details, such as where you may store practice records. You will need to attest that the information you are providing is true and accurate, and to provide paper proof of your licensure and malpractice coverage. Time frames for a written response to your application vary, and the process may take many months. The reliability of companies' follow-through may also vary, but the provider enrollment department ought to be able to give you an estimate of stated time to review and respond, and you may need to correspond in the interim or to ask about the status of the application.

You may find that entering your credentials and other information into a database maintained by the Council for Affordable Quality Healthcare, or CAQH (http://caqh.org), is worthwhile, because you can then make them available to MCOs, licensing boards, hospitals, or others you choose. Many panels require the CAQH and its yearly updating ("recredentialing"). It is rather complex, but the process is well described by Centone (http://www.counseling.org/news/blog/aca-blog/2012/12/17/getting-on-insurance-panels-preparing-for-the-process). Additional practice information can be included, and there is no cost. Incidentally, never pay a fee to join a panel or to be recertified; charging such a fee is a sure sign of a weak company.

Try to offer the MCO a practice name with a first letter that is early in the alphabet, as MCO case managers usually go down an alphabetical list when referring phone calls from potential clients. You may find some MCO criteria burdensome, such as completing clinical evaluations and the paperwork for "initial certification for treatment" within a day or two, or being able to see referred clients "immediately." MCO staffers have been known to make calls to clinicians while presenting themselves as clients and asking to be seen as soon as possible, to check on your compliance with the latter point.

All communication with any insurance company should be conducted in writing, because lost messages, unrecalled verbal agreements, and documents "not received" are common. Keep copies of everything, document all phone calls, and never send originals. Important documentation (such as required proofs of licensure, education/training, and malpractice insurance) should be sent via a form of U.S. mail requiring proof of receipt and a signature. Emails will have "date and time" information, but they can go astray, and you may have no certainty they were received.

In addition to the application itself, try to get the following information from the insurance company:

1. The number of subscribers the company has in your geographic region (usually the ZIP code or codes for the area where you will practice). The company may respond that it "does not have" information about how many subscribers it has in your area, or that this is "proprietary" information. In that case, because you may have no way to gauge whether you might be inundated with clients with this coverage, or have no referrals, consider applying later to that company.

2. The company's fee schedule, showing reimbursement amounts for mental health services (by CPT codes) you are able to provide. Although a fee schedule should be available to an applicant, some companies may say that this will not be provided until a clinician is approved, or ask you to promise not to reveal the information once it is provided to you.

3. All mental and behavioral health policies regarding coverage, determination of "medical necessity," treatment documentation and case reviews that may be required, and similar policies. These are the company's "manuals" and may be available online. The company's "medical necessity" policies will be critically important in enabling you to understand whether your services may be covered, and how those determinations are made. See Form 3.2 (discussed later) to understand the logic.

## Your Contract with the Insurer or MCO

You will be asked to sign a contract with the company, and its terms will, for all practical purposes, not be negotiable. This contract will govern such factors as how much notice you or the company must provide in order to end the contract; the time frame in which you must submit claims and in which the company agrees to provide reimbursement; the length of time for which, and conditions under which, you will be responsible for clients after the contract ends; and whether the company may **"resell" your contract to another company** that may purchase the MCO or insurer. Many contracts will have this latter possibility, as the "provider panel" is essentially considered an "asset" of the company. We have heard many reports of clinicians' being called by prospective clients or referrers saying that they are certain the clinicians accept their insurance, as this is what is shown on the company website or in printed materials, when the clinicians never enrolled with that particular company. These confusions often turn out to be instances of insurance company mergers and acquisitions. You may be contractually obligated to honor an obligation to a company with which you never enrolled or even decided against joining and at different payment levels, so be cautious.

### Complexities in Your Contract with the MCO

We strongly recommend that you **not sign any contract without having it reviewed by an attorney** who specializes in health care contracts. By all means, ask the attorney questions and read the contract yourself. *You must understand every part of the contract you sign.* This may seem obvious, but you will need to do repeated readings, as well as obtain the assistance of peer consultation and your practice lawyer to grasp the implications of the contract's language (see Stout et al., 2001, for an introduction to the language of MCOs). Here are some examples:

- Do not assume that you are offered a contract identical to what other clinicians like yourself have been offered in your area, or that this year's is identical to the one you signed last year. Note that "evergreen renewals" allow an MCO to renew your contract without any negotiation with you.

- Read not only the contract but all of its "attachments," such as the provider manuals in which more obligations and responsibilities are spelled out. These are in "incorporated by reference" statements.

- Understand the risks you assume by agreeing to "withholds" (payments for your services that are not paid to you unless you provide services the way the MCO wishes).

- An indemnification or "hold harmless" agreement states that if the MCO is sued by a client for the actions of the provider, then the provider cannot hold the MCO responsible in any way for the outcome. Generally, your professional liability insurance will cover your actions and those of any employees you have included in your insurance application, but not the actions of your nonemployees (such as the MCO). If you cannot avoid such agreements, try to add the MCO to your insurance policy as an additional insured.

- Beware of "noncompete" or "exclusivity" clauses, which prevent you from having business relationships with competing insurers or MCOs, even after you have left the first MCO.

- "No-disparagement" and "gag" clauses can prevent you from criticizing the MCO, discussing treatment options that the MCO won't pay for, mentioning financial incentives given to you or other providers, criticizing adverse decisions made by the MCO, or the like. These may limit your ability to practice as you believe best, advocate for your clients, and appeal a denial of payment. These "gag" rules may be disappearing because of new laws, but do read your MCO contracts carefully. The risk to you is that you may be sued or complained against for failure to treat properly when you knew or should have known that a different kind of service was needed, and yet you could not recommend or refer for it because of your MCO contract. You are still responsible for your clients' care.

- "Termination without cause" provisions allow an MCO to remove you from its panels with 60 or 90 days' notice for any reason. This could be a financial disaster to you, could limit the continuity of your care, and might not be in your clients' best interest. Best would be allowing only termination with a list of specified causes, but also ask about the MCOs appeals process for these types of termination, and try to make them work both ways.

- "Severability" clauses keep the rest of the contract binding, even if one part is declared illegal or unenforceable. These are almost universal, but ask your lawyer about any risks.

- You cannot bill MCO clients for their missed but uncanceled appointments—and, by the way, you cannot deduct your losses due to missed appointments on your income taxes, even if you work outside managed care.

- In evaluating your profit from MCO cases, add your administrative time in dealing with the MCO over authorizations, lost paperwork, case reviews, and appeals of denials. This may be quite substantial.

- Be aware that MCOs do **retrospective case reviews** as well as the ongoing ones (through continuing authorization requirements). An MCO can, after examining paid-for (often closed) cases, decide that you did not document need or improvement; if this occurs, the MCO will require you to return money paid to you. If you have a large MCO caseload, prepare for such demands. Typically the MCO will review a few cases, find a few with questionable documentation, deny those, and scale that percentage to all of their cases, and demand a refund for all those cases. These retrospective denials (so-called "claw-backs") can end a practice.

- Beware of contract language that requires your contractual obligations to survive contract termination but does not require the same of the MCO; allows the MCO to interpret your nonresponse to contract changes as acceptance of them; defines your case records as its proprietary information; or requires you to provide inappropriate 24-hour/7-day coverage—coverage all night or when you go on vacation. In some cases, the MCO may require you to employ only other panel members for such coverage.

The list above is not exhaustive, and other issues will arise over time. A review by your business attorney is highly recommended before you sign any managed care contract.

### Resigning from Panels

You may increase your overall income, and your happiness, by resigning from low-paying panels or resigning from those with the most administrative burdens. If you simply stop accepting referrals, the panels may terminate you, and then you will have to explain the situation when some credentialing agency asks if you were ever terminated. To resign, read your contract's sections on ending the contract. Second, notify the MCO in writing by certified mail of your intentions. Keep copies, as you will probably have to resubmit your letter (and their acknowledgment). Notify new and current clients with a 3- to 6-month window. Many of them will simply finish up with their therapy, but you may continue to see the MCO's clients for some months. You may offer to see them at the reduced rate you received from the MCO, or you may need to refer them.

Be aware that your name is unlikely to be removed from the MCO's lists of providers, and so you will get calls for appointments for years. Insurers want to have large panels to show potential customers (companies that buy insurance for their workers). These calls are opportunities to do some public education on managed care; make it clear to callers that the fault for this misinformation lies with the MCO and not with you. You might explain why you have resigned, but check your contract for "gag" clauses forbidding such discussions even after resignation.

## The Special Case of Enrolling with Medicare

Medicare is the federal health insurance program for people who are 65 or older, certain younger people with disabilities, and people with end-stage renal disease. Government programs can be intimidating, but do not reject providing services to Medicare-covered clients too quickly. Although there are some bureaucratic complexities, there are many benefits (see below for details), and you will have grateful clients and families. A short introduction to being a Medicare provider can be found at this site (http://www.ama-assn.org/ama/pub/physician-resources/solutions-managing-your-practice/coding-billing-insurance/medicare/medicare-participation-guide.page). Some of the legal and ethical issues are discussed by Harris (https://www.trustinsurance.com/Portals/0/documents/medicare.pdf). Medicare Part B covers services provided by physicians and other health practitioners (physician assistants, nurse practitioners, etc.), as well as clinical psychologists and clinical social workers (http://www.medicare.gov/coverage/doctor-and-other-health-care-provider-services.html). Counselors may well be added to this list in the next few years.

The American Psychological Association (APA) Practice Organization has a free and very comprehensive *Medicare Handbook,* available only for those APA members who pay the Practice Organization dues. This is the single best source of information for psychologists, and reading its approximately 35 pages will be well worth your time. The APA Practice Organization's site (http://www.apapracticecentral.org) has other relevant resources, such as "The Basics of Medicare Audits," "State Medicaid Reimbursement Standards for Psychologists," and "Medicare Private Contracting: Plus or Minus?"

There are a number of reasons to consider enrolling with Medicare even if you do not join any other insurer:

- Medicare accepts "any willing provider" who meets its licensure criteria. For example, Medicare defines a "clinical psychologist" as a person who (1) holds a doctoral degree in psychology; and (2) is licensed or certified, on the basis of the doctoral degree in psychology, by the state in which he or she practices, at the independent practice level of psychology to perform diagnostic, assessment, and treatment services directly to individuals. As long as the applicant meets these basic criteria (and has no relevant adverse legal or administrative events), the psychologist will be accepted. Where the applicant got his or her education and internship is not of concern. Psychologists will apply under and be assigned Medicare Specialty 68, which will allow provision of diagnostic and treatment services to Medicare beneficiaries. Medicare also has a category of "independently practicing psychologist" (Specialty 62), which allows only provision of diagnostic (i.e., testing) services. Psychiatrists use Specialty Code 26, or 86 for neuropsychiatry, and clinical social workers use Specialty Code 80.

- Payments are reliable and fast. Many more *Current Procedural Terminology* (CPT) codes can be used for more complete and realistic reimbursement. Medicare reimbursement rates are quite good and are the same for all doctoral mental health professionals for services that both psychiatrists and psychologists may provide. Clinical social workers are reimbursed at 75% of the fee schedule for doctoral professionals. Medicare's fee structure varies by locality and is determined objectively (the process is amazingly complex and so is not discussed here), although unfortunately the process has become increasingly politicized. Even in this context, reimbursement amounts are public information available for all procedures including for mental health at the Centers for Medicare and Medicaid Services (CMS) website (https:// www.cms.gov). These fees are announced annually once federal budget issues are settled. This contrasts with the challenge of obtaining fee information from private insurance companies.

- Medicare is minimally intrusive and offers greater privacy in the client–mental health practitioner relationship. Preauthorizations, reauthorizations, and ongoing case reviews are not required. However, companies hired for Medicare's Recovery Audit Program have been quite aggressive in pursuing reviews and recovering payments previously made. When working with Medicare it is essential that complete, legible documentation is made according to Medicare's standards. Medicare places the burden and expectation of knowing its standards on the clinician, but these are readily available (https://www.cms.gov/Outreach-and-Education/Medicare-Learning-Network-MLN/MLNMattersArticles/downloads/MM8378.pdf) for both national-level and local policies.

Enrolling in Medicare requires only the following:

- An identified physical location where you will provide services (not, e.g., a post office box as the only contact location). Service and payment addresses can be different.

- An identified location where you will store client health care records—either the treatment location or an off-site place.

- An NPI, as previously discussed. It may be possible to use an Employer Identification Number (EIN) for the application, but you will not be able to submit claims without an NPI.

- A copy of your license, proof of your degree, and (if you are applying with an EIN) IRS documentation regarding that number.

Medicare is regionally administered by Medicare Administrative Contractors (MACs), and your application will be processed by the contractor who is your local Medicare carrier. Enrolling is possible by paper application or online (the main online location for resources is https://www.cms.gov/Medicare/Provider-Enrollment-and-Certification/ MedicareProviderSupEnroll/index.html

**You can also check on your application and make changes to your status at this site.** You can download forms directly from links on the website, and the Enrollment Applications page will tell you which form you need. If you are enrolling (or updating your information), you will submit Form 855I. This will establish you as an individual practitioner with Medicare. If you are applying as a clinic or group practice, you will submit Form 855B, which establishes the corporation with Medicare.

You may also submit Form 855R, Reassignment of Medicare Benefits. This "reassigns" benefits to a corporation, if that is your arrangement with the group practice or clinic. Under this arrangement, when you bill Medicare, both the individual practitioner's NPI and the company's NPI go on the claim form. The reimbursement checks will be made out to the corporation. If you are applying as a practitioner in a group that already has established ties with Medicare and has a group number under which you will bill, you will submit Form 855I to establish yourself with Medicare, and Form 855R to reassign reimbursement to the group. You may also need to submit Form CMS-460, the Medicare Participating Physician or Supplier Agreement, which identifies you as a Medicare participant, defines "accepting assignment" (of Medicare payments), and establishes the term of the agreement (which essentially lasts until you or Medicare terminate the agreement in writing). Check with your local carrier whether this form is required or not.

It will be wise to seek out any specific requirements that may be particular to the Provider Enrollment Unit of your local carrier. If you call with a question you may get a feel for how helpful or vague representatives of your local carrier may be, and perhaps to establish a good working relationship with the person(s) who may help you through the application process.

Do not be intimidated by the apparent length of the applications. The Form 855I packet is 28 pages, but fewer than half of these pages require information, and even fewer are likely to apply to you (e.g., some are related to adverse legal events associated with health care delivery or billing that you or employees you manage, any companies that manage your practice, or any electronic billing clearinghouse you may use may have had). The information requested is straightforward, and the instruction pages are actually intelligible.

Carriers may take up to 60 days to process your application if they have all the information they need; the wait may be longer if they have to request additional information, and it may also depend on your location and how backlogged the system is. However, turnaround typically is quicker (in the 30- to 45-day range). You may see Medicare clients between the time you apply and your application is approved. This is not uncommon, for example, in situations in which recently licensed or relocated practitioners must immediately get up to speed with providing services. However, you will not be able to *bill* Medicare for those services until your application is approved. Once your application is approved, you may bill for services previously provided. For more on billing Medicare, see Section 3.8.

## What about Medicaid?

Medicaid "is a joint federal and state program that helps with medical costs for some people with limited income and resources. Medicaid also offers benefits not normally covered by Medicare, like nursing home care and personal care services" (http://www.medicare.

gov/your-medicare-costs/help-paying-costs/medicaid/medicaid.html). It is thus a "public" insurance plan. Medicaid regulations vary considerably by state, so you will need to contact your state Medicaid office to find out the requirements and process for enrolling, fee schedules, documentation, and similar requirements. Not all states cover the services of psychologists or social workers, and the relationship between PPACA and Medicaid programs is a work in progress at this writing.

## 3.6 Beginning to See MCO Clients

### Verifying Coverage, Eligibility, and Benefits

Assuming you have been accepted by an insurance company to provide covered services (i.e., you have been "empaneled," "enrolled" or "joined the network"), the next step will probably occur when you encounter a person covered by that insurer who calls you to schedule or comes to an intake. Prospective clients will call their MCO and the MCO staff will refer them to you (and probably several other providers), or clients will call you because they see your name in the MCO's pamphlet of provider names. Those referred by the MCO have had a session or two "preauthorized," but before you see a self-referred client, you usually must obtain preauthorization from the MCO for being paid. This will involve at least one phone call to certify or verify the client's benefits and current coverage status.

You should assume that clients are woefully uninformed or misinformed about their actual coverage. Clients are also not in the best position to learn the intricacies of behavioral health insurance when they come for help, and many simply give up seeking services or payments (which is something MCOs apparently count on). You or your staff members are usually better motivated, better informed, and more persistent, and your clients will be grateful for your relieving them of this burden.

When a new client arrives, you will be well advised to copy both sides of the client's insurance card. This will include all the account numbers for your client. It may also contain contact information for the company (e.g., a phone number to call to verify coverage, a billing address to submit claims) and other "fine-print" information (such as whether mental and behavioral health benefits need to be verified with or are managed through a company other than the main insurance company). Recall that some insurance companies "carve out" both the mental health benefits and their management to secondary companies, separately from "medical" benefits.

It will be very costly to provide services for which a client is not eligible for insurance coverage. It is very helpful to have a standard "interview" format for verifying benefits, so that you or office staff members who are doing this for you do not leave out the relevant questions to ask. Form 3.1 includes many of the questions we have found through trial and error to be relevant. Note that when you or your staff members are talking to the clerks who will "verify" your client's benefits, such "verifications" always come with the disclaimer that the "information provided is the best current information available and is not a guarantee of payment, which determination will be made at the time the claim is submitted." **FORM 3.1** Therefore, Form 3.1 allows you or your staff to record information about the call. The form also asks whether the client is current with paying his or her premiums, because if the person stops paying, any services rendered in the last 60 or 90 days will not be covered. A client's credit card authorization for you to bill can lower this risk.

Another scenario is the possibility that a client wants to use health insurance with

## Questionnaire for Determining Behavioral Health Insurance Benefits

Today's date: ____/____/____

### Information needed before a call to the insurer

Patient's name: _____  Date of birth: ____/____/____  ID #: _____

Policy holder's name (if different from patient's): _____

Policy holder's date of birth: ____/____/____  Policy holder's ID #: _____

Policy holder's employer: _____

Address of employer: _____

Name of insurer: _____  Name of policy: _____

Name of any behavioral health subcontractor: _____

Where are claims forms to be sent? _____

Phone #: _____  Member ID #: _____  Plan #: _____

Policy #: _____  Group #: _____  Other #: _____

### When you call, try to get an answer to each question, and make notes of anything unclear.

Date coverage began: ____/____/____  Date coverage will end/be renewed: ____/____/____

| Phone # | Buttons or prompts, extension | Date(s) called | Name(s) of representative(s) spoken with | Title | Who called? |
|---|---|---|---|---|---|
| | | | | | |
| | | | | | |
| | | | | | |

*(continued)*

## Eligibility

a. Does this specific patient have any coverage under this policy?   ❑ Yes   ❑ No

b. Coordination of benefits: Is this insurance   ❑ Primary?   ❑ Secondary?   ❑ Other insurance?:

c. Are services for treating "mental and nervous disorders" covered?   ❑ Yes   ❑ No

d. Are services for treating "drug and alcohol disorders" covered?   ❑ Yes   ❑ No

e. Is "outpatient psychotherapy" or "outpatient mental/behavioral health treatment" covered?   ❑ Yes   ❑ No

f. Is preauthorization required for any mental/behavioral health services?   ❑ No   ❑ Yes

   If yes, which services? _____

   _____

   If yes, what is the process? _____

   _____

## Provider

a. Is this therapist a "participating" provider under this particular health care plan?   ❑ No   ❑ Yes

b. Will the insurance plan pay out-of-network providers?   ❑ No   ❑ Yes (see below for costs)

c. Is referral by a physician required?   ❑ No   ❑ Yes   Is supervision by a physician required?   ❑ No   ❑ Yes
   Is consultation with a physician required?   ❑ No   ❑ Yes

d. How are payments computed? _____

## Treatments

a. Will the insurance pay for these kinds of treatments?   Individual psychotherapy   ❑ Yes   ❑ No
   Group therapy   ❑ Yes   ❑ No   Family therapy   ❑ Yes   ❑ No   Drug and alcohol treatment   ❑ Yes   ❑ No
   Psychological testing   ❑ Yes   ❑ No   Other: _____

b. If the spouse, the parents of a child patient, or the whole family is seen, are these visits covered differently
   from visits of the patient alone?   ❑ No   ❑ Yes   If so, how? _____

   _____

c. If we must meet for two sessions on a single date, will insurance pay for it or for only a single session per
   day?   ❑ Double   ❑ Only one session

d. Will insurance pay for more than one session per week?   ❑ No   ❑ Yes, but only _____ sessions per week
   ❑ Yes, as decided by the professional

## Diagnoses

Are there excluded diagnoses? (Ask about ADHD, learning disorders, personality disorders, conduct disorder,
chronic pain, or others as relevant.)   ❑ No   ❑ Yes   If so, which? _____

## Allowable reimbursements/payments

a. Is there a limit on the amount the insurance will pay for mental health services in a year?   ❑ No   ❑ Yes:
   $_____   per   ❑ Calendar year?   ❑ Policy year?   How much of this remains available today? $_____

b. Is there a limit on the amount the insurance will pay for these services in a lifetime?   ❑ No   ❑ Yes:
   $_____   How much of this remains available today? $_____

*(continued)*

c. Does the insurer pay the entire amount of allowable charges for mental health services, or does it reduce the coverage for mental health services? ❑ No reduction ❑ Yes: By how much? $_____ or ____ %

d. Is there a limit on the number of visits/sessions per year or by diagnosis? ❑ No ❑ Yes: ____ per year

   ❑ Yes, for these diagnoses: _____

e. Are visits reimbursed by ❑ percentage of clinician fee? If so, what percent? _____% or by ❑ set fee for these CPT codes:

| 90791 | 90832 | 90834 | 90837 | 90846 | 90847 | 96101 | 96118 | | |
|-------|-------|-------|-------|-------|-------|-------|-------|---|---|
|       |       |       |       |       |       |       |       |   |   |

f. What are the limitations on hospitalization? _____
_____

g. Can inpatient hospital days be converted into outpatient sessions? ❑ Yes ❑ No

h. What other considerations affect charges/fees/payment amounts? _____
_____
_____

## Costs to the patient

What is the patient's *deductible* before the insurance company will pay anything?

$_____ ❑ per policy year ❑ per calendar year ❑ per person/patient ❑ per family ❑ per diagnosis

How much of this has been met? $_____ as of ____/____/____

What is the client's *copayment* per session after the deductible is met? $_____ ❑ No copayment

**Are there any other rules, requirements, forms, or procedures** that we should be aware of? _____
_____
_____
_____
_____

Treatment authorization #: _____ Authorizer: _____

Starting date: ____/____/____ Number of sessions: ____ Dollar limit: $_____

Authorization renewal date: ____/____/____

Authorization to be faxed to clinician: ❑ No ❑ Yes If yes, date received: ____/____/____

which you are not enrolled, so you are OON, as discussed earlier. In that instance, first determine whether the policy allows and will reimburse for OON care. If not, your client will be responsible for the full cost of your services. Before initiating treatment, in order to provide fully informed consent, you will need to discuss financial arrangements and discover limitations on benefits (such as a deductible or cap on payments).

Note that because clients may continue in treatment beyond the calendar year or the policy year of their insurance policy, it will probably be smart to set up a reminder and process for verification of benefits at least annually. As you know from going to your own doctors or dentists, or to the hospital, many health professional offices do this at the time of every visit with the simple question "Have there been any changes in your insurance?" or, more directly, "Is your insurance still with X Company?" Clients have come to expect this as a standard part of the "check-in" process.

### An Option: Treating an MCO Client without Using MCO Benefits

Regardless of whether or not a client wants to use his or her insurance, you are contractually obligated if you are on that insurer's panel to accept the fee you agreed to as full payment, and not to bill the client for the difference between that charge and your (usually much higher) regular fee. However, if the service you will provide is not covered by your or the client's MCO contract (e.g., telephone therapy, executive coaching, parenting skills, and almost all assessments) or is only partially covered (e.g., half the number of hours of professional time required for a testing battery), or if the benefits have been used up or have been denied, then you and the client can work out any mutually agreeable financial arrangement. Make sure to document this with a letter of agreement, or use Medicare's Advance Beneficiary Notice of Noncoverage form (see Section 3.8).

## MCOs and Treatment Plans

After meeting a self-referred client, you may have to complete and submit an assessment and treatment plan—often called an "initial treatment plan" or "individualized treatment plan"—with a great deal of information on the client's history and functioning. A few MCOs may require a clinician to provide a diagnosis, treatment plan, evaluation of the client's level of performing activities of daily living, assessment of substance use/abuse, and evaluation of the lethality of any suicidal plans, so that the "medical necessity" (see below) of treatment may be determined. It is not uncommon for MCOs to take some time to decide to accept or refuse your proposed treatment plan, during which time you may suffer the financial risk of unpaid treatment and your client may undergo emotional hardship. Such delays place both you and your client in anxious limbo.

### Problems with the Use of a Highly Structured Treatment Plan Format

Most of the large MCOs now use their own check-off forms, at least for reauthorizations. Although this reduces the MCOs' processing costs (compared to having a human read and understand a narrative), they may increase your vulnerability, for several reasons:

1. You have to reduce complex issues and judgments to only a few options. The list of symptoms, signs, or impairments may allow you only to indicate their presence or

absence, or to rate them as mild, moderate, or severe. These may not reflect the variations and interactions accurately. The few boxes for indicating substance use may
force you to report use that is not problematic or not currently problematic.

2. The choices presented on these forms may not fit your goals or aims very well. For
   example, the Outpatient Review Form from Value Options offers these four choices:
   "Reasons for continued treatment: . . . 1. Remains symptomatic, 2. Maintenance, 3.
   Prepare for discharge within coming month, 4. Facilitate return to work" (see http://
   www.valueoptions.com/providers/Forms/Clinical/Outpatient-Review-Form.pdf). A
   similar form from Mutual of Omaha offers under "Treatment Plan" these options:
   "Improved functioning/symptom reduction and discharge from treatment;
   Transfer to support groups or self-help and discharge from treatment; Provide ongoing supportive counseling and maintain stabilization of symptoms; Provide ongoing medication management; and Other" (see http://www.mutualofomaha.com/
   healthcareprofessionals/index.html).

3. The choices presented may not fit a client very well. The forms do not allow more
   than two diagnoses. When you are seeking more treatment sessions, each symptom
   has to be neatly rated as either "worse," "same," "improved," or "resolved." What
   degree of progress are you agreeing to with "improved," and are you ever sure a
   symptom is fully "resolved"?

4. These kinds of data can more easily be entered into computerized databases and
   thus accidentally disclosed, shared with other organizations, and used for profiling
   providers.

5. The choices may not be mutually exclusive or accurate. For example, doesn't the
   intended use of a selective serotonin reuptake inhibitor as an "antidepressant,"
   "mood stabilizer," "anxiolytic," or "other" depend on the client's situation and not
   the drug's "class"?

In light of these risks, we suggest not only the usual thoughtfulness and attempts to
foresee the consequences, but also recording comments and qualifications in your case
notes.

   If your proposed treatment is acceptable to the MCO, you will have a small number of
visits "authorized." Before these are used up, you must decide whether your client will need
more treatment; if so, you must submit an "outpatient treatment report" (OTR), which is a
kind of progress note on how the client is functioning and a revised treatment plan. Generally, you must indicate progress toward treatment goals for the authorization of further services. Because you ethically may not lie on an OTR about levels of functioning, treatment
may be denied to those who could benefit from it but who are not severely incapacitated.
After all, MCOs' therapeutic goal is only a "return to previous level of functioning," by
which they mean reduction of symptoms to a baseline level before treatment began. This is
not what we mean by "mental health" or even "remission."

   After you begin seeing clients (which may not be soon—most clinicians receive only a
few referrals per year), the MCO will start a "profile" on you. This will include how many
sessions you typically use per case (and perhaps how frequently you see clients); how much
difficulty you cause the MCO when seeking authorization for services; and how you meet
many other undisclosed criteria. This profile will be used to decide whether or not to offer
you referrals and a further contract. Lastly, despite your timely submission of forms and

information to the MCO, there may be extensive delays before you receive payment, even after authorization. This delay burdens you and your clients, but many states have enacted laws to require timely payment of "clean" (errorless) claims.

## Initial Discussions with the Client about MCO-Related Ethical Issues

Securing informed consent involves discussion with any potential client prior to treatment about its risks and benefits (see Chapter 5). Managed care brings additional risks beyond the clinical ones, such as those concerning confidentiality and continuity of care.

Having a client read and review any needed OTR form[1] will make more concrete and believable the information sought by MCOs and the concerns you raise in your discussion. The form will also be a stimulus for the client to weigh the use of insurance benefits. Although some forms are fairly simple, others are quite intrusive, requiring the collection (and, effectively, the disclosure) of a great deal of information not clearly relevant to treating the presenting issues. An example of an OTR form is the one offered by Value Options (http://www.valueoptions.com/providers/Forms/Clinical/Outpatient-Review-Form.pdf and http://www.valueoptions.com/providers/Forms/Clinical/Outpatient_Review_Form_instructions.pdf).

### Informing the Client about MCO Confidentiality

Potential clients must be informed before treatment begins of the risks and consequences of treatment to give them the right of informed refusal of treatment. This should include the implications for MCO confidentiality.

Under HIPAA, all MCOs are CEs (included in "health plans") and must conform to the Privacy and Security Rules. However, CEs are allowed to design their own internal processes within the general HIPAA privacy and security regulations. At this writing, investigations of HIPAA compliance occur only upon a complaint of an "unauthorized disclosure." Although the future will bring inspections, they will not be common. The almost universal experience of the "loss" of protected health information (PHI) materials sent by clinicians to MCOs should constitute the presumption of an unauthorized disclosure, but this has not been pursued legally. The skills and training of those evaluating the PHI you submit are uncertain. These people are not controlled by the laws and ethics that apply to licensed clinicians. Reviewers are not (at least at the initial levels) mental health professionals; even at higher levels, they may not be clinicians or therapists, and are rarely specialists. Few MCOs require a professional of your discipline ("a peer") to review your treatment. Given these factors, we advise the following:

❑ You should have a detailed discussion with the client of the issues described here, have the client read Handout 3.1, and get a more specific release-of-information (ROI) form (e.g., Form 8.2 or 8.3) signed before talking to an MCO reviewer. The MCO will assert that you do not need more authorization to send PHI, because the client

---

[1]Since the MCO will not pay you for the time you need to complete OTRs, you might consider doing so with the client during your billable face-to-face time (if this is not forbidden by contract). An alternative is to bill the client for your time, as it is a "noncovered" service you provide. But be aware of possible acting out of negative feelings about the MCO.

signed an ROI form when he or she enrolled for the health insurance. However, this occurred before any PHI was created, and so it hardly represents informed consent. Consider offering clients the one-page glossary available at the following website for client education (http://www.theshouldercenter.com/wp-content/uploads/pdf/ Understanding-Insurance-Speak.pdf).

❑ You should discuss with the client the probable consequences of releasing this information to the MCO, where it will become part of a permanent medical record.[2] It is likely that this record will be accessible to many other organizations over time, such as when the client applies for disability or life insurance (so the client should get these before therapy starts), security clearances, mortgage loans, or jobs. Of course, this information will not be shared for these purposes without the client's signature. The issue here is that once the information is in a record, its disclosure will be required, or the client will have to forgo ordinary opportunities like getting a job or a mortgage. Such honest discussion may or may not lessen the tendency of clients to be forthcoming and self-disclosing when advised of an MCO's confidentiality rules (Kremer & Gesten, 1998).

❑ Releasing detailed information may be countertherapeutic for some clients with borderline or paranoid personality disorder diagnoses, as well as with those in the public eye. You should decide what to do and may have to forgo MCO payments with these clients. See below for more about treating MCO clients without using insurance.

### Informing the Client about an MCO's Coverage, Benefits, and Limitations on Treatment

Clients must make informed decisions about their costs under their MCOs' coverage. This should include not only the written limits, but your own experience of the services frequently authorized and the limitations on those from whom they can receive treatment without having to pay more out of pocket.

- The client must accept the MCO's intention to pay only for treatment to return the client to *baseline* levels of functioning. When this has happened, you and the client must renegotiate your contract, including goals, methods, and payment for further services.

- MCOs tend to approve only very brief treatment, which may not be clinically appropriate for all clients. In the experience of many clinicians, this seems to prevail no matter what a client's diagnosis, history, or needs may be. Again, however, this prejudice may be changing for some diagnoses, and it depends on definitions of "medical necessity." MCOs' definition of "brief" is often too short (6–10 sessions) to be effective according to the literature (which suggests 20–30 sessions for effectiveness with anxiety disorders and depression).

---

[2]The Medical Information Bureau is the most likely repository, but the information is not in your words or in a narrative format. It is simplified and coded for the use of insurers, and thus open to misinterpretation. Also, when MCOs and similar organizations merge, their data systems must merge too, and so data may be lost or jumbled. Lastly, when mental health data are recorded in medical databases, the level of confidentiality may be lowered to that of the routine medical data.

- MCO staff members are not your consultants or your supervisors, and therefore are legally unable to offer direction for treatment. However, MCOs' position is that they are not prescribing or proscribing treatment (that can only be decided by professionals like us); they are only deciding what they will pay for.

- Some plans will reimburse for services provided by those not on their panels (OON). If you are not on an MCO's panel, and if no empaneled provider is available in the area (or none has your specific skills), and if a client assertively seeks your services, then you could be paid at higher than the empaneled rate. You must negotiate each such case with the MCO and could be authorized as an OON provider, but only if the client's contract allows such an increasingly rare arrangement.

- A client's insurance coverage and MCO may change during your treatment; reviewers and other staff members at the MCO may give you inaccurate information; or they may later deny payment for previously authorized service ("retroactive denials," "recoupment")—all of which change the true costs of treatment for the client. Clients should be informed of these possibilities and (in your experience) their likelihood, and they must agree to pay for services they received and for which payment has been retracted. Indeed, they would have paid for them then if the policies were correctly known. Some contracts will prevent your billing the clients in these cases and, in cases where Medicare is involved, simply pay up, investigate, and consider a later appeal.

## A Client Education Handout about Managed Care

**HANDOUT 3.1** Handout 3.1 is designed to inform clients of the practical, financial, legal, and ethical implications of managed care. Before using it, read and decide whether it is accurate for your location, contracts, profession, and experience, and tailor it to your setting. For example, if a patients' bill of rights is passed in your state or nationally, or if your state has legal precedents like the *Jaffee v. Redmond* (518 U.S. 1, 1996) case (see http://www.jaffee-redmond.org; DeBell & Jones, 1997; and Shuman & Foote, 1999), you should modify the statements about confidentiality in this form. Some sentences in the handout are highly critical of managed care, and you might choose to delete them if your practice is dependent on MCOs. A few sentences are adapted from Higuchi (1994), who provides a good review of the legal issues. Jackson Rainer, PhD, of Norcross, GA, and Charles H. Steinmeyer, PhD, of Warren, PA, have improved this section and handout through their reviews. Therapists have also posted similar patient education materials on the effects of using one's insurance. You might look at these:

> http://judykoehlertherapist.com/2012/05/using-insurance-for-counseling
> http://boulderpsychotherapistsguild.com/Information%20for%20Therapists.php

Therapists have an ethical responsibility to inform clients of the main issues in using managed health care, including the fact that some research on the effects is not very positive. For example, in an analogue study, independent practitioners informed student nonclients of the impacts of managed care on therapy. It had negative effects: "Participants were significantly more likely to believe that managed care would have a negative impact on treatment and significantly less likely to see an independent practitioner, use insurance

## What You Should Know about Managed Care and Your Treatment

Your health insurance may pay part of the costs of your treatment, but the benefits cannot be paid until a managed care organization (MCO) authorizes payment. The MCO has been selected by the insurer your employer chose, not by you or me. The MCO sets some limits on us, and you need to know what these are before we go further.

### Confidentiality

If you expect to use your health insurance to help pay for psychotherapy, you must allow me to tell the MCO about your problem or problems and give you a psychiatric diagnosis. You must also permit me to tell the MCO about the treatment I am providing, about your progress during treatment, and about how you are doing in many areas of your life (your functioning at work, in your family, your social life, and in activities of daily living). I am not paid separately for collecting, organizing, or submitting this information, and I cannot bill you for these services. All of this information will become part of the MCO's records, and some of it will be included in your permanent medical record at the Medical Information Bureau, a national data bank. It is not open to the public, but it will be examined when you apply for life, disability, or health insurance, and it may be considered when you apply for employment, credit/loans, a security clearance, or other things in the future. You will have to release this information or you may not get the insurance, job, loan, or clearance.

All insurance companies and MCOs claim to keep the information they receive confidential, and there are federal laws about its use and release. Those laws apply to me as well as other laws and codes of ethics that are much stricter. If you are concerned about who might see your records now or in the future, we should discuss this concern more fully before we start treatment. You should evaluate your situation carefully in regard to confidentiality. For some people and some problems, extreme privacy of their communications to their therapist is absolutely essential to their working on their difficulties. For others, their problems are not ones that raise much concern over confidentiality and they are comfortable with the usual protections.

### Treatment and Payment

If I have a contract with your MCO, I am one of its providers, and so I am "in network" and must charge you the fee that the MCO and I have agreed to. You will pay me the full fee until your payments reach the yearly "deductible" of your health insurance. After that, you will pay me only the copay at each session.

I am not on all insurance panels, and it is possible that your insurance plan has coverage or benefits payable to providers who are "out of network." If so, it may be possible for me to negotiate a special fee arrangement between me and your MCO.

The MCO will review the information I send it and then effectively decide how much treatment I can provide to you. *The MCO can refuse to pay for any of your treatment, or for any treatment by me. Or it may pay only a very small part of your treatment's cost (because of deductibles, coinsurance, and copayments), and later it can prevent me from charging you directly for further treatment we agree to pursue.*

- The MCO may verify your eligibility for payment and then later decide that this was in error and require you (or me, if it paid me) to return the payments received (these are "retroactive denials").

*(continued)*

- The MCO will almost always require you to see a psychiatrist for medication evaluations (and prescriptions), *whether you or I think this is appropriate.*
- It can set limits on the kinds of treatments I can provide to you by refusing to pay for them. It will decide which are not "medically necessary." The ones it authorizes may not be the best suited to your difficulties or in your long-term best interest, and it may not agree to pay for those that we might consider most beneficial.
- Not all services may be covered, including phone meetings, video conferencing, and sessions that are deemed medically unnecessary. If you request or agree to services that are not covered, you will be expected to pay for them, and we will sign an additional contract.
- The MCO will approve treatment aimed at improving the specific symptoms (behaviors, feelings) that brought you into therapy. It will usually not approve any further treatment, even if you and I believe it is needed to fully relieve your problems, or if we believe that undertreating your problems may prolong your distress or lead to relapses (worsening), or if we feel that more sessions will help you function much better than before.
- The MCO may stop its payments because it believes that you have made sufficient progress and no longer need treatment. If the MCO denies payment before either of us is satisfied about progress, we may also need to consider other treatment choices, and those may not be the ones we would prefer.
- When it does authorize our treatment, the MCO is likely to limit the number of times we can meet. Your insurance policy probably has a maximum number of appointments allowed for outpatient psychotherapy (per calendar or per policy year, and there may be a lifetime limit), or the limit may be in dollars, but the MCO does not have to let you use all of those.
- Even if we send all the forms and information to the MCO on time, there may be long delays before any decisions are made. This creates stressful uncertainty and may alter our earlier beliefs about the costs and nature of your treatment.
- We can appeal the MCO's decisions on payment and number of sessions, but we can only do so within the MCO itself. We cannot appeal to other professionals, to your employer, or through the courts.
- This state does not have laws regulating MCOs' decisions—that is, laws about the skills or qualifications of their staff members, about access to medical and psychological records by employers and others, or about the appeals process. These are all decided by each MCO.
- The particular MCO in charge of your mental health benefits can change during the course of your treatment. If this happens, we may have to go through the whole treatment authorization process again. It is also possible that the benefits or coverage for your treatment may change during the course of our therapy, and so your part of the costs of treatment may change.
- I will discuss with you any efforts the MCO makes to get me to limit your care in any way.
- You should know that my contract or your employer's contract with a particular MCO prevents us from taking legal actions against the MCO if things go badly because of its decisions.

## Our Agreement

If, after reading this handout and discussing it with me, you are concerned with these issues, you may have the choice of paying me directly and not using your health insurance. This will create no record outside of my files. This possibility requires that I don't have a contract with your insurer or MCO.

My signature below indicates that I have read and understood the issues described above, and willingly enter treatment accepting these conditions and limitations. I give my therapist permission to submit information in order to secure payment for the mental health services to be provided to me.

❏ Yes, I want to review any written materials you send to my MCO.    ❏ No, that is not necessary.

_____    _____    ____/____/____

Signature of client                                      Printed name of client                                Date

benefits, expect to benefit from treatment, expect to form a strong working relationship, and trust that the practitioner would work in their best interest" (Pomerantz, 2000, p. 159). These results suggest that therapists should make certain to provide accurate, current, and balanced information about managed care, and that they should be especially sensitive to the effects of insurance use on the therapeutic relationship.

If you have a financial and legal arrangement that involves capitation (payments to you of a fixed amount—a "per member, per month" [PMPM] rate—to provide for all the mental health needs of the "covered lives") or a case rate system (in which you are paid a lump sum per case no matter what kinds of care the client needs), you should disclose this to all new clients. Why? Because these arrangements, like other cost controls, serve to constrain and ration the care available (Miller, 1998). Clients should be informed of these limitations to be able to consent to enter treatment. For example, Rosenthal (2000) found that case rate payments resulted in reduction of numbers of sessions by 20–25%, compared to sessions for clients seen on a fee-for-service basis (payments for each session).

## 3.7 Submitting Claims to Get Paid

It is crucial to distinguish your fee from your charges when you are dealing with insurers. You set a fee for each of the services you provide. Let's say that this fee is $150. If you then contract with an MCO for a payment of, say, $70, that is all you will receive. On your bill, however, always indicate your full fee and then add an "adjustment" of, say, $80, which brings your charge to the insurance company down to the contracted $70. If your bill shows only what you expect to collect (the $70), then the payer will consider that your full fee and discount their payments from that. Clients without insurance will pay your full fee unless you arrange and indicate an adjustment.

Although we recommend submitting the claims for clients, the client can submit the bill if you are OON. The easiest way to provide the client with all the information needed by the insurer is to generate a Superbill (see Section 2.3). Many such forms are available online, and there are simple programs to generate them as well.

### Ethical and Legal Considerations in Billing Insurers or MCOs

❑ Do not try to bill for double sessions at your usual MCO fee, so that when the insurance company pays for both at its discount, you will then receive about your full fee. Similarly, do not bill for an hour and a half hour session for 1 hour of your work. "It's dishonest, and you're telling the client that you think it is fine for both or you to become criminals for the price of a few sessions" (Reid, 1999, p. 63).

❑ Don't be greedy. Do not bill two insurers for the same service by billing for both members of a couple when each has separate insurance coverage. However, it may be acceptable to bill the second insurer for the part not paid by the first; read what the contract says about "coordination of benefits."

❑ Do not mislead the insurance company into believing that you provided a service when in fact a trainee or assistant did, even if the insurance company will not pay for services provided by others under your supervision. This is a limitation we should take up with lawmakers.

❑ Charge a client only the copayment you and the MCO have agreed to. If clients really cannot afford that amount, (1) see them *pro bono*, or (2) refer them to another provider or clinic they can afford. See the APA Practice Organization's advice about this (http://www.apapracticecentral.org/update/2009/09-30/caution-waiving.aspx).

❑ If you agreed to a fee with the insurer of $N, and later you accept less as full payment because you are not collecting the client's part (the copayment), this acceptance is considered fraud, submission of a false claim, or violation of the anti-kickback provisions of your contract with the payer. Do not advertise or state in your client information brochure that "Insurance is accepted as full payment."

You must make good-faith efforts to collect the client's part of the fee and document your collection efforts. These are burdens, but the risks are high. It would be best to write an office policy about waiving the copayment only for indigent clients or those undergoing hardship, and define your criteria for "hardship" or "indigent." Do not offer the waiver; let clients ask for it. Medicare's policy on occasional waivers can be found in the middle of this document (http://oig.hhs.gov/fraud/docs/alertsandbulletins/121994.html). Investigate and document the client's income and insurance coverage before waiving the copayment.

Your contract usually states that if the MCO rejects your claim for payment for services you have rendered, you can only collect from the client the copayment and not the rest of the fee (for which you had billed the MCO). Read your contracts very, very carefully.

❑ Do not change the diagnosis or the CPT code (the numerical code for the service being billed) so that the insurance company will pay for your services or pay more (this is called "padding the bill" or, more currently, "upcoding"). For example, do not label what is truly an ICD-10-CM Z-code situation as an "adjustment disorder," or turn "adjustment disorder" into "major depressive disorder."

❑ Don't "cream and dump." That is, don't see those with good insurance until their coverage is exhausted and then refer them away.

❑ Do not try to explain that you were "too busy with clinical issues to worry about the paperwork," or say that you "trusted your assistant," or use other excuses for fraudulent billing.

The federal government has cracked down on fraudulent health care billing by creating the Health Care Fraud Prevention and Enforcement Action Team (HEAT), so if you plan to accept Medicare, you will need to protect yourself from accusations of fraud, waste, and abuse with a compliance plan (for more about this, see http://www.stopmedicarefraud.gov).

**Failure to follow these rules can result in your being prosecuted.** You may then be convicted of insurance fraud, perjury to commit fraud, or collusion with the client; these are all felonies and you can subsequently be fined and jailed. It will usually cost you your license and livelihood. Psychologists have served time for insurance fraud.

## What You Need to Know for Insurance Claim Processing

• Know what forms and terms to use. You will need the CMS-1500 or the insurer's own billing form, or the insurer may offer an online claims submission option. Be familiar with the jargon of billing ("duration of session," "place of service," "coin-surer," "effective date," etc.) and what must be entered into each blank on the CMS-1500. Understand deductibles, copayments, maximum out-of-pocket payments, panels and OON status, coordination of benefits, and percentage coverages, as well as how they are computed.

Barnett and Walfish (2011) cover the basics, but there does not appear to be a more sophisticated resource for learning about insurance claim processing. Therefore we recommend using a biller or buying an EHR program, rather than developing billing as an exhausting hobby.

- Know which of your services are reimbursable and for what amounts. Each MCO decides which services, as indicated by CPT numerical codes, it will cover and who can provide them (physicians can be paid for many more services, such as phone calls, than nonphysicians). Because clinicians use only perhaps a dozen codes and they are often revised, we suggest searching for the currently acceptable ones online (see http://psychcentral.com/lib/cpt-codes-for-psychology-services/0001187, http://www.quicdoc.com/docs/PsychotherapyCodesChanges.pdf, and http://www.apapracticecentral.org/reimbursement/billing/psychotherapy-codes.pdf). The whole "reimbursement" section of the APA's site is a helpful and reliable resource. For a fuller discussion, see the rich website of psychology's long-term representative to the CPT coding authority, Anthony Puente (http://psychologycoding.com).

- Similarly, each insurer decides which diagnoses it will pay for from each kind of clinician. As of October 2015, the diagnoses are from ICD-10-CM—the Clinical Modification of the current (10th) revision of the *International Classification of Diseases*, created by the World Health Organization and licensed to the Centers for Disease Control and Prevention (CDC) in the United States. The very long, very inclusive official version can be downloaded from the CDC (http://www.cdc.gov/nchs/icd/icd10cm.htm) and edited down with significant effort.

  ICD-10-CM includes about twice as many diagnoses as the current (fifth) edition of the standard psychiatric manual, the *Diagnostic and Statistical Manual of Mental Disorders* (DSM-5). The DSM and ICD codes (numbers) and diagnoses (names, labels) are not always identical, and care should be used when entering this information into any record. Generally use DSM to determine the diagnosis, and ICD names and numbers to record information anywhere.

- If you are treating a psychological condition related to a medical one, or if you are doing neuropsychological evaluations or treatments, use the *medical* ICD codes. They are reimbursed more routinely, with less resistance, and often at higher rates by Medicare, Medigap policies, commercial carriers, and MCOs. The related psychological CPT codes may allow you more hours for assessment or services. If you are treating a psychological condition and using psychological methods, use both a psychological CPT code and a mental ICD diagnosis code. Do not use the psychological procedure codes with a medical diagnosis, and vice versa. Different procedures can be provided to the same client for different diagnoses; this is why there is a space on the CMS-1500 form for a diagnosis code next to each procedure code's space. There may be limits on similar procedures performed during the same visit.

- Obtain precise information concerning lifetime and annual deductibles or limitations, so you can estimate the likely costs to a client, but make it clear that this estimate is not a final calculation and that the final figure depends on the MCO's decisions. Become smart about how to use time of billing to your advantage. For example, are yearly deductibles based on calendar years or on 365-day periods from diagnosis or initiation of service?

## The Concept of "Medically Necessary" Care

"Medical necessity" is the term universally used to limit payments to providers. It is a concept created by MCOs and has no history or basis in economics, research, medicine, psychiatry, or psychology. It was based on the belief that services were being overused (i.e., that treatment was being provided when it was not necessary), and that this overuse was the cause of the great increases in health care costs in the 1970s. MCOs sold employers the idea that they could substantially reduce health care costs by limiting care to "medically necessary" services. Indeed, some services were exploiting insurance (e.g., treating substance abuse with months-long residential care and hospitalizing adolescents were far too common). For about a decade, health care costs to employers did indeed grow more slowly or level off. Providers, especially hospitals, were paid a lot less, and MCOs made huge profits. Cost cutting peaked in the early 1990s.

The criteria for "medical necessity" vary both among disorders and across MCOs. They are generally considered proprietary information, and so they may not be made publicly available but do search the Internet. They have also not been subjected to empirical evaluation. One list of such criteria is available (http://www.magellanprovider.com/MHS/MGL/providing_care/clinical_guidelines/MNC.asp?leftmenu=5&sub=child5_4). Note that outpatient, office-based treatment is addressed in just 2 of this list's 105 pages. An informative recent paper by two reviewers for Cigna (Papatola & Lustig, 2015) indicates that the presence of symptoms is necessary but not sufficient, because meriting a diagnosis is not sufficient reason for supplying services. They note that therapists often report "life events" or "stressors," but that these "are not symptoms," and that the severity of the symptoms must impair specific day-to-day functioning to make treatment necessary.

The definitions of "medical necessity" are crucial for payment and client care decisions, and so the concept has been argued, but without much agreement (see http://store.samhsa.gov/product/Medical-Necessity-in-Private-Health-Plans/SMA03-3790 for an overview). Also note that the definitions for children under state-administered Medicaid may differ greatly across states and may be much broader than the definitions for adults, even under Medicaid. In practice, the MCO reviewers' opinions of what is "medically necessary" care will be based on their training by the MCO and their internal documents.

**FORM 3.2**    Form 3.2, a checklist for documenting the necessity of providing psychotherapy, is modified from one by Allan J. Comeau, PhD, of West Los Angeles, CA, and is used with his kind permission. It was designed to improve documentation to third-party payers and to assist clinicians with thinking through decisions about continuing, reducing, or ending treatment. Because MCOs use the language of "medical necessity" in dealing with their reviewers, it may be advantageous to discuss a case from this perspective. This form summarizes your conclusions and (ideally) will lead the reviewer to see the case in the way you indicate.

In order to establish the necessity of a level of care (e.g., inpatient, partial, or outpatient), MCO reviewers will seek much more information than is available on the OTR. Under HIPAA, because they are CEs, they can ask for the entire file you have created, all notes,

# Checklist for Assessing the Medical Necessity for Psychotherapy

Patient's name: _____ ID #: _____

Based upon my ongoing assessment, the above-named patient requires continuing psychotherapy and or psychotherapeutic case management for the following reasons:

❑ This patient has a history of regression to a lower level of functioning without ongoing psychotherapy services.

❑ This patient has improved considerably in the past, but his or her functioning and condition have deteriorated following a reduction of frequency in therapy visits.

❑ This patient has a history of noncompliance with other essential components of his or her care (medications, treatment program attendance, abstinence, etc.), and psychotherapy will help this patient to improve his or her level of adherence to planned and effective treatment.

❑ This patient's current level of functioning is such that psychotherapy and/or case management services are needed to support maintenance at this (lower) level of functioning.

❑ This patient's current WHODAS 2 (World Health Organization Disability Assessment Schedule) score, or other similar instrument's score, indicates moderate or greater difficulties in social, occupational, or school functioning. Psychotherapeutic treatment is essential to support stabilization or improve functioning.

❑ This patient's functioning score indicates severe difficulty in social, occupational, or school functioning. Psychotherapeutic treatment is essential to assist with achieving stabilization. Additional information ❑ is or ❑ is not attached.

I have reviewed the "medical necessity" policies of the patient's health insurance plan or company [name of company]: _____, at [website URL]: _____, and/or the written policies numbered _____, and have determined that this patient/client's condition meets the relevant criteria for medical necessity as per those policies. I therefore recommend these methods and frequency of treatment:

❑ Individual psychotherapy at the rate of ____ sessions per week/month.

❑ Group psychotherapy at the rate of ____ meetings per week/month.

❑ Collateral therapy at the rate of ____ meetings per week/month.

❑ Clinical case management at the intensity of _____

❑ Other: _____

Thank you for your attention to this matter.

Sincerely,

_____     ____/____/____
                        Signature of clinician                                              Date

**FORM 3.2. Medical-necessity-for-psychotherapy checklist.** Adapted from a form devised by Allan J. Comeau, PhD, of West Los Angeles, CA, and used by permission of Dr. Comeau. From *The Paper Office for the Digital Age, Fifth Edition*. Copyright © 2017 Edward L. Zuckerman and Keely Kolmes. Published by The Guilford Press. Permission to reproduce this material is granted to purchasers of this book for personal use or use with individual clients (see copyright page for details).

and other information in it. While HIPAA suggests that we can send only the "minimum necessary information," it also allows an insurer to decide what that is and protects us by saying we can rely on the insurer's decisions about this. Of course, this protection for a HIPAA complaint does not protect us from complaints to our licensing boards about loss of confidentiality.

## Assignment of Benefits

Some clients may receive payments from their health insurance for services you have provided and then fail to pay you. You can prevent this, as well as simplify the financial part of their lives, with the very standard procedure that the sample letter below supports. In addition, when you experience problems with receiving payment, having such a letter may allow you legitimate access to a client's benefit information and previous records, or if the client has left treatment, as is likely, to respond to denials.

[Your Letterhead]

[Date]

[Name of insurer]
[Addresses]                                    [Client's or insured's identification number or Social Security number]

Dear [Name of Client or Insured]:

Your health insurance may cover part of the costs of your treatment here. I would prefer that the insurance company pay its obligations directly to me, rather than paying you and then having you pay me. In order to make that arrangement, I need your signature below. Please read the next two paragraphs and sign where indicated. If you have questions or would like to discuss this, please give me a call.

**AGREEMENT**

**This is a direct assignment of my rights and benefits under this policy.**

I, _____, the client, hereby request that payment of authorized Medicare and/or other health insurance plan benefits be made on my behalf to the therapist named above for services provided. I authorize this therapist to release to my third-party payer/insurer and/or to the Centers for Medicare and Medicaid Services and its agents, as necessary, any medical information needed to determine the benefits payable for related services. This authorization shall be considered valid for the duration of the claim. A photocopy of this authorization will be considered as effective and valid as the original.

I understand that I will be personally responsible for any amount denied, or any remaining amount owed for services partially covered by my third-party payer/insurer. This payment will not exceed my indebtedness to the above-mentioned assignee, and I agree to pay, in a current manner. I agree to pay any costs incurred by this therapist in collecting such fees.

_____        ___ /___ /____

Signature of client (or insured, parent, guardian, or legal representative)                Date

❑ Copy received by client or   ❑ Copy held by therapist

## Making the Claim on the CMS-1500

The HCFA-1500 is the standard form for filing health insurance claims. Despite the intended uniformity (which sets a "minimum required" dataset), individual insurance companies may have peculiarities and additions in what they may expect on the form, so check with the individual companies. The red ink is required; printing must be precise; and the forms are widely available at many office supply companies, typically for a few cents each when bought in packets of 100 or more.

Claims submitted on paper and by mail are increasingly being given lower priority than electronic claims submission (ECS) so are likely to require more time for a response from the insurance company's claims processor ("claim adjudication"). It often takes considerably more than 30 days before you receive a "remittance advice" or "explanation of benefits" (EOB), much less actual payment. Some states do have "timely payment" laws that set a time limit within which "clean claims" (i.e., claims without errors such as missing or incorrect information) must be paid. However, unless you intend to pursue companies that do not meet this standard with legal action or complaints, we highly recommend moving up to an ECS program. Some insurers, such as Medicare (with few exceptions; see below), require ECS (see https://www.cms.gov/Medicare/Billing/ElectronicBillingEDITrans/ASCAWaiver.html). CMS also provides a fact sheet with guidance on Medicare billing forms and procedures (https://www.cms.gov/Outreach-and-Education/Medicare-Learning-Network-MLN/MLNProducts/downloads/form_cms-1500_fact_sheet.pdf).

The advantages of ECS include the following:

- A greatly increased likelihood that the claim submitted will be "clean" (because the software will flag inconsistencies and omissions so you can fix them before submission) and will be accepted by the insurance company.

- Quicker processing of the claim by the insurance company, and so perhaps quicker payment.

- Freedom from paper records, as the entire process is tracked electronically, with digital records of the transactions maintained essentially forever.

## How to Submit Claims Electronically

There are several ways to submit claims electronically:

1. "Do it yourself," using software that will produce and upload the electronic claim to a clearinghouse or to the insurer. There are simple software programs that allow you to enter the basic information only once. Add the dates and specifics each time you bill, and print these onto the CMS form, which you can then mail. These programs are available from various sources (e.g., http://www.ezclaim.com and http://www.littleguysoftware.com). Doing ECS yourself may be the least costly in terms of necessary equipment and access, but the greatest cost in terms of the time investment and delays. At a minimum, you will need a computer with Internet access and the software. You will also need a subscription to an online "clearinghouse" (see item 3 below).

2. Enter claim data online on the individual insurance companies' portals. Many insurance companies allow ECS at no cost through their websites, and some (e.g., Tricare/Champus) allow clients to complete the form online and submit the claim (http://www.dtic.mil/whs/directives/forms/eforms/dd2642.pdf).

3. Enter claim information through a central online claim portal—a "clearinghouse"—that allows submission to multiple insurance companies. This is a business that receives your claim, checks it for errors that would cause the claim to fail (such as missing information), and either returns it to you for corrections or sends it on to the claim-processing location for the insurer. Some clearinghouses charge on a per-claim basis, but most charge a monthly fee for a maximum number of claims. Some clearinghouses are offering their service at no cost, for a limited or even unlimited number of claims, with the service supported by other products the clearinghouse promotes such as online EHRs. We believe that the time and stress saved will make using a clearinghouse well worth its costs.

4. Hire a billing company to submit claims for you and to monitor their progress. These are mostly small offices and you will receive personal services.

5. Move to an EHR program, because all of these include claim processing mostly with a monthly additional cost.

These methods will have different costs in terms of both infrastructure (computers, space, programs) and your time, so you will have to decide on what best fits the ways you want to practice.

## When Should You Hire a Biller?

Deciding to use a billing company will involve tradeoffs among costs, your time, and the emotional frustrations. Most clinicians report that they or their staff members spend several hours per week on the phone with MCO staff members, trying to resolve unpaid bills and sending/resending forms and other documents to them. The level of frustration is high, as is the cost of direct time and the time lost for earning money or developing the clinicians' practices. Hiring a biller will very likely cost much less than these lost opportunities. That is the major benefit.

The billing company will usually supply a simple format for you to enter data about sessions and the client's insurance. Most are digital and not complicated, but typing errors, missing information, and a learning curve are involved. Many companies specialize in mental health claims billing and provide service to multiple mental health practitioners and small- or large-group practices. Many will perform claims tracking for unpaid claims and are well worth the cost.

## Checklist for Evaluating a Potential Billing Service

❑ How much does it cost? Specifically, is there a cost to sign up for training, and is there a monthly charge for a certain number of claims submitted or a per-claim cost? Does the service bill by the hour or accept a percentage of the amounts collected, or are there other ways it gets paid? Ask several times for any "hidden" costs (e.g., costs if you have to call for tech support or to resubmit claims). **In order to evaluate whether it's a good deal for you, you should have an idea of what it costs you now to submit claims.**

❑ Ask the billing service if it can work with all the most frequent insurers you submit claims to. If not, you'd be paying for ECS with it and still submitting paper claims to other companies. How does it add companies?

    ❑ Does the service automatically submit claims to the secondary insurer? If yes, it could be a good deal, as you only have to submit once electronically. If no, you'll likely be submitting the second claim on paper, as noted above.

    ❑ How does the service deal with its own billing mistakes? Is it responsive and nondefensive? How does it deal with your mistakes?

    ❑ How does it deal with insurance company denials? Does it simply pick the "low-hanging fruit" of easy cases to collect, or is it persistent but not too aggressive in resubmitting and arguing claims?

❑ Determine that the claim submission process will work with any client information software you use. Evaluate the forms the biller wants you to use to enter data for how well they match your current workflow.

❑ A billing service will "do it all" for you (as described above) or will do as much as you purchase. Some of these services will even do the most onerous parts of things, such as collections (tracking down recalcitrant insurance companies and clients who are not paying), if you want them to.

❑ How can you end your relationship with the service?

❑ Confirm how long the service has been in business and how many clients it has.

Among the negatives of using a billing service or clearinghouse, Walfish and Barnett (2009) note these:

- The cost to therapists is based on a percentage of the amount collected; the range is 4–12%.

- Your account will be just one of their many accounts, and you may not receive optimal attention.

- There may be substantial costs in leaving one company and joining up with a second biller.

- You will spend time monitoring the service's performance.

- Legal and ethical lapses by the biller can become the responsibility of the clinician. Remember, you will be held responsible for the biller's actions—if not legally, then ethically (APA, 2010, Standard 6.06).

Additional guidance is available online (http://www.hashdoc.com/document/11102/how-to-select-a-billing-service).

Because a billing service will receive your PHI, you will need to have a business associates contract with it to comply with HIPAA; it will usually supply the form.

There is another option for billing electronically that appears to be increasingly available and popular: Many EHR systems integrate their billing ledger with electronic claim generation and ECS. In these systems, when a clinician documents a visit, a charge is automatically generated to the billing portion of the program. The program accesses all necessary billing information, a rate sheet, and individual client variables necessary for the claim. Claims are produced either individually or in a batch and uploaded to the associated clearinghouse, which submits them to the insurer.

EHRs for mental health practices are proliferating, and so you should periodically evaluate their suitability to your practice. Most EHRs will allow "free trial" periods so that you can get a feel for the systems. Costs of ownership (actually, subscribing to the service) are reasonable (a dollar or two a day) and most require Internet access. Developers are well aware of and attending to security requirements. Be aware that nonmedical practices and those not serving Medicare clients will not receive financial support from the HITECH Act funds to pay for EHRs.

# 3.8  Billing for Medicare Clients

According to the 1989 Medicare law, you must notify a client's primary physician after treatment has begun, unless the client specifically requests that no notice be given. You should discuss the desirability of this notification, carry it out by letter or phone rather than email (for confidentiality reasons) if the client agrees, and document these steps and this decision in your notes (see Section 4.2).

## Providing Noncovered Services to Medicare Beneficiaries

Medicare clients can be billed for any services agreed to but not covered by Medicare, and these can include no-shows and recommended further evaluations. The form for doing this is called the Advance Beneficiary Notice of Noncoverage (which can be seen at https://www.cms.gov/Medicare/Medicare-General-Information/BNI/ABN.html). More information is provided in a 15-page booklet from CMS (https://www.cms.gov/Outreach-and-Education/Medicare-Learning-Network-MLN/MLNProducts/Downloads/Items-and-Services-Not-Covered-Under-Medicare-Booklet-ICN906765.pdf). You might even consider offering other services that would be beneficial and affordable although not covered.

## How to Opt Out of Medicare and See Medicare-Covered Clients as Private Pay Clients

Clinicians are not allowed to treat Medicare beneficiaries unless they are registered as Medicare providers *or* they have gone through the necessary procedures to opt out of Medicare. It is not necessary to enroll in Medicare before one opts out (http://www.apapracticecentral.org/update/2013/10-24/medicare-enrollment.aspx).

There are several steps involved in opting out of Medicare, but they are not overly burdensome. First, you must tell any Medicare beneficiaries you are presently seeing that you will be opting out and what this will mean to them financially. Next, complete an affidavit promising not to bill Medicare, and provide a letter or contract to each Medicare beneficiary explaining that he or she will have to pay you and that you won't bill Medicare. More information for mental health clinicians is provided by the American Psychiatric Association (https://www.psychiatry.org/psychiatrists/practice/practice-management/coding-reimbursement-medicare-and-medicaid/medicare/opting-out-of-medicare).    The Association of Physicians and Surgeons has an excellent guide for physicians (http://www.aapsonline.org/index.php/article/opt_out_medicare). Patient education on this is available through Medicare (http://www.medicare.gov/your-medicare-costs/part-a-costs/assignment/costs-and-assignment.html).

## 3.9    Tips for Dealing with Managed Care

The relationship between clinicians and MCOs has ranged from grudging cooperation to implacable hostility. The relationship has evolved from MCOs' automatic denials of payment, and clinicians' arrogant hostility, to a mutual recognition that there is an inherent opposition in what is just a business arrangement (setting aside professional issues). MCOs differ in their methods and emphases, and we cannot describe a typical relationship, but we can offer some tips. You will have to decide which, if any, apply to your relationships

### Late Payments from Insurers

In most states, insurers must either pay or deny a claim within a limited time period (usually 30 days) after it is submitted. You can threaten to report insurers to the state insurance commissioner if they are too slow. Therefore, you should monitor the progress of all claims you submit, and keep after the insurers on old claims. Computerized billing programs and EHRs can do this automatically. For more serious delays, it can be very productive to have a client complain to the employer's department that bought the insurance. You may receive calls from companies you have never heard of, promising quicker payment if you will accept less than your charges. There is no reason to accept these offers.

### Continuity-of-Care Concerns

As soon as you accept clients, you have a duty to provide high-quality care until you discharge them. But because of MCOs' limitations on treatment, you may have clients for whom MCOs refuse to authorize more treatment but who are not ready for discharge. Therapists have the ethical obligation—and may, under managed care, have a contractual obligation—to continue to treat clients whose benefits become unavailable or are exhausted. There are three aspects of maintaining continuity of care.

First, ethically, you cannot abandon a client in crisis, regardless of the financial situation. Second, as a therapist, you have the additional **obligation to appeal an MCO's decisions** to deny services that you have recommended. If your client could benefit from more treatment but is not severely incapacitated, authorization may be denied, and ethically you may not falsify levels of functioning. In appealing the MCO's decision, note that the process is entirely under the auspices of the MCO, which makes all the rules. You should make some effort at the initial appeal level. A decision on whether to continue to secondary levels of appeal needs to be made in consultation with the client. A page of advice on how to appeal a denial by an insurer can be found online (http://www.theshouldercenter.com/wp-content/uploads/pdf/HowtoAppealAnInsuranceDenial.pdf).

Third, since an appeal is rarely successful, alternative treatment resources must be considered. You should ask yourself and the client:

- Can the client afford to obtain care from an OON provider at higher cost?

- Can the client pay out of pocket for your therapy?

- Is the client willing to proceed with your therapy during the appeals process, risking being held responsible for all the charges accrued in the interim?

- Are there free or less expensive alternative sources of care to which the client can be referred, if you find them competent to treat the client, and if the client finds this referral acceptable?

- Are you willing to continue your care at a reduced rate or without payment?

- Are you willing to terminate the client?

However, read your MCO's contract carefully. It may in fact require you to discharge the client. Or it may require you to continue to treat the client after benefits are exhausted, if he or she still needs treatment; it may even prevent you from charging the client for this treatment.

## Dealing with MCO Reviewers

Some MCOs "micromanage" therapy by requiring frequent, detailed telephone consultations with their "care coordinators" or reviewers and submissions of OTR forms in order for you to receive reauthorization of payment for a small number of continuing treatment sessions. For clinicians to protect themselves against MCOs' disorganization, mistakes, and deceit, the late John Roraback, PhD, of Moline, IL, suggested that clinicians record their calls to MCO reviewers. If you decide to do so, notify the reviewer at the start of the call; otherwise, your audio recording might be illegal. Although MCOs record such calls, this approach could be seen as hostile by the MCO if you adopt it, but it should serve to protect you in cases of legal actions over adverse consequences to a client, so you might be selective. Always get the full name(s) and any other identifier(s) of the reviewer(s) you speak to, use these during the call, and record the date and time of the call and the number(s) called. You can record wait times as well. Note the contents of the call for later support or negotiations. Reviewers generally cannot make significant changes, but their supervisors can.

From the other side, Papatola and Lustig (2015)—describing the policies at Cigna, a huge insurer—list common triggers for a review: treatment lasting beyond 6–8 months; individual treatment by more than one therapist, or of more than one family member at a time; failure to employ well-established practices; and offering too many diagnoses.

Clinicians should remember that MCO reviewers are simply doing the job they were trained to do: to carry out their employers' policies in a very complex system of rules. The guidelines below are designed to make the process of dealing with MCO reviewers more efficient and effective. They are offered by Bruce Barrett, MA, LMHC, of Duxbury, MA, who was a medical reviewer; they are reproduced with his kind permission.

1. Always assume that reviewers really do have clients' interests in mind. They really believe that short-term treatment in the least restrictive setting works best, and that they have the research studies to support their positions. They also see payments to you as the clients' money (which it is—it's part of the compensation package at their employment), and see their job as making sure it is spent wisely.

2. Don't confuse a life-threatening diagnosis with life-threatening client status. For example, bulimia nervosa can be fatal, but the status of a client with bulimia nervosa may not currently be life-threatening. You'll need to document the current facts to show that the client's present condition warrants the treatment you're planning now.

3. Failure in outpatient treatment is often necessary before inpatient treatment will be approved. Documenting client *behavior* that shows this failure is what reviewers look for (rather than therapists' impressions, feelings, or anticipations, accurate as they may be).

4. Make sure you are really doing what you tell a reviewer a client really needs. Reviewers remember you, and they keep notes.

5. Be ready to appeal decisions of payment denial. It may be that your client has to do this, but you can help by knowing the procedure. Insurance companies have higher-skilled professionals to review denials and appealed claims, although in our experience the first-line reviewers are pretty sharp, too. Overturned denials are typically the results of clearer documentation of the need for treatment.

6. Learn the "medical necessity" criteria for admission, continued stay, and the various other levels of treatment (partial hospitalization, outpatient care, etc.) for the various conditions you treat. Learn them as well as you would if you were a reviewer, or a consultant to an insurance company. Then learn (from the reviewers, if possible) what manner of documentation—what type and quality of case facts—they use to make their decisions (see Form 3.2).

7. Rely on objective and behavioral data in your case notes. "Spouse reports client binged and purged three times in last 24 hours" is much more useful than "This client is getting worse and needs an inpatient stay." Client self-report helps, too, even when there is clear evidence of denial (e.g., "Client reports feeling better than ever, despite evidence of repeated purging").

8. Psychological denial and other forms of client-based unreadiness for treatment can be tricky, but reviewers know that, too. Showing evidence that a client's degree of denial is colossal, and might be broken through with intensive treatments (specialized outpatient treatments or partial hospitalization), can be impressive to a reviewer.

9. Make sure that everything fits together: diagnosis, need for treatment (client condition), intensity of treatment planned, and intensity of treatment delivered. Hyperbole about the absolute need for treatment, when coupled with routine scheduling

of appointments (or even scheduled gaps in treatment), stands out like a sore thumb. A life-or-death client condition calls for urgent action and timing from a therapist.

## 3.10  The Future of Insurance in Mental Health Care

Predictions about the future of insurance in mental health care are, of course, uncertain, but what follows are some likely future trends based on current influences.

Given the U.S. Supreme Court's June 2015 decision to uphold the PPACA, it will continue to influence health care greatly for many years. The main implication is that more and more Americans will have insurance coverage. Most Americans will maintain their employer-based plans, but some will shift to individual plans and will have a wider choice of benefits, including better coverage for mental health and substance abuse treatment. Insurers have reacted by raising the deductible threshold and copayments to lower utilization and their costs.

A key question for practicing mental health clinicians is the extent to which clients will expect to use their benefits for covered services that will include mental health disorder assessment and treatment, behavioral health treatment, and substance use disorder treatment. Also, how many clients will be interested in or willing to purchase noncovered services on a fee-for-service basis? This is part of the equation that mental health practitioners must take into account when weighing "whether or not to take insurance" and which insurance.

Teletherapy or telemental health is too cost-efficient to be ignored and will come to at least partially allow practice across states, despite not being licensed in all states.

New formats for organizing practitioners will come to dominate the market. Consider joining local ones which support the kind of work you prefer to do. There are many new structures and payment methods being developed: ACOs in both private and public domains, primary care or patient-centered medical homes (PCMHs), independent practice associations (IPAs), and many more. Private insurers will continue to manage care through HMOs and MCOs but will limit and exclude the current fee-for-service models and practices.

As a matter of federal law and national policy, the U.S. health care system is moving beyond transparency in care to measurement and ultimately to improved performance. We can see the beginnings of this in the Physician Quality Reporting System (PQRS), in which providers are encouraged to provide some simple (for now) assessments of their clients in order to measure improvements in overall health and population health. Failure to monitor client care will result in lower payments for Medicare claims. CMS provides more details about the PQRS (https://www.cms.gov/Medicare/Quality-Initiatives-Patient-Assessment-Instruments/PQRS/index.html?redirect=/pqri). Before you decide to participate in the PQRS, consider what proportion of your income stems from Medicare Part B payments. If this proportion is small, participation may not be worth the efforts required; just accept the few percentage points of loss in reimbursement. To see if you are eligible, see another CMS document (https://www.cms.gov/Medicare/Quality-Initiatives-Patient-Assessment-Instruments/PQRS/Downloads/PQRS_List-of-EligibleProfessionals_022813. pdfv). The APA Practice Organization also provides guidance (http://www.apapracticecentral.org/update/2015/02-12/pqrs-measures-codes.aspx).

As payment methods shift from fee-for-service to pay-for-performance models, many clinicians will need to participate in systems that assume responsibility for care and demonstrate positive outcomes for groups of clients in order to obtain reimbursement. "Insurance reimbursement" for individual visits will decrease over time as the dominant payment model. If so, this will render the question "Should I take insurance?" less relevant than "Should I join that [small/large] group or system?" The agile, entrepreneurial mental health clinician will be watching closely and acting in light of these changes.

On balance, it is probably fair to state that mental health professionals who emphasize the privacy of the treatment relationship and independence in practice should limit their involvement with "managed care" arrangements, but that others have developed satisfactory working relationships with these companies.

# CHAPTER 4

# Reducing Malpractice Risk by Operating Ethically

## 4.1 Ethics and Malpractice

### Why Are Ethical and Legal Issues So Complicated?

Abstract ideas of right and wrong can be simple statements, but the real world can be quite complicated:

- "Should" and "must" are often too vague to direct specific actions; actions require precision ("when," "how," "where," etc.).

- Principles must be stated abstractly to be comprehensive, and yet each case and situation is unique.

- Ethics and laws can sometimes conflict, such as when the client's best interests require confidentiality but the law requires disclosure (Knapp et al., 2007). These are ethical "problems."

- Two ethical imperatives can be in conflict in a particular situation and create a "dilemma," which will not have a right and a wrong answer.

- Therapy's goals may conflict with ethical guidelines. For example, full disclosure of a treatment's risks is necessary for informed consent, but may weaken a client's motivation for therapy. Offering success rate data may make the client disappointed with the therapist or hopeless about therapy's outcome.

- There are many ways to view a case and its issues; we cannot know all of them. Even experts will differ in their interpretations, recommendations, and judgments, as each can have different conceptual bases. Keith-Speigel (2013a) recounts many cases in all their complexity.

- The fields of mental health keep evolving. Laws and court decisions keep changing. Each state has different laws; departments within a state government can have different rules; and there are gaps and overlaps in the laws and rules (for examples, see Knapp & VandeCreek, 2001).

In addition to the points made above, keep in mind that written standards for ethical behavior can be of two kinds: ethical "standards," which are mandatory, with punishment for violations; and more general "principles," which are aspirational and do not involve punishment for violations, but toward which we are expected to strive. Thirty-plus years ago, Haas et al. (1986) found that "When psychologists are faced with a variety of ethical dilemmas, they will often make decisions based on their personal value systems and not on the basis of defined ethical principles" (p. 321). This is still probably the case. Such decisions may "feel right," but can we be sure that this is good enough to protect us legally and ethically?

## The Formula for Risk and Risk Management

The consequences to us of our decisions and actions constitute an inseparable part of ethical discussions. These are usually discussed as "risks," and we are expected, as professionals, to manage the risks we face. The theory behind risk management is not complex. The formula is shown in Figure 4.1.

This simple formula is heuristic: By asking the questions, we sort dangers into categories for protective interventions. "Risk management" is reducing any of the components of the formula, and if any can be reduced to zero, the total risk becomes zero, since risk is the product of all components. For example, when we buy insurance, we limit the impact of a threat to what we have paid for a premium, and so the overall risk is greatly reduced. This book offers hundreds of way to reduce vulnerability and the likelihood of damage.

## The Licensing Board Risks for Clinicians

As professionals committed to empiricism, let's look at the data. Our most likely threat is of complaints to licensing boards, not of malpractice liability suits. Complaints are much more common and as damaging, although they lack the financial costs of a judgment against us. Complainants do not have to spend much time or any money (the board will do the investigation and prosecution), and they do not need to employ a lawyer. Complainants do not have to prove damage or loss (proof of "harm" is needed for malpractice), only a violation of

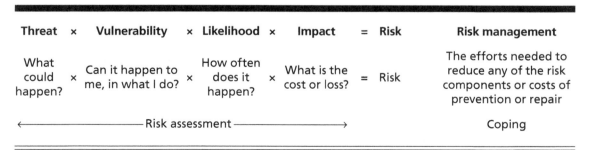

**FIGURE 4.1.** The formula for risk and risk management.

**TABLE 4.1.  Most Common Types of Disciplinary Actions by APA Ethics Committee, 1994–2003: Cases with Multiple Categories**

| Category | Number of cases | Percent of cases |
|---|---|---|
| Sexual misconduct (adult) | 198 | 34 |
| Nonsexual dual relationship | 72 | 13 |
| Insurance/fee problems | 72 | 13 |
| Child custody | 65 | 11 |
| Confidentiality | 40 | 7 |
| Outside competence | 28 | 5 |
| Inappropriate follow-up/termination | 20 | 3 |
| Test misuse | 20 | 3 |
| Termination/supervision | 21 | 4 |
| False, fraudulent, or misleading advertising | 17 | 3 |
| Sexual misconduct (minor) | 10 | 2 |
| Inappropriate response to crisis | 10 | 2 |
| Total | 578 | |

*Note.* Adapted from Table 1.A of Bennett et al. (2006). Copyright © 2006 the American Psychological Association Insurance Trust. Adapted by permission.

the board's rules. They will not be cross-examined or have their past made public in court, and a complaint can provide much the same satisfactions as a suit. Furthermore, in states that incorporate your profession's national code of ethics into the licensing law, an ethics violation can be grounds for revoking your license.

Reviewing the best available data,[1] Van Horne (2004) concluded: "It appears that about 40 in 10,000 licensed psychologists will face any action by a licensing board [in any year], while fewer than 13 in 10,000 licensed psychologists will face a formal discipline reported to the ASPPB [Association of State and Provincial Psychology Boards] Disciplinary Data System" (p. 175). This is a real-world rate of almost 4 psychologists in 100 who are disciplined in a 30-year career. Even so, almost 10% of psychologists will be complained against, and that is a major stressor.

Table 4.1 (adapted with permission from Bennett et al., 2006) provides an overall picture of actions taken by the American Psychological Association (APA) Ethics Committee based on data from 1994 to 2003, and so it may not be accurate for any one state or province and the rates of the categories may have changed somewhat. These are disciplinary *actions* taken against psychologists, not simply the *complaints* filed, which are much more numerous but less damaging. The most common categories are listed, but there are dozens of less frequent issues. Furthermore, different states' boards use different names for what appear to be the same issues and actions; there is no consistency across states, across boards, or over time. States differ greatly in how many complaints they ultimately punish and which actions they take. In some, many complaints lead to severe disciplinary actions like loss of

---

[1]While there is a national organization of psychology boards, the Association of State and Provincial Psychology Boards (ASPPB), we know of no parallel sources of data for board actions in social work, counseling, or psychiatry.

license; in others, complaints are handled informally, with consequences such as required education.

## The Major Malpractice Risks for Clinicians

Pope (1989) reviewed the data on malpractice suits against psychologists from January 16, 1986, to July 1, 1988, and found 27 major causes for successful suits. His findings are summarized in Table 4.2. The major issues and causes found by Pope are ranked by the percentage of claims each represents. Note how few "failure to warn" cases there were (ranked 23rd), although such cases generate a lot of therapist anxiety. These data are for the late 1980s, by

TABLE 4.2.  Major Causes of Successful Malpractice Suits against Psychologists

| Cause | % of costs | % of claims |
|---|---|---|
| 1. Sexual impropriety | 53.2 | 20.4 |
| 2. Incorrect treatment (i.e., using treatments the therapist was not qualified to perform by lack of training or experience) | 8.4 | 13.2 |
| 3. Loss (to the patient) from evaluation (performed by the psychologist) | 2.6 | 8.5 |
| 4. Breach of confidentiality or privacy | 1.3 | 6.4 |
| 5. Countersuit for fee collection (improper fee setting, billing, or fee collection methods) | 1.3 | 6.2 |
| 6. Suicide of patient | 11.2 | 5.8 |
| 7. Diagnosis: Failure to or incorrect | 3.7 | 5.4 |
| 8. Defamation: Libel/slander | 0.7 | 4.4 |
| 9. Improper death of patient or others | 2.0 | 3.2 |
| 10. Miscellaneous (the meaning of this category was unclear to Pope) | 0.8 | 3.1 |
| 11. Premise liability (e.g., a client was hurt in the office by falling) | 0.1 | 2.4 |
| 12. Violation of legal regulations | 0.5 | 2.6 |
| 13. Bodily injury | 1.6 | 2.2 |
| 14. Loss of child custody or visitation | 0.2 | 2.2 |
| 15. Violation of civil rights | 1.1 | 2.1 |
| 16. Licensing or peer review | 0.2 | 2.1 |
| 17. Poor results | 0.1 | 1.7 |
| 18. Undetermined (i.e., the causes of action were undetermined) | 7.9 | 1.5 |
| 19. Breach of contract | 0.1 | 1.4 |
| 20. Assault and battery | 1.5 | 1.2 |
| 21. Failure to supervise properly | 0.3 | 0.9 |
| 22. Undue influence (these are basically dual relationships) | 0.4 | 0.6 |
| 23. Failure to warn | 0.6 | 0.4 |
| 24. Abandonment | 0.1 | 0.3 |
| 25. False imprisonment/arrest | 11 cases, average cost $935 | |
| 26. Failure to refer | 1 case, cost $2,141 | |
| 27. Failure to treat | 2 cases, average cost $38 | |

*Note.* The data are from Pope (1989). The comments in parentheses are by ELZ.

which time the classic case *Tarasoff v. Regents of the University of California* (1976) had been decided, and so the boards and therapists knew all about it. Note also how relatively many problems were related to fee collection (ranked 5th), despite which many therapists vigorously pursue monies owed them.

There are additional areas of concern (Sam Knapp, personal communication, October 2, 1996). First, child custody evaluations, which by their nature leave one side unhappy, have produced a large number of complaints on the issues of breach of confidentiality and violations of the ethics of assessment. Second, those who are unhappy with decisions about their fitness for duty or disability will complain fairly often to a board about the clinicians who offered professional opinions about this fitness. Third, a survey by Montgomery et al. (1999) indicated that issues of supervision may be a largely unrecognized area of increased risk (see Section 4.9 for ways to reduce this risk) and, in fact, disciplinary actions over supervision have apparently increased in the last decade. Lastly, services such as custody evaluations or other forensic evaluations that may leave a client disgruntled have more recently led to negative comments and reviews on consumer sites such as Yelp.com. In addition to board complaints, a clinician's online reputation on consumer review sites can be a significant source of stress in our connected world.

These tables may seem like a long list of risks. Do you have to worry about everything you do as a therapist? The answer is no. Nearly all malpractice complaints stem from just a few issues, and most are in areas over which you have excellent control. Over 60% of the claims in Table 4.2 (and the majority of complaints noted by the APA Committee on Ethics) originated in sexual improprieties, dual relationships, substandard diagnosis or treatment, lapses in the duty to protect, and poor office administration. You can reduce or eliminate the vast majority of risks in these areas if you are clinically competent and self-aware, if you consult fully with others, and if you create an adequate written record to document your actions and the reasons for them. Here is the good news in all this: **Almost all malpractice cases arise not from unforeseeable problems, but from ones that could have been avoided if only they were recognized and anticipated** (Bennett et al., 1990).

In some cases, the issues are so clear that lists of "dos and don'ts" can be created for them. We have included these in this book where appropriate. More importantly, some principles are so clearly formulated that they can be incorporated into your practice simply by using the forms, handouts, sample documents, guidelines, and checklists in this book. In fact, that is the major concept underlying this book: **If you build the ethics into your paperwork and procedures, you greatly reduce your risk of errors, complaints, and malpractice.**

## Four Steps toward Ethical Self-Protection

1. **Be realistic.** Ethical problems will happen to you. One barrier to improved ethical practice is arrogance. "Pride goeth before a fall," but arrogance is hard to avoid when capable people are asking your advice every day, listening carefully, paying you, and being grateful. Do not let false pride, denial, panic, ignorance, or rumors cause you to avoid acting to protect yourself and your clients.

2. **Learn the rules.** The fact that you have the client's best interests at heart, are well intentioned, or like the client does not ensure that you are acting ethically. Don't assume that ethical niceties and picky little rules can be ignored; these rules have been carefully worked out after painful experiences.

First, get, read, and keep available copies of your state's licensing law and all the ethical codes you operate under. You need to be mindful of the legal context in which you operate. There are many codes of ethical standards. Which apply to you? They will be the codes of the group you align with by education, by licensure, and by the title or description you offer of your services. You will also, perhaps surprisingly, be held to the standards of any group an ordinary citizen would see you as belonging to. Even if you are not certified by the American Association for Marriage and Family Therapy, a court is likely to hold your practice to this group's standards if you identify yourself as a "marriage counselor" or "family therapist."

Second, buy a recently published book on ethics and risks (e.g., Knapp et al., 2013) every once in a while. Skim it, and especially note new risks and threats, among other developments. This is especially important when your discipline's code has been revised. You can most easily find links to about 150 codes at Kenneth S. Pope's site (http://www.kspope.com/ethcodes/index.php).

Third, take courses on ethics. Conversations and discussions about ethical issues in these courses will keep you abreast of new issues and the evolving standards of care.

Fourth, join your profession's associations. Their newsletters and online discussion groups will keep you ahead of changes in laws, regulations, and court decisions. Their boards, ethics committees, and professional staffs are available to offer protective guidance.

3. **Develop an ethical consciousness.** Ethics education should result in feeling a "learned unease." This is an awareness of vulnerability, complexity, and multiple perspectives. It is almost an operational definition of an ethical consciousness. It will give you a "little nagging voice" to guide and warn you. This anxiety should motivate thoughtfulness, consultation, conservatism, foresight, contingency planning, and empathy. The development of an ethical sensitivity will help alert you to the ethical aspects and implications of all your professional activities. It will also help you to know when consultation is necessary. Consultation with an ongoing group of colleagues, with a recognized expert, or with your state association's ethics committee is essential to any private practitioner's welfare. While comments on your profession's online discussion groups cannot replace consultations, listserv members may offer names of appropriate consultants for your particular issue.

   In addition, write your notes with the awareness that you will not be able to keep them away from anyone with a good reason to access them. Be discreet. Be especially careful about novel or uncommon practices. If what you are considering doing with a client is unusual among your peer professionals, get at least one consultation on its ethical correctness *before* proceeding. A good rule is this: If you don't personally know any other professional who is doing what you are considering doing, don't do it! Some of the worst errors are made by lone wolves.

4. **Tighten up your procedures.** Checklists, forms, and similar procedural devices can head off problems efficiently. Such procedures can remind you of legal obligations, shape the issues you pursue, and offer easily incorporated risk management strategies. Read each section of this book that applies to your practice, evaluate the forms and sample documents, make copies, and *use them* with every one of your clients for a few months. Then evaluate and modify them to your practice.

# 4.2  Legal Aspects of Malpractice

## When Do Clients Sue?

Lawsuits represent about the last stage of breakdown in human relationships. They tend to occur in therapeutic contexts under the following conditions:

- When clients are disappointed with the outcome of treatment and attribute it to their therapists' incompetence or negligence.

- When clients feel disrespected, believe that they are being treated with indifference, or feel that their concerns are not being heard.

- When clients are presented with bills larger or later than they expected.

- When clients believe they have been exploited or "used" financially, emotionally, or sexually.

- When clients additionally want to prevent others from being harmed.

## What Is Malpractice?

"Malpractice is a form of civil law whereby parties who are injured in a professional relationship may seek monetary compensation for their damages" (Bennett et al., 2006, p. 18). There are four elements of a malpractice claim, but the key issue is a deviation from the "standard of care" (sometimes called the "standard of practice").

"The 'medical standard of care' is typically defined as the level and type of care that a reasonably competent and skilled health care professional, with a similar background and in the same medical community, would have provided under the circumstances that led to the alleged malpractice. An 'average' standard would not apply because in that case at least half of any group of practitioners would not qualify" (retrieved from http://www.nolo.com/legal-encyclopedia/what-the-medical-standard-care-malpractice-case.html).

This definition needs to be fully understood. It requires prudence and foresight. Our training and experience give us the ability to understand circumstances and accurately anticipate many consequences. **The standard of care consists of those diagnostic and treatment processes clinicians actually do or believe should be done for a certain type of client, illness, or clinical circumstance.** Of note, the standard of care is not the same as guidelines from organizations, not what experts consider "best practices," not the opinions of licensing boards, not what is legally required, not what the research indicates, not the majority's opinions, not risk management recommendations, not bound to any one theory, not based on good outcomes, not determined by cost, not aspirational (i.e., not "should do," but "is done" and "would do"), and not perfection—although all of these and more (Zur, 2010) may contribute (Alban, 2010b). And there are no exceptions to the standards for beginners or for those in rural or underserved areas.

To win a malpractice case, the plaintiff must demonstrate all of what are called the "four D's": duty, dereliction, direct cause, and damage. Each must be proved to the standard for conviction in a civil suit—"the preponderance of the evidence" or "more true than not." These are quite high thresholds.

1. Because a clinician–client relationship existed, the clinician/defendant owed a **duty** of care to the client/plaintiff. This is only rarely in dispute.

2. The performance of that duty was **derelict**; that is, it fell below the standard of care expected of the typical clinician. This standard used to be determined on a local basis, but is now interpreted by the courts on a regional or national basis. The comparison may be based on the specialty advertised or offered to the client, or on the care offered by other practitioners of a particular school of thought (Knapp et al., 2013).

3. The clinician's dereliction of duty was the **direct cause** of some harm. Causation is a complex legal point, but a clinician is rarely seen to cause harm without the client's or others' acting between the clinician's statements and the resulting damage.

4. There was some demonstrable **damage.** A jury of average citizens must appreciate the kind and severity of this harm.

And there is usually a necessary fifth criterion: **deep** pockets—assets available as compensation given the nature of the plaintiff's bar.

Many kinds of clinician behaviors have resulted in liability: negligence, breach of contract, battery, intentional infliction of emotional distress, defamation, invasion of privacy, failure to prevent an injury, and so on. Wilkinson (1982) adds liability for self-inflicted injuries and suicide, harm by the client to third parties, errors in judgment concerning client management, harmful treatment methods, and sexual misconduct. Perhaps it should be emphasized that neither a bad outcome nor a mistake is proof of malpractice, according to the New Jersey Courts (n.d.).

## The Good News (for Us): The Real Risks Are Small

Despite the impression given by media reports, actual malpractice cases against mental health clinicians are surprisingly rare. Among mental health clinicians, psychiatrists are sued much more frequently than any others, and yet they are the least often sued among types of medical specialists, with a rate of 2.6% sued each year (Anupam et al., 2011). However, only about half a percent lose their cases and must make any kind of financial settlement (usually paid by insurance). A clue to your risks may be found by comparing your insurance premiums with those of professionals in other disciplines.

Winer (n.d.), an experienced malpractice lawyer, notes many factors that make cases against mental health clinicians hard to pursue. There is rarely one piece of key evidence of guilt (the "smoking gun"), as happens in medical cases; clients may have mental illnesses that make them poor witnesses; almost any kind of treatment is acceptable; given the other stressors in a client's life, it is usually very difficult to prove that the client was injured by the clinician's actions (the argument is that "but for" the clinician's actions, the client would have been fine). And these cases are very time-consuming and expensive (need for expert testimony) to pursue. Winer (n.d.) indicates that cases involving inpatient suicides and sexual relationships are the ones most likely to be lost.

Data on the outcomes for sued mental health practitioners are not readily available, and the numbers appear too small to generalize from. However, we can find some trends in medical malpractice suits that are likely to apply in mental health. Cases are rarely successful. Although 100% of clients who consult malpractice attorneys are disappointed and angry at their doctors, only 20% are deemed by the attorneys to have winnable cases. Only 30% of lawsuits against physicians go to trial, and in them defendants are exonerated 70–90% of the time; only a few percent of physicians lose. Sixty percent of the lost cases are resolved without payment to the clients, and in only 1% do physicians pay beyond what the insurance covers (Kane, 2013).

## The Bad News (for Us): Malpractice Accusations Hurt

As the saying goes, "You can't win a malpractice lawsuit, but you sure can lose one." And you can do so very badly. The actual costs, losses, and hassles pale before the self-doubt, public humiliation, and anxiety. You can be sued for more money than you have or will ever have, or than your spouse has or will earn, or than either of you might inherit. Your insurer will try to settle the case early. If this effort is successful, you may be seen as guilty by your peers even if you are innocent. You will spend countless hours gathering evidence, being deposed, conferring with lawyers, getting support from friends, and engaging in endless self-examination and self-reproaches. If you are convicted of a felony, you will lose your license and have to find a new line of work. Yet another consequence is being entered into the National Practitioner Data Bank/Healthcare Integrity and Protection Data Bank (P.O. Box 10832, Chantilly, VA 20153-0832; http://www.npdb.hrsa.gov). Maintained by the U.S. Department of Health and Human Services (DHHS), it lists those practitioners who have had medical malpractice payments made on their behalf; actions taken against their licenses or clinical privileges; actions taken by professional societies against them; and judgments or convictions for health care fraud, criminal convictions, and similar decisions. Although those entered can get information on their entries, the public cannot and may never be able to. However, health care organizations, licensing boards, lawyers, and insurers can access this list, and so being placed on it may greatly limit your future ability to practice.

Charles and Frisch (2005), Thomas (2005), and Sanbar and Firestone (2007) have described and offered counsel about coping with a "litigation stress syndrome" or "malpractice stress syndrome"—a pattern of behaviors, feelings, and thoughts that is likely to appear in those professionals involved in malpractice cases. The sued professionals are more likely to feel depressed, ashamed, misunderstood, defeated, tense, angry, and frustrated. They may experience headaches, insomnia, and similar symptoms; drink alcohol excessively; and have suicidal ideation. They may stop seeing certain kinds of clients, consider retiring earlier, and discourage their children from entering their profession. A majority of psychologists who had sexual relationships with clients reported "significant impacts on their professional work" (p. 102) and reported that "the relationship was not worth having" (p. 104) (Lamb et al., 2003).

## Where to Get Advice on Legal/Ethical Problems

### How to Prepare Beforehand

1. Get an attorney familiar with professional and business practices; do not rely on your personal attorney. Your practice attorney can review your procedures, forms,

letters, and other documents, as well as be on call for advice and legal services should you need them. You will pay by the hour.

2. If you think that suits or complaints are likely because of the kinds of work you do (e.g., custody evaluations), get a specialist attorney on a retainer. Malpractice specialists are not necessarily specialists in licensing board complaints.

3. If you think you can benefit from legal advice on many issues, consider buying a legal consultation plan. In Pennsylvania, up to 3 hours per year of consultation with one of the three attorneys who are also psychologists costs $137 per year.

### When You Recognize That a Legal or Ethical Risk Exists

1. The professional affairs officers at your discipline's state association are underused resources. They know the persons and facts of recent cases, board members and judges, and understand how the system works. If you are not a member of this association, join it.

2. You can ask (discreetly) on professional online discussion groups, bulletin boards, or forums for terms, resources, experiences, and names of attorneys. Reveal as little as possible, because these postings can be legally "discovered" at trial.

3. Call your professional liability insurance agency's risk managers. You are contractually required to notify them of risky situations, and you must immediately notify them of any legal action. They will have lawyers available as consultants.

4. Use your legal consultation plan, if you have it. That lawyer will know many specialist attorneys.

## What to Do If You Are Complained Against: A Checklist

The following checklist concerns having a complaint alleged against you with an ethics or licensing board. It is based on recommendations from Wright (1981a, 1981b), Woody (2000), the American Professional Agency (1992), Pope and Vasquez (2011, Chap. 16), and others. However, be aware that boards' operations differ widely and are not necessarily consistent over time. Boards are generally not transparent about their procedures and decision making, and so reading your board's licensing laws and rulings will not always provide answers on what to expect, although such a reading should be your first action to orient yourself.

❑ **It is possible that you will be surprised by a licensing board complaint,** because administrative law's rules do not include the same due process protections as those of the U.S. Constitution (Williams, 2001). Boards can investigate without telling you about the investigation, and you may not have to be given a copy of the complaint until later.

❑ **If you are served a summons or a subpoena, accept it, but don't overreact to it.** Control your anxiety; don't panic. Keep these points in mind:

Do not assume that you know the outcome of the process and in a panic surrender your license (Indest, 2013).

It is common practice to list many allegations, but most of the time they are all settled at once.

Exaggeration and intimidating "legalese" are to be expected from opposing attorneys.

Boards are set up to receive and process complaints; it is their job. They have their procedures to follow.

Resolution may take years (1–3 years, usually).

The best attitude, and one that will help you avoid feeling intimidated, is to treat the complaint as an invitation from your board to hear your side of the story. They know they have heard only one side.

❑ **Do not contact the client** in an attempt to "therapeutically resolve" the issues or to "negotiate" a resolution. The client is now an ex-client, because he or she has deliberately entered the legal arena. Also, the reason you would be calling is to get the client to stop the action. These communications could be deemed harassment, are not privileged, and can be used against you. In some settings, this kind of *ex parte* communication is illegal.

❑ If the client is a current client, **end the therapy immediately with a letter** (created with the help of your attorney) advising the client to seek service elsewhere, and offering a few referral names. See Section 7.3 on termination.

❑ **You have the right to a lawyer** at every stage, even before you meet with the board's investigator. This is simply common law and is not mentioned in the regulations. A good rule is that you need legal input unless the situation is a simple mistake and you are certain that it will be corrected after a simple exchange. Having your own lawyer deal with the board does not indicate wrongdoing and will not worsen your situation.

❑ **Call your professional liability insurance agency immediately, and supply the information its staff members request.** They will open a file, assign a claims manager at their office, and probably assign you a local lawyer if they believe your case is one they must defend. They may have clinician lawyers available as consultants, or have other options.

❑ **Consider hiring your own lawyer.** Your professional liability insurance company is the employer of the lawyer the company sent you to, and your goals and those of the insurance company may not be identical. Your goal is to keep your license, and the insurance company's goal it to settle the case as quickly and cheaply as possible.

For a licensing board complaint, you will want a lawyer experienced in administrative law and boards, not just a civil law or a malpractice attorney. Sources for such specialized attorneys include your practice's or business's attorney, your profession's state association's professional affairs officer, your state bar association's referral lists, and various websites (e.g., http://www.martindale.com). Your professional lawyer can serve as a consultant to monitor the case and advise you on options, even if he or she does not represent you at the hearing, negotiations, or trial.

❑ **Meet with your attorney as soon as possible.** Remember that these contacts with a lawyer *are* privileged communications. But do not make any notes until you have established a relationship, as these documents are *not* privileged unless they are created for an attorney.

☐ **Assemble all relevant documents and records.** Show your records to no one except your lawyer. Do not release any documents unless your attorney instructs you to do so. Make and keep copies and originals of everything. Do not offer more than is relevant except to your lawyer. With your lawyer's guidance, aim to assemble a case so well organized and clear that it will cause the board's investigator to think, "No problem here; time to move on to my next case."

☐ **Do not alter or destroy any documents.** "Alter" means to make the original unrecoverable or even just ambiguous. Do not line out, white out, black out, or cut out any entry. Should you find errors or omissions, you can *amend* the record. This means to add new information to the record. Do not do this in the margins of the document. Instead write, near the text you wish to amend, a statement like "See entry of [today's date]," and then make a new entry at the end of the record such as "[Today's date.] Upon reviewing my records of [the date of the entry you are amending], I find that I forgot to mention . . . " or " . . . I have learned that my entry was incomplete, and so . . . " Similarly, if a client wants you to remove or modify entries, decline and offer the opportunity to submit his or her versions, which you will incorporate into your records. The Health Insurance Portability and Accountability Act (HIPAA) requires this procedure and notes that you do not have to send the client's amendments to those to whom you previously sent the client's records, but only include them in future releases.

☐ **Educate your lawyer about the strengths and weaknesses of your case.** If this is a complaint to the licensing board, consult with your lawyer, and prepare a carefully considered and structured reply to the board. The client is likely to read this reply, so be circumspect. In order to make the complaint, the client has released your records, but do not go beyond what your attorney decides is relevant.

☐ **Assume a defensive stance.** Admit nothing and make no self-incriminating statements to *anyone* not covered by privilege. As noted above, your client has become your adversary by entering the inherently adversarial legal area. Many states have "I'm sorry" laws protecting health care professionals who admit errors from having such admissions used against them in a later suit. Although these laws have been effective in reducing such cases, they have not been applied to nonmedical professionals.

☐ **Do not talk openly to the investigator of the complaint.** Be aware that the investigator has been trained to gather information from people like you, so be very careful. A professional investigator's actions will not be swayed by your friendliness, and you may reveal too much. These conversations are not privileged or confidential and can be used against you.

☐ **Do not "play lawyer."** Don't meet or talk with the ex-client or the opposing lawyer unless your attorney is present. Such interactions open you to being manipulated. Every communication with the other side should go through your attorney, and every action should be approved by him or her.

Even if you are told that another therapist is the target of potential litigation, follow this rule: Inform the client's attorney, and "Bill the [client's] attorney for your time, just as you would bill the client. To not bill might imply that you owe the client something because of improper care" (Barge & Fenalason, 1989).

❑ **Do not discuss your case with *anyone* (except perhaps your legal spouse) without the agreement of your personal attorney, because privilege laws vary with states.** This includes not discussing the facts via email with anyone or on professional online discussion forums, no matter how well the facts may be disguised! Consultation with a trusted colleague or close friend may be valuable, but such conversations are *not* privileged and could later be used against you. If you do talk to experts in ethics, any lawyers other than your own, or any institutional colleagues, do so only in hypothetical terms. Limit discussions with colleagues to the process of being sued or ways to cope with the stress, and do not discuss details of the case, the care you provided, or any other legally relevant information. **Personal therapy** for the stress and other personal issues related to a claim may be valuable, and such conversations *are* considered privileged communications because you are then a client.

❑ **Continue to work at your profession to the same high standards.**

Do not feel ashamed because you have had a complaint. Remember (as you have no doubt told clients), the fact that someone didn't like what you did does not prove you did anything wrong.

Don't let yourself get depressed or overly concerned. Control your anger as well. Learn to compartmentalize your life.

You will not be able to work as well the day after receiving the complaint as you did the day before, so make all the needed adaptations to cope before the stress impairs you.

Remember that being complained against doesn't mean you are a jerk, stupid, or incompetent.

The death rate from licensing board complaints is very low; you will survive and can even flourish afterward.

You might create a diary to record contacts, ideas, and experiences for the long haul. Do not discuss the facts of the case in it, because it is subject to subpoena as a professional document relevant to the case.

❑ When it is all over, **create a summary of the case and its outcome.** You may need this in the future, when you apply for panel membership, train others, or other opportunities. "When the ordeal is over and the dust settles, celebrate your survival and get on with your life. Acknowledge the lessons you've learned, make amends where you need to, and move on" (Boedecker, 1995, p. 3).

## 4.3  Professional Liability ("Malpractice") Insurance[2]

*Disclaimer:* These issues are complex; needs are individual; and policies differ in many details. The following is intended as an overview, so do not base your insurance decisions

---

[2]This section has benefited greatly from the comments and suggestions of Eric C. Marine, Vice President for Claims of the American Professional Agency.

solely on this summary. Examine the actual policies (not the summaries or advertisements), ask questions, and consult.

## Introduction

You may ask, "Do I really need professional liability insurance?" It covers more than "malpractice," the name that is often used by clinicians. Such insurance also addresses such issues as premises liability (e.g., liability if someone is injured in your office), slander and libel, invasion of privacy, and many other professional activities.

You could buy no insurance (an option informally called "going bare"). It will save a few hundred tax-deductible dollars a year and *might* reduce your risk of some kinds of suits (because plaintiffs' lawyers look for those with "deep pockets" to make a case worth taking on). However, this option offers no protection for your personal assets, and no assistance with the high expenses of defending yourself in either a suit or the much more likely licensing board complaint. Without insurance, you assume all the risks of practice by yourself; buying insurance is a way of risk sharing. If you are considering "going bare," read more about the risks, assess your exposures and assets, and consult your colleagues. If a court judgment goes against you, you can lose all your current assets and future resources (inheritance, future income, spouse's income, etc.). You could also lose your license and thus your profession. Lastly, most employers will require you to have your own insurance.

## Occurrence-Based versus Claims-Made Policies

There are two types of liability policies: "occurrence-based" and "claim-made." Either one may be a better fit for you, depending on your needs. Most of us, to save money, buy claims-made plans without much to worry about. Problems generally arise only if we wish at a later date to switch to an occurrence-based plan or wish to change carriers (insurance companies). As we go through this discussion, refer to Figure 4.2.

### Claims-Made Policies

Simply put, a claims-made policy covers claims (accusations of professional liability) made against you during each of the years you paid premiums for the policy. It does not matter when the incident occurred on which a claim is based, only when the claim is made. More technically, it covers most of your professional activities that occurred after the effective date (when you started to pay premiums) of your initial policy (or the retroactive date of a successor policy), or after the termination date if you purchased a "tail."

A "tail" or "extended reporting period" covers the time period starting with the end of your claims-made policy (when you stopped paying the company's premiums) and moving forward in time. The language is confusing, because we usually think of a tail as being behind us in time, but here it is understood as the continuing tail of risks assumed by the insurer as you move forward in time. You can buy a tail from your previous claims-made carrier. They are often free or not very expensive if you have been insured for 5–10 years. Their costs are low, because you will no longer be adding to their risks by seeing clients, and the risk assumed by the insurer actually declines over time as your old cases age.

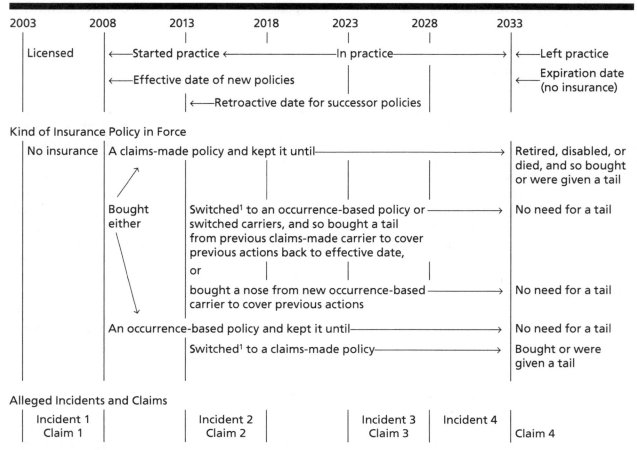

**Kind of Insurance Policy in Force**

**Alleged Incidents and Claims**

[1]Or were canceled/dropped, or the claims-made policy's company stopped writing professional liability coverage or went bankrupt or was bought out and changed its business, or any other reasons.

Incident 1 would be covered only if you had bought prior-acts "nose" coverage in 2013. It would not be covered under the occurrence-based policy or even a claims-made policy bought in 2008, because it occurred before the effective dates of either kind of policy.

Incident 2 would be covered under either the claims-made policy (if the claim was made after the effective date, 2008, and before the expiration date, 2033, of the policy) or the occurrence-based policy (no matter when the claim was made).

Incident 3 would be covered under either claims-made policy (the 2008–2033 policy or the 2013–2033 policy), but only if the policy were in force when the claim was filed (after the retroactive date—2013). If it were reported after 2033, it would only be covered under the tail coverage bought in 2033. It would be covered under the occurrence-based policy bought in either 2008 or 2013.

Claim 4 would be covered by an occurrence-based policy, or only if you bought or received a tail (since you last had a claims-made policy).

**FIGURE 4.2.  An illustration of your coverage in claims-made and occurrence-based policies over time.**

### Occurrence-Based Policies

If you are accused of an incident that is alleged to have occurred after your policy's effective date (the first day of coverage) and before its termination date (when you canceled it or stopped paying for it), an occurrence-based policy will cover it even if the claim is made years later (and would not be covered by a claims-made policy that ended). See below for more on this.

### Changing from One Type of Policy to the Other

A change may be forced upon you by a policy's cancellation, a carrier's withdrawal from the professional liability business, your need for a policy that better addresses your activities, or other changes in the world of insurance. If you choose or are forced to switch from a claims-made to an occurrence-based policy, you will need coverage for the previous years of practice no longer covered by a claims-made policy. You may be able to buy a tail from the claims-made carrier that you are leaving, or you can buy the same "nose" coverage from your new occurrence-based carrier. This is called a "prior-acts rider," and covers those actions you took before being covered by the new occurrence-based policy.

## Points of Comparison and Advantage

### Costs

The premiums will usually be higher for occurrence-based coverage, because you are essentially paying for built-in tail coverage. Also, when the policy is first issued, the carrier must estimate its costs 10 or more years out and so will build in more income for itself. On the other hand, after you stop paying for your occurrence-based coverage, there is no need to purchase a tail whose price or availability you cannot anticipate years in advance.

To compare policies, compute the costs for at least 5 and preferably 10 years. Add the increase in premiums of each year until a claims-made policy matures, and add the costs of a tail to compare the policies. These figures are available from each company, no matter what the person who answers the phone says, because all companies are registered with your state's insurance commissioner and have provided these data.

### Limits of Liability Coverage

A valuable advantage of claims-made policies is that you can purchase higher liability coverage (more dollars) at any year's renewal to protect you against any rising cost of defense and awards. With an occurrence-based policy, there is no way to make your coverage for past incidents retroactively larger; you specified the limits for each year each time you renewed the policy.

The two types of policies are not equivalent in dollars of protection, so evaluate your needs and risk tolerance. There is a large difference in the pool of money you are buying to cover claims lost, as described by Bogie (2002):

> Say you have a $1 million occurrence[-based] policy and you renewed it each year for ten years. You would have $1 million coverage for each and every one of those ten years. Compare it to a $1 million claims-made policy with an unlimited tail . . . which you renewed for ten years. You would have $1 million in total covering the entire ten-year period.

A disadvantage of occurrence-based policies is that a claim may be made many years after the alleged act occurred, and therefore it would be covered under a policy written many years ago. This has several limitations: (1) The policy probably had lower liability limits, and so fewer dollars are available to pay all the claims made under your policy; (2) it may have had different features, no longer matching today's types of risks and claims; and (3) it may have been with a carrier that is no longer in this market and not eager to defend a claim about a professional who is no longer a customer.

## Guidelines and Issues to Consider When Purchasing Liability Insurance

Specific information on policies is not easy to acquire. Insurers offer nonoverlapping information, and the agencies (listed in Appendix B) vary in their enthusiasm for providing information before you sign up. Below are listed the main points and guidelines you should consider when examining the an insurer's offerings; there may be others, depending on your practice, local laws, history, and projected needs.

❑ **Never lie or omit anything on an application,** as the insurer can easily deny coverage later because of false statements or failure to stay within policy limitations (such as your not really being in "part-time" practice).

- Examine the application form for these characteristics: complexity and burden (because you will be redoing it every year); specific language of history questions, especially if you have had an ethical problem; intrusiveness and history requested. (Some states allow questions to discover whether your "personal habits" constitute a "moral hazard.")

❑ **Become well informed. Read your current policy** or that of a friend. Review the resources listed in Appendix B of this book.

- **Do ask each insurer you are considering for a "specimen" policy,** because its marketing materials and "summaries" may not give you enough information for your particular practice, may make misleading simplified comparisons, and may incorrectly describe competitors' products. If there is a problem, you will be held to the language of your policy. Some policies seem to be almost unchanged from a general business liability form or one for all professions, whereas others understand and speak to therapists.

- **Examine the differences between the policies** to see which are relevant for your practice, history, and future professional plans. Attend to what is not covered, the "exceptions," the definitions, and other limitations.

❑ **Liability limits numbers are stated as two different dollar amounts**—for example, "$1 million/$3 million." The first is the maximum to be paid for a single claim (even if it includes more than one person), and the second is the maximum to be paid for all claims filed against the policy in any one policy year (the "aggregate"). If the first claim settles for, say $250,000, the policy retains $2,750,000 for other claims.

- Buy the coverage limits to protect your personal assets, present and future, as well as the risks of your practice activities. If you need even higher limits (e.g., for a group practice), talk with the agency.

- Higher coverage is not much more expensive than the lower coverage. Buy the best.

- The most commonly purchased coverage is the $1 million (per claim)/$3 million arrangement, but some employers may require you to buy higher coverage.

❑ **Choose the program administrator or agency that provides the best service.** This is the office that sells the policy you buy, bills you and collects your payments (premiums), evaluates claims made against you, and so forth. It is not the insurance company, the "carrier." Call each agency and ask a few simple questions. Learn the following:

- Can you reach informed and experienced persons when you have questions? Are their answers accurate and complete? Are they educating you, or just selling policies? Are they forthcoming about any limitations?

- When you have policy questions, can you speak to a licensed agent or only to a salesperson, or are there delays and barriers in gaining access to experts? Can you speak with a lawyer or a peer clinician?

- Can you understand the answers? Can you use the answers in your decisions?

- What do the agency's personnel say about the other companies' policies? Do they know the differences?

- Do they send you any materials they promised? How helpful are they?

- You might ask about their policy regarding "tails" to evaluate their options and responsiveness.

❑ **Consider the stability and size of the insurance company (the "carrier")** that actually provides the coverage.

- Look for A. M. Best ratings of A++ or A+, and similar high ratings by other raters. If there is any doubt that a company will still be solvent in 15 years, do not consider its occurrence-based policy. In recent years, several insurers have become insolvent.

- Some insurers are not "admitted carriers" in your state, although most are. If a company becomes insolvent and is not admitted, your state's guaranty fund will not pay its claims. Lloyd's underwriters are not usually admitted, so avoid "surplus lines coverage" policies.

- Evaluate the number of years the carrier has been insuring your kind of professional, the number of states it operates in, and the number of professionals it insures; longer, larger, and more will make the carrier more skilled in handling such claims and less likely to pull out of the business.

- Insurance companies new to the professional liability area can offer lower rates because they have fewer payouts. This factor must be balanced against such a company's ratings of size and financial security.

- You may want to stay with the same carrier and program administrator out of loyalty to the professional association, or in order to avoid a reexamination of a closed complaint against you.

❑ **Check into the availability or size of discounts** offered to the following:

- Those who have taken continuing education courses in ethics or risk management.

- Part-time practitioners (usually working 20 hours per week or less). Find out how this status is determined by each insurance carrier, as it can differ. Do not misrepresent your work.

- Members of the National Register, the diplomates of the American Board of Professional Psychology (ABPP), or other certifying boards.

- Different types of employees in your practice. You will be charged the "insured" rate; employees with a master's degree or higher may be charged a "professional" rate; others may be charged a "paraprofessional" rate and clericals are not usually charged. Can you get different limits for each therapist ("severability of limits")? If one member of the group has a practice that requires high-limit coverage, he or she can get that without having everyone else pay the same (higher) premiums. These are all for W-2 employees; your independent contractors ("1099s") are not usually covered and need their own policies.

❑ If the premium is substantial, **evaluate the availability of periodic payments** throughout the year.

❑ **Investigate the costs and availability of coverage for agencies, facilities, or other organizations for which you work** (called "additional insureds") and which may require you to have insurance to protect them.

- Generally, if you are the sole employee of a professional corporation, you do not need to buy additional coverage for your corporation; however, if there are other practitioners, discuss your situation with the agency. There may be an additional charge for partnerships or corporations.

- If you are in a partnership or joint practice that has a claims-made policy, and you then leave the practice, you should be covered by the policy for work done before you left.

❑ Having **coverage for prior acts** is becoming more important, because the courts are now accepting suits beyond the old statutes of limitations, and if you work with children they may file claims when they become adults. Even if you are not near retirement, you might have to quit practice due to disability or other reasons. For these reasons, **investigate the cost of a tail** and the guarantee of its availability. If you will be practicing for only a few years, consider an occurrence-based policy, which will save you the costs of buying a tail—but do the math. Some tails are written to cover you only for a limited number of years into the future, so consider whether you might need longer coverage. When you buy a tail, the size of the tail fixes the total amount of money available to pay all the claims that may be made against you in the future. Since the tail's size can depend on the liability limits you chose in your last renewal, consider raising these limits substantially if you anticipate leaving practice. Caution and inflation will be well served.

❑ **Generally, policies will not pay fines, penalties, or some damages (punitive, exemplary, or multiplied), or coverage when a criminal act is alleged or proven.** These are simply excluded and will be levied against your assets if awarded (the bad news). These are very, very rarely imposed in our area, as malice and repetition ("intentional damage") must be proven (the good news). However, when "sex" is involved, such awards are much more likely—and policies do not cover these. If there is coverage, it is usually a maximum of $25,000 for the claim. Insurers use the rationale that their policies don't cover intentional or knowing misconduct or dishonest or fraudulent acts, and that your ethics code and the literature have put you "on notice" that these are wrong.

❑ **Understand how the policy pays the costs of defense** in either a lawsuit (investigation, bonds, legal fees, court costs, cost to you of your deposition and testimony, costs of expert testimony, etc.) or defenses before licensing and other regulatory bodies.

- In lawsuits, the defense costs' coverage tends to be unlimited (great news). Only a few insurers would deduct those costs from the indemnity limits, but do check. Unlimited defense costs usually applies even in sexual misconduct claims, but some policies limit the defense costs to the indemnity maximum (usually $25,000). You should know that these payments only last up until admission of guilt or conviction.

- Check to see how the costs of defense against a HIPAA complaint are covered. Newer policies offer some coverage for the investigation and initial remediation. This is an area of increasing risk.

- The common limits of payments (e.g., $5,000) for defending licensing board complaints are easily exceeded. (How many hours of attorney time would those dollars cover?) "It usually costs between $10K and $20K to defend a board action that goes beyond the initial inquiry stage. If you are in the custody evaluation business or do personnel screening you have a great chance of needing the higher limits because of the increased chance of someone not liking your conclusions" (E. C. Marine, personal communication, 2010). When costs exceed your limit because the case is or becomes complex or longer, you will have to pay the attorney yourself, and it is unlikely that you will want to switch to another attorney and start all over at your expense. In fact, a licensing board complaint is many times more likely than a civil suit, say, alleging malpractice, and most experts recommend raising defense coverage to $25,000 or more through purchase of a "defense rider."

- Will the policy cover **the income lost** when you are defending a claim against you by giving depositions, consulting with your lawyer, and attending hearings or a trial? What is the limit to these payments per day or in total? A limit of $5,000 per insured is common. If you expect more lost income, you should consider buying a "business interruption" policy.

- Are your other costs included (hotels, transportation, etc.)?

- The coverage for defense in a hearing before a state licensing board may not be as advantageous as it seems. With some boards, the involvement of lawyers from the beginning may make the process adversarial and litigious when it otherwise might have been more collegial, Remember, many complaints are dismissed or resolved at this early stage. On the other hand, having an attorney may support some due process and further investigation, which the board may not offer you otherwise.

- As soon as you notify your plan administrator/agency of a complaint or suit, it will assign to you an attorney from its panel of attorneys who have the appropriate experience. You can ask about how the attorney is being paid by the insurer (capitation, discounted fees to get the referral [managed legal care], billing against a retainer, salary, fee-for-service billable hours, etc.) but you may not be told. Use this information to evaluate how much service you may get before you use up your coverage, and ask what will happen then. Use this information to evaluate any financial pressures on the attorney to settle. This may be too cynical, because lawyers have ethical duties to protect their clients (us) or face legal malpractice claims.

❑ These policies exclude **business exposures**—that is, those that do not arise out of the practice of, say, psychology. They don't cover actions that do not require a license, such as firing a secretary or problems with workers' compensation insurance.

❑ **Examine statements about the location(s) of your services.** Are you covered for providing services outside your office? If you practice in several states, or outside the United States, make sure your activities are covered.

❑ **How does the policy define your work?** Aim for a policy that covers all the work you do or are legally allowed to do (including, e.g., teaching, consulting, or coaching), and not one that defines your work more narrowly. **What kinds of activities are excluded from the coverage?** Read the specimen policy critically, and don't rely on a summary or advertising. Evaluate which exclusions you can live with.

- **The policy should cover "all your professional activities" and exclude none.** It may only cover those specified. Check the coverage for special treatments (hypnotism, biofeedback, divorce mediation, group therapy, telepsychology, coaching, or whatever you do). Other complex risks are collaborating with physicians and other disciplines, and forensic testimony.

- **Does the policy offer coverage when you act as a supervisor** (to nonemployees), and if so, what is its cost? Claims for negligent supervision can be made against you even if you never saw a client yourself. Is the number of your supervisees larger than the policy allows?

- **You can have "vicarious liability"** for actions of your students, supervisees, employees, and independent contractors. This is most important in group practices and in collaboration with other professionals. If you have any uncertainties, seek professional guidance. You can ask the licensed representative at the agency. Your state's rules on kinds of liability will matter as well.

- If you serve as a peer reviewer or on an ethics panel, make certain you are covered against claims of negligence or maliciousness by either the sponsoring organization's policy or your own liability policy.

- Examine the coverage for **"Good Samaritan" acts** if you might provide this kind of service during a disaster or emergency.

❑ **Examine the policy for coverage of these other situations:**

- Personal injuries (slander, violation of rights of privacy, malicious prosecution, assault and battery, etc.).

- Advertising and publication injuries (false advertising, libel, copyright infringement).

- Premises medical payments ("slips and falls") liability. Try to get this included (see the discussion of other kinds of insurance, below).

- Contractual or fee disputes (e.g., breaking a contract, conflicts with a managed care organization [MCO]).

- And others: employment practices liability; discriminatory acts; nonprofessional administrative activities; cases against another professional with the same insurance carrier; dishonest, criminal, fraudulent, or malicious acts; assault and battery, and any business relationship problems.

- Confirm the availability and cost of any of coverage for any risks relevant to your way of practicing.

❑ **Sexual misconduct liability coverage** (not just the costs of defense before a licensing board or in a civil suit, but for payment of judgments against you), if any, is usually small—a "sublimit" of $25,000. Your employees should be covered, as well as yourself. There does not appear to be any consistent definitions of sexual actions; definitions have progressively been expanded from genital contact to other forms of touching, and more recently to words such as seductive talk or fantasy sharing.

❑ **Evaluate each policy's "consent to settle" options. Read all of the policy.**

- The best policies require your agreement before settling, which is called "unlimited consent to settlement." In the worst case, you may have no choice but to accept any settlement your carrier agrees to (a "hammer clause"). Try for some language that allows you some leeway and power.

- Generally, if you refuse to accept a settlement that the insurance company recommends (and that the plaintiff, suing you, accepts), the carrier will not cover any further defense costs, and you will have to pay those. Furthermore, if you then lose the case, the company will not pay more than it could have settled for. Newer policies offer arbitration of these situations.

❑ **What kind of support does the insurer or agency offer?** Does it offer high-quality, low-cost risk management seminars and educational efforts? Does it offer continuing education credits for such training? Is telephone risk consultation available when you are worried? If so, how good is it?

❑ If you are a psychologist, the American Psychological Association Insurance Trust, now called simply "The Trust" is a major insurer. Its **"endorsement" is a value that is difficult to weigh.**

- The Trust offers legal and ethical consultation to those buying its insurance. Many clinicians have found this service of great value, and other insurers may offer it as well.

- As of 2014, you do not have to be an APA member, nor need you pay APA dues, to buy a policy through The Trust.

- By the way, you will not see booths from other professional insurance companies at APA conventions, because APA will not allow competition for any "member benefits" it offers. Similarly, you will not see competitors' ads in APA journals, and so you will have to make the effort to get information from other agencies. See Appendix B.

If you do have more complex arrangements, consult a licensed agent or broker.

## Other Kinds of Insurance to Consider

### *Disability Protection*

You are much more likely to become disabled than to die, and your disability will disrupt your career almost as much as an adverse malpractice judgment will (if not more so), so prepare for it with disability insurance. Disability insurance is moderately expensive, but less so if you buy it at a younger age.

### *Income Protection*

Be aware that loss of income if your license is revoked due to malpractice is not covered by your professional liability/malpractice insurance.

### *Office Overhead/Expense Protection*

If your office expenses (rent, loans, advertising, car, staff) consume a large part of your income, and you *must* pay them because of contracts you signed, you can buy insurance to pay these expenses if you are ill or injured.

### *Business Owner's Policy*

A business owner's policy is a comprehensive policy like homeowner's insurance, and so it covers a number of other and nonspecified risks (the costs of reconstructing paperwork after a disaster, electronic media risks, etc.).

### *Premises Liability*

If anyone (not just a client) is injured while in your office, premises liability insurance can protect you. Many professional liability policies include this coverage (usually limited to $2,500), and the better ones include it free of charge, but do ask. If you need this coverage for a home office where you see clients, see your home insurance agent about a "rider," which is inexpensive.

### *Office Property Protection*

Finally, consider insurance to cover your office equipment, such as computers and furniture. Select more than you think you'll need, because prices rise and the replacement process is costly. "Replacement cost" is much better than "current value" when you have a loss. If you work at home, you will need a separate policy or a rider on your homeowner's policy to cover the cost of replacing your office equipment. As noted above, such insurance is inexpensive.

## 4.4   Ways to Reduce Your Risk of Malpractice

*Note:* For a discussion of reducing your risk of malpractice in billing, see Section 2.4.

## Twenty-Four Steps for Risk Reduction

As long as you are practicing, you can never totally eliminate your risk for malpractice, but here are 24 concrete steps that can significantly reduce your risk. These steps pertain to psychotherapy with *adults;* the assessment and treatment of children raise other issues. An excellent yet brief introduction to how the ethical principles play out for child and adolescent clients can be found in Barnett et al. (2001).

1. **Assure the continuity of each client's care.** You do not have to accept everyone as a client, but once you have accepted a client, don't neglect or abandon him or her. Abandonment is not just failing to provide services (dereliction of the duty owed a client by a clinician), but failure to be available in an emergency. See Section 7.3 on termination for a discussion of how to do it properly. Discuss with clients early in treatment and during the treatment process how and when treatment will end. Let them know that it is OK to bring this up and discuss what their expectations, hopes, and needs are, as well as to make it clear to you when they feel disappointed by things that arise during treatment.

2. **Perform within the standard of care or practice.** The standard of care has been discussed at the start of Section 4.2. When we perform above it, we and our clients are fortunate. If we perform below it, we become vulnerable to accusations and legal procedures, and so this concept is central to considerations of malpractice and ethics. Therefore, you must know the rules that apply to you. First, you must know the appropriate standards and guidelines of your discipline. Professional organizations have published many guidelines with which you should be familiar when they apply to your work or the populations you serve. Generally, you will be held to your national organization's standards, so learn them and provide services at a high level of quality and integrity.

3. **Practice competently.** A central protective rule of ethics is to stay within what we understand and know how to do. However, it is hard to know what we don't know, or to know beforehand what we don't know well enough. A severe impediment to good practice is that we usually cannot know what we do not know. In a series of experiments, Kruger and Dunning (2002) found that the least capable individuals greatly overestimated their abilities and the most capable slightly underestimated theirs. More striking is that unless we are highly competent in an area, we cannot judge our own or others' competence accurately. Let this serve as a humbling warning. Keep the following guidelines in mind:

   - Never do what you are not legally entitled to do. Do not practice medicine, law, or pharmacy if you are not so credentialed.

   - Do not try to do everything you *are* legally allowed to do. Don't do everything you are licensed, trained, or even degreed to do. You are *not* competent to handle everything that walks in your door.

   - Moreover, you are probably not really competent to do some things you know about, unless you received the necessary quality and intensity of training *recently.*

- Make clear the real areas of your competence in your communications to clients, both orally and in writing. Inaccurate expectations can be the basis for dissatisfaction, treatment failure and a complaint.

- If you do assessments, use "a well-defined and systematic method of interpreting test findings and be able to support your findings in court" (Cohen, 1983/1990, p. 660).

- Don't use shortcuts (sending tests home with clients, or depending excessively on computerized test interpretations).

- Do not, through defensiveness or arrogance, go beyond your data. The APA ethics code reminds us that psychologists must recognize the "limitations of their interpretations" of assessment results (APA, 2010, Standard 9.06), and the same should apply to all other data.

- Do not do custody evaluations without considering the inherent conflicts and the potential for dissatisfied clients. Doing custody evaluations will result in a high frequency of licensing board complaints because of a base rate of about 50% unhappy clients. Take many precautions. Glassman (1998) reviews the issues and makes many useful suggestions. A publication of the APA Committee on Professional Practice and Standards (2010), *Guidelines for Custody Evaluations in Family Law Proceedings,* includes many resources and definitions as well as suggested behaviors. Finally, the APA code of ethics (APA, 2010) requires the psychologist to "clarify at the outset . . . the probable uses of the services provided or the information obtained" in family work (Standard 10.02).

- If you operate in the areas of health psychology or behavioral medicine, or work in a primary health care setting, be especially careful not to "practice medicine without a license." For most mental health clinicians, this means at least not telling a client to start taking, stop taking, or take differently a medication. Maintain full, continual, and two-way communication with physicians, and define your roles and knowledge base carefully.

- Be alert to biasing factors both in you and in others who provide information. Seek out and attend to personal, social, and cultural factors that can bias your judgments (as we discuss more fully later in Section 4.4). These may include communication deficits (hearing, speech, English as a second language, reading skill, etc.); ageism; "beautyism" (the influence of weight, height, coloring, and prettiness); ethnic preferences and beliefs; racism; sex-role stereotypes; your socioeconomic status; "personal allergies" to some people; your financial gain from some findings or diagnoses; sympathy with the "victim"; hostility to the "aggressor"; blaming the "victim"; supporting the "downtrodden"; your personal liberalism or conservatism; feelings about those who smoke, drink, abstain, and/or are "in recovery"; biases for or against various religions or degrees of religiosity; and other, less well-recognized feelings that can interfere with careful analysis.

- Understand and always give full weight to the "low base rate" phenomenon, which can severely limit the accuracy of any variable's identification. Similarly, appreciate the effects of a high base rate, and know the local base rates of the phenomena of interest.

4. **You must know the current state and local laws that apply to you.** Conflicts between what you promise a client (such as confidentiality) and what the governing laws require can be avoided if you know all the applicable laws, such as, those concerning clients with both substance abuse and developmental disabilities. Another example: Which takes precedence, workers' compensation law or mental health law? If your state's rules are less stringent in protecting privacy than those of HIPAA, or if the state does not address an issue that HIPAA does, the rules and procedures of HIPAA will apply, so you must be familiar with them as well.

5. **Get fully informed consent.** Always require and obtain voluntary and fully informed consent from a competent person. Consent is so important that we devote a whole chapter of this book to its ramifications. See Chapter 5.

6. **Maintain confidentiality.** Know the limits of the confidentiality you can offer, and do not promise more than you can deliver. For example, inform clients fully about the exceptions to confidentiality, *before* they reveal something you cannot keep confidential. See Chapter 8 on confidentiality.

7. **Communicate completely.**

   - Keep your clients' expectations reality-based with two-way discussions and information sharing.

   - Communicate openly. Become curious about misunderstandings and failures of communication. Be willing to hear complaints nondefensively.

   - Communicate honestly. Don't pretend to have clarity or certainty you don't have; the best direction is not always clear, and each case is a little different. Issues and decisions can remain clouded. We can only use our best judgment based on our knowledge, skill, and experience, but we can use all of it and share our concerns.

   - Communicate clearly, especially in regard to money, fees, and insurance.

   - Communicate regularly. Your client handouts, forms, and regular feedback on progress are crucial here.

   - Don't be distant. Always listen and be kind where appropriate. Show that you genuinely care about the client's welfare.

8. **Supervise fully.** When you supervise, be thorough and be available. Monitor your students, teammates, and employees with as much effort as needed. Supervision is always a difficult balance between a quasi-parental role and the encouragement of autonomy, between risk tolerance and self-protective fears. Have your supervisees obtain their own professional liability insurance, if possible. If not, you must provide it under your policy. Remember that you will be held responsible for their actions. Bear in mind that your professional employees can commit malpractice, and that nonprofessionals can cause other harms for which you are legally responsible. Prevention should include training in confidentiality, collections, scheduling, and any other areas that occur to you. See Section 4.9 for more guidance.

9. **Keep abreast of new developments on both the clinical and legal fronts.** You must know the standard of practice in your field, so you have to keep up with current developments. Put aside time and money each year for professional development

(more than the minimum required for continuing education credits). Continuing education on both your methods *and alternative ones* is essential; go to the presentations of those you disagree with. Remember that the half-life of the knowledge base gained in a PhD program is about 10 years (Neimeyer et al., 2014). Keep aware of new developments in the legal aspects of professional work as well.

10. **Consult frequently and formally.** Get consultation when things aren't going well with a client, whenever you have some unease about something, and definitely when you are considering breaking any rule. If you have doubts or are uncomfortable about your conceptualization or treatment, consult with a colleague and/or your attorney. Do not delay! Thomas Gutheil (2007) suggests this rule of thumb: "Never worry alone." "Consult" with clients' former therapists by getting records and asking questions. Nonmedical therapists (and many medical therapists) should consult clients' physicians about any possible medical interactions. Consultation is legally protective as well, probably because when we consult we share and learn each other's ideas of the standard of practice, and so are more likely to stay within it.

11. **Take seriously and evaluate thoroughly any evidence of suicidal ideation or intent.** See Sections 4.7 and 4.8.

12. **Have a contingency plan for threats.** It is much more difficult to protect after a client becomes dangerous to self or others. Your plan should include resources for family or support system contact, special consultations for both you and the client, medications, referrals, hospitalization, police contacts, contacts with your lawyer, and so on. Tell your clients from the beginning about your duty to protect and your options (see Section 4.8).

13. **Refer carefully.**
    - Refer clients when the problem they present is one with which you have little experience or training.
    - Refer only to other professionals who have the necessary areas of competence. Get feedback from those clients you refer and respect, so that you learn about the competencies among your possible referral resources. There is a kind of malpractice called "negligent referral."
    - Ethically, a client who does not improve under your care should be referred elsewhere, even when a colleague with the necessary competence seems hard to find or the client is reluctant to start again. At the minimum, the client must be informed and allowed to choose. Document the options, the choices made, and their rationales.

14. **Be conservative in your treatments.** You are required by the ethics of your profession to act prudently and reasonably, at the standard of care. If you do not, you are exposing yourself to risk, because you are exposing your client to substandard treatment.

    Having a theoretical rationale for a treatment does not automatically make it ethical; nonetheless, base all your psychotherapeutic interventions on well-established theory (Woody, 1988, p. 211). This does not mean that you must *only* follow a recognized "school," but do not offer services for which you are the only expert or practitioner. Your treatment does not have to have an empirical justification, but it must be seen as acceptable by a significant number of your peers—and, in some states, this is part of the licensing laws. In general, it will be hard for a court to find fault with the prudently reasoned use of a new and professionally or scientifically supported method by a therapist with strong credentials and no personal gain in sight.

If your treatment lacks this prudence, call it "experimental," tell the client of other treatment options, get more detailed informed consent, and discontinue it at the first sign of harm to the client. It is a continuing and difficult professional struggle to balance the use of a scientifically tested method, which (in theory) protects the client, against the need to tailor a method to the unique client and the need to innovate (for future clients' benefit). This balancing is an inescapable ethical dimension of high-quality practice.

15. **Don't promise a cure.** Be careful in discussing the effectiveness of your treatment approach, and do not allow a client to develop expectations that will not be fulfilled. Promote realistic expectations of treatment outcomes, not overly optimistic expectations of a total change.

16. **Document.** Get a relevant case history, especially of substance use, violence, self-injury or suicide; all previous episodes and treatments; lawsuits; and the like (see the intake materials in Chapter 6). Keep clear, concise, and complete records. Use behavioral descriptions, not just diagnoses, labels, or shortcut jargon. Record the essentials. Pressman and Siegler (1983) suggest: "One way to think about what the medical record should contain might be to think about what you would want to see if you were called in as a new consultant on the case in order to understand the history and to start a course of treatment" (p. 109). Record diagnoses, prognoses, progress, and evaluations of outcome. Record your instructions to clients, handouts given to clients, and after-hours calls. Document no-shows (and your responses), consultations, and your arrangements for another professional's covering for you, and for which clients.

In risky circumstances, document your understanding, reasoning, and judgments. This is called **"thinking out loud for the record."** See Chapters 6 and 7 for a full discussion of clinical record keeping.

17. **Diagnose.** If you do health care, you *must* diagnose, but in other cases a good history *may* be all that is necessary and *reasonable* (the key word). The extent and nature of this evaluation process depends on your professional discipline as well.

A care provider has an obligation (a) to diagnose accurately and thus treat properly; (b) to ensure that a client who presents with an emotional problem does not suffer from an undiagnosed and untreated coexisting or contributing medical illness; and, if so, (c) to arrange for adequate biological treatment. This burden is especially heavy on care providers who are biased against, lacking proficiency in, or reluctant to obtain consultation for such treatment. One can make mistakes in diagnosis without committing malpractice, but one must not do less than the standard in one's procedures and judgments. In order to supplement your own clinical judgments, administer psychological tests (if you have the appropriate training) as necessary.

18. **Avoid fee disputes and the accumulation of a large debt.** Your payment policy

should be stated clearly and enforced regularly. Never turn a debt over for collection without a personal conversation by you (not your secretary or office manager) with the client (not a spouse or other person).

19. **Be alert to a client's dissatisfaction with you, as it may escalate into legal actions.** Dissatisfaction may be why the client is not paying your bill, attending sessions regularly, or complying with treatments. Other early warning signs of dissatisfaction may include a client's seeming overconcerned with your fees; being overly critical of a previous therapist or treatment (and therefore likely to be dissatisfied with yours); and having unrealistically high expectations of therapy's outcome (which are bound to be dashed). Of course, all of these should be dealt with as issues in therapy. Entering therapy under external pressure may direct a client to seek a way out of therapy, to gain revenge, and to make a profit all at the same time—by filing a complaint or suit.

    Any client's dissatisfaction or disappointment should be responded to immediately. If you are distant, arrogant, not readily available, or hard to talk to, then a client may begin to question your competence. Remember that clients are usually not qualified to judge your clinical competence. This is why testimonials from clients were forbidden until the 1992 revision of the APA code of ethics, and even now testimonials from current clients are not allowed (APA, 2010, Standard 5.05). You may be surprised to discover highly negative comments and evaluations from your disgruntled clients on Internet review sites if dissatisfaction is not addressed.

20. **Consider screening clients for litigiousness.** You might think about excluding from your practice clients you believe are likely to file lawsuits at some point. Few data are available to guide us in this regard, but wealthier clients are more likely to sue. Take a legal history, and note the client's comments about previous therapists.

    Be very careful about your intake and assessment of "fit" with new clients. If you anticipate that someone will be a poor fit, or if things feel strange or just "off" during the intake, consider referring this person elsewhere to lower the likelihood of complaints, negative Internet reviews, poor outcomes, and so on. Most of us were never encouraged to develop or trust these instincts in our training, but they are protective in private practice, where we are much more vulnerable.

21. **Respect the complexities of families and couples.** Be aware that family and couple therapies raise sticky complexities regarding the therapist's responsibility to each person, particularly regarding confidentiality and informed consent. The therapist's own values (about preserving a marriage, extramarital affairs, polyamory, sex roles, secrets, etc.) add to the complexities and create opportunities for misunderstandings, failed expectations, and ultimately complaints (de Becker, 1999).

22. **Don't work if you are impaired.** Exhaustion, drugs and alcohol, personal crises, illness, sleeplessness, and pain will limit your ability to do good work. If you engage in malpractice, it will be much more damaging than just your poor functioning. Self-care comes before other care. Do not let your desire for income or other pressures lead you to do below-standard work. This can be a difficult lesson for those just starting a private practice, who may be struggling with a low caseload and school debt. Please take our advice and learn to implement self-care practices early so they can become good habits.

    A significant risk factor for unethical practice is **therapist burnout.** If you identify with several of the items on the short list below (or see http://www.proqol.org), read some of the books on therapist burnout (e.g., Maslach & Zimbardo, 2003; Figley, 2002; Rothschild & Rand, 2006), and seek consultation.

- Do you feel pessimistic or even cynical toward clients?
- Have you experienced persistent and interfering daydreams during sessions?
- Have you had hostile thoughts toward any client?
- Are you bored with your clients? Do they all sound the same?
- Do you find yourself overly quick to diagnose?
- Are you overusing medications/alcohol/stimulants to tolerate your work?
- Are you blaming the client?

Most professional organizations have "colleague assistance" programs that can help you recover and are confidential. The APA Practice Organization (2006) offers its members a superb manual for effective programs, *Advancing Colleague Assistance in Professional Psychology*. It also offers "Tips for Self-Care," with many good resources (http://www.apapracticecentral.org/ce/self-care/acca-promoting.aspx). If you notice a colleague's problematic or risky behaviors, Keith-Spiegel (2013b) offers clear advice on confronting an unethical colleague.

23. **Terminate properly.** See Section 7.3 for guidance in avoiding abandonment and other problems.

24. **Consider limiting the scope of your practice.** You might accept as clients only those with some diagnoses or problems, or who can benefit from a specific approach of yours. This is a variation on staying within your areas of competence.

## Sensitivity to Differences in Culture, Religion, Gender, and Other Dimensions of Diversity

In no other profession do culture, socialization, roles, and worldview matter more than in clinical work. We should be aware and respectful of clients' customs, parenting styles, acculturation, expectations of therapy and healing, and many other factors that play major roles in our work. We have both an ethical obligation (APA, 2003; APA, 2010, Principle E) and a clinical need to be sensitive and competent in dealing with those of different backgrounds from our own. It goes without saying that we should be aware of the common cultural, ethnic, religious, racial, and sexual orientation differences. However, we also need to examine our beliefs about body size, alternative sexual practices, aging, gender variations, income/other aspects of socioeconomic status, disabilities, illiteracy, language use, and other areas of difference.

We are required to examine our own values, biases, and prejudices. Goode (2000) offers a fine checklist to raise awareness. Enlarging our sensitivities to these issues can help us avoid limiting our clients' potentials. Sensitivity includes noticing our own lack of cultural competence and the need for consultation or referral to a clinician with the necessary expertise. New writings on microaggressions note that clinicians may unwittingly communicate bias to clients, which can have a negative impact on the therapy relationship or lead clients to terminate early (Sue, 2010).

Lists of culture-specific characteristics that affect psychological functioning are available for many subcultures and ethnicities (Paniagua, 2005; D'Avanzo & Geissler, 2003). Although such information is often valuable, assuming that all members of a group will have all these characteristics is stereotyping; there is much variation within any group. It is probably best to use these characteristics as hypotheses to be modified or discarded during treatment.

Becoming more multiculturally competent is difficult, but many resources are available for assessing and altering beliefs that limit effectiveness with clients outside our own cultural and racial groups. Hansen et al. (2006) is highly recommended. Besides general resources such as Sue and Sue (2008) and Paniagua (2005), others address personality assessment (Dana, 2005), substance abuse treatment (Straussner, 2001), and family therapy (McGoldrick et al., 2005). Seek out materials suited to your practice. For difficult self-change, see Sue (2003). The Multicultural Toolkit (http://goo.gl/plNpF0) is a set of tables with dozens of books, articles, and other kinds of resources for ethnicity and race; lesbian, gay, bisexual, transsexual, questioning, intersex, asexual (LGBTQIA), and other gender-nonconforming status; and multicultural, religion, and women's issues.

In addition, we offer these suggestions:

- The largest minority population consists of those with disabilities, and competence to work with them is required. Artman and Daniels (2010) offer specific suggestions for therapists.

- Those for whom English is a second language may be able to participate in therapy in English, but may be better informed about legal and ethical details by reading some materials in their primary language. Look online for non-English versions of the Notice of Privacy Practices (NPP) forms and consent forms (see Chapters 6 and 7). Non-English educational materials on disorders and substance abuse are available from the Substance Abuse and Mental Health Services Administration (SAMHSA), the National Institute of Mental Health (NIMH), and hospitals serving minorities. Programs available on the Web can translate your materials or those of others into workable versions in clients' languages (see, e.g., http://translate.google.com and https://www.bing.com/translator).

- Review all your forms, handouts, and other paperwork for clients, with an eye to cultural assumptions and possible stereotypes. Although clearly racist, ethnocentric, and unscientific content is unlikely, insensitivity to all the variations of the human condition may make your practice less comfortable to diverse populations.

- Consider replacing check boxes with fill-in blanks for items such as ethnicity, sex/gender, preferred pronoun, disability status, and sexual orientation. Providing what you assume are the only possible responses (e.g., male and female for gender) may indicate ignorance on your part and lead a client to assume that you lack sensitivity to human diversity.

- If your practice is not accessible to persons with different abilities, such as those who use wheelchairs, you may want to indicate this to avoid frustrating potential clients. Written materials in larger typefaces, efforts to reduce background noise and other distractions, larger or different seating, and other modifications for clients with physical differences will be appreciated. For guidance on meeting the standards for online accessibility, Kenneth S. Pope's separate site called Accessibility & Disability

Resources for Psychology Training & Practice (http://www.kpope.com) is comprehensive and authoritative.

## 4.5  Boundary Issues

We all inhabit many roles in life, such as being therapists, and each one comes with expectations—what is to be done and not done in performing that role. Some of those expectations are unique to a role, and some are shared with other roles. Different roles have different rules. For example, in regard to touch, generally therapists are expected not to touch clients, but the friend role can include touch, and the sexual partner role requires touch. Other expectations of the therapy relationship include having specific meeting times, a private meeting place, limits on therapist self-disclosure, restrictions on gifts/money, and so on. The rules for therapists on the Internet are still developing. For example, is it legitimate for a therapist to learn about a client through online searching and not just the usual client-provided information? How "network-friendly" should we be with ex-clients? These issues are discussed in further detail in Chapter 9.

Using a Venn diagram allows us to integrate the concepts of boundaries and roles. Gutheil and Gabbard (1993, 1998) proposed a now widely accepted model of roles and boundaries to understand and guide ethical decision making. We present a version of this model as Figure 4.3.

In Figure 4.3, each circle contains a collection of behaviors expected of one of these roles: therapist, friend, sexual partner. The edges of the circles represent each role's boundaries. These are the stated rules about what is to be included in the role (shoulds, oughts, musts, appropriates) and what is excluded (shouldn'ts, the forbidden, etc.). The excluded behaviors are likely to be part of another role or roles. When these role boundaries are respected and a person stays in a single role, then the relationship is made predictable and safe. Boundaries are **crossed** when a person in one role performs a behavior belonging to another role. This is the definition of a "dual relationship." Examples include a therapist who is also a business partner, teacher, consultant, or sexual partner. Such dual relationships are represented by the overlap of the circles in Figure 4.3.

Gutheil and Gabbard (1993, 1998) make the crucial point that crossings can be helpful, neutral, or harmful to the client. They introduced the term **"boundary violations"** for crossings that harm a client. For example, imagine a professional woman who dresses and speaks well, but whose hair is a mess. As her therapist, should you refer her to a hairdresser? According to this model, the first question would be "Is suggesting a hairdresser part of my role?" In some therapies, such as those dealing with vocational advancement, such a referral might easily be understood by both parties as part of the therapist's role. In these cases, there is no boundary crossing. However, in most psychotherapies (such as for a phobia), a referral to a hairdresser is outside the therapist's role and would be better understood as part of a friend's role. In this case, making such a referral would be a boundary crossing. A second question then arises: "Will this action help the client, be neutral, or harm the client?" If causing harm is likely, a therapist should not proceed, or he or she will have engaged in a boundary violation.

Boundary violations are not linear and simple, but must be weighed along many facets, because we have many sets of rules: the therapist's intent (desire to be helpful vs. self-interest and benefit); the relevance of the action to the treatment (outside meetings as part of *in vivo* desensitization vs. socializing); the client's interpretation of the behaviors (a hug

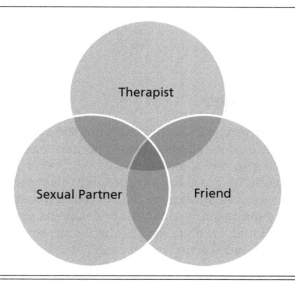

**FIGURE 4.3.** Gutheil and Gabbard's model of crossed role boundaries.

intended by the therapist to be congratulatory may be seen as intrusive or sexual by the client); current, evolving, and local professional standards (first-name-basis conversations were once considered inappropriate); and others. Furthermore, a boundary crossing may be seen as a violation if the client feels it is unwelcome or if the client's history, diagnosis, or values shape it as stressful.

Gutheil and Brodsky (2011) offer extensive discussions of all aspects of boundaries, including self-disclosure, behaviors in and out of the office, and dress, as well as harms, vulnerabilities, warning signs, and the legal aspects. Pope (2014) has gathered hundreds of resources on "Dual Relationships, Multiple Relationships, and Boundary Decisions."

Barnett et al. (2007b) suggest that before acting, clinicians should

> work to be sure that (a) their intention is motivated by the client's treatment needs and best interests and not by their own needs; (b) the boundary crossing is consistent with the client's treatment plan; (c) the boundary crossing is sensitive to the client's diagnosis, history, culture, and values; (d) the boundary crossing—and the reasoning supporting it—is documented in the client's record; (e) the boundary crossing is discussed, if possible, with the client in advance to ensure his or her comfort with the plan and to prevent misunderstandings; (f) the power differential present is considered, and the client's trust is not exploited; and (g) consultation with a respected colleague is used to guide the psychologist's decision. (p. 403)

To deepen your awareness of times when the risks of crossings and violations are increased, take the time to complete the questionnaire presented in Figure 4.4. To gain the most from it, consider all your clients when answering the questions, not just the one the questionnaire asks about. We are indebted to Estelle Disch, PhD, of Cambridge, MA, for her permission to reprint it, and to Sam Knapp, EdD, of Harrisburg, PA, for suggesting the addition of the last four items. Dr. Disch has a more extensive and specific list, designed for clients, that can also raise our awareness (available at http://www.survivingtherapistabuse.com/treatment-abuse-checklist).

Other self-educational questionnaires for therapists include the Exploitation Index (Epstein & Simon, 1990), which explores the consequences of boundary confusion.

Keith-Spiegel (2013a, pp. 4–7) offers a sensitive list of "red flags" for many kinds of difficulties.

All current professional ethics codes incorporate the concepts of boundaries and roles, but some do not use both words. In the most recent revision of the American Counseling Association's (ACA's) ethics code (ACA, 2014), Section A.6 discusses boundary crossings as boundary "extensions" and urges informed consent, consultation, and documentation of the thinking process. The relevant portion of the APA code of ethics (APA, 2010) is Standard 3.05.

Please note that **the requirements and prohibitions of the therapist role are also the standard of care** (a consensus about those rules) and so are enforceable.

Boundary issues stemming from "dual relationships" in general are discussed more fully in the remainder of this section. Those stemming from client–therapist sexual intimacy in particular are discussed in detail in Section 4.6.

## Why Avoid Dual (or Multiple) Relationships?

Dual relationships can have many negative effects. Specifically, they can:

- Lead to conflicts between your interests and the client's.

- Impair your unselfish judgment, and limit your comfort with necessary confrontations.

- Limit the effective handling of the relationship variables.

- Create confusion and ambiguity. (If, as the therapist, you perform one behavior customary to the friendship role, what other friendship behaviors might the client expect?)

- Usually close the door to future therapy that might be needed.

One core concept is this: The therapist's promise to forgo all other relationships with the client is a gift to the client. It creates confidentiality and trust, and gives the client the **safety** to reveal, explore, feel, and do almost anything without fear of consequences, because the consequences would only arise in the other relationships.

A second core concept arises from the fact that all relationships have power differences because one party has more knowledge, social status, money, or the like than the other. If the more powerful party decides to put the needs of the other ahead of his or her own, it creates a **fiduciary relationship.** At the heart of the therapeutic relationship is the therapist's promise to put the client's interests ahead of the therapist's. It is a major element of being a professional in our society, and it is part of why we are to be trusted by clients and why professionals are allowed to operate independently.

The power differential inherent in the therapy relationship may be exploited through seducing, intimidating, or otherwise influencing the client into the other relationship. When clients are exploited in dual relationships, complaining about it is much more difficult for them than complaining about most other issues, like fees. The clients must overcome the power differential and positive feelings in order to assert their own needs. The risks to a client are usually much greater than the risks to a therapist. For example, in a complaint, confidentiality may be broken and the therapist can say, allege, or deny almost anything about the client's life, thus putting the client on trial.

# Are You in Trouble with a Client?

The purpose of this checklist is to alert you to boundary issues that might be interfering with your ability to work effectively with a particular client. Be particularly attentive if the situation persists even after you have attempted to change it. Answer either true or false to each question, and add any explanations or details on another page.

Client's initials or pseudonym: _____     Date: ____/____/____

| | | |
|---|---|---|
| 1. This client feels more like a friend than a client. | ☐ True | ☐ False |
| 2. I often tell my personal problems to this client. | ☐ True | ☐ False |
| 3. I feel sexually aroused in response to this client. | ☐ True | ☐ False |
| 4. I want to be friends with this client when therapy ends. | ☐ True | ☐ False |
| 5. I'm waiting for therapy to end in order to be lovers with this client. | ☐ True | ☐ False |
| 6. To be honest, I think the good-bye hugs last too long with this client. | ☐ True | ☐ False |
| 7. My sessions often run overtime with this client. | ☐ True | ☐ False |
| 8. I tend to accept gifts or favors from this client without examining why the gift was given and why at that particular time. | ☐ True | ☐ False |
| 9. I have a barter arrangement with this client. | ☐ True | ☐ False |
| 10. I have had sexual contact with this client. | ☐ True | ☐ False |
| 11. I sometimes choose my clothing with this particular client in mind. | ☐ True | ☐ False |
| 12. I have attended small professional or social events at which I knew this client would be present, without discussing it ahead of time. | ☐ True | ☐ False |
| 13. This client often invites me to social events, and I don't feel comfortable saying either yes or no. | ☐ True | ☐ False |
| 14. This client sometimes sits on my lap. | ☐ True | ☐ False |
| 15. Sometimes when I'm holding or hugging this client during our regular therapy work, I feel like the contact is sexualized for one or the other or both of us. | ☐ True | ☐ False |
| 16. There's something I like about being alone in the office with this client when no one else is around. | ☐ True | ☐ False |
| 17. I lock the door when working with this client. | ☐ True | ☐ False |
| 18. This client is very seductive, and I often don't know how to handle it. | ☐ True | ☐ False |
| 19. This client owes me/the agency a lot of money, and I don't know what to do about it. | ☐ True | ☐ False |
| 20. I have invited this client to public or social events. | ☐ True | ☐ False |
| 21. I am often late for sessions with this particular client. | ☐ True | ☐ False |
| 22. I find myself cajoling, teasing, or joking a lot with this client. | ☐ True | ☐ False |
| 23. I am in a heavy emotional crisis myself, and I identify so much with this client's pain that I can hardly attend to the client. | ☐ True | ☐ False |

**FIGURE 4.4. Are you in trouble with a client?** Questionnaire for assessing boundary issues, devised by Estelle Disch, PhD, of Cambridge, MA, and reprinted here by permission of Dr. Disch. Items 48–51 were suggested by Sam Knapp, EdD, of Harrisburg, PA.

| | | |
|---|---|---|
| 24. I allow this client to comfort me. | ❏ True | ❏ False |
| 25. I feel like this client and I are very much alike. | ❏ True | ❏ False |
| 26. This client scares me. | ❏ True | ❏ False |
| 27. This client's pain is so deep I can hardly stand it. | ❏ True | ❏ False |
| 28. I enjoy feeling more powerful than this client. | ❏ True | ❏ False |
| 29. Sometimes I feel like I'm in over my head with this client. | ❏ True | ❏ False |
| 30. I often feel hooked or lost with this client, and supervision on the case hasn't helped. | ❏ True | ❏ False |
| 31. I often feel invaded or pushed by this client and have a difficult time standing my ground. | ❏ True | ❏ False |
| 32. Sometimes I hate this client. | ❏ True | ❏ False |
| 33. I sometimes feel like punishing or controlling this client. | ❏ True | ❏ False |
| 34. I feel overly protective toward this client. | ❏ True | ❏ False |
| 35. I sometimes drink or take drugs with this client. | ❏ True | ❏ False |
| 36. I don't regularly check out what the physical contact I have with this client means for the client. | ❏ True | ❏ False |
| 37. I accommodate to this client's schedule and then feel angry/manipulated. | ❏ True | ❏ False |
| 38. This client's fee feels too high or too low. | ❏ True | ❏ False |
| 39. This client has invested money in an enterprise of mine or vice versa. | ❏ True | ❏ False |
| 40. I have hired this client to work for me. | ❏ True | ❏ False |
| 41. This client has hired me to work for her/him. | ❏ True | ❏ False |
| 42. I find it very difficult not to talk about this client with people close to me. | ❏ True | ❏ False |
| 43. I find myself saying a lot about myself with this client—telling stories, engaging in peer-like conversation. | ❏ True | ❏ False |
| 44. If I were to list people in my caseload with whom I could envision myself in a sexual relationship, this client would be on the list. | ❏ True | ❏ False |
| 45. I call this client a lot and go out of my way to meet with her/him in locations convenient to her/him. | ❏ True | ❏ False |
| 46. This client has spent time at my home (apart from the office). | ❏ True | ❏ False |
| 47. I'm doing so much on this client's behalf I feel exhausted. | ❏ True | ❏ False |
| 48. I have given this client a ride home. | ❏ True | ❏ False |
| 49. We have had lunch/dinner during sessions. | ❏ True | ❏ False |
| 50. This client has performed minor favors for me, such as returning library books or picking up dry cleaning. | ❏ True | ❏ False |
| 51. I have accepted valuable gifts from this client. | ❏ True | ❏ False |

**FIGURE 4.4** (*continued*)

Harmful dual relationships usually stem from "subtle, gradual, and innocuous beginnings" (Pope, 1988a, p. 17). They may arise from inattention to the dynamics of the therapeutic relationship or from a desire to be of even more help to a client. They can also arise from the client's own manipulation (because of pathology, transference, or other sources); in these cases, "dual" relationships often become "duel" relationships.

## Examples of Multiple Relationships

There are many types of dual or multiple relationships, and therapists must be alert to all the possibilities. Pope (1988a) lists 18 real-life scenarios, and below we have adapted some of these and added some others.

- Being a therapist as well as a supervisor, teacher, dissertation committee member, evaluator, or research supervisor to the same person. You should refer your current students seeking therapy, and should be careful about other relationships with those who might become your students. It may even be better to remain somewhat distant, have only casual contacts, or meet only at social events associated with the university until a student graduates and one of your roles terminates, before entering a closer friendship with this person (Koocher & Keith-Spiegel, 2008).

- Providing therapy to current social acquaintances or business contacts, or to former ones when the old relationship was intense.

- Being both a therapist and a friend. A "friend" is someone with whom one socializes outside the therapy office. There are many distinctions between friendship and therapy, and Handout 4.1 (see "Preventing Boundary Crossings and Violations," below) describes some of them. A policy statement is also included in the sample client information brochure (Section 5.2). You may wish to make additions to these from your own experience.

- Being a "friend" or "contact" on a social networking site, which may blur boundaries or otherwise confuse clients about the nature of the therapy relationship. The most recent revision of the ACA code of ethics (ACA, 2014) specifically prohibits virtual relationships (e.g., "friending") with current clients (Section A.5.e) and cautions about others (Section H.6 on social media). We may see other professional associations make similar rules.

- Having any kind of sexual relationship with a former or current client (see Section 4.6).

- Having any kind of business relationship with a former or current client (such as that of employer, coauthor, consultant, advisor, mentor, partner, lender, debtor, etc.).

- Providing any kind of psychological services to the children of your employees; to children of colleagues, friends, or frequent social, political, or business contacts; or to children you coach in an athletic activity.

- Serving in a second professional capacity with your clients, such as practicing law/medicine/financial advising (or any other profession) with or without a license.

- Providing assessments to therapy clients for disability, return to duty, custody, parenting fitness, or similar activities.

- Serving as an advocate for a client (e.g., writing letters to support receiving clinically relevant special services and accommodations) can be consistent with being a therapist but can easily compromise confidentiality. However, serving as an expert witness is likely to compromise the therapeutic relationship, because it raises conflicts: Experts are expected to be objective and skeptical, whereas therapists are more supportive and subjective; the focus of treatment will likely shift from clinical to forensic issues; and the working alliance may be harmed if the client sees the therapist being examined and cross-examined in court, or discussing areas where the therapist might not support the client's case.

- Engaging in several types of financial relationships. Extending credit by allowing payment over time can become conflictual. Trading or bartering therapy for legal or professional services (e.g., tutoring), goods, or discounts—on either a dollar-for-dollar value basis or a task-for-task basis—puts you into an additional commercial role. In this role, your goals are, or appear to be, in conflict with those of your clients. That is, you seem to be providing services at the lowest cost to you but the highest cost to them.

## When Dual Relationships Are Unavoidable: Weighing Their Effects

In small towns and other close populations (such as some religious groupings), multiple relationships are necessary and so boundary crossings may be unavoidable. Schank and Skovholt (2005) thoroughly cover these issues.

The relevant ethical principle is **nonmaleficence**—avoiding harm to the client. The APA ethics code notes that "Multiple relationships *that would not reasonably be expected to cause impairment or risk exploitation or harm* are not unethical" (APA, 2010, Standard 3.05; emphasis added). Thus the code does not forbid dual or multiple relationships, but puts the burden of keeping them harmless on the psychologist.

Some unavoidable boundary crossings will be helpful and some neutral, but the goal is to prevent a crossing from becoming a violation and harmful. With advance warnings and patient education, harm can often be averted. For example, you can offer a "Walmart speech" to clients early in the relationship: "If we should meet in Walmart or some other public place, I will make eye contact to acknowledge you and then look away, because I want to maintain the privacy of our relationship. I don't know whether the person standing next to you is your nosy neighbor or a curious relative. Also, it is unlikely that we can say much of therapeutic value in such a setting."

In a thoughtfully clarifying article, Gottlieb (1993) has proposed that the effects of a dual relationship ought to be weighed on three dimensions: "power," "duration," and the clarity of the time limits of the relationship, which he calls "termination." Essentially, relationships with low power differentials, briefer contacts, and clear time boundaries are less risky for exploitation, require less consultation, require less extensive and detailed informed consent, need less documentation, and so on. For example, vocational testing is lower on all three dimensions than intensive psychotherapy. For carefully reasoned arguments and suggestions about defining which multiple relationships are harmful and which are not, see Younggren and Gottlieb's (2004) elaboration of Gottlieb (1993), as well as Sonne (2006).

The Markkula Center for Applied Ethics (https://www.scu.edu/ethics/practicing/decision) has educational materials. Staal and King (2000) have adapted Gottlieb's model for military psychologists, and Younggren's (2002) article is helpful in evaluating the ethics of a dual relationship.

### Preventing Boundary Crossings and Violations

**HANDOUT 4.1** A client handout on dual relationships is presented as Handout 4.1. It is intended to be used for patient education, and thus to lessen troubles in this area. It can be left in your waiting room or handed to a client when questions or a potentially risky situation occurs.

## 4.6   Sexual Intimacies in Therapy

Sexual relationships with clients, students, and supervisees are a particularly toxic sub-type of multiple relationships, and they constitute a plague in the health care professions. We must greatly extend our efforts to prevent them through consciousness raising, training, supervision, investigation, and punishment. The APA code of ethics (APA, 2010) says flatly in Standard 10.05 that "Psychologists do not engage in sexual intimacies with current therapy clients/patients," and in Standard 10.08 that they do not do so "with a former client/patient for at least two years after cessation or termination of therapy." (See our later discussion in this section for clarification of this latter prohibition.)

### What Is Meant by "Sexual Intimacies"?

Although there is no precise agreement on the definition of "sexual intimacy," the following statements are made in the professional liability insurance policies of several professional organizations.

The American Professional Agency's (2015) policy offers this definition:

> Sexual Misconduct means any type of actual, alleged, attempted, or proposed physical touching or caressing, or suggestion thereof by You or any person for whom You may be legally responsible, with or to any of Your past or present patients or clients, or with or to any relative or any person who regularly resides with any such patient or client, or with or to any person with whom such patient or client or relative has an affectionate personal relationship, which could be considered sexual in nature and/or inappropriate to any psychological services being provided.

According to the CNA Group (https://www.cna.com), "sexual misconduct" means:

> • any type of physical touching or caressing, or attempt thereof, or suggestion thereof by you or by any person for whom you may be legally responsible, which could be considered sexual or erotic in nature, including consensual sexual activity or sexual activity in contravention of any professional code of ethics or conduct; or any act of sexual assault, harassment, abuse or molestation.

And from CPH and Associates (https://www.cphins.com) come these exclusions of their responsibility: "Arising out of sexual therapy, where sexual contact is used as a form

## Limits of the Therapy Relationship: What Clients Should Know

Psychotherapy is a professional service I am able to provide to you. However, because of the nature of therapy, our relationship has to be different from most other relationships. It may differ in how long it lasts, in the topics we discuss, or in its goals. It must also be limited to the relationship of therapist and client *only*. If we were to interact in any other ways, we would then have a "dual relationship," which might be harmful and may not be legal. The different therapy professions all have rules against such relationships to protect us both. Let me explain why having a dual relationship is not a good idea.

Dual relationships can set up conflicts between your best interests and my best interests. What is best for you might not be what is best for me, and I must put your interests before my own, because you are my client. So we must have only one relationship.

Because I am your therapist, dual relationships like these are improper:

- I cannot be your supervisor, teacher, or evaluator for custody, disability, or similar issues.
- I cannot serve as your advocate or take your side in any legal matter or court action.
- I cannot be a therapist to my relatives, friends (or the relatives of friends), people I know or knew socially, or business contacts.
- I cannot have any other kind of business relationship with you besides for therapy. For example, I cannot employ you, lend to or borrow from you, trade or barter your services (such as for tutoring, repairing, child care, etc.) for mine, or trade goods for therapy.
- I cannot give legal, medical, financial, or any other type of professional advice.
- I cannot have any kind of romantic or sexual relationship with a current or former client, or with any other people close to a client.
- We should not exchange gifts.
- I will not "friend" clients on social media or accept clients' "friend" requests.

There are important differences between therapy and friendship. While I expect us to be friendly and respectful, as your therapist I cannot be a typical friend. Friendships are two-way exchanges, but in therapy I will offer very little about myself and my feelings, because our focus is on you and your needs and development. Friends usually see you only from their personal viewpoints and experiences, and I will try to be more objective and nonjudgmental. Friends may want to find quick and simple solutions to your problems so that they can feel helpful, but these responses may not be in your long-term best interest, which is our goal. Therapists can focus on issues and motives that are not apparent and that require persistent exploration for change to occur. Friends do not usually follow up on their advice to see whether it was useful; therapists do follow up to be more helpful. Friends may feel a *need* to have you do what they advise; a therapist offers you options and helps you choose what is best for you. A therapist's responses to your situation are based on tested theories and proven methods of change, not just personal experiences. To preserve your confidentiality, therapists are required to keep the identity of their clients private. Therefore, I will let you take the lead on whether to acknowledge or recognize me if we meet in a public place, and I will decline to attend your family's gatherings if you invite me. Lastly, when our therapy is completed, I will not be able to be a friend to you like your other friends.

In sum, my duty as a therapist is to care for you and all my clients, but *only* in the professional role of therapist. Please note any questions or concerns on the back of this page so we can discuss them.

of treatment thereof, or where any surrogate sexual therapy related to sexual dysfunction is employed," and "Physical abuse, sexual abuse or licentious, immoral or sexual behavior whether or not intended to lead to, or culminating in any sexual act, whether caused by, or at the instigation of, or at the direction of, or omission by any of you."

As you can see, policies are very broadly written and include your employees and supervisees. In addition, state laws differ in defining sexual behaviors. Bear in mind that some years ago what was prohibited was only genital contact, but the prohibitions have since been expanded to include nongenital contact like kissing and caressing, and they now include conversation such as seductive talk or fantasy sharing and intentions—not just actions.

## With Whom Are Sexual Intimacies Prohibited?

Sexual intimacies are not allowed with "patients" or "clients" of any kind. In this context, the term "clients" includes supervisees, trainees, students of yours, or any persons in a professional relationship with you (e.g., business partners or employees). In parallel, the APA ethics code (APA, 2010) says that you should not do therapy with your former sexual partners (Standard 10.07).

Standard 10.06 of the APA code (APA, 2010) also forbids sexualized relationships with "individuals [whom psychologists] know to be the close relatives or significant others of current clients/patients." This definition includes all members of a client's household, and it may even include anyone (such as an ex-spouse or a boyfriend or girlfriend) with whom any of these persons has or had a close emotional relationship.

Stromberg and Dellinger (1993) raise the question of how state regulations define "patient" or "client." This may be of considerable importance to psychologists, who often have a wider spectrum of possible professional relationships than do other professions. For example, besides doing therapy, psychologists may see assessment subjects, organizational clients, and/or research participants; counsel some persons about employment; and coach many kinds of people. Obviously, psychologists have to know how "client" or "patient" is locally defined and be circumspect; regulators tend to think in polarities, whereas psychologists may evaluate "clienthood" in terms of the intensity, duration, and intimacy of the relationship. Haspel et al. (1997) provide both excellent discussions of the definitional issues and quote definitions from many states' laws.

## The Damage to the Client and to Therapy

Therapist–client sexual intimacies are universally prohibited because they betray the trust the client has in the therapist's putting the client's needs first—the fiduciary responsibility, as defined earlier. The resulting harm to the client can be extensive.

Frequently reported consequences to clients (Bouhoutsos et al., 1983) include ambivalence, distrust of men or women, and distrust of therapy. The clients preyed upon in this way become "therapeutic orphans," unable to participate in potentially healing therapy. They may have flashbacks, nightmares, and other recollections, and/or depression, hospitalizations, and suicides. They may exhibit relationship problems, with confusion about identity, boundaries, and roles. They may experience feelings of anger, abandonment, exploitation, devastation, guilt, emptiness, and isolation; they may also show suppressed rage, emotional dyscontrol, and mood swings.

Pope (1988b and at http://www.kspope.com/sexiss/sexencyc.php) has described the "therapist–patient sex syndrome" as similar both to posttraumatic stress disorder and to the sequelae of child or spouse abuse, rape, and incest. According to Pope, this syndrome involves "(a) ambivalence, (b) a sense of guilt, (c) feelings of emptiness and isolation, (d) sexual confusion, (e) impaired ability to trust, (f) identity, boundary, and role confusion, (g) emotional lability . . . , (h) suppressed rage, (i) increased suicidal risk, and (j) cognitive dysfunction" (1988b, p. 222). Folman (1990) has suggested that 11 psychotherapy processes are all affected negatively by sexual contacts: transference, countertransference, trust, confidentiality, resistance, privacy, intimacy, boundaries, self-disclosure, use of touch, and termination. Theory suggests that the effects may differ for men and women, may be worse if the therapist initiates the intimacies and is married, and may also be worse if the client has been victimized before.

In summary, if any of the negative consequences described here is likely to occur, they are so serious that taking the chance that a client *won't* be harmed is unethical. As clinicians, we do have a minimal ethical duty: "At least do no harm."

## Is Sexual Intimacy with a Client *Ever* Acceptable?

Sexual intimacy with a client is *never* acceptable, even if the therapy is over; this is the safest guide. The American Psychiatric Association (2006) says, "Sexual activity with a current or former patient is unethical" (Section 2, No. 1), and other professional groups have gone further.

For psychologists, the code of ethics (APA, 2010, Standard 10.08) sets a 2-year post-therapy time limit (because the data indicate that a majority of relationships begin within 2 years), but after that the psychologist is still fully responsible for demonstrating that the relationship is not exploitative (Standard 10.08b) and does no harm. This is slippery; a therapist in love/lust/loneliness is likely to be a poor judge of these issues. It is educational to read the APA code's list of criteria for evaluating potential exploitativeness: the length of time since termination; the nature, duration, and intensity of the treatment; the circumstances of termination; the client's personal history and present mental status; the chances of adverse impact on the client; and any statements or actions by the therapist during the course of therapy *suggesting or inviting* the possibility of a posttermination sexual *or romantic* relationship with the client (APA, 2010; modified and emphasis added).

Individual states, however, are enacting laws concerning the time limits (Haspel et al., 1997). Some consider the therapy relationship to continue in perpetuity (Fla. Stat. Chapter 21U-15004), while others have adopted the 2-year rule. There is also much uncertainty about the statute of limitations for suing. Generally it has run from the time of the incident, but courts are now accepting the idea that the statute may not start until the harm is discovered or recognized, and this may be many years later.

Because of the many options and factors involved, therapists who are sexually involved with clients or ex-clients can never be sure that they will not be sued for sexual intimacies, no matter how long it has been since the termination of therapy. Winer (n.d.) asserts that therapists should expect to lose these suits. For all these reasons, "never" is safest for both you and your clients.

**It is always our responsibility to say "No."** If you need reinforcements for abstaining from sexual intimacies, here are some from Keith-Spiegel (1977) and others:

- Subsequent therapists will support and encourage your ex-client to complain to the licensing boards and pursue a suit.

- Your client/lover will expect commitment, or at least a continuation of the relationship, from you; you will then have to deal with a spurned lover, not a helped client.

- The mass media love these cases. You will be publicly pilloried.

- Most states, through their licensing boards, make ethical violations illegal, so you can lose your license.

- At least 24 states have criminalized sexual contact between therapists and clients (McArdle, 2003). It is a felony, and the maximum sentence is often 20 years in prison and a fine of $150,000.

- The three types of legal proceedings feed into each other: Having lost at a licensing board hearing is evidence that attorneys will see as support for their winning at a civil trial (perhaps for intentional infliction of emotional harm) with severe costs. And in many states the authorities can pursue a criminal trial, with fines, prison time, and subsequent placement on a sexual predator/sex offender registry.

- You cannot really win if you are sued, no matter what happens. You will experience excruciating stress, loss of reputation, and conflict with your significant others even if you are exonerated. And these will go on for years.

## A Checklist of Preventative Measures

- ❏ Inform clients early in therapy about ethical limits on the client–therapist relationship. (See Handout 4.1 and Section 4.5.)

- ❏ Reduce your vulnerability by doing nothing but therapy in the office, keeping the office businesslike, and perhaps never being alone in the office suite with some clients.

- ❏ Be sensitive to how each client may interpret your nonsexual or affectionate behaviors, conversation about sexual topics, jokes, efforts to be helpful, and so forth. Even simple touches and expressions of concern can be misinterpreted. Consider how the client will interpret your touching him or her. Explain what you are doing and why before you do it, so that it will not be seen as a sexual overture (Bennett et al., 1990).

- ❏ Monitor your feelings throughout the therapy. If your attraction or fantasies become distracting, seek consultation immediately.

- ❏ Ask yourself: What effects will a sexual relationship with this client have on my other important relationships?

- ❏ Remind yourself: You really need this career. You have worked hard and long for it, and you are, or will be, very good at it. Don't throw it away for a little "fun" or passion. Even "true love" does not create an exception to the prohibition.

## What to Do If a Client Asks You for Sex

If a client asks you for sexual contact, plan your reaction carefully, because this is a high-risk situation for you and a high-vulnerability time for the client.

- Step back and ask yourself whether this presentation has previously been a strategy of the client's for getting his or her needs met. Examine how such a strategy plays into your own needs and situation.

- One response (suggested by KK) is a reframe, such as "I'm glad therapy feels safe enough for you to express your sexual feelings, which are an extremely important part of who you are. But we need to be very clear that sexual intimacies will not happen between us." The response should consider the developmental stage of the client (adolescent vs. psychotic adult vs. high-functioning adult, etc.). If you as a clinician are feeling flustered, flattered, excited, or frightened by these expressions, then ongoing consultation is essential. Some possible questions are these: Is the client attracted to your role or power, or to you as a person? Are there transference, avoidance, authority, abuse, or parental issues? Is the client subverting the therapy to avoid confrontation and change? Is the client setting up another defeat of a therapist, failure of treatment, or failure of his or her own efforts? Rutter (quoted in Foster, 1996, p. 27) offers this observation:

  > A client trying to seduce a therapist may be repeating past injuries, but is also most likely searching for a response that will discourage this repetition. The client is doing exactly what clients are supposed to do when they see their doctors: bringing her [sic] illness to her therapist, her self-destructive pattern, in the only way she knows how, by repeating it with her therapist, right there in the room. Along with her hunger for warmth and affection, she is showing her therapist that she has always been out of control of her own sexual boundaries. The therapist can either victimize her as others have, or he [sic] can offer her a way to begin recovering from her past injuries.

- When you say "No" to the client (as you must), make the "No" solid. Do not be ambiguous. Don't say "Only if . . . ," or "When . . . ," or even "No, but. . . . " Say, "It would be harmful to you. Not after therapy is over. Never, under any conditions." Saying that it is unethical is a weaker and, to the client, irrelevant argument. Set boundaries and keep them rigid, but also use this incident as grist for the therapy mill.

## What to Do If You Are Attracted to a Client

"Attraction" means finding a client strikingly physically attractive, amazingly witty or sensitive, alluringly comfortable for you, or the like. Here are some guidelines for what to do if you find yourself feeling attracted:

- Consider your own issues, such as rescue fantasies and needs to be admired, found attractive, be in control, or be depended upon. In addition, how are your intimate relationships going now?

- How have you previously resolved such attractions? Remember, therapists should meet clients' needs, not vice versa.

- Irvin P. R. Guyett, PhD, of Pittsburgh, PA, advises (personal communication, 2014): If you find yourself fantasizing about a client outside the session, or your fantasies are amplified in the next session, consult someone with expertise in working with sexual transference and countertransference.

- If you are attracted, do *not* discuss this attraction with the client until you have consulted a peer first. You must fully understand your side before putting anything more on the client.

- It is likely to be better in the long run to process these feelings with your supervisor or consultant and to resolve them. But you must be willing to be open about these feelings to a colleague and willing to change. If you cannot resolve the feelings, then terminate the therapy and refer the client, before you get into deeper trouble.

- It is still your responsibility to deal with your urges, fantasies, and attractions in a therapeutically productive way, or you may be at risk of negligence even without the sexual contact.

- Some advise immediately referring a client to whom you develop romantic feelings; however, besides resembling abandonment and punishing the client, this is avoidance of your or the client's feelings.

Keith-Spiegel (2013a) fully examines many cases. The literature on romantic and sexual feelings and behaviors has been thoroughly reviewed by Sonne and Johai (2013).

## Reporting Another Therapist

What if you learn that your client had a sexual relationship with a previous therapist? Do you have to report it? Your discipline's ethical code may direct you to report it, because you have a duty to care for the client, and harm is assumed. However, doing so would involve a violation of the client's confidentiality and may be experienced as another loss of control. These factors create an ethical dilemma (conflict of ethical values). The state of California, for example, does not make it mandatory to report another therapist, but requires the current therapist to give the client a document (on which Handout 4.2 is partly based) to support the client's decision-making processes.

In general, our ethical codes require us to confront colleagues whose actions seem to violate the codes, and Brodsky and McKinzey (2002) offer specific guidance. Some states require reporting colleagues because fewer than 3% of such cases are reported to licensing boards (Parsons & Wincze, 1995). However, Zur (2012) advises caution in judging another therapist's actions without full information and consultation.

What if a client *falsely* accuses a previous therapist of sexual misconduct? Good sources for considering this possibility are Gutheil (1992), Sederer and Libby (1995), Williams (2000), Hall and Hall (2001), and Thompson (2007), which review the impacts of false complaints on clinicians.

## Client–Therapist Intimacy: Appropriate and Inappropriate Conduct

**HANDOUT 4.2** The purposes and functions of Handout 4.2 are as follows: (1) to reduce the rate of inappropriate sexual behaviors on the part of clients; (2) to increase the rate of clients' reporting

# Client–Therapist Contact: Proper and Improper Conduct

This brochure has been written to help you understand what is proper and improper conduct for a therapist, and what responses are available to you as a consumer. It may raise issues that you have not considered before. However, if you are well informed, you will be better able to make sure your needs get met in therapy.

Although almost all therapists are ethical people (that is, moral and law-abiding) who care about their clients and who follow professional rules and standards in their practice, there are a very few who do not always do what is best for their clients and who behave unethically. They may be any kinds of mental health workers: psychologists, psychiatrists, social workers, counselors, clergy, nurses, marriage and family therapists, and so on.

## Attraction to Your Therapist

It is normal for people in therapy to develop positive feelings, such as admiration, affection, or even love, toward a therapist who gives them support and caring. These feelings can be strong and may sometimes take the form of sexual attraction. There will be times in your therapy when it might be important, even if it is uncomfortable, for you and your therapist to discuss your feelings and concerns about sex. Sometimes such discussions may be needed if you are to benefit from your therapy. However, a caring, ethical therapist would never take advantage of your feelings by suggesting sexual contact during therapy, or by ending therapy in order to have a romantic relationship with you.

**Sexual contact is never a proper part of any psychotherapy, sex education, or sex therapy.** Sexual contact in therapy has been found to be harmful to a client in many ways, including damaging the client's ability to trust. The harmful effects may be immediate, or they may not be felt until later. For this reason, sexual contact with clients is clearly against the rules of all the organized mental health professions.

## Therapist Behaviors That May Not Be OK

Caring therapists may sometimes show their feelings through touch. These forms of physical contact in therapy, such as a handshake, a pat on the back, or a comforting hug, may not concern you. But you are the best judge of the effects that any touching may have on you. If your therapist engages in any kind of physical contact that you do not want, tell him or her to stop, and explain how you feel about that contact. A responsible therapist will want to know about your feelings and will respect your feelings without challenging you. Keep in mind that your therapist might not know your feelings without your talking about them.

If your therapist makes sexual comments or touches you in a way that seems sexual to you, you are likely to feel discomfort. Trust your feelings. Do not assume that your therapist must be right if it feels wrong to you.

There are some warning signs that a therapist may be moving toward sexual contact with you. The therapist may talk a lot about his or her own personal problems; give you gifts; write letters, send electronic messages, or make phone calls to you that are not about your therapy work; or dwell on the unique nature of your relationship. Or the therapist may create the idea that he or she is your only source of help by criticizing you for standing up for yourself, or by telling you how to behave with a sexual partner when advice about that is

*(continued)*

not what you are seeking. A red flag should definitely go up if your therapist discusses his or her own sexual activities or sexual attraction to you. Other signs include making remarks intended to arouse sexual feelings, or forms of physical seduction, such as sexual touching.

### Actions You Can Take If You Believe That Your Therapist's Actions Are Not OK

Any time you feel uncomfortable about a part of your therapy, including therapist behaviors that you think are improper, discuss this with your therapist. Your therapist should not try to make you feel guilty or stupid for asking questions, and your therapist should not try to frighten or pressure you. If your therapist will not discuss your concerns openly and helpfully, or continues to behave in ways that are not OK with you, you have reasons to be concerned.

When a discussion with your therapist about these behaviors does not help, you have the right to take some further action. You may wish to find another therapist and/or to file any of several types of complaints. It is important for *you* to make the final decision about what course of action is best for your concerns and needs.

Many therapists work in agencies or other offices with supervisors. Consider talking to your therapist's supervisor or agency director to see what can be done.

It may be very hard for you to think about making any kind of complaint against your therapist. You may worry that he or she will find out about your complaint and feel angry or hurt. You may also be concerned about possible harm to a therapist you care about. There are several points to consider when you are trying to decide what is the best thing to do:

- Sexual contact between a therapist and a client is never a proper form of treatment for any problem.

- A therapist who suggests or engages in sexual contact in therapy is showing a lack of concern for you.

- Sexual contact in therapy is never your fault, regardless of the particular things that have happened or whatever has been said. The responsibility for not having sexual contact is always the therapist's.

- You have placed your trust in the therapist, and it is his or her duty not to take advantage of that trust. If the therapist does this, you have been betrayed.

- A therapist who engages in sexual contact with a client may do so more than once and with more than one client. If no one reports this behavior, other people could be harmed by the same therapist.

### Specific Courses of Action

Remember that you have the right to stop therapy whenever you choose. At the same time, you may also wish to make some type of complaint against a therapist who has acted improperly.

If you choose to make a complaint against your therapist, the process may become long and difficult. Some clients taking such action have felt overwhelmed, angry, and discouraged. It is very important that you have support from people you can depend upon. Good sources of support may be family members, friends, support groups, a new therapist, or some type of advocate. Identifying and using good sources of support will help you feel more confident about the plan of action you have chosen.

You may wish to see another therapist to help you continue with your therapy, including dealing with problems resulting from the experience with the unethical therapist. It would not be unusual for you to have confusing thoughts and feelings about your experience and your previous therapist. It would also be understandable if you felt frightened about finding a new therapist or had difficulty trusting him or her.

You may also want an advocate to help you decide on what to do and taking those actions. Try to locate a mental health worker who has had experience with other clients who have been victims of therapist sexual misconduct. He or she will be able to understand your situation, provide you with important information, and support you in your choice of action.

To get a referral to an advocate or therapist experienced in working with victims of sexual misconduct, or to obtain information on filing a complaint, call or write to this state's professional organization.

There are groups in many communities to help victims of sexual abuse, and you can usually find them

*(continued)*

through online searches for "sexual misconduct by therapists."

Here are the addresses of some of the national organizations that can help and direct you:

American Counseling Association
6101 Stevenson Avenue
Alexandria, VA 22304
800-347-6647
http://www.counseling.org

American Psychiatric Association
1000 Wilson Blvd., Suite 1825
Arlington, VA 22209-3901
703-907-7300
http://www.psychiatry.org

American Psychological Association
750 First Street NE
Washington, DC 20002-4242
800-374-2721
http://www.apa.org

National Association of Social Workers
750 First Street NE, Suite 800
Washington, DC 20002-4241
202-408-8600
http://www.naswdc.org

You may want to contact the state and/or national professional group to which your therapist belongs. For example, many practicing psychologists are members of this state's Psychological Association and the American Psychological Association. These organizations have specific rules against sexual contact with clients, and they will refer you to ethics committees that listen to complaints. The state and national professional associations do not license their members to practice psychotherapy, but they can punish an unethical therapist, sometimes by expelling that person from membership in these associations. Such an action can make it more difficult for the therapist to get or keep a license to practice.

If your therapist is a licensed professional, you may want to contact your state's licensing board, which gave the therapist a license to practice. It has the power to take away or suspend the license of a professional found guilty of sexual misconduct. *Be aware that unlicensed persons have no legal oversight and no board to whom you can complain. They may not subscribe to any code of ethics.* However, you can search online and find many support groups and other assistance including another professional who can help you deal effectively with what has happened to you if you feel that would be useful to you.

[Insert addresses of your state's licensing boards here.]

Another option is to file a civil suit for malpractice, which can be done through a lawyer. But this is a complicated procedure, so discuss it with your professional advocate or support persons.

Please write your questions on the back of this handout so we can discuss them. Thank you.

of sexual exploitation by all kinds of professionals; and (3) to protect you if you are misunderstood or even accused of sexual improprieties, because this form states your rules of practice. The handout is valuable because it is written for consumers in a narrative and casual style. Its message and tone are empowering; it addresses questions of ethics, harm, love, and discomfort with sexual behavior in therapy; and it offers options for handling the emotions stirred up by sexual behaviors in therapy and taking action.

This handout is not suitable for routine distribution to every client, because the reading may be burdensome for those who have not had ideas or experiences along these lines. Also, it may stimulate inappropriate thoughts in clients who have weak boundaries.

You should be the one to bring up the subject of this handout, because the client may be feeling too ashamed, confused, or guilty to do so. It can be given to a client when it is topically appropriate; it can also be made available in a three-ring binder (along with other client education materials and some of your forms) in your waiting room, or on your website in a section called "Helpful Materials for Psychotherapy Clients" or "Information for Clients: Please Read." You might routinely suggest to all clients that they "look through the book [or this section of the website] when you have a chance, because I want you to have this information." Perhaps 3–5% of new female clients will have had a sexual relationship with a previous therapist or other trusted professional. Although you should ask about this possibility in the first history taking (this is why questions about it are included in the intake interview questions and guide—see Form 6.15), the client may not be ready to reveal this. You generally cannot ask this question repeatedly but by leaving Handout 4.2 in your waiting room or posting it on your website, you have "normalized" the question, done some education, and told the client you are ready to hear about this relationship whenever the client is ready to reveal it. The same reasoning applies to domestic violence.

Thorn et al. (1993) found that the use of a brochure or handout such as Handout 4.2 raised clients' consciousness about specific kinds of sexual abuse, and was very likely to prevent such abuse by therapists. Furthermore, Thorn et al. (1996) showed that the use of this brochure did not decrease trust in therapists or increase the likelihood of filing a false complaint, as some might fear. Some of your clients who read this handout or similar materials may come to recognize that a previous therapist was sexually exploitative. You should be prepared to deal with this contingency legally, emotionally, and professionally through education and/or referral.

Handout 4.2 is based on one authored by the Alabama Psychological Association's (n.d.) Committee to Prevent Sexual Misconduct. This was in turn adapted from a longer brochure published by the APA's Committee on Women in Psychology (1989), entitled "If Sex Enters the Psychotherapy Relationship." This handout has been revised from several versions available online from many sources and is written in plain English. Modify it for your location, profession, and preferred wordings before you copy it for distribution. Because problems may have arisen with a previous therapist of a different discipline, all the national organizations are listed, and you may include all your state's licensing boards.

## 4.7   Assessing a Client's Dangerousness to Self and Others

This section covers the assessment of dangerousness—an assessment that underlies any protection efforts. If you have *any* reason to suspect any risk, a comprehensive evaluation of the risks of violence is necessary. Be sensitive to your feelings, which may lead you toward or away from full and accurate assessment. Chapter 7 of Bennett et al. (2006) helpfully demonstrates the application of their comprehensive risk management model. For assessment through skilled interviewing, Shea (1999/2011) is highly recommended, especially Appendix A on documentation. Simpson and Stacy (2004) offer practical guidelines of documenting suicide risk assessments from a legal standpoint. The books by Bongar (2013) and Maris et al. (2000) are comprehensive and well written. For the management of suicidal clients, Jobes (2016) is both informative and supportive. Some ideas on risk documentation from these sources have been incorporated below.

Here are the steps you should ideally take in dealing with the risk of violence.

## Preparing Ahead of Time

It is essential to become educated in risk assessment, stay current with developments in the field, and be conversant with the laws of your jurisdictions. On a tactical level, collect information on resources for interventions. For example, you should obtain continuing education and otherwise keep up to date on working with domestic violence. Also, indicate the limits of confidentiality in your educational procedures at the beginning of therapy (see Sections 5.2 and 8.1).

## Gathering Information to Assess Risk

Request and review records of the client's current and prior treatments. You need not obtain all previous records. If a record is very old, if it concerns problems irrelevant to the risks at hand, or if it is likely to be unobtainable, you do not need to obtain it to be seen as acting like a responsible professional. However, it is advisable to obtain any record known to be relevant to violence, and to obtain the usual records and read them for violence-related information. In addition, it may be advisable to ask the client for a release to question others who may know of the client's behavior, history, or motives (you can amend Form 8.2). If the client refuses, document this refusal, and use your clinical judgment on how to proceed.

## The Issues and Risk Factors of Suicide

If adults not adjudicated incompetent are responsible for their own behavior, why are mental health workers held responsible when their clients commit suicide? While in some cases clients have been seen as negligently contributing to their deaths (Appelbaum, 2000), more often courts have concluded that a suicide occurred within the context of "diminished capacity" due to a client's mental illness, and so have held clinicians more responsible.

Although courts usually recognize that suicide cannot be well predicted, "professionals have been held liable when they ignored or failed to assess indicators of suicide" (Knapp & VandeCreek, 1983, p. 18). "Courts usually consider two fundamental issues: (a) Did the professional adequately assess the likelihood that a client was suicidal? and, (b) If an identifiable risk of harm was determined, did the professional *take sufficient precautions* to prevent suicide?" (Knapp & VandeCreek, 1983, p. 18; emphasis added). The assessment of a client's suicidality must be an ongoing process throughout treatment, because many factors can rapidly raise or lower the chances of a suicide attempt. To perform ethically, you must collect all the relevant information, weigh this information to the best of your ability and in line with the standards of care, and document your conclusions and decisions. **You are not expected to predict the future perfectly, only to do your job well—that is, to the standard of care.**

Your assessment can be based most securely on different sources of information and different ways of acquiring it. For example, you can assess known risk factors, which produce a general probability or likelihood of suicide but can't predict the specific likelihood for an individual (Motto, 1999). The checklist of suicide risk factors we present here (Form 4.1) facilitates the recording of the most widely recognized risk factors. A second, and essential, source of information is your interviewing of the client. However, what the client tells you may be distorted for a variety of reasons (a wish to avoid hospitalization, cognitive deficits, inability to assess future impulses, etc.), and so additional sources of information should be consulted, such as family members, previous treaters, or other records. Your efforts to gather such information and its results should be indicated in your records. Finally, you can integrate all the information you have obtained on the suicide risk assessment summary and recommendations (Form 6.19 in Chapter 6). It is designed not only to summarize the risk factors and interview information, but to document your professional judgments about suicide. You may not need to use both of these forms, especially when early indications are that the suicide risk is not great, but they are desirable when the risk appears to be high. This form does not address Non-Suicidal Self Injury (NSSI).

**FORM 4.1** *(margin label)*

## Assessing Suicide Potential:
## Risk Factor Analysis versus Predictions of Suicide

Although the research on suicide risk factors is helpful, it does not allow us to predict who will actually commit suicide. Why not? First, the research is based on group data, which will not necessarily apply to a particular individual. Second, the main obstacle is well recognized: Suicide is quite rare. Although the total number of suicides was 38,364 in 2010, which makes it the tenth leading cause of death, only about 11 in 100,000 persons per year commit suicide in the United States (Centers for Disease Control and Prevention [CDC], 2014). It is so rare that even a highly accurate test for suicide potential results in unacceptably high levels of false positives (which mean that time and money are wasted in investigating low or no risk cases) and false negatives (which mean, tragically, that interventions are not offered when they might help).

Although we can't predict suicide, we can assess risk. Risk factors are those variables that are significantly correlated with suicide. Using them, we can design levels of intervention appropriate to the level of risk. For example, risk factors of sex, race, and sexual orientation are significant. There are about four times as many deaths for males as for females. In regard to race, "In 2010, the highest U.S. suicide rate [per 100,000 persons](14.1) was among Whites and the second highest rate (11.0) was among American Indians and Alaskan Natives. Much lower and roughly similar rates were found among Asians and Pacific Islanders (6.2), Blacks (5.1) and Hispanics (5.9)" (CDC, 2014). And people who self-identify as LGBTQIA are at significantly increased risk of suicide. Among LGBTQIA adolescents, the risk is double that of heterosexual peers (Russell & Joyner, 2001), and they are three to four times as likely to make suicide attempts (http://www.thetrevorproject.org/pages/facts-about-suicide).

Pope and Vasquez's (2016) chapter on responding to suicide risk is an essential resource in this area. They describe 21 risk factors and 10 steps to reduce risk, as well as pointing

# Checklist of Suicide Risk Factors

Client: _____ Date: ____/____/____

The following ratings are based on my:

❑ Review of records (specify): _____

❑ Interview with staff, friends, relatives (circle and name): _____

❑ Observations of this individual over the last ❑ interview ❑ day ❑ week ❑ month

❑ Other (specify): _____

## Demographic risk factors

❑ European American or Native American ❑ Suicidal partner ❑ Male

❑ Lower socioeconomic status ❑ Protestant ❑ Never-married or widowed status

❑ Divorced status (especially repeated divorce or divorce in last 6 months)

❑ Age: Young adult (15–24) or very elderly (75–85 or older) ❑ LGBTQIA

❑ Health care professional, law enforcement officer, veteran, other: _____

## Social/interpersonal risk factors

❑ Irrevocable losses:
    ❑ Relative or close friend died by suicide ❑ Loss of a child or spouse
    ❑ Relationship loss by marital separation, etc. ❑ Permanent dependence on others
    ❑ Major physical illness(es) with losses or limitations (dialysis, physical integrity) _____
    ❑ Unrecoverable loss of social status
    ❑ Other loss:_____

❑ Severe or persistent financial or legal problems ❑ Unwanted pregnancy

❑ No/poor therapeutic alliance ❑ Family instability ❑ Leaving, not facing, life crises

❑ Strained, absent, or only painful relationships with family of origin

| | | | | | | | |
|---|---|---|---|---|---|---|---|
| ❑ Stressors (social, financial, health, bereavement, shame) | Low | 1 | 2 | 3 | 4 | 5 | High |
| ❑ Social support system (local friends, therapist, partner) | Strong | 1 | 2 | 3 | 4 | 5 | Weak |
| ❑ Anomie (no sense of connection or continuity) | Low | 1 | 2 | 3 | 4 | 5 | High |

❑ Other possible risk factors:_____

*(continued)*

## Recent suicidal behaviors

Check applicable boxes and enter a code for time period at the "T" as follows: 24 = within last 24 hours, ds = last few days, w = last 7 days or week, m = last 30 days or month, ms = last few or 2–4 months, y = last 12 months or year.

❏ Had passive death wishes   T: _____

❏ Had fleeting ideation   T: _____   ❏ Had persistent ideation   T: _____

❏ Made realistic threats   T: _____

❏ Has made multiple statements   T: _____

❏ Engaged in rehearsals   T: _____

❏ Actions as pleas for help   T: _____

❏ Reports recent/relevant media reports   T: _____

❏ Talked with therapist or other staff about suicide intentions/impulses/ruminations   T: _____

❏ Made suicide plans that involve a highly lethal method and a time without interruption   T: _____

❏ Clearly intended to die in an attempt of   ❏ high   ❏ medium   ❏ low lethality   T: _____   but was rescued

❏ Secretive attempt with   ❏ high   ❏ medium   ❏ low potential for rescue   T: _____

❏ Multiple attempts of   ❏ high-lethality method   ❏ high medical severity

❏ Anniversary attempts   T: _____

❏ Described a practical/available method or plan   T: _____

❏ Established access to means/methods   T: _____

❏ Has given away an important personal possession   T: _____

❏ Made funeral arrangements   T: _____

❏ Made a will   T: _____

❏ Written a suicide note   T: _____

❏ Drastic behavior changes   T: _____

❏ Social withdrawal   T: _____

❏ Loss of interest in previously valued activities   T: _____

❏ Lessened self-care   T: _____

❏ Took unnecessary risks   T: _____

❏ Other suicidal behaviors:_____

## Current personal psychological risk factors

❏ Major psychiatric disorder (bipolar disorders, schizophrenia, eating disorders, substance use, some personality disorders)

❏ Unchangeable chronic pain   ❏ Debilitating chronic illness   ❏ Noncompliance with treatment

❏ History of abuse (physical, sexual, of long duration, during childhood, etc.)

❏ Checked "suicide" on intake form or other assessments   ❏ Self-mutilating or parasuicidal behaviors

❏ History of significant substance use with negative consequences   ❏ Frequent accidents   ❏ Living alone

❏ Criminal behaviors   ❏ Inconsistent work history   ❏ Recent inpatient/prison discharge

*(continued)*

| | | | | | | | |
|---|---|---|---|---|---|---|---|
| ❑ Hopelessness, no plans for future | Hopeful | 1 | 2 | 3 | 4 | 5 | Hopeless |
| ❑ Psychological pain | Little | 1 | 2 | 3 | 4 | 5 | Intolerable |
| ❑ Sleep disturbances: decreased or increased | Mild | 1 | 2 | 3 | 4 | 5 | Severe |
| ❑ Depression (blunted emotions, anhedonia, isolating) | Low | 1 | 2 | 3 | 4 | 5 | High |
| ❑ Restlessness, agitation, irritability, rages, violence | Low | 1 | 2 | 3 | 4 | 5 | High |
| ❑ Problem-solving ability, dependency, helplessness | Good | 1 | 2 | 3 | 4 | 5 | Poor |
| ❑ Involved in treatment, progressing, adherent | Yes | 1 | 2 | 3 | 4 | 5 | No |
| ❑ Self-regard | Positive | 1 | 2 | 3 | 4 | 5 | Negative |
| ❑ Felt burden to others | Low | 1 | 2 | 3 | 4 | 5 | High |
| ❑ Attraction to death (ruminations, online searching) | Constant | 1 | 2 | 3 | 4 | 5 | None |
| ❑ Impulsivity (low self-control, distractibility, mood volatility) | Low | 1 | 2 | 3 | 4 | 5 | High |
| ❑ Indirect self-destructive behaviors, parasuicidal behaviors | None | 1 | 2 | 3 | 4 | 5 | Many |
| ❑ Cognitive disorganization (organic brain syndrome, psychosis, intoxication, head injury) | Low | 1 | 2 | 3 | 4 | 5 | High |
| ❑ Feels ready and confident of carrying out plan | Low | 1 | 2 | 3 | 4 | 5 | High |
| ❑ Other factors (homicidal intent, few/weak deterrents, motivated by revenge or attention getting, etc.) | Low | 1 | 2 | 3 | 4 | 5 | High |

Additional information on the items checked can be found in/at: _____

**Protective factors/Skills/Reasons for living**

❑ Married or in committed relationship     ❑ Has young children     ❑ Supportive family relationships

❑ Consistent/supportive employment or schooling     ❑ Self-efficacy     ❑ Has plans for future

❑ Enjoys leisure, friendships, hobbies, recreation, family     ❑ Positive spiritual/religious beliefs

❑ Other: _____

**Additional risk factors for a child or adolescent**

❑ Female (more likely to attempt)     ❑ Male (more likely to succeed when attempting)

❑ Age above 15     ❑ Rural resident     ❑ Strained family relationships

❑ Other stressors (legal difficulties, unwanted pregnancy, change of school, birth of a sibling, etc.)

Therapist: _____ Supervisor: _____

*This is a strictly confidential patient medical record protected by state and national laws.*

to a number of pitfalls in managing suicide risk as identified by 16 expert therapists. This chapter is available online (http://www.kspope.com/suicide/index.php#copy). Simon (2012) discusses many risk factors and intervention options, and an extensive list can be found in Zuckerman (2010). There are many suicide risk assessment forms available, but Simon (2009) has criticized relying on these. Similarly, the FDA's requiring a black box label on antidepressants due to a supposed increase in suicide by adolescents on these meds appears to be not just an overreaction but an erroneous interpretation, and perhaps quite costly in terms of lives lost (Jureidini, 2007).

### Risk Factors for Suicide among Psychiatric Clients

Psychiatric clients have greatly elevated suicide rates. Raoof (2013) has clearly summarized the risks by diagnosis:

> Although all mental disorders are associated with an elevated risk of suicide, certain disorders carry with them remarkably high lifetime risk. In fact, 80–90% of people who commit suicide have a mental illness. [Having had a] Hospitalization for a psychiatric disorder is quite prevalent in the suicidal population. The main disorders associated with a higher risk for suicide include depressive disorder, bipolar disorder, schizophrenia, anxiety disorders, namely post-traumatic stress disorder (PTSD) and phobias, and substance use problems. The highest risk increase . . . is among people with mood disorders and anxiety disorders. Organic mental disorders, dementia and mental retardation have the lowest increase in suicide risk.
>
> 1. Two thirds of people who die by suicide have symptoms consistent with major depression at the time of death, and people with major depression have a suicidal risk of twenty times that of people with no mood disorder.
> 2. People with bipolar disorder have a suicide risk of fifteen times that of people with no mood disorder. Studies show that in the majority of cases suicide occurs in the depressed phase with the most powerful predictors of suicide being a previous suicide attempt and feelings of hopelessness.
> 3. People with schizophrenia come next in increased risk of suicide with about 5% lifetime risk. Predictors of suicide among people with schizophrenia include a past history of suicide attempt; co-morbid mood disorders and substance abuse; multiple admissions during the past year; distressing persistent symptoms; fear of deterioration with hopelessness and loss of faith in treatment, and having hallucinations, often auditory, such as voices commanding them to kill themselves (command hallucinations).
> 4. About 40% of those with alcohol dependence will attempt suicide, and up to 7% will die by suicide.
> 5. Comorbidity is common in psychiatric disorders and that increases the risk of suicide. That includes substance abuse co-morbid with any other major mental disorder, and depressive disorder co-morbid with schizophrenia.

There are many studies on risk factors, but Hall et al.'s (1999) findings are impressive. They found the following to be "excellent predictors" of severe suicide attempts: "Severe anxiety, panic attacks, a depressed mood, a diagnosis of major affective disorder, recent loss of an interpersonal relationship, recent abuse of alcohol or illicit substances coupled with feelings of hopelessness, helplessness, worthlessness, global or partial insomnia, anhedonia, inability to maintain a job, and the recent onset of impulsive behavior" (p. 17). Note also that "Patients with managed care were overrepresented by 245% in the study" (p. 2). The report of this study can be found online (http://www.drryanhall.com/Articles/suicide.pdf).

There are many clusters of risk factors for suicide, and several of these have been incorporated into Form 4.1. Bear in mind that these factors have to be weighted, but lack established weights for a prediction equation; they change over time; they have different meanings for different individuals; they may not be linearly additive; and they must be integrated with other data. Thus Form 4.1 is only a guide. The purposes of this form are (1) to evaluate the recognized risk factors for suicide, (2) to ensure and document the thoroughness of this evaluation for ethical and protective purposes, and (3) to initiate appropriate treatment of the suicidal client. A clever reorganization of such data by Sanchez (2001) separates them into acute and chronic states, and so a time frame is introduced into Form 4.1. Caution in the use of the term suicide "gesture" is urged by Heilbron et al. (2010), due to ambiguity and historical meanings.

## Responding to a Suicidal Crisis

There is no one simple plan to follow in dealing with a suicidal client, but comprehensive assessments and plans offer the best treatment and protection. Precautionary measures could include the following:

- Hospitalization.

- Close, repeated, and continuing observation, through scheduling more frequent sessions and/or recruiting family and friends of the client. Consider calls between sessions. Work to instill hope.

- Referring the client for all appropriate services.

- Preventing access to means of self-harm (e.g., letting the client have only small doses of risky medications, removing guns and other highly lethal means from the client's home). See Bryan et al. (2011) and Jobes (2016) for specific guidance about this very protective action.

- Providing backup services when you are unavailable.

- Obtaining thorough and well-documented consultation.

- Reviewing and keeping complete records.

Weighing the multiple factors and forming judgments about the degree of suicidality as a clinical process may be assisted by using the continuum of suicidality (from nonexistent to extreme) developed by Rudd et al. (1999). It takes into account eight factors: predisposition, precipitants, symptomatic presentation, hopelessness, nature of suicidal thinking, previous suicidal behavior, impulsivity, and protective factors. For example, assess the client for lessened internal controls that may be due to psychosis, paranoid suspiciousness, organic brain syndrome, or substance use (Beck, 1990, pp. 702–703). Bennett et al. (1990, p. 66) note that the following may also lower internal controls: a history of impulsiveness or volatile temper, affective illness, beliefs in justified revenge or the appropriateness or efficacy of violence, and medication interactions.

Be cautious with "no-suicide contracts," because evidence that they reduce suicides by themselves is lacking (Reid, 2005). They also have no legal validity and have not protected professionals in lawsuits (Lewis, 2007). However, refusal or reluctance to sign such a contract may be informative and may open the way for discussions. Such an agreement can strengthen the "alliance for safety" as part of a comprehensive plan. In the context of a strong therapeutic relationship, agreements can support open communication about suicidality, and restate shared goals and commitments. For a suicidal client who (you believe) understands the issues and is competent to sign, you might consider a "safety agreement" starting with "What actions can we plan to keep you safe?" and revising it as conditions change. Rudd et al. (2001) offer a sensitive sample. The Department of Veterans Affairs (Stanley & Brown, 2008) has developed a 20-page "safety plan" for brief interventions, which is "a prioritized written list of coping strategies and sources of support that patients can use during or preceding suicidal crises."

## The Risk Factors for Interpersonal Violence

Most of the risk factors for suicide also are risks for interpersonal violence, so here we do not offer two forms with lists of factors. Instead, below, we provide some lists of risk factors for violence that are not addressed in Form 4.1 on suicide risk. Note that these factors are not presented in order of their importance, and that they are based on grouped data rather than data on individuals, so use them with circumspection. In fact, a survey of clinician-identified risk factors not only found differences due to the clinicians' disciplines, but noted that the factors clinicians offered did not in fact predict who became violent (Odeh et al., 2006). There does not appear to be any reliable differences in violence factors between psychiatric and nonpsychiatric populations (Rueve & Welton, 2008), so both are included here.

### Demographic Risk Factors

❑ Male under age 40 (especially age 16–25)   ❑ Lower intelligence

❑ Prior arrest; young age at time of first arrest   ❑ School truancy   ❑ Foster home placement

❑ Access to/possession of firearms/other weapons; other means available; history of weapons use

❑ Living or growing up in a violent subculture or familyHaving been a victim of violence

❑ Having appeared in court for violence, or having had inpatient psychiatric treatment for violence

### Social/Interpersonal Risk Factors

❑ History of cruelty to animals and people      ❑ History of fire setting

❑ Risk-taking behaviors      ❑ Behavior suggesting loss of control or impulsivity

❑ Child/adolescent behavior problems, particularly aggression

❑ A significant other and/or caregiver who is either provocative or not protective

❑ Peers who support criminal/aggressive behavior

❑ Impending losses (e.g., likely loss of home, job, friend, family member)

### Recent Violent Behaviors

❑ History of violence (this is the best indicator)—fighting, hurting others, and violence against animals (evaluate violence against property separately for motivation and degree of control)

❑ More severe, recent, and frequent violent acts

❑ Threats of violence          ❑ Reporting own acts of violence

❑ Having previously identified potential target persons who are available or accessible

### Current Personal Psychological Risk Factors

❑ Personality disorder (e.g., antisocial, borderline)

❑ Cognitive impairment      ❑ Impulsive behaviors

❑ Behavior marked by anger, agitation, hostility, tension, suspiciousness, excitement, stress

❑ Command hallucinations to harm others; paranoid delusions

❑ Intoxication (slurred speech, unsteady gait, flushed face, dilated pupils, etc.)

❑ Acute symptoms of mania, schizophrenia, psychosis, delirium

❑ Lack of concern over consequences of violent acts        ❑ Lack of compassion/empathy

❑ View of self as victim          ❑ Intention to harm          ❑ Unrealistic plans

## Analyzing the Information Gathered

Although the *legal* risks to us as clinicians from suicide and interpersonal violence are not very different, we treat those clients differently *in clinical practice*. So we must consider what additional information is needed and obtain the assessments. Examples may include assessments of paranoia or sociopathy, or of membership in a social grouping that condones or promotes violence. Richard E. Jensen, PhD, of St. Charles, IL, helpfully suggests considering all potential problematic behaviors: aggression (verbal as well as physical, threatened, historical), arson, elopement, suicide, robbery, property destruction, terroristic threats, and any other situation-specific behaviors. Jensen also suggests attempting, from records or other data, to assess these intervention-relevant factors: the "triggers" of the negative behaviors; the client's compliance with previous treatment and likely compliance with future treatment; and the client's attitude toward therapists, programs, staff, members, and so on. Webster et al. (2009) offer thoughtful guidance and links to scales for special populations, all in just four pages. Finally, the subject is treated in two books: Maden (2007) reviews the different methods of risk assessment and offers his procedures, and Webster et al. (2013) integrate structured judgment with treatment.

Be alert to threats. If a client makes any threats toward either self or others, Bennett et al. (1990) advise evaluating their purpose. Is a threat real or manipulative? Is it self-justifying or self-protecting, or is it made in order to avoid some other consequence? Be especially alert to threats with specific details. Beck (1990) cautions that mention of time, method, contingency, location, victim (of interpersonal violence), and use of the active voice are all indicators of greater likelihood in a threat.

Get consultation as well. The demonstration of a consensus, especially among professionals of several disciplines, proves that your care did not fall below the standard. You may need someone's assistance if pharmacotherapy or hospitalization is necessary.

Finally, it may be valuable, but is not generally necessary, to consider other foreseeable victims (such as coworkers) beside those identified by a client who is threatening interpersonal violence.

Berman (2006) summarizes the issues and responses in suicide risk management, and Bongar et al. (1999) is also widely recommended. Form 6.19, Suicide Risk Assessment

Summary and Recommendations, can assist in documenting your conclusions and the steps you will take.

## Documenting the Situation and Your Actions

**The rule for documenting is to "think out loud for the record."** You are a trained clinician. You have to do as good a job as your peers would (at the standard of care). Slow down your thoughts and record them. Because it is a risky situation, the rule is "More risk, more notes." Quote and date the client's statements and answers to your questions, and note your understandings. Your records should show how you considered the facts and issues in an ongoing and thorough way; your conclusions; the options you considered, and their pros and cons; risk–benefit analyses and other rationales; your well-reasoned course of actions; the client's involvement; the treatment plan to reduce risk factors; what happened, and so on. All of these are what our peers would do; they constitute the standard of practice.

## Managing the Risk

Make any **environmental manipulations** (e.g., removing guns) that may reduce the danger of impulsive actions. Introducing obstacles and delay between impulse and access to highly lethal methods—"means restriction"—has been shown to be a powerful risk reduction technique. "Although some individuals might seek other methods, many do not; when they do, the means chosen are less lethal and are associated with fewer deaths than when more dangerous ones are available" (Yip et al., 2012, p. 2393). But consider also the possible negative consequences of environmental manipulations. For example, removing guns could paradoxically raise the level of risk, because it humiliates a person who has lived with guns safely for years or is proud of a collection.

**Before you break confidentiality, weigh the costs against the benefits.** The costs can include losing the client's trust, or even the opportunity to continue to work with the client and help with the risky situation. Discuss the issues with the client before disclosure. This discussion is rarely unproductive when it is handled as a part of therapy, and harm seems more likely when disclosure is not discussed.

This may sound strange, but you should attempt to get a release (see Form 8.2) to break confidentiality if a serious threat is made, particularly a threat of violence against others. Most violent people are both desperate and ambivalent about their aggression, and are still competent to consent. Violent behavior does not, in and of itself, justify breaking confidentiality. Do not break confidentiality when you have only suspicions but no client words or deeds. If you are uncertain, use judgment, consultation, and thorough, honest documentation. Do not act to warn simply for fear of a *Tarasoff* suit.

As an alternative to breaking confidentiality, **consider intensifying the therapy** and documenting the alteration and its rationale. The following are good ideas:

- Increase the frequency of sessions. They need not be longer unless this seems justified. Perhaps call the client between sessions.

- Focus on anger, aggression, controls, consequences, alternatives to suicide or violence, and topics that stimulate violent thoughts.

- Pay more attention to minor threats.

- Work with the client to attend to the "triggers" and to change the behaviors and risks, but be aware that the client may lie to you about his or her changes.

- Follow up on any lack of compliance with treatment (Monahan, 1993).

- Do anything that will increase the "therapeutic alliance."

In addition, it is wise to **develop various protective interventions** when interpersonal violence is threatened:

- Develop a safety plan for both the potential target and the perpetrator.

- If the client's spouse is a possible target, consider couple therapy, but only if safety issues can be adequately addressed and documented.

- Work with family members who can more closely observe the client.

- Consider hospitalizing the client or notifying the police—actions that would serve to incapacitate the client (Monahan, 1993).

- Monahan (1993) also suggests "target hardening," or making the target less vulnerable (by decreasing salience or accessibility, hiring bodyguards, etc.). This is not a therapy area, so get consultation.

- "Communicate information and concerns about violence to the person responsible for making decisions about the client, and make important items salient" (Monahan, 1993, p. 245).

- Be wary of your desire to trust and believe your client, and try to avoid naïveté.

**Gather your resources now; do not wait for an emergency situation.** We suggest that you determine *this week* the referral and support resources in your community; trying to find them with a crisis on your hands is certainly more stressful and may be too late. Make it a goal for this week to ask all your peers, and anyone else you can think of, which persons and agencies to contact for help in *any* crisis (suicide, domestic violence, homicidal threats, animal cruelty, etc.). Collect names, phone numbers, addresses, and any procedural details for contacting the following:

- ❑ Police in your and the client's area
- ❑ Psychiatric or other inpatient or residential facilities
- ❑ Consulting psychiatrists
- ❑ Local mental health authorities who can authorize inpatient evaluations or hospitalization
- ❑ Lawyers and legal organizations you can consult with
- ❑ Colleagues familiar with the local scene and with the treatment of potentially suicidal/violent individuals
- ❑ Support groups and shelters
- ❑ Any other persons who, or agencies that, may be helpful

For a specific client, routinely gather information on who is medicating or can medicate him or her; on friends and family members who can intervene, house the client, or separate him or her from potential targets; and on insurance coverage for emergency hospital care and/or other intensive treatment.

It is always possible that the client will not agree to your efforts to reduce the likelihood of suicide or interpersonal violence. You might consider getting a more specific **waiver of your responsibility** any time a client refuses to cooperate with important treatment recommendations (Liberman, 1990). You could create a letter to be signed by the client to the effect that (1) he or she has been fully informed about your treatment recommendations; (2) refusing your specific treatment recommendations may seriously compromise his or her health, or have other adverse personal, social, vocational, medical, legal, or other consequences, some of which have been discussed fully with the client and other consequences of which may be presently unforeseeable; and (3) the client, voluntarily and with full understanding, is choosing to refuse or not to cooperate with your recommendation(s). Examples offered by Liberman (1990) include a client with severe bipolar disorder who refuses or discontinues mood-stabilizing medications; a client with severe anorexia nervosa who refuses inpatient treatment; and those with signs of serious medical conditions who refuse evaluation, consultation, or treatments.

## Doing Damage Control

If suicide or violence has occurred, do not make public statements of responsibility, and do not alter the record (Monahan, 1993). See Section 4.2. The whole story is probably unclear and certainly unavailable to you at this point. Although many states have "I'm sorry" laws that prevent the use of physicians' statements to clients or their families of what went wrong to further a malpractice claim, these laws have not been extended to mental health professionals.

Suicides by clients of trainees is not uncommon. A summary of some emotional and ethical issues can be found in Coverdale et al. (2007).

# 4.8    The Duty to Protect (and Warn)

If you believe that a client is dangerous (to others, but also to self), you can use your professional judgment and position to *protect*—not just the narrower duty simply to *warn*. Your duty is to take appropriate action, which is not confined to warning. You have a less clear but more general obligation as a citizen to protect your fellow citizens. Threats and risks concern future actions but the law imposes no similar requirement as to *completed* criminal conduct, "dangerous" or not (Goldman & Gutheil, 1994). Some cases are just too ambiguous—for example, a client's threat is to rob a specific store but to threaten the clerk with an unloaded gun, or to use a date rape drug at some time. Document and consult extensively.

You need to know your local rules and obligations about victims. Victims of abuse such as children, elders, or other vulnerable persons require a lower threshold—reason to suspect—for taking protective actions. As a further example of the need for knowing local and current rules, the *Ewing* decision (*Ewing v. Goldstein*, 2004) in California expanded the need for *Tarasoff* (duty-to-warn) protections when family members communicate the threats (Letter in Support of Petition for Review, 2004).

## The Legal Basis

A California's court's two decisions in the famous *Tarasoff* case (*Tarasoff v. Regents of the University of California*, 1976) established therapists' duty to protect. Since then, court cases have sent mixed messages about the limits of therapists' liability and required behaviors. But they have only rarely held a therapist liable, and never when a professionally proper response was made. (This is good news for therapists.) **You will not be held responsible for a negative outcome if you have done what a good clinician should have—proper evaluation, planning, and implementation—which is the standard of care.** A review (Appelbaum, 1996) of suits against clinicians for warning others concludes that therapists should warn potential victims in order to avoid liability for subsequent violence, even though doing so opens the therapist to allegations of breach of confidentiality.

When adopting *Tarasoff*, the courts have usually followed three principles in assessing liability. These principles are the (1) foreseeability of harm (a verbal threat or action taken), (2) identifiability of a victim, and (3) feasibility of therapist intervention (see more below). *Tarasoff* warning duties vary with states. As of 2009, 24 states have enacted a duty to protect by statute, and another 9 by court decision; 6 require a warning to the victim and/or law enforcement 10 states permit but do not require a warning, and the others have not decided (Werth et al., 2009).

On the other hand, some states have adopted "anti-*Tarasoff*" (or pro-confidentiality) legislation or immunity statutes, which hold a therapist not liable if he or she fails to warn a victim. Every state with a requirement to warn also protects clinicians from any liability from the consequences of warning. Obviously, you must know your state's rules in detail. It is illuminating to note the arguments against a *Tarasoff* duty. In a case in Pennsylvania (*Emerich v. Philadelphia Center for Human Development*, 1998), the APA and the Pennsylvania Psychological Association argued in their "friends of the court" brief

> that there is no sound basis for imposing a unique duty to warn on mental health workers because: (1) no other person (e.g., criminal defense attorneys) in the same or similar position is charged with such a legal duty or subject to litigation and potential liability; (2) mental health workers are not in a better position to protect third parties than others since they have neither special ability to predict who will commit violent acts nor any special means to control dangerous people; (3) imposing a duty to warn on therapists cannot be expected to increase public safety since a duty to warn has not been shown in the scientific literature to reduce violence and, instead, imposing such a duty to warn disserves broader public safety goals; and (4) alternatively, if the court were to find a duty to warn, such duty should be limited in a manner least destructive to public safety and the continuing availability of effective psychotherapy by being imposed only when there is a specific threat to an identified or reasonably identifiable victim and an imminent threat of serious bodily injury or death. (Brief for the APA and the Pennsylvania Psychological Association as Amici Curiae, 1996)

The brief urged the court to adopt the "professional judgment rule" as the applicable standard of care. Indeed, Edwards (2014) statistically estimated that the imposition of such warnings resulted in an increase in homicides of 9%.

## When Do You Have a "Duty to Warn"?

In most jurisdictions you have a "duty to warn" when you have reasonable cause to believe that a client is dangerous to a specifiable person. But what are the characteristics of "reasonable cause" that trigger your duty? Here are the most common criteria.

First, there must be a *threat*. This may be simple and direct, implied, or part of a larger picture. It may arise through the client's contemplation of a criminal act, so be attentive to all the consequences of such statements. Second, the threat must be toward *an identifiable target*. This must be a particular person or persons, or sometimes property, rather than a general group or category. The threat may also be toward the client's self, as in self-mutilation, suicide, or possibly self-neglect (such as failing to eat or drinking alcohol to the point of unconsciousness) Third, the threat has to be *believable*. It should be explicit, not vague, and motives count, as does history, in assessing the potential for violence. Fourth, the threat has to be *imminent,* so that you must take action and cannot wait for others to learn of the risk and act to prevent the damage. Last, the threat must be by a *client* of yours. Your state's statutes and case law may qualify all of these. See also the lists of risk factors for violence in Section 4.7.

In determining whether reasonable cause exists, you must use good judgment, professional skill, and knowledge at levels usually provided by your peers. You do not need to be a perfect predictor of dangerousness—only to exercise a standard of care that a reasonable member of your discipline, in your local community and in these particular circumstances, would use. Such a professional should have current knowledge in the areas of evaluating dangerousness and violence. You must "take whatever other steps are reasonably necessary under the circumstances" (*Tarasoff,* 1976). In a related situation, where a client appears too intoxicated to drive home, would there be a duty to warn? No, because of the lack of a specific victim. However, a more general civic duty as well as our ethical principles would suggest taking some protective actions.

## What to Do When You Decide to "Warn"

"Discharging your *Tarasoff* duties" (as the lawyers call it) depends on many factors. You must take "reasonable" and "necessary" steps to protect the potential victim(s). These will, of course, vary with the circumstances and the local laws, but *may* include the following options. Good sense suggests that you should implement as many of these options as possible, based on local rules and professional consultation:

- To the extent you decide, discuss the warning with the client.
- Warning the intended victim about the threat and the sources of the threat.
- Contacting people who can apprise the potential victim of the danger.
- Notifying local law enforcement authorities.
- Initiating voluntary or involuntary psychiatric commitment. (This will shift the burden of decision making to the legal and medical systems.)
- Taking whatever other steps seem appropriate and necessary under the unique circumstances.
- Documenting all your thoughts and efforts. As recommended earlier, "Think out loud for the record."

## Suicide

The duty to protect often extends to protecting clients from themselves, as noted above. Although courts have rarely held therapists responsible for outpatient suicides, this situation is now changing, especially where the situational facts are clear. In general, the therapist is protected by performing the proper professional activities—thorough evaluation, thoughtful consideration, and appropriate interventions.

## Domestic Violence and Abuse

Clinicians must be prepared to respond to their ethical and legal responsibilities to protect spouses/partners and children from abuse by doing the following. (The last four steps are from Cervantes, 1992.)

- Develop a list of resources for yourself as therapist, including consultation, coordination of treatments, and referral options.

- Gather the information of relevance from clients and others who might know the facts.

- Develop a safety plan with clients. Know your local and national resources for protection.

- Know the legal protections available in your community and how to access them quickly.

- Assess for and report child abuse. You must know your local laws and procedures.

- Assess for and report cruelty to animals, which may be a mandated report.

The National Coalition Against Domestic Violence (http://www.ncadv.org) and the National Online Resource Center on Violence Against Women (http://www.vawnet.org) have extensive resources and connections.

Precautionary measures should include the following:

- Examine all situations coming to your attention that might involve abuse.

- Just as people with hypochondria can get sick, even people with paranoia and people who lie can be victims. Be thorough.

- Keep your assumptions about perpetrators open. People of all races, ages, and socio-economic levels assault other people. In particular, be alert to your reactions to a possible perpetrator when he or she is your client. If these continue to interfere with your objectivity, refer the case. Similarly, attend to your rescue fantasies.

- Understand in detail your local laws' requirements about reporting abuse, obey them, and prepare your response thoughtfully. You must also know about child abuse reporting time frames for your state and similar legal issues.

- Get thorough consultation if you are not familiar with the perpetrator's or other family members' coping and personality patterns and choose not to refer.

- Document fully and sensitively the claims, your evaluation, and your actions. Because perpetrators or other family members may pressure abused persons to recant or modify their statements, be certain to record verbatim the information offered to you (about occurrences, circumstances, sequences, etc.).

## Limiting Your Personal Vulnerability to Violence

Therapists are more vulnerable to violence than others. Simon (2011, p. 16) reported:

> The annual rate of nonfatal violent crime for all occupations between 1993 and 1999 was 12.6 per 1,000 workers. For physicians, the rate was 16.2. The rate for nurses was 21.9 (80% of nurses were subject to violent crime during their career). For psychiatrists, the rate was 68.2 per 1,000. For custodial staff, the rate was 69 per 1,000. The rate for other mental health workers was 40.7. Of psychiatrists responding to surveys, the average rate during their careers was 40%.

Pope and Vasquez (2011) reported that almost one in every five psychologists reported having been physically attacked by at least one client, over 80% of the psychologists reported having been afraid that a client would attack them, over half reported having had fantasies that a client would attack, over one out of four had summoned the police or security personnel for protection from a client and about 3% reported obtaining a weapon to protect themselves against a client. Purcell et al. (2005) and Anderson and West (2011) have discussed the dangers posed by clients who stalk psychologists. Kenneth S. Pope offers links to many resources for therapists who are stalked, threatened, or attacked by clients (http://www.kspope.com/stalking.php).

As a result of such experiences, many therapists have taken protective measures and organized them into a comprehensive safety plan. Such measures may include taking a more detailed history of violence; asking clients to estimate their risk of violence, and discussing the issue fully; specifying intolerable client behaviors; refusing to treat certain clients; terminating a threatening client; refusing to disclose personal data to clients; always using the word "we" when talking about office issues, whether there is someone else around or not; creating the illusion of another person in the office area with a desk, name plate, clothing, and suggestions that this person has just stepped out; requiring all new clients to bring a driver's license to the first meeting to confirm identity; getting to know local police; introducing yourself and your routines to your office's neighbors, and checking in regularly; relocating one's office to a "safer" building; avoiding isolated practice; removing objects that could become weapons; making sure the office has more than one escape route; developing contingency plans for summoning help at the office; learning conflict deescalation skills; avoiding working alone in the office, and perhaps never leaving it alone; hiring a secretary or just a student to work in an outer office; installing a video monitor to see who has entered the waiting room; installing an office alarm system (you can add a hand-held remote control "panic button" to such a system at small cost—keeping this in public display as well as reach makes good sense); learning to use nonlethal weapons, such as wasp spray that shoots 20 feet; keeping a weapon at home and/or at the office, and maintaining training in its use; hiring a security guard; obtaining training in management of assaultive behaviors and self-defense for yourself and your loved ones; discussing safety issues with your loved ones and developing a safety plan; prohibiting clients from appearing at your home; developing a contingency plan for family members if a client appears at the home; having no home address listing in directories; installing a home security alarm system; and other measures (Guy et al., 1992). It may be in your best interest to consider each of these for yourself and implement some of them today, before trouble strikes.

# 4.9   Legal and Ethical Aspects of Supervising and Being Supervised

As clinicians, we all participate in clinical supervision[3] during our careers, often both as supervisees and as supervisors. We do this because of our faith in the necessity of face-to-face assessing, teaching, monitoring, and mentoring to raise skill levels, model sophisticated skills and attitudes, socialize novices into a profession's world view, and so on.

Being supervised is like an apprenticeship with a master: It enables a novice to integrate the theory learned in training (in school as well as self-education) with the development and application of skills to the needs of real-world clients. In contrast to "consultation" with an independent peer or organization, "supervision" includes the monitoring, responsibility for, and control of the supervisee's practice by the supervisor. The supervisor retains full responsibility for the welfare of the client, as well as complete control over the actions of the supervisee. On a legal level, requiring formal supervision is the way our society protects citizens from amateurs who are learning a profession. Barnett and Molzon (2014) cogently review the ethical dimensions of supervision of psychotherapists.

Formalizing the supervision relationship by means of a contract with peers, associates, or others from whom you can learn or to whom you teach is a legally protective step, and it is implied by Standard 7.06 of the APA ethics code (APA, 2010). We provide an example of such an agreement later in this section as Form 4.2.

Most supervision takes place either on a one-to-one basis or in a seminar format. However, it can also include the use of cotherapy and team therapy, formal assignments and teaching, modeling by the supervisor, and formalized mentoring outside the classroom. The Internet and the technological revolution have created other possibilities, such as live video supervision with sufficient assurances of privacy. APA updated its guidelines in 2014 (see http://www.apa.org/about/policy/guidelines-supervision.pdf).

## Risks and Responses

**Supervising is a special set of skills.** Some circumspection is needed by clinicians who are considering becoming supervisors. A high level of clinical skill is a necessary but not sufficient qualification for a supervisor, because students need more than demonstrations to learn sophisticated procedures. Some clinicians may be well able to do, but not to explain well or teach. Knowledge alone is insufficient to assure its being passed on, because "telling is not teaching," and showing does not address the situation of learners. Also, clinicians may approach supervising from the perspective of their favorite school of therapy, which may not be appropriate or sufficiently flexible for the demands their supervisees face. Lastly, supervision based on a supervisor's own training experiences may simply pass on poor-quality or obsolete skills. A brief but sophisticated overview is provided by Barnett et

---

[3]This is not related to having a "supervisor" as part of being employed, as this "administrative supervision" concerns aspects such as hiring, promotion, salaries, schedules and other non-clinical activities.

al. (2007a). Formal training in supervision skills and models can benefit supervisors and is probably necessary to reduce risk as well.

Carol A. Falender and Edward Shafranske have written two excellent books on supervision, one for supervisors (2004) and a second for supervisees (2011). Supervisors (and supervisees) may find useful the American Association of State and Provincial Psychology Boards' *Supervision Guidelines,* which may be found at the Association's website (http://www.asppb.net/?page=Guidelines). It may also be useful to check a specific state's or province's psychology practice act or similar legislation, to see what regulations it may have relevant to supervision. There are links to each state's and province's psychology laws on a page of Kenneth S. Pope's site (http://www.kspope.com/licensing/index.php). A fine example of paperwork to support the ongoing development of interns and the evaluation of the processes involved can be downloaded as well (http://www.appic.org/Portals/0/docs/ElementsofContinuousInternshipProgramEvaluationJanWiller6-25-03.doc).

**Be aware of vicarious liability.** There is an old legal concept, *respondeat superior,* in which the master is held responsible for the actions of the servant; thus some clinicians may shy away from supervising, fearing its unpredictable consequences. However, a careful selection process, comprehensive discussions and training, continual monitoring, a clear contract, and inclusive liability insurance can greatly reduce the supervisor's risk. Supervision should be timely, frequent, and of sufficient duration to allow competent monitoring of the supervisee. More clinically, it should allow all necessary mutual understanding of the case and evaluation of the treatment. A rather thorough discussion of the legal issues and the theory behind them can be found in two articles by Saccuzzo (both n.d., but apparently written about 2002). Both can be found on the website of the National Register of Health Service Providers in Psychology (http://www.nationalregister.org).

**Do not exceed your areas of competent practice or the supervisee's.** Just as you would not employ a method you didn't know well or treat a condition you were unfamiliar with, you should not attempt to supervise in a clinical area in which you do not have demonstrated competence or to perform the kinds of supervision for which you lack sufficient skills. Supervisees must have been adequately trained to execute each treatment prescribed by the supervisor. This may require you to refuse some supervisees or some clients for a supervisee.

**Be aware of informed consent issues.** There are two issues here: the client's consent to be treated by a clinician who is being supervised, and the supervisee's consent to be supervised. First, according to Standard 10.01c of the APA ethics code (APA, 2010), clients must be informed about, understand the consequences (risks and benefits) of, and voluntarily agree to treatment by your supervisee. Specifically, they must be told that you are supervising, what your credentials are, that you will be reviewing the supervisee's records (and probably recordings of the sessions), and so on (see Form 5.8 for more details). Second, your supervisee must be fully informed and voluntarily consent to the supervision process you will pursue. A full discussion of this issue with the contents for a contract (and citations to other contracts) can be found in Thomas (2007).

According to Standard 7.06 of the APA ethics code (APA, 2010), the processes for evaluating performance and providing feedback to students and interns are required to be specified. Vespia et al. (2002) offer a list of 52 supervision behaviors from which you could develop your own rating forms. Saccuzzo (n.d.-b) offers an informed consent form for supervisees.

**Consider confidentiality issues.** Understand that neither consultations nor supervision create privileged communications, so you and your notes could be dragged into court.

**Avoid exploitation and dual relationships** with a supervisee. As discussed earlier in this chapter, sexual relationships between supervisors and supervisees are forbidden in psychology (by Standard 7.07 of the APA ethics code; APA, 2010). Supervising with business partners, relatives, spouses, friends, or prior clients should also be avoided where there is a risk of harm, although some multiple relationships may not be avoidable (Gottlieb et al., 2007). For example, the emotional safety that needs to be established in a supervisory relationship can sometimes conflict with the need for the supervisor to function as a gatekeeper for the profession.

Moreover, a supervisee should pay a fee (in states where this is not forbidden by board regulations) for each hour, and this fee should not be a percentage of the fees received from the clients, which might be seen as fee splitting and is still (usually) unethical. One pays for supervision in Minnesota, West Virginia, Kentucky, and other states, but it must not be paid for in California, Massachusetts, Illinois, and Louisiana. Check your local rules.

**Do not become your supervisee's "therapist," as this is a dual relationship.** If a supervisee needs assistance on a case with significant legal implications, refer him or her to a lawyer. Similarly, if he or she needs therapy for anxiety or depression arrange for a therapist with the usual privacy protections.

**Supervising can be harmful.** Ellis et al. (2013) found that a third of supervisees rated their supervision as harmful, and almost all rated it as inadequate. Careful monitoring and open feedback could improve these results. **Advice to supervisees:** Your sessions should be constructive, so if you are not sure you are getting what you value, seek out another consultant. You can outgrow your teacher, you know.

## A Formal Agreement

A formal agreement can incorporate consent issues, clarify and harmonize expectations, and support the development of ethical and competent professionals. Form 4.2 is a written agreement, but it is not a legal contract between supervisor and supervisee. It addresses many issues and should greatly reduce the risks of poor communication. This form incorporates some ideas from a form developed by Kathleen Quinn, EdD, of Cheyenne, WY, for which we are most grateful.

**FORM 4.2**

Since supervision can take place at many levels, some of the terms in Form 4.2 have been placed in parentheses where they would apply only to those being supervised for pre- or postdoctoral internships or for licensure. The agreement is written for psychotherapy supervision, so other clinical functions (such as diagnostic testing, case management, school consultation, mentoring, and group supervision) may require additional or substitute paragraphs. If the supervision is taking place to enable the supervisee to qualify for licensure or to meet some other formal goal, make sure that the frequency, duration, and intensity are sufficient to meet the requirements by incorporating them into the form's text. The means of emergency contact should include all usable numbers and addresses. The form states that addenda or modifications can be attached to it. These addenda may include descriptions of the nature or style of supervision—for example, observation, group supervision, reviews of the supervisee's products (such as test protocols and reports or recordings of therapy sessions), discussions of the supervisee's work concerns, and discussions of selected topics in sessions.

The form deliberately does not address the model of therapy, school, discipline, or

## Agreement for Professional Supervision Services

### Introduction

This agreement has been created to address the legal, ethical, practical, and clinical issues of the supervision relationship. It can be added to or modified as the supervision process unfolds over time and across cases, and these addenda will be indicated on the last page. This agreement is intended to articulate and clarify the complex mutual responsibilities of the parties involved, the procedures of the supervision, and the personal development needed to become a capable and responsible professional deserving of ethical, safe, and effective independent professional practice.

### Parties

We, _____ (hereinafter called the "supervisee"), and _____ (hereinafter called the "supervisor"), agree that the supervisor will provide professional supervision services starting on ____/____/____ and continuing until ____/____/____, as outlined below.

### Meetings and communication

The supervisee agrees to meet with the supervisor in person as mutually arranged or this way:

Location: _____  Days, hours: _____

Location: _____  Days, hours: _____

It is the supervisee's responsibility to initiate meetings as often as necessary to meet the goals of supervision, to meet his or her training needs, to provide high levels of care to the clients involved, and to address other needs that may arise.

Besides our face-to-face meetings, we may use postal mail, telephone, video, email, or other means to communicate and the privacy and security of these must be confirmed before use. Electronic recordings will require the written consent of the clients involved. Because we need to be able to reach each other easily, and because emergencies may arise, the following arrangements for contact are made.

*Supervisee:* _____  _____  _____
             Days and hours of availability  Means of routine contact  Means of emergency contact

*Supervisor:* _____  _____  _____
             Days and hours of availability  Means of routine contact  Means of emergency contact

When the supervisor is unavailable due to vacation or other events, the supervisor will assure adequate availability of a substitute supervisor and will inform this person of the supervisee's needs and situation.

### Frequency and financial concerns

The supervisee agrees to pay for services provided, up until the time either of us informs the other (in person or by written means) of his or her plans to end the relationship. The supervisee agrees to pay the fee of $____ per session for these services, starting on or about ____/____/____ and continuing at about the rate of about ____

*(continued)*

meetings per _____. Vacations and other planned absences from supervision will be negotiated at least 30 days in advance.

## Confidentiality

The nature and limits of confidentiality between supervisor and supervisee will be clarified at the beginning of supervision, and as supervision proceeds and issues arise.

## Records

1. We both agree to keep records of our meetings, which will document the following:
   - The dates and times we met face to face or otherwise communicated.
   - The cases involved by name or case number.
   - The results of clinical efforts and interventions, the progress of each case, the client's needs, and similar concerns.
   - Other relevant issues, such as ethical, legal, procedural, interpersonal, or organizational ones.
   - The supervisee's areas or skills in need of enhancement and progress toward mastery.
   - The recommendations and assignments given by the supervisor and assumed by the supervisee.
   - Discussion of the supervision process, procedures, and progress.
2. We will maintain these records in the same ways as we maintain clinical case records (as to confidentiality, availability, security, etc.).
3. We are both aware that these records are not legally privileged.

## Supervisee's responsibilities

1. Presentations to clients and informed consent.
   - The supervisee agrees not to misrepresent or advertise him- or herself in any way that might imply a competence, credential, or independence he or she does not have.
   - In dealing with clients and the public, the supervisee agrees to explain his or her professional achievements, status, and legal title; to make it clear that he or she is being supervised; and to provide the name of the supervisor. The supervisee will explain the supervision process and the supervisor's activities, profession, and credentials. The supervisee will explain that clients in therapy with the supervisee are legally considered to be clients of the supervisor.
   - The supervisee assures that clients will read and agree to the supervisor's Information for Clients or Practice Description brochure, Notice of Privacy Practices, and other client educational materials as needed.
   - The supervisee will obtain informed consent of clients to the use of protected health information and sharing of records involved in this supervision. Where direct observations and/or audio or video recordings will be made, the supervisee will obtain fully informed consent, using forms provided by the supervisor.
2. Risk management.
   - The supervisee will inform the supervisor of any concerns or problems with any clients or cases as soon as possible. Any interactions with a client that raise any level of concern about any risk to the client, family, peers, or others must be discussed with the supervisor immediately.
   - The supervisee will abide by the relevant state and national professional codes of ethics and their guidelines, and other similar materials, as appropriate to the kinds of services being rendered to clients and the characteristics of those clients.
   - The supervisee will abide by the current rules and regulations of this state's professional licensing board.
   - The supervisee will adhere to the policies and procedures of the employers of the supervisor and supervisee.
   - The supervisee will obtain and maintain his or her own professional liability insurance coverage (unless otherwise provided) for the duration of the supervision.

*(continued)*

3. Supervisee's education and development as a professional.

   - The supervisee recognizes that a major value of supervision is the learning of professional roles and associated behaviors.

   - The supervisee agrees to use his or her best abilities to remain responsive to suggestions and recommendations.

   - The supervisee agrees to bring to the attention of the supervisor any deficits the supervisee recognizes in his or her ability to perform the clinical functions involved in therapy or other clinical activities with clients.

   - The supervisee agrees to complete readings and other educational assignments made by the supervisor. The supervisee may be asked to summarize or in other ways demonstrate the learning of the contents of these materials.

4. Clinical procedures.

   - The supervisee agrees to meet with clients and perform psychotherapeutic or other clinical functions in a professional, reliable, and responsible manner.

   - The supervisee agrees to implement to the best of his or her ability the recommendations made by the supervisor for the handling of each case.

   - The supervisee agrees to develop adequate, appropriate, and current written treatment plans and will remain responsible for such. These will be reviewed at scheduled times with the client(s) and supervisor, and changes will be incorporated as needed.

**Supervisor's responsibilities**

1. Sensitivity, responsiveness, and flexibility.

   - The supervisor agrees to try always to bear in mind issues of diversity, hierarchy, and privilege in their many dimensions and influences, and to be sensitive and respectful of all differences among the client(s), the supervisee, and him- or herself.

   - The supervisor agrees to attend to the boundaries, balances, and potential multiple relationships between the supervisor and supervisee. In all cases, the interests of the supervisee will be held primary.

   - The supervisor agrees to maintain awareness of the sometimes fine line between doing supervision and providing psychotherapy. If the supervisor should decide that the supervisee can benefit from psychotherapy, he or she will make referrals.

   - The supervisor agrees to continue to learn about supervision.

   - The supervisor agrees to remain current in the model(s) and methods of assessment, therapy, legal and ethical issues, and similar clinical concerns.

2. Evaluation.

   - The supervisor agrees to conduct an initial evaluation of the supervisee's knowledge, attitudes, and skills relevant to the clinical activities that the supervisee intends to undertake and the supervisor to supervise. Other areas, as proposed by either party, may be assessed as well. Based on this comprehensive evaluation, both parties will formulate specific goals and methods for the content and nature of the supervision.

   - The supervisor agrees to explain and obtain fully informed consent of the supervisee to any and all methods and procedures for the evaluation of the supervisee, their nature and timing, and any other persons who will also review the evaluations and results, before implementing any of them.

   - If disagreements should arise that the supervisor and supervisee cannot resolve, they will take these difficulties to the supervisee's educational supervisor if the supervisee is in supervision as part of an educational program, and if not they will consult with appropriate members of the local or state professional association or others agreed to by both parties.

3. Monitoring and risk management.

   - The supervisor will assure compliance with written policies about client record keeping and client access to records; confidentiality and its exceptions; and similar concerns as described by the supervisor's Information for Clients or Practice Description brochures and Notice of Privacy Practices.

   - The supervisor will review the supervisee's treatment plans, written notes, and audio and/or video recordings of selected treatment sessions on a periodic basis, as decided by the supervisor. Direct

*(continued)*

observation of the services provided by the supervisee will be arranged if at all possible.

- The supervisor has legal responsibility for the supervisee's clients and will take all appropriate actions in their best interests.
- Supervision will include examination of and education in legal and ethical issues, as well as client treatment issues.
- The supervisor agrees to abide by the related state and national codes of ethics for his or her profession and their guidelines, and other similar materials, as appropriate to the kinds of services being rendered to clients and the characteristics of those clients.
- The supervisor agrees to abide by the current rules and regulations of this state's professional licensing board.
- The supervisor agrees to adhere to the policies and procedures of employers of the supervisor and/or supervisee.
- The supervisor will maintain current professional insurance coverage and include the supervisee as required by law, regulation, or the insurer.

4. Administrative responsibilities.

- The supervisor will create all appropriate and necessary records of the experiences and services provided to and by the supervisee for licensure or certification, and will ensure that the criteria are met.
- The supervisor will file reports as required when any condition of supervision changes.
- The supervisor will file a final supervision report within 2 weeks after termination of supervision.
- The supervisor will provide evaluations, letters of recommendation, and similar documents about the supervision and supervisee as requested by the supervisee.
- The supervision will retain supervision records for 7 years from date of last session, or indefinitely if ethical or legal actions are pending
- The supervisor will provide or arrange for appropriate space, equipment, and support services for the supervisee. Any additional resources for the supervisee are listed in an addendum.
- The supervisor will provide resources for and instruction in all billing and payments procedures for supervised clients.
- Arrangements for termination or transfer of clients will be arranged well ahead of the end of supervision.

Modifications to this agreement can be made with consent of both parties, and shall be made in writing and attached to this agreement.

I, the supervisee, have read the supervisor's office policy statements as well as the supervision statement above. I agree to act according to everything stated there, as shown by my signature below. I understand that this agreement can be terminated if either party does not live up to his or her responsibilities as outlined above. I agree to adhere to the contents of this agreement, until otherwise negotiated and formalized as addenda to this agreement.

_____     ___/___/____

Signature of the supervisee indicating agreement                     Date

I, the supervisor, have discussed the issues above with the supervisee. I hereby agree to adhere to the contents of this agreement, until otherwise negotiated and formalized as addenda to this agreement.

_____     ___/___/____

Signature of the supervisor indicating agreement                     Date

❑ Copy accepted by supervisee or   ❑ Copy kept by supervisor

approach, as these are likely to differ widely across supervision situations. The following points have also been omitted from Form 4.2 because they are too dependent on the circumstances, but should be articulated for informed consent and clarity: the purposes of the supervision; the work the supervisee is to perform (assessment, counseling, consulting, etc.); the location of the services; and the payment to the supervisee for services rendered to the clients of the supervisor, and payments to the supervisor if allowed. This form is not appropriate for online or peer-to-peer supervision. Lastly, it is not designed for specialized supervision, such as that of "burned-out," traumatized, or otherwise impaired professionals, or of professionals who are being rehabilitated or under supervision prescribed by their licensing boards.

Thomas (2007) cogently suggests incorporating clarity and informed consent into any approach to supervision, and describes an agreement. She has expanded the 2007 article into a book on examining and coping with the ethical issues of supervision (Thomas, 2010). Those engaged in supervision might also take a look at the literature review, discussion, and extensive sample contract provided by Sutter et al. (2002). Similar contracts are also available online. The Saskatchewan College of Psychologists has posted its 2003 Supervision Agreement for Provisional Practice Psychologists on its website (http://www.skcp. ca/forms/supervision-agreement.pdf). An important author in the area of clinical supervision, Carol A. Falender, PhD, has placed an outline of a sample contract online (http:// www.cfalender.com/super.pdf). Note that Dr. Falender's form is copyrighted (as you should assume all online materials are, unless they specifically indicate otherwise). A summary of a supervisory contract by the APA can also be found (http://supp.apa.org/books/Essential-Ethics-for-Psychologists/summary.pdf). California has a standard form for psychologists that asks the basic questions (http://www.psychology.ca.gov/applicants/sup_agree.shtml), and North Carolina's spells out responsibilities (http://www.ncpsychologyboard.org/Office/ PDFiles/SupvContWeb.pdf). An excellent supervision contract that is sensitive to technology has been devised by Stretch et al. (2013), and Barnett (2011) should be consulted as well.

## A Record of Supervision Meetings

A format for recording supervision is offered below, but you should create a customized format for your goals, methods of practice, and types of contacts. Both the supervisor and supervisee should agree to this format, and both should get copies of the eventual form.

Notes can be written into the spaces provided, or the numbers can be used to organize narrative notes recorded on a separate page. This format provides a space for the supervisor's name and location, but it is best if more detailed information is also recorded. For example, it could indicate the following for each supervisor in full on the back of the first of these forms you use: the supervisor's agency, type of agency, or setting (e.g., private practice); full business address; telephone numbers (regular, home, emergency, fax, pager, email, etc.); Social Security number; and any other information that might be needed in the future to substantiate that the supervision occurred.

## Supervision Record

1. Supervisor: _____          Supervisee: _____

   Agency/location: _____

2. Session's date: ____/____/____   Meeting number: _____   Duration: _____

   Individual or group? _____   Live or case consultation? _____

3. Preparation: (a) Supervisee's progress on tasks or homework from last session with client; (b) client case materials collected (paper and electronic records, genograms, consultations); (c) other materials collected (literature); (d) supervisee's concerns/issues to be addressed (personal, family, case, theoretical, practical, organizational, ethical, conflicts); and (e) goals for the session.

   _____

   _____

4. Clients discussed (use initials): For each, discuss (a) problematic behaviors or concerns/main issues/ progress/questions; (b) themes; (c) hypotheses; (d) treatment decisions made/tasks assumed.

   _____

   _____

5. Supervisee's views of session. Possible eliciting questions: "What were you working on as a therapist in this session? What did you think went well? Where did you struggle? What might you do differently? What do you want me to listen for?"

   _____

   _____

6. Supervisor's comments/evaluations about the following: supervisee's conceptualization of case/ treatment/problems; interventions/implementation of treatments; handling of issues; self-awareness; process, clinical, or theoretical areas; evaluation of treatment; and other factors as agreed upon.

   _____

   _____

7. Skill development/training recommendations or suggestions made. If supervisee's performance is deficient, this must be made clear, and a remediation plan must be developed and implemented.

   _____

   _____

8. Our signatures indicate agreement to perform the tasks described above.

   _____

   _____

   Signature of supervisor: _____

   Signature of supervisee: _____

   *If recordings are to be made, client agreement is necessary. Use Form 5.9.

For other options, Falvey and Cohen (2003) review many templates for supervisors' record keeping and discuss their benefits.

## Consultation

Consultation differs greatly from supervision. A consultant offers his or her expertise to an independent fellow professional who is not obliged to comply with any advice and retains full responsibility for his or her own actions and clients. If there might be misunderstandings or ambiguities, get a letter of agreement about roles and responsibilities.

Going it alone in murky waters is risky, if not self-destructive. The rule from Thomas Gutheil, mentioned earlier in this chapter, is widely quoted: "Never worry alone." ELZ gives himself 2 days of solitary worrying. If he has not resolved the issue by then, he knows it is time to consult because he lacks the resources to resolve the concern. Continuing professional consultations are essential for good clinical care; no one knows everything. However, without *scheduled* consulting relationships, you are less likely to actually obtain advice when a question (clinical or ethical) comes up. Furthermore, again as noted earlier in this chapter, frequent and formal consultation with a respected peer is seen as powerful protection against a malpractice verdict.

It is in your best interest to keep notes on your consultation sessions. ELZ prefers to keep these separate from any case notes that would go into a client's chart. You may choose not even to note in the chart that you consulted, so as to keep your notes more under your control. These notes can be stored with readings, diaries, handouts, and anything else to support the consultation relationship and professional learning. These notes will document the sessions (perhaps for a credential) and their content for defense if you are accused of an ethics or malpractice violation.

# CHAPTER 5

# Getting Informed Consent

## 5.1   The What and Why of Getting Informed Consent

The relationship of therapist and client is complex and multidimensional. It evolves interpersonally, therapeutically, and economically. If this relationship is not spelled out, the client, therapist, ethics committees, insurance companies, and courts are all quite likely to interpret it quite differently. The relationship should thus be clarified as soon as clinically feasible; this process of clarification and of obtaining informed consent is not optional, but inherent. The relevant parts of the American Psychological Association (APA) ethics code (APA, 2010) are primarily Standards 3.10 and 3.11, as well as 9.03 for assessment and 10.01 for therapy.

Please note that this chapter does not deal with consent for forensic evaluations or services, including custody and legal competence. These issues are so complex that they go beyond our ability to discuss them here. Also, the Notice of Privacy Practices (NPP) required by the Health Insurance Portability and Accountability Act (HIPAA) is covered in Chapter 6.

How can you be sure you have obtained informed consent? What specific methods can you use to obtain it? This chapter answers these questions and offers five paths, or methods, you can use with clients to secure their informed consent. Let us start with a definition, and then discuss the four components of fully informed consent.

### What Is Informed Consent?

Two aspects of informed consent are relevant for therapists. First, "Informed consent is actually a statement about the moral atmosphere of the relationship between clinician and client. In more practical terms, informed consent is a dyadic process, or dialogue that begins at the moment of eye contact and continues throughout the relationship" (Gutheil, 1993, p. 1005). The moral atmosphere includes respecting each party's autonomy and the differences in power between the two parties.

Second, informed consent is not merely a signature on a form; the signature is only the public acknowledgment of consent. **Informed consent is a mental state** arrived at through the sharing of information, discussion, questions, answers, and dialogue. It is actually a common experience. For example, when deciding to purchase a car, we visit dealers but are not usually ready to buy until we have consulted several dealers. We also read reviews and talk to friends. At some point we feel ready to purchase, because we have enough relevant information about cars and our needs and resources. This mental state is fully informed consent. Consent for therapy involves an understanding of the processes and rules, as well as an agreement to proceed.

## What Informed Consent Requires

Informed consent requires a **mentally competent** person who has a **good understanding** of what will occur in treatment, who **freely chooses** to be treated, and who has his or her consent **documented.** If any of these components is lacking, its absence must be documented, explained, and addressed. Let's look more carefully at each of these elements.

### Mental Competence

Mental competence is presumed for all adults unless a court has decided that an adult is incompetent, or the adult has manifested clear signs of incompetence to you as a well-trained and responsible clinician. Some indicators of *possible* incompetence are psychosis, dementia, severe depression, suicidal behavior, and the like. Receiving a severe diagnosis or even being involuntarily hospitalized is not automatically create incompetence. In such cases, consult or refer if you lack the professional skills to evaluate the impact of these symptoms on the client's competence. Appelbaum (2007) reviews the issues and guidelines.

If you need formal assessments of competence to make decisions about treatment, the three scales developed by the MacArthur Treatment Competence Study are sophisticated and specific. They address denial of symptoms, assessment of cognitive functioning, and understanding of the explanations offered of treatments. An introduction can be found in Grisso et al. (1997). More information is available at the MacArthur Treatment Competence Study Archive (http://macarthur.virginia.edu/treatment.html). The use of the scales is also described by Grisso and Appelbaum (1998). The scales and manuals are available from Professional Resource Press, P.O. Box 3197, Sarasota, FL 34230 (1-800-443-3364; http://www.prpress.com).

"Competence" and "incompetence" are the common legal terms and so are used often in this discussion, but the term "capability" is often recommended by experts in mental health law—both because of its narrowed focus (e.g., the presence of a mental disability does not render one unable to make all decisions) and for its suggestion of empirical determination of such components as understanding decision-relevant information, appreciating the nature of one's own situation, reasoning with information, and expressing a choice. Bear in mind also that competence is not "all or nothing." A client may be competent to consent to some treatments and not to others; the latter may require resources the client does not possess, now or at any time, such as the ability to foresee specific or personal consequences. And lastly, the outcome of a choice, its harm to the client without adequate benefit, or its seeming irrationality (resulting in harms without balancing benefits or without adequate rationales) is unrelated to the competence to make the choice.

Competence is generally denied to minors, but local laws differ. A "minor" is usually anyone under 18 years of age. By law and presumption, minors cannot give consent or waive privilege, because they are considered to have children's minds and so are deemed unable to anticipate the consequences of their actions. Proxy consent must therefore be obtained from their parents or guardians. Residing with a minor does not assure legal custody or make an adult that minor's legal guardian, and being a parent does not assure the parent's legal status to consent. If you need consent for a minor, determine who can give it.

In order to reduce barriers to treatment of minors, there are some legal exceptions concerning their competence to consent to treatment. For example, minors can generally seek treatment for sexually transmitted diseases or pregnancy without parental consent. Some states have extended these exceptions to include drug and alcohol treatment and other diagnoses, or have allowed treatment in some settings. The tendency is to give more weight to the thinking abilities of older adolescents and less to those of younger adolescents. **You must know your local laws.**

### *Knowledge*

Note that knowledge has two aspects: (1) giving adequate information and (2) ensuring that the client understands it. We need to examine each aspect in turn. First, how much information needs to be disclosed? Must every *possible* effect be described?

Courts have held that we are required to disclose "the material information a reasonable person in the patient's position would want to know in order to make an informed decision," and some courts have added "the consequences of not consenting to the treatment procedures" (Simon & Shuman, 2006, p. 60). Reid (1999, pp. 27 and 77) suggests balancing significance and likelihood. Although rare or benign effects of treatment may not require discussion, the more dangerous or more common an effect is, the more weight and time its discussion will deserve. Haas and Malouf (2005) recommend that if you are in doubt, it is probably better to give information and thus support the autonomy of the client than to withhold it and be accused later of failing to support such autonomy. Making this decision is clearly subtle and complex in real-life practice, but some effort must be made toward achieving a balanced discussion with every client.

Full knowledge involves giving the information that a reasonable and prudent person would want to have before making a decision. This usually requires you as the therapist to explain the following:

❑ Your approach and your qualifications.

❑ All procedures to be used, and any changes of methods during treatment.

❑ The aims of treatment—both the long-term and the short-term or immediate goals.

❑ Discomforts to be expected (e.g., temporary increases in anxiety when confronting conflicts or denied or disregarded issues).

❑ Foreseeable negative consequences, or "harms." "The harms which concern rational persons are death; pain (physical and mental); various disabilities; and loss of freedom, opportunity, or pleasure" (Group for the Advancement of Psychiatry [GAP], 1990, p. 80). They may also include some side effects of treatment.

❑ The option of no treatment and its consequences.

❑ The anticipated benefits of this treatment.

❑ Alternative treatments. A useful guideline for alternatives is to ask yourself whether some very differently trained but fully competent therapist might suggest some other treatment in this situation (GAP, 1990, p. 81).

A discussion of clients' expectations as these relate to the points raised in the informed consent materials can be both informative and liberating. Such a discussion can clarify points about a client or a proposed course of therapy for you as well. O'Neill (1998, as quoted in Pope, n.d.) puts it this way:

> While most therapists recognize that negotiation can clear up clients' misconceptions, fewer recognize that negotiation is also a vehicle for clearing up the therapist's misconceptions. An open dialogue can make the therapist aware of features of the case that depart from both the therapist's model and his or her previous experience, and thus it serves as a corrective to the representativeness and availability biases.

Even though a more general informed consent to treatment was obtained early in treatment, if specialized techniques (such as biofeedback or hypnotherapy) are later introduced, additional informed consent seems necessary. Those who use paradoxical methods should proceed with caution; these methods raise some serious questions about consent and require a more extensive consent-getting process.

As mentioned above, the second requirement is that **the client must understand how the information applies to him or her** at the present time (GAP, 1990, p. 13). Low levels of literacy are common, and conversational ability is not a good indicator of the ability to understand and use written health information. You should consider the possibility of low literacy when clients have had fewer than 8 years of schooling; may have had lower-quality schooling; are members of any "minority" group; were imprisoned; have limiting chronic conditions; and/or have experienced repeated work failures. Obviously, these factors are not determinative. But bear in mind that about a third of the population will not understand (much less remember) common written materials in health care (National Center for Education Statistics, 2006).

Unless your clients are all college graduates, aim for a seventh- to eighth-grade reading level in your client materials. This is necessary for informedness. Microsoft Word and Office include readability tests, and others are available online (see, e.g., https://readability-score.com). Clear explanations of these tools are also available (http://blog.raventools.com/ultimate-list-of-online-content-readability-tests). Generally aim for a Flesch Reading Ease Score of 60–70; having a Flesch–Kincaid grade level below 8 is excellent.

To increase the client's understanding, remember these guidelines:

- Use simple, usually short, declarative sentences.

- Avoid jargon. Use ordinary words to describe special meanings, whether clinical, legal, or bureaucratic.

- Give explanations in "plain English" or a language the client understands sufficiently well for conducting therapy. Make special efforts if English is the client's second language, or if there are hearing or cultural barriers.

- Understanding may be enhanced by the use of analogies and metaphors or even case vignettes, but beware of the client's drawing unrealistic conclusions from the parallels between the client in the story and him- or herself. Visual aids and graphics such as Venn diagrams and flow charts may help explain how things have worked and will work in causal terms.

- Respect the client's levels of cognitive functioning (especially memory abilities). One pitfall is that information overload can prevent the obtaining of informed consent, perhaps as much as under-disclosure (Haas & Malouf, 2005).

- Communicate that any questions the client may have now or in the future will be answered whenever they occur.

- Ask questions that probe the client's understanding, in addition to inviting and answering his or her questions.

- Couch your risk–benefit statements to the client in terms like these (GAP, 1990, p. 10):
  - " . . . while no completely satisfactory statistics are available, [I] believe that this combination of treatments offers the best chance of success."
  - "The success rate of this treatment is about ____%. That is, about ____% of all clients receiving this treatment experience complete or substantial relief of their symptoms."

### Choosing Freely

Treating clients without their consent is one type of "paternalism"—that is, clinician behaviors that limit clients' autonomy (the right to decide for oneself) (see GAP, 1990, pp. 27–44). Freely choosing to be treated, or "voluntariness," requires that the consent must be free from coercion from negative consequences. There should be a clear absence of coercion on your part, but bear in mind that other people, as well as social reality, may exert coercion. Pressure is not the same as coercion; arguing forcefully for a course of action and voicing a degree of challenge may be quite appropriate at times (GAP, 1990, p. 82), especially when you believe that the client's best interests are not being attended to.

The other side of the coin is that the client must know that he or she can withdraw from treatment at any time without being punished or suffering any consequences other than the loss of any benefits derived from the treatment. If there are other negative consequences, they must be described fully.

Clients (except children) can, of course, refuse treatments. When appropriate, document a client's **"informed refusal"** or noncompliance (with your advice, recommended treatments, consultations, workups) and any nonrecommended client actions. In private practice, you can (and perhaps should) discharge a client for refusal to adhere to your best treatment recommendations.

### Documentation

All of this therapist–client communication and rapport usually lead to the signing of a form, but the form cannot substitute for the interpersonal process of gaining informed consent. The form is not itself the consent; it is at best, the public written evidence of the discussion and agreement. The APA code of ethics (APA, 2010) requires that "Psychologists appropriately document written or oral consent, permission, and assent" (Standard 3.10d). If you do not get a signed form, you must carefully document in your notes what you have told the client about treatment, to demonstrate that you have indeed obtained informed consent and why you did not get written consent.

If you cannot obtain consent before beginning treatment, document the reason why not (e.g., emergency, incompetence/proxy consent, court-ordered treatment, etc.) The APA ethics code (APA, 2010) recognizes this issue and details responses in Standard 3.10b. When "consent" does not apply, this kind of agreement is termed "assent." Consent forms can include clinically valuable leverage, as noted by Beahrs and Gutheil (2001): "Optimally, they also should mention the necessary role of clients' self-therapeutic activity, which in certain cases can be elaborated to include voluntary abstinence from specific problem-maintaining behaviors such as abuse of controlled substances" (p. 8).

## Informed Consent in Three Steps

We reiterate that a signed form, by itself, is not a guarantee that informed consent has been obtained. Vaccarino (1978) has reported that "legal actions for lack of informed consent have been brought despite the existence of a signed consent form" (p. 455). He emphasizes that **consenting is an interpersonal, face-to-face, rapport-based, continual discussion process, and not a mechanical, paper-based one.** Furthermore, studies of medical patients given written consent forms suggest that at best 60% of the information is retained, and so the discussion process is essential (Grunder, 1980; Ley, 1982).

How can you be sure you have obtained fully informed consent? The following three-step process offers the best procedures.

**The first step is to have discussions covering the issues,** because discussion is the foundation of informedness. Use your memory—or, better, one of the following—as a basis for the topics to cover in your discussion:

- The topics covered in the client information brochure (see Section 5.2).

- The questions in "Information You Have a Right to Know" (see Section 5.3).

- The contents of clients' rights statements (see Section 5.4).

- The contents of treatment contracts (see Section 5.5).

- A checklist made up from any of the materials above and your own understanding and ideas about the nature of your treatment, the context of treatment, and the client as an individual.

**The second step is to document the client's agreement** with one (or, in complex situations, both) of the following:

1.  A signed consent form. Use one of these:
    - The client information brochure (see Section 5.2).
    - A treatment agreement or contract (see Section 5.5).
    - Consent-to-treatment forms (see Section 5.6).
2.  Your notes concerning each of the relevant issues. The notes must document the following about both the discussions and the client's consent:

- That you and the client discussed all the relevant issues (for informedness).
- That you answered all the client's questions to the client's satisfaction (again for informedness).
- That the client signed the form voluntarily.
- That the client was competent to consent. Perhaps use a statement such as this: "In my professional judgment, and after interacting with the client for _____ minutes, observing his or her behavior, and noting his or her responsive discussion of many topics, I found no reason to suspect that the client was not competent to consent to treatment."

**The third step is to keep the discussions about your treatment and their documentation ongoing.** This is especially important when there are difficulties or when you change the treatments you offer.

### The Five Paths to Informed Consent

Now we come to the subject matter the client is to be informed about. The lists below contain what we believe to be the most important items, but a few cautions are in order. First, while we have, as you will see, incorporated many, many issues, each clinician's work setting will raise a few more. Your board's rules, state's legal decisions, payment methods, and client characteristics, among others factors, should be used to modify the list. Second, we do not incorporate here HIPAA's required NPP, because it is complex and must be tailored to each practice. The NPP is covered in Section 6.4. Third, the contents offered in one method or path are not duplicated in all others, and so before following the path you prefer, please skim the others for any relevant points. Fourth, some states or disciplines require you to furnish clients with a brochure often entitled "Disclosure Statement" or "Informed Consent." The paths below are not substitutes for these legally required documents, but additions with more detail and specifics. Lastly, we encourage you to develop your own additional client education materials to expand on issues of particular relevance, such as confidentiality or insurance payments.

The remainder of this chapter offers five methods for conducting the informed consenting process. In essence, they are five differing *paths* to fully informed consent. These are (1) giving and discussing a client information brochure; (2) offering clients a list of questions to guide discussion (here called "Information You Have a Right to Know"); (3) offering a list of clients' rights as a basis for discussion; (4) using a psychotherapy treatment contract; and (5) using a consent-to-treatment form.

## 5.2   The First Path to Informed Consent: The Client Information Brochure

### Kinds of Brochures

There are at least three kinds of brochures in wide use. Each serves a different purpose—namely, to market your practice; to educate clients on conditions and procedures; and to initiate clients into, and assure informed consent for, therapy. The marketing brochure, for example, could be the core of a package mailed or emailed to potential referrers. (See Chapter 9 for more on marketing.) Table 5.1 offers a more detailed description of each brochure type and distinguishes their contents. We avoid the ambiguous term "practice brochure," because it describes only some aspects of the practice.

In this section, we describe in detail the third type, the client information brochure. This brochure needs to be as comprehensive and protective as possible, in order to achieve the purposes listed in Table 5.1. It is a social contract, the formalization of a unique human relationship; as such, **it is the core document of therapy.** It establishes the boundaries of your way of practicing—what you will do and won't do. It initiates and structures your relationship with the client, which is the medium of therapy. And it is a legal and ethical contract creating, when the client has read and understood it, the fundamental informed consent.

Beyond these purposes, this document can enhance the process of therapy. Based on open exchange, it models an ongoing negotiation process between persons with recognized rights. Transparent collaboration with an informed client facilitates the trust needed for therapy. The brochure can also help correct client misconceptions. Clients typically enter treatment with fantasies and erroneous beliefs; if these are not addressed, they could hinder therapy. The client information brochure permits identification and handling of these issues earlier, and in a manner divorced from later emotional contexts. Finally, this document serves to "socialize" or introduce clients into the procedures and expectations of therapists.

## How to Use the Model Client Information Brochure

After some introduction, we offer an exhaustive model client information brochure. It attempts to include the full range of topics, not all of which may be relevant to your practice. It is designed to allow you to create a comprehensive and detailed brochure suited for your own practice, in just an hour or two of editing the electronic version. Spending the time to tailor a brochure to your work will be a good investment, both ethically and professionally. Even weighing the parts you decide are inessential can raise your awareness.

**TABLE 5.1. Types and Purposes of Brochures Used in Psychotherapy**

| Type | Purpose | Possible contents |
|---|---|---|
| Marketing brochure | Describing your services in a very positive light so as to attract new clients.<br><br>This type of brochure is discussed more fully in Chapter 9 on marketing. | Your credentials, experience, and specialties; addresses, ways to reach you, office hours, and so on; may also include testimonials (from former clients), maps, photographs of your building, office, and the like. |
| Topical brochure | Teaching and telling clients about individual clinical topics (e.g., diagnoses and treatments). This is called "patient education" in medical settings. | Treatable conditions and the methods and benefits of therapy; health insurance's costs and rules; medications; child development and schooling; and many other common concerns. |
| Client information brochure | Assuring informed consent; demonstrating conformance to ethical and legal standards; creating a therapeutic alliance and rapport; reducing malpractice risks; socializing clients into therapy; modeling openness; and so on. | Office procedures, such as intake, financial arrangements, appointments, clinical records, and the release of records. Also, your professional qualifications, the nature of therapy, appropriate goals, treatment planning, and assessment of progress. |

This brochure is highly detailed, so as to be legally and ethically correct. It is written in standard U.S. grammar and word choice to make it widely applicable. Terms unfamiliar to the average client are explained in language the client can understand. We have chosen a personal "I" style over an institutional, passive voice or a formal "we" version. You may prefer one of the other two; choose what feels most comfortable for you, but be consistent across all your documents.

You can change the format or margins, and add suitable wording to tailor it to your working methods, your locality, your clients, and your understanding of your practice. Here we call the model brochure "Information for Clients," but alternative titles include "Welcome to the Psychological Practice of [Name]," "Introduction to the [Name] Clinic," or "New Client Introductory Information." Others might prefer "Starting Our Work Together" or "How I Do Therapy."

Having the brochure conveniently available on your computer is advantageous, because you can then print or email copies when needed, revise the versions on your website, and update it as your practice evolves. To keep versions clear, add a creation date somewhere. As a rule, when you find yourself telling three clients the same information, you should probably add it to your version of the brochure.

We recommend the use of a client information brochure as the most comprehensive method for getting informed consent. However, the use of even a very complete brochure has some drawbacks:

- There is no way to be certain that a client has understood what he or she has read, or even that the client has read all of the brochure, unless you open a discussion.

- Risks and alternative treatments for an individual's particular difficulties are very difficult to convey in a generic, prepared document.

- The client has effectively lost the right to refuse information.

- Most of these brochures require too high a level of psychological sophistication and reading skill to assure understanding. Therefore, it is worth considering the alternative methods or paths presented later.

## The Model Client Information Brochure

The model brochure now begins, with our suggested wordings set off in a different font than the rest of the text and on a gray background. The headings and most of the subheadings below can be used in your own brochure. As you will see, our comments and suggestions are interwoven throughout. On the CD you will find the Sample Client Information Brochure, without the comments, so it is easier for you to customize.

### INFORMATION FOR CLIENTS

Welcome to my practice. I appreciate your giving me the opportunity to be of help to you.

This brochure answers some questions that clients often ask about therapy. I believe that our work will be most helpful to you when you have a clear idea of what we are trying to do.

This brochure talks about the following:

- What will be the goals of therapy?
- What are my methods of treatment?
- How long might therapy take?
- What are the risks and benefits of therapy?
- How much do my services cost, and how do I handle money matters?
- What are some other important concerns?

After you read this brochure, we can talk together about how these issues apply to you. This brochure is yours to keep. Please read all of it. Mark any parts that are not clear to you. Write down any questions you have, so we can discuss them at our next meeting. When you have read and fully understood this brochure, I will ask you to sign it at the end. I will sign it as well and make a copy, so we each have one.

### About Psychotherapy

I strongly believe that you should feel comfortable with the therapist you choose and hopeful about the therapy. When you feel this way, therapy is more likely to be most helpful to you. Let me describe how I see therapy.

My theoretical approach is based on . . .

The most central ideas in my work are . . .

The methods or techniques I use most are . . .

In the blank spaces in this part of the brochure, you should create a general statement about therapy as you see it. Tailor your statement to your conception of the nature and value of your services. It can include the general aims appropriate to therapy as you understand it. Include your model of working with clients (e.g., collaboration, education, problem solving, solution focus, insight into dysfunctional patterns, acceptance and commitment, relearning through transference, body work, etc.). It is also appropriate to describe, under a separate heading, other services you offer (such as consulting with the client's primary care provider [PCP] or a child's teachers, court testimony, relationship counseling, or psychological assessment, etc.) and their costs. If these service descriptions become quite detailed, you should make them into separate handouts. Services you do *not* offer can also be specified, such as custody evaluations for therapy clients.

It may be useful to indicate, if applicable, that you are not a physician (or "medical doctor," not just the ambiguous "doctor"), and so you do not use physical interventions such as medications, massage, herbs, injections, surgery, or electroshock. Psychologists, psychotherapists, and counselors should find ways of clearly but not pejoratively distinguishing themselves from psychiatrists. You can indicate that when medications are appropriate, you will work closely with the client's PCP or other prescribers. It may be helpful in discussing medical care to evaluate the client's attitude toward psychotropic medications. Irrational fears, overly optimistic expectations, and general ignorance (e.g., "chemical imbalance") are widespread; having information about your client's thoughts (from a discussion of your brochure or from responses on your intake forms) may usefully guide later treatment.

### Addressing Values

Hare-Mustin et al. (1979) suggest specifying and elaborating on any technique that might be at odds with clients' values. For example, if you do relationship counseling, you might indicate your views on divorce as a response to marital distress, or make it clear that your obligation is to the mental and emotional health of the individuals, not to the relationship. If your treatment methods are experimental or even controversial, you should make this section even more detailed or prepare a special consent form.

Because psychiatrists are the least religious of medical specialists (and psychologists are not likely to be very different), a gap in religiousness between a client and clinician is not uncommon (Curlin et al., 2007). An aspect of fully informed consent arises when you are asked whether you do "Christian counseling" or have "Christian values." It is both ethically appropriate and potentially therapeutic to clarify what the client expects before you reply. The caller may be seeking a Bible-based therapy (involving praying together, references to Bible stories, the teachings of Jesus, etc.). This is pastoral counseling, and you should either be so qualified or refer the client if he or she is uninterested in therapy based on secular theories, principles, or research. McMinn et al. (2010) helpfully and briefly clarify the several approaches of Christian counselors and trace the implications for psychologists, as well as offering focused resources.

For those of us who are psychologists, there are several concerns in discussing "Christian values." First, we have an ethical requirement to respect the values of others (Principle E of the APA ethics code; APA, 2010). Second, because value-free therapy does not exist, we must make our own values and beliefs clear to clients from the beginning, so that clients can give informed consent to treatment. Third, we have an ethical requirement for cultural competence (Principle E). It seems clear that evangelical or especially devout Christians constitute subcultures, so we must have the same level of cultural competence we require for working with other special populations. Lastly, the research shows that therapy is more successful when the client and therapist share more expectations. This suggests the benefits of exploring values early in the therapy process.

The following is the way ELZ's brochure describes his approach, its central ideas, and its goals to clients:

> The type of therapy I do is called "rational–emotive behavior therapy," or REBT. It was developed by Albert Ellis, PhD, and is described in his dozens of books and hundreds of professional articles.
>
> We often believe that our actions and feelings are caused by what happens in the real world. However, this is not quite true. When we have any kind of experience, it does not affect us directly. Instead, we first give it a meaning through our beliefs about it. For example, if I hear a sound in the kitchen and believe that it is made by my wife, I am not bothered at all. But if I believe that I am alone in the house, the same sound can bother me a great deal. Here we see that my feelings and actions about the sound come from my own thinking and my adding a meaning to the actual event (the sound).

Dr. Ellis separates beliefs into two kinds: "rational" beliefs, or ones based on reality and logic, and "irrational" beliefs, or ones based on false or unrealistic ideas. When we have irrational beliefs, we suffer from strong negative emotions (like rage, depression, and anxiety). When we act on the basis of irrational beliefs, our actions are often not effective and can be harmful. If we have rational beliefs, we will feel the milder versions of the negative emotions (like irritation, sadness, and concern); we will experience more of the positive emotions (like pleasure, hope, and joy); and our behaviors will be more effective.

My approach to helping people with their problems is an educational one. Anyone can learn to recognize irrational beliefs, challenge and argue with them, and replace them with more rational beliefs. This is what I mean by an educational approach. We can, with practice, unlearn irrational beliefs and become happier persons who function better in the world.

I want you to become able to use REBT without me. I will encourage you to learn more about what methods are used in REBT, how well it works, and what possible problems or side effects it may have. I can lend you books and articles that explain how it works. Please return them when you no longer need them, so I can lend them to other clients. I may also give you copies of articles or handouts that are yours to keep.

You may want to include the URLs of websites that explain and document your methods. This is not only educational, but supports therapeutic optimism and client motivation. For example, the National Association of Cognitive-Behavioral Therapists has a three-page overview suitable for clients (http://www.nacbt.org/whatiscbt.htm). A description of emotionally focused therapy is also available online (http://www.iceeft.com/index.php/about-us/what-is-eft). The Gottman Institute provides descriptions of marital/couple therapy (http://www.gottman.com/marriage-couples). You probably should include links to sites like these on your own website.

I usually take notes during our meetings. You may find it useful to take your own notes, to remember important points or the steps you plan to take. You may also wish to take notes outside the office.

By the end of our first or second session, I will tell you how I see your case at this point and how I think we should proceed. I view therapy as a partnership between us. You define the problem areas to be worked on; I use my specialized knowledge to help you make the changes you want to make. Psychotherapy is not like visiting a medical doctor for a shot. It requires your very active involvement. It requires your best efforts to change thoughts, feelings, and behaviors. For example, I will expect you to tell me about important experiences, what they meant to you, and what strong feelings were involved. This is one of the ways you are an active partner in therapy.

I expect us to plan our work together. In our treatment plan, we will list the areas to work on, our goals, the methods we will use, the time and money commitments we will make, and some other things. I expect us to agree on a plan that we will both work hard to follow. From time to time, we will look together at our progress and goals. If we think we need to, we can then change our treatment plan, its goals, or its methods.

An important part of your therapy will be practicing new skills that you will learn in our sessions. I will ask you to practice outside our meetings, and we will work together to set up homework assignments for you. I might ask you to do exercises, keep records, and read to deepen your understanding. You will probably have to work on relationships in your life and make long-term efforts to get the best results. These are important parts of personal change. Change will sometimes be easy and quick, but more often it will be slow and difficult and will need repetitions, and so you will need to keep trying. There are no instant, painless cures and no "magic pills" for changing well-learned habits. However, you *can* learn new ways of looking at your problems that will be very helpful for changing your feelings and reactions.

### How Long Therapy Might Take

Those new to therapy have little accurate knowledge of what it involves and are likely to have much misinformation from the mass media. Sandra L. Ceren, PhD, of Del Mar, CA, tells her clients this:

> "No one can estimate how long it will take for you to achieve benefit. Some people come away from some sessions without feeling they have gained, but later on things begin to fit into place. Others gain from the start. Some take a few steps forward, then retreat. It is not unusual to resist making changes. After all, you have been the way you are for a long time."

The research on the duration of therapy is extensive. While the modal number of sessions has long been precisely 1, the average appears to be 7–8 sessions; this number may be sufficient for clarification, advice, directions, and support, which is all many clients may expect. Well-informed clients may stay longer. A recent review of research (Swift et al., 2012) using a risk–benefit model indicates that most clients get the most benefit from 18–20 sessions.

Most of my clients see me once a week for 3–5 months. After that, we meet less often for several more months. Therapy then usually comes to an end. The process of ending therapy, called "termination," can be a very valuable part of our work and well worth spending our time on. Stopping therapy should not be done casually, although either of us may decide to end it if we believe it is in your best interest. If you wish to stop therapy at any time, I ask that you agree now to meet then for at least one more session, to review our work together. We will review our goals, the work we have done, any future work that needs to be done, and our options. If you would like to take a "time out" from therapy to try it on your own, we should discuss this. We can often design such a "time out" to be more helpful.

KK asks clients on her intake form how many sessions they expect they will need to resolve their problem, and incorporates this information into the informed consent and assessment process. She then regularly checks with her clients about where they are in their goals and vision for treatment, and will tell clients when they may need longer to meet those goals. This process supports both an informed and collaborative exploration if longer-term work is desirable, and a clear conversation about the new goals that emerge.

### The Risks and Benefits of Therapy

As with any powerful treatment, there are some risks as well as many benefits of therapy. You should think about both the benefits and risks when making any treatment decisions. For example, in therapy there is a risk that clients will, for a time, have uncomfortable levels of sadness, guilt, anxiety, anger, frustration, loneliness, helplessness, or other negative feelings. Clients may recall unpleasant memories. These feelings or memories may bother them for a while. A few uninformed people in the community may mistakenly view anyone in therapy as weak, or perhaps as seriously disturbed or even dangerous. Also, clients in therapy may have problems with people important to them, like relatives and peers. Family secrets may be told. Therapy may disrupt a marital or couple relationship, and may even lead to a separation or divorce. Sometimes, too, a client's problems may worsen after the beginning of treatment. Risks like these are temporary and should be expected when people are making important changes in their lives. Finally, even with our best efforts, there is a risk that therapy may not work out as you would like. All of these should be weighed against the costs of not changing and continuing as you are.

KK tells clients this in her brochure:

During the initial evaluation or the course of therapy, you may remember unpleasant events, and experience considerable discomfort, such as strong feelings, anxiety, depression, and insomnia. I may challenge some of your assumptions or propose different ways of thinking about or handling situations. This may cause you to feel upset, angry, or disappointed. Attempting to resolve issues that brought you into therapy may result in changes that you did not originally intend. Psychotherapy may result in decisions to change behaviors, employment, substance use, schooling, housing, or relationships. Change can sometimes be quick and easy, but more often it can be gradual and even frustrating. There is no guarantee that psychotherapy will yield positive or intended results.

A risk–benefit statement can be written to encourage efforts by emphasizing the collaborative nature of therapy: Therapy's success is a result of efforts by both therapist and client.

Psychotherapy is known to harm a not insubstantial number of clients. It may be educational to become familiar with some of this literature (Dimidijian & Hollon, 2010; Barlow, 2010; Lillenfeld, 2007); with client guidelines such as those by Aimes (2011); and with some websites (e.g., http://www.therapyabuse.org and the list and comments at http://www.goodtherapy.org/blog/warning-signs-of-bad-therapy).

The benefits of therapy are extensively documented and can be the scientific basis both of our work and of what we tell clients.

While you consider these risks, you should know also that many benefits of therapy have been shown by scientists in hundreds of well-designed research studies. Most clients will find their symptoms greatly lessened, will feel more confident and relaxed, and will improve their daily functioning. People who are depressed may find their mood lifting. Other clients may no longer feel afraid, angry, or anxious. In therapy, people have a chance to talk things out fully until their feelings are relieved or the problems are resolved. Clients' relationships and coping skills can improve greatly. They may get more satisfaction out of social and family relationships. Their personal goals and values may become clearer. They may grow in many directions—as persons, in their close relationships, in their work or schooling, and in the ability to enjoy their lives.

I do not take on clients I do not think I can help. Therefore, I will enter our relationship with optimism about our progress.

You might also want to cite Martin Seligman's (1995) *Consumer Reports* research on the effectiveness of psychotherapy, which is quite readable. A summary of Seligman's study has been written for clients by Larry M. Friedberg (http://www.drlarryfriedberg.com/psychotherapy-works). Additional evidence of the effectiveness of psychological interventions can be harvested from Kenneth S. Pope's list of more than 150 recently published meta-analyses (http://www.kspope.com/hospices/meta-analyses.php). A 30-page booklet reviewing the literature, *The Efficacy and Effectiveness of Psychological Treatments,* is available (http://www.cpa.ca/docs/File/Practice/TheEfficacyAndEffectivenessOfPsychologicalTreatments_web.pdf).

In your description of the benefits of psychotherapy (either orally or in writing), be careful not to promise a cure or benefits so substantial that they approach a problem-free future. Realistically, do not promise even a specific outcome. We are not in control of all or even most of the factors determining our clients' outcomes, and we especially do not wish to cause disappointment. However, recommending (even energetically) is not insisting and is not coercion, so don't be shy about the therapy you offer.

To fully inform a client and support choice, you should discuss **alternative treatments** to your preferred methods. This is difficult for most of us to do fairly or comfortably, but practice helps. Also, the major alternatives are medications. You might want to review the literature on the limited effectiveness, high costs, and adverse short- and long-term effects of psychiatric medications. There are book-length examinations, such as those by Whitaker (2010a, 2010b) and Kirsch (2011). That said, be aware that there are times when medications can be appropriate complements to psychological treatment, and knowing when to refer a client for a medication evaluation is essential.

Try to present alternative treatments even-handedly for two reasons: (1) to present yourself as truly having the client's best interests at heart; and (2) to keep the client from thinking that, because you are discussing other helping programs so enthusiastically, you do not really want to work with the client (Hare-Mustin et al., 1979).

Formal assessments or testing may be helpful to therapy and may be required for some external purposes, so some notice of these should be included in your brochure. For a consent form for assessment or testing, see Section 5.7.

Psychological assessment (with or without administering tests) can increase our understanding of your personality, psychological dynamics, intellectual and emotional resources, or other areas, and so it may help us design or improve your therapy. If this seems beneficial, I will discuss it with you and get your consent before proceeding.

### Consultations

Depending on your practice, you might indicate that you sometimes will suggest the need for psychological, educational, or vocational testing; for medication evaluation and prescription; or for other therapies. If you are likely to refer clients to other professionals for services such as nutrition evaluation and counseling, exercise or martial arts training, vocational guidance, cosmetic surgery for scars or deformities, credit counseling, shelters and protection agencies, or the like, this would be a good place to describe those options briefly as well. You might indicate that you will discuss any approximate costs of such assessments and treatments and your usual arrangements for these referrals. Do not accept fees for making (or receiving) such referrals because they would create possible conflict between your financial interests and the best services for the client's needs.

> If you could benefit from a treatment I cannot provide, I will help you to get it. You have a right to ask me about such other treatments, their risks, and their benefits. Based on what I learn about your problems, I may recommend a medical exam or use of medication. If I do this, I will fully discuss my reasons with you, so that you can decide what is best. If you are treated by another professional, I will coordinate my services with him or her and with your own medical doctor if you want me to.

### What to Expect from Our Relationship

Sam Knapp, EdD, of Harrisburg, PA, offers the following wording in his brochure as an introduction to this topic:

> Psychological services are best provided in an atmosphere of trust. You expect me to be honest with you about your problems and progress. I expect you to be honest with me about your expectations for services, your compliance with medication, and any other barriers to treatment.

The wording of this section of the brochure (both here and on the CD) reflects our own professional status as psychologists; tailor it to your own discipline as appropriate.

> As a professional, I will use my best knowledge and skills to help you. This includes following the standards of the American Psychological Association, or APA. In your best interests, the APA puts limits on the relationship between a therapist and a client, and I will abide by these. Let me explain these limits, so you will understand that they don't apply just to you and me.
>
> First, I am licensed and trained to practice psychology—not law, medicine, finance, or any other profession. I am not able to give you good advice from these other professional viewpoints.
>
> Second, state laws and the rules of the APA require me to keep what you tell me confidential (that is, just between us). You can trust me not to tell anyone else what you tell me, except in a few unusual situations. I explain what those are in the "About Confidentiality" section of this brochure. For example, I try not to reveal who are my clients. This is part of my effort to maintain your privacy. If we meet on the street or socially, I may not say hello or talk to you at all. I am not ignoring you; it is a way to maintain the confidentiality of our relationship.

In the paragraph above, it would be appropriate to add any rules you have that the client might inadvertently break or misinterpret. For example, some therapists have a rule never to touch a client, mainly to avoid miscommunication. Or you may have a rule that you will examine the client's motivations for any expressions of racism or sexism. Such clarifications are especially useful for clients with histories of abuse or manipulation.

### Exclusion from Legal Proceedings

It is possible that a client or couple that you see may become involved in a lawsuit in the future. If a custody battle or other legal situation develops, it is likely that lawyers will attempt to obtain your records and/or testimony. Serving in both a therapeutic and a forensic role creates a dual relationship with conflicting priorities and mixed obligations. The APA code of ethics (APA, 2010, Standard 10.02b) suggests that you address this point. You can add the paragraph below to your brochure (it is included on the CD). For more on this point, see the part of Section 5.6 about Form 5.7, and the discussion about Handout 8.1 in Chapter 8.

> If you ever become involved in a divorce or custody dispute, or any other legal matters (such as a lawsuit over injuries), I want you to understand and agree that I will not provide my records, or evaluations, depositions, or testimony in court. There are several reasons for this: (1) I may not possess the professional skills to make decisions about issues besides those we deal with in therapy; (2) therapy often involves full disclosure of information that you might not want to have revealed in court; (3) if you are holding back information because of that fear, our work will not be as productive as it could be; (4) my statements will be seen as biased in your favor because we have a therapy relationship; and (5) what I might say in testifying or being deposed might change our therapy relationship, and I must put that relationship first. If you want custody evaluations and recommendations, I will be happy to refer you to those with this expertise.

Serving as both a therapist and a forensic expert is usually counterproductive, and we strongly recommend avoiding it. Steve Eichel, PhD, of Newark, DE, suggests adding the following clarifications to your contract form, and we quote it here with his kind permission:

> I, the parent, am aware that requesting the release of treatment notes or plans, reports, or evaluations (which you made as this child's therapist) for forensic purposes (such as in separation, divorce, or custody actions), or subpoenaing them or your testimony about the content of my child's treatment, will interfere with the therapy relationship so necessary for progress and so will greatly jeopardize my child's health and well-being. Therefore, I knowingly and freely waive my right to request the release of information (beyond the attendance, dates, and length of our meetings, and your charges) to my attorney or any other officer of the court. I understand that release of clinically significant information to any officer of the court shall only be in response to a court order signed by a duly appointed judge.

A potential problem with such a blanket agreement is that the records have not yet been created, and so the client cannot provide informed consent to withholding or releasing their unknown contents. However, even requiring clients to read a statement like this puts them on notice if they were contemplating using your therapy in a legal conflict. Their subsequent asking about it may be revealing.

A therapist who has an agreement from the parents not to involve the therapist or request his or her notes in litigation will have to contend with HIPAA's perspective that the client owns the content of the records, not the therapist, and that all releases of information

(ROIs) allow for the client to control the release of records—meaning that a client can change his or her mind about releasing or withholding records.

Our reluctance to go into court because of the pain this can cause us should not be the primary reason to ask clients not to drag us and our records in. Balancing the costs and benefits of our ethical obligations is part of our work. For example, the welfare of a child may indeed be furthered by our records' information, and this information may be unavailable from any other source, may confirm or deny a parent's allegations of violence or drug use, or may contradict a parent's statements about a child's feelings about a situation. Experienced custody evaluators report that judges are quite willing to support a psychologist's request to keep a child's therapy notes confidential, despite lawyers' requests. They appear to recognize the necessity of supporting a child's confidentiality for therapy.

### Social Gatherings and Gift Giving

You might also want to add more specific information on the following points to your client brochure (these statements are also included in the Sample Client Information Brochure on the CD):

> Even though you might invite me, I will not attend your family gatherings, such as parties or weddings.
>
> As your therapist, I will not celebrate holidays or give you gifts. I may not notice or recall your birthday and may not receive any of your gifts eagerly.

Haas and Malouf (2005) offer excellent guidelines on the subject of gift receiving: Express positive and caring feelings; do not immediately process the giving clinically; suggest an alternative (such as a gift to charity); and relax about most of these situations.

### About Confidentiality

The section of the client information brochure on confidentiality is one of crucial legal concern. The APA ethics code (APA, 2010, Standard 4.02) requires that the limits of confidentiality be communicated explicitly and in advance to all clients (both clinical and organizational). It requires that you discuss the limits of confidentiality at the beginning of treatment and as new circumstances warrant. The HIPAA Privacy Rule requires that you immediately furnish clients with an NPP, which is all about privacy (see Section 6.4 for more on this form). Several states, including Colorado and Massachusetts, require therapists to furnish a handout to each client explaining the limits of confidentiality, so this section of the brochure addresses this issue in detail. You might want to provide selected clients with a separate handout concerning only this issue; see Section 8.1 for such a handout and for more information.

> I will treat with great care all the information you share with me. It is your legal right that our sessions and my records about you be kept private. That is why I ask you to sign a "release-of-records" form before I can talk about you or send my records about you to anyone else. In general, I will tell no one what you tell me. I will not even let anyone know that you are in treatment with me without your agreement.

In all but a few rare situations, your confidentiality (that is, the privacy of what you tell me) is protected by federal and state laws and by the rules of my profession. Here are the most likely situations where your confidentiality is *not* protected:

1. If you were sent to me by a court or an employer for evaluation or treatment, the court or employer expects a report from me. If this is your situation, please talk with me before you tell me anything you do not want the court or your employer to know. You have a right to tell me only what you are comfortable telling.

2. Are you suing someone or being sued? Are you charged with a crime? If so, and if you tell the court that you are seeing me, I may then be ordered to show the lawyers my records. Please talk to your lawyer about what to say to me.

3. If you make a serious threat to harm yourself or another person, the law requires me to try to protect you or that other person. I simply cannot promise never to tell others about threats you make.

4. If I believe that a child, older adult, or other dependent person has been or will be abused or neglected, I am legally required to report this to the authorities.

Under the second exception above, you might consider noting that your records may be brought into divorce, custody, or adoption proceedings (this is important if you see couples or families), or into any other legal case in which a judge decides that a client's mental or emotional condition is an important element. Disability cases and workers' compensation hearings usually require release of our complete records, and civil and criminal cases may do so as well.

In the fourth exception above, we use the phrase "If I believe that a child. . . . " State laws about **mandated reporting** differ in their language; you must know the rules that apply to you. The word "believe" may not be accurate in your state. For example, in jurisdictions where the legal criterion is "what a reasonable person would suspect," this means that the level of evidence required for reporting is lower than in jurisdiction where the law says "believe." Moreover, note that a therapist is not expected or required to investigate or validate allegations of abuse; only suspicion or belief is necessary for a report. This is not a judgment call, but a legal demand placed on therapists to protect children and other vulnerable persons by a society that values such protection more than confidentiality. You must know your local rules. You might post a copy of the law in your waiting room, as suggested by David Clovard, MD, of Raleigh, NC, so as to try to prevent a client's unknowing disclosure (which you would then have to act upon). Incidentally, therapists are not under legal obligation to report past crimes disclosed to them, although they may have a moral or societal duty. Mandated reporting laws usually include some protections for the reporter from prosecution for breaking confidentiality, mistaken reporting ("in good faith"), and other retaliations, but they vary in protecting the reporter's identity and may not apply to those in independent practice. Know your local laws. A useful discussion and listing of some states' rules can be found online (https://www.childwelfare.gov/topics/responding/reporting/mandated/examples), but you will need to know your state's exact language and expectations. You can search two other sites for these (http://www.ndaa.org/pdf/Mandatory%20Reporting%20of%20Child%20Abuse%20and%20Neglect-nov2012.pdf and http://www.ncsl.org/research/human-services/child-abuse-and-neglect-reporting-statutes.aspx).

An alternative phrasing for the third and fourth exceptions above is this:

> As a therapist, my legal and moral duty is to protect your confidentiality, but I also have a duty under the law to the wider community and to myself if there is harm, threat of harm, or threat of neglect.

Obviously, you need to tailor the confidentiality section of your brochure to your specific situation. For example, does your state have other exceptions to confidentiality besides those listed above? Be sure as well to modify this statement in light of your title, your profession's legal status, the state in which you practice, and the type of therapy you are doing. For example, if you see clients for neuropsychology or rehabilitation, and your state requires you to notify it of impaired drivers, you should indicate this rule.

### Ground Rules for Minors and Parents

If you see children, you should set the ground rules with minors and their parents before therapy.

> Parents and/or guardians with legal custody can be told about their child's diagnoses, the counseling methods used and recommended, significant safety concerns, and the progress of treatment, either as needed or when requested.

See also Forms 5.2 and 5.3 for treatment contracts for minors, and Form 5.6 for a consent-to-treatment form for a child.

### Covering Colleagues and Consultations

Below are statements about confidentiality when you consult and when a colleague covers for your vacations or other absences from practice. Your practice might require a different or fuller statement, so see Handout 8.1.

> There are two times when I might talk about you with another therapist. I ask you now to understand and agree to let me do this in these two times.
>
> First, when I am away from the office for a few days, a trusted fellow therapist will be available to you in emergencies. He or she will need to know some things about your situation. Of course, this therapist has the same laws and rules as I do to protect your confidentiality.

Your "covering" colleague may need information on and plans for handling clients with serious problems. Also have your colleague document any calls received and actions taken, and have him or her send this documentation to you for your case files. It is probably best never to be completely unreachable, but you cannot provide all services from a distance, so carefully document your thinking, decision making, and actions in an emergency. As usual, "Think out loud for the record" is the relevant rule. Save your travel documentation (such as tickets and hotel receipts) for a while as self-protection in case a malpractice problem develops.

> Second, I sometimes talk with other therapists or other professionals about my clients, because it helps me to provide high-quality treatment. These professionals are also required to keep your information private. I maintain your privacy with them. I never tell them your name, I change or skip some facts about you, and I tell only what they need to know to understand your situation and help me.

An alternative phrasing for consultation is offered by Constance Fischer, PhD, of Pittsburgh, PA:

> We consult with colleagues and specialists about our ongoing work. This pursuit of quality assurance never involves your name or any specifics through which you might be identified.

The brochure then goes on to cover recordings:

> For the purpose of these consultations, I may want to make audio or video recordings of our sessions. I will review the recordings with my consultant to assist with your treatment. I will ask your permission to make any recording. I promise to destroy each recording as soon as I no longer need it, or, at the latest, when I destroy your case records. You can refuse to allow this recording, or can insist that the recording be edited.

You might add information about how you will protect this electronic protected health information (EPHI) under HIPAA. Relatedly, Form 5.8 is a consent form for electronically recording sessions and using them or other data for research or teaching.

While HIPAA allows the sharing of PHI with other clinicians without any other consent beyond the initial NPP, state laws and licensing boards are often more restrictive. Clients may also object, and they have some ability under HIPAA to restrict the sharing of their information (see below). If in doubt, complete an ROI form so that all the facts are clear.

> If your records need to be seen by another professional, or anyone else, I will discuss this with you. If you agree to share these records, you will need to sign a release-of-information form. This form says exactly what information is to be shared, with whom, and why. You may read this form at any time. If you have questions, please ask me.

Knapp (1992b) has made a number of suggestions about communicating with a client's PCP, both in general and when the client is a Medicare client. He suggests discussing the desirability of notifying the PCP, doing so in the most efficient way, and documenting this in the chart. If the client has refused, note this and the reasons offered. Knapp (1992b, p. 7) suggests this wording for your brochure:

> It may be beneficial for me to confer with your primary care physician *(sic)* with regard to your psychological treatment or to discuss any medical problems for which you are receiving treatment. In addition, Medicare requires that I notify your physician, by telephone or in writing, concerning services that are being provided by me unless you request that notification not be made.

Because you cannot foretell the needs for your records, ELZ suggests retaining them for 10 years, and keeping some records forever (see Section 1.6 on retention of records). Your clients should be advised of your policy on record retention.

> It is my office policy to destroy clients' records 10 years after our last meeting. Until then, I will keep your case records in a safe place and make them available when you authorize their release.

An addition might be:

> After I destroy your records, I will retain, for up to 25 years, a one-page summary of the dates of treatment, number of sessions, why you came to see me, diagnoses, and any outcome information I have.

Because HIPAA requires that our records must be available even when we cannot provide them (see Section 1.6), include a statement like this in your brochure:

> If I must discontinue our relationship because of illness, disability, or other presently unforeseen circumstances, I ask you to agree to let me transfer your records to another clinician who will make sure they are kept safe, confidential, and available when you want them, and then destroy them someday.

Keeping records forever may protect you, but they are discoverable by opposing lawyers. The information in records can become outdated and invalid, and thus useless or even misleading. We think that therapists cannot refuse to furnish records just because they might be invalid, so we suggest adding the statement above to your cover letter (see Form 8.4) and placing it in the brochure.

## Treating Couples and Families

The APA ethics code (APA, 2010, Standard 10.02) addresses confidentiality issues in treating couples or families, and HIPAA allows one person to release records of couples and families. However, you might want to insert a notice like the following to allow for greater privacy.

> If we do family or couple therapy (where there is more than one adult present), and you want to have my records of this therapy sent to anyone, all of the adults present will have to sign a release of information.

Family therapy and couple therapy may result in divorce and custody hearings, and such hearings may bring your records into an open court. Secrets may be revealed, or information that is irrelevant but damaging may be made public. The most protective record keeping is to generate separate records for each adult and for the family as a whole. This allows for some privacy, but does not guarantee it in a legal contest. If you do this, both parents should release family records, but each can release his or her own records, such as for seeking life insurance or a security clearance.

In over 30 years in practice, ELZ was contacted twice by the FBI when clients sought security clearances. However, this is not the only risk of receiving mental health treatment; other situations should be fully explored before a record is created and it is too late. For example, when all client records are computerized, there is likely to be no way of segregating old records, created under assumptions of confidentiality, from new ones with lower or just different confidentiality rules (e.g., HIPAA). Records from other states may have different confidentiality rules. In addition, almost everyone's medical diagnoses and treatments received have been recorded in the Medical Information Bureau's (http://www.mib.com) files, in a very simplified format; these records are accessed whenever a person applies for life, health, disability, or long-term care insurance, as well as for other purposes like financial credit. Routinely, diagnoses of depression affect people's eligibility for life insurance, the cost of such insurance, and hiring for security-sensitive jobs. You should decide whether you need to educate your clients about this issue before creating a record that would become included in permanent, semipublic records.

> As part of cost control efforts, health insurance companies will ask for information on your symptoms, diagnoses, progress, and outcomes. My policy is to provide only as much information as the insurance company will need to pay your benefits. This information will become part of your permanent medical record. I will let you know whether a company has asked for this and what it has asked for. If the company does not get the information it asks for, it may refuse to pay your benefits for our treatment. Please understand that I have no control over how these records are handled once they leave my office. For more on these issues, please read my Notice of Privacy Practices.

These are lively issues and of great concern. Federal laws like the HIPAA regulations and the Employee Retirement Income Security Act of 1974 interact with state laws, regulations, and our codes of ethics concerning privacy issues. The computerization of medical records, storage in multiple databases with very different access rules, the possibilities of hacking and breaches, and other pressures and events not foreseeable at present will necessarily shape our ways of creating records. You will have to craft (and update) guidelines for your practice that you believe are in your and your clients' best interest.

### Clients' Access to Their Own Records

Few states have laws concerning clients' access to their own records, and even those rarely apply to private practice. For example, federal law is silent on clients' inspection of their drug and alcohol treatment records (e.g., the Drug Abuse Office and Treatment Act of 1972), even when such clients are seen in private practice. But it defers to stricter state laws. These laws (and HIPAA) usually concern the following points: A client has a right to inspect records; to request amendments to correct inaccurate, irrelevant, outdated, or incomplete information; and to submit rebuttal information or memoranda, all of which you must incorporate into your records. If your state laws do not offer clients the opportunity to review and modify your records, the HIPAA regulations on accessing and amending records (164.524 and 164.526, respectively) are very likely to apply (see Section 8.1).

> You can review your own records in my files at any time. You may add to them to correct errors or provide more information, and you can have copies of them (but you will have to assume the risks of loss of confidentiality when you receive and store your copies). If I believe that it might be in some way harmful for you to view your records, I may suggest that we review them together or that I provide you with a summary of the records in place of the entire record. I ask you to understand and agree that you may not examine records created by anyone else that you have had sent to me.

You can charge a reasonable fee for copies and mailing (see http://www.lamblawoffice. com/medical-records-copying-charges.html for acceptable charges), but usually not for just locating records; the accessibility of records is part of our legal responsibility of record keeping. When a client asks ELZ to send copies of records to another treater, he does so and does not charge; however, when the records are to be used in a nonclinical situation that might benefit the client, his policy is to provide a copy to the client and have him or her make copies for others. This makes the contents known to clients and places the responsibility for release with the clients. KK prefers to send a summary to subsequent treaters, because it is more likely to contain the pertinent points for the sole purpose of continuity of care, and reduces any potential bias or countertransference leakage from her longer records (although she strives to avoid this in her records).

Technically, no authorization is needed to give clients their own records, but filling out an ROI documents exactly what has been copied and sent, to whom, for what purpose, when, and so forth.

HIPAA allows a professional or an agency manager to remove part of the record temporarily, if he or she determines that it might be detrimental to the client. This professional must document the removal and its rationale. The client may appeal any limitation of access, all under HIPAA. If you design your procedures to work within these guidelines, and indicate your rules in your brochure, you will reduce your risk of problems. A notice about this may only apply in some unusual situations and so is optional.

> In some very rare situations, I may temporarily remove parts of your records before you see them. This may happen if I believe that the information will be harmful to you, but I will discuss this with you.

HIPAA gives clients the right to ask for some limited restrictions on the disclosure of their records.

> You have the right to ask that your information not be shared with family members or others, and I can agree to that limitation. You can also tell me if you want me to send mail, or phone you at a more private location or number than, say, your home or workplace. If this is of concern to you, please tell me so that we can make arrangements.

Note that email is not mentioned in the paragraph above, because risk exists with unencrypted email, and so more secure methods are preferable. See the discussion of the NPP in Chapter 6. As an alternative to this paragraph, you can provide spaces on the intake data form (see Form 6.6) for the client to supply a different address or different phone numbers (including answering machine or voicemail numbers) for contacts.

## My Background

This section of the brochure or website gives your clients information about your professional experience and training. In the paper version, be brief. Mention only your clinically relevant background; do not list social or political accomplishments unless relevant to being a therapist. You can include your areas of special professional interest, your publications, your supervisor status, and/or positions you hold in professional organizations. If you present yourself as having any specialty, you will have to perform at, and conform to, the standards of those with full certification in that specialty. See Section 1.2 on the ethics of self-presentation. On your website, you can be more expansive on the topics above and others. Few people are knowledgeable about therapists' credentials, so it may be helpful to offer explanations of such matters as licensure or levels of certification. You can also mention major training, such as internships, qualifications, supervision, education, and positions held. KK posts her full curriculum vitae (CV) on her website and on LinkedIn.

It is not unethical to include a statement of experience such as this: "I have over 20 years of experience in the delivery of psychotherapy, psychological assessment, and consultation to children, adults, and families." You can also list the full range of services you offer such as group, individual, relationship, and/or family therapy; evaluations of various kinds; consultations with schools, other clinicians, or lawyers; hospital and home visits; and so on.

The following are ELZ's credentials, presented here and on the CD as an example. Please tailor this section of the brochure to your personal information.

> I am a psychologist with 35 years of experience. For the past 18 years, I have had my own office for the independent practice of clinical psychology. I am trained and experienced in doing one-on-one and couple therapy with adults (18 years of age and over). Earlier in my career, I worked in clinics and similar settings. I hold these qualifications:
>
> I have a doctoral degree in clinical psychology from the University of Pittsburgh, whose program is approved by the American Psychological Association (APA).
>
> I completed an internship in clinical psychology, approved by the APA.
>
> I am licensed as a psychologist in Pennsylvania.
>
> I am a member of the American Psychological Association and of the Pennsylvania Psychological Association.

You can use any explanatory terms. Just make certain that they are accurate, supported by credentials, and not misleading. ELZ prefers the term "independent practice" to "private practice," and KK is comfortable with "private practice."

Do not hesitate to list (and perhaps explain) which credentials require the demonstration of your areas of competence. Although most organizational memberships do not certify competence, listing them informs the client of your understanding and adherence to the organizations' codified ethical and other standards. Therefore, the client can be informed and reassured, as well as having recourse to organizations' ethics committees. This model brochure addresses this later under the heading "Statement of Principles and Complaint Procedures."

### Disclosure of Supervision

If you are being supervised, ethics and laws require that you inform clients of this fact. In addition to giving the supervisor's name, we suggest adding his or her license number, address, and phone number, with the intention of addressing problems early on.

### Disclosure of Financial Conflicts of Interest

One last point for fully informed consent concerns financial conflicts of interest between the client's needs and your professional relationships. For example, if you recommend or refer the client to a program or agency of which you are an owner (or even an employee who might benefit indirectly from the program's or agency's profitability), you are bound to disclose this relationship. See also the discussions of fee splitting in Sections 2.1 and 2.4.

---

**About Our Appointments**

The very first time I meet with you, we will need to give each other a lot of basic information. For this reason, I usually schedule 1–2 hours for this first meeting. Following this, we will usually meet for a 50-minute session once or twice a week, then less often. We can schedule meetings at times convenient for both of us. I will tell you at least a month in advance of my vacations or any other times we cannot meet. Please ask about my schedule in making your own plans.

---

The paragraph above describes the general time frame for brief therapy. You might want to be more detailed about the first session. It could be called an "initial evaluation session," for example, and you could specify that it includes open discussion of problems and concerns, history gathering, testing or questionnaires, and completion of forms (e.g., Form 6.10, the financial information form).

As a marketing tool, some clinicians offer a free first session (calling it a consultation, but that term is usually reserved for communications between peers); others see the professional activities and risks involved as worth compensation. See Chapter 9 for more on this.

### Scheduling

The scheduling of weekly appointments is traditional but not empirical. In a fascinating article, Zhu and Pierce (1995) suggest that to the degree that the learning in therapy resembles the learning–forgetting curves seen in laboratory studies, the schedule of meetings ought to be negatively accelerated. As an example, they suggest meetings at 1, 3, 7, 14, and 30 days for optimal prevention of relapse. ELZ strongly encourages you to consider such a schedule.

We suggest above that appointments can be scheduled "at times convenient for both of us." An alternative wording might be "Changes in appointments should be made with as much advance notice as possible, as a sign of our mutual respect." Or "While I am willing to be flexible, I have found that therapy is more effective when it occurs at a regular time each week. I hope we can work toward this regularity in our schedules." Or "Appointments can be scheduled during my office hours, Monday through Friday, 11:00 A.M. to 9:00 P.M." If you use this last format, you could indicate that appointments or calls outside these times will be charged at twice your usual rate. You might schedule clients for 3–4 months in advance, for simplicity and the saving of lots of negotiating time.

Be careful not to use "session" and "hour" interchangeably (unless your session length truly is 60 minutes). Doing so may mislead some clients. You might choose the length of your session on the basis of your style of doing therapy and the client's clinical benefit, not just tradition. Keep in mind your needs for your breaks and for time to write notes, as well as your office's location and the lengths in *Current Procedural Terminology* (CPT) billing codes. Therapists often schedule 50-minute sessions for individuals and 75- or 90-minute sessions for couples. Due to insurance coverage policies and CPT codes, these times may vary. If you treat both individuals and couples, you can include both lengths at this point in your materials.

> ### Cancellations and No-Shows
>
> We agree to meet at my office and to be on time. If I am ever unable to start on time, I ask your understanding and promise that you will receive the full time agreed to or be charged proportionately. If you are late, we will probably be unable to meet for the full time, because it is likely that I will have another appointment after yours.
>
> I am rarely able to fill a cancelled session, so you will be charged the full fee for sessions cancelled with less than 72 hours' notice, for other than the most serious reasons. Your insurance will not cover this charge.

Repetition of your cancellation policy on your appointment cards, on your bills, and on a sign in the office is recommended. A longer discussion on preventing missed sessions is included in Section 6.3.

Most managed care contracts prevent you from charging the insurer or the client for a no-show or late cancellation, or a full fee for late arrival. However, if you are able, should you try to collect your fee? It may be best to say on paper that all missed sessions will be fully charged, and then evaluate each situation and client before implementing the policy. You might say that you are "allowed to discount this charge, but one time only." Licensed psychologist Sheila Carluccio, MA, of Dickson City, PA, has made some excellent suggestions about this issue:

> Although it specifically states in my guidelines for treatment that I reserve the right to charge for cancellations, I reduce the charge for a missed session to $40.00 and am very specific that the charge is (1) not reimbursable through insurance and (2) charged in the event of frequent cancelling/no-shows, etc. We talk about the circumstances for missing the session. For instance, if you'd rather go to the mall/keep forgetting to show up/don't "feel like" coming to a session, I'd have to charge. You have a sick child/got called to work mandatory overtime/you're snowed in and can't make it, no charge. The guidelines are then signed as a treatment contract. In the event that difficulties arise, I refer back to this contract and we discuss it. Clients know from the beginning that being charged is something that they are choosing; at the same time, I am giving clients the clear message that they need to be responsible for their own benefit (consistent treatment), that I have a respectable boundary, and that my time and their treatment [are] valuable. For most families living in my area, $40.00 is nothing to sneeze at.

KK deals with the first missed session by offering clients "one free pass." She explains that they can use this "freebie" this one time or choose to use it at another date in the future if clients need to cancel within 48 hours. This allows the process to be collaborative, can help assess commitment to therapy, and can help strengthen the alliance early in treatment.

Consider offering phone sessions or HIPAA-compliant, secure video sessions when you can't meet face to face. Another option for a cancelled session is to make it up in the next few days by scheduling an additional session and, of course, billing for both. In this case, ELZ recommends offering to charge only half the fee for the missed session. This creates a "win–win" situation, in that the momentum of treatment is not lost through a 2-week delay, clients feel they got a bargain, and he gets to fill an otherwise empty hour. It can also provide invaluable information to a clinician regarding a client's motivation to do the work of psychotherapy. Other clinicians waive a missed session if the client and clinician are able to reschedule the same week and use the freed-up time productively.

For some therapists, the minimum advance notice for cancellation is 24 hours; this might then make a provision for weekends necessary, such as "Cancellations for a Monday appointment should be made no later than Thursday morning." If you treat families or couples, you need to make clear what you will do when everyone does not attend. (See Section 5.5 for some points concerning family therapy contracting.)

Besides interference with therapy process, missed sessions can raise therapists' frustration and fears of losing income, losing a client for charging, being exploited, or being accused of lack of compassion or competence. Processing the last reaction with the client is best, but when doing so would be countertherapeutic, consult your supervisor and colleagues. Many clients will be angry at being charged, and some will leave treatment. Those angry clients who stay often benefit from exploring their belief that the therapist's sacrifice means love or some other important schema.

Clients may sometimes object to "paying for a session that did not take place," but it is better reframed as honoring the clients' commitments and the choices they have made in managing their responsibilities. Modeling firm boundaries can be highly therapeutic for a client and therapist alike.

Some therapists add, "A retainer against such sessions, or for the closing session, will be requested at the initial meeting." Alternatively, getting credit card information to charge for missed sessions has been found to be very effective. If you do not charge for the missed appointment, consider requiring a deposit and apply it against the second appointment. As part of a consistent policy of charging for missed appointments, do not reschedule after a missed appointment unless it has been paid for.

Charging for missed sessions can be complicated by your agreements with managed care organizations (MCOs), which generally forbid your charging a client for anything but the copayment. Read your contracts before including such a statement. Medicare allows a client to be charged for missed sessions, as long as you also charge all your other clients for missed sessions (see https://www.cms.gov/Regulations-and-Guidance/Guidance/Transmittals/downloads/R1279CP.pdf).

What if you yourself are unable to make it to the session? A free next session would seem fair, but some clients may be made uncomfortable by such an offer, and this is worth exploring clinically. If you have forgotten the session or are late, do consult to examine any countertransference issues.

## Fees, Payments, and Billing

You may want to specify different fees for activities with different time needs or costs. For example, fees for supervising may be lower as a commitment to your profession. Fees for conducting in-service or other training sessions may be higher because of the preparation time involved, or lower because they may be a good source of referrals. Court testimony is often priced by the half-day, since schedules may be uncertain. If you write reports for lawyers or others, you may want to state that these "must be fully paid for before they are provided in legally signed form or released to any third party," to prevent payment problems when the conclusions are not what the lawyer wanted or so that your opinions cannot be altered by the payer.

> Payment for services is an important part of any professional relationship. This is even more true in therapy; one treatment goal is to make relationships and the duties and obligations they involve clear. You are responsible for seeing that my services are paid for. Meeting this responsibility shows your commitment and maturity.
>
> My current regular fees are as follows. I reevaluate my fees each January, based on changes in the cost of running my business, and implement the change in April. You will be notified several months in advance of any changes.

Raising fees in midyear may lessen the impact of yearly deductibles and so may make adjustments easier for clients. If you anticipate long treatment periods and significant inflation, you should state your rationales. Consider applying the higher price only to new clients, because it may appear that you are exploiting established relationships (and this may trigger complaints).

> *Regular therapy services:* For a session of _____ minutes, the fee is $_____.

If you offer lower fees for hours that are harder to fill, or have a set number of lower-fee or *pro bono* hours, you can indicate that here.

> Please pay for each session at its start. I have found that this arrangement helps us stay focused on our goals and works best. It also allows me to keep my fees lower, because it cuts down on my bookkeeping costs. I suggest that you make out your check or ready your credit card before each session begins, so that our time will be used fully. Other payment or fee arrangements must be worked out before the end of our first meeting. I accept cash, checks, credit and debit cards, and health care spending cards in the office or by phone. I do not store your card's numbers in any file.

You could offer planned "phone sessions" with set time limits billed to a credit card, or invite clients to call as follow-up on an intervention.

> *Telephone consultations:* I believe that telephone consultations may be suitable or even needed at times in our therapy. Some insurers will pay for these services, but many will not. If so, I will charge you our regular fee, pro-rated over the time needed.
>
> If I need to have telephone conferences with other professionals as part of your treatment, you will be billed for these at the same rate as for regular therapy services. We will discuss this in

advance, so we can set rules that are comfortable for both of us. Of course, there is no charge for brief calls about appointments or similar business.

*Extended sessions:* Occasionally it may be better to go on with a session, if possible, than to stop or postpone work on a particular issue. This extension time will be charged on a pro-rated basis. It is also likely that your insurance will not pay for extra time, and so I will bill you.

You should clarify the payer's policy before deciding to include this. Many therapists simply waive payment for occasional longer sessions.

*Psychological testing:* Services are $_____ per hour. Psychological testing fees include the time spent with you, the time needed for scoring and studying the test results, any consultations necessary, and the time needed to write a report on the findings. The amount of time involved depends on the tests used and the questions the testing is intended to answer.

The paragraph above does not tell how much a full evaluation might cost; if that were posted, it might well frighten off some clients. Potential clients do not understand what assessments they might need, and so you might just say, "Costs vary by individuals' needs."

*Reports:* I will not charge you for my time spent making routine and simple reports to your insurance company. However, I will have to bill you for any extra-long or complex reports the company might require. The company will not cover this fee.

*Other services:* Charges for other services, such as hospital visits, consultations with other therapists, home visits, or any court-related services (such as consultations with lawyers), will be based on the time involved in providing the service at my regular fee schedule. Some services may require payment in advance.

Other professionals charge for travel time (door-to-door), postage, phone calls, and making copies. Make rules about your charges that you can live with comfortably, or you may feel resentment and taken advantage of.

I realize that my fees involve a substantial amount of money, although they are well in line with similar professionals' charges. For you to get the best value for your money, we must work hard and well.

You may wish to offer variations in your fee structure, but be careful to avoid seeming to have two sets of fees—one for those who have health insurance and a lower one for those who do not—because the insurance company will see this as fraud. Instead, you can offer a discount on your regular fee, just as you do when you sign onto a panel of an MCO. You could offer a discount to self-paying clients for payment in full at the time of billing or for payment in advance, but not for those who pay slowly. All of this must be explicitly stated in your information brochure for clients.

Other points that may need clarification can be included here:

- For health insurance clients, will you expect the payment of a portion of the fee (the copayment) at the time of services, with the rest to be paid by the insurance company at a future date? Or will the client pay the whole charge and await reimbursement from the insurance company?

- Will you lower your charges if the MCO lowers the amount it pays you (when your contract is renewed), or if a client's insurance coverage is exhausted, or if a client's income is greatly reduced? (See Section 2.1 on financial policies.) You should decide and include a statement in the brochure.

- It is a good idea to place the following in all your materials, in large lettering: "You, the client, are responsible for paying all charges for our services, regardless of payments from health insurance or any other sources." It's also a good idea to repeat that payment is due at each session by hanging a sign about this in your waiting area (if it is exclusively yours). You can also have it printed on your appointment cards. Among other benefits, it deals with a situation where you unfortunately see a client before your receive an authorization or the authorization is voided, and yet his or her MCO's policy requires preauthorization of services or they will not be covered. Another potentially sticky situation can occur when parents are paying for an adult child's therapy and family issues may affect their willingness to pay.

- If you offer payment by credit card, say so in this section. If you don't offer it, you may want to consider doing so (see Section 2.3).

- If your charge varies with the client's MCO contract, you should indicate that this is so, or you may be seen as misrepresenting your fee.

- If you make any other extra charges, such as a double rate outside your usual hours, put it here.

> I will assume that our agreed-upon financial arrangements will continue as long as I provide services to you. I will assume this until you tell me in person, by telephone, or by certified mail that you wish to end it. You have a responsibility to pay for any services you receive before we end the relationship.

If you decide to bill some clients, you probably should put something like the following paragraphs into your brochure:

> Because I expect full payment at the time of our meetings, I usually do not send bills. However, if we have agreed that I will bill you, I ask that the bill be paid within 10 days of the billing date. If your insurance company does not pay us within a reasonable period of 60 days, I will expect you to pay the full amount and wait for your insurance company to reimburse you. Of course, if I receive a payment from the company after you have paid me, I will refund your overpayments.
>
> At the end of each month, I will send you a statement. The statement can be used for health insurance claims, as described in the next section. It will show all of our meetings, the charges for each meeting, how much has been paid, and how much (if any) is still owed. At the end of treatment, and when you have paid for all sessions, I will send you a final statement for your tax records.

The paragraphs above should obviously be tailored to fit your own office procedures. If you provide a Superbill (see Section 3.7) at the end of each session, this is what a client should submit to the insurance company, and you won't need to send a statement. As regards tax deductibility, you could add, "Depending on your financial circumstances and total medical costs for any year, therapy may be a deductible expense," and "Consult your tax advisor."

Charging interest or extending credit requires you to comply with federal and state laws and forms, which are burdensome. Therefore, we recommend that you use late fees or charge no interest. You can state, "A late fee of 1.5% of the unpaid balance will be charged each month," or "A late payment fee of $____ will be charged each month that a balance remains unpaid." You may want to indicate that you do not give refunds to unsatisfied customers (or to explain when you do give refunds).

> If there is any problem with my charges, my billing, your insurance, or any other money-related point, please bring it to my attention immediately. I will do the same with you. Such problems can interfere greatly with our work. They must be worked out openly and quickly.

It is best not to allow a large debt to accumulate. An alternative is to set a session limit rather than a dollar limit.

If you have decided to use collection agencies or legal methods (see Section 2.4), you should inform clients of this in your brochure (see the APA code of ethics—APA, 2010, Standard 6.04e), including the fact that they will have to pay the costs of collection. However, some clinicians feel that stating this adds a negative quality to the relationship at its beginning.

> If your account has not been paid for more than 60 days and arrangements for payment have not been agreed upon, I have the option of using legal means to secure the payment. This may involve hiring a collection agency or going through small-claims court. In most collection situations, the only facts I release regarding a client's treatment are his or her name, the kind of services provided, and the amount due. If such legal action is necessary, its costs will be included in the claim.
>
> If you think you may have trouble paying your bills at times, please discuss this with me. If your unpaid balance reaches $____, I will notify you by mail. If it then remains unpaid, I must stop therapy with you. Again, fees that continue unpaid or without a payment plan after this may be turned over to small-claims court or a collection service.

You may want to advise some clients to look into medical or health *savings* accounts (MSAs or HSAs) or flexible *spending* accounts (FSAs), because they can cover psychotherapy costs. The clients or their employers buy high-deductible health insurance and then fund an MSA or HSA. An FSA for medical expenses cannot be used to pay insurance premiums, but it can pay for deductibles, copayments, and most medical expenses not covered by insurance, which could include psychotherapy. HSAs allow clients to save money for future expenses, whereas FSAs forfeit unspent money back to the employer each year. The costs are low and the tax advantages are high for any client who can afford to pay several thousand dollars a year to fund such accounts.

Many potential clients believe that therapy's costs are unaffordable. A course of treatment (15 sessions at $150 each) may cost $2,250—but "While not a trivial amount, it is within the reach of the same families who spend discretionary income on vacations, restaurants, designer dogs, amusement parks, sporting events, weddings, tattoos, prom night,

Christmas gifts, electronics, alcohol, tobacco, and other non-necessities," says Pauline Wallin, PhD, of Camp Hill, PA (personal communication, May 1, 2012). Reluctant clients may be educated to appreciate the value of therapy (see http://www.ethicalpsychology.com/2012/12/is-psychotherapy-too-expensive.html).

Those who call seeking a therapist want to know your fees as soon as possible to help them make their decision, and you should help them with information. Your comfort with transparency and full information or other personal factors will also shape your actions.

Should you post your fees on your website? Posted fees may screen out those whom you cannot afford to see and may prepare those who do call. Some potential clients may think your fees too high, or posting fees may even dissuade callers who think that everyone must pay full fees and that you won't negotiate. On the other hand, the absence of fee information may dissuade some from even calling. Some clinicians do not post fees so that when potential clients call, they can explain their policies (full fee, some *pro bono* slots, sliding scale, insurance, credit cards, etc.) that would make therapy more affordable. As a result, you will spend some time discussing their problems with those who ultimately cannot afford your services and so must be referred. Many clinicians feel that this time is not wasted, but constitutes a public service. If you have such discussions, it is advisable to make clear that they do not create a therapist–client relationship:

You might consider adding this paragraph if your typical client seems to need this clarification.

> I will not be your therapist and we will not have an ongoing relationship just because of this kind of discussion. This way, I can help you make the best choice for your needs.

### If You Have Health Insurance

You should be prepared to deal with the inevitable question "Do you take insurance?" If you say "No," prospective clients probably won't immediately hang up, and you could ask, "But are you certain that you want to use your insurance?" They are unlikely to have examined the costs of it use in terms of loss of confidentiality and the small value of its payments. Your version of Handout 3.1 could be offered as an email courtesy (and posted on your website), and you may get these prospects as clients because you will be seen as well informed, helpful, and generous.

> Because I am a licensed psychologist , many health insurance plans will help you pay for therapy and other services I offer. Because health insurance is written by many different companies, I cannot tell you what your plan covers. Please read your plan's booklet under coverage for "Outpatient Psychotherapy" or "Behavioral Health," or under "Treatment of Mental and Nervous Conditions." Or call your employer's benefits office to find out what you need to know.
>
> Because your health insurance may pay part of my charge, I will help you with your insurance claim forms. However, please keep the following in mind:
>
> 1. If you subscribe to a health maintenance organization (HMO) or preferred provider organization (PPO), or have another kind of health insurance with a managed care organization (MCO), decisions about what kind of care you need, from whom, and how much of it you can receive will be reviewed by the plan. The plan has rules, limits,

and procedures that we should discuss. Please bring your health insurance plan's wallet card or description of services to our first meeting, so that we can talk about it and decide what to do.

2. Your health insurance policy is a contract between you and your insurance company, and does not guarantee payment for my services. I had no role in deciding what your insurance covers. Your employer decided which services will be covered, which will not be covered, and how much you have to pay. You are responsible for checking your insurance coverage, deductibles, payment rates, copayments, and so forth. Your insurance coverage is between you and your company; it is not between me and the insurance company.

3. You—not your insurance company or any other person or company—are responsible for paying the fees we agree upon. If you ask me to bill a separated spouse, a relative, or an insurance company, and I do not receive payment on time, I will then expect this payment from you.

You should insert here whatever procedures you will perform (such as doing all the verification of coverage, billing insurers, billing for copayments, etc.) and what the responsibilities of the client are.

4. As a service to you, I will provide information about you to your insurance company only with your informed and written consent. My office will try its best to maintain the privacy of your records, but I ask you to understand that I have no control over what happens to your records after they leave my office.

It may be helpful to list in your brochure the panels of MCOs and similar organizations to which you belong, and then describe the procedures they require you to follow.

Your MCO can ask for and review all my records as part of its regular audits of providers and services. It may be satisfied with a phone discussion or a summary. It will usually be looking to see that the services are compatible with the severity of your limitations and diagnoses. This is called "evaluating the medical necessity of treatment." I will tell you if this happens.

Managed care issues are complicated, so see Chapter 3 for a fuller discussion. If you think that the loss of confidentiality, lessened professional control of treatment, and the impact of a psychiatric diagnosis are significant concerns for clients, consider giving them Handout 3.1 and having a discussion of alternatives. Ackley (1997) also has excellent educational handouts about fees and insurance and about payment plans.

If you do not participate in managed care programs, you might want to say something like this:

I have chosen not to join or participate in any health insurance plans or panels. If you choose to use your insurance, I will not file claims for you, but I will give you a receipt for my services with the information the insurers need to pay you back if allowed by your contract. This information will include standard diagnostic and procedure codes, the times we met, my charges, and your payments

Because I do not have a contract with your insurance company, it may pay a part of my fees as an out-of-network provider. Please check here to allow me to speak with your insurance company if it contacts me, to provide information to help you collect reimbursement benefits (if any):  ❑ Yes  ❑ No

### If You Need to Contact Me

I cannot promise that I will be available at all times. Although I am usually in the office _____ through _____, from _____ to _____, I do not take phone calls when I am with a client. You can always leave a message with my [assistant/answering service], or on my [answering machine/voicemail], and I will return your call as soon as I can. Generally, I will return messages daily except on _____ and holidays. During times I am scheduled to be away for a few days, another professional will be available for urgent issues.

If you have an emergency or crisis, mention this when you are leaving a message, and ask that I be contacted. If you have a behavioral or emotional crisis and cannot reach me or my assistant immediately by telephone, you or your family members should call one of the following community emergency agencies: the county mental health office at _____ or the crisis center at _____; your PCP; or the nearest hospital emergency room.

Some answering services record all calls, and some transcribe them and send you an email. Depending on what yours does, you might add to your message some variant of the following:

This call may be recorded, and it will be treated with the same confidentiality as any other information you share with our office.

Setting boundaries to your availability that are appropriate to the client, the circumstances, and your own needs is fully reasonable and can be therapeutic. Clinicians in private practice are not clinics or hospitals. Many therapists have instructions on their answering machines that in emergencies clients should call 911 or go to a hospital emergency department. Simon (2008) has criticized this practice as "worse than useless," because (1) it is likely to be perceived as creating a barrier ("Don't bother me!"); (2) it won't be implemented because of (a) the embarrassment of having the police arrive as a result of a 911 call or (b) the inability of a client in crisis to follow directions; and (3) emergency departments often fail to provide rapid enough care or even good mental health care. He indicates that continuous availability, or arranged competent coverage by a colleague, is the standard of care. Client phone calls should be returned rapidly to assess and intervene, to preserve and enhance the therapeutic alliance, to manage the risk, to avoid legal abandonment, and to reduce suicide. Simon suggests making a "pre-need" plan with a safe place for the client to go to while awaiting the return call, and the inclusion of the use of suicide hotlines.

Many therapists offer their cellphone numbers "for urgent issues" with few problems, as most clients can distinguish when they truly need help and the therapists are glad to be available earlier rather than after conditions worsen. Having a therapist's number can be very comforting to some clients. Consider having a discussion with each client as to what might or might not constitute an emergency.

An option is to have two voicemail boxes: one for routine calls, and the other only for emergencies. This second one would call your cellphone immediately. For the first, caution clients that you may not pick up the messages the same day and that calls may not be returned for 24 hours, especially if they are left in the evening or on weekends. Communication technology changes rapidly, so explore your options every few years.

You might indicate (only if it is true, of course) that you expect to return all calls and emails within 24 hours. This rule of return is a good one to make, even if you have to work hard to keep it. If you do this, consider adding this to your message:

> If I don't return your message within 24 hours, please assume that a mechanical problem has occurred and call back.

You probably should indicate that responding to a message outside some hours will be treated as an emergency and charged accordingly. If it fits your style of practice to reduce "telephone tag," you could specify a particular time each day during which you will return calls, or consider adding an online scheduling system to your site. Callers can then leave a number where they can be reached during that time, and you can confirm or reschedule.

The following are some possible additional phone policies:

> I find that telephone therapy does not work as well as face-to-face therapy, and so I discourage it. I will generally suggest our meeting if you call with a problem that is not critical.
>
> I have found that brief telephone calls work quite well for some purposes, and I am willing to arrange this.
>
> If I feel that our work together calls for it, I will make special arrangements for telephone contact, and this service will be charged at my usual rate.

A last point concerns returning a call from a client in crisis. An abusive partner may learn that the abused partner has sought help, and may be able to discover your phone number (and identity and location) if you do not block your number or use a calling card. Call blocking may not work on business phone lines.

---

**If I Need to Contact Someone about You**

If there is an emergency during our work together, or I become concerned about your personal safety, I am required by law and by the rules of my profession to contact someone close to you—perhaps a relative, spouse, or close friend—to protect you. I am also required to contact this person, or the authorities, if I become concerned about your harming someone else. Please write down the name and information of your chosen contact person in the blanks provided:

Name: _____    Relationship to you: _____

Address: _____

Home phone: _____    Cell: _____    Work: _____

You may give me more than one person.

_____

_____

_____

### Social Media

We recommend that each clinician develop a comprehensive "Communications Policy" section of the brochure to address social media, email, and so forth, rather than tackle each issue separately. See Sections 8.6 and 9.6 for suggestions. Will you have Facebook pages and "friend" clients, post Tweets, accept email, or Google clients and so learn more than what they have chosen to offer face to face or on paper? Or will you promise never to look or ask them not to Google you? For a comprehensive and current social media policy for therapists, see KK's policy on her website (http://drkkolmes.com/social-media-policy) and the fuller discussion in Chapter 9. A recent brief overview of electronic communication policies for therapists may be helpful (http://www.psych.on.ca/OPA/media/Members/Guidelines/Guidelines-for-Best-Practices-in-Electronic-Communications.pdf?ext=.pdf).

### Other Points

You might include a discussion of these points to head off some troubles.

You may not make any kind of electronic recording of our sessions without my written consent.

Many clients use email and text messaging, but these are not secure and could lead to a loss of confidentiality. If you would like to use email to communicate with me, please read my Social Media Policy.

I will charge you at my regular rate for letters, reports, and similar documents you ask me to create for you.

As part of the confidentiality that I offer you, I ask you not to disclose the name or identity of any other client being seen in this office.

Depending on your methods, you might supply other information for clients, such as suggesting comfortable dress, requesting no smoking, or asking that they avoid bringing food or drinks. If you have an office pet, offer a note about your dog's or cat's presence. In addition, consider clients' allergies and histories with animals, and make sure your pet has a safe retreat. Make sure your office building allows animals in the building, other than service animals. Your insurance will not cover harms to the client, but if your dog has been certified as a therapy dog, you can buy insurance coverage from the certifying organization.

### Children and Property Issues

If you treat children, a few additional points can be addressed here. Will you allow a parent to drop off a child and then do errands, or leave siblings in your waiting room? Both of these situations seem to create legal risks. And what about possible property damage or theft?

> I request that you do not bring children with you (other than a child I am seeing for treatment) if they are young and need babysitting or supervision, which I cannot provide. I do not have toys, but I can provide reading materials suitable for older children. You will be charged for any damage to, or theft of, property in this office or outside by you or anyone for whom you are legally responsible. I cannot be responsible for any personal property or valuables you bring into this office.

### Intoxicated Clients

If you treat clients for addictions, they may show up intoxicated at some point. Handling this is best done with paragraphs in your brochure having them agree to attend treatment clean and sober, giving consent to random drug or alcohol tests, and emphasizing the value of and need for honesty. Then you can immediately confront them when you suspect substance use and explore it therapeutically, rather than dismissing them from therapy (temporarily or permanently)—or, worse, ignoring slips. Also consider a plan of action for intoxication (calling a friend to drive the client home, calling a cab, taking the client's keys, etc.).

### Shared Office Space

If you share office space with other therapists under any kind of financial arrangement, and especially if you operate together under an assumed business name such as Therapy Associates, you will need to make clear to every client that you each operate separately as independent professionals. This is done mainly to avoid becoming involved in a complaint or suit against one of your office mates, but also to assure your clients of confidentiality.

> Although I share this office space with other professionals and we use some office equipment together, we are not in business together as partners, employers, or employees. I do not routinely consult with them on cases, or make referrals to or receive referrals from them. We are all independent licensed professionals.

### Collecting Information on Progress and Outcomes

> As a professional therapist, I naturally want to know more about how therapy helps people. To understand therapy better, I must collect information about clients before, during, and after treatment. Therefore, I ask you to help me by filling out some questionnaires about different parts of your life—relationships, changes, concerns, attitudes, and other areas. I ask your permission to take what you write on these questionnaires and what I have in my records, and to use it in research or teaching that I may do in the future. If I ever use the information from your questionnaire, it will always be included with information from many other clients, and you will never be identified. All personal information will be disguised and changed. After the research, teaching, or publishing project is completed, all the data used will be destroyed.

KK believes that the use of such information for research and teaching (not just simple data on outcomes) should be explained and authorized on a case-by-case basis, with the client knowing that he or she has the right to opt out without any negative penalty or effect on therapy. Form 5.8 will support this process. But if you are going to assess only progress and outcomes, you could say:

> I will send you a brief set of questions about 6 months after our last session. These questions will ask you to look back at our work together and tell me how you are doing. Sending them to you is part of my duty as a therapist. I ask that you agree, as part of entering therapy with me, to return this follow-up form and to be very honest about what you tell me then.
>
> *Records Issues*

A rare client may ask you to return, remove, or destroy some materials with the intention of removing your means of defense, and then complain against you or institute a lawsuit. Never alter your records, but instead invite clients to offer additional information to amend your records, or offer to return materials to them but to retain copies.

> If, as part of our therapy, you create and provide to me records, notes, artworks, or any other documents or materials, I will return the originals to you at your written request but may retain copies.

Since you have made provisions for your records availability and release if you are no longer able to do so (see Section 1.7), you might mention this in your brochure.

> If I am unable to provide continuing care to you due to my illness or disability, I have made arrangements with other fully qualified and confidential clinicians for your immediate care and for maintenance of your records.

Because you can never know what will happen, you might add a statement like this:

> These arrangements are in effect as long as I am in practice.

If you use an electronic health record (EHR) program in your office, you should tell clients about it. The American Counseling Association's (ACA's) code (ACA, 2014) requires this disclosure in its Section H. Topics to be covered at least are security measures, encryption, cloud storage, and retention times. For more, see the website of Roy Huggins, MS, NCC (http://www.personcenteredtech.com), and sign up for the newsletter to access the forms he has created for this and other purposes.

### Other Special Rules

You can also indicate in this section any special rules you have—for example, about treating criminal or court-referred clients, clients accused or convicted of partner/child abuse, suicidal clients, clients with paranoid disorders, and so on.

Finally, you can leave a space here to write in any additional issues that bear on each individual case.

> ### Statement of Principles and Complaint Procedures
>
> It is my intention to abide by all the rules of the American Psychological Association (APA) [or other professional organization] and by those of my state license.

The APA's rules include its ethical principles and code of conduct, its standards for providers of psychological services, and its guidelines for delivery of specialty services. If you are not a psychologist, mention the applicable rules and codes of your profession. This may enhance your perceived ethicality and competence.

> Problems can arise in our relationship, just as in any other relationship. If you are not satisfied with any area of our work, please raise your concerns with me as soon as possible. Our work together will be slower and harder if your concerns with me are not worked out. Some issues that arise between us may be clinically relevant to other relationships in your life. I will make every effort to hear any complaints you have and to seek resolution. If you feel that I (or any therapist) have treated you unfairly or have broken a professional rule, please tell me. You can also contact the state licensing board for the discipline under which any therapist practices (psychologist, psychiatrist, licensed professional counselor, or social worker). Staff members there can help clarify your concerns or tell you how to file a complaint.

Some therapists would consider it unnecessary, pessimistic, or even masochistic to tell clients how to lodge a formal complaint. But this information is essential for fully informing the consumer, and it is required by the HIPAA regulations. See Section 8.9 for more on this, and Form 8.6 for a sample complaint form (reframed as "Is There a Problem?"). Vinson (1987) found that the low level of reporting of sexual and other abuses by therapists was not attributable to lack of motivation, but to lack of information on how to file a complaint. Hare-Mustin et al. (1979) say that clients need to know what the legitimate grounds for complaints are, as well as what options are available for resolving them. Brown (personal communication in Branscomb, 1996) reported that in the state of Washington, where providing such information has been required since 1987, there was no increase of complaints (frivolous or otherwise) as of 1996. If a concern or complaint of any sort arises, document it. Do this even if you think it trivial or baseless. See Section 4.2 on what to do if you are complained against.

> In my practice as a therapist, I do not discriminate against clients because of any of these factors: age, sex/gender, sexual orientation, marital or family status, race, color, religious beliefs, ethnic origin, place of residence, veteran status, physical disability, health status, or criminal record unrelated to present dangerousness. This is a personal commitment, as well as being required by some federal, state, and local laws and regulations. I will always take steps to advance and support the values of equal opportunity, human dignity, and racial, ethnic, and cultural diversity. If you believe you have been discriminated against, please bring this matter to my attention immediately.

In the list above of groups that can be discriminated against, we have tried to be comprehensive—including, for example, "health status" to cover HIV-positive individuals, and "place of residence" in regard to low-socioeconomic-status areas or community mental health center catchment areas. You should add to this list anything else applicable to your practice, or delete anything from it that is not applicable.

---

### Our Agreement

I, _____ (name of client or person acting for the client), indicate by my signature below that I have read or had read to me the issues and points in this document. I have discussed those points I did not understand, and have had my questions answered to my satisfaction.

I understand that no specific promises have been made to me by you, the therapist, about the results of treatment, the effectiveness of the procedures you use, or the number of sessions necessary for therapy to be effective.

I understand that any of the points mentioned above can be discussed and may be open to change. If at any time during the treatment I have questions about any of the subjects discussed in this brochure, I can talk with you about them, and you will do your best to answer them. I understand that after therapy begins, I have the right to withdraw my consent to therapy at any time, for any reason. However, I will make every effort to discuss my concerns with you before ending therapy with you.

By signing below, I agree to act according to the points covered in this brochure, but this does not waive any of my rights.


_____     ____/____/____
Signature of client (or person acting for client)                                        Date


_____
Printed name

Relationship to client:

   ❑ Self   ❑ Parent   ❑ Legal guardian
   ❑ Health care custodial parent of a minor (less than 14 years of age)
   ❑ Other person authorized to act on behalf of the client: _____

---

Besides the signature, for your additional protection and assurance that the client has read every page, you could ask the client to initial each page at the bottom by including a statement like this: "Initial here to show that you have read this page."

---

I, the therapist, have met with this client (and/or his or her parent or guardian or others related to this person's situation) for a suitable period of time, and have informed him or her about the issues and points raised in this brochure. I have responded to his or her questions. I believe this person fully understands the issues, and I find no reason to believe that this person is not fully competent to give informed consent to treatment with me. I agree to enter into therapy with the client, as shown by my signature here.

_____   ____/____/____
                         Signature of therapist                                Date

I truly appreciate the chance you have given me to be of professional service to you and look
forward to a successful relationship with you. If you are satisfied with my services as we proceed, I (like any professional) would appreciate your referring other people to me who might
also be able to make use of my services.

❏ Copy accepted by client   or        ❏ Copy kept by therapist

## 5.3   The Second Path to Informed Consent: The Question List as a Guide to Discussion

The second method for obtaining informed consent comes from the work of Pomerantz,
Handelsman, and others. ELZ considers it the most elegant and effective solution to the
need for obtaining fully informed consent.

> First, it informs clients what information they have a right to [ask about] but preserves their
> right to request it or not. Second, it may be less overwhelming for clients. . . . Third, because
> the answers are not spelled out, the form requires a conversation between therapist and client
> to take place. . . . Fourth, the form has a fourth-grade readability level. (Handelsman & Galvin,
> 1988, p. 224)

In short, this approach is an admirably respectful, flexible, and effective solution to a
thorny problem.

The give-and-take of discussion used in this approach *is* the process of informing for
consent. In practice, you can give the question list to the client any time in the first session
or to take home and read. **It is a structured interview the client conducts with you.** After
answering the client's questions, you can write a note such as this: "I believe I have obtained
fully informed, voluntary, and competent consent to proceed with treatment because we
have addressed everything on my [question list] that this client has concerns about." This
procedure simultaneously (1) meets your legal responsibility to get an informed consent
form signed; (2) meets your ethical responsibility to have the dialogue (questions and
answers) that must logically and legally underlie informed consent; and, most importantly,
(3) is clinically elegant, as it starts therapy off with openness—putting everything on the
table not only by answering the client's questions, but by even showing the client the most
important questions to ask. It even respects the client's right not to know.

Because the questions are in simple English, and because the client signs the list to
affirm that he or she has had a discussion of the points and understands them, this procedure makes a legal challenge that the client simply signed a form (and that therefore the
consent was not really informed) far less likely to succeed.

The questions offered in this section and in Handout 5.1 are adapted with permission from the list by Pomerantz and Handelsman (2004), which is based on several earlier
researched versions. You may want to introduce some issues with your clients besides those
based on their work. For example, if you think it is important to have your clients know

more about your way of practicing, their insurance, or other services you can offer, you can add questions designed to elicit this information. Similarly, you can add questions about clinical issues (e.g., homework expectations), cultural differences, values, or diagnoses. You could review the points raised in the client information brochure (see Section 5.2 and the Sample Client Information Brochure on the CD) for additional topics to include in these questions. Do rehearse your answers so that they flow easily to convey your professional expertise.

**HANDOUT 5.1**

Some of the key questions based on Pomerantz and Handelsman's work are discussed below. The full list is presented at the end of this section as Handout 5.1. You might want to create an expanded version for yourself, with suggested answers and important points you want to make sure you explain. You can use that expanded version to respond during the interview. KK suggests that many of these answers can be placed on a Frequently Asked Questions (FAQ) page on your website.

### Information You Have a Right to Know

When you come for therapy, you are buying my professional services. Therefore, you need information to make a good decision about entering therapy with me. Below are some questions you might want to ask. You can ask me any of these questions and others, and I will give you the best answers I can. If my answers are not clear or complete enough, please ask me again.

1. Tell me about yourself.
   a. Are you a social worker? Psychologist? Psychiatrist? Family therapist? Counselor?
   b. What are some of the advantages and limitations of your profession?

Be prepared to compare the different mental health disciplines in an even-handed and nondefensive way, with some indications of their respective strengths. Do not either brag or be too humble, but be confident in your areas of provable competence. Clarity will either build hope in the client or lead to a referral to someone better able to serve the client's needs.

As noted in Section 5.2, some clients seek out therapists of specific religions, believing that these therapists will share their values. All therapists have a moral philosophy, as do all therapies, so you should probably discuss value-related issues that are most relevant to the presenting problem (e.g., loyalty to family and marriage, honesty despite the fear of consequences, gender roles and preferences, respect for age and authority, adherence to values and principles).

2. Tell me about therapy.
   a. How does your kind of therapy work?

You can emphasize your theory of change and describe what each of you will do in therapy. You might say something along these lines:

"We will discuss fully what brought you to see me; explore your history and background, to understand where problems may have come from and what might be keeping them going; talk about all areas of your life, especially where you have problems; and discuss anything else that is important, so that I can fully understand your situation."

You could then describe various treatment approaches.

You could describe your expectations and assumptions as follows:

"I will expect you to be open and honest about your thoughts and feelings; to help design homework and practice to change things; to complete the homework to the best of your ability; to try out new ways of dealing with your feelings, thoughts, and other people; to keep records of your feelings and behaviors . . . " (add anything else you think appropriate).

### e.  Are there negatives or possible risks in this therapy?

This question and the next few open discussion of possible losses and harms, as well as of the effectiveness of therapy. For content, see "The Risks and Benefits of Therapy" in Section 5.2 and the Sample Client Information Brochure on the CD. Do mention that almost every therapy client is concerned about these things, but that the great majority of clients do get better—even much better.

Having outcome data based on your clients and your setting is ideal, and its collection might be considered an ethical requirement for high-quality practice (see Section 7.5). In its absence, do not paint too rosy a picture or promise a cure. Many studies have demonstrated the effectiveness of therapy. You might offer a few statistics that you can explain easily. Do explain the costs and losses associated with *not* entering therapy. DSM-5 (American Psychiatric Association, 2013) has information on the life course of some diagnoses, which you can draw upon for this discussion.

### f.  About how long will therapy take?

The response to this question will depend on the client's presenting problems and prognosis. Be realistic. Don't try to offer a low number of sessions just because that is all the client's insurance will pay for, especially if you suspect that those will be insufficient to relieve the client's distress or improve functioning. You can discuss this in terms of long-term and short-term goals.

### g.  What will I notice when I am getting better?

ELZ has often told his clients that they should feel increased optimism in a few sessions; increased self-confidence, energy, and courage in a few more; and consistently less anxiety or depression in 10–15 sessions. He has also told them that others may notice changes before they do. You can also focus the client's attention on specific areas chosen for their clinical utility. You might suggest that symptoms change in frequency, duration, intensity, or latency, but that which aspect will change first cannot be predicted. For strategic purposes consider warning of the predictable "flight into health"—that is, feeling much better after a session or two, discontinuing therapy (but without the changes to support it), and then backsliding and becoming disappointed with therapy. KK sometimes explains to clients with no prior therapy experiences that they may feel a bit exposed and vulnerable in therapy after sharing so much at first, but that this is a normal response to opening up so much in a one-sided way with a relative stranger. However, over time, feelings of comfort and safety should emerge, along with a sense of optimism and belief in one's ability to improve. She also notes that improvement does not always proceed in a straight line or always move up; it can happen in waves, and week-to-week fluctuations are normal.

> h. What should I do if I feel therapy isn't working?

You might say this:

"You should discuss this with me first. Our expectations might have been incorrect or unrealistic. We may need to add more treatment sessions or different methods. If we are not making progress, I will consult other professionals, and I may recommend that you talk to another therapist for a consultation."

You might add that you do not take clients you don't think you can help, although sometimes it takes some work together to see that you and a particular client might not be the best fit, and that you have an ethical obligation to refer those clients who are not benefiting. You might mention placebo effects and "buyer's remorse," but decide how much of this to explain to maintain motivation and momentum.

> i. Is there someone I can talk to if I have a problem or a complaint about therapy that we can't work out?

If you are being supervised, this is an opportunity to explain that. HIPAA requires you to have a complaint process for breaches of confidentiality and to explain this to clients (see Section 8.9). Your state or your ethics code may require you to explain complaint procedures or to post them visibly in your office.

> j. Will I have to take any kind of tests or answer questionnaires?

Obviously, the answer to this depends on your approach and discipline, but checklists may be useful for assessing and documenting progress and outcome for both insurers and clients.

> k. Do you follow a therapy manual with planned steps?

You have an ethical obligation to use the most appropriate and effective treatments, and so you should know about them and adopt approaches suitable for your clients.

> l. Do you do therapy over the phone? Over the Internet?

For some situations where weather or transportation limit attendance, you might offer phone or online sessions as options. If you are a clinician who is providing telemental health services regularly, this is a chance to explain the circumstances in which you provide this service.

> 3. Tell me about other kinds of therapy and help.
>    a. What other types of therapy or help are there for my kind of problems?

This is often a hard question for a therapist to answer, because of interdisciplinary rivalry, ignorance of others' approaches, and fears of one's own inadequacy in regard to training and skill. However, this is the kind of information you would want when choosing therapy for yourself or a member of your family. If you become informed about other approaches and share what you know openly, clients will appreciate your honesty and trust you more, and therapy will be more effective. You can describe counseling, medications, group therapies, support groups, self-help, readings, agencies, private organizations, schools, and other practitioners.

> f. Will I have to take medications? Do you prescribe them? Do you work with others who do that?

Explain how you handle a need for psychiatric medications. Explain how managed care may require an assessment and push for prescriptions, how adherence is crucial, and what your role will be in relating to the client's prescriber. Delay discussions of the relative value of medications versus therapy and combined treatment, of the misuse of drugs, and of their limitations ("Pills don't teach") for clinically determined teachable moments.

> 4. Tell me about appointments.

Your response to this item (and its subitems) should be a straightforward presentation of how you run your practice.

> 5. Tell me about confidentiality.
>    a. What kinds of records do you keep?

Describe your records, or, better yet, show the client the forms you use. You can put the forms and educational materials on your website, as well as putting them in a three-ring binder and placing this binder in your waiting room. ELZ titles his binder "Information for Clients. Please Read."

> b. Can members of my family, or the group [in group therapy], see my records?
> c. Who else will see my records or know about me?

Some possibilities to be explained are these: how the client can read (and can also amend) his or her own records; what the client's MCO (if there is one) has the right to know; what information is provided to collection agencies; and how lawyers and courts might become involved. This may be a good time to explain the process and show the client the form for authorizing the release of records, and describe how this release protects privacy. If you have not given the client your NPP and gotten the consent form signed, this should be done at this point. (See Section 6.4.)

> #### d. When do you have to tell others about the things we discuss?

It is essential that you explain the limits of confidentiality, because what is revealed in confidence cannot be unheard. The usual situations are suicidal or homicidal threats, child or elder neglect and abuse, and court-referred cases. Your intake may suggest other areas worth exploring.

> #### 6. Tell me about money matters.

You should provide a straightforward presentation of your practice's rules about money. Rehearse this, so that you can be comfortable asking for money.

> #### 7. Tell me about health insurance and managed care.
> #### a. What kind of information do you have to give my health insurance company about me?

You can explain this by showing Form 7.2. Chapter 3 describes dealings with MCOs.

> #### b. What will the insurance company decide about my therapy?

Your answer can be as simple as recounting some recent experiences. You can review some key points of your contracts with the MCOs to whose panels you belong.

> #### c. What if you or I disagree with the insurance company about the best treatment?

It is widely accepted that you have an ethical obligation to appeal an MCO's decisions with which you disagree, at least to the first level. Experience suggests exhausting all appeals.

> #### d. How would therapy be different if I did not use insurance and just paid you myself?

This is an invitation to discuss the clinical advantages of a fee-for-service practice in terms of confidentiality, additional treatment options, and expanded goals. Be aware that MCOs' contracts and Medicare rules forbid you to see their clients on a fee-for-service basis.

Be sure to ask at the next session—and, indeed, periodically throughout treatment—whether any new questions have arisen.

## Information You Have a Right to Know

When you come for therapy, you are buying my professional services. Therefore, you need information to make a good decision about entering therapy with me. Below are some questions you might want to ask. You can ask me any of these questions, and I will give you the best answers I can. If my answers are not clear or not complete enough, please ask me again.

1. Tell me about yourself.
   a. Are you a social worker? Psychologist? Psychiatrist? Family therapist? Counselor?
   b. What are some of the advantages and limitations of your profession?
   c. What is your training and experience? Are you licensed by the state? Supervised? Board-certified?
   d. What is the name of your kind of therapy?
   e. How did you learn how to do this therapy? Where?
   f. How many people like me have you worked with? Clients with my cultural or ethnic background? Clients of my sexual orientation or gender identity? Clients with my kind of problem or diagnosis?

2. Tell me about therapy.
   a. How does your kind of therapy work?
   b. What percentage of clients improve? In what ways? How do you know?
   c. What percentage of clients get worse? How do you know?
   d. What percentage of clients improve or get worse without this therapy? How do you know?
   e. Are there negatives or possible risks in this therapy?
   f. About how long will therapy take?
   g. What will I notice when I am getting better?
   h. What should I do if I feel therapy isn't working?
   i. Is there someone I can talk to if I have a problem or a complaint about therapy that we can't work out?
   j. Will I have to take any kind of tests or answer questionnaires?
   k. Do you follow a therapy manual with planned steps?
   l. Do you do therapy over the phone? Over the Internet?
   m. Who else should be involved in my therapy?
   n. Are there any other things I should do to help with my problems?

3. Tell me about other kinds of therapy and help.
   a. What other types of therapy or help are there for my kind of problems?
   b. How does your kind of therapy compare with other kinds of therapy?
   c. How often do they work? How do you know?
   d. What are the risks and benefits of these other approaches?
   e. What are the risks and benefits of not getting therapy?
   f. Will I have to take medications? Do you prescribe them? Do you work with others who do that?

*(continued)*

4. Tell me about appointments.
   a. How do we arrange appointments?
   b. How often do we meet?
   c. How long are sessions? Do I have to pay more for longer ones?
   d. How can I reach you in an emergency?
   e. If you are not available, is there someone I can talk to?
   f. What happens if the weather is bad so I can't come to your office, or if I'm very sick?

5. Tell me about confidentiality.
   a. What kinds of records do you keep?
   b. Can members of my family, or the group [in group therapy], see my records?
   c. Who else will see my records or know about me?
   d. When do you have to tell others about the things we discuss?
   e. What do the laws and government regulations, like HIPAA, say about the privacy of my records?

6. Tell me about money matters.
   a. What is your fee?
   b. Will you ever charge me more?
   c. How do you want to be paid?
   d. Do I need to pay for cancelled or missed appointments?
   e. Do I need to pay for telephone calls, letters, or emails?
   f. If I lose my job or have less income, can my fee be lowered?
   g. If I do not pay the fee, what will you do to collect?

7. Tell me about health insurance and managed care.
   a. What kind of information do you have to give my health insurance company about me?
   b. What will the insurance company decide about my therapy?
   c. What if you or I disagree with the insurance company about the best treatment?
   d. How would therapy be different if I did not use insurance and just paid you myself?

We have now talked about some aspects of our work together, and I expect that this should have answered most of your questions. I will be happy to answer other questions you have as we go along. This will help make your decision a good one.

I have also given you some written information. This has included a Notice of Privacy Practices, the consent form, my Information for Clients brochure, and other papers. You can keep these, and please read them carefully at home.

I, the client (or his or her parent or guardian), have gone over this list with the therapist, and I understand these questions and the therapist's answers.

_____     _____     ____/____/____

Signature of client (or parent/guardian)          Printed name                    Date

I, the clinician, have discussed these issues with the client (and/or his or her parent or guardian). I believe this person fully understands the issues, and I find no reason to believe that this person is not fully competent to give informed consent to my treatment.

_____     ____/____/____

Signature of clinician                                                              Date

❑ Copy accepted by client or   ❑ Copy kept by therapist

223

## 5.4   The Third Path to Informed Consent: Lists of Clients' Rights

The third path to informed consent is more abstract and fluid, and therefore better suited to some therapists and clients than the question list may be. It is the offering of a list of clients' basic rights in psychotherapy.

If you are going to use this approach, you should review the available online lists cited below. Add your own ideas, and then devise a list tailored to the style and needs of your practice. You must also modify these rights statements to fit your local and current legal circumstances before you distribute the list. You should keep it current by consulting with your local ethics committee.

The Patient Bill of Rights from the Mental Health Bill of Rights Project is available from the National Association of Social Workers (http://www.naswdc.org/practice/behavioral_health/mental.asp). A more readable version can be found at another site (http://blogs.psychcentral.com/therapy-soup/2010/05/therapy-patients-bill-of-rights).

In addition, the Psychology Clinic at Western Illinois University has posted its excellent clients' rights statement online (http://www.wiu.edu/users/psyclin/Client_Rights.html). A long but complete listing with attention to the therapist's side has been written for physical therapists, but can be adapted (with permission, of course) and is posted at the site of the World Confederation for Physical Therapy (http://www.wcpt.org/policy/ps-patients-rights). An Internet search will find many similar statements from other settings and organizations. Please examine each rights statement and modify it (with permission) to suit your locale and style of practice. For example, telling a client that he or she cannot refuse court-ordered testing or therapy may insert you into a conflict between the client and the court, which would be better handled by the court (Sam Knapp, personal communication, October 2, 1996).

New Hampshire requires all licensed clinicians to give all clients a copy of a two-page Mental Health Bill of Rights (http://www.nh.gov/mhpb/documents/bill_of_rights.pdf). The five-page original version of Florida's Patient's Bill of Rights and Responsibilities, Florida Statute 381.026, can be found here (http://scmsociety.typepad.com/patients/files/patient_bill_of_rights.pdf), while a one-page summary can be downloaded from here (http://uhs.fsu.edu/docs/patient_rights.pdf).

## 5.5   The Fourth Path to Informed Consent: Psychotherapy Contracts

Contracts are formal statements of exchanges and obligations. They document who is to do what, and so they can establish a different quality of relationship from the other paths by focusing on more specific aspects of therapy activities. The contract forms offered here expand information on the techniques or methods of therapy, and some focus more on the goals of treatment, the "rules" for therapy, or the risks of treatment versus the probability of success.

A treatment contract is evidence of consent, but it is not a substitute for it. The client must still be fully informed through discussions if consent is to be effectively and legally given. Only then should a contract form be completed and signed. As treatment evolves, the terms may be renegotiated and redrafted. If you prefer less legalistic-sounding terminology than "contract," you can call such a form an "understanding" or an "agreement."

We make a distinction between the more detailed "treatment contract" and a more general "consent-to-treatment form." A consent-to-treatment form leaves out many of the goals, problem definitions, methods, and tactics; only the most critical items are stated, so it should not be considered a psychotherapy contract. These pared-down consent forms constitute the fifth path to consent and are covered in the next section. This section offers the more detailed and specific contract approach.

## The Nature of Contracts

Contracts have many advantages, as pointed out by Hare-Mustin et al. (1979):

- They reinforce equality, mutuality, and cooperation because they require negotiation.
- They clarify the relationship's goals, boundaries, and expectations.
- They "prevent misunderstandings about the responsibilities, methods, and practical arrangements of therapy" (p. 8).
- They clarify the roles of each person in the relationship: the therapist as possessing special skills, the client as offering personal knowledge.
- They increase both parties' accountability.

Volk et al. (2012) offer a very brief but thoughtful discussion of the consequences of making relationships with clients into contracts; we recommend reading this before proceeding.

Contracts can also be made therapeutic for some clients by the planned placement of ideas under headings such as "Responsibilities" (e.g., completing all homework assignments) or "Possible Negative Effects of Treatment" (e.g., disappointment with therapy for not making the client's life better without the client's making any efforts). For a contract phrased in terms of the responsibilities of the clinician and of the client, Dr. William McDonald's is simple and clear (http://billmcdonaldonline.com/contract.html). The APA's insurance Trust provides a good example of a contract for working with children (https://www.trustinsurance.com/resources/download-documents).

In phrasing a contract, as in phrasing a client brochure, do not underestimate the difficulties of therapy or promise changes over which you have little control. Continually reevaluate progress and modify the goals as issues become better understood.

Contracts should be tailored to your practice and to the client's individual situation. Sample contract forms are offered in the following pages: a contract for individual psychotherapy, two for treating children and adolescents, and one for group therapy. We also discuss important issues for contracts with families and couples.

## Checklists for Psychotherapy Contracts: Elements and Options

The contracts offered here do not cover all possible variations, and as written they may not suit your way of practicing. Therefore, we offer checklists of the basic elements that a contract should include, with a few additional options. These checklists are designed to help you create your own contracts. You can use one of the several forms as a general model and then adopt items from the checklists. Any items included in the client information brochure (see Section 5.2) could also be incorporated into a contract; however, those are not duplicated here.

The checklists are partially based on ideas developed by the Health Research Group (Adams & Orgel, 1975), as modified in Kachorek (1990, p. 105). They also incorporate ideas from Stromberg et al. (1988, pp. 164–165), Hare-Mustin et al. (1979), Bennett et al. (1990, p. 54), and Stuart (1975).

### Agreement and Consent

❑ Does the form indicate clearly that this is an informal "agreement" and not an exhaustive, complete specification of all treatment variables and issues? Its purpose is to indicate an understanding, or set of mutual expectations, between the client and therapist; its goals are clarification and communication.

❑ Does it fully inform the client of all relevant aspects and decisions, so that the client can consent to treatment as an autonomous adult? Does it state that the client's consent to treatment is voluntary, and that he or she is free to discontinue treatment without penalty (besides the loss of the benefits of treatment)?

❑ Does it tell the client that the contract will become part of the treatment record?

❑ Is there space for the signatures of both client and therapist indicating agreement, and for the dates of the signatures?

### Goals

❑ Are both long-term goals and short-term objectives of the psychotherapy with this client stated?

❑ Have means for measuring progress and outcomes been included?

### Listing and Description of Techniques

❑ Does the form describe treatment techniques, or confirm that the client has been informed of them through discussion with the therapist or reading materials?

❑ Are any uncommon, unexpected, or experimental techniques fully explained with their risks and benefits?

❑ Has the client been informed of any techniques that might be at odds with his or her values?

### Risks and Benefits

❑ Are the likely benefits to the client described fully, accurately, and without any promise of specific outcomes, results, cures, or guarantees?

❑ Are the likely risks to the client described, including contraindications, side effects, and undesirable or negative effects, including the risks of receiving no treatment?

### Client Responsibilities

❑ Does the form state that the client will "cooperate fully" and "to the best of my ability"?

❑ Are specific client responsibilities indicated?

### Therapist Responsibilities: Treatment

❑ Does the form state that the therapist will use his or her best efforts, skills, resources, training, experience, in good faith, in the best interests of the client?

❑ Does the form state that the therapist will operate responsibly and respect professional standards and ethics?

### Therapist Responsibilities: Confidentiality

❑ Does the form indicate the exceptions to confidentiality (see Chapter 8)?

❑ Does the form make it clear that written permission will be needed to disclose information about any specific clients to anyone (with any exceptions listed)?

### Meetings and Fees

❑ Are the location, frequency, and length of meetings indicated together with how they are arranged?

❑ Are fees and charges explicitly stated, including fees for missed sessions?

❑ Is the form clear about when payment is expected?

### Changing the Contract and Terminating Treatment

❑ Does the form state that any of the contract's contents may be renegotiated, but must be honored until changed?

❑ Does it state that the contract may be terminated by either party, but with some explicit advance notice?

## A Contract for Individual Therapy with an Adult

**FORM 5.1**   Form 5.1 is a generalized agreement for adult clients. Modify it to suit your way of working.

## Contracts for Couples and Families

When you go from individual to couple and family therapies, the number of ways of interacting, and thus the number of ethical complexities, increase enormously. Although these complexities cannot be detailed here, there are two excellent reviews available, one by Patten et al. (1991) and one by Hansen et al. (1989).

A brief but pointed discussion of the issues of couple therapy, including secrets and

# Agreement for Individual Therapy

I, _____, the client, agree to meet with the therapist named below at the appointment times and places we agree on, starting on ____/____/____ for about ____ sessions of ____ minutes each.

I have read the following materials on therapy, which have been provided to me by this therapist:

1. _____    3. _____

2. _____    4. _____

I believe I understand the basic ideas, goals, and methods of this therapy. I have no important questions or concerns that we have not discussed. In my own words, I understand the following:

1. According to this therapy, the causes of my problems lie in: _____

2. The main methods to be used in this therapy are: _____

3. During these sessions, we will focus on working toward these goals:

   a. _____

   b. _____

   c. _____

   d. _____

   I understand that reaching these goals is not guaranteed.

4. I understand that I will have to do the following things or take the following actions:

   a. _____

   b. _____

   c. _____

   d. _____

With enough knowledge and understanding, and without being in any way pressured, I enter into treatment with this therapist. I will keep my therapist fully up to date about any changes in my feelings, thoughts, and behaviors. I expect us to work together on any difficulties that occur, and to work them out in my long-term best interest. This commitment also shows my therapist's willingness to use and share his or her knowledge and skills in good faith.

At the end of ____ meetings, we will evaluate progress and may change parts of this agreement as needed. Our goals may have changed in nature, order of importance, or definition. If I am not satisfied by our progress toward goals, I will work to revise this agreement, and I may stop treatment after meeting with the therapist for one last time.

This agreement shows my commitment to pay for my therapist's services. I agree to pay $____ per session at the beginning of each session. I agree to pay for uncanceled appointments or those where I fail to give the agreed-upon notice that I will not attend. I understand and accept that I am fully responsible for this fee, and that my therapist will help me in getting payments from any insurance coverage I have. I understand that this agreement will become part of my record of treatment.

I also give my permission for the therapist to take notes and to make electronic recordings of our sessions

*(continued)*

for personal review and use with a consultant, who is also bound by the legal framework of privacy and confidentiality. I understand that any information in this recording that could identify me in any way will not be published or given out without my written consent.

My signature below means that I understand and agree with all of the points above and on the previous page.

_____     ____/____/____

Signature of client                                                                          Date

I, the therapist, have discussed the issues above with the client. My observations of this client's behavior and responses give me no reason, in my professional judgment, to believe that this person is not fully competent to give informed and willing consent.

_____     ____/____/____

Signature of therapist                                                                       Date

❑ Copy accepted by client or   ❑ Copy kept by therapist

*This is a strictly confidential patient medical record. Redisclosure or transfer is expressly prohibited by law.*

defining the client, can be found in Pukay-Martin (n.d.). The two most common ethical problems are the situations when only one partner comes for therapy and when there are secrets in the family. Your contracts should address both in detail. More specifically, the contract should state your policy on nonattendance by a family member or one member of a couple. It should state your policy on handling family secrets (e.g., an affair or financial information), including information shared with you when you cannot refuse it (e.g., voice-mail). The contract should also make clear who can release records of joint sessions, as well as carry protection against clinical records' being sought for forensic purposes.

## Contracts for Therapy with Minors

### A Contract for Parental Consent to Therapy with a Minor

Before treating minor children, you should have the consent of both parents, or nonparents who have legal authority—but in some cases obtaining this consent can become problem-atic. What if one parent refuses consent or withdraws it after treatment has begun? What if a parent plans to use your assessments and notes for a custody fight, but reveals this only after treatment is underway? Does your state's board have rules about complicated consent-ing, or does your location have relevant laws defining some youngsters as adults or about minors seeking treatment on their own? What effect would a custody decree, an accusation, or a finding of abuse have on your treatment?

When one parent brings a child to your office, always ask about the other parent's involvement. You need to consider whether the other parent might have any objections; this can help you prevent later disagreements and perhaps board complaints from feuding parents. Our advice about the various possibilities in this situation (keep in mind that we are not lawyers) is as follows.

**Always ask about marriage, separation, divorce, and custody on intake.** If there has been a custody decision, require the parent to bring the paperwork to the first meeting. It may be sufficient to get an oral agreement to treatment from the other parent (and docu-ment this in your notes), but if the parents seem to be in conflict, litigious, or unsure about custody or treatment, get both parents' formal written consent before going further. Laws and regulations differ, but in general, you can evaluate or treat children from intact families with the permission of either parent and can do so until there is a custody decree. In reality, the one with the legal authority to agree to treatment may be a parent or relative with sole legal custody, a state agency with custody, a guardian *ad litem,* or another person or agency. Clarify this issue by reading the legal agreements; if these are old, call a representative of the court to confirm that they are still in force and have not been superseded.

If only one separated parent asks for treatment and says the other parent will agree but is not present, you might consider seeing the parent and child for just a single evaluation session to help clarify the issues, with the understanding that you will be allowed to contact the other parent and discuss his or her perceptions and the request for your services. Do not offer any findings or recommendations, but perhaps discuss how you might help both parents to work with their child in regard to custodial changes and visitation. Be sensitive to the likelihood that you may be contacted with the agenda of supporting a custody battle or other accusation. Make an effort to clarify and resolve the issues with all involved par-ties. Weigh the impact of treatment on the family, its possible benefits to the child, and your own legal and ethical risks before proceeding. What are the risks of not treating the child?

Which treatment configurations are going to be more distressing to the child, and which less? It may be best to refuse to treat a child during a custody struggle or divorce proceeding unless you get a court order to do so (always the best risk management strategy).

After a divorce or custody decree, you must get the permission to treat the child from the child's legal custodian, who may or may not be the physical custodian. Shared legal custody, which is by far the most common arrangement, will require permission from both parents. If both originally agreed to treatment and one parent later objects, the picture is cloudy. Generally, you can proceed with treatment, but be very careful. Do not initiate treatment of a child over the objections of a parent unless there is an emergency or there has been a court order for therapy. After a custody decision, it is best to have the court write your treatment into the decree. (See also the discussion of Form 5.7 in Section 5.6.)

As long as the other parent's rights have not been terminated, you should get the agreement of both parents that you will provide the noncustodial parent with general information (when you saw the child, his or her overall functioning and progress, treatment goals and plans, etc.). But what if the other parent cannot be located due to homelessness or abandonment? You or the custodial parent must make reasonable efforts, such as sending certified mail to the other parent's last known address, or making some calls to find out whether anyone has a more recent address. The Social Security Administration may assist in cases where the parent is using its services. What if the other parent refuses to consent, refuses to pay for treatment or to consent to the use of his or her insurance (typically feeling that the other parent should pay because he or she brought the child for treatment), or sets up other barriers to treatment? This is a time for consultation and judgment. Always document the facts, your observations, and the thought processes leading to your decisions. If possible, get these issues resolved by including them in the custody or divorce agreements.

**FORM 5.2**    Form 5.2 includes the minimum for written parental consent to assessment and/or treatment of a child, as suggested by Morris (1993). He indicates the need for a written consent unless the evaluation is court-ordered, the situation is a true emergency, or the child is committed to an institution employing you.

Other considerations for a contract include statements on parents' or guardians' legal rights to certain information, on a minor's right to a private life, and on your use of discretion in communicating with parents. You may also include your policy on disclosing a minor's drug use, sexual behavior, or risky/illegal actions, as well as confessions and similar privacies. Will you require children you see to be current on vaccinations (to protect yourself, family, and clients)?

### A Contract for Therapy with an Older Minor

It is important to clarify the legal status of young people in your caseload. Young people may become "emancipated" or be "mature minors" and have adult rights when they marry, graduate from high school, join the military, or live on their own. Other likely exceptions to the need for parental consent are emergencies, treatment for drug and alcohol abuse, and some sensitive medical conditions. Incidentally, it is customary that if people can legally consent to treatment, they have the legal ability to access and to release the records of that treatment, and this custom applies to minors as well.

When you are dealing with any minor, who cannot give consent, obtain substitute ("proxy") consent from the properly informed parent or guardian. In addition, the APA code of ethics (APA, 2010) encourages seeking minors' assent and considering their preferences (Standard 3.10b).

# Agreement for Psychotherapy with a Minor

I, _____, the parent/legal guardian of the minor, _____, give my permission for this minor to receive the following services, procedures, treatments, or assessments:

1. _____

2. _____

3. _____

These are for the purpose(s) of:

1. _____

2. _____

3. _____

These services are to be provided by the therapist named above, or by another professional as the therapist sees fit. The fees for these services will be $____ per session of service, or $____ for the all the planned services. This therapist's office policies concerning missed appointments have been explained to me.

I have been told about the risks and benefits of receiving these services and the risks and benefits of *not* receiving these services, for both this minor and his or her family.

I agree that this professional may also interview, assess, or treat these other persons:

1. _____

2. _____

A report or reports concerning the therapist's findings will be available after this date: ____/____/____. Progress in this minor's treatment will be reviewed on or about this date: ____/____/____ and on a regular basis after that.

I am the legal custodian of this child, and there are no court orders in effect that would prohibit me from consenting to the treatment of this child.

My signature below means that I understand and agree with all of the points above.

_____     ____/____/____
Signature of parent/guardian                                                                 Date

I, the therapist, have discussed the issues above with the minor client's parent or guardian. My observations of this person's behavior and responses give me no reason, in my professional judgment, to believe that this person is not fully competent to give informed and willing consent to the minor client's treatment.

_____     ____/____/____
Signature of therapist                                                                        Date

❑ Copy accepted by client or   ❑ Copy kept by therapist

*This is a strictly confidential patient medical record. Redisclosure or transfer is expressly prohibited by law.*

**FORM 5.2. Contract with parent/guardian for psychotherapy with a minor.** From *The Paper Office for the Digital Age, Fifth Edition*. Copyright © 2017 Edward L. Zuckerman and Keely Kolmes. Published by The Guilford Press. Permission to reproduce this material is granted to purchasers of this book for personal use or use with individual clients (see copyright page for details).

A major concern in treating older children and adolescents is **balancing the degree of legal confidentiality available (little or none) with a minor's needs for privacy and trust in a professional.** No perfect solution exists, but clarity about your rules, stated at the initiation of therapy, is essential. The parents can consent and the child can assent to the treatment and some ground rules about confidentiality. Form 5.3 offers a model that addresses most of the problems. A signed and negotiated "letter of agreement" concerning specifics of confidentiality is advantageous at the onset of treatment, but is difficult to construct before the issues are explored. A well-worded consent form for adolescents, with good examples of behaviors of concern, has been developed by Sherry Kraft, PhD (see http://www.centerforethicalpractice.org/Form-AdolescentConsent).

**FORM 5.3**

Below are paragraphs addressed to parents from Beverly Celotta, PhD, of Gaithersburg, MD, and modified with her kind permission.

> Many children will not share critical information with me if they believe I will tell their parents. For therapy to be helpful, we need open communication and trust in confidentiality. If I betray their trust, then neither you or I would learn about their concerns, and therefore no one would be able to provide the guidance and support they need. Teens especially need to be assured that I will not discuss their sexual activity, substance abuse, eating patterns, and similar issues with their parents, in order to work on these problems in therapy.

Some parents, new to the therapy process, understandably are concerned about the idea of confidentiality for their children. Here is my way of protecting both of you:

- Although I may need to withhold the specifics of conversations I have with your child, I always provide parents with continuing progress reports.
- I always encourage children to share important information with you.
- When you are interested and willing, I can teach you some useful communication techniques so that you may be better able to find out about important issues in your child's life.
- I will share information about any life-threatening, imminent risk to your child or to others.
- By law, I must report any suspected past or present physical or sexual abuse or neglect.

> If you have a concern about these and similar serious issues, please discuss them with me. You might also want to talk with your child's pediatrician, who can do substance abuse and pregnancy tests and other tests as appropriate. By signing below, you agree to give up access to specific, personal information in your child's records.

Form 5.3 is designed to be understood and signed by an older child or adolescent. It was originally written by Glenn W. Humphrey, OFM, PhD, of New York, NY, and is adapted here with his kind permission. To make it fit the client, replace or select the gender pronouns, and perhaps replace "the therapist" with your name and title. You should add to the end of the third paragraph your state rules about sexual contacts with minors if you think it appropriate.

## A Contract for Group Therapy

Orienting a client to a group experience is complex, and only the legal and ethical issues are addressed here, not the clinical ones. You may want to construct one or more additional

# Agreement for Meetings with My Therapist

I, _____, agree to meet with the therapist named below, for _____ time(s) per _____, starting on _____/_____/_____. Our meetings will last about _____ minutes. When we meet, we may talk, draw pictures, play games, or do other things to help this therapist get to know me better and understand my problems, strengths, and goals.

I understand that my parent(s) or guardian(s) have a right to know about how I am doing in therapy, and that this therapist may talk with them to discuss this. They may also talk about concerns and worries they may have about me. They may talk about things the therapist and I decide my parent(s)/guardian(s) need to know about. Sometimes this therapist may meet with my parent(s)/guardian(s) without me. At other times we may all meet together.

The things I talk about in my meetings with the therapist are private. I understand that this therapist will not tell others about the specific things I tell him or her. He or she will not repeat these things to my parent(s)/guardian(s), my teachers, the police, probation officers, or agency employees. But there are two exceptions. First, because of the law, the therapist will tell others what I have said if the therapist comes to believe I might seriously hurt myself or someone else. This therapist will have to tell someone who can help protect me or the person I have talked about hurting. Second, if I am being seriously hurt or threatened by anyone, this therapist has to tell someone for my protection.

Sometimes coming to meetings may interfere with doing other things I would prefer to do. But I also understand that coming to therapy should help me feel or act better in the long run. I understand that sometimes I may not feel good about some things we may talk about in our meetings. Some things we talk about may make me feel angry or sad or frightened. I may feel uncomfortable talking to this therapist because I don't yet know him or her very well. I may feel embarrassed talking about myself or what I have done or what has happened to me. But I understand that these unpleasant feelings may be necessary to make good changes and they will often be temporary. I may find that over time, I will come to trust this therapist and can talk about things that I can't talk to anyone else about. I may learn some new, important, and helpful things about myself and others. I may learn some new and better ways of handling my feelings or coping with my problems. I may feel less worried or angry or depressed and come to feel better about myself.

Any time I have questions or am worried about the things that are happening in therapy, I know I can bring these concerns and worries to this therapist and get explanations I can understand and use. I also know that if my parent(s)/guardian(s) have any questions, the therapist will try to answer them.

I understand that my parent(s)/guardian(s) can stop my coming to therapy if they think that is best. If I decide therapy is not helping me and I want to stop, this therapist will discuss my feelings with me and with my parent(s)/guardian(s). I understand that the final decision about stopping is up to my parent(s)/guardian(s).

Our signatures below mean that we have read this agreement, or have had it read to us, and agree to act according to it.

_____    _____/_____/_____

Signature of child assenting to treatment    Date

*(continued)*

---

**FORM 5.3. Contract for psychotherapy with an older child or adolescent (p. 1 of 2).** Adapted from a form devised by Glenn W. Humphrey, OFM, PhD, of New York, NY, and used by permission of Dr. Humphrey. From *The Paper Office for the Digital Age, Fifth Edition.* Copyright © 2017 Edward L. Zuckerman and Keely Kolmes. Published by The Guilford Press. Permission to reproduce this material is granted to purchasers of this book for personal use or use with individual clients (see copyright page for details).

_____     ____/____/____

_____     ____/____/____

Signature(s) of parent(s)/guardian(s) consenting to treatment      Date(s)

I, the therapist, have discussed the issues above with the minor client and his or her parent(s)/guardian(s). My observations of their behavior and responses gives me no reason, in my professional judgment, to believe that these persons are not fully competent to give informed and willing consent.

_____     ____/____/____

Signature of therapist      Date

❑ Copy accepted by client and parent(s)/guardian(s) or    ❑ Copy kept by therapist

*This is a strictly confidential patient medical record. Redisclosure or transfer is expressly prohibited by law.*

handouts. These may cover the "ground rules," ways members work to promote growth, the roles of leaders, contacts with members' partners, use of drugs and alcohol, violence, and permission to make recordings.

There are some unique risks and benefits you might discuss with the group or add to the contract we present here. **Some possible risks**, according to Soreff and McDuffee (1993, p. 492), include "disclosure of one's name or other information by a group member; emergence of extreme reactions, including disruptive behavior, in response to the intensity of the group experience; acquisition of others' symptoms and behavior from exposure to their psychopathology." **Some possible benefits**, also according to Soreff and McDuffee (1993, p. 492), include "insight into one's relationships; opportunity to practice interpersonal communication skills; recognition of how [one affects] others (group feedback); diminished isolation; increase in sensitivity to the reactions and feelings of others." You could emphasize the processes of member-to-member interactions; feedback from multiple perspectives, and from peers as well as therapists; the potential for exploring socially uncomfortable topics; members' discovering that they are not alone; trying out interactions that are possible only in a group; and the like. Some members may benefit from explanations of the normality of uncomfortable feelings of puzzlement about how this therapy can benefit them; reluctance and concerns with exposure; and the roles of members as audience or "witness bearers," even when they have little to contribute. You might indicate what the leader will do (e.g., serve as "referee" and coordinator, interrupt some kinds of criticism and attacks) and will not do (e.g., take sides, play "the authority").

Many of the issues are the same in group therapy as in other therapy formats, so you might review the other paths to informed consent described above. However, there are important differences. **The legal and ethical rules of confidentiality do not apply to group therapy,** because the members are not professionals (or even cotherapists in the professional/ ethical sense). The legal model in HIPAA and in most states' applicable laws is that information shared with anyone besides a therapist, or a therapist's employee, is no longer protected.

To increase the likelihood of confidentiality's being maintained, you can stress the rationale and importance of maintaining it from the first meeting onward, and model it in the discussions of early group interactions. Repeat the rationale when any new member joins or when the topic comes up in a session, even in an indirect way. Offering many examples of breaking confidentiality seems to help people control their natural desire to gossip. If you see a member of the group in individual therapy as well, be especially cautious when raising issues with this person in the group, to make certain that the information was not given to you in the confidence of the individual session. If it was, generally do not share it or act on it in group sessions without specific authorization. Keep separate records for each kind of therapy.

**FORM 5.4**   Form 5.4 is a contract designed for groups. It may need to be modified or amended to be appropriate for a particular group. Consider the following points carefully:

- This contract is designed to be used with elements from the other paths to informed consent, because it does not cover issues of emergency contact, consultations, and the qualifications of the leader(s).

- Decide on a time-limited or number-of-sessions-limited group format, and include a statement about this in the first paragraph. Requiring a commitment to six sessions for the leaders to assess members and for members to discover benefits is fairly common.

# Agreement for Group Therapy

As a group member, I have rights as well as duties or responsibilities, and I understand that some of them are described in this agreement.

This group will be called _____ and will meet from ____ to ____ on _____ at _____. The total cost of this group is $____, or $____ per session. I agree to pay this fee even for group meetings I do not attend, unless I make other arrangements with the leaders.

The purpose of this group is to provide me with the opportunity to achieve the following goals:

1. _____

2. _____

3. _____

I agree to work in this group. This means openly talking about my thoughts and feelings, honestly reporting my behaviors, keeping my promises, offering helpful feedback (being clear and direct about my reactions to others), and listening as fully and carefully as I can to other members' reactions to me. I have had this process explained to me and understand that it is the core process of group therapy.

I will attend all meetings of this group for the full time period, even if I do not always feel like it. If I cannot attend, I will tell the group a week in advance (at the beginning of that meeting), or, if it is an emergency, call one of the leaders as soon as I know I cannot attend. If I decide not to continue or am unable to continue with the group, I will discuss my reasons with the group and its leaders, and I will attend two sessions after the date of the discussion.

I will not socialize outside the group with any of its members or leaders. This is needed so that everyone will be equals in the group. If I happen to meet a member outside, I will tell the group at our next meeting. I promise not to socialize with members for at least 6 months after the group terminates or I withdraw.

I will also not become a "friend," "follower," or "contact" with any of the other group members on social media for at least 6 months after the group terminates. I also promise to refrain from looking up other members on social media, since this can dilute the value of what we share and disclose to one another in the group. If I fail to keep this commitment, I will discuss it with a group leader so that we can explore how this may affect the group dynamics. I will also notify the group leader if another group member makes contact with me outside the group.

I understand that this group experience is not a replacement for individual therapy. If issues arise for me that are not suitable for the group's process, I may benefit from individual therapy sessions, for which I will have to pay separately from the cost of the group therapy. I will discuss this with the group's leader(s).

I understand that the leaders are required by law to report any suspected child or elder abuse, or credible threats of harm to myself or another person, to the proper authorities and take actions to prevent harm.

With full understanding of the need for confidentiality (respecting and supporting the privacy of what all members share with the group), I accept these rules:

1. We will use only first names. I promise to tell no one outside the group the names of the group members, or in any other way allow someone not in the group to learn their names.

*(continued)*

2. We will permit no children, spouses, partners, significant others, relatives, journalists, or other visitors in our sessions.

3. We will not permit any kind of recordings (audio or video) or photographs of our members or sessions, even by our members or leaders, except for clinical notes made by the leaders.

4. I promise not to seek information beyond what is offered by members during the group about other members, either online or through any other methods.

5. I promise not to tell anyone outside the group about any of the problems, histories, issues, or other facts presented by any group member, even if I conceal the name of the member.

6. I understand and agree that if I break rules 1–5 even without meaning to, I may be asked to leave the group. If I ever break one of these rules on purpose, I will be asked to leave the group. I will also face a possible lawsuit in which I may have to pay damages. If I reveal private information, I give the offended person or persons the right to recover for damages to his, her, or their reputation or other losses or harms. Also, this person or persons may recover for any other damages, losses, or harms that can be proven.

7. I understand and agree that the leaders will keep progress notes on each individual member, and that this record will not contain information by which any other members can be identified. This record, kept in each member's name, can be shared with other professionals only with the member's written consent or to meet legal requirements.

8. I understand that the leaders will keep another record about the group's meetings and the interactions of the members, and that this record will not be included in any member's records. This record may not be shown to anyone without the written agreement of all the members involved and the leaders involved.

9. Other points: _____

I have read the points stated above, have discussed them when I was not clear about them, and have had my questions answered fully. I understand and agree to them, as shown by my signature below.

_____     _____     ____/____/____
Signature of member (or parent/guardian)          Printed name                    Date

Please return a completed and signed copy of this agreement to one of the group's leaders, and you will receive a copy for you to keep.

I, a leader of this group, have discussed the issues above with the client (and/or his or her parent or guardian). My observations of this person's behavior and responses give me no reason to believe that this person is not fully competent, informed and willing to consent to this treatment.

_____     _____     ____/____/____
Signature of leader                              Printed name                    Date

❑ Copy accepted by group member or  ❑ Copy kept by leader

*This is a strictly confidential patient medical record.*

- If you charge a down payment to reserve a place in the group, you may want to include that in your discussion of costs. You may also want to indicate that some fees are not refundable or are negotiable, describe how you handle insurance, and note the costs for missed or cancelled sessions.

- The form includes a prohibition on socializing outside the group meetings, but this may not be appropriate for some support groups. Or you might alter it to require continuing disclosure of all members' relationships to the group.

- If the group concerns domestic violence perpetrators, you might want to add a paragraph giving permission for your full and continuing contact with each group member's partner.

- You may want to require each individual to meet separately with the leaders on a regular basis.

- The provision for a monetary payment for damages in rule 5 is to support a breach-of-contract suit in the future if a member should reveal the contents of group discussions, identity of group members, or other confidential matters. This paragraph is loosely based on one from Morrison et al. (1975) as quoted in Bindrim (1980). You might consider adding a clause to rule 5 that if a group member sues another member for breaching confidentiality, slander or libel, the one being sued will "hold harmless" the therapist for any consequences of the breach. Because state laws vary; consult your practice lawyer for the proper terms.

- In regard to attendance, you might add more on the effects on the group of absent members, tardiness, leaving early, vacation arrangements, and so forth. Discussing expected attendance as a personal commitment one makes to others, each member's irreplaceability, and so on may be useful at this early point. Similarly, the impact on the group's process of adding a new member or having one leave is usually an important clinical topic and may be noted here as such.

- Rule 6, about access to the group notes, might be modified so that this record can be reviewed by any member without needing specific permission of the other members. If so, you will need to write the record in such a manner that it does not identify members or their issues, but documents the topics and conclusions, interaction patterns, and other aspects you deem important to record. You may choose to record the group's process so that you can hypothesize and test dynamics, recall significant statements or important interactions, and so forth, entirely for your own use as a therapist. This kind of record could very probably be protected as a "psychotherapy note" under HIPAA (see Section 7.2 on psychotherapy notes).

## 5.6    The Fifth Path to Informed Consent: Consent to Treatment and Other Services

The "consent-to-treatment forms" presented next are for occasions when a contract would be too detailed or comprehensive, but agreement to participate in treatment must be documented for legal or therapeutic reasons. These consent forms leave out many of the goals, problem definitions, methods, and tactics, and they state only a few of the most critical items.

This section and the next offer several consent forms, covering the following:

- Generic consent to the treatment of an adult.

- Generic consent to the treatment of a minor child.

- Consent to counseling for a child whose parents are separating or divorcing.

- Permission to make electronic recordings of sessions, and to make various uses of case material.

- Consent to psychological testing and assessment.

## Generic Consent to an Adult's Treatment

*Nothing blocks a patient's access to help with such cruel efficiency as a bungled attempt at informed consent. . . .* The doors to our offices and clinics are wide open. The resources are all in place. But not even the most persistent patients can make their way past intimidating forms (which clerks may shove at patients when they first arrive), our set speeches full of non-informative information, and our nervous attempts to meet externally imposed legalistic requirements such as the Health Insurance Portability and Accountability Act. A first step is to recognize that informed consent is not a static ritual but a useful process. (Pope & Vasquez, 2007, p. 135; emphasis added)

**FORM 5.5**   Form 5.5 is a brief form for obtaining consent to the treatment of an adult. It may be useful as a preliminary agreement for a client who would be frustrated and likely to abandon treatment if confronted immediately with a longer and more complex document, such as the client information brochure (Section 5.2 and on the CD). It can be used when simple attendance is not viewed as sufficient consenting to treatment.

## Generic Consent to a Minor Child's Treatment

**FORM 5.6**  Form 5.6 is a brief form for generic consent by a parent or legal guardian to the treatment of a child. Essentially, it certifies that you and the parent have had discussions on the issues relevant to the treatment, but it does not address confidentiality or legal concerns. It is probably best when you sense reluctance and want a signed document before proceeding. With more clarity later, you can use a more extensive document like Form 5.7.

The consent of minors who are allowed to agree to treatment without parental consent (such as for substance abuse) should be documented as well with a variant of this form; add paragraphs tailored to your state's laws.

## Consent to Counseling for a Child of Separation or Divorce

The roles of therapist and forensic evaluator (e.g., of custody, suitability for parenting, eligibility for services) are different, because the clients are different. As a therapist in court, you are an advocate for the child. As a forensic evaluator, your duty is likely to be to the court. Never try to serve in both capacities—it is the classic dual relationship with all its risks (Greenburg & Shulman, 1997).

# Consent to Treatment

I, _____, acknowledge that I have had all my questions about treatment answered fully and to my satisfaction.

I seek and consent to take part in treatment with the therapist named below. I understand that developing a treatment plan with this therapist and regularly reviewing our work toward meeting the treatment goals are in my best interest. I understand and agree to play an active role in the therapy processes.

I understand that no promises have been made to me about the results of treatment or of any procedures provided by this therapist.

I am aware that I may stop my treatment with this therapist at any time. If I do, I will have to pay for the services I have already received. I understand that I may lose other benefits or may have to deal with other problems if I stop treatment. (For example, if my treatment has been court-ordered, I will have to answer to the court.)

I know that I must call to cancel an appointment at least 72 hours (3 business days) before the time of the appointment. If I do not cancel and do not show up, I will be charged for that appointment.

I am aware that my health insurance company or other third-party payer may be given information about my diagnose(s) and life functioning, as well as the type(s), cost(s), date(s), and providers of any services or treatments I receive. I understand that if payment for the services I receive here is not made, the therapist may stop my treatment.

My signature below shows that I understand and agree with all of these statements.

_____    _____    ____/____/____
Signature of client or legal representative            Printed name                              Date

_____    _____
Printed name of legal representative                    Relationship to client

I, the therapist, have discussed the issues above with the client (and/or his or her parent, guardian, or other representative). My observations of this person's behavior and responses give me no reason to believe that this person is not fully competent to give informed and willing consent.

_____    ____/____/____
Signature of therapist                                      Date

❑ Copy accepted by client or   ❑ Copy kept by therapist

*This is a strictly confidential patient medical record. Redisclosure or transfer is expressly prohibited by law.*

# Consent to Treatment of a Child

Name of child client: _____ Date of birth: ____/____/____

The therapist named below and I have discussed my child's situation. I have been informed of the risks and benefits of different treatment choices. The treatment chosen includes these actions and methods:

1. _____

2. _____

3. _____

These actions and methods are planned to move toward these goals:

1. _____

2. _____

3. _____

I have discussed these issues, had my questions answered, and believe that I understand the planned treatment and its likely consequences. Therefore, I agree to make sure my child attends therapy and to play an active role in this treatment as needed, and I give this therapist permission to begin this treatment, as shown by my signature below. I agree to pay for these services, regardless of any other resources that might be available.

I am this child's ❏ Parent ❏ Legal guardian ❏ Other: _____ and have the legal authority to make medical and treatment decisions on behalf of this child.

_____ ____/____/____

_____ ____/____/____

Signature(s) of parent(s)/guardian(s)/other                                      Date

I, the therapist, have discussed the issues above with this child's responsible party. My observations of this person's behavior and responses give me no reason, in my professional judgment, to believe that this person is not fully competent to give fully informed and willing consent to the child's treatment.

_____ ____/____/____

Signature of therapist                                                                    Date

❏ Copy accepted by parent/guardian/other or   ❏ Copy kept by therapist

*This is a strictly confidential patient medical record. Redisclosure or transfer is expressly prohibited by law.*

**FORM 5.6. Form for generic consent to treatment of a child.** From *The Paper Office for the Digital Age, Fifth Edition.* Copyright © 2017 Edward L. Zuckerman and Keely Kolmes. Published by The Guilford Press. Permission to reproduce this material is granted to purchasers of this book for personal use or use with individual clients (see copyright page for details).

Steve Eichel, PhD, of Newark, DE, suggests adding the following clarifications to your contract form, and we quote it here with his kind permission. If you intend to add it to Form 5.7, use it instead of the first paragraph under section 5.

- I, the parent, am aware that requesting the release of treatment notes or plans, reports, or evaluations (which you made as this child's therapist) for forensic purposes (such as in separation, divorce, or custody actions), or subpoenaing them or your testimony about the content of my child's treatment, will interfere with the therapy relationship so necessary for progress and so will greatly jeopardize my child's health and well-being. Therefore, I, by signing below, knowingly and freely waive my right to request the release of information (beyond the attendance, dates, and length of our meetings, and your charges) to my attorney or any other officer of the court. I understand that release of clinically significant information to any officer of the court shall only be in response to a court order signed by a duly appointed judge.

The children of divorcing parents often have an obvious need for treatment. Yet a therapist can easily stumble into a minefield of unresolvable conflicts, so, again, we strongly advise that you do not serve as both treater and evaluator. Even an evaluator with a comprehensive understanding of family dynamics and developmental issues should also have very good understanding of family law and legal procedures. Garber's (2015) book can be highly recommended because of its integration of these areas in its multidimensional fam-
**FORM 5.7** ily evaluation tools. Form 5.7 is designed to educate the parents and inform them about the role you will assume. It asks parents and other concerned adults to agree to the treatment of their child, support full and open communication, and not disrupt the therapeutic relationship with personal or legal concerns. It is adapted from a form by Garber (1994) that addresses the important points.

If the parents endorse this agreement beforehand, this should greatly reduce your exposure to complaints, in addition to supporting meaningful therapeutic interventions. Before using the form, modify the language to suit your state's rules on confidentiality and legal discovery and on mandated reporting.

Caroline Danda, PhD, of Prairie Village, KS, has a very assertive two-page Agreement which addresses privacy and court involvement at her website (http://www.carolinedanda. com), under Forms. Mary Alice Fisher, PhD, of Charlottesville, VA, has posted a brief informed consent form for the treatment of children of separated or divorced parents at her site (http://www.centerforethicalpractice.org/ethical-legal-resources/practice-resources/ sample-handouts/informed-consent-form-child-therapy-separateddivorced-parents).

**If it is too late to warn parents about the difficulties of a therapist's providing testimony in a custody case,** here are some protective steps you can take (partly based on Saunders, 1993):

1. Make your relationship with each person clear to all parties, especially the lawyers. Assert that you have no opinion about custody (or other legal matters); that your role is therapist and not advocate, evaluator, or the like, and such roles would conflict with the nonjudgmental attitude and the openness and trust necessary for therapy; and that you have already established with the client the rules about confidentiality (with some well-known exceptions) necessary for therapy to operate.

2. Make clear the limits of what you can testify to. You can clarify the child's needs, but cannot offer opinions on parenting skills, because you have not evaluated these

# Letter of Agreement for Parents

Psychotherapy can be very helpful for children of a family where there has been or is going to be a separation or divorce. The therapy relationship can:

- Allow a child to safely learn about and express strong and natural feelings (such as guilt, grief, sadness, fears, and anger) that accompany changes in the family.
- Help children understand their realistic part in these transitions, and prevent inappropriate feelings of guilt and misplaced responsibility.
- Help children work out their part in the new family arrangements and learn how to deal with each member of the rearranged family.
- Give observations, feedback, and recommendations to a child's caregivers. These would be based on accurate scientific knowledge of children's emotional needs and the abilities typical of their ages. These recommendations would be tailored to how your child is dealing with the big changes.

*However,* the value of this therapy will be undermined if the therapy becomes just another issue over which the parents argue and fight. Because of this possibility—and so that I can best help your child—I strongly recommend that each of the child's caregivers (e.g., parents, stepparents, day care workers, guardian ad litem [GAL], etc.) accept and agree to the following terms before therapy is started:

1. My main focus as your child's therapist is on the best way to respond to your child's emotional needs. To do this best, I will, at a minimum, need to meet with your child and each of his or her caregivers. At these meetings, I will gather the information I need to understand how others (e.g., pediatrician, teachers, counselors, other psychologists, social workers) see your child functioning emotionally and behaviorally, alone and with others. I may recommend that you consult your pediatrician or other specific professionals.

2. I ask that all the caregivers frequently and openly talk to each other (in person, by email, by telephone, in writing, or by other means) about how the child is behaving and feeling. I will, of course, be available for open sharing of information and observations as well.

3. I will not align myself in any way with or against any party to any dispute, and I ask you all to recognize this position, understand it, and make it clear to the child. My allegiance is to the best interest of your child.

4. I strongly recommend that parents and caregivers get involved in psychoeducational groups for parents who are separating or divorcing. There, each member can learn how to conduct a divorce in a way that causes the least amount of upset, distress, or harm to the child. I will refer you to these programs.

5. Privacy and confidentiality for this kind of therapy has some limits, which you need to know about:
   - I take notes about each therapy session. I also record all contacts I have with any people involved with your child. It is possible that these will be subpoenaed by any of you and your attorneys.
   - If you have information you want kept confidential, please ask me about the legal rules about confidentiality *before* you tell me the information, because I may not be able to keep it confidential.
   - Any information that any of you give to me may be revealed to any other caregiver or involved persons.
   - I am legally required to act to protect a child if I should come to suspect harm to the child's health or safety. I may also have to act to protect others from harm.

6. I will not be offering any kind of custody recommendations based on this therapy, because the attitudes and

*(continued)*

---

goals, techniques and methods, and kinds of information needed for custody recommendations are different from and may be opposed to those of a child's psychotherapist.

I strongly urge people legally disputing custody of a child to try other ways to resolve the dispute (such as negotiation, mediation, or custody evaluations) and not try to use the courts.

If, despite the limitations listed above, I am called to appear in court for any reason related to your divorce or separation, please be aware that my fees for both preparation and time in court are $\_\_\_\_ per hour, due to the time these tasks take me away from my practice. These fees must be paid in advance of my work.

7. I expect to be paid at the time I provide services. Fees for any services that create a balance due (for example, consultations with attorneys, teachers, GAL, or other professionals) must be paid promptly and in full as soon as billed.

An initial retainer of $\_\_\_\_ is required before I will start therapy. It will be used against charges for my services, but will be returned at the conclusion of this therapy if not used.

I have made this list because I have come to believe that clarity about these points will prevent difficulties that commonly arise. Your signature below indicates that you have read, understand, and agree to the points made above.

| | | |
|---|---|---|
| _____ | _____ | ___/___/___ |
| Caregiver's signature | Printed name | Date |
| _____ | _____ | ___/___/___ |
| Caregiver's signature | Printed name | Date |
| _____ | _____ | ___/___/___ |
| Caregiver's signature | Printed name | Date |

_____     ___/___/___   _____
Child's name     Date of birth     Age

_____     ___/___/___
Mental health professional     Date

❑ Copy accepted by client or   ❑ Copy kept by therapist

*This is a strictly confidential patient medical record. Redisclosure or transfer is expressly prohibited by law.*

with the methods required for ethical practice. Suggest independent evaluations of all parties, and make referrals where necessary to court-appointed custody evaluators or other evaluators.

3.  The parties did not enter therapy having consented to your testifying, and so may have offered information that they would now not consent to your revealing. With a lawyer's support, you can try to invoke the privileged communication statute (to avoid revealing the contents of therapy).

4.  Explain to the parents' attorneys that your testifying could easily lead to termination of the therapeutic relationship. Either parent might be offended by what you might reveal and might end his or her consent to treatment, and the consent of both parents is legally required to treat (in the absence of a sole legal custody decision). State that in your professional opinion, continued therapy is in the child's best interest, and causing such termination would harm the child and could embarrass that parent's attorney in court.

5.  If you are compelled to testify, ask the judge to limit your testimony to only the questions the judge and you agree are appropriate to your role as therapist. You might ask to receive and answer questions in writing.

6.  If you are compelled to testify, withhold any opinions and serve only as a fact witness. In that role you can only report dates of service, note costs, and affirm that you provided the services to the client. You can say what the client said and did, but not why. If you are testifying to more than this, all your statements are professional judgments and opinions, and so you are testifying as an expert witness and deserve preparation time and higher fees.

7.  If your records have been subpoenaed, an option is to ask the judge to redact your records to exclude content irrelevant to the issues at hand *and* potentially harmful to the clients.

8.  A way to discourage your being dragged into legal proceedings over a child you are treating, even after parents sign an agreement not to do so, is to inform them that they will be billed at your much higher forensic rates for all your time spent on legal issues (e.g., responding to the attorneys to explain why you will not be providing some information, answering phone calls and mail, reading reports, writing reports and case note documentation, conferring in person or by phone, traveling from your office to the court, waiting to testify). Indicate that such payments must be received before depositions or testimony.

## 5.7   Other Consents

### Authorization to Record Sessions and Use Case Materials

There is an inescapable conflict of values between protecting your clients' privacy and publishing your clinical work to advance the educational and scientific needs of the field. Do consider the effects on the treatment relationship, address issues of the "ownership" of the material, and weigh the possibility of complaints.

Most situations are covered through simply making identification impossible by altering or omitting the facts of the case, but sometimes these facts cannot be changed, and sometimes information slips through. Sieck (2012) offers a very thoughtful discussion of the options of disguise versus obtaining consent. The use of a fully informative consent form provides better protection for both clients and clinician, with little additional effort. Other methods include using case composites and grouping the data.

If you think you will ever use any of your clinical notes or cases in any future professional work, you should probably get Form 5.8 signed during treatment (but not at the beginning, because the client will not be able to give informed consent without knowing what will come up in therapy). It is also inadequate to ask for the client's consent as you start an electronic recording; the client will not know what will be discussed or revealed, and so cannot give informed consent. Explain this, get verbal consent to proceed (and to stop the recording), and use this form afterward.

Form 5.8 combines a consent-to-record form with a consent to use any materials for any professional purposes. Combining these functions gives you more options for future use of case materials, while addressing the confidentiality concerns of clients.

A decision to be made and then documented in the form concerns whether the recording should be made part of the client's clinical records. If so, it needs to be maintained for many years, in accord with the record retention rules in place. Why be concerned with this? If the client should seek "all" of his or her records in the future, should the recording be released? It will contain very different material from that in the clinician's notes. What if the client reports on an incident that triggers a mandated report? What if a trainee's behavior falls so far below expectations that supervisory intervention is required and this event is preserved? When and how can these be removed?

**FORM 5.8** Form 5.8 is based on ideas from two forms: Release and Permission to Tape Form (by Elizabeth A. Schilson, PhD) and Client Informed Consent for Videotaping. Both forms are included in Piercy et al. (1989).

Under HIPAA, you must distinguish PHI for use in treatment or training from **PHI for use in research.** The former does not require a separate authorization, because such use is covered under normal "treatment, payment, and health care operations," and consent would have been obtained with the NPP (see Section 6.4) during the intake process. Form 5.8 supports recording sessions before you decide on using them in research, which would need additional documenting under HIPAA or institutional research board rules.

## Consent to Psychological Testing and Assessment

The APA code of ethics (APA, 2010) specifically requires obtaining "informed consent for assessments, evaluations, or diagnostic services, . . . except when (1) testing is mandated by law or governmental regulation; (2) informed consent is implied because testing is conducted as a routine . . . organizational activity . . . or (3) one purpose of the testing is to evaluate decisional capacity" (Standard 9.03a).

Form 5.9 does not refer to the confidentiality of the test materials (such as questions) or test results (such as responses, transcripts, protocols, and scores). Their legal protection from disclosure resides with your state's laws and court decisions. Current practice is to allow the release by clients of their test results, but not to provide the copyrighted testing materials. If the court orders these materials to be provided, an agreement among the

# Consent and Authorization to Record Sessions and to Use Case Materials

As a clinician, I naturally want to know more about how therapy helps people. To understand therapy better, I must collect information about clients before, during, and after therapy. Therefore, I ask you to help by allowing me to record our sessions, and also by filling out some questionnaires about different parts of your life (relationships, changes, concerns, attitudes, etc.). Video and audio recordings are often used as aids in the therapy process, in the education of mental health professionals, and in research. I need to have your written permission to make and use these recordings and materials for these purposes.

I would also be grateful for your consent to use your case material in my other professional activities. It is possible that I would use your material in teaching, supervision, consultation with other clinicians, or scientific research and professional publishing. For these purposes, I might use any of the following. Please check the boxes below to indicate which uses you consent to. (You may revoke your consent at any time.)

- ❑ Clinical or case notes that I or other professionals have written during or after our sessions.
- ❑ Psychological test responses and scores, and responses to questionnaires, checklists, and similar data collection forms.
- ❑ Electronic or other recordings (such as audio and/or video recordings, transcriptions, physiological monitoring, or any other recording method) of any interview, examination, or treatment with me, my employees, or other professionals. These recordings may include clients, clinicians, or others, and may be made in my office or in other settings by other professionals.
- ❑ Observation of our meetings by professionals or student professionals, using video recordings or adjacent observation rooms.
- ❑ Other: _____

For simplicity, everything listed above will be referred to as "materials" in the rest of this form.

Materials will be presented only to other health care professionals and to students in the health professions. All of these persons are bound by federal and state laws and by professional rules about clients' privacy.

When I use materials from my testing or therapy work, I do not want anyone who hears, reads, or sees them to be able to identify you or any other clients involved. Therefore, I would conceal all identities by using one or more of the following methods:

- ❑ Removing (or, if this is not possible, greatly changing) names, dates, places, descriptions, or any other information by which you or anyone else involved could be identified. In particular, I will not use, or allow anyone else to use, your real name in any presentation of any of these materials.
- ❑ Reporting the results as grouped data (that is, publishing only numbers like averages, and not publishing any individual's scores, names, or case numbers).
- ❑ Using any other methods for maintaining confidentiality appropriate to the medium, such as electronically concealing a person's face or altering his or her voice.
- ❑ Using other methods (including those not presently available) that would be consistent with my professional code of ethics and professional guidelines for the maintenance of confidentiality.

I will keep all these materials in a secure location and destroy them when they are no longer needed.

*(continued)*

Therefore, I am asking you to read and agree to the following:

I, _____, the client (or his or her parent or guardian), consent to the recording of sessions and/or the collection of data for the purposes described above. The purposes and value of recording and data collection have been fully explained to me, and I freely and willingly consent to this recording.

I understand that I am fully responsible for my own or my child's participation in any and all exercises and activities suggested by the clinician. I agree not to hold the clinician legally responsible for the effects of these activities on me/my child, either during the session or later.

I give the clinician named below my permission to use the materials for research, teaching, and advancing other professional purposes. I understand that they will be used as an aid in the process of improving mental health work or training health care workers. I agree that the materials may be sold or otherwise made available to health care professionals for educational, training, and/or research purposes.

This consent is being given in relation to the professional services being provided by the clinician named below. I agree that I am to receive no financial benefit from the use of the materials.

By signing below, I give up my rights to any and all interests that I may have in the materials which I have authorized above. I agree to let the clinician be the sole owner of all the rights in these materials for all purposes authorized above. There are no other agreements between us besides this one, and it can only be changed in writing.

I understand that if I do not agree to the uses of these materials or the recording of meetings as indicated, I will not be penalized in any way, and it will not affect the care I am to receive in any way. I understand that I may ask for any recording to be turned off or recordings to be erased at any time during my sessions. I also understand that within 5 business days following a session, I may choose to request a viewing of the recording with the clinician or other appropriate staff members and I can then ask for the recording to be destroyed. If I choose to ask this, I will deliver a written statement to this effect to the clinician within 5 business days following the viewing.

❑ I give permission only for the use of video conferencing via the Internet to provide therapy or assessment or other clinical purposes to me or my child. I ❑ do or ❑ do not give permission to record the sessions or consultations. I understand that while all reasonable precautions will be taken to insure confidentiality it cannot be guaranteed, and I will not hold the clinician responsible for any consequences or harms. I understand that I can withdraw this consent at any time.

_____     _____     ___/___/___
Signature of client  (or parent/guardian)                    Printed name                              Date

I, the clinician, have discussed the issues above with the client (and/or his or her parent or guardian). My observations of this person's behavior and responses give me no reason to believe that this person is not fully competent to give informed and willing consent.

_____     ___/___/___
                              Signature of clinician                                              Date

❑ Copy accepted by client or   ❑ Copy kept by clinician

This is a strictly confidential patient medical record. Redisclosure or transfer may be prohibited by law.

attorneys to limit access to those materials to professionals can be sought. However, sadly, almost all test materials can be found on the Internet with a little searching by those motivated to do so.

HIPAA does not specifically address these materials. However, one might argue that these should be included in "results of clinical tests," and thereby should go into the general medical record rather than into HIPAA-protected psychotherapy notes (see Section 7.2).

**FORM 5.9**   Form 5.9 is both a consent form for testing and an agreement to pay for such evaluations; it covers the most common and simplest cases. This form is based on one created by the late John M. Smothers, PhD, ABPP, of Bethesda, MD.

Additions could include the following:

---

- I understand that questions may involve personal and private matters that could revive painful memories. I recognize that the evaluator does not intend to cause any discomfort, but is simply doing a professional evaluation.

- I understand that I am being seen for a psychological, neuropsychological, vocational, or _____ evaluation. The evaluation will include an interview, review of records, and testing with various measures of attention, motivation, motor and sensory abilities, language and spatial skills, problem solving, memory, emotional or personality functioning, and similar or related tests. I can ask for more explanations and information about any of these.

- This evaluation is scheduled for a [full day/____ hours]. I can ask for breaks, and, if needed, I may return on another day to give my best performance. Feedback will be provided at the completion of testing, or arrangements will be made to provide feedback at a later date.

---

## Consent to Being Evaluated for a Third Party

Problems may arise when either a child or an adult is referred for an evaluation whose results are to be used by the referrer (such as a court, lawyer, or disability agency) for its own purposes, which may not overlap with the client's preferences or even best interests. If you take such a case, you may be placed in a position where your obligations (to the client, to the referring agency, to the payer, to principles of beneficence, etc.) conflict. For fully informed consent in such cases, you should advise clients whom you are testing that the results may not be in their favor. A form is needed that combines the elements of consent to be evaluated and release of the results of the evaluation. Such a consent form can be found online (http://riverhillsneuro.com/wp-content/uploads/2012/12/NP-Behav12_12.pdf).

## Consent and Agreement for Psychological Testing and Evaluation Services

I understand that the purpose of this evaluation is to provide information about ❑ me or ❑ _____ for this purpose:

❑ Treatment planning ❑ A civil or criminal case, or other legal proceedings

❑ Entry into a program ❑ Eligibility for services (specify): _____

❑ Other (specify): _____

I understand that a report of the findings of this assessment will be sent to _____.
This person or organization or designate will be responsible for disclosure or distribution of this report.

I, _____, agree to allow the psychologist named below to perform the following services:

❑ Psychological testing, assessment, or evaluation ❑ Report writing

❑ Consultation with ❑ School personnel ❑ Lawyers ❑ Other (specify): _____

❑ Deposition (that is, written or oral testimony given to a court, but not made in open court) ❑ Testimony in court ❑ Other (specify): _____

I understand that these services may include face-to-face interviewing or administering tests, questionnaires, checklists, and other assessment methods. They may also include the psychologist's time required for the reading of records, consultations with other psychologists and professionals, scoring of tests, interpreting the results, constructing a report about the results and findings, and other activities to support these services. If I have questions or concerns about this assessment, the psychologist agrees to discuss these although some answers may be deferred until after completion of the testing and interview.

I understand that the fee for this (these) service(s) will be $____ per hour, or a total of $____, and that this is payable in two parts: a deposit of $____ payable before the start of this (these) service(s), and a second payment of the balance due on the completion and delivery of any report. For forensic functions, all charges must be paid before the assessment begins by means of a retainer of $____ against the final costs. I understand that I am fully responsible for payment for these costs and payments.

I also understand the psychologist agrees that the procedures for selecting, administering, and scoring the tests, interpreting the results, and maintaining my privacy will be carried out in accord with the rules and guidelines of the American Psychological Association, other professional organizations, and with the applicable state and federal laws.

I agree to cooperate and help as much as I can by supplying full and accurate answers and making a sincere effort. I understand that I may refuse to answer any question or terminate the evaluation whenever I wish. I understand that whatever I say during this evaluation may later be the subject of inquiry. I understand that the evaluator is required to notify authorities if the evaluator believes or suspects that a child is abused, or if the evaluator has reason to believe that I may harm others or myself.

_____     ___/___/___
Signature of client (or parent/guardian)                             Date

I, the psychologist, have discussed the issues above with the client (and/or his or her parent or guardian) and answered any questions raised. My observations of this person's behavior and responses give me no reason, in my professional judgment, to believe that this person is not fully competent to give informed and willing consent.

_____     ___/___/___
Signature of psychologist                                             Date

❑ Copy accepted by client or ❑ Copy kept by psychologist

*This is a strictly confidential patient medical record. Redisclosure or transfer is expressly prohibited by law.*

# CHAPTER 6

# Intake and Assessment Forms and Procedures

## 6.1 Creating the Client's Chart

Most clinicians dislike the burden of paperwork, but the keeping of clinical records is not optional. How, then, can it best be done with the least time and effort? How can you be sure that your records are legally and ethically adequate to protect you? How can you best document your effectiveness for supervisors or third-party payers? Besides these legal, ethical, and practical questions, there are the clinical ones: What do you need to learn about your client to be most helpful? What questions produce responses most relevant to your way of working? Because such clinical information varies so much with each client, we offer basic but complete standardized forms in this chapter.

### The Chronology of Record Making

This chapter and the next one offer standards for making clinical case records, and detailed suggestions for how to meet those standards. **The forms we offer follow the natural chronology of an episode of treatment.** We cover various types of records at the places in the chronology where you need to give them attention.

- We start where you will almost always start with a case—at the first telephone contact and the agreement to meet as therapist and client. You collect the information essential for intake. We call this Phase 1.

- Next, in Phase 2, we offer materials that can constitute a "new-client package," to be mailed, emailed, or downloaded before the first meeting. These include various histories, financial and insurance data, reasons for seeking services, and so forth. If time is short, the client can complete these in the office before the first meeting (Phase 3).

- Phase 3 occurs during the client's first office visit, just before the interview with the client. The main goal is to assure that the more general forms have been completed, but it may also involve completion of additional forms selected because of what was learned from the more general forms. Some of these forms may be completed by the client in the privacy of the office, and some may require the greater confidentiality of the interview.

- Phase 4 is the actual interview. We offer forms for structuring the collection of more detailed data. This information is often sensitive, and its collection requires face-to-face interaction with the client. Examples include information on self-injury, physical or sexual abuse, and mental status. The interview should also include screening questions, where the client's reactions may suggest to the clinician that clinically significant information may be obtained by probing further.

- In Phase 5, the last phase of intake, the data collected are integrated and summarized. We offer forms for summarizing suicide risk, drug and alcohol use, and the formulation of the client's case. These form the basis for the next chapter, Chapter 7, which continues the chronology through treatment planning, treatment progress notes, and termination.

### The Contents of the Record

It is a challenge to keep all of this information logically separated and yet easily accessible for different purposes at different times. See Section 1.4 for more on structures for organizing your records, and Section 7.2 for more on structuring the contents of what you record in your notes.

## 6.2    Phase 1: The Initial Telephone Contact

The client's record should begin at the beginning—with your first contact with him or her as a prospective client. This is almost always by telephone. This initial conversation should have the following goals:

- Assessing whether you are an appropriate clinician to treat this person and problem. This assessment has both clinical and interpersonal aspects.

- Discovering whether there are reasons for refusing this person as a client (see below).

- Making efforts to increase the likelihood that the person will continue in treatment long enough to benefit. This includes rapport building and role socialization. (Section 6.3 discusses this in greater detail.)

- Beginning the chart or record of your relationship (if you accept the caller as a client) so that this record is professional, efficient, and helpful.

- Answering any questions the client may have about your practice or your approach to treatment of his or her issue(s), in order both to achieve informed consent and to deepen the relationship.

Your first contact with future clients can be a source of both satisfaction and income; do it right. Ideally, you should sound competent, efficient, and eager to listen. As the saying goes, you have only one chance to make a good first impression. Practice until you are comfortable, smooth, and confident when offering information and answering common questions. Be prepared to give information about office hours, the types of insurance you accept, your fees, and your credentials. Practice until your statements are anxiety-free and almost routine, so that you can attend to the more subtle aspects of the questions.

Remember, confidentiality extends to this first contact, so make sure no one can overhear you or the client. If you suspect that some highly sensitive information is about to be revealed, make sure to defer it until you can meet with your caller and discuss the implications of its disclosure more fully.

## Reasons for Refusing a Caller as a Client

A caller may not be an appropriate client for you, for a variety of reasons:

- The client has problems outside your areas of expertise. Remember, you are not a master of every effective treatment, and therefore you are not competent to treat every problem or every person seeking treatment (because of a person's special needs, language skills, history, etc.).

- You do not have the time available, and placing the caller on a waiting list is inappropriate or unacceptable. Unless you know the prospective client well (such as when a former client requests to return to treatment), or you have carefully evaluated her or his ability to delay treatment, it is probably best to refer the caller elsewhere immediately. Placing someone on a waiting list might entail some liability if harm comes to the person or to another because of the delay in care.

  If you decide to keep **a waiting list,** a protective written policy could include at least two points. First, state your decision-making criteria—for example, "Priority for being given appointments is based on client need (serious emergencies are given higher priority)." Potential clients should be told to "call if you are experiencing an emergency." Second, indicate the length of your waiting list with an estimate that depends on the number of emergencies, and assumes no staff illnesses or resignations. (This paragraph's ideas are from Sam Knapp, EdD, Professional Affairs Officer of the Pennsylvania Psychological Association, email list posting, November 6, 2006.)

- You and the caller are not able to establish a working relationship for some reason (e.g., your personalities, expectations, or belief systems differ sharply).

- The caller is a relative, coworker, trainee, or the like. (See Section 4.5 on dual relationships.)

- The client cannot afford your fees (and your low-fee and *pro bono* hours are filled).

- The client may not be suitable for outpatient or voluntary treatment because he or she has a significant or recent history of violence, is in an acute medical crisis, has an active and severe substance use disorder, is too cognitively disorganized, is unable to consent to treatment, has repeatedly discontinued treatment against professional advice, or has refused prescribed treatments.

Note that if a deaf client will require an interpreter, or a client whose first language is not English requires a language translator, "to ensure effective communication," you generally may not refuse the client. In the former case, you may have to bear the cost of an interpreter (one is required by the Americans with Disabilities Act), as insurers will not pay for this. Also, get a confidentiality agreement, which professional interpreters will have available. An online article offers more details about interpreters for deaf clients (http://www.trustinsurance.com/resources/articles/ADADeafInterpreters.pdf).

If you decide you need to refer a caller elsewhere, you might say something like this:

> "I want to make sure you get the best treatment possible, and I know now that given my training and experience, I'm not able to provide that for you. I do know of someone who is an expert in the kind of problems you are having, and I think that you'll really be pleased with this professional and what he [she] can do for you."

## Getting the Essential Data

**FORM 6.1**  The simplest way to ensure the collection of basic data is to fill out the first-contact record (Form 6.1) as you talk to the caller. You might keep blank copies in your briefcase, datebook, laptop, or tablet device, so as to have one always available when you get a referral. Using the sequence of Form 6.1 will assure that cover these essential points:

1. Get the client's name and address, spelled correctly (ask), and obtain a private and secure means of contact. This means will be essential if the client fails to keep the appointment or if you have to contact the client (or another person) to cancel, reschedule, or respond. (See Section 6.3.) Since confidentiality begins here, when you ask for phone numbers, email, or street address, ask whether it is all right to call and ask for the client by name or send mail to the address. If not, make some other arrangement (e.g., perhaps call only during certain hours).

2. Identify the referrer by asking, "And how did you get my name?" This answer is needed for some insurance; more importantly, however, it tells you about your reputation and professional network, and perhaps about the client's understanding of the problem. If doing so is appropriate later, you can ask for permission to send thanks to the referrer and confirmation that the referral was completed. Having the caller offer a name may also increase the likelihood of his or her coming in if the referrer is someone the client will see again, such as a primary care provider (PCP), who may ask about the referral. If the client got your name from an advertisement or presentation you made to a group, ask, "What moved you to call?" or "Why did you call me in particular?" These are the clinically important "Why now?" questions. The answers are clinically useful (see Section 6.3), are relevant to your marketing efforts, and are natural bridges to discussing the presenting problem. Such questions might be informative even in cases where clients got your name from a managed care organization's (MCO's) panel or staff person, or if they simply did an Internet search.

3. Ask about the chief complaint or chief concern, so that you can decide whether the caller has reached the wrong type of helper, and you can then make a better referral. Elicit this information by asking the caller, "Please tell me briefly what problem has caused you to call me," or "Please tell me about what is troubling you," or "Please try to tell me the problem in one sentence." Ask whether the client has had

# First-Contact Record

Date: ____ / ____ / ____    Time: ____ A.M./P.M.    **Case record #:** _____

## Identification

Caller: _____    Client (if not caller): _____

Caller is   ❑ client   ❑ spouse/partner   ❑ parent   ❑ legal guardian   ❑ referrer   other: _____

## Phones

Home or evening number: _____    Work: _____    Cell: _____

Client gives permission to be called or to leave messages at:   ❑ Home   ❑ Work   ❑ Cell   ❑ Email

Restrictions on messages or contact: _____

Client's private email address: _____    Password for encrypted email: _____

**Street address:** _____

_____

May we send mail to this address?   ❑ Yes   ❑ No, use this address: _____

_____

**Referral source:** _____    ❑ Personal   ❑ Professional

❑ Other: _____

**Chief complaint** (in client's exact words): _____

_____

**Previous treatment** (where/with whom, nature, outcome): _____

_____

**Urgency estimate:**   ❑ Emergency; immediate interventions   ❑ Serious disruption of functioning; act in next 24 hours   ❑ Treatment needed; act soon/routine   ❑ Wait for: _____

**Triage:** Referral to: _____    for: _____

**Any questions?** _____

_____

_____

*(continued)*

**Follow-through**

First appointment scheduled for _____/_____/_____ at _____ A.M./P.M. at (location): _____

❑ Bring goals to first meeting?  ❑ Bring meds?  ❑ Directions?  ❑ Map?  ❑ Cancellation costs and method?

❑ New-client package:  ❑ Told client to download  ❑ Sent by email  ❑ Sent by postal mail  ❑ Not sent

❑ Fees explained. Name on credit card: _____  Card #: _____
   Exp. date: _____/_____  CVS: _____  Billing address for card if different from client's: _____

❑ Preauthorization initiated.  ❑ Call: _____  at: _____

**Performance monitoring**

Return call: Date: _____/_____/_____  at: _____ A.M./P.M. to: _____  Initials of call returner: _____

Call response latency: Days: _____  Hours: _____  Appointment latency: Days: _____  Hours: _____

*This is a strictly confidential patient medical record. Redisclosure or transfer is expressly prohibited by law.*

treatment for this concern before or whether it is new; if it has been treated before, ask about that treatment. Was it helpful? Why or why not?

4. Determine the urgency of the problem. Ask whether the caller feels that he or she is in crisis, or whether he or she will be all right until the appointment. Has there been harm? Get enough information about the situation so that you can decide whether you can accept the client or refer for emergency care.

5. Ask, "Do you have any questions?" The most usual question is about fees. Prepare a short and simple explanation and rehearse it several times, *today*. Most of us are uncomfortable talking plainly about money. Determining the ability to pay your fees at this time may save time interviewing. If you say "No" to the insurance question, the caller probably won't immediately hang up, and you could ask, "Are you certain that you want to use your insurance for therapy?" They are unlikely to have examined the costs of its use in terms of loss of confidentiality and uncertainty of payments. Handout 3.1 can be offered as an email courtesy, and you may get the caller as a client, because you will be seen as knowledgeable. In addition, many policies with high deductibles and large copays (both of which are becoming more common) substantially reduce the benefit of using health insurance. A health savings account (HSA) or flexible spending account (FSA) can help to offset these costs. For more on insurance, see Chapter 3. If the client wants to use insurance, you may need preauthorization or precertification *before* seeing the client, so collect the information you will need during the first call. Use the top half of Form 3.1 or Form 6.10 to gather this information.

6. Ask for the financial information indicated in Form 6.1. It can serve two purposes:

   a. If you suspect that something is not quite right in this call or that there is unstable or insincere motivation for treatment, it is wise to gather financial information (such as credit card numbers) as a means of screening the client, as well as to state clearly that you will charge the client the full fee if he or she does not show up for appointments including the first session.

   b. Raising these issues and making this statement will indeed enable you to charge for your (lost) time and effort if the client fails to keep the appointment.

7. If the insurance situation is clear, and *only* if you are comfortable with the client and feel competent to deal with the problems, schedule the first appointment. Write its date and time in your appointment book. The longer the caller has to wait to see you, the less likely he or she is to come in. (See the discussion of reducing dropout in Section 6.3.) Less than 24 hours is ideal service (you would want that for yourself), but it does not allow enough time to mail out the new-client package, unless you are emailing it or the person can download it from your site.

   You could take this opportunity to negotiate a unique password to be used for encrypted communications with the person (via services such as Hushmail.com). For instance, the person can use this type of service to return your forms, and you can use it to send bills privately, email the client, or deal with other presently unforeseen circumstances. If the client forgets the password, do not email it to him or her, as this negates the security measures you have taken. Contact the client by phone to remind him or her of the password, or give the client a new one. Be aware that if the client uses certain voice services, a message may transcribe your voicemail—texting or emailing the password you left on a voice message, and thus negating this security step in another way.

8. Tell the client you want to use the first meeting to get an understanding of his or her situation or history, the problem, and the ways the client has been coping with the situation. A useful phrasing is "This will be an opportunity for you to find out if I can understand your situation in a way that is useful to you." You can ask the client to bring a "list of issues" to provide some focus.

    Some clinicians tell clients, "We will not have a professional relationship until after our first meeting and evaluation. I will not be your therapist until then. I cannot offer you any professional services such as guidance or advice until I complete an evaluation, because I do not have enough information." We believe that this is not always a legally supportable distinction about when the treatment relationship legally begins, but the statement is still protective.

9. You might ask whether the client has any "reservations" or "reluctance" about entering treatment with you now. This is accepting, sensitive, and normalizing of resistance; builds rapport; allows you to address misconceptions; and is very likely to lower the rate of cancellations.

10. Explain your cancellation policy as it applies to first sessions, and make sure it is understood and agreed to. Some clients may need to hear that "This time is set aside exclusively for you," and that if they cancel it will be "impossible to fill this time." KK's practice is to request that clients pay for missed first sessions via Pay-Pal. Explain the costs if this appointment is not kept (delay in resolving problems, getting clarity or relief, or taking action; continued suffering, etc.).

11. Briefly tell the caller how to cancel if an absolute necessity or emergency arises, so you won't be waiting in your office at 10 P.M.

12. Ask whether the caller needs directions to your office. Keep in mind the time of day (for light, landmarks, and safety), the parking situation, and public transportation specifics. Your website should have a map.

13. The bottom of Form 6.1 reminds you of what needs to be done before the first meeting. Make notes here and follow up immediately by making calls, sending your new-client package, directing the client to your website for forms and policies, or whatever is most appropriate to each case. If you will need a translator or interpreter, you must make those arrangements, as noted earlier.

If you need more room for responses, you can use the back of the form. After the first interview, in which other client information forms are completed (see Phases 3 and 4), place the first-contact record at the back of the new chart. The form has a place for entering a case number. If you file records by name, you don't need to use a number; however, if you want to keep all the records for members of a family together, or if the client's name changes, then an anonymous case number may be useful.

To recap, the purposes of Form 6.1 are to enable you to gather data (both demographic and clinical) for the initial appointment, and to support clinical decision making (triage) as early as possible. In addition, when completed, the form can be used for "performance monitoring" of your practices at a later time. You can discover how long it takes to set up an appointment after an inquiry—information that MCOs believe to be important. You can also evaluate the distributions of your clients by age, gender, location, presenting problem, referral source, and so forth, in order to expand or focus your practice.

**6.3**   **Phase 2: The New-Client Package and Other Preappointment Contacts**

The purposes and functions of having the client read and complete some paperwork before the first appointment include the following:

- It provides material evidence of your responsiveness to the client's needs; it solidifies the relationship, demonstrates your caring, and helps initiate the client's attachment to treatment.

- It confirms the existence of an appointment and so the beginning of treatment.

- Because it provides this evidence, it is likely to reduce the rate of no-shows.

- It presents you in a very professional manner—as organized, attentive, responsive, and thorough, and thus ultimately trustworthy.

- It can help you to collect the basic information you need about the client.

- Sending the financial information form (Form 6.10) can get the client used to the idea of paying directly for your services, and can provide necessary information about insurance coverage. Other forms, discussed in Section 6.4, can also be included in the new-client package.

- Seeing how the client fills out the forms can give you information on motivation and competence for therapy.

- Including the client information brochure (see Section 5.2) in the package can help to socialize the client into the role of client, answer unasked questions, and give him or her permission to express further concerns. It can also teach about informed consent, confidentiality, and your way of doing therapy.

- The Health Insurance Portability and Accountability Act (HIPAA) requires that new clients have access to your Notice of Privacy Practices (NPP) at the "first contact." This means that they should be able to **read your NPP on your website** if your site is more than simply educational. So if you direct a new client to your site to fill out other forms, post your NPP there; if you instead mail or email your new-client package, include your NPP. For more on the NPP see the next section. The new-client package and other ways of making contact with a new client are discussed next.

### Ways to Respond Before the Initial Appointment

#### *An Appointment Confirmation Note*

If there is time, confirming the appointment by means of a form letter allows you to give detailed instructions or to express your feelings. This letter can be included in the new-client **FORM 6.2** package, sent by mail, emailed, or downloaded. Form 6.2 is an appointment confirmation letter that you can modify for your practice. It includes language designed to prevent a no-show because of ambivalence and anxiety. It incorporates some ideas from Browning and Browning (as applied in a book of forms by Berk et al., 1994). If you put your forms online, use this as the first page of the package.

### The New-Client Package

Receiving the new-client package confirms the client's intention to enter therapy and lays the groundwork for it. The package should include the client information brochure (see Section 5.2), several of the preliminary assessment forms provided in Section 6.4, and the NPP with its related consent form. A cover letter might say, "In order to get a head start on our work, I would like some information. Please complete the enclosed forms and bring them to our first meeting," or "Please read through the Information for Clients brochure and write any questions you have on it." For specifics on what to include, see below under "Ways of Collecting Further Client Information."

Including a self-addressed stamped envelope with the package, or providing instructions to bring the forms to the first meeting (if time is short), will increase the likelihood that the client will complete the forms. KK has all of her forms on her website with clear instructions for what clients should read before they come in, and what to "print, complete, and bring to your first session."

## Ways of Dealing with No-Shows

If a client does not show for a first appointment, there is not yet a treatment contract with, or a *strong* legal obligation upon, a therapist. It is legally unclear whether setting a first appointment (necessarily based on relatively little information) creates a "doctor–patient relationship," but there is certainly some ethical obligation to provide care appropriate to the initial stages of a professional relationship. Making a phone call is better than sending a note. If you reschedule, arrange prepayment for the missed session(s). You could express your belief in the benefits of treatment and offer referrals. Most clinicians can tell of many clients who went on to work successfully, despite missing initial appointments. Be hopeful.

Many therapists will not call a client who did not show for a regular appointment (or failed to keep or cancel an appointment), out of fear that they will hear complaints about their competence, helpfulness, or methods. Therapists should be more tough-skinned, realistic, and aware of client issues. They should follow up on every missed appointment—ideally during the appointed time, indicating that they are present and still available to be contacted during this time. We advise never waiting more than 24 hours to make this important contact.

There are many reasons for calling, including the ethical responsibility for continuity of care and the need to avoid the possible abandonment of a client. KK says something like this when she calls:

> "I understood [or thought] that we were to meet today at [time]. It's 20 minutes past the hour, and I haven't heard from you. I hope everything is OK. Please get in touch with me as soon as possible and let me know what happened and also if you'd like to confirm our next meeting or reschedule."

Dear _____,

First, let me thank you for choosing me for help with your concerns or problems. I intend and expect to provide you with high-quality professional services.

Your first appointment is scheduled as follows: Day: _____ Date: ____/____/____
Time: _____ A.M./P.M.

Your first appointment may take ____ hours or more, because I will ask you to fill out some paperwork. Please make sure you have enough time scheduled.

Please note the location of your appointment: _____

_____

If you are absolutely unable to keep this appointment, please reschedule it at least ____ hours/days in advance by calling _____.

It is common for those new to therapy to feel both eager to get going and uncomfortable about starting the work of therapy. Do not let some discomfort keep you from beginning what you know will be best for you in the long term. If you have some questions and you believe you need answers before this appointment, please call and let us discuss these. I hope that, as in most situations in life, you will find that if you forge ahead, your worries will soon resolve.

Over the years, my clients have found it very helpful to think ahead about what they want to get from treatment or therapy. Please make some notes about your goals and what is most important to you, so that we can be sure to consider these when we meet.

In order for us to serve you best, please bring a list of *all* your current and recent medications. Please also bring *all* of your health insurance cards, so my staff and I can help determine your coverage, find out whom to bill, and give you an idea of what your costs will be.

The fee for this first visit will be $_____. My office policy is that payment must be made or insurance coverage must be arranged at the time of each visit. Even when you or the person legally responsible for the bill gives information about insurance coverage or other methods of payment, paying the charges for therapy is your responsibility.

I look forward to a productive and successful relationship.

Yours truly,

---

**FORM 6.2. Letter of appointment confirmation.** From *The Paper Office for the Digital Age, Fifth Edition.* Copyright © 2017 Edward L. Zuckerman and Keely Kolmes. Published by The Guilford Press. Permission to reproduce this material is granted to purchasers of this book for personal use or use with individual clients (see copyright page for details).

Even though you are frustrated, if you express acceptance of the client's anxiety and ambivalence, you will always be remembered fondly. Of course, you should not try to solve large (or even medium-sized) problems on the phone or in a message. Calling is a way you can practice your assertiveness (just what a therapist usually preaches) in the face of (fears of) rejection and overconcern with others' opinions, anger, or disappointment.

The client may have had an attack of resistance or reactance, forgotten, "felt better," or had an emergency; may be expressing problematic disorganization; or may simply be ashamed for not showing up and too embarrassed to call. In our experience, about 50% of no-show cases can be attributed to a mix-up in appointment times or some other easily resolvable or nonrecurring cause.

## Minimizing Dropouts

When clients drop out of treatment early, or even before the first appointment, it wastes time and energy, depresses new therapists, limits the interpretation of therapy research, and (of course) fails to benefit the clients. Such clients can often be encouraged to continue in therapy with appropriate interventions like those described below. At a minimum, you need to protect yourself legally from complaints of abandonment. (For issues of termination and procedures for managing it, see Section 7.3.)

Getting clients to show up, to attend longer, or not to drop out may be aided by the following procedures (partly from Pekarik, 1985, and Kobayashi et al., 1998):

- Some clients call and schedule when in a crisis, but lose interest when the crisis passes. Carefully consider the type of crises that you are willing to treat at the start of therapy.

- The phone intake is the time to do more than provide information; it is also the time to assess this person's readiness for and commitment to therapy. Asking about previous treatment, and about the current impetus to come in *now,* may provide information that helps you decide whether this person is a good fit for your practice.

- Carefully screening referrals from generic lists and managed care panels can reduce no-shows.

- Requiring a PayPal or credit card payment at the time of scheduling to "hold" the appointment, and reminding the client that your cancellation policy applies to first sessions, can also help.

- Consider offering services at alternative hours or days (e.g., seeing clients on Sundays or at 7 A.M. or 10 P.M.).

- Consider using electronic appointment reminder technology.

- You might try shortening the waiting time for an appointment or between appointments.

- Provide usable feedback (video can demonstrate progress) and positive reinforcement for continued attendance.

# 6.4 Phase 3: The New Client's Arrival for a First Meeting

## The Notice of Privacy Practices and the Related Consent Form

HIPAA requires that new clients see your NPP at first contact, which is why it is explained in this section. For informed consent, they should see how you will handle their information before any information is collected, so put the NPP first when you offer these forms or ask clients whether they have read it on your website.

As noted throughout this book, HIPAA requires all **covered entities** (CEs) who provide treatment to tell clients how they will safeguard the client's **protected health information** (PHI) from unauthorized disclosures, and how PHI is **used** in your practice and **disclosed** to others for purposes of **treatment, payment, and health care operations** (TPO). All of these terms are important.

Your NPP (Forms 6.3 and 6.4) should be designed to inform the client about your policies and procedures designed to maintain privacy. The consent form (Form 6.5) that the client signs is not necessarily an agreement to your privacy policies or a consent to release of information (ROI) that is sufficient for your profession and state; it simply indicates that the client agrees that he or she has been exposed to your NPP. Treatment will require much more consenting, and releasing PHI will require an ROI form.

### What Your NPP Must Contain

The NPP is an official and legally required document, but HIPAA deliberately does not offer a standard version of it. Instead, your NPP should reflect your way of working, just as your practice brochure does. It should be integrated into your client intake, education, and orientation forms. The U.S. Department of Health and Human Services (DHHS), which sets rules for HIPAA, says that CEs are "encouraged to provide individuals with the most specific notice possible." (http://www.hhs.gov/hipaa/for-professionals/privacy/guidance/privacy-practices-for-protected-health-information/index.html) The NPP must include and explain at least the following required items if it is not to be considered legally defective:

❑ It must describe all the uses and disclosures of PHI that you are *permitted or required* to make for TPO *without* authorization[1], including those uses or disclosures subject to the consent requirements, such as to law enforcement and public health agencies. You must include at least one example of each type of uses and disclosures you can make in terms of TPO.

❑ It must list the client's rights to do the following things:
  - Request restrictions on certain uses and disclosures (although it must also include a statement that you are not required to agree to a requested restriction).
  - Receive confidential communications of PHI. This means that the client can arrange for you to send mail or bills to certain addresses, or limit phone calls to retain privacy. (In practice, we are accustomed to making these arrangements, so we have not included a form for documenting them; continue to record in your progress notes any arrangements to which you agree.)

---

[1]While HIPAA may allow such disclosures without more authorization, our state laws and ethics require higher privacy protection and so prevail over HIPAA. We should use an ROI for all releases.

- Have "access" to his or her PHI by any means agreed to. HIPAA deliberately does not define "access."
- Amend his or her PHI to correct or provide additional information (although the client cannot require you to alter or delete anything).
- Receive an accounting of disclosures of PHI beyond those used for TPO. These will be very few.
- Receive a paper copy of the NPP upon request.

❏ It must cxplain your legal duty and current practices to maintain the privacy of the client's PHI (use of an ROI form, methods of storing records, etc.) and inform the client that you will abide by the terms of the current NPP.

❏ It must describe how the client can lodge a complaint if the client comes to believe that his or her privacy rights have been violated.

❏ It must state that you will not disclose the PHI for purposes other than TPO without the client's written authorization.

❏ It must inform the client that your business associates (BAs) will comply with the HIPAA regulations and procedures. BAs are your nonemployees who create, receive, use, or transmit PHI on your behalf. They, as well as you, have to do risk assessments and will be held liable for impermissible uses and disclosures. However, you are ultimately responsible and so have to obtain satisfactory assurances of HIPAA compliance through BAs' contracts, and BAs must do the same for their subcontractors.

❏ It must offer the name of and contact information for your privacy or compliance officer.

❏ It must show the date on which the NPP became effective.

There are some more detailed contents, which are included in Forms 6.3 and 6.4.

HIPAA's privacy protection rules interact with your state and other laws, court decisions, local practices, and professional ethics. The versions of NPPs presented in this book are based on HIPAA and have to be considered and modified in light of other, more stringently protective state or federal laws and regulations, as required by Section 164.520(b)(1)(ii)(C) of HIPAA. Please keep in mind that this "cross-walking" of federal and state rules is an evolving process as new laws, court decisions, unintended consequences, and ramifications come to light. Therefore, we recommend that you schedule a reexamination and possible revision of your NPP at yearly intervals.

### Other Required Procedures

❏ **Separate the NPP from the consent form.** The HIPAA Privacy Rule prohibits the NPP and consent form from being combined into a single document. Therefore, put your consent form (Form 6.5) on a separate page, and give it a title making it clear that it is not a continuation of the NPP.

❏ **Post the NPP prominently on your website.** If your practice's site offers or explains any of your clinical services (not, we believe, just information about disorders or other topics), you must direct clients to read your NPP before receiving your service.

If a client has a phone intake and makes an appointment, having your NPP on your website can be wise, since HIPAA requires that you prominently display this information and it should be available at first contact. You must indicate that clients can obtain a paper copy of the NPP and tell them how to do so.

❑ **Post the NPP prominently in your office.** Placing copies in your waiting area is probably sufficient if it is practical to do so. You can laminate the NPP and put it in a three-ring binder with other client education materials, or put it in a rack if you share a waiting area.

❑ **The client must review the NPP and sign the consent form by the first meeting.** This must be done "no later than the date of the first service delivery," so you could supply the NPP before you see the client by making it part of your new-client package. This gives the client time to receive what the regulations call "adequate notice." In any case, the client should be made to review the NPP and sign the consent form before you interview him or her.

❑ **Provide any revised NPP to new clients within 60 days of the changes, and post it.** For current clients, you do not have to document that you provided the revised version nor get a new acknowledgment of receipt of the notice (consent form) but might choose to do so for simplicity or transparency.

❑ **Use understandable language.** HIPAA requires the NPP to be written in "plain language," so that an average reader will understand his or her rights. It does not state a reading level. It does not state "in English," nor does it require versions in any other language or use of an alternative form of communication. However, other laws do mandate non-English versions (e.g., Title VI of the Civil Rights Act of 1964). You should make the effort to provide a version your clients can understand; without this, the goal of having clients understand their rights may not be achieved, and the clients' confidence in your commitment to privacy may be weakened. Versions in many languages are available from many organizations, which you can find by searching the Internet. Although you are not required by law to do so, you should print the NPP in at least 12-point type (like this) or 14-point type (like this) so that everyone can read it.

### An Unabridged NPP

As noted above, the HIPAA regulations do not provide an example of an NPP, but only specify its contents, so each CE is free to choose its own format and wording. A very complete version of an NPP can be found in Form 6.3. We have simplified and condensed the required language for the clients of a typical mental health professional and a small practice. Please do not adopt it uncritically; your NPP should be tailored to the way your office actually works, so that you are only promising what you will deliver. The HIPAA regulations specifically require this adaptiveness, which is the reason why they offer no standard NPP.

**FORM 6.3**

• This version uses the plural "we" to refer to your practice, but you may want to substitute a less formal or more precise "I" for your practice.

• The initial paragraph in all capitals is required to be included verbatim and prominently displayed near the top of the page.

# Notice of Privacy Practices

**THIS NOTICE DESCRIBES HOW MEDICAL INFORMATION ABOUT YOU MAY BE USED AND DISCLOSED AND HOW YOU CAN GET ACCESS TO THIS INFORMATION. PLEASE REVIEW IT CAREFULLY.**

Privacy is a very important concern for all those who come to this office and who work here. It is also complicated, because of the many federal and state laws and our professional ethics. Because the rules are so complicated, some parts of this notice are very detailed, and you probably will have to read them several times to understand them. If you have any questions, our compliance officer [insert name, phone number, and email address of compliance officer here] will be happy to help you understand our procedures and your rights.

**Contents of this notice of privacy practices**

A. Introduction: To our clients

B. What we mean by your medical information

C. Privacy and the laws about privacy

D. How your protected health information (PHI) can be used and shared

    1. Uses and disclosures with your consent

        a. The basic uses and disclosures: For treatment, payment, and health care operations

        b. Other uses and disclosures in health care

    2. Uses and disclosures that *require* your consent and authorization

    3. Uses and disclosures that *don't require* your consent or authorization

        a. When required by law

        b. For law enforcement purposes

        c. For public health activities

        d. For matters relating to deceased persons

        e. For specific government functions

        f. To prevent a serious threat to health or safety

    4. Uses and disclosures where you have *an opportunity to object*

    5. An *accounting* of disclosures we have made

E. Your rights about your protected health information

F. If you have questions or problems

## A. Introduction: To our clients

This notice will tell you how we handle your medical information. It tells how we *use* this information here in this office, how we *disclose* (share) it with other health care professionals and organizations, and how you can see it. We want you to know all of this so that you can make the best decisions for yourself and your family. If you have any questions or want to know more about anything in this notice, please ask our compliance officer for answers or explanations.

*(continued)*

## B. What we mean by your medical information

Each time you visit us or any doctor's office, hospital, clinic, or other health care provider, information is collected about you and your physical and mental health. It may be information about your past, present, or future health or conditions, or the tests or treatment you got from us or from others, or about payment for health care. All this information is called "PHI," which stands for "protected health information" which means its privacy must be protected. This information goes into your medical or health care records in our office.

In this office, your PHI is likely to include these kinds of information:

- Your history: Things that happened to you as a child; your school and work experiences; your marriage, relationships, and other personal history.
- Your medical history of problems and treatments.
- Reasons you came for treatment: Your problems, complaints, symptoms, or needs.
- Diagnoses: These are the medical terms for your problems or symptoms.
- A treatment plan: This is a list of the treatments and other services that we think will best help you.
- Progress notes: Each time you come in, we write down some things about how you are doing, what we notice about you, and what you tell us.
- Records we get from others who treated you or evaluated you.
- Psychological test scores, school records, and other evaluations and reports.
- Information about medications you took or are taking.
- Legal matters.
- Billing and insurance information

There may also be other kinds of information that go into your health care records here.

We use PHI for many purposes. For example, we may use it here:

- To plan your care and treatment.
- To decide how well our treatments are working for you.
- When we talk with other health care professionals who are also treating you, such as your family doctor or the professional who referred you to us. When we do this, we will ask for your consent. Almost always, we will also ask you to sign a release-of-information form, which will explain what information is to be shared and why.
- For teaching and training other health care professionals or for medical or psychological research. If we do this, your name will never be shown, and there will be no way they can find out who you are. Before we do this we will ask for your consent and ask you to sign an authorization, so that you will know what information will be shared and why.
- To show that you actually received services from us, which we billed to you or to your health insurance company.
- For public health officials trying to improve health care in this area of the country.
- To improve the way we do our job by measuring the results of our work.

When you understand what is in your record and what it is used for, you can make better decisions about what other persons or agencies should have this information, when, and why.

## C. Privacy and the laws about privacy

We are required to tell you about privacy because of a federal law, the Health Insurance Portability and Accountability Act of 1996 (HIPAA) and the HIPAA Omnibus Final Rule of 2013. [Insert any state laws that apply.] HIPAA requires us to keep your PHI private and to give you this notice about our legal duties and our privacy practices.

This form is not legal advice. It is just to educate your about your rights and our procedures. It is based on current federal and state laws and might change if those laws or court decisions change. If we change our privacy practices, they will apply to all the PHI we keep. We will also post the new Notice of Privacy Practices in our office

*(continued)*

where everyone can see. You or anyone else can also get a copy from our compliance officer at any time. It is also posted on our website at [insert the URL]. We will obey the rules described in this notice.

## D. How your protected health information (PHI) can be used and shared

Except in some special circumstances, when we use your PHI in this office or disclose it to others, we share only the *minimum necessary* PHI needed for those other people to do their jobs. The laws give you rights to know about your PHI, to know how it is used, and to have a say in how it is shared. So now we will tell you more about what we do with your information.

Mainly, we will use it here and disclose (share) your PHI for routine purposes to provide for your care, and we will explain more about these below. For other uses, we must tell you about them and ask you to sign a written Release of Information form. However, the HIPAA law also says that there are some uses and disclosures that don't need your consent or authorization which we will explain below in section 3. However, in most cases we will explain the PHI and who it will go to and ask you to agree to this by signing a release-of-information form.

### 1. Uses and disclosures with your consent

We need information about you and your condition to provide care to you. In almost all cases, we intend to use your PHI here or share it with other people or organizations to provide treatment to you, arrange for payment for our services, or some other business functions called "health care operations." You have to agree to let us use and share your PHI in the ways that are described in this Notice of Privacy Practices. To agree, we will ask you to sign a separate consent form before we begin to treat you. If you do not consent to this, we will not treat you because there is a risk of not helping you if we don't have some information.

#### a. The basic uses and disclosures: For treatment, payment, and health care operations

Here we will tell you more about how your information will be used for these purposes.

*For treatment.* We use your information to provide you with psychological treatments or services. These might include individual, family, or group therapy; psychological, educational, or vocational testing; treatment planning; or measuring the benefits of our services.

We may share your PHI with others who provide treatment to you. We usually try to share your information with your personal physician, unless you tell us not to. If you are being treated by a team, we can share some of your PHI with the team members, so that these providers will work best together. The other professionals treating you will also enter their findings, the actions they took, and their plans into your medical record, and so we all can decide what treatments work best for you and follow a treatment plan.

If we want to share your PHI with any other professionals outside this office, we will need your permission on a signed release-of-information form. For example, we may refer you to other professionals or consultants for services we cannot provide. When we do this, we need to tell them things about you and your conditions. Later we will get back their findings and opinions, and those will go into your records here. If you receive treatment in the future from other professionals, we can also share your PHI with them. We can do this only when you give your permission by signing a release-of-information form. This is so that you will know what information is being shared and with whom. These are some examples so that you can see how we use and disclose your PHI for treatment.

*For payment.* We may use your information to bill you, your insurance, or others, so we can be paid for the treatments we provide to you. We may contact your insurance company to find out exactly what your insurance covers. We may have to tell them about your diagnoses, what treatments you have received, and the changes we expect in your conditions. We will need to tell them about when we met, your progress, and other similar things. Insurers may also look into a few of our patient records to evaluate the completeness of our record keeping.

*For health care operations.* Using or disclosing your PHI for health care operations goes beyond our care and payment for services. For example, we may use your PHI to see where we can make improvements in the care and services we provide. We may be required to supply some information to some government health agencies, so they can study disorders and treatment and make plans for services that are needed. If we do, your name and all personal information will be removed from what we send.

*(continued)*

*b. Other uses and disclosures in health care*

*Appointment reminders.* We may use and disclose your PHI to reschedule or remind you of appointments for treatment or other care. If you want us to call or write to you only at your home or your work, or you prefer some other way to reach you, we usually can arrange that. Just tell us.

*Treatment alternatives.* We may use and disclose your PHI to tell you about or recommend possible treatments or alternatives that may be of help to you.

*Other benefits and services.* We may use and disclose your PHI to tell you about health-related benefits or services that may be of interest to you.

*Research.* We may use or share your PHI to do research to improve treatments—for example, comparing two treatments for the same disorder, to see which works better or faster. In all cases, your name, address, and other personal information will be removed from the information given to researchers. We will discuss this with you, and we will not use your PHI unless you give your consent on an authorization form. If the researchers need to know who you are, we will discuss the research project with you, and we will not send any information unless you sign a special release-of-information form.

*Business associates.* We hire other businesses to do some jobs for us. In the law, they are called our "business associates." Examples include a copy service to make copies of your health records, and a billing service to figure out, print, and mail our bills. These business associates need to receive some of your PHI to do their jobs properly. To protect your privacy, they have agreed in their contracts with us to safeguard your information just as we do.

## 2. Uses and disclosures that require your consent

If we want to use your information for any purpose besides those described above, we need your permission on a release-of-information form. If you do allow us to use or disclose your PHI, and then change your mind, you can cancel that permission in writing at any time. We will then stop using or disclosing your information for that purpose. Of course, we cannot take back any information we have used here already or disclosed to anyone with your permission.

As a [member of profession/discipline] licensed in this state, and as a member of this state's [professional association] and [these national associations], I maintain your privacy more carefully than is required by HIPAA. The HIPAA rules are described below, but we will almost always discuss these with you and ask you to sign a release of information so that you are fully informed.

## 3. Uses and disclosures that don't require your consent or authorization

The HIPAA laws let us use and disclose some of your PHI without getting your consent or authorization in some cases. Here are some examples of when we might do this. We will almost always notify you if any of these situations occur.

*a. When required by law*

There are some federal, state, or local laws that require us to disclose PHI:

- We have to report suspected abuse [or neglect] of children [elders, frail/disabled persons, etc.] to a state agency.
- If you are involved in a lawsuit or legal proceeding, and we receive a subpoena, discovery request, or other lawful process, we may have to release some of your PHI. We will only do so after telling you about the request and will suggest that you talk to your lawyer.
- We have to disclose some information to the government agencies that check on us to see that we are obeying the privacy laws, and to organizations that review our work for quality and efficiency.

*b. For law enforcement purposes*

We may release medical information if asked to do so by a law enforcement official to investigate a crime or criminal.

*c. For public health activities*

We may disclose some of your PHI to agencies that investigate diseases or injuries.

*(continued)*

### d. For matters relating to deceased persons

We may disclose PHI to coroners, medical examiners, or funeral directors, and to organizations relating to organ, eye, or tissue donations or transplants.

### e. For specific government functions

We may disclose PHI of military personnel and veterans to government benefit programs relating to eligibility and enrollment. We may disclose your PHI to workers' compensation and disability programs, to correctional facilities if you are an inmate, or to other government agencies for national security reasons.

### f. To prevent a serious threat to health or safety

If we come to believe that there is a serious threat to your health or safety, or that of another person or the public, we can disclose some of your PHI. We will only do this to those people who can prevent the danger.

If it is an emergency, and we are unable to get your agreement, we can disclose information if we believe that it is what you would have wanted and if we believe it will help you. When we do share information in an emergency, we will tell you as soon as we can. If you don't approve, we will stop, as long as it is not against the law.

## 4. Uses and disclosures where you have an opportunity to object

We can share some information about you with your family and anyone else you choose, such as close friends or clergy. We will ask you which persons you want us to tell, and what information you want us to tell them about your condition or treatment. You can tell us what you want, and we will honor your wishes as long as it is not against the law.

## 5. An accounting of disclosures we have made

When we disclose your PHI, we will keep a record of whom we sent it to, when we sent it, and what we sent. You can get an accounting (a list) of many of these disclosures. We may charge you a reasonable fee if you request more than one accounting in any 12-month period. If the records were sent as electronic medical records, we will always record that, and there will be no charge for an accounting.

## E. Your rights about your protected health information

1. You can ask us to communicate with you about your health and related issues in a particular way or at a certain place that is more private for you. For example, you can ask us to call you at home, rather than at work, to schedule or cancel an appointment. We will try our best to do as you ask, and we don't need an explanation. Sending your information in emails has some risk that these emails could be read by someone else. We can set up a password-protected email service to prevent this, or you may just accept the risk of using emails just for simple messages like changing appointments, and not use it for any PHI or sensitive information. We ask that you be thoughtful before you put any information in an email and not use email for anything you want kept private. By signing the separate consent form, you agree to this use of email. Please note that anything you send us electronically becomes a part of your legal record, even if we do not place it in the chart. Be mindful of this, and please do not forward us emails from third parties or others in your life. It is better to print those out and bring them in to discuss them.

2. You have the right to ask us to limit what we tell people involved in your care or with payment for your care, such as family members and friends. You can ask us face to face, and we may then ask for your written permission. We don't have to agree to your request, but if we do agree, we will honor it except when it is against the law, when there is an emergency, or when the information is necessary to treat you.

3. You have the right to prevent our sharing your PHI with your insurer or payer for its decisions about your benefits or some other uses, if you paid us directly ("out of pocket") for the treatment or other services and are not asking the insurer to pay for those services unless we are under contract with your insurer (on their panel of providers).

4. You have the right to look at the PHI we have about you, such as your medical and billing records. In some very unusual circumstances, if there is very strong evidence that reading this would cause serious harm to you

(continued)

or someone else, you may not be able to see all of the information.

5. You can get a copy of these records, but we may charge you a reasonable cost-based fee. If your records are in electronic form, not on paper, you can ask an electronic copy of your PHI. Contact our compliance officer to arrange how to see your records. <u>Generally we do not recommend that you get a copy of your records, because the copy might be seen accidentally by others. We will be happy to review the records with you or provide a summary to you, or work out any other method that satisfies you.</u>

6. You have the right to add to (amend) your records to explain or correct anything in them. If you believe that the information in your records is incorrect or missing something important, you can ask us to make additions to your records or to include your own written statements to correct the situation. You have to make this request in writing and send it to our compliance officer.

7. You have the right to a copy of this notice. If we change this notice, we will post the new one in our waiting area, and you can always get a copy from the compliance officer.

8. If you have a problem with how your PHI has been handled, or if you believe your privacy rights have been violated, contact our compliance officer. We will do our best to resolve any problems and do as you ask. You have the right to file a complaint with us and with the Secretary of the U.S. Department of Health and Human Services at 200 Independence Avenue SW, Washington, DC 20201, or by calling 202-619-0257.

9. We will not in any way limit your care here or take any actions against you if you complain or request changes.

You may have other rights that are granted to you by the laws of our state, and these may be the same as or different from the rights described above. We will be happy to discuss these situations with you now or as they arise.

**F. If you have questions or problems**

If you have any questions or problems our health information privacy policies, please contact our compliance officer [insert name, phone number, and email address of compliance officer here].

The effective date of this notice is ____/____/____.

- Under the "For treatment" heading in section D (part 1a) of Form 6.3 is the sentence "We usually share your information with your personal physician unless you tell us not to." You may want to clarify or constrain this statement.

- Under the "Other uses and disclosures in health care" heading in section D (part 1b) is a paragraph on "Other benefits and services." This marketing use of PHI is controversial and rare for mental health work, so you may decide to modify this statement.

- You may need to make a number of adjustments to section D (part 3a). In regard to mandatory reporting of various abuses, note that some states use a "suspicion" standard and others a "belief" standard, so make the appropriate alterations. Regarding lawsuits and legal proceedings, if you are ever subpoenaed by lawyers or receive a court order, you, as the knowledgeable professional, can assert on your clients' behalf their right to privilege (their legal ability to keep some information given to you in confidence out of legal proceedings) if maintaining confidentiality is seen as necessary by the clients and their lawyers. See Section 8.1 for more on this. The risks are sometimes substantial, so see Borkosky and Smith (2015) for guidance.

- On preventing a serious threat to health or safety (section D, part 3f), you should review your state's handling of duty-to-warn situations and then decide on your phrasing of this point.

- The rules of access to records after death are entirely state-specific so edit section D, part 5, as necessary for your state. HIPAA says only that it no longer applies to records older than 50 years after the client's death and may not be worth mentioning for most practices.

- Section E1 allows clients to agree to use email, but only for information that is not PHI. Sending PHI in unencrypted email is allowed after you have advised clients of the risks (as this sentence does) and document their acceptance of the risks. (See the HIPAA Omnibus Final Rule, 2013, with commentary.) However, there are still risks to therapists from unauthorized disclosures, and so we recommend using email only if it is encrypted not just password protected.

- Section E, part 5, concerns clients' access to their records. Here you should consider whether or not you allow clients access to your (HIPAA-protected) psychotherapy notes if you have decided to keep them (see this book's Section 7.2 for more on this subject). In Form 6.3's section E, part 4, the last paragraph reads: "In some very unusual circumstances . . . you may not be able to see all of the information." You might discuss the kinds of information in your progress notes, but you do not need to tell clients or anyone else that you keep psychotherapy notes, unless you are asked in a legal proceeding.

- You should (but are not required to) notify current clients of substantial changes to your NPP, as indicated in section E, part 7. You can add other ways to those listed such as posting to your website or sending it by email.

- At the end of section F, you must indicate a date upon which the form started to be used. Your first version of the NPP would be dated when your practice became HIPAA-compliant.

### Other Versions of the NPP

- The DHHS now provides **model NPPs in English and Spanish.** They are worded for most readers, but this material cannot be made too simple. These versions are designed for medical settings and do not address any state rules, so consider modifying them. They do not include a consent form, but do offer the advantage of nice layouts (they can be found at http://www.hhs.gov/ocr/privacy/hipaa/modelnotices.html). Four versions of the text are offered:

    1. The notice in the form of an eight-page "booklet" nicely laid out, with white spaces, color, and some graphics.

    2. The notice with the design elements found in the booklet, but formatted for five full pages.

    3. The information in a different layout with a summary of the information on the first page, followed by the full content on the following four pages. DHHS calls this the "layered" version.

    4. A text-only version of the notice, the summary first page, and some instructions in seven pages.

    All four versions are arranged under the headings of "Your Rights," "Your Choices," "Other Uses," and "Our Responsibilities." The text is consistent with the HIPAA Omnibus Final Rule of 2013. Unless you have special software, the first three model forms are not editable. If you prefer to revise them for your language preferences and for mental health records, start with the fourth version. If you are simply going to use what is provided, select the first or second version, but read the separate instruction page.

- Medicare's HIPAA website has a suggested and sample NPP, *but only for Medicare clients* (you can see it at http://www.medicare.gov/privacypractices.asp). It is about two pages long and has a reading level of 9th–10th grade. If you intend to use it, you will need to add any variations imposed by more stringent laws in your state and adapt it to your office procedures.

- A long and formal version of the required contents, entitled *HIPAA Privacy Rule Checklists, Section 164.520, Notice of Privacy Practices for Protected Health Information*, is available (http://nchica.org/resources/hipaahitech). This checklist can be helpful if you are designing your own NPP or struggling to integrate the NPP's contents with your current client information materials and procedures.

- Because NPPs must be posted to many client-oriented websites, you can find dozens of versions online with a simple search if you want to see how others are coping with this regulation. Be aware, through, that most of these are written at too high a reading level for many clients to understand (Walfish & Ducey, 2007).

- There was a recent contest to design the most usable NPPs, and the winners have been posted online (http://oncchallenges.ideascale.com/a/pages/digital-privacy-notice-challenge-winners). Most are actually programs or websites designed to be interactive and not printable, but the third winner generates an NPP based on the model NPPs at the DHHS site described in the first bullet point above.

### A Briefer NPP

The federal government recognizes that an unabridged NPP can be intimidating to clients and so allows you to offer **a shorter version,** which must be accompanied by the longer version. This is called a "layered approach." We recommend sending the briefer version with your introductory materials to new clients, and offering them the opportunity to read or receive the longer version when you first meet.

**FORM 6.4**      Our briefer version is provided here as Form 6.4. It may be more suitable when your local rules are more stringent and protective than HIPAA's. It is also suitable if you do not want to offer clients more text that might confuse, distract, or alarm them, but it should not be used as a substitute for the longer version, which you are required to offer or make available.

The paragraph in capitals cannot be altered and must be displayed prominently near the top of the page. The NPPs in Forms 6.3 and 6.4 have both been reorganized and reworded from the way the contents are presented in the regulations, to make reading and understanding them easier for clients.

Your shorter versions should be tailored to the needs of the clients you see in your practice. For example, if your population has lower reading skills, a simplified version might be more appropriate, along with the offer of a fuller (and documented) discussion of the issues. If you see a population whose information is likely to be highly sensitive, you can emphasize or expand the sections (and incorporate local laws) about what information is shared with whom under what conditions.

### Documenting Consent to Privacy Practices

After clients have been notified of their rights (though reading the NPP or having it read or explained to them), a formal acknowledgment of having been informed of your procedures and their rights is sought. This is accomplished by having them sign what is called a "consent" form—but this is *not* a consent to treatment or a legally sufficient (in most situations) authorization for having PHI used or disclosed. It is simply an indication that the client has been exposed to your rules for handling PHI. It would more properly be called an "assent" or "acknowledgment" form. According to the DHHS, no more is required, because clients' consent to the sharing of information is implied by their seeking treatment. HIPAA, which is almost entirely medical in its understandings, incorporates this common-sense view.

**FORM 6.5**      The regulations concerning the consent form can be found at Section 164.506(c) of HIPAA, which specifies all the required contents of such a form. Form 6.5 incorporates all of these.

- The client's PHI may be used and disclosed by the CE to carry out TPO. Actually, you have to specify which uses and which disclosures your office requires to perform specific parts of TPO.

- For more information on uses and disclosures, the client is referred to the NPP.

- The client has a right to review the NPP before signing the consent form.

- The client has a right to request restrictions on uses and disclosures of PHI for TPO (see below). The client must be told that you do not have to agree to these requests, but that if you do, the agreement is binding.

## Notice of Privacy Practices (Brief Version)

THIS NOTICE DESCRIBES HOW MEDICAL INFORMATION ABOUT YOU MAY BE USED AND DISCLOSED AND HOW YOU CAN GET ACCESS TO THIS INFORMATION. PLEASE REVIEW IT CAREFULLY.

### Our commitment to your privacy

As part of providing professional care to you, we will do all we can to maintain the privacy of what is called your "protected health information" (PHI). We are also required by law to keep your PHI private. These laws are complicated, and we must give you this important information. This page is a shorter description of what we do to maintain your privacy. If you would like to read the more detailed version, please ask any staff member for a copy. If you have any questions about our practices, please contact our compliance officer, whose information is listed at the bottom of this page.

### How we use and disclose your protected health information (PHI) with your consent

We will use the information we collect about you mainly to provide you with treatment; to arrange payment for our services; and for some other business activities called, in the law, "health care operations." We will ask you to sign a separate consent form to show that you understand these ways we handle your information. If you do not agree and won't sign this consent form, we will not treat you. If we want to use or send, share, or release your PHI for other purposes, we will discuss this with you so you fully understand it, and ask you to sign a release-of-information form to allow this.

### Disclosing your health information without your consent

There are some times when the laws require us to share your information without getting your consent. They are described in the longer version of our Notice of Privacy Practices, but here are the most common situations:
1. When there is a serious threat to your or another person's health or safety or to the public. We will only share information with people who are able to help prevent or reduce the danger.
2. When we are required to do so by lawsuits and other legal or court proceedings.
3. When a law enforcement official requires us to do so.
4. For workers' compensation and some similar programs if you seek these benefits.

### Your rights about your health information

1. You can ask us to communicate with you in a particular way or at a certain place that is more private for you. For example, you can ask us to call you at home, rather than at work, to schedule or cancel an appointment. We will try our best to do as you ask.
2. You can ask us to limit what we tell people involved in your care or the payment for your care, such as family members and friends.
3. You have the right to look at the health information we have about you, such as your medical chart, case file, and billing records. You can get a copy of these records, and we can charge you for it. Please talk to our compliance officer to arrange how to see your records.
4. If you believe that the information in our records is incorrect or missing something important, you can ask us to make additions to your records to correct the situation. You have to make this request in writing and send it to our compliance officer.
5. You have the right to file a complaint if you believe your privacy rights have been violated. You can file a complaint with our compliance officer and with the Secretary of the U.S. Department of Health and Human Services. All complaints must be in writing. Filing a complaint will not change the health care we provide to you in any way.
6. You have the right to a copy of this notice.

Also, you may have other rights that are granted to you by the laws of our state, and these may be the same as or different from the rights described above. Our compliance officer will be happy to discuss these situations or answer any questions now or as they arise. Here are the officer's name and contact information: [insert name, phone number, and email of privacy officer here].          The effective date of this notice is ____/____/____.

## Consent to Use and Disclose Your Health Information

This form is an agreement between you, _____, and me/us, _____.
When we use the words "you" and "your" below, this can mean you, your child, or a person for whom you are the legal or personal representative if you have written his or her name here: _____.

When we examine, evaluate, diagnose, treat, or refer you, we will be collecting what the law calls "protected health information" (PHI) about you. We need to use this information in our office to decide what treatment is best for you and to provide this treatment to you. We may also share this information with others to arrange payment for your treatment, to help others provide other treatment to you, or to carry out certain business or government functions.

By signing this form, you are agreeing to let us use your PHI here and to send it to others for the purposes described just above. Your signature below acknowledges that you have read or heard our Notice of Privacy Practices, which explains in more detail what your rights are and how we can use and share your information. If you do not sign this form agreeing to our privacy practices, we cannot treat you, because we need to use your PHI to evaluate, diagnose, and treat you.

In the future, we may change how we use and share your PHI, and so we may change our Notice of Privacy Practices. If we do change it, you can get a copy from our website [insert website URL here], or from our compliance officer, [insert officer's name here], who can be reached at [insert officer's phone number and email here].

After you have signed this consent, you have the right to revoke it by writing to our compliance officer. We will then stop using or sharing your PHI, but if we have already used or shared some of it, and we cannot change that.

_____     ___/___/___
Signature of client or personal representative                Date

_____     _____
Printed name of legal representative              Relationship to client

_____
Description of personal representative's authority

_____
Signature of authorized representative of this office or practice

❑ Copy given to the client/parent/personal representative          [Insert date of NPP here]

**FORM 6.5. Consent to privacy practices.** From *The Paper Office for the Digital Age, Fifth Edition.* Copyright © 2017 Edward L. Zuckerman and Keely Kolmes. Published by The Guilford Press. Permission to reproduce this material is granted to purchasers of this book for personal use or use with individual clients (see copyright page for details).

- The client can revoke the consent in writing, but not retroactively for PHI that has been released.

- The consent form should be signed and dated.

Other points about HIPAA consents:

- Because clients have to read the current version of your NPP, there is a space on the consent form to indicate what version (by date) of the NPP they have seen.

- The consent form must be visually distinguishable and organizationally separate from the NPP and any other consents, such as a consent for assignment of benefits or the more traditional ROI or request for records. Putting it on a separate page should do.

- You must retain this consent form for 6 years from the last date it was in effect—the date of your last treatment contact.

- Consents do not have a specified duration, and so should be considered to be in effect for at least the duration of an episode of treatment. However, they can be revoked.

Form 6.5 is a sample consent form written to be a more explicit agreement to the procedures in the NPP. It is written in plain language, which you should tailor to your own practice and needs. Some clients may have not read or understood the NPP and will be surprised to see how much of their privacy they are surrendering. Some clients hesitate or even refuse; they may not want so little control over their information, especially when they do not yet know what information you will be collecting. It may be best to draw every client's attention to these procedures and explain how *you always* ask clients for an authorization to release information and do not rely solely on this consent. By reviewing your ROI, they will know exactly what will be released and to whom.

## Ways of Collecting Further Client Information

For simplicity, we have separated personal and identifying information (on Forms 6.1 and 6.6) from more clinical information (on Form 6.7), although these obviously interact and only together provide the basis for a meaningful biopsychosocial case formulation. Since you can easily modify these forms, consider recombining their items if that might better suit your way of working with clients and conceptualizing cases.

The initial telephone call with a prospective new client should give you guidance for the additional information you need to gather. You can note the specific forms you want to have completed at the bottom of the first-contact form (Form 6.1). Ask the client to arrive 20–30 minutes before the interview "to complete some necessary paperwork." Be aware of the need for confidentiality, and do not leave anything with the client's name on it where others can see it or allow the client to do so. If there is insufficient time and the client cannot stay, ask him or her to return the forms by mail the next day. Including a self-addressed stamped envelope will increase the likelihood of return.

Having this information before you first meet the client face to face is very desirable. For example, without the financial information form (Form 6.10), you might start a relationship with a client whom you really cannot afford to see. Also, the client's clinical information form (Form 6.7) will tell you whether you need to ask the client to fill out more detailed information on his or her drug and alcohol use or legal problems.

Information materials and forms suitable for completion by the client in the waiting room (or in the new-client package) include the following:

- As discussed earlier, your NPP (Forms 6.4 and perhaps 6.3) must be provided, and the related privacy practices consent form (Form 6.5) must be signed at the first contact between client and clinician.

- The adult client demographic information form (Form 6.6) collects more identifying information, although it does also include a few basic clinical questions. It expands on the first-contact form (Form 6.1) with minimal duplication.

- The adult client clinical information form (Form 6.7) asks for more sensitive information, and so it may be better in some situations to offer it only when the client is alone as in your waiting room.

- The health information form (Form 6.8) collects information on medical problems, medications, and treatment sources. The chemical use survey (Form 6.9) collects more specific data on alcohol and drug use.

- The financial information form (Form 6.10) collects essential information about insurance and other resources and authorized payment to the clinician.

- The agreement to pay for professional services (Form 6.11) clarifies payment obligations.

- Problem checklists efficiently survey the client's functioning and understanding of problem areas; they also encourage the identification of difficulties, which the client may be reluctant to state during the initial call. We offer two such forms: an adult checklist of concerns (Form 6.12) and a child checklist of characteristics (Form 6.13). For children, there is also a child developmental history record (Form 6.14).

These clinical forms are not intended as empirically supported screening tools, but only as means of easily surveying for any symptoms relevant to psychotherapy and then of focusing your discussions with the client.

## Obtaining the Client's Demographic Information

**FORM 6.6**  When completed, the adult client demographic information form (Form 6.6) expands the first-contact form, because it is more complete and can be placed first in the client's file, thus becoming a "face sheet." Again, it can be included in the new-client package to be downloaded and completed at home or given to the client in the waiting room at the first meeting. As its name implies, it is straightforward, is primarily demographic, and can easily be filled out by the client at any time. By contrast, the adult client clinical information form (Form 6.7, discussed below) seeks more private and detailed information that may need your guidance, and so may be better completed with the client during your first interview.

*Note:* If you include the second part of section A in Form 6.6, it may be useful also to include here the "no discrimination" clause from the client information brochure (Section 5.2 of this book).

# Adult Client Information Form 1

**Today's date:** ___/___/___

*Note:* If you were a patient here before, please fill in only the information that has changed.

## A. Identification

Your legal name: _____ Date of birth: ___/___/__

Other names you have used (maiden, nicknames, aliases): _____

Address: _____ City: _____ State: ____ Zip: _____

Home phone number: _____ Work number: _____

Email: _____

❑ Driver's license #: _____ ❑ Other ID #: _____ State: _____

❑ Disability status: _____ ❑ Talk about later

❑ Gender identity: _____ ❑ Talk about later

❑ Sexual orientation: _____ ❑ Talk about later

❑ Racial/ethnic identities: _____ ❑ Talk about later

❑ Religious/spiritual traditions or identity: _____ ❑ Talk about later

Other ways you identify yourself and consider important: _____

## B. Emergency information

If some kind of emergency arises and we cannot reach you, whom should we call?

Name: _____ Phone: _____ Relationship: _____

## C. Referral

Who gave you my name to call? Name: _____

Address: _____ Phone: _____

How did this person explain how I might be of help to you? _____

Is this person's relationship with you ❑ personal or ❑ professional?

If professional, may I let this person know that you have come to see me? ❑ Yes ❑ No

## D. Current problems or difficulties

Please describe the main difficulties that led to your coming to see me: _____

_____

When did these problems start? _____

*(continued)*

What makes these problems worse? _____

What makes these problems better? _____

With therapy, how long do you think it will take for these to get a lot better? _____

## E. Your medical care

From whom, or where, do you get your medical care? Clinic/doctor's name: _____

Address: _____ Phone: _____

Results of your last physical exam: _____

If you enter treatment with me for psychological problems, may I tell your medical doctor so that he or she can be fully informed and we can coordinate your treatment?  ❑ Yes  ❑ No

Rate your general level of health:  ❑ Excellent  ❑ Good  ❑ Fair  ❑ Poor  ❑ Extremely poor

| Current medications | For what condition? | Prescribed and supervised by: |
|---|---|---|
|  |  |  |

## F. Your education and training

How many years of school have you had (including elementary and high school)? _____ years

Degrees/certificates: _____ Field(s) of study: _____

## G. Employment and military experiences

Current occupation: _____

Current employer: _____ Date hired: ____/____/____

Address: _____

City: _____ State: _____ Zip: _____

Previous employment history

| From (date) | To (date) | Name of employer | Job title or duties | Reason for leaving |
|---|---|---|---|---|
|  |  |  |  |  |
|  |  |  |  |  |
|  |  |  |  |  |
|  |  |  |  |  |

Present salary: $_____ Total family income: $_____ How much debt do you have? $_____

*(continued)*

Have you ever declared bankruptcy?  ❏ No  ❏ Yes. When? _____ Why? _____

Have you been in the military?  ❏ No  ❏ Yes: From: _____ to: _____ Highest rank held? _____

## H. Family-of-origin history

### 1. Members of your family as you grew up

| Relative | Name | Current age (or age at death) | Illnesses (or cause of death, if deceased) | Education | Occupation |
|---|---|---|---|---|---|
| Parent/Guardian 1 | | | | | |
| Parent/Guardian 2 | | | | | |
| Stepparents | | | | | |
| | | | | | |
| Brothers | | | | | |
| | | | | | |
| | | | | | |
| | | | | | |
| Sisters | | | | | |
| | | | | | |
| | | | | | |
| | | | | | |
| Grandparents | | | | | |
| | | | | | |
| Uncles/aunts | | | | | |
| | | | | | |
| | | | | | |

If you were adopted or raised by other than your biological parents, how old were you when this started? _____

Briefly describe your relationship with your brothers and/or sisters: _____

_____

Which of the following best describes the family in which you grew up?  ❏ Warm/accepting  ❏ Average
❏ Hostile/fighting  ❏ Other: _____

### 2. Parent/Guardian 1     Name: _____

Please describe this caregiver: _____

_____

(continued)

How did this person discipline you? _____

How did this person reward you? _____

How much time did this person spend with you when you were a child?  ❑ A lot  ❑ Average  ❑ Little

How did you get along with this person when you were a child?  ❑ Poorly  ❑ Average  ❑ Well

How do you get along with this person now?  ❑ Poorly  ❑ Average  ❑ Well  ❑ Does not apply

Did this person have any problems (e.g., alcoholism, violence) that may have affected your childhood development?  ❑ Yes  ❑ No  ❑ Don't know

Is or was there anything unusual about this relationship?  ❑ No  ❑ Yes: _____

### 3. Parent/Guardian 2      Name: _____

Please describe this caregiver: _____
_____

How did this person discipline you? _____

How did this person reward you? _____

How much time did this person spend with you when you were a child?  ❑ A lot  ❑ Average  ❑ Little

How did you get along with this person when you were a child?  ❑ Poorly  ❑ Average  ❑ Well

How do you get along with this person now?  ❑ Poorly  ❑ Average  ❑ Well  ❑ Does not apply

Did this person have any problems (e.g., alcoholism, violence) that may have affected your childhood development?  ❑ Yes  ❑ No  ❑ Don't know

Is or was there anything unusual about this relationship?  ❑ No  ❑ Yes: _____

## I. Your significant nonmarital relationships (past and present)

| Name of other person | Person's age when started | Your age when started | Your age when ended | Reasons for ending |
|---|---|---|---|---|
|  |  |  |  |  |
|  |  |  |  |  |
|  |  |  |  |  |
|  |  |  |  |  |
|  |  |  |  |  |

## J. Marital/couple relationship history

|  | Spouse's/partner's name | His/her age at marriage | Your age at marriage | Your age when divorced/ widowed | Has he/she remarried? |
|---|---|---|---|---|---|
| First |  |  |  |  |  |
| Second |  |  |  |  |  |
|  |  |  |  |  |  |

*(continued)*

## K. Children

In the last column below, indicate those from your current marriage with "Y," those from a previous marriage or relationship with "P," and your current stepchildren with "S.")

| Name | Current age | Sex | School | Grade | Adjustment problems? | Yours? Previous? Step? |
|------|-------------|-----|--------|-------|----------------------|------------------------|
|      |             |     |        |       |                      |                        |
|      |             |     |        |       |                      |                        |
|      |             |     |        |       |                      |                        |
|      |             |     |        |       |                      |                        |
|      |             |     |        |       |                      |                        |
|      |             |     |        |       |                      |                        |

## L. Religious concerns

What role, if any, does faith or spirituality play in your life? _____

_____

What is your present religious affiliation, if any? _____

## M. Other

Is there anything else that is important for me to know about, and that you have not written about on any of these forms?   ❏ No   ❏ Yes, and I have written about it on another sheet of paper.

*This is a strictly confidential patient medical record. Redisclosure or transfer is expressly prohibited by law.*

Section E of Form 6.6 ends with a question about **a client's expectations of the duration of therapy.** The answer could be the basis for client education, and it may be helpful in preventing dropout and motivating progress. KK, who works outside managed care, asks clients on her intake forms how long they believe this treatment will take to resolve their issue. She offers options of 1–10 sessions, 10–20 sessions, 20 or more, and longer-term ongoing therapy. She finds that this information can help frame what a client is looking for and helps her to structure the treatment approach to the client's particular needs and preferences. She and the client can track how they are moving toward the client's goals and whether their expectations are being met. Sometimes, after the immediate goals are addressed, clients choose to move to longer-term ongoing therapy. But this is a collaborative conversation.

For both efficiency and privacy, try not to seek more information than you need for your work. Do you need the specific employment or educational history? You might substitute questions relevant to your setting or practice, such as language spoken in the home, sources of income, living situation, additional relationships of interest, and so on.

We believe that some items that are part of informed consent are so important they are worth raising face to face with a client before therapy proceeds, even if they are mentioned explicitly in your paperwork. These items include the limits of confidentiality and fees, including cancellation, insurance, and yearly fee increases. Making sure that the client knows these details before you begin can help you strengthen the alliance and bypass troubles down the road.

## Obtaining the Client's Clinical Information

**FORM 6.7** As noted earlier, the adult client clinical information form (Form 6.7) asks for more personal and detailed information, and so perhaps should be completed when others are not present. Because it is useful to have this information *before* the first interview, it can be completed in the waiting room if you decide the client would not be uncomfortable doing so, or it can be posted on your website for download.

Section B asks about previous treatments, including medications, and the last column on the outcomes of these treatments can be very informative. Of course, what has worked can be reapplied, and what has not can be forsworn, but the client's memory of the qualities of the relationship can be an even better guide to your treatment decisions. Section B asks about treatments and medications for identified psychiatric conditions, which is appropriate for this screening form. More information on *all* medications is sought in Form 6.8.

Section D of Form 6.7 asks about various kinds of abuse and neglect. Do not let anyone skip this section, but do use judgment in inquiring. When adults disclose their abuse as children, it is painful for everyone involved. Abuse shatters our assumptions about the world as a safe place, and so professionals may avoid asking about it (Becker-Blease & Freyd, 2006). This mirrors the silence of the victims, who were groomed by perpetrators not to tell anyone (Veldhuis & Freyd, 1999). Clients may find that being asked straightforwardly on a form is normalizing (because it is apparently common enough to be on a printed form), relieving (because someone cares enough to ask and presumably will attend to this information), or frightening (because the pain will be reexperienced). But it can be therapeutic if handled well (see Ullman, 1999; Sullivan & Cain, 2004). Indeed, we *must* ask about abuse; see Section 4.8.

In Section E, questions 4 through 7 ask the CAGE criteria for alcoholism, described by

# Adult Client Information Form 2

*Note:* If you were a patient here before, please fill in only the information that has changed.

## A. Identification

Name: _____    Date: ____/____/____

## B. Treatment history

Have you ever received inpatient or outpatient psychological, psychiatric, drug/alcohol treatment, medications, or counseling services before?   ❑ No   ❑ Yes. If yes, please describe:

| When (dates)? | For what (diagnosis)? | What kind of treatment? | Where or from whom? | With what results? |
|---|---|---|---|---|
|  |  |  |  |  |
|  |  |  |  |  |
|  |  |  |  |  |

Has any relative had inpatient treatment for a psychiatric, emotional, or substance use disorder?   ❑ No   ❑ Yes. If yes, please describe:

| Name/relationship | For what (diagnoses)? | What kind of treatment? Where or from whom? | When (dates)? | With what results? |
|---|---|---|---|---|
|  |  |  |  |  |
|  |  |  |  |  |
|  |  |  |  |  |

What medications, herbs, or supplements are you taking for mental, emotional, or psychiatric conditions?

| Name of medication | For what condition? | Who prescribes this? | What have been the effects on you? |
|---|---|---|---|
|  |  |  |  |
|  |  |  |  |
|  |  |  |  |

*(continued)*

## C. Relationships in your family of origin

Please describe the following:

1. Your parents' or stepparents' relationship(s) with each other: _____
_____

2. Your relationship with each parent and with any other adults present when you were growing up: _____
_____
_____

3. Your parents' physical health problems, drug or alcohol use, and mental or emotional difficulties: _____
_____

4. Your relationship with your brothers and sisters (or stepsiblings), in the past and present: _____
_____
_____

## D. Abuse history

*Note:* Please be aware as you answer these questions that if I suspect there is a risk of abuse, I have to report it. You may leave this section blank for discussion later.

❏ I was not abused in any way.   ❏ I may have been abused in some way.

❏ I was abused. Please indicate the following. For kind of abuse, use these letters: P = physical, such as beatings; S = sexual, such as touching/molesting, fondling, or intercourse; N = neglect, such as failure to feed, shelter, or protect; E = emotional, such as humiliation, etc.

| Your age | Kind of abuse | By whom? Intimate partner? Relative? Sibling? Other (specify)? | Effects on you? | Whom did you tell? | Consequences of telling? |
|---|---|---|---|---|---|
|  |  |  |  |  |  |

## E. Chemical use

1a. How many caffeine drinks (coffee, tea, colas, energy drinks, etc.) do you use each day? _____

1b. How often each week do you use medications (prescription or over-the-counter) or chemicals to be more alert or sharper? _____

2a. How much tobacco do you smoke or chew each week? Amount: _____    Kind: _____

2b. Do you use vapor or e-cigarettes?   ❏ No   ❏ Yes. How many per week? _____

3. How many drinks of beer, wine, or hard liquor do you consume in a typical week? _____

4. Have you ever felt the need to cut down on your drinking?   ❏ No   ❏ Yes

5. Have you ever felt annoyed by criticism of your drinking?   ❏ No   ❏ Yes

6. Have you ever felt guilty about your drinking?   ❏ No   ❏ Yes

7. Have you ever taken a morning "eye-opener"?   ❏ No   ❏ Yes

*(continued)*

8. Did you ever drink to unconsciousness, or run out of money because of drinking?   ❑ No   ❑ Yes

9. Have you ever used inhalants ("huffing"), such as glue, gasoline, or paint thinner?   ❑ No   ❑ Yes. If yes, which and when? _____

10. Which drugs (not medications prescribed for you) have you used in the last 10 years? _____
_____

11. Do you think that you have a drug or alcohol problem?   ❑ No   ❑ Yes

## F. Legal history

1. Are you presently being sued, suing anyone, or thinking of suing anyone?   ❑ No   ❑ Yes. If yes, please explain: _____

2. Is your reason for coming to see me related to an accident or injury?   ❑ No   ❑ Yes. If yes, please explain: ____
_____

3. Are you required by a court or probation/parole officer to have this appointment?   ❑ No   ❑ Yes. If yes, please explain: _____
_____

4. List all the contacts with the police, courts, and jails/prisons you have had. Include all open charges and pending ones. Under "Jurisdiction," write in a letter: F = Federal, S = State, CO = County, Ci = City. Under "Sentence," write in the *time* and the *type* of sentence you served or have to serve: CD = Charges Dropped, AR = Accelerated Release or Alternative Resolution, CS = Community Service, F = Fine, I = Incarceration (jail or prison), PR = PRobation, P = Parole, R = Restitution, O = Other.

| Date | Charge/arrest | Jurisdiction | Sentence Time | Type | Probation/parole officer's name |
|------|---------------|--------------|---------------|------|-------------------------------|
|      |               |              |               |      |                               |
|      |               |              |               |      |                               |
|      |               |              |               |      |                               |

5. Your current attorney's name: _____   Phone: _____

6. Have you ever declared bankruptcy?   ❑ No   ❑ Yes. If yes, when: _____

7. Have you had any other legal involvements?   ❑ No   ❑ Yes. If yes, please explain: _____
_____

## G. Other

Is there anything else that is important for me as your therapist to know about, and that you have not written about on any of these forms?   ❑ No   ❑ Yes. If yes, please tell me about it here or on another sheet of paper:
_____
_____

**Please do not write below this line.**

## H. Follow-up by clinician

Based on the responses above and on   ❑ interview data   ❑ records I reviewed   ❑ other information:
_____, I have requested the client to complete and/or I have completed the following forms:   ❑ Chemical use   ❑ Risk assessment   ❑ MSE   ❑ Other: _____

*This is a strictly confidential patient medical record. Redisclosure or transfer is expressly prohibited by law.*

Ewing (1984). Depending on the client's answers, your observations, and any referral information, you may want to have the client complete the chemical use survey (Form 6.9). The CAGE questions are widely used, but may not be the most sensitive measures of change or of physiological dependence. There are a few dozen brief and validated substance abuse screening tools available for different populations (who have different abuse patterns and base rates), so you should select one or two for your typical clientele. Much useful advice and links to tools are available at a Kentucky Board of Medical Licensure website (http://kbml.ky.gov/substance-abuse/Pages/default.aspx). The Substance Abuse and Mental Health Services Administration (SAMHSA) has many kinds of screening tools available (http://www.integration.samhsa.gov/clinical-practice/screening-tools), including 10 for substance use with links. The CRAFFT is a tool designed for adolescents, and a 24-page CRAFFT booklet for professionals is available (http://www.ceasar-boston.org/CRAFFT/). Risk assessment tools for opioid use with a good discussion are also available (http://www.opioidrisk.com/node/774). Finally, the National Institute on Drug Abuse provides 15 tools and more information (http://www.drugabuse.gov/nidamed-medical-health-professionals/tool-resources-your-practice/screening-assessment-drug-testing-resources/additional-tools-screening-assessment-drug).

Some further questions can be added to section G of Form 6.7:

- What are your major strengths?
- List five of your behaviors you hope to change.
- Have any anniversaries of important or stressful events in your life occurred recently, or are any due to occur soon?
- List any major problems or stressful events that other family members or close friends are currently dealing with.
- What solutions have you tried for the problems that bring you here?
- Can you tell me of your hopes and dreams? For yourself? For others?
- What things worry you the most? Do you have significant fears we should be addressing?

Many health care providers routinely ask new clients whether they keep guns in the home, whether their friends do, and what safety precautions are being taken. Some may see such questions as intrusive, and others as preventative of violence.

### Obtaining the Client's Medical Information

Gathering health-related information about a client in psychotherapy has several goals:

- A key goal is making as sure as possible that the client does not have an undiagnosed or untreated medical condition that is causing the psychological symptoms you observe; this presentation is called "psychiatric masquerade." For a summary of medical conditions that may result in such "masquerade," see Reed (2013) for a moderate list; the prime resources are Taylor (2007) and Morrison (2015). It is not always possible to place the cause of symptoms into clear organic *or* psychological categories. By being sensitive and informed about the psychological presentation of medical conditions, the competent therapist (medical as well as nonmedical) can make appropriate referrals for evaluation and treatment.

- Mental health clinicians can contribute to the psychological management of clients' medical conditions. For example, diabetes has painful and complex management needs that are sometimes psychologically resisted, and depression is a frequent comorbidity.

- Through gathering health information, clinicians may also be able to discover and thus to treat psychophysiological disorders with specific interventions. For example, temperature biofeedback can be very effective for migraine and Reynaud's phenomenon. More general techniques, such as stress management, mindfulness, or family therapy, can be helpful for hypertension and irritable bowel syndrome.

- Psychological techniques can lessen suffering from physiological conditions such as chronic pain, which may be managed with hypnosis or behavioral treatments. There are other benefits of behavioral medicine for specific conditions; these are too numerous to describe here, but they are well worth the efforts of the professional therapist.

- Depression and anxiety may be hidden in the presentation of medical complaints or very frequent help-seeking patterns. When they are discovered, their treatment becomes possible, and the reduced overutilization of medical resources (called "medical cost offset" from providing psychological services) becomes a very significant financial benefit (mostly to payers).

**FORM 6.8**    The purposes and functions of Form 6.8, the health questionnaire form, are (1) to gather useful information on the client's *health* status; (2) to document that this information was gathered; (3) to support consultation with the client's medical caregivers; and (4) to assess psychobiological conditions for intervention. Open-ended questions put the responsibility for naming, recall, and organization on the client. Check boxes provide the cues, but might miss important unlisted issues. A strategy might be to offer Form 6.8 and follow up with more specific checklists if you are unsatisfied with what the first form produced.

Many detailed checklists and forms for gathering medical information about clients are available from publishers and online. These ask clients to indicate their symptoms, histories, surgeries, and similar medical data. However, those who cannot interpret this data probably should not acquire it. The form offered here asks only for general health problem areas (to be further investigated by both medical and psychological means), diagnoses that have already been established, and the names of the client's medical care providers. Form 6.8 is not a substitute for a medical evaluation, a thorough history, or any appropriate consultations with physicians and other medical personnel.

Whether you are a physician or not, consultation with the client's PCP is appropriate both before and during your treatment. Of course, do not make such contact before getting the client's agreement and a signed ROI form.

A word about **medication** is in order here. Littrell and Ashford (1995) argue that both ethically (there is a requirement for coordination of treatment) and legally (cotreating nurses and pharmacists already do it), nonphysician therapists can and should discuss medications with clients. However, unless they have the ability to prescribe medications, clinicians

# Health Information Form

## A. Identification

Client's name: _____   Date: ____/____/____

## B. Medical caregivers

List at the top your current doctor or primary care provider (PCP) or medical agency. Then list other health care providers, agencies, or clinics treating you in the last 5 years.

| Name | Specialty | Address | Phone # | Date of last visit |
|------|-----------|---------|---------|--------------------|
|      |           |         |         |                    |
|      |           |         |         |                    |
|      |           |         |         |                    |
|      |           |         |         |                    |

## C. Medical history

1. Starting with your childhood and proceeding to the present, list *all* illnesses, accidents/injuries, surgeries, hospitalizations (including ones for mental illness or substance abuse), periods of loss of consciousness, convulsions/seizures, and any other medical conditions you have had. (Describe pregnancies in section E.)

| Age | Illness, injury, or other condition | Treatment received | Treated by | Results |
|-----|--------------------------------------|--------------------|------------|---------|
|     |                                      |                    |            |         |
|     |                                      |                    |            |         |
|     |                                      |                    |            |         |
|     |                                      |                    |            |         |

*(continued)*

| Age | Illness, injury, or other condition | Treatment received | Treated by | Results |
|-----|-------------------------------------|--------------------|------------|---------|
|     |                                     |                    |            |         |
|     |                                     |                    |            |         |
|     |                                     |                    |            |         |

2. Are you allergic to medications or anything else?   ❑ No   ❑ Yes. If yes, please describe here.

| To what? | Reaction you have | Allergy medications you take |
|----------|-------------------|------------------------------|
|          |                   |                              |
|          |                   |                              |
|          |                   |                              |

3. List *all* medications, drugs, or other substances you take or have taken in the last year—prescribed medications, over-the-counter vitamins, supplements, herbs, and others.

| Medication, drug, or other substance | Dosage and how often | For what condition? | When started | Effects | Prescribed and supervised by: |
|---|---|---|---|---|---|
|  |  |  |  |  |  |
|  |  |  |  |  |  |
|  |  |  |  |  |  |
|  |  |  |  |  |  |
|  |  |  |  |  |  |
|  |  |  |  |  |  |

4. Have you ever been exposed to toxic chemicals?   ❑ No   ❑ Yes. If yes, please describe here.

| Dates | Kind of work or location | Kinds of chemicals | Effects |
|-------|--------------------------|--------------------|---------|
|       |                          |                    |         |
|       |                          |                    |         |
|       |                          |                    |         |

## D. Health habits

1. How much physical exercise do you get? I (do) _____, for _____ (length of time), _____ days per week.

*(continued)*

2. Do any of the following describe you?  ❑ Very conscious of eating healthily  ❑ Tend to overeat (binge)  ❑ Eat a balanced diet most of the time  ❑ Watch my weight very closely  ❑ Eat junk foods  ❑ Other: _____

3. How was your appetite in the last month?  ❑ Normal  ❑ Very good  ❑ Low

   Do you try to control your eating in any way?  ❑ No  ❑ Yes. If yes, how (special diets, medications)?

   _____

   Why? _____

4. I have  ❑ gained  ❑ lost ____ pounds within the last 6 months.

5. What hobbies do you enjoy? _____ How often? _____

6. What problems do you have with sleep? _____

   What do you do to help you sleep? _____

7. Have you ever injected drugs?  ❑ Yes  ❑ No  ❑ Talk about later

   Ever shared needles?  ❑ Yes  ❑ No  ❑ Talk about later

8. Have you had HIV testing in the last 6 months?  ❑ No  ❑ Yes  ❑ Talk about later

## E. For women only

1. Menstruation: At what age did you start to menstruate (get your first period)? ____ years old.

   How regular are your periods? _____ How long do they last? _____

   How much pain do you have? _____ How heavy are your periods? _____

   Other experiences during periods? _____

2. Please list all of your pregnancies and attempts to get pregnant:

| Your age? | What happened with this pregnancy? Miscarriage, abortion, stillbirth, child born, etc. Other problems? |
|-----------|------------------------------------------------------------------------------------------------------------|
|           |                                                                                                            |
|           |                                                                                                            |
|           |                                                                                                            |
|           |                                                                                                            |

3. At what age did you first notice signs of menopause? _____

   If you are in or around the age of menopause: What signs or symptoms do you have now (hot flashes, mood swings, menstrual period changes, body pain, etc.)? _____

   _____

   At what age did menstruation stop? _____

## F. Other

Are there any other medical or physical problems that you are concerned about, or that you think I should know about?  ❑ No  ❑ Yes. If yes, describe: _____

_____

*This is a strictly confidential patient medical record. Redisclosure or transfer is expressly prohibited by law.*

should avoid telling clients (even indirectly) to start, discontinue, or change medications; this would be "practicing medicine without a license," as well as exceeding the boundaries of most nonphysicians' competence. Many prescription medications are taken by people who become therapy clients, and these may cause psychiatric symptoms, which may mislead the unwary professional assessing or treating these persons.

Of course you will monitor psychiatric symptoms. Consider whether the onset of any change in the client appears to correlate with the initiation of or change in a medication. If such a correlation appears to exist, obtain a signed ROI to contact the client's prescriber, or help the client to do so.

## Assessing Chemical Use

Chemical use is a complex biopsychosocial and historical phenomenon, and so there is no checklist (no matter how large) that will substitute for a comprehensive evaluation by an experienced clinician. If you want interview questions, there is a very complete set of questions to evaluate most aspects of chemical use in Zuckerman (2010). Form 6.9 can be given to clients to complete when there is any indication—from the referrer, from your observations, or in responses to your screening interview questions—that chemical use may be a problem.

**FORM 6.9**

The purposes and functions of Form 6.9, the chemical use survey, are as follows: (1) to screen all new clients for chemical use problems; (2) to document that information on these issues was sought, whether and which information was obtained, and that options were weighed; and (3) to assist with the formulation of the case in its full biopsychosocial context. The first three questions in section G of the form ask about consequences and can be supplemented with motivational interviewing. Other commonly used screeners are the Michigan Alcoholism Screen Test (MAST; Selzer, 1971), the Drug Abuse Screening Test (DAST; Skinner, 1982), and the Alcohol Use Disorders Identification Test (AUDIT; Babor et al., 1992).

Because of the denial and shame centering around chemical use problems, it is especially important to get objective or confirmatory data beyond what the client tells you. Try to interview a friend or family member of a person suspected of drug or alcohol misuse. Later in this chapter, Form 6.18, a case formulation for chemical users, is provided to aid you in summarizing all of your findings, formulating a case in a biopsychosocial context, and planning treatment for a client with a substance use problem.

Because chemical use can be understood from many perspectives, Form 6.9 offers several ways to document the findings; you can add or delete elements according to your preferences. Furthermore, the individual's patterns of use/overuse/misuse/abuse/dependence may change with availability, finances, setting, decision, treatment, and aging, and may involve cross-addictions, temporary substitutions or preferences, and many other factors, so a detailed, current, and individualized history is desirable. Obviously, denial will significantly affect your information gathering. Therefore, follow your clinical intuition and the client's lead (or avoidances) in history taking to get all the relevant facts.

There are many publications on assessment and treatment of substance abuse available from both the National Institute on Alcohol Abuse and Alcoholism (http://www.niaaa.nih.gov/publications/clinical-guides-and-manuals) and SAMHSA (http://store.samhsa.gov). Chapter 4 of *Substance Abuse Treatment for Persons with Co-Occurring Disorders* (SAMHSA, 2005) has tools and a particularly valuable discussion of complexities and subtleties of

# Chemical Use Survey

Name: _____   Date: ____/____/____

In order to treat you effectively, I need full and accurate information about the ways you and your family have used alcohol, drugs, and/or other chemicals that can affect you psychologically, so please answer these questions honestly. If you have concerns about privacy please raise them with me.

## A. What have you used?

1. Please recall *all* the chemicals you have used, and indicate how much you used *and* how often. Then write all the effects each had on you (mental, physical, family, legal, etc.).

| Chemical | Age or ages started | Date of last use | How much and how often in the last 30 days | Effects/consequences | See question 3, below |
|---|---|---|---|---|---|
| Caffeine | | | | | |
| Tobacco (smoked or chewed), vapor | | | | | |
| Alcohol | | | | | |
| Marijuana/THC | | | | | |
| Cocaine | | | | | |
| Heroin | | | | | |
| Amphetamines, "meth" | | | | | |
| Barbiturates | | | | | |
| Inhalants ("huffing") | | | | | |
| Hallucinogens | | | | | |
| Prescribed pills | | | | | |
| Others (specify): | | | | | |

2. Write "Main" above next to the name of your main drug of choice.

3. For each of the chemicals you have used in the last month, what causes you to stop? Enter one or more of these letters in the last column above: A = The money runs out. B = I use up my supply. C = Personal decision. D = I become unconscious. E = I have achieved my purpose. F = Other reasons: _____

_____

*(continued)*

4. What are or were your sources of money for buying the chemicals you have used? _____

_____

## B. Effects of use

Which of these have you had? ❑ Blackouts ❑ Withdrawal symptoms ❑ Cravings ❑ Overdoses
❑ Detoxification in a hospital ❑ Tolerance ("Could not get high no matter how much I took")
❑ Preoccupation (spent all your time finding and using chemicals) ❑ Failed attempts to cut down or control
use ❑ Other problems: _____

_____

## C. Family patterns of chemical use

Please describe the chemical(s) used by current family members.

| Relative | Name | Chemical | Age started | Last use | Amount and how often in the last 30 days | Effects |
|---|---|---|---|---|---|---|
| Father | | | | | | |
| Mother | | | | | | |
| Brothers/ sisters | | | | | | |
| Spouse/ partner | | | | | | |
| Other relatives | | | | | | |
| Children | | | | | | |
| Friends | | | | | | |

Please add any other information you think is important: _____

_____

*(continued)*

## D. Treatments for chemical use

In the table below, use these codes in the "Methods used" column: AA/NA = Alcoholics Anonymous/Narcotics Anonymous; O = Outpatient counseling; ID = Inpatient Detoxification; IT = Inpatient Treatment (e.g., 28-day); O = Other treatments (please specify).

Use these codes in the last "Effects of treatment" column: W = made situation Worse; N = No change; U = better Understanding of addiction; R = Reduction of use; BA = Brief Abstinence (up to a month); LA = Long-term Abstinence (several months or more); O = Other effects (specify).

| From (date) | To (date) | Agency/provider | Type of program | Voluntary? (yes or no) | Length of treatment | Methods used | Participation in aftercare programs (which? or not) | Effects of treatment |
|---|---|---|---|---|---|---|---|---|
| | | | | | | | | |

## F. Self-description of use

1. Would you say you ❑ are a social drinker? ❑ are a heavy drinker? ❑ have alcoholism? ❑ have a drinking problem? Or how would you describe your use? _____

2. Would you say you ❑ are a recreational drug user? ❑ have a drug problem? ❑ have an addiction? Or how would you describe your use? _____

## G. Other

Has your drinking/drug use caused you any social problems? _____

Has your drinking/drug use caused you any problems at work? _____

Has your drinking/drug use caused you any spiritual problems? _____

What triggers do you have for re-starting your drug/alcohol abuse after being sober/abstinent for a while? _____

What has been most helpful to you in maintaining sobriety? _____

*This is a strictly confidential patient medical record. Redisclosure or transfer is expressly prohibited by law.*

assessment. The tools include an 18-item Simple Screening Instrument for Substance Abuse (SSI-SA), which addresses the issues in Form 6.9 as sentences with only "yes–no" responses.

## Obtaining Financial Information

**FORM 6.10**  The purposes and functions of Form 6.10, the financial information form, are as follows:

1.  It collects all the essential data you need for evaluating the client's insurance benefits, and thus the truer costs to the client of your services;

2.  It allows you to decide whether a client can afford your charges. If you do not use it before seeing the client, you should discuss fees and resources early in the interview, to avoid engaging anyone in a process and relationship that must then be disrupted. That is why it is best to mail this form to new clients or to give it to them while they wait for their first visit.

3.  It reinforces the client's ultimate obligation to pay for services.

**Do not expect or trust clients to understand their coverage or the technicalities of today's insurance marketplace.** You will have to decide whether you are going to see clients who have insurance, in which case we recommend that you follow all the steps in Chapter 3. When they come in, make copies of any insurance wallet cards they have. With those numbers and the clients' Social Security numbers, you can call the insurers to verify their coverage. Try not to start therapy without such verification.

You may need to make some changes to this form. For example, if your state has a special name for its health insurance program, or you see a lot of clients covered by a specific carrier, you may need to change some of the wording.

For efficiency, section G of Form 6.10 contains condensed legal statements addressing the release of records to an insurer, acceptance of financial responsibility, and assignment of the payment of the client's benefits to you. If you are going to use other forms for these purposes (such as Form 6.11 about paying for services, or the letter in Section 3.7 about assignment of benefits), you might mention them here.

The question asking for any secondary insurance company (section F) is for "coordination of benefits," in which insurers set priorities about who will cover services first. Ideally, the secondary insurer will cover any remaining amount due you. Karen Davison, PsyD, of San Francisco, CA, contributed her experience and perspectives to this form, for which we are grateful.

## Assuring Financial Responsibility

**FORM 6.11**  The purpose of Form 6.11, the agreement to pay for professional services, is to formalize a client's (or other person's) assumption of financial responsibility for therapy or other services. You may wonder, "Isn't the client's stated promise to pay sufficient?" Simon (1992) indicates that an oral contract is valid and enforceable in circumstances where a client makes a simple promise such as "I will pay for this treatment," but where there is a condition such as "I will pay if someone else fails to pay," a written contract is needed. The client may harbor hidden assumptions—for example, that he or she will need only a few sessions,

# Financial Information Form

I truly appreciate your choosing to come to me for treatment. As part of providing high-quality services, I need to be clear with you about our financial arrangements.

If you have health insurance, it may pay for a part of the cost of your treatment here. To find out if this is so, I need the information requested below in sections D, E, F and G. I will explain any part of this form that is not clear to you.

A. Please select one or more of the following options:

    1. ❑ I intend to use any insurance benefits available to pay for part of the services I receive here. (Please complete sections E, F, and G of this form.)

    2. ❑ I decline to use the health insurance I have with _____ (company). (Please select options 4, 5, or 6 below.)

    3. ❑ I have no health insurance coverage.

    4. ❑ I intend to use a health savings account (HSA), flexible savings account (FSA), or similar. (Please discuss this with me so that I can supply you with the forms you will need.)

    5. ❑ I will use a credit card to pay my copays or other fees. (Please discuss this with me so that I can supply you with the information and forms you will need.)

    6. ❑ I will pay by cash or check at each visit.

B. If you ask me to, I can submit claims to your health insurance plan or managed care organization (MCO) for you, but you must authorize me to receive any payments the insurer makes. Because I have a contract with your plan, I am "in network" and must charge you only the fee that the insurer and I have agreed to. You will pay me the full fee until your payments reach the yearly deductible of your health insurance. After that, you will pay me only the copayment or "copay" for each time we meet.

C. The use of health insurance to pay for all or part of therapy involves many considerations. You can learn more about these in my handout entitled "What You Should Know about Managed Care and Your Treatment." The major concerns include these:

- When an insurance company pays for part of your treatment, the company has a right to review your records, limit treatment, and deny claims for payment.

- Not all services may be covered, including phone meetings, videoconferencing, and any services the company decides are not "medically necessary." If you request and agree to services that are not covered, you will be expected to pay for them, and we will sign an additional contract.

- If your insurance changes, you agree to provide me with an update as soon as possible. If you become eligible for additional or different insurance such as Medicare, you must inform me.

- This office will submit claims in a timely manner and will provide an update to you if the insurance company or MCO denies the claim.

*(continued)*

**D.** Please give us this information as it appears on your insurance policies or cards.

Your name: _____ Date of birth: ___/___/___ Age: _____

Home phone #: _____ Cell #: _____

Home street address: _____

City: _____ State: _____ Zip: _____

**E.** If you are covered under someone else's insurance plan, please provide this information.

Policy holder's name: _____ Date of birth: ___/___/___

Relationship to the patient: ❑ Spouse ❑ Child ❑ Other: _____

Name of the insurance company: _____ Health plan: _____

Policy #: _____ Group #: _____ FECA #: _____ Effective date: ___/___/___

Reciprocity number: _____ Phone number of plan: _____

Address to send claims: _____

Any other information on the card? _____

**F.** If you or the policy holder (if different from you) have a second kind of health insurance, please fill in the numbers and names for it.

Policy holder's name: _____ Date of birth: ___/___/___

Relationship to the patient: ❑ Self ❑ Spouse ❑ Child ❑ Other: _____

Name of the insurance company: _____ Health plan: _____

Policy #: _____ Group #: _____ FECA #: _____ Effective date: ___/___/___

Reciprocity number: _____ Phone number of plan: _____

Address to send claims: _____

Any other information on the card? _____

**G.** Release of information and assignment of benefits:

I, the client (or the policy holder), by my signature below authorize the release by this office of any information obtained during evaluations and treatment that is necessary to support and process any insurance claims, determine medical necessity, support any clinical or financial audits, or requests for additional sessions. I hereby assign medical benefits, including those from government-sponsored programs and other health plans, to be paid to the clinician or organization above. Medicare regulations may apply.

I understand that I am responsible for all charges, regardless of insurance coverage or other payments. I understand that I will be responsible to pay the full session fee if I fail to cancel my appointment at least three business days in advance.

A photocopy of this assignment is to be considered as good as the original.

_____     _____     ___/___/___

    Client's (or policy holder's) signature              Printed name             Date

My signature indicates my agreement to and accuracy of all of the statements above

*Please bring your (or the policy holder's) health insurance card(s) with you to your first session.*

## Agreement to Pay for Professional Services

I request that the clinician named below provide professional services to me or to _____,

who is my _____ and I agree to pay this clinician's fee of $_____ per session for these

services or the fee of $____ for _____.

I understand and agree that I am responsible to pay the charges for services provided by this clinician to me (or this client), although other persons or insurance companies may make payments on my (or this client's) account.

I agree to pay for services provided to me (or this client) up until the time we end the relationship. We will discuss ending, and a date will be agreed to and recorded in this client's medical records; or I will inform the clinician, in person or by certified mail, that I wish to end it. I agree to meet with this clinician at least once before stopping therapy.

I have also read this clinician's "Information for Clients" or practice brochure and agree to act according to everything stated there, as shown by my signature below and on the brochure.

_____     ___/___/___
Signature of client (or person acting for client)                         Date

_____
Printed name of client (or person acting for client)

I, the clinician, have discussed the issues above with the client (and/or the person legally acting for the client). My observations of the person's behavior and responses give me no reason to believe that this person is not fully competent and able to give informed and willing consent.

_____     ___/___/___
Signature of clinician                                                      Date

❑ Copy accepted by client or   ❑ Copy kept by clinician

or that psychotherapy services will be fully paid for by insurance or a government program, or that he or she won't have to pay if the problem is not fixed. Presenting this form (or using the first paragraph as part of another form) brings these assumptions to the surface for clarification and resolution.

If any of the following situations apply, make certain to get a responsible person's signature before you become too involved in treatment:

- A noncustodial parent brings a child in for services. Because legal and physical custody are not identical, and because there are various kinds of agreements and custody rights, ask before therapy begins for the paperwork supporting the legal authority to give permission to treat. States' rules differ, but the safest way is to get permission to treat from both parents unless the child's treatment is court-ordered.

- A divorcing spouse whose assets are likely to be in dispute, or perhaps inadequate to pay for services, comes for treatment.

- An adolescent without assets seeks your services.

- Treatment is going to be long or expensive, and you want someone besides the client to share the cost.

- You suspect that the client isn't sincere in offering to pay for your services.

- You sense that the client doesn't fully appreciate the responsibility involved.

Note that a statement indicating acceptance of financial responsibility is included at the end of the financial information form (Form 6.10, section G): "I understand that I am responsible for all charges, regardless of insurance coverage or other payments." It is always a good idea to repeat this point, and if you have any doubts about the client's full appreciation of this point, Form 6.11 can then be used.

Form 6.11 indicates that the client has read and agreed to the client information brochure (see Section 5.2), because the client cannot be expected to assume financial responsibility without knowing basic information about therapy (its duration, probable costs, etc.). It is best to include this form with the new-client package.

The American Academy of Family Physicians has a brief document similar to Form 6.11 online (http://www.aafp.org/fpm/20040400/samplepaymentpolicy.doc). This document cleverly includes definitions of the terms and procedures involved in using health insurance.

Another option to ensure payment is to ask for a credit card to be used to pay balances after the insurer has paid its share. The card could also be used to pay the copayments you have to collect. The details and options can be added to Form 6.11.

## Problem Checklists

People come for "help" for many reasons (physician referral, threat of divorce, intolerable pain, desire for the cure of symptoms, need for answers or advice, support for their views, failure of previous efforts, etc.) and with many different understandings of the cause and possible cure of their difficulties. It has been shown repeatedly that the more closely client and therapist agree on the nature, cause, and methods of relieving the presenting problem, the better the outcome of therapy. Yet the professional's role often involves relabeling or reformulating the "chief complaint" or "referral reason" into something he or she understands as a professional and has the skills to relieve.

The intent of problem checklists is to offer new clients the widest range of possible difficulties to select from. This allows the exploration of all concerns early in therapy. If you simply ask, "What brings you here today?" you will get an abridged list of only the most salient items (probably the most recent or currently distressing) or "critical incidents," but not necessarily the most limiting or treatable. Or you might get the "referral reason," which is simply the problem as defined by another professional, or a request for a specific treatment method (such as hypnosis). Although clients may come seeking a particular kind of therapy, this should be a professional's well-considered decision.

For precise information and documentation of symptoms or conditions, thousands of **specific tests, checklists, and scales are available,** and we encourage their valid use. An excellent starting point is the volume by Corcoran and Fischer (2013).

For an emphasis on a child or teen's functioning, rather than symptoms, the Child and Adolescent Functional Assessment Scale (CAFAS) offers eight subscales and an overall dysfunction score. It has been widely used, offers a full list of strengths, and is very comprehensive although therefore long (http://vinst.umdnj.edu/VAID/TestReport.asp?Code=CAFAS). A very simple yet quite large form for adolescents, with 208 questions in 12 areas, is the Personal Problems Checklist (Schinka, 1984); this is available from Psychological Assessment Resources (http://www4.parinc.com).

The checklists offered here are labeled to avoid excessive pathologizing of a client's experience. The adult's version (Form 6.12) is called a checklist of "concerns" rather than "problems." The child's version (Form 6.13), called a checklist of "characteristics," offers both problematic and helpful behaviors so that you will have at least some positives to build upon, and is to be completed by a caregiver. If you wish to focus on character strengths, the Values in Action Classification of Strengths assesses 24 positive characteristics under 6 broad virtues (Peterson & Seligman, 2004); also see Rashid (2013) for more on the clinical application of this approach.

You can, of course, tailor these two lists to your own practice by adding some items. If you do so, we suggest removing some, so that the lists do not become burdensome for clients. For example, if you do more behavioral health work, you can add "Headaches," "High blood pressure," and the like, and delete less relevant items. You can also change the instructions to ask clients to "Circle any of the following if they were a concern in the past, and <u>underline</u> those that are presently of concern to you." If you have a client complete Form 6.12, or a caregiver complete Form 6.13, before the first meeting, you can follow up on checked items to clarify exactly what is understood by each term and what difficulties are being presented.

Finally, note that under "Abuse" on Form 6.12, cruelty to animals is included; this is illegal in all states and is highly correlated with violence against humans. For more information or resources, contact the Latham Foundation (http://www.latham.org).

**FORM 6.12** (margin label)

**FORM 6.13** (margin label)

## Obtaining Information on Child Clients

Most of the forms discussed above have been designed for adults. If you see adolescents, you can use the information form for young adults (Form 6.16) instead of the adult versions (Forms 6.6 and 6.7), and either the adult or child checklist (Form 6.12 or 6.13).

# Adult Checklist of Concerns

Name: _____ Date: ____/____/____

Please mark all of the items below that apply to you (or the client), and feel free to add any others at the bottom under "Other concerns or issues." You may add a note or details in the space next to the concerns checked. For a child, mark any of these and then complete the Child Checklist of Characteristics. When you are done, please read the note at the end.

❑ I have no problems or concerns at this time
❑ Abuse—physical, sexual, emotional; neglect; cruelty to animals
❑ Adjusting or adapting poorly
❑ Alcohol/drugs (for myself): Prescription medications, over-the-counter meds, street drugs
❑ Alcohol/drugs (in my family): Prescription meds, over-the-counter meds, street drugs
❑ Anger, hostility, arguing, irritability
❑ Anxiety, nervousness, worrying
❑ Attention or concentration difficulties, distractibility
❑ Childhood issues (your own childhood)
❑ Codependence
❑ Confusion, disorganized thoughts
❑ Compulsions, having to say or do certain things
❑ Custody of children
❑ Decision making, indecision, mixed feelings, putting off decisions and actions
❑ Delusions (false ideas)
❑ Dependence
❑ Depression, low mood, sadness, crying, inactivity
❑ Eating problems: Overeating, undereating, appetite, vomiting (see also "Weight and diet issues," below)
❑ Emptiness feelings
❑ Failure
❑ Fatigue, tiredness, low energy, low stamina
❑ Fear of losing control
❑ Fears or phobias
❑ Feeling "too good," unrealistic happiness
❑ Financial or money troubles, debt, impulsive spending, low income
❑ Friendships
❑ Gambling
❑ Gender identity concerns or questions
❑ Grieving, mourning, deaths, losses, divorce
❑ Guilt, shame
❑ Hallucinations (hearing, feeling, or seeing things not present)
❑ Headaches, other kinds of pains
❑ Health, illness, medical concerns, physical problems

*(continued)*

❑ Hoarding, excessive collecting
❑ Hopelessness
❑ Housework/chores: Quality, schedules, sharing duties
❑ Inferiority feelings
❑ Injuring oneself deliberately
❑ Immaturity, irresponsibility, poor judgment, lack of motivation
❑ Impulsiveness, loss of control, risky actions
❑ Legal involvements, charges, suits
❑ Loneliness
❑ Marital conflict, distance/coldness, infidelity, remarriage, disappointments
❑ Memory problems, forgetting
❑ Menstrual difficulties, PMS, menopause, perimenopause, hormonal changes
❑ Mood swings
❑ Nervousness, tension
❑ Obsessions, repeated thoughts or memories
❑ Pain management, chronic pain
❑ Panics or anxiety attacks
❑ Parenting, child management, single parenthood
❑ Perfectionism
❑ Pessimism
❑ Procrastination, "laziness"
❑ Relationship problems with friends, with relatives, or at school or at work
❑ Self-centeredness, selfishness
❑ Self-esteem, self-confidence
❑ Self-neglect, poor self-care, poor hygiene
❑ Separation or divorce
❑ Sexual issues, dysfunctions, conflicts, desire differences, other problems
❑ Shyness, oversensitivity to criticism or rejection
❑ Sleep problems: Too much, too little, insomnia, nightmares
❑ Smoking and tobacco use
❑ Spiritual, religious, moral, ethical issues
❑ Stress, relaxation, stress management, stress disorders
❑ Suspiciousness
❑ Suicidal thoughts
❑ Temper problems, low frustration tolerance, irritability, outbursts
❑ Threats, violent actions, aggression
❑ Traumatic events
❑ Unconsciousness, "knocked out"
❑ Unusual thoughts or behaviors
❑ Weight and diet issues
❑ Withdrawal, isolating
❑ Work problems: Employment, "workaholism," can't keep a job, dissatisfaction, ambition
❑ Other concerns or issues: _____

Now go back to each concern you checked, and rate how much difficulty it causes you (or the client): 0 = none or not present now; 1 = mild (lowers quality of life but doesn't limit day-to-day functioning); 2 = mild/moderate (lowers quality of life and functioning); 3 = moderate (worse than 2); 4 = fairly severe impacts and limitations on quality of life and functioning; 5 = severely lowers quality of life and ability to function.

*This is a strictly confidential patient medical record. Redisclosure or transfer is expressly prohibited by law.*

# Child Checklist of Characteristics

Name of child: _____ Date: ___/___/___ Age: ____

Person completing this form: _____

Many concerns can apply to both children and adults. If you have brought a child for evaluation or treatment, review this checklist, which contains concerns (as well as positive traits) that apply mostly to children, and mark any items that describe the child. Feel free to add any others at the end under "Other characteristics."

❑ Affectionate
❑ Angry, often irritable, easily angered
❑ Artistic
❑ Assertive
❑ Bullies/intimidates, teases, inflicts pain on others, is bossy to others, picks on, provokes
❑ Careful, thorough
❑ Cheats
❑ Creative, imaginative
❑ Cruel to animals, "teases," "plays tricks on them"
❑ Concerned for others, sensitive to others' feelings
❑ Conflicts with parents over breaking rules, chores, homework, grades, choices
❑ Confident, independent
❑ Complains, criticizes everything and everybody, sarcastic
❑ Cries easily, feelings are easily hurt
❑ Dawdles, delays, procrastinates, wastes time
❑ Defiant, resists, refuses, does not comply
❑ Dependent, clinging, timid
❑ Demands attention
❑ Developmental delays
❑ Dissatisfied with body, weight
❑ Disobedient, uncooperative, doesn't follow rules
❑ Disrupts family activities
❑ Distractible, inattentive, can't concentrate, daydreams, slow to respond
❑ Drug or alcohol use
❑ Eating and diet: Poor manners, refuses food, appetite increase or decrease, odd
❑ combinations, overeats, weight changes, overconcern with weight
❑ Exercises, active in sports
❑ Extracurricular activities interfering with academics
❑ Feels inferior, low confidence
❑ Fearful, anxious, cries
❑ Fighting, hitting, violent, aggressive, hostile, provokes, threatens, destructive
❑ Fire setting
❑ Friendly, outgoing, makes friends easily, gets along with most people and family

*(continued)*

- ❑ Gender identity concerns
- ❑ Good looking, attractive, handsome, pretty
- ❑ Graceful, well coordinated
- ❑ Not healthy, always complains of feeling sick
- ❑ Healthy, energetic, has stamina, rarely sick
- ❑ Hurts or harms self, bites or hits self, bangs head, scratches self, bites nails
- ❑ Immature, "clowns around," has only younger playmates
- ❑ Imaginary playmates, extensive fantasy play
- ❑ Imaginative, creative
- ❑ Impatient, low frustration tolerance, interrupts, talks out, yells
- ❑ Isolates, likes to be alone, withdraws, does not socialize
- ❑ Intelligent, ahead of peers in school, solves problems, smart, quick to learn
- ❑ Lacks organization, unprepared
- ❑ Learning disability
- ❑ Legal difficulties: Truancy, loitering, drinking, vandalism, stealing, fighting, drug sales
- ❑ Lies often, not trustworthy
- ❑ Mature beyond his or her years, responsible, trustworthy
- ❑ Nervous, tense, worries excessively, startles easily
- ❑ Needs a lot of supervision at home over play/chores/schedule
- ❑ Obedient, helpful
- ❑ Overactive, restless, hyperactive, out-of-seat behaviors, restlessness, fidgety, noisy
- ❑ Prejudiced, bigoted, insulting, name calling, intolerant
- ❑ Polite, well mannered
- ❑ Pouts, sulks, moody
- ❑ Recent move, new school adjustment, loss of friends
- ❑ Rocking or other repetitive movements
- ❑ Runs away
- ❑ Sad, unhappy, down, often blue, tearful, cries
- ❑ School problems: Grades, attendance, class cutting, failing out of school
- ❑ Sexual issues: Sexual preoccupation, public masturbation, inappropriate sexual behaviors
- ❑ Shy, timid, refuses to speak
- ❑ Socially smart, understands others
- ❑ Sleep difficulties, bedtimes, excessive sleep, sleep walking, nightmares
- ❑ Stubborn
- ❑ Suicide talk or attempt
- ❑ Swears, blasphemes, bathroom language, foul language
- ❑ Thumb sucking, finger sucking, hair chewing, scratches or picks at skin
- ❑ Tics (involuntary rapid movements, noises or words)
- ❑ Teased, picked on, victimized, bullied
- ❑ Underactive, slow-moving or slow-responding, lethargic
- ❑ Uncoordinated, accident-prone, gets hurt a lot, falls, drops things
- ❑ Violent, breaks things, hurts others, temper tantrums, rages
- ❑ Well groomed, dresses with care
- ❑ Wetting or soiling the bed or clothes
- ❑ Other characteristics: _____

Please look back over the concerns you have checked off, and choose the one that you most want the child to be helped with. Which is it? _____

*This is a strictly confidential patient medical record. Redisclosure or transfer is expressly prohibited by law.*

However, when a child has a significant clinical problem, current and more detailed
**FORM 6.14** information is best acquired during an interview. The purposes and functions of Form 6.14,
the child information form, are (1) to gather and record information about major historical
issues in development; (2) to direct the interview process; and (3) to support the later sum-
marization of information to support treatment planning and initiation. Some items are
adapted from a very complete set of forms by Robert E. McCarthy, PhD, of Myrtle Beach,
SC.

On the last line, the item "Entered into birthday book" pertains to the sending of birthday cards, which may be appropriate for some child clinicians.

You could add to this package symptom checklists (e.g., the Pediatric Symptom Checklist; see http://www.massgeneral.org/psychiatry/services/psc_home.aspx) or specialized
questionnaires (e.g., for attention-deficit/hyperactivity disorder), or pre–post measures sensitive to change.

For child and adolescent clients, Caroline Danda, PhD, of Kansas City, MO, has generously placed her very comprehensive and gorgeous (to appreciators of forms) 11-page New
Patient Information Form online (http://www.carolinedanda.com/forms).

## 6.5  Phase 4: First Meeting with a New Client

Should you use a questionnaire or checklist to ensure that you have missed nothing in the
range of possible presenting symptoms, or should you rely on both your interviewing skills
(noticing "clinical flags") and the conscientious client to discover all important aspects of
the case? Each approach has advantages and disadvantages, and so we offer materials to
support a combination approach, which is a multistep process.

*Step 1.* Use standard questionnaires to survey all of the current concerns, such as the
two adult client information forms (Forms 6.6 and 6.7), the two checklists (Forms
6.12 and 6.13), and the child information form (Form 6.14). At least some of these
forms can be filled out by the client (or the child's caregiver) before the first meeting.

*Step 2.* Do an interview to follow up on what the questionnaires found and to explore
history and presenting problems in more detail, so that you and the client can come
to a shared understanding of their nature and priority, and can establish a positive
alliance.

*Step 3.* Because there may be other clinical issues that the client has not identified or
was unwilling to indicate initially, do a survey interview with questions directed at
some areas of known importance to all clients. The intake interview questions and
guide (Form 6.15) can provide structure when structure is desired, without impos-
ing it.

*Step 4.* Follow up any new concerns with focused interviewing methods. A very complete list of questions, organized according to clinical symptoms or syndromes, can
be found in the *Clinician's Thesaurus* (Zuckerman, 2010).

*Step 5.* Use very specialized and focused questionnaires, behavioral schedules, and
checklists only when the presentation is very complex or detailed documentation is
essential. These syndrome-specific materials are beyond the scope of this book, but

# Child Information Form

**Today's date:** ___/___/___

*Note:* If your child has been a patient here before, please fill in only the information that has changed.

## A. Identification

Child's full name: _____ Date of birth: ___/___/___

Nicknames: _____

Child's legal guardian: _____ Person(s) completing this form: _____

Disability status: _____ ❑ Talk about later

Gender identity: _____ ❑ Talk about later

Sexual orientation: _____ ❑ Talk about later

Racial/ethnic identities: _____ ❑ Talk about later

Religious/spiritual traditions or identity: _____ ❑ Talk about later

Other ways you identify your child and consider important: _____

## B. Family information

Mother/guardian: _____ Age: ____

Best phone number: _____ Other phone number: _____

Address: _____

Email: _____ Occupation: _____

Employer: _____ Location: _____

Father/guardian: _____ Age: ____

Best phone number: _____ Other phone number: _____

Address: _____

Email: _____ Occupation: _____

Employer: _____ Location: _____

Parents are currently: ❑ Married ❑ Divorced ❑ Separated ❑ Remarried to others ❑ Never married
❑ Other: _____

Patient lives with: ❑ Mother ❑ Father ❑ Relative ❑ Guardian ❑ Other: _____

Who has legal custody* of this child? ❑ Mother ❑ Father ❑ Both/either/shared ❑ Relative
❑ Guardian ❑ Other: _____

*Please bring custody or court papers to the first appointment if they exist.

*(continued)*

FORM 6.14. **Child information form (p. 1 of 7).** From *The Paper Office for the Digital Age, Fifth Edition.* Copyright © 2017 Edward L. Zuckerman and Keely Kolmes. Published by The Guilford Press. Permission to reproduce this material is granted to purchasers of this book for personal use or use with individual clients (see copyright page for details).

Members of the household and other important persons in the child's life:

| Name | Relationship | Age | Sex | Health, behavioral or learning difficulties? | Last grade in school completed, or works as a . . . | How does this person get along with the child? |
|------|-------------|-----|-----|---------------------------------------------|---------------------------------------------------|-----------------------------------------------|
|      |             |     |     |                                             |                                                   |                                               |
|      |             |     |     |                                             |                                                   |                                               |
|      |             |     |     |                                             |                                                   |                                               |
|      |             |     |     |                                             |                                                   |                                               |
|      |             |     |     |                                             |                                                   |                                               |

## C. Emergency information

If some kind of emergency arises and we cannot reach you directly, or we need to reach someone close to you, whom should we call?   Name: _____   Phone: _____

Relationship: _____   Address: _____

## D. Referral

Who gave you my name to call?   Name: _____   Phone: _____

Address: _____

How did this person explain how I might be of help to you? _____

Is this person's relationship with you   ❑ personal or   ❑ professional?

If professional, may I have your permission to thank this person for the referral?   ❑ Yes   ❑ No

Should I consult with this person about the referral?   ❑ Yes   ❑ No

## E. Current problems or difficulties

Please describe the main difficulties that led to your bringing this child to see me: _____

_____

When did these problems start? _____

What makes these problems worse? _____

_____

What makes these problems better? _____

_____

With therapy, how long do you think it will take for these to get a lot better? _____

## F. Development

### 1. Pregnancy and delivery

Prenatal medical illnesses or problems: _____

Maternal substance use:   ❑ Alcohol   ❑ Tobacco   ❑ Medications   ❑ Other drugs

Maternal stressors: _____

Was the child premature?   ❑ No   ❑ Yes, by ____ weeks. Birth weight: ____   Birth length: ____

Birth complications or problems? _____

*(continued)*

### 2. The first few months of life

Breast-fed? ❑ No  ❑ If yes, for how long? _____  Feeding problems? _____

Allergies? _____  Sleep patterns or problems: _____

Relationship with mother: _____

### 3. Milestones

At what age did this child do each of these?

Sat without support: _____  Crawled: _____  Walked without holding on: _____  Helped when being

dressed: _____  Ate with a fork: _____  Stayed dry all day: _____  Didn't soil his or her pants during

day: _____  Stayed dry all night: _____  Tied shoelaces: _____  Buttoned buttons: _____

Slept alone: _____  Rode bicycle: _____

### 4. Speech/language development

Age when child said first word understandable by a stranger: _____  Said first sentence understandable to a
stranger: _____

Any current speech, hearing, or language difficulties? _____

### 5. Any other current concerns about development? _____

_____

### G. Homes/residences

If the child was ever placed out of a home, see item 10 under section I, below.

| Child's age when moved | Location | Lived with whom? | Reason for moving | Problems there |
|---|---|---|---|---|
|  |  |  |  |  |
|  |  |  |  |  |
|  |  |  |  |  |

### H. Education

How many years of schooling has your child had (including preschool and kindergarten)? ____ years.

| From (date) | To (date) | School's name and district | Teacher | Special classes or supports? | Did your child graduate? |
|---|---|---|---|---|---|
|  |  |  |  |  |  |
|  |  |  |  |  |  |
|  |  |  |  |  |  |

May I call and discuss your child with the current teacher?  ❑ No  ❑ Yes  If yes, phone number: _____

### I. Health and medical care

1. How is your child's general level of health?  ❑ Excellent  ❑ Good  ❑ Fair  ❑ Poor

2. Pediatrician/PCP/Clinic/doctor's name: _____

   Phone: _____  Address: _____

*(continued)*

- If your child enters treatment with me for psychological problems, may I tell your child's medical doctor/PCP, so that he or she can be fully informed and we can coordinate your child's treatment?  ❑ Yes  ❑ No
- If your child sees other doctors or clinics, please check here  ❑ and write their names, addresses, and phone numbers on the back of this page.

3. List all childhood illnesses, hospitalizations, medications, allergies, important injuries, surgeries, periods of loss of consciousness, convulsions/seizures, and other medical conditions.

| Condition | Age, or from-and-to ages | Treated by whom? Mark the primary care provider (PCP) with a star. | Effects/outcome |
|---|---|---|---|
|  |  |  |  |
|  |  |  |  |
|  |  |  |  |
|  |  |  |  |
|  |  |  |  |

4. List *all* medications, drugs, or other substances your child has taken in the last year—prescribed medications, over-the-counter vitamins, supplements, herbs, and others.

| Medication | Dosage? And how often? | For what condition? | When started? | Effects/outcome | Prescribed and supervised by whom? |
|---|---|---|---|---|---|
|  |  |  |  |  |  |
|  |  |  |  |  |  |
|  |  |  |  |  |  |
|  |  |  |  |  |  |

5. Describe your child's allergies to medications or anything else.

| Allergic to | Allergic reaction | Treatment and medications |
|---|---|---|
|  |  |  |
|  |  |  |
|  |  |  |

6. Has you child ever received inpatient or outpatient psychological, psychiatric, drug or alcohol treatment, medications or or counseling services before?  ❑ No  ❑ Yes. If yes, please indicate:

| For what (diagnoses)? | From (date) | To (date) | Name of doctor, provider, or agency and location | What kind of treatment? | With what results? |
|---|---|---|---|---|---|
|  |  |  |  |  |  |
|  |  |  |  |  |  |

*(continued)*

| For what (diagnoses)? | From (date) | To (date) | Name of doctor, provider, or agency and location | What kind of treatment? | With what results? |
|---|---|---|---|---|---|
|  |  |  |  |  |  |
|  |  |  |  |  |  |
|  |  |  |  |  |  |
|  |  |  |  |  |  |

7. Has any other family member been hospitalized for a psychiatric, emotional, or substance use disorder?
   ❑ No   ❑ Yes. If yes, please indicate:

| Name of family member | For what (diagnoses)? | What kind of treatment? | From (date) | To (date) | With what results? |
|---|---|---|---|---|---|
|  |  |  |  |  |  |
|  |  |  |  |  |  |
|  |  |  |  |  |  |

8. Describe any substance abuse or mental illness in family members (who, relationship, disorder, currently active?): _____

_____

9. Has the child had any residential placements, institutional placements, or foster care?   ❑ No   ❑ Yes. If yes, please indicate:

| Age entered | Age left | Program's name | Reason for placement | Problems there |
|---|---|---|---|---|
|  |  |  |  |  |
|  |  |  |  |  |
|  |  |  |  |  |
|  |  |  |  |  |

10. Other important family issues (losses, adoption, stepparents, other relatives): _____

_____

## J. Abuse history

*Note:* If I suspect that there is or has been abuse, I have to report that. Please be aware of this as you answer the questions below, or leave them blank.

❑ This child was not abused in any way.   ❑ This child may have been abused.

❑ This child was abused. For the kind of abuse, use these letters: P = Physical, such as beatings; S = Sexual, such as touching/molesting, fondling, or intercourse; N = Neglect, such as failure to feed, shelter, or protect; E = Emotional, such as humiliation, etc.

*(continued)*

| Child's age | Kind of abuse | By whom? Intimate partner? Relative? Sibling? Other (specify)? | Effects on the child? | Whom did the child tell? | What happened then? |
|---|---|---|---|---|---|
| | | | | | |
| | | | | | |
| | | | | | |
| | | | | | |
| | | | | | |
| | | | | | |
| | | | | | |

## K. Chemical use by your child

1a. How many caffeine drinks are consumed by your child each day (coffee, tea, colas, energy drinks, etc.)? ____

1b. How often each week are medications (prescription or over the counter) or energy drinks or other chemicals used for alertness? _____

2. How much tobacco is smoked or chewed each week? Kind: _____  Amount _____

3. How many drinks of beer, wine, or liquor are consumed by your child in a typical week? ____

4. Did he or she ever drink to unconsciousness, or run out of money because of drinking?  ❑ No   ❑ Yes

5. Has your child ever used inhalants ("huffing"), such as glue, gasoline, or paint thinner?  ❑ No   ❑ Yes. If yes, which and when? _____

6. Which drugs (not medications prescribed for the child) have been used in the last 5 years? _____
_____

7. Do you think that your child has a drug or alcohol problem?  ❑ No   ❑ Yes. If yes, what kind? _____
_____

## L. Legal history

1. Are you or your child presently being sued, suing anyone, or thinking of suing anyone?  ❑ No   ❑ Yes. If yes, please explain: _____
_____

2. Is your reason for bringing the child to see me related to an accident or injury?  ❑ No   ❑ Yes. If yes, please explain: _____
_____

3. Are you or your child required by a court, the police, or a probation/parole officer to have this appointment?  ❑ No   ❑ Yes. If yes, please explain: _____
_____

4. List any contacts with the police, courts, and jails/prisons that  ❑ you have had, or  ❑ your child has had. Include all open charges and pending ones. Under "Jurisdiction," write in a letter: F = Federal, S = State,

(continued)

CO = County, CI = City. Under "Outcome," write in the *time* and the *type* of sentence you or the child served or must serve: CD = Charges Dropped, AR = Accelerated Release or Alternative Resolution, CS = Community Service, F = Fine, I = Incarceration (jail or prison), PR = PRobation, P = Parole, R = Restitution, O = Other.

| Date | Charge/arrest | Jurisdiction | Outcome | Probation/parole officer's name | Attorney's name |
|------|---------------|--------------|---------|-------------------------------|-----------------|
|      |               |              |         |                               |                 |
|      |               |              |         |                               |                 |
|      |               |              |         |                               |                 |

5. Your current attorney's name: _____ Phone: _____

6. Are there any other legal involvements? ❑ No ❑ Yes. If yes, please explain: _____

_____

## M. Special skills or talents of the child

List hobbies, readings, sports, recreational, musical, TV, and toy preferences, etc.: _____

_____

_____

## N. Friends of the child

How many? ____ Their gender: ❑ Only same ❑ Both ❑ Only other

Their ages: ❑ About the same as my child ❑ Mostly older ❑ Mostly younger

Activities with friends: _____

_____

Influence of friends on child: ❑ Positive ❑ Negative. Specifics: _____

_____

## O. Other

Is there anything else that is important for me as your child's therapist to know about, and that you have not written about on any of these forms? ❑ Yes, and I have written about it on the back of this page or another sheet of paper.

**Please do not write below this line.**

## P. Follow-up by clinician

Based on the responses above and on ❑ interview data ❑ records I reviewed ❑ other information: _____
_____, I have requested the client's parent/guardian to complete and/or I have completed the following forms: ❑ Chemical use ❑ Risk assessment ❑ MSE ❑ Other: _____

❑ Entered child and parent/guardian into phone book ❑ Entered child into birthday book

*This is a strictly confidential patient medical record. Redisclosure or transfer is expressly prohibited by law.*

several sources are listed above under "Ways of Collecting Further Client Information."

*Step 6.* Summarize and organize your data, using the forms provided in Section 6.6 for
suicide risk, chemical use, and overall case formulation.

In summary, the purposes and functions of the forms presented in this section and
in Section 6.6 are as follows: (1) to enable you efficiently to identify and assess the client's
problems in clinical terms and decide how to intervene; (2) to document your assessment so
that it is concise, accessible, productive, and professional; and (3) to help you begin building
a productive therapeutic alliance.

## Preparing the Client for the Intake Interview

Some routine and some critical information has to be exchanged, and organizing this process is advantageous for both sides. You can streamline the process by specifying what
information clients need to provide to you (by sending your intake forms or making then
accessible online); giving them enough time to collect and record the information; encouraging them to note down any questions and areas of uncertainty; and (during the first interview) complimenting them on the quality of their work, and emphasizing that their efforts
are appreciated and augur well for the therapy enterprise.

Since most people get "nervous" in a professional's office, they are likely to fail to disclose important material or to pursue answers to some of their questions. If you appear
rushed, this will compound the problem; make it clear to clients that the session will not be
interrupted, and remind them how much time you have made available. You might encourage some clients to take notes and support this with paper, pens, and a clipboard: "Write
down what you think is most important in what we say today, the answers to your questions, and my recommendations and suggestions." If you have any doubts about the clarity
and fullness of the communication, say, "I want to be sure we are understanding each other,
so tell me what you remember about. . . ."

Another way to collect many of these data is to have the client write his or her own
history, using a comprehensive outline given by you. Joan Anderson, PhD, of Houston, TX,
suggests that this is especially useful in any case you expect may go to court, because you
will have the data in the client's own words (and often in his or her handwriting as well).

## Using the Intake Interview Questions and Guide

Rather than use a printed form (which always seems to have either too much or too little
space) for recording the responses to interview questions, you can ask questions from the
**FORM 6.15** intake interview questions and guide (Form 6.15) and record the client's responses, numbered to correspond to the questions asked, on paper or on a laptop or tablet. Consider the
use of a genogram (Petry & McGoldrick, 2013) to record the information and to assist with
treatment. Here are a few more suggestions about the use of Form 6.15:

- The introductory questions repeat some of those in the adult client information
  forms (Forms 6.6 and 6.7), and so it may not be necessary to ask these again. However, if it has been a while since the first contact, the questions can be asked as a way

# Intake Interview Questions and Guide

Client's name:_____  Date: ____/____/____  Interviewer's initials: ____

## Introductory questions

1.  Who suggested that you come to see me? _____  Referral code: _____

    OK to acknowledge referral (if professional)?  ❑ No  ❑ Yes  ❑ With limitations of

    _____

2.  What is the problem, in your own words? How do you see the situation?
    a.  Symptoms—frequency, duration, intensity, latency, recurrence, course; distress caused.
    b.  Change efforts.
    c.  Why seeking help *now*—precipitants, stressors, consequences.

## Essential information

3.  Previous psychological episodes, treaters, and treatments.
    a.  For what?
    b.  Where/by whom?
    c.  Treatment?
    d.  When (from–to)?
    e.  Outcome?
    f.  Satisfaction/difficulties? (Problems/abuse by therapists—e.g., dual relationships, sexual intimacies, litigation?)
    g.  Release(s) for records signed?  ❑ Not needed  ❑ Yes  ❑ Not yet

4.  History of abuse? (Interview partners separately: Disagreements and decisions; verbal, emotional, physical, sexual abuse; marital, elder, childhood, family-of-origin abuse; kinds of violence; coping and protections; actions taken against abuser; fears, danger.)

5.  Follow-up of responses to client information forms.
    a.  Health problems. (Injuries, illnesses, allergies, eating, exercise, sleep, sexual; medications.)
    b.  Legal history. (Involvement with the law/police, arrests; charges lodged [civil and criminal]; eviction, fraud, violence; consequences, sentences; litigation anticipated, pending or in past, especially against therapists; lawyer's name and phone number.)
    c.  Family of origin. (Make genogram. Parents: ages, health, education, etc. Sibs: number, ages, relationships, etc. Important friendships. For all relatives: issues of abuse, affection, control, discipline, expectations, aspirations, personalities, mental health, religion, schooling, occupations, marriages, legal issues.)
    d.  Substance use history. (For client, family of origin, current family: Alcohol, drugs [street and prescription], chemicals, caffeine, tobacco; current and past use.)
    e.  Current relationship/family situation. (How client met current partner; attraction, closeness, warmth, conflicts; family's role; duration, transitions, stressors; number and ages of children; concerns about children.)

*(continued)*

---

**Optional questions**

6. What changes do you hope therapy will lead to? (Realism, readiness; psychological mindedness, changes in self vs. others.)

7. What do you want to change about yourself? (Locus of responsibility, control.)

8. How will therapy help you make these changes? (Understanding, sophistication, dependence.)

9. What do you think a therapist should do/be like?

10. How long do you think these changes will take? (Realism of time frame.)

11. What are your major strengths? (Abilities, resources, skills, education, employment, personality, feelings, habits, relationships.)

12. What have been your major crises, and how have you handled them? (Precipitants, coping mechanisms/skills, defenses.)

13. What are your long-term goals? (Ambitions, family/school/work situation and satisfaction.)

14. What persons, ideas, or forces have been most useful or influential to you in the past?

15. When are you happy? What are the positive factors in your life now?

16. What spiritual/religious issues are important to you?

17. How does your culture/heritage influence you?

18. Is there anything we haven't talked about that that you feel I should know about?

19. Examiner's confidence in accuracy of information obtained (high, adequate, marginal, poor).

20. Add other questions that seem called for or appropriate, or that you prefer:

of reestablishing rapport and making sure you and the client agree on the problems to be dealt with. You may also discover changes that have occurred since the earlier contact. Finally, if you have doubts or concerns about what the client indicated earlier, ask these questions again to gain more detailed information or discover inconsistencies.

- As always, you should add or delete questions to this form to suit your clientele or practice. If you prefer to use a written questionnaire, you can rephrase, reformat, and delete some of the questions in Form 6.15 for your clients to complete it in writing.

## Collecting Information from Young Adults

**FORM 6.16** Form 6.16 is designed to supplement the information sought in other forms. It should be acceptable to and productive with adolescent clients, who are often reluctant to divulge information, unfamiliar with anyone's ability to keep information confidential, hostile to seeing a "shrink," and otherwise resistant (Rubenstein, 2013). It asks initial questions, which are then followed up during the interview for more detailed information. For example, the question "Do you party?" is a lead into alcohol consumption, sexual activity, use of contraception, and so forth. Alternative phrasings for the question "Why do you think you are here?" include "What do you understand about why you are coming here?" and "Are you coming here because of a problem that is mainly someone else's?" If so, ask, "Whose?" or "What is the problem?" Validation of feelings, especially negative ones is important to adolescents. This form is based on one designed by Nora Fleming Young, PhD, of Pocatello, ID, and is adapted here with her kind permission. The confidentiality statement at the top may need to be modified for your state and the young person's age.

## Special Considerations for Interviewing a Child

During your interview of a child client or his or her caregiver(s), you might want to consider collecting data and your impressions about these points:

### Social Context

1. Relationship between this child and each parent or significant adult.

2. Ways affection is shown and emotions are expressed and controlled.

3. Parenting skills. (Empathy, appropriateness of expectations, methods of control/discipline, by whom.)

4. Chores expected and performance.

5. Autonomy. (Age-appropriateness; allowances; selection of clothes, friends, music; etc.)

6. Relationships with siblings, relatives.

7. Social skills. (Friendships, peers, older vs. younger playmates, skill level.)

8. Social context. (Cultural, ethnic, religious, economic, immigration status, etc.)

9. Other.

# Young Adult Information Form

*Note:* Unless there is a serious risk of injury to you or someone else, what you say on this form is confidential between us. I will not discuss it with your parents or anyone else without your consent.

## A. Identification

Your name: _____ Today's date: ___/___/___ Your age: ___

What name do you prefer to be called? _____ Gender preference: ____ Pronoun preference: ___

## B. Health

How tall are you? _____ How much do you weigh? _____ What do you think is your ideal weight? _____

What kind of exercise do you do? _____ How often? _____

Which of these have you used in the last year? ❑ Tobacco ❑ Alcohol ❑ Marijuana
❑ Ritalin/other stimulants ❑ Steroids ❑ Hormones ❑ Emetics (to vomit) ❑ Laxatives
❑ Other chemicals: _____

## C. Family

Main female caregiver: _____ Main male caregiver: _____

Are these your ❑ birth parents? ❑ adoptive parents? ❑ stepparents? ❑ Other? _____

How would you describe their relationship? _____

Do your caregivers have legal issues? _____

What kinds of problems are you having with:
  Your parents/stepparents/guardians/partners of parents? _____
  Your brothers or sisters (or stepbrothers or stepsisters)? _____
  Other members of your family? _____

What are your responsibilities at home? _____

How do your caregivers discipline or punish you? _____

How important is religion/spirituality to your family? ❑ Highly ❑ Not too much ❑ Not important

How important is religion/spirituality to you? ❑ Highly ❑ Not too much ❑ Not important

## D. School

Which school do you go to? _____ Grade level/year: _____

Which subjects are hardest for you? _____

Are you having problems in school? If so, describe: _____

What are your plans after you graduate? _____

*(continued)*

**FORM 6.16. Information form for young adults (p. 1 of 2).** Adapted from a form devised by Nora Fleming Young, PhD, of Mayer, AZ, and used by permission of Dr. Young. From *The Paper Office for the Digital Age, Fifth Edition.* Copyright © 2017 Edward L. Zuckerman and Keely Kolmes. Published by The Guilford Press. Permission to reproduce this material is granted to purchasers of this book for personal use or use with individual clients (see copyright page for details).

## E. Work

Do you work?   ❑ No   ❑ Yes. If yes, how many hours a week? ____

What do you do? _____   Where? _____

Are you having problems at work? If so, describe: _____

## F. Special skills or talents

What are your hobbies? _____

What sports do you play? _____

What do you enjoy doing most? _____

What are your greatest accomplishments and strengths? _____

## G. Your friends and social activities

| Names of best friends | Age | Gender | What do you do together? |
|---|---|---|---|
| | | | |
| | | | |
| | | | |
| | | | |

Do you party?   ❑ Never   ❑ Some   ❑ Often. If so, when and where? _____

Do you have a cellphone?   ❑ No   ❑ Yes. Is it a smartphone?   ❑ No   ❑ Yes

How many hours a day do you spend online? ____   Watching TV? ____   Listening to music? ____   What kinds of music do you like best? _____

Circle any of these you use: texting, email, Facebook, Instagram, Twitter, other (specify): _____

## H. Concerns

Would you like information or answers in any of these areas:   ❑ Sex   ❑ Body changes   ❑ Birth control
❑ Alcohol   ❑ Drugs (if so, which?): _____

❑ Adult relationships   ❑ Love   ❑ Training and jobs   ❑ Other: _____

What worries or upsets you? _____

Why do you think you are here? Please tell me in your own words. _____

What would you like to see happen or change because of this counseling? _____

What would you like me to let your parents know? _____

Is there anything else I should know that doesn't appear on this or other forms, but that is or might be important? _____

Your signature: _____

*Parental Understanding of Problem(s)*

1. Parent's view of child's main problem.

2. Parental efforts to cope with, change, or cure the child's problems.

3. Parental ideas of what the school or consultant can do for the child.

A very complete and practical guide to collecting and using information on child clients is Braaten's (2007) *The Child Clinician's Report Writing Handbook.*

## The Evaluation of Mental Status

There is no paper substitute for a comprehensive evaluation by an experienced clinician, because mental status is a complex biopsychosocial phenomenon.

**FORM 6.17**     Form 6.17 is a mental status checklist adapted from Zuckerman (2010), which contains detailed resources for evaluating and describing every aspect of mental status. This book also has a large collection of mental status questions in all categories, and hundreds of words and phrases describing all aspects of cognitive functioning commonly evaluated in a mental status evaluation.

The purposes of Form 6.17 are as follows: (1) to record observations about the customarily noted aspects of functioning in a systematic way; (2) to document the client's current mental status for baseline and treatment planning; and (3) to help a treating therapist, who may not be experienced in comprehensive and precise mental status evaluations, to document observations.

# 6.6   Phase 5: Summarizing the Intake Information

During the previous phases of the intake process, you have collected data about the client from the client, your observations, forms, and perhaps other sources. Now it is time to review, sift, and integrate those data. This section offers three forms to assist with this process.

## Summarizing Chemical Use and Suicide Risk Data

The processes of assessing clients' chemical use and suicide risk have already been dis-
**FORM 6.18** cussed in Sections 6.4 and 4.7, respectively. Form 6.18, the chemical user's case formulation,
**FORM 6.19** and Form 6.19, the suicide risk assessment summary and recommendations, are designed to assist you in summarizing and integrating the relevant information in cases where one or the other of these factors plays a significant role.

## Formulating the Whole Case

When the information presented by a new client has been collected, the data must be organized for the making of clinical decisions. What should be the disposition of the case?

# Mental Status Evaluation Checklist

**Directions:** Rate current observed performance (not reported, historical, or projected, which can all go into a narrative).

## A. Identification

Client: _____    Date: ___/___/___    Age: ____ years

Highest grade completed: _____    ❑ GED?   ❑ Special education: Type _____    for ____ years

Primary occupation: _____    Others: _____

Native language: _____    Evaluator: _____

## B. Informed consent

Informed consent was obtained about:   ❑ The recipient(s) of the report   ❑ Consequences of this assessment
❑ Other: _____

By means of:   ❑ Evaluator's NPP   ❑ Interactive discussion   ❑ Other: _____

## C. Evaluation methods

1. The information and assessments below are based on my observation of this client during:   ❑ Intake interview   ❑ Individual therapy   ❑ Formal mental status testing   ❑ Other: _____

2. We interacted for a total of ____ minutes.

3. Setting of the contact:   ❑ Professional office   ❑ Inpatient room   ❑ Clinic or agency office   ❑ Jail/prison
❑ School office   ❑ Home/residence   ❑ Work   ❑ Other: _____

## D. Mental status descriptors

Circle the most appropriate descriptive terms, and write in others as necessary. If an aspect of mental status was not assessed, ~~cross it out~~.

### 1. Appearance and self-care

| | | | | | |
|---|---|---|---|---|---|
| *Stature* | Average | Small | Tall (for age, if a child) | Height of ____ inches | |
| *Weight for size* | Average weight | Overweight | Obese | Underweight | Weight of ____ pounds |
| *Clothing* | Neat/clean | Careless/inappropriate | Disheveled | Dirty | Meticulous |
| | Appropriate for age, occasion, weather | | Inappropriate | Seductive | Bizarre |
| *Grooming* | Normal | Meticulous | Neglected | Inappropriate | Unusual | Bizarre |
| *Cosmetic use* | Appropriate | Inappropriate for age | Excessive | Unusual | None |
| *Use of perfume/cologne* | None | Some | Excessively scented | Body odor | |

*(continued)*

| *Posture/gait* | Normal | Tense | Rigid | Stooped | Slumped | Bizarre | Other: _____ |

*Motor activity*   Unremarkable   Tremor   Tics   Slowed   Restless   Jumpy   Agitated   Gestures

*Other aspects:* _____

## 2. Sensorium

*Attention*   Alert   Inattentive   Unfocussed   Wanders   Unaware   Vigilant

*Concentration*   Normal   Distractible   Drowsy/tired   Lethargic   Confused   Bewildered

Anxiety interferes   Focuses on irrelevancies   Preoccupied

*Orientation*   To all five   Time   Person   Place   Situation   Object

*Recall/memory*   Normal   Defective in:   Immediate/short-term   Recent   Remote

and severity is _____   Confabulates   Gaps   Amnesia   Hallucinated

## 3. Affect and mood

*Affect*   Appropriate   Full range   Dramatic   Labile   Restricted   Blunted   Flat

Teary   Anxious   Apathetic   Other: _____

*Mood*   Euthymic   Irritable   Pessimistic   Dysphoric   Hypomanic   Elated   Euphoric

Other: _____

## 4. Thought and language

*Speech flow*   Normal   Mute   Blocked   Paucity   Slowed   Pressured   Flight of ideas

Loud   Soft   Whispered

*Organization*   Normal   Goal-directed   Simplistic   Loose   Circumstantial

Tangential   Incoherent

*Thought content*   Congruent (mood and circumstances)   Incongruent   Ideas of reference   Suspicions

Delusions of _____   Ideas of influence   Illusions   Monomania

Perseverations   Personalizations   Other: _____

*Preoccupations*   Indecision   Phobias   Somatic   Suicide   Homicide   Guilt   Religion

Other: _____

*Hallucinations*   Auditory   Visual   Tactile   Olfactory   Other: _____

Content: _____

## 5. Executive functions

*Fund of knowledge*   Average   Above average   Impoverished by: _____

*Intelligence*   Average   Below average   Above average   Needs investigation

*Abstraction*   Normal   Concrete   Functional   Popular   Abstract   Overly abstract

*Judgment*   Normal   Common-sensical   Fair   Poor   Dangerous

*Reality testing*   Realistic   Adequate   Distorted   Variable   Unaware

*Insight*   Uses connections   Gaps   Flashes of   Unaware   Denial

*Decision making*   Normal   Only simple   Impulsive   Vacillates   Confused   Paralyzed

*(continued)*

### E. Relating

*Eye contact*          Normal     Fleeting     Avoided     None     Staring

*Facial expression*          Responsive     Tense     Anxious     Sad     Exhausted     Angry     Mask-like

*Attitude toward examiner*          Pleasant     Cooperative     Approval-seeking     Dramatic     Passive     Bored

Silly     Resistant     Critical     Irritable     Hostile     Sarcastic

Argumentative     Provocative     Demanding     Threatening     Suspicious

Guarded     Defensive     Manipulative     Other: _____

### F. Social functioning

*Social maturity*     Responsible     Thoughtful     Irresponsible     Self-centered     Impulsive     Isolates

*Social judgment*     Normal     "Street-smart"     Naive     Heedless     Victimized     Impropriety

### G. Stress

*Stressors*     Pain     Income     Housing     Family conflict     Work     Grief/losses

Illness     Transitions

*Coping ability*     Normal     Growing     Resilient     Exhausted     Overwhelmed

Deficient supports     Deficient skills

*Skill deficits*     None     Education     Communication     Interpersonal     Decision making

Self-control     Persistence     Self-care     Activities of daily living

*Supports*     Usual     Family     Friends     Church     Service system     Other: _____

Needed: _____

### H. Other aspects of mental status

*Risk of harm to self/others*     Denies     Passive     Plans     Means     Threat     Preoccupation     Gesture

Attempt     Other: _____

[Write additional observations, clarifications, and quotations on a new page.]

*This is a strictly confidential patient medical record. Redisclosure or transfer is expressly prohibited by law. This report reflects the patient's condition at the time of consultation or evaluation. It does not necessarily reflect the patient's diagnosis or condition at any subsequent time.*

# Chemical User's Case Formulation

Based on the data collected during this evaluation process, these are my conclusions:

## A. Identification

Client's name: _____  Date: ____/____/____  Case #: _____

## B. Observations and consequences

| | | | | |
|---|---|---|---|---|
| Client was intoxicated at interview: | ❏ Not at all | ❏ Possibly | ❏ Mildly | ❏ Clearly | ❏ Hung over |
| Consumption history was | ❏ Acknowledged | ❏ Minimized | ❏ Denied | ❏ but confirmed |
| Legal consequences were | ❏ Acknowledged | ❏ Minimized | ❏ Denied | ❏ but confirmed |
| Financial consequences were | ❏ Acknowledged | ❏ Minimized | ❏ Denied | ❏ but confirmed |
| Health consequences were | ❏ Acknowledged | ❏ Minimized | ❏ Denied | ❏ but confirmed |
| Spiritual consequences were | ❏ Acknowledged | ❏ Minimized | ❏ Denied | ❏ but confirmed |
| Vocational consequences were | ❏ Acknowledged | ❏ Minimized | ❏ Denied | ❏ but confirmed |
| Academic/school consequences were | ❏ Acknowledged | ❏ Minimized | ❏ Denied | ❏ but confirmed |
| Familial consequences were | ❏ Acknowledged | ❏ Minimized | ❏ Denied | ❏ but confirmed |
| Consequences to other relationships were | ❏ Acknowledged | ❏ Minimized | ❏ Denied | ❏ but confirmed |

What brought the client in now? _____

_____

The patient's goals (and their realism, comprehensiveness, resources needed): _____

_____

_____

## C. Degree of identification/denial as having alcoholism/addiction/dependence

❏ Denies any intemperate use; denies need for treatment

❏ Minimizes consequences of drinking/use

❏ Is "treatment-wise" or "just going through the motions"

❏ Identifies self as "alcoholic/addicted," "in recovery"; has made sobriety his or her first priority

❏ Is willing to and did do whatever is necessary to maintain sobriety

❏ Has a positive and optimistic attitude toward the future

*(continued)*

## D. Stage in the progression of the disease (for alcoholism only)

❑ Unclear   ❑ Prealcoholism   ❑ Prodromal   ❑ Crucial   ❑ Chronic   ❑ Periodic excessive drinking

❑ Blackouts   ❑ Sneaking drinks   ❑ Loss of control over drinking   ❑ Remorse and rationalization

❑ Changing the pattern of drinking   ❑ Morning drinking   ❑ Benders/binges   ❑ Defeat

## E. Personal variables

| | |
|---|---|
| *Religiosity* | ❑ Not relevant   ❑ Minimal   ❑ Important   ❑ Crucial |
| *Ethnicity/heritage* | ❑ Not relevant   ❑ Minimal   Important   ❑ Crucial |
| *Sense of efficacy* | ❑ Normal   ❑ Control in other life areas   ❑ Helpless/passive/defeated |
| *Identity/Self* | ❑ Blames others/denial   ❑ Ashamed   ❑ Guilty   ❑ Self-destroying |
| *Impact of abuse* | ❑ None   ❑ Mild   ❑ Significant   ❑ Severe/prolonged |
| *Attitude toward treatment* | ❑ Eager for   ❑ Hopeful   ❑ Neutral   ❑ Pessimistic |

Other personal findings: _____

## F. Social variables

| | |
|---|---|
| *Residence* | ❑ Comfortable, stable   ❑ Safe   ❑ Unsafe   ❑ Unstable   ❑ Temporary   ❑ None |
| *Employment* | ❑ Regular   ❑ Underemployed   ❑ Irregular   ❑ Tenuous   ❑ None |
| *Friends* | ❑ No friends   ❑ Only substance abusers   ❑ Some abusers   ❑ No abusers |
| *Addiction of close relatives* | ❑ Not current   ❑ Minimal   ❑ Important   ❑ Crucial |
| *Spouse/significant other* | ❑ None   ❑ Supportive   ❑ Uncooperative   ❑ Not involved   ❑ In denial |
| | ❑ Enabling   ❑ Codependent   ❑ Addicted   ❑ In recovery |
| *Family involvement* | ❑ None   ❑ In denial   ❑ Cooperative   ❑ Exhausted   ❑ Punitive |
| *Support system for sobriety* | ❑ Excellent, stable, broad   ❑ Some   ❑ Minimal   ❑ Counterproductive |

Other social factors: _____

## G1. Alcohol use diagnosis

ICD-10 diagnosis is on intake summary.

❑ Abstaining   ❑ In recovery   ❑ Social/controlled drinking   ❑ Heavy drinking   ❑ Problem drinking

❑ Uncontrolled drinking/alcohol addiction/compulsive drinking   ❑ "Dry drunk" syndrome   ❑ At risk

❑ Cross-addicted   ❑ Other: _____

## G2. Nonalcohol substance use diagnosis

ICD-10 diagnosis is on intake summary.

❑ Abstaining   ❑ In recovery   ❑ Social/recreational/controlled use   ❑ Heavy use

❑ At risk   ❑ Cross-addicted   ❑ Other: _____

*(continued)*

## H. Additional assessments needed

❑ Mental status exam    ❑ Neuropsychological    ❑ Neurological    ❑ Medical    ❑ Educational/vocational

❑ Diagnostic evaluations for presence of concurrent psychiatric disorders

❑ Assessment of relationship/marital/sexual difficulties

❑ Assessment of risk for suicide, homicide, abuse, violence

## I. Prognosis

The prognosis, with treatment as specified in the individual treatment plan, is considered to be:

| | | | | | |
|---|---|---|---|---|---|
| For participation in and benefit from treatments: | ❑ Optimistic | ❑ Good | Guarded | ❑ Poor | ❑ Negative |
| For improvement of symptoms: | ❑ Optimistic | ❑ Good | Guarded | ❑ Poor | ❑ Negative |
| For recovery to previous level of functioning: | ❑ Optimistic | ❑ Good | Guarded | ❑ Poor | ❑ Negative |
| For growth and wellness: | ❑ Optimistic | ❑ Good | Guarded | ❑ Poor | ❑ Negative |

## J. Other

Enter any other observations here: _____

_____

*This is a strictly confidential patient medical record. Redisclosure or transfer is expressly prohibited by law. This report reflects the patient's condition at the time of consultation or evaluation. It does not necessarily reflect the patient's diagnosis or condition at any subsequent time.*

## Suicide Risk Assessment Summary and Recommendations

Client's name: _____ Date: ____/____/____

*This assessment reflects the patient's condition at the time of consultation or evaluation. It does not necessarily reflect the patient's diagnosis or condition at any subsequent time.*

This assessment is based on information collected from the following, on the following dates:

❑ My interview(s) with this person/these persons:

    ❑ The client. Dates: _____

    ❑ Family members: _____ Dates: _____

    ❑ Friends: _____ Dates: _____

    ❑ Other persons: _____ Dates: _____

❑ Reading of records (specify): _____

❑ Knowledge from previous client contacts at: _____

❑ Other sources: _____

It is my professional judgment offered with a reasonable degree of clinical confidence, in line with other similar judgments, that this person currently presents the following risk of suicide:

❑ Almost nonexistent. No direct or indirect evidence for suicidal ideation, rumination, or behaviors from client or others. (It is against strongly held beliefs; the client has many or valued reasons for living.)

❑ Low. Only passive/death wishes (fleeting ideation, ambivalence, wondering, considering).

❑ Moderate. Ideation without plan, means, motivation (tired of living/pain; not wanting to be a burden ).

❑ Significant/likely. Persistent ideation, making plans, acquiring means. (The client has made statements, rehearsals, threats, gestures, or low-lethality/symbolic/ineffective attempts. The client has discussed suicide.)

❑ Very high. Serious/high-lethality attempt is likely in near future. (The client has arranged some affairs, has acquired some means, and has some plan of action and privacy.)

❑ Acute and immediate. Persistent and preoccupying thoughts, continual efforts. (The client has acquired high-lethality means and is deliberate and focused. The client has one or more effective plans of action and the necessary privacy.)

Therefore, I recommend the following interventions:

❑ No intervention at present.

❑ Reevaluation by this date: ____/____/____

*(continued)*

---

**FORM 6.19. Suicide risk assessment summary and recommendations (p. 1 of 2).** From *The Paper Office for the Digital Age, Fifth Edition.* Copyright © 2017 Edward L. Zuckerman and Keely Kolmes. Published by The Guilford Press. Permission to reproduce this material is granted to purchasers of this book for personal use or use with individual clients (see copyright page for details).

❑ Consultation with these people or organizations:

   ❑ Relatives: _____

   ❑ Other professionals: _____

   ❑ Mental health authorities: _____

   ❑ Others: _____

❑ Changes to therapy or new therapeutic interventions:

   ❑ Exploration of issues and motives   ❑ A safety agreement and comprehensive plan

   ❑ More frequent or longer psychotherapy sessions   ❑ Consultations and other evaluations

   ❑ Changes in medications   ❑ Intensive family interventions and support

   ❑ Crisis intervention team   ❑ Intensive outpatient treatment program

   ❑ Partial hospitalization with intensive treatment   ❑ Contacts with police or other authorities

   ❑ Psychiatric inpatient hospitalization (involuntary if necessary)

   ❑ Other recommendations:_____

| | | |
|---|---|---|
| _____ | _____ | ___/___/___ |
| Signature | Printed name | Date |

A copy of this form should now be sent to _____ at _____.

*This is a strictly confidential patient medical record. Redisclosure or transfer is controlled by state and national laws.*

Should the client be referred elsewhere, be sent for further assessments or consultations, receive treatment from you, or be sent to a specialized treatment program? If treatment is appropriate, what should be the goals, and what methods should be used? A treatment plan is needed.

**FORM 6.20**    The purposes and functions of Form 6.20, the intake summary and case formulation, are to gather and formulate the findings so as to (1) record the findings; (2) prioritize the client's most important and immediate problems; (3) facilitate all appropriate referrals for evaluation or treatment; (4) support consultations and coordination with other professionals (integrated care); (5) document the need for services to funding sources (e.g., health insurers and MCOs—medical necessity); (6) concentrate the data needed to develop a treatment plan; and (7) provide for continuity and comprehensiveness of care. If your client requires an MCO's approval, complete this form first and then use Form 3.2, the Chapter 3 checklist for MCOs of medical necessity for psychotherapy.

Section D, part 1, of Form 6.20 offers check boxes for the assessment of risks. Some of the items can be modified or expanded if your setting needs greater precision, as in these examples:

---

a.  *Suicide*:  ❑ Not assessed   ❑ No indications   ❑ Passive death wish   ❑ Ideation without plan   ❑ Threat   ❑ Preoccupation   ❑ Plan   ❑ Prior gesture   ❑ Prior attempt   ❑ Plan without means   ❑ Access to means   ❑ Other: _____

b.  *Homicide*:  ❑ Not assessed   ❑ No indications   ❑ Ideation without plan   ❑ Threat   ❑ Identifiable victim   ❑ No identifiable victim   ❑ Preoccupation   ❑ Plan   ❑ Prior attempt   ❑ Plan without means   ❑ Access to means   ❑ Access to victim   ❑ Additional information:

---

Other categories of risk can be added:

---

*Nonsuicidal self-injury*:  ❑ Not assessed   ❑ No indications   ❑ Ideation without plan   ❑ Threat   ❑ Preoccupation   ❑ Plan   ❑ Access to means   ❑ Access to privacy   ❑ Prior injuries: _____

*Isolation*:  ❑ Self-preoccupation   ❑ Avoidance   ❑ Seclusion   ❑ Self-neglect   ❑ Refuses supports   ❑ Harm or injury from neglect   ❑ Other:

---

In the "self-injury" category, distinguish acts of suicidal intent from culturally associated body modification (tattooing, piercing, scarification, acts motivated by psychopathology (relief of psychic pain through self-cutting and blood), sexual or power exchange activities (knife play, dominant and submissive that involve whipping, spanking, etc.). If you do not know the difference between self-harm and marks or bruises from consensual bondage/dominance-and-submission activity, now is the time to learn more. This site offers basic information (https://ncsfreedom.org/key-programs/consent-counts/consent-counts/item/467-sm-vs-abuse.html), and this one is much more detailed (http://www.evilmonk.org/a/bamm03.cfm).

Another revision you could make is that you could add or substitute a visual scale for each of the risks in section D, part 1:

# Intake Summary and Case Formulation

Where space is insufficient, use the section's letter and number for reference, and write the information on additional pages with name and date.

## A. Basic information

Client: _____ Date: ___/___/___ ID #: _____

*Purpose of this intake:*

❑ New client evaluation ❑ Readmission; previous intake on ___/___/___

❑ Consultation; copy to be sent to _____ ❑ Reevaluation/review

❑ Other: _____

## B. Dynamics of difficulties

| Presenting complaint(s): Thoughts, behaviors, emotions | Stressors Acute/chronic | Strengths/resources |
|---|---|---|
|  |  |  |

## C. Present level of functioning/limitations/impairment

Use the 12- or 36-question WHODAS, with each response on a scale of 0 = no difficulty to 4 = extreme difficulty or cannot do. Enter sum of each area, and calculate the total.

| Area of functioning (domain of WHODAS 2.0) | Domain sum |
|---|---|
| Cognition—understanding and communicating |  |
| Mobility—moving and getting around |  |
| Self-care—hygiene, dressing, eating, and staying alone |  |
| Getting along—interacting with other people |  |
| Life activities—domestic responsibilities, leisure, work, and school |  |
| Participation—joining in community activities |  |
| Total of all domains (with a maximum score of 24 or 72). Convert to score of 0–100 for disability assessment. |  |

*(continued)*

## D. Assessment conclusions

1. Assessment of currently known **risk factors:**
   a. *Suicide:* ❑ Not assessed    Risk is ❑ Very low  ❑ Low  ❑ Moderate  ❑ Significant  ❑ Very high
   b. *Homicide:* ❑ Not assessed  ❑ No known behaviors  ❑ Fleeting ideation  ❑ Persistent ideation
      ❑ Plan  ❑ Intent without means  ❑ Intent with means
      Risk is ❑ Very low  ❑ Low  ❑ Moderate  ❑ Significant  ❑ Very high
   c. *Impulse control:*  ❑ Not assessed  ❑ Sufficient control  ❑ Moderate  ❑ Minimal  ❑ Inconsistent
   d. *Domestic violence:*  ❑ Not assessed  ❑ No indications  ❑ Denied  ❑ Victim  ❑ Perpetrator  ❑ Both
      ❑ Threats  ❑ Emotional/psychological  ❑ Physical  ❑ Sexual  ❑ Financial exploitation
      ❑ Children involved  ❑ Pets involved  ❑ Safety plan in place  ❑ Other: _____
   e. *Physical or sexual abuse as victim:*  ❑ Not assessed  ❑ No  ❑ Yes
      Legally reportable?  ❑ No  ❑ Yes (see section E5, below)
   f. *Child/elder neglect or abuse:*  ❑ Not assessed  ❑ No evidence or suspicion  ❑ Yes
      Is client  ❑ Victim?  ❑ Perpetrator?  ❑ Both?  ❑ Neither, but abuse exists in family
      Legally reportable?  ❑ No  ❑ Yes (see section E5, below)
   g. *Substance use:*  ❑ Not assessed  ❑ No evidence  ❑ Unstable remission  ❑ Full, sustained remission
      ❑ No harmful use/misuse  ❑ Overuse  ❑ Use disorder
   h. *Adherence to previous treatments:*  ❑ Not assessed  ❑ Full adherence  ❑ Variable
      ❑ Minimal nonadherence/moderate adherence  ❑ Little or no adherence
   i. *If risk exists:* Client  ❑ can  ❑ cannot validly agree to a contract not to harm  ❑ self  ❑ others  ❑ both

2. **Urgency estimate:**  ❑ Emergency; immediate interventions  ❑ Serious disruption of functioning; act in next 24 hours  ❑ Treatment needed; act soon/routine  ❑ Wait for: _____

3. **Diagnoses** (current best formulation): Besides F codes, include Z codes and medical conditions. Place diagnosis you will treat first at top of the list:  ❑ DSM-5 or  ❑ ICD-10

| Code # | Name of diagnosis |
|--------|-------------------|
|        |                   |
|        |                   |
|        |                   |
|        |                   |

4. Significant and relevant **medical conditions,** including allergies and drug sensitivities:

| Condition/diagnosis | Treatment/medications | Care provider | Current condition |
|---------------------|----------------------|---------------|-------------------|
|                     |                      |               |                   |
|                     |                      |               |                   |
|                     |                      |               |                   |
|                     |                      |               |                   |

*(continued)*

**E. Recommended program of evaluations and coordinated services, liaisons, consultations**

1. Psychotherapy: ❑ Cognitive ❑ Behavioral ❑ Family/systems ❑ Play therapy ❑ Mindfulness/relaxation ❑ Support/maintenance ❑ Environmental change ❑ Multisystemic therapy (MST) ❑ Assertive community treatment (ACT) ❑ Therapy group: _____ ❑ Clinical hypnosis ❑ Biofeedback ❑ Couple/relationship ❑ Other: _____

2. Groups:
   a. Support groups: ❑ Twelve-Step program: _____ ❑ Grief ❑ Sexual orientation or gender support ❑ Other social support: _____
   b. Psychoeducational groups: ❑ Parenting skills/child management ❑ Communication skills ❑ Assertiveness ❑ Stress management ❑ Women's issues ❑ Other: _____

3. Residential treatment: ❑ Partial hospital ❑ Psychosocial rehab ❑ Facility-based crisis ❑ Child/adolescent day treatment ❑ Respite care ❑ Other: _____

4. Substance abuse services: ❑ Intensive outpatient program ❑ Comprehensive outpatient tx. ❑ Nonmedical community residential ❑ Medically monitored community residential ❑ Halfway house ❑ Detoxification services ❑ Non-hospital-based medical detox ❑ Medically supervised Alcohol and Drug Abuse Treatment Center (ADATC) detox/crisis stabilization

5. Legal services: ❑ Offender program ❑ Victim support ❑ Referral to advocates: _____ ❑ Child abuse (or other) call/report made by _____ on ___/___/___ at ____ A.M./P.M.

6. Referrals for ancillary and continuing services:

| Referred to: | For (kind of service): | Date of referral |
|---|---|---|
|  | Psychotropic medication evaluation |  |
|  | Physical medical care |  |
|  | Patient education |  |
|  | Nursing care |  |
|  | Social services coordination |  |
|  | Educational/vocational services |  |
|  | Occupational or physical therapy |  |
|  | Pain clinic or "back school" |  |

7. Further assessments, based on current clinical evaluation, are needed to answer these concerns or rule out these possible coexisting conditions:
   ❑ Psychological presentation/symptoms of medical condition. Considerations:
   ❑ Thyroid ❑ Diabetes ❑ Alcohol/drug misuse ❑ Circulatory problem ❑ Neurological problem ❑ Poor nutrition ❑ Medication interactions ❑ Toxin exposure ❑ Other: _____
   ❑ Sexual dysfunctions ❑ Factitious disorders
   ❑ Psychophysiological disorders ❑ Learning disabilities ❑ Genetic disorders/counseling
   ❑ Other: _____

*(continued)*

8. Documents to be obtained:

| Type of record | Source | Date of first request |
|---|---|---|
| ❑ Medical/physician/hospital | | |
| ❑ School | | |
| ❑ Agency | | |
| ❑ Other | | |

Clinician completing this form:

| | | /    /    |
|---|---|---|
| Signature | Printed name | Date |

When compared with this practice's/agency's typical client population, the risk this client presents is judged at this time to be:

| | | | | |
|---|---|---|---|---|
| Very low | Low | Medium | High | Very high |

For section E, you could substitute a statement or checklist with options of the services you have available, in order of intensity of service/need:

E.  Recommended level of care/medical necessity
- ❑  Emergency/immediate psychiatric hospitalization
- ❑  Regular, 24-hour psychiatric hospitalization
- ❑  Residential treatment center
- ❑  Inpatient medical detoxification
- ❑  Inpatient substance abuse/dependence program
- ❑  Specialized inpatient program for:
- ❑  Group or supported housing   ❑ Shelter
- ❑  Partial hospitalization/day treatment program
- ❑  Structured/intensive outpatient program for: _____

Or, depending on the likely needs of your clientele, you can add these to the present section E:

Educational/vocational services:   ❑ Agency evaluation   ❑ GED classes   ❑ Work hardening   ❑ Sheltered workshop   ❑ Special school services   ❑ Other: _____

Economic supports:   ❑ Full-time employment   ❑ Part-time employment   ❑ Welfare/AFDC   ❑ Soc. Sec. Disability   ❑ SSI   ❑ Other: _____

# CHAPTER 7

# Planning and Then Documenting Treatment

After intake and assessment have been completed and recorded, the next clinical and record-keeping tasks are planning treatment, documenting its progress, and finally terminating the case. This chapter of *The Paper Office for the Digital Age* covers these aspects in detail.

## 7.1 Treatment Planning

The whole subject of treatment planning is in flux. There is neither a widely accepted set of essentials for a plan, nor any universally accepted format in use. The following general guidelines, as well as the forms and formats offered in this chapter, are intended to provide ideas and a framework rather than to be prescriptive or final.

### Issues

Some therapists resist the planning of treatment, because they believe it interferes with the immediacy and spontaneity they value in therapy. It also seems to require the prediction of what they see as unpredictable—the evolving, branching dance of client and therapist, problem and intervention.

The research has not resolved the question of whether a planful or a spontaneous approach is better, and it may never. Funding sources, manualized treatment methods, and clinical experience all suggest that at least some degree of organized anticipation is beneficial.

Highly organized treatment plans soon succumb to the vagaries of the clinical process and need constant revision. But more generic plans may fail to maintain the focus and momentum of therapy. A treatment plan serves to limit distractions from the central goals. Without a plan, sequence, or map, both you and your client can easily be distracted by the immediate from what is most important. You can both easily lose your "vision" in the welter of endless information, intercurrent events, levels of analysis, and so on, and fail to integrate the immediate into the important. As the saying goes, when we are up to our ears wrestling alligators, it is hard to remember that we came here to drain the swamp.

Developing a treatment plan jointly with each client requires the kind of thoughtful, individualized, and insightful effort that ensures successful therapy. It can be a productive focusing of therapeutic time. This process can be used cooperatively to involve the client in planning, homework/self-monitoring, revisions of methods, and overall evaluation. Such a model of joint decision making strengthens the connections among consultation, planning, treatment, and evaluation. It also implements beliefs in mutuality and equality.

## Guidelines for Treatment Planning

Typically, a client comes in with complaints or problems, some ideas of their causes, and some desired outcomes. The client's presentation is reformulated (fitted to a diagnosis, formulated into a "case," with its presumed dynamics) by the therapist within a professional framework that allows for intervention and anticipates change. The therapist's favorite (or even just familiar) methods are offered to the client, and progress is assessed irregularly and mainly unreliably. A more systematic and yet realistic sequence for treatment planning would proceed as follows:

1. Do a **biopsychosocial assessment** of all the current problematic or symptomatic behaviors, affects, or cognitions. Review all areas of functioning. Gather data from different sources and integrate them.

2. Create an agreed-upon limited **list of problems.** You may call them "concerns" or "issues to focus on," to be even less pathologizing. Select a primary and some secondary problems to address. Others will have to be delayed or disregarded. Attend to your capabilities and expertise. Set priorities collaboratively.

3. **Refine the definitions of the problems.** Most treatment plans emphasize the functional costs of problems (the favorite definition of payers) as against the psychic pain and problems defined by observable behaviors although psychological problems are most subjective. Chapter 6's forms support this process, and formats for a problem list are offered in Section 7.2.

4. **Define the outcomes desired**—both long-term "goals" and short-term "objectives." The client takes the lead in this with the assistance of the clinician.

5. **Goals** can be global as well as long-term, and can involve significant changes as well as problem resolution. They do not need to be couched in behavioral terms.

6. To construct **objectives,** ask, "If we are to achieve this long-term goal by this specific date [such as next year], what smaller steps would have to be accomplished and by when [such as next month]?" These smaller steps, or objectives, should be behavioral, measurable, and concrete. Generally each goal should have at least two objectives. A way to create objectives is to consider that behaviors can change in at least four ways: frequency ("More often . . . " or "Decrease rate . . . " or "Relieve . . . "), intensity ("mumble instead of scream," "scratch instead of cut"), duration (shorter anxiety attacks), or latency ("When $X$ happens, client will be able to delay response $Y$ for $Z$ minutes").

7. **Consider the interventions and resources needed** to achieve the goals. Each objective should have at least one intervention. The selecting and sequencing of interventions are usually the responsibilities of the therapist. For precision, the objectives should answer the questions of who is going to do what when and how, with what resources.

8. Provide reliable ways to **assess progress and outcomes.**

These steps are considered in more detail below.

## Systems and Formats of Treatment Planning

If you are seeking a comprehensive system of planning treatment, consider the following models. Some are more comprehensive or more detailed than others, and some will suit your setting or needs better.

### The Problem-Oriented Record

The "problem-oriented record" (POR) is a comprehensive and logical method that is widely used in medicine. It is discussed in detail in Section 7.2.

### Impairment Profile

Goodman et al. (1992) have cleverly suggested using a "client impairment profile" to document and communicate treatment needs, to develop a rationale for treatment and a treatment plan, and to predict outcome of care. The list of impairments (in their Appendix A) becomes a common language for helpers from different disciplines. When combined with a severity rating, it suggests an appropriate level of service or care. They add outcome objectives, selections from a list of interventions (their Appendix B), and progress measures to assess the effectiveness of treatment (basically, changes in the ratings of severity). Their system is neat and complete, but requires a new focus—not problems or complaints, but impairments. However, the functional approach is the basis of current managed care models and has been adopted by the World Health Organization as the *International Classification of Functioning, Disability and Health* (ICFDH). This, coordinated with the ICD, is likely to substantially displace the DSM for most psychotherapy and rehabilitation in the future, so it is well worth your monitoring and attention. It can be searched, browsed, and downloaded at its own website (http://www.who.int/classifications/icf/en).

### Content Resources

Arthur E. Jongsma, Jr., PhD, with colleagues, has produced a series of books called *Treatment Planners, Progress Notes Planners,* and *Homework Planners,* as well as a computer program to aid in the development of treatment plans. They offer very specific language for these topics, which can be used to create plans from hundreds if not thousands of statements.

## Other Points in Planning Treatment

### Taking Account of Resistance

If a treatment plan is to be truly effective, it must anticipate and respond to the obstacles to change. A great deal of the elegance and effectiveness of psychotherapy is found in its sophistication about handling "resistance." Here are some questions ELZ likes to ask a client in the course of planning treatment. The client's responses to these questions can be built into the plan and can thus increase the chances of a successful outcome.

"What would happen if you were to make the changes you say you want? How would these changes affect your partner, family, and friends? What would be the negative consequences?" (This question identifies demotivators, obstacles, and blind spots.)

"What do you see as preventing the changes? What are the blockages and obstacles to change?" (This lets you see how the client conceptualizes the work to be done.)

"What has not worked in the past?" (This might keep you from repeating unsuccessful approaches.)

"What *has* been helpful in the past in dealing with these problems?" (You can then build on these.)

"When were there situations like this, and you were able to manage them successfully?" (This is a solution-focused approach.)

"Who are your best allies in helping you deal with problems like these?" (This question identifies the client's social and other supports.)

"Who do you know who has successfully dealt with these same problems?" (This identifies potential role models.)

"What do you think is necessary to make things better, and how long might each of these take?" (This question explores the client's conceptualization of treatment, so that you can blend into it or work to change it.)

### Coordinating Treatment Efforts

If treatments must be simultaneous, you will need to communicate the relevant information among providers. Traditionally, case and team conferences have borne this function; however, unless they are very well organized, they make poor decisions (Meehl, 1973) and waste everyone's time and a lot of money. For many purposes, phone call consultations are sufficient and confidential. When multiple providers are involved in a client's care, video conference calls (using online resources such as http://www.GoToMeeting.com, http://www.VSee.com, and http://www.WebEx.com) are easy, but they may not be effective without structure and a clear agenda. Compliance with the Health Insurance Portability and Accountability Act's (HIPAA) security standards are essential for these online conferencing sites and those that allow document sharing. Scheduling can be difficult, although a site such as http://doodle.com (without any confidential information posted, of course) can help with group scheduling.

## *Evaluating Outcomes with Goal Attainment Scaling*

How can you assess the changes a client makes? The methods of planning described earlier generally use symptom reduction as the criterion of change. However, alternative, more flexible models exist. The best-known of these is "goal attainment scaling" (GAS), which is a very simple but powerful method of documenting progress toward goals (Kiresuk et al., 1994). A website (http://www.marson-and-associates.com/GAS/GAS_index.html) makes it all very easy and fun. GAS consists of just the following components:

1. Specifying at least five goals. Goals can be described in *any* terms or areas or levels of abstraction; this is a major strength of this method.

2. Choosing a date in the future when progress toward the goals is to be evaluated.

3. Defining at least three of five possible outcomes for each goal. They must be observable to be reliably ratable by a third party, not just the client or clinician. The five levels of goal attainment are as follows (slightly reworded):

    –2 = The worst outcome that is likely to occur.

    –1 = An outcome less successful than expected.

     0 = An outcome that achieves the expected level of success.

    +1 = An outcome more successful than expected.

    +2 = The most favorable outcome thought likely.

4. At the previously decided point or points in time, the level of attainment of each goal is scored by a disinterested party.

5. A simple statistical test (Student's *t*-test) can be applied to this score to decide how likely these outcomes are to have happened by chance.

Scores can be compared over time, across clients, or across programs. Some difficulties will arise if expectations are set too low, but repetitions of the process will correct these over time. The method is simple, easily learned (by a client), and widely applicable. Its greatest advantage is that it can be applied to almost any kind of goal, and is thus independent of any theory or orientation, and yet produces statistically meaningful evaluations of progress and outcoime.

Two other well-regarded measures are Duncan and Miller's Session Rating Scale (SRS) and Outcome Rating Scale (ORS), which can be found online (http://www.myoutcomes.com) and can be used via monthly subscription. The SRS (also discussed in Section 7.5) assesses shifts in the alliance *during* treatment, and the ORS is an outcome measure when therapy is completed. The website also offers paper versions, which can be handed to clients at the end of sessions.

## Formulating Treatment Plans for Managed Care Organizations

We should not let the current and substantial differences between the objectives of managed care organizations (MCOs) and those of many clinicians obscure the commonalities. Thoughtful planning of treatment interventions is always desirable and in the client's best interest. Keeping an eye on treatment plans was managed care's preferred method for tracking "quality and appropriate care," according to Scott Harris, PhD, who was codirector of the Center for Behavioral Health Care in Los Angeles (Harris, 1993, pp. 5–6). "It provides a structured mechanism for periodic review and authorization, monitoring providers for appropriateness, competence, and effectiveness."

Although most MCOs do not require treatment plans for initiating treatment, some do after a small number of approved sessions. Most require completion of their own forms, almost always online. Although this reduces the MCOs' processing costs (compared to having a human read and understand a narrative), they may increase your vulnerability for several reasons, as discussed in Section 3.5. You can see what 50 or so treatment plans and requests for treatment forms look like at http://www.psychbiller.com/forms.

## 7.2    Documenting Treatment's Progress

After treatment has been planned and initiated, records of its implementation need to be kept. The treatment-planning formats offered earlier in this chapter often include ways to monitor the progress of the case. This section discusses those and other options in more detail. Specifically, it extensively discusses the following options for keeping treatment records:

- Guidelines for note taking, including when and how to take notes.

- HIPAA's rules on the contents of the medical record and psychotherapy notes, with sample forms.

- Structured progress notes for individual and for group therapy.

- The POR (mentioned in Section 7.1), including an example of a POR progress note form.

- A structured form for group therapy.

- Client-generated records and those co-created by clinician and client.

### Note Taking: Guidelines and Suggestions

The purposes of a progress note form are (1) to document the progress of your treatment and the client's response to it (for clinical and legal reasons); (2) to enable you to do this with as little time and effort as possible (by using check boxes *and* short narratives); (3) to support evaluation of the treatment by you, the client, and other interested parties; and (4) to ensure continuity of care, if treatment is transferred.

Although notes should be concise, they must also be coherent, accurate, current, relevant, and handled in ways to assure and maintain confidentiality. Your narratives should be guided by these principles.

Most clinicians write narratives in terms of the sequence of events and observations as they are happening in the therapy hour or what they recall, and so their notes only partially describe the important facts of the therapy. Such notes will probably not protect these therapists or support understanding of their therapy, because they don't indicate a guiding framework for treatment (thus the need for the additional treatment plan). If this description applies to you, find or invent a system you can live with—one that makes sense for your way of working, helps you do your job, and protects you. The following ideas may help.

### When to Write Notes

ELZ does not recommend waiting until the end of the day to write notes. Writing so far removed from the experience can lead to contamination of your memories of one client by those of other clients or events, as well as to other errors or distortions in your recollections. This is not fair to you or your clients. KK, however, finds that while some details may fade, the bigger picture may become clearer if she waits to write up notes.

It's good to take notes immediately after a session. This allows for perspective on the whole session, as well as for the identification of themes and the most important events. Make certain to schedule enough time and to include this time in your charge to the client (although your managed care contract may forbid your charging the MCO for non-face-to-face work). When time between clients is too short for a note, KK sometimes writes some "bullet points" in a sticky note for later expansion into a progress note.

Writing notes during a treatment session saves time, but may lead to incompleteness and (because of lack of reflection or excess brevity) later incomprehensibility. It also reduces eye contact and rapport with the client. Other therapists find that taking notes uses little time, is seen as thoroughness, and gives them time to consider what is happening and to weigh their responses. Here are some additional suggestions about note taking during a session:

- Take notes about the major issues in a "headline" or "telegraphic" format, leaving space. As soon as the session is over, write in the details and your considered formulations. You can certainly use a shorthand method or Speedwriting™, which essentially omits all vowels. However, notes that are illegible or too telegraphic will not serve to defend you by demonstrating your assessments, thought processes, and decision making, and will not support any of the other functions of clinical notes.

- Take real-time notes of things you suspect you will forget or any factual data that you may not remember accurately without a reminder (Wilson, 1980, p. 7).

- Be aware of your client's reactions to your note taking. It is rumored that despite his efforts to be nondirective, Carl Rogers's occasional note taking was thought by his clients to indicate what he considered important. Saying, "Let me just make a note of that," or even the minimal cue of writing after a client says something, may reinforce that topic, mood, or pattern even when you don't want to increase symptomatic behavior. Some clients will be flattered by your making a permanent record that you might review between sessions. Others may suspect that you are recording judgments of them that you won't share. Some clients may want or need your undivided attention. Note taking can be either a barrier or an opportunity to process your thoughts without creating an uncomfortable silence.

- If a client becomes uneasy, discontinue your note taking and offer to share the notes with him or her.

- Find a way to ensure that you document all nontrivial phone calls. Date, time, person, content, decisions, and actions should be noted. Some argue that the trivial ones should also be recorded, as patterns may emerge that you would not otherwise recognize.

- Consider dictating your notes. Dragon's products (http://www.nuance.com/dragon/index.htm) are not expensive and will convert your dictation to printable text very accurately, despite accents or idiosyncrasies. The programs do require learning their commands for punctuating, which will take some time. If you adopt dictation, consider adding protective statements to all your reports, such as "Dictated but not read. Errors may be present." Dictating with a cellphone is free but raises privacy concerns. Your speech is uploaded to servers and a computer to be transcribed and then returned to you, all over cellphone networks. While Apple, at least, says that it uses these messages as data only to improve its speech-to-text function, these companies do not sign business associate contracts. We do not know how long this material is stored or who sees what parts of it, so, at the very least, don't identify the client by name. You might dictate a summary or just some stems and later edit the note, or listen and transcribe it on your computer for a permanent record. There are also ways to keep the dictation Mac-based without sending the dictation to Apple's servers (see http://support.apple.com/kb/HT5449?viewlocale=en_US&locale=en_US).

- *Not* keeping notes is not an option; you are ethically required to have such records. (See Section 1.4 for information on record-keeping obligations.). Whatever note-taking schedule you adopt, always keep your notes current. Periodically, or when you are closing a case, you can revise your working notes into formal records.

### What to Write Down: Guidelines

You may have heard, "If it wasn't written down, it didn't happen," but what does this mean? Taken literally, it is nonsense. A lot goes on that we don't record—the client's clothing, the back pain we felt, the room's temperature. Why not? Because it isn't relevant, and so we didn't need to record it. A rational response to this imposition could be "I did not record that because it was not relevant to my work, purpose, intent, or conceptualization of this case at that time."

When there is a change in the client's condition (a new problem develops or is recognized, there is a response or a lack of response to adequate treatment, etc.), be sure to record any event or decision that preceded it. For justification of continuing treatment ("medical necessity"), it could be advantageous to record a mini-assessment perhaps every 6 months.

Document your clinical decision making for your own later review. Ask yourself, "Will I need to know this later? For the next session? Later in treatment or after treatment, for another purpose?" **If having this information will not change some aspect of treatment, do not bother to record it.**

Klein et al. (1984) (as summarized in Soisson et al., 1987) recommend the **documentation of *all* significant decisions during therapy.** Specifically, the record should include the following:

1. What the treatment choice is expected to accomplish (goals, objectives).

2. Why you believe it will be effective (a rationale).

3. Any risks involved and why they are justified.

4. Which alternative treatments were considered.

5. Why they were rejected or deferred.

6. Any steps taken to improve the effectiveness of the chosen treatments.

7. Evidence of informed consent, as provided by the client's statements or your own observations supporting the client's consent.

8. The rationales for any referrals made.

Make a record of your clinical decision making for good clinical care, your professional development, and perhaps self-defense. A useful rule of thumb may be **"If it might make a mess, make a note."** In a similar vein, Gutheil (1980, p. 482) intelligently suggests that when taking any risky actions, you should "think out loud for the record" so that if the unfortunate happens, it can be traced only to an error in judgment and not to negligence. The following specific pointers may be helpful:

- Explicitly note where information isn't clear.

- Document all clinically significant events, such as nonroutine calls, missed sessions, consultations with other professionals, threats, and suspicions.

- When forensically significant events or possible malpractice situations are anticipated, the record should be written from the perspective of future readers (Gutheil & Appelbaum, 2000), especially unfriendly readers. An example of such a situation might be a suicidal client.

- Emergency treatment situations are responsible for a disproportionately large share of malpractice claims, and so should be documented with extra care (Gutheil & Appelbaum, 2000). Get full consultations, and document any resistance from significant others, so that responsibility can be placed accurately (Cohen, 1979).

- Your statements about the limitations of a treatment should be noted; its success should not be guaranteed, and excessive optimism should be shunned to avoid responsibility for a failure (Gutheil & Appelbaum, 2000). Underpromise and overdeliver.

- Don't omit sexual material; doing so may leave you with little defense against an accusation of impropriety during a session.

- Do not hesitate because of modesty to **record a client's statements of appreciation** for your work or **reports of successes and improvements during therapy.** These will be clinically valuable when the inevitable failures and frustrations surface in the normal course of an episode of therapy, and protective in the case of a complaint.

### What Not to Write Down: Guidelines

Do not record anything that is unnecessary for or irrelevant to treatment. We suggest that you generally exclude the following:

- Excessive detail.

- Gossip and hearsay.

- Statements that the client would find insulting, embarrassing, or overly critical.

- Informal diagnoses such as "heavy drinker," "criminal," or "wife beater."

- Reference to clients solely in terms of their diagnoses or other problems ("person-first" language is currently favored, such as "people with schizophrenia").

- Moral or personal value judgments (especially negative ones) about the client or others (e.g., "fat," "lazy," "weak," or "acted stupidly"). Similarly, moralizing, preaching, or editorializing.

- The client's political, religious, or other personal beliefs.

- Names of illicit partners (perhaps even just use first initials?) or specific indicators of affairs.

- Reports of most illegal activity in the past and incriminating information about illegal activity in the present (e.g., details of drug use), except when you are treating the use or in situations where you are a mandated reporter.

- New medical diagnoses or other judgments that your training and experience do not qualify you to make.

- Most sexual practices, unless you are providing sex therapy and so the information is essential.

If you feel the need to record sensitive data to guide your therapy such as the types described above or the items listed below, put them in a HIPAA-protected psychotherapy note (where they legally belong), not the regular progress note:

- Hunches and hypotheses, unconfirmed diagnoses, suspicions.

- Countertransference ideas.

- Difficulties you had with other professionals or agencies in this client's case.

- Criticisms of other professionals or services received by the client, based on the client's complaints.

- Anything else that is highly sensitive, that is only for your management of the case, and that you want to record details of or are likely to forget.

### A Checklist of Tips for Clinical Notes

❑ If you find yourself entering the same data on many notes, creating codes will require less recording time and space. Examine your current notes to decide what might be coded. For example, you might use this format for "Change since ____/____/____ (date)": < < to indicate much worse; < for worse; 0 for no change; > for improved; and > > for greatly improved. For "Treatment provided," you could code with "sm" for stress management, "resoc" for resocialization/social skills, and the like.

❑ It is best to avoid nonstandard or idiosyncratic **abbreviations and acronyms.** If you must use them, keep a list of them somewhere in your records so you won't forget what they stand for, and so a court can't misinterpret your intentions. If you use a lot of these, perhaps make it a practice to include your list whenever you send out records.

❑ Although HIPAA and likely payers require us to document **a client's medications,** most of us are not prescribers; thus the usefulness of this information to us is very limited, and it may be misinformation. What are we to make of finding that a client is on more than the usual adult daily dosage? Dosages and drugs are frequently changed, so such notations will often soon be inaccurate. Instead, we recommend simply noting who is prescribing and monitoring the client's medications, and asking the client about changes and main and side effects, which we then document and which can be shared with the prescriber. On the other hand, messages left by prescribers that note changes to medication should absolutely be documented.

❑ All entries should be dated, sometimes timed, and signed. A signature may be unnecessary when the notes are in your handwriting, but initials should indicate where a particular note ends. Every page should have the client's name on it. Indicate the date and time of your next meeting when it is scheduled, so as to document continuity of care.

❑ Formatting is your friend if you handwrite your notes. Consider subheadings of the session's notes for clarity. <u>Underline important information if you will have to search for it later</u>. (See how well it works?) Number issues and subjects in your notes. You can circle some contents and draw arrows. If you use a problem list, you can cross-reference each entry to a problem (by its number—P1, P2, etc.). See the discussion of the POR, below.

❑ Whenever confusion might arise, write paragraphs giving fuller explanations, which are better than phrases or cryptic notations. Terms such as "No change" or "Improving" are too open to varying interpretations.

❑ For whom are you writing your notes? Most payers and treatment plan reviewers want behavioral language and not imprecise, subjective, general statements, or even technical terms. As readers, they want words that help them visualize, so make your words a camera.

❑ Ignore set lengths as required on a printed form. The forms in this book can be adapted to allow entry of any amount of text. Write as complete a note as necessary to achieve the record's purpose, but no more.

❑ The sources of all information recorded should be indicated. Never state as "fact" what a client reported. Remember that in court witnesses testify to their "truth," and that the jury, judge, and other officers of the court are the "finders of fact." Use direct quotations to indicate the client's experiences and thought processes. Separate your judgments and conclusions from the facts and observations. A simple and practical notation scheme is as follows:

> ❑ All unmarked notations are the client's ideas and reports.
>
> ❑ Quotes from the client are indicated by standard double quotation marks: " ".
>
> ❑ Statements from others reported to you by the client are indicated by single quotes inside double quotes, such as: " ' ' ".
>
> ❑ Words in parentheses are (your statements to the client).

❑ Words in square brackets are [your unspoken hypotheses or conclusions]. Consider using HIPAA-compliant psychotherapy notes when you do not want clients to access to these.

❑ Using "HW" for homework assignments and "Tx" for topics to be addressed later supports easy review in the next session.

❑ Information related to the treatment, including consultation regarding steps to take, belongs in the client's chart. ELZ recommends keeping such consultation information in a separate file, to retain control of this until it must be introduced. Do not make entries in your progress notes (which can easily become public) criticizing another caregiver, or enter anything about countertransference, liability, malpractice, or attorney contacts. Other information that is more closely related to a clinician's functioning and needs (including liability issues, attorney advice, discussion of clinician errors, etc.) belongs in a separate place.

❑ **Never alter your notes.** Never erase, write over, "black out," or "white out" anything you have written. Draw a single line through an error, date and initial it, and either write in the correct information (if there is generous space) or indicate nearby where you placed the correct information into the record. If you later want to add anything to your notes—that is, to **amend them**—do it by indicating that there is a change and where in the chart the new material or changes can be found. For example, write, "See entry of [today's date], [initials]." On the current day's page, write out the full amendment: for example, "My present recall differs, in that . . . " or "I was misinformed at that time, and now believe . . . " or "Upon reading this entry, I realize I forgot to mention . . . " and sign your name. At any time, more or newer information can be incorporated into your records in this format.

### Special Considerations for Keeping Notes in Family or Couple Therapy

If you see several members of a family, or a couple, you will have particularly complex decisions to make about record keeping.

You can keep separate records (separate folders or sections of a folder, not just separate pages) on each person involved in a conjoint session, so that you do not have to release all the records when just one client is involved. Confidentiality can then be maintained. On the other hand, separate records create a fiction that there were not several interacting people in the room. Because the family members' issues involve each other, separate notes on each person cannot be considered truly independent and so cannot logically be read separately.

The suggestion that all participating members must give permission for the release of a singular record seems logical. However, this must be implemented before the therapy is begun, by means of a paragraph in your client information brochure and paragraphs in your release-of-information (ROI) forms. Problems may arise when one member does not consent to the release that another member seeks. Therefore, consider including in your practice brochure a statement allowing any adult to release the records of his or her family or couple sessions. There is no ideal solution to these issues. Some providers are able to negotiate a redacted file or a summary of one person's contributions to treatment when notes are combined and consent is not given by all parties.

### Two Kinds of Clinical Notes:
### Routine Progress Notes and Psychotherapy Notes

Our training talked of "therapy notes, "case notes," "process notes," "progress notes," and other terms, but because these were rarely identified in state laws, HIPAA's concepts of notes have therefore become the standard. HIPAA's Privacy Rule considers clinical records to be of two kinds. The first consists of the "medical chart" and includes many kinds of documents (lab reports, histories, discipline-based progress notes, records received from others, etc.). For our present discussion and consideration of how we work, we simply call these "routine progress notes." The second kind of record, called "psychotherapy notes," is given special privacy protections. In the discussion that follows, **"psychotherapy notes" means only these HIPAA-protected notes.** HIPAA restricts its use and disclosure, even to clients, beyond that of other protected health information (PHI). As explained by the Secretary of the Department of Health and Human Services (DHHS),

> [The] *rationale for providing special protection* for psychotherapy notes is not only that *they contain particularly sensitive information,* but also that *they are the personal notes of the therapist, intended to help him or her recall the therapy discussion* and are of little or no use to others not involved in the therapy. Information in these notes is not intended to communicate to, or even be seen by, persons other than the therapist. Although all psychotherapy information may be considered sensitive, we have limited the definition of psychotherapy notes to only that information that is *kept separate by the provider for his or her own purposes.* It does not refer to the medical record and other sources of information that would normally be disclosed for treatment, payment, and health care operations [TPO]. (Emphasis added. This and all other quotations about psychotherapy notes in this discussion that are not otherwise directly attributed come from "Standards for Privacy . . . ," 2000, pp. 82497, 82622–82623, 82652–82654.)

The special status of psychotherapy notes was partly a response to the many state laws establishing psychotherapist–client privilege, and partly a response to the U.S. Supreme Court decision in *Jaffee v. Redmond* (518 U.S. 1, 1996), which held that statements made to a therapist during a counseling session were protected against civil discovery under the Federal Rules of Evidence. In HIPAA, psychotherapy notes are similarly protected. Some states (New Jersey, Illinois) offer extensive protection to such notes. However, court decisions and laws will clarify the extent of this privacy protection, so do not assume that they offer permanent or complete privacy protection.

Keep in mind that **no record can be completely secret,** even as the obligation remains to try to keep information private. If you work in a setting covered by federal law, the Privacy Act of 1974 (Public Law 93-579) and the Freedom of Information Act of 1974 (Public Law 93-502) give clients rights of access to all your notes about them. Furthermore, state law or case law, or the filing of a suit against you, will also give them access through discovery procedures. Obviously these laws and decisions have to be integrated with the *Jaffee v. Redmond* (1996) decision, and with the HIPAA rules that deny clients access to your "psychotherapy notes." without your permission. Your clients may someday see your notes, so consider their psychological and legal implications. On the other hand, vague and generic documentation serves no useful purposes. We have to balance the pressures on us.

Only mental health clinicians can create psychotherapy notes, and they can choose to create or not to create them. In fact, they do not need to tell anyone that they are creating psychotherapy notes. If you are being deposed in a legal matter you will almost certainly be asked if you have any other notes beside the chart notes you offered. You could handle this by creating a rule to destroy your psychotherapy notes when you close a case or at some interval afterward. If you do this, record your procedure in your HIPAA Policy and Procedure Manual.

The distinctions between psychotherapy notes and routine progress notes are legally defined, and so some conditions must be met if you wish your notes to have these special protections. Below we review each kind of note in terms of the dimensions along which they differ.

## A Comparison of Routine Progress Notes and Psychotherapy Notes

### Definition by Contents

**Routine progress notes:** By exclusion, these contain all the other usual contents of mental health notes. Since these notes are part of the regular record, they are used and disclosed for TPO, so an MCO or **insurer may have all of the following information:**

>    Medication prescription and monitoring
>    Counseling sessions
>        Start and stop times (not just duration)
>        The modalities of treatment (individual, family, couple, group)
>        Frequencies of treatment furnished
>    Summaries of:
>        Diagnosis
>        Functional status
>        Treatment plan
>        Symptoms
>        Prognosis
>        Progress to date
>        Results of clinical tests

Of note, the important term "summaries" is nowhere defined, and so these may be of any length or detail.

**Psychotherapy notes:** According to Section 164.501 of HIPAA, psychotherapy notes are those "recorded (in any medium) by a health care provider who is a mental health professional documenting or analyzing the contents of conversation during a private counseling session or a group, joint, or family counseling session."

Their content is clarified as follows: "These process notes capture the therapist's impressions about the client, contain details of the psychotherapy conversation considered to be inappropriate for the medical record, and are used by the provider for future sessions. . . . [They] contain sensitive information relevant to no one other than the treating provider."

These notes are for material that is not to be seen by others—for instance, the therapist's fantasies and emotional reactions to the client; tentative formulations, hypotheses, or speculations; some themes; and so on. These notes may also include aspects of the psychotherapist's life that he or she believes may have an impact on the therapy, such as illness, pregnancy, the illness of a family member, or other major life events.

### Location

**Routine progress notes:** These are part of the client's regular health care record or chart. Nothing more specific is offered.

**Psychotherapy notes:** "These are separated from the rest of the individual's medical record" (HIPAA, Section 164.501). "Separated" is not defined in HIPAA, but see "Requirements for Creating Psychotherapy Notes," below.

### Conditioning of Services

**Routine progress notes:** Failure to consent to a release of these notes for TPO is an allowable reason to deny services or payment. Requiring the release of PHI is called "conditioning" benefits upon consent to release information and is allowable.

**Psychotherapy notes:** Failure to authorize the release of psychotherapy notes cannot be a reason to deny payment from a health plan. The intent of disallowing this "conditioning" is to prevent the release of highly personal information to insurance companies and other nonclinical operations. Thus clinicians can prevent the access by some payers to some information.

### Type of Consent Needed to Release

**Routine progress notes:** Under HIPAA, only the initial consent form is required, although state rules usually require more informedness. We recommend the routine use of an ROI form. See Sections 8.3 and 8.5 for more discussion.

**Psychotherapy notes:** According to HIPAA's regulations, a treating covered entity (CE) can rely on the previously signed Notice of Privacy Practices (NPP) consent form to

> use and disclose psychotherapy notes, . . . to carry out its own limited treatment, payment, or health care operations as follows: (1) Use by the originator of the notes for treatment [in the treater's offices], (2) Use or disclosure for the covered entity's own training programs for its mental health professionals, students, and trainees, and (3) Use or disclosure by the covered entity to defend itself in a legal action or other proceeding brought by the individual.

A special authorization is required for all uses beyond these, according to Section 164.508(a)(2) of HIPAA, but this should be very rare.

- If you should need an ROI to release psychotherapy notes, use Form 8.3. Write in "Psychotherapy notes" in section C and cross out all the other options.

- An ROI for psychotherapy notes cannot be combined with other ROIs except those for other psychotherapy notes, according to Section 164.508(b)(3)(ii) of HIPAA.

- Psychotherapy notes can still be released by a clinician without an ROI to Social Security Disability Insurance and to workers' compensation, but not to Medicare.

### Redisclosure

"Redisclosure" is the forwarding by a second CE to a third CE (such as a successor therapist) of records created by a first CE and released to and now in the possession of the second CE.

**Routine progress notes:** Redisclosure is permitted by HIPAA once the generic consent is signed

The routine redisclosure of PHI is a much looser privacy safeguard than that in most states' laws, and so the state laws are likely to preempt HIPAA. If the state law does not address redisclosure, HIPAA will prevail.

**Psychotherapy notes:** Redisclosure is not automatically permitted. A second client authorization is required for a second CE to disclose psychotherapy notes to a third CE.

### Client Access

**Routine progress notes:** Clients have rights to access, copy, and amend these, because these are part of their medical records.

**Psychotherapy notes:** There is no right of client access. It is allowed but not required; it is a choice by the notes' writer.

### Discoverability in Litigation

**Routine progress notes:** These are routinely discoverable either with consent or a court order.

**Psychotherapy notes:** These are probably not routinely discoverable. It depends on several factors, including the type of suit or charges, the venue, previous decisions, and other factors. Consult your legal counsel.

Note that no client authorization is required for disclosure of psychotherapy notes when a client brings legal action against his or her therapist, according to Section 164.512(e) of HIPAA. This is logical, because the alternative is to have to ask the now-suing client to cooperate and sign an authorization to release the notes. The HIPAA regulations only go so far as allowing release of these notes to the therapist's lawyer for preparing a defense.

### Requirements for Creating Psychotherapy Notes

First, the two kinds of notes must be kept separated. But how "separate" must these notes be? HIPAA doesn't say. Develop ways to distinguish the two kinds of notes to prevent an accidental disclosure of psychotherapy notes—which would be a prosecutable violation of the client's privacy, and which might occur when other records are being released. Certainly use different sheets of paper (do *not* put each type of notes on different sides of a single page). Keep them in different folders if they are in the same file drawer or computer, but even more separation will be protective. KK recommends not identifying the clients in psychotherapy notes that focus on your personal processes. You might keep psychotherapy notes by hand on paper, and all other information in a computer. Or use a different name or code for each type of note, so they are not easily confused or accidentally combined. Starting this bifurcation now can protect you later, because if there is a legal involvement, you cannot separate out these notes later without altering the record (which can be disastrous for your case). However, current legal opinion is that any "memorialization of our work" in any format (untranscribed dictation) or location (a diary) can be discovered in litigation.

ELZ argues that ways of postponing this disgorgement allows our arguing in court for some exclusions, and that the legal climate may change.

Second, the *information* in psychotherapy notes must be kept nowhere else and must not be shared with other treaters, or it loses its special protection.

Third, the form of the information is irrelevant. Notes that are handwritten, typed into your computer, or audio-recorded, and even conversations and the like, are all protected from unauthorized access.

## Deciding Whether to Keep Psychotherapy Notes

Look at your current records. Find a dozen notes that are typical and of good quality. Ask these questions:

1. Is there material that you believe you must record, and yet you don't want it shared with . . .
   - The client, because it includes your working hypotheses and was of value only at one time?
   - Insurance companies or others who are not required to protect its confidentially as carefully as your profession requires you to do?
   - Anyone else, because it is too sensitive and potentially damaging to you, the client, or others?
   - Other treaters, because they are not and will not be doing the kind of work you are with the client?

2. But you . . .
   - May want to share the information with professional students for training or for your own supervision.
   - Find value and meaning in these notes as you review them.

If you answered yes to any of these, then the information should be kept separate in psychotherapy notes.

The main advantages of keeping psychotherapy notes are the facts that the client has no access to them; that you don't have to reveal them to insurers; and that you can think freely for the record in terms of both clinical hypotheses and risk management, but need not reveal this content. The main disadvantages are that psychotherapy notes require maintaining separate records; are likely to be discoverable in some legal proceedings; take additional time to create; and don't protect the kind of information that must be placed in the routine notes.

### Other Options

- If you mainly record the formalities of the therapy (such as your interventions and the client's responses), and you are comfortable disclosing this information to an insurer or other CEs, you have no need for records beyond the routine progress note.

- Keep psychotherapy notes for some clients, but not all. Keep in mind, however, that doing so for only some sessions may look suspiciously like destroying notes, so make some entry for every session.

- In some unusual practices, keep only psychotherapy notes, don't release them, and (in the rare situation when you have to or wish to share PHI) generate a simple routine progress note by referring to them.

### Examples of the Two Types of Notes

Here are examples of the two types of notes, made about treatment of the same transgender female client with a diagnosis of panic disorder who is also grieving for the end of a relationship.

*Routine Progress Note*

7/16/14

Sess #8         45 mins         Individual p/t interpersonal insight-oriented.

- Client consulted Dr. Smith re breast implants. Discussed pros and cons (aware of risks). Client exploring her feelings about breast implants to be able to present as more feminine to the partners she wishes to attract, but also struggles with submission to male cultural definitions; still, is pleased she is able to do this for herself now.

- Successful contract on her project at work.

- Deflected realistic praise from boss and me, but will address next time (3rd recurrence).

- Still stuck on ex. She still speaks of ex-boyfriend longingly, and it is difficult to see her both empowered in her transition and yet still stuck on this person who treated her with such indifference.

- Has excitement and fear about living in a "new body" that he did not touch. Feelings of loss, excitement, potential liberation.

*Psychotherapy Note*

7/16/14

- Client accepts confrontation fairly well, but she is not ready for interpretation of core issues and fragility of self. I want very much for her to be able to feel integrated with her body as a transgender woman, and I know she has waited a long time for this and given it a great deal of thought.

- I find that her struggles and identity issues raise memories of my adolescent issues. Reviewing memories of friendships, what I read, clothing selections, etc. and reexperiencing threats and losses, terrors, loneliness. Revisiting old "lessons."

## Format for a Psychotherapy Note

To meet legal requirements, psychotherapy notes must be identified as HIPAA-defined and so should be explicitly labeled "Psychotherapy Notes." There is no prescribed format for psychotherapy notes, so by adding the paragraph below to the pages you use for your current method of note taking, you are likely to meet the labeling requirements.

## Psychotherapy Note

Name of client: _____  Date: ____/____/____  Case/ID #: _____  Page #: __

NOTICE: This page is a psychotherapy note under the HIPAA regulations. It must not be included in or attached to any other part of the client's health care records except other psychotherapy notes.

Any information recorded here that is also in the rest of the client's records is not protected.

Date and sign every entry. Disclosures of these notes may require special authorization.

## A Basic Format for Routine Progress Notes

Although narratives are standard practice, formats with check boxes can simplify and shorten some aspects of record keeping. Ideal practice may be your thoughtful combination of check boxes for simple data and narratives for dynamic, subtle, and complex information. Below we offer several forms and many additional components from which you can compose a form that fits your ways of working. If you do several kinds of work, you may be happiest with creating more than one progress note format.

### A Minimal but HIPAA-Compliant Progress Note

HIPAA asks us to record a minimum set of data in the "medical chart" and states that this is all a payer is able to require for purposes of deciding on payment. Particular payers may ask for more information, depending on your contract with them, the ways they conceive "summaries," and their definitions of the "minimum necessary information" they **FORM 7.1** can request. Form 7.1 records only minimum data that HIPAA requires for a medical chart note. It protects privacy very well, because since "summaries" is not defined in HIPAA, so you can choose how little to write. However, we believe that most clinicians will require the recording of more information to meet their own documentation needs, state laws, and discipline guidelines, and so it can be used as the foundation for generating your own tailored note.

### A More Detailed Progress Note

**FORM 7.2**  Form 7.2 is somewhat more complex, but still basic. It collects all the HIPAA-required information, but offers more detail. As it stands, it includes a simplified mental status, which is often required by payers but not by HIPAA. You can delete it to provide more space for notes or to insert other components. Depending on your clientele, your local legal situation, or the MCOs you deal with, you may want to add or expand its sections.

### Additions and Modifications to Form 7.2

You might find the modifications listed below useful. If you do several kinds of very different work, you may find that having more than one format is more efficient.

# Case Progress Note

Client's name: _____ Case #: _____ Page number: ____

Date: ___/___/___ Starting time: ____ A.M./P.M. Ending time: ____ A.M./P.M. CPT code: _____

Modality: ❑ Individual therapy ❑ Family ❑ Couple ❑ Group ❑ Consultation ❑ Other: _____

Frequency of current treatment: ____ per ❑ week or ❑ month or in ____ weeks or ❑ PRN

Medications prescribed: _____

_____

❑ Client reports no changes made to medications since last session here.

## Summaries

Diagnoses (ICD code #s): _____

Symptoms: _____

_____

_____

_____

Functional status: _____

_____

_____

_____

_____

Tests administered and results: _____

_____

Treatment plan: _____

_____

Prognosis: _____

_____     _____  ___/___/___
Mental health clinician's signature              Printed name                    Date

*This is a strictly confidential patient medical record. Redisclosure or transfer is expressly prohibited by law.*

**FORM 7.1. HIPAA-based case progress note.** From *The Paper Office for the Digital Age, Fifth Edition*. Copyright © 2017 Edward L. Zuckerman and Keely Kolmes. Published by The Guilford Press. Permission to reproduce this material is granted to purchasers of this book for personal use or use with individual clients (see copyright page for details).

# Case Progress Note

Client's name: _____ Case #: _____ Page number: ____

Date treatment provided: ____/____/____ Starting time: ____ A.M./P.M. Ending time: ____ A.M./P.M. CPT code: ___

Modality: ❑ Individual therapy ❑ Family ❑ Couple ❑ Group ❑ Consultation ❑ Other: _____

Session #: ____ of ____ by ____/____/____. Current frequency: ____ per ❑ week or ❑ month or in ____ weeks or ❑ PRN

Diagnoses (ICD code #s): _____

Medications: Changed? ❑ No ❑ Yes, by _____. Effects reported: _____

_____

Reports of benefits, side effects/adverse reactions/complaints: _____

_____

Participation level: ❑ Active/eager ❑ Attentive ❑ Variable ❑ Only responsive ❑ None ❑ Resistant

Treatment adherence: ❑ Full ❑ Partial ❑ Low/nonadherent ❑ Resistant ❑ Denial of disorder/need for treatment

**Target symptoms**

| Behavioral description | Progress (in words and/or symbols) | Rating of changes since [date] |
|---|---|---|
|  |  |  |

*(continued)*

**FORM 7.2. Case progress note, structured (p. 1 of 2).** From *The Paper Office for the Digital Age, Fifth Edition*. Copyright © 2017 Edward L. Zuckerman and Keely Kolmes. Published by The Guilford Press. Permission to reproduce this material is granted to purchasers of this book for personal use or use with individual clients (see copyright page for details).

**Follow-through**

Homework: _____

Prognosis/expected course: ❑ Guarded ❑ Improvement ❑ Recovery ❑ Fluctuating ❑ To be determined

Modality: ❑ As above ❑ Added/changed to: _____

Intended frequency: ____ per ❑ week or ❑ month or in ____ weeks or ❑ Client will call

Next appointment: ____/____/____ at ____ A.M./P.M. with _____ at _____

**Brief mental status examination**

Mood: ❑ Normal/euthymic ❑ Anxious ❑ Depressed ❑ Angry ❑ Elevated ❑ Restless ❑ Other: _____

_____

Affect: ❑ Normal/appropriate ❑ Intense ❑ Blunted ❑ Inappropriate ❑ Labile ❑ Other: _____

_____

Consciousness: ❑ Normal ❑ Lessened awareness ❑ Memory deficiencies ❑ Disoriented

❑ Disorganized ❑ Vigilant ❑ Delusional ❑ Hallucinating ❑ Other: _____

Substances used/quantity: ❑ Tobacco/_____ ❑ Caffeine/_____ ❑ Alcohol/_____ ❑ Opiates/_____

❑ Marijuana/_____ ❑ Over-the-counter drugs: _____ ❑ Herbals/supplements: _____

❑ Other: _____

(For each substance used, mark in space: D = denies; U = current use; E = episodic use; UD = use disorder; R = in recovery)

Suicide/violence risk: ❑ None observed ❑ Ideation only ❑ Passive death wish

❑ Engaged in prevention program ❑ Threat/rehearsal/gesture/attempt, documented in _____

Sleep quality: ❑ Refreshing ❑ Delayed ❑ Broken ❑ Hypersomnia ❑ Daytime sleepiness

❑ Total sleep time: ____ hours. Planned treatment: _____

**Functional status**

WHODAS today: ❑ 12Q or ❑ 36Q version. Totals for Cog: ____ Mobil:____ Self-care: ____

Getting along: ____ Life acts: ____ Participation: ____ Overall total: ____

More specific functioning: _____

_____

Notes: _____

_____

_____

_____

_____

_____

_____    _____    ____/____/____

     Mental health clinician's signature            Printed name            Date

*This is a strictly confidential patient medical record. Redisclosure or transfer is expressly prohibited by law.*

1. Next to "CPT code," you could offer some code numbers typical of your practice, each with a check box, or with instructions to circle numbers as appropriate.

2. If the form will be used by several clinicians, print each person's name, degree, and title, across the page so that each can sign over his or her printed information.

3. You can add to the page, "If a check box is insufficient information,  ❑ check here and write additional information on a separate page." The additional information can be numbered to each topic.

4. To describe target symptom progress, you can use words or symbols like these, as suggested earlier: < <, much worse than expected; <, worse than expected; 0, as expected; >, better than expected; and > >, much better than expected. If you want to indicate the amount or intensity of a symptom, you could place a number next to it which represents **intensity** (e.g., 1 = mild, 2 = moderate, 3 = severe) and **frequency** (e.g., 0 = never, 1 = rarely, 2 = sometimes, 3 = frequently, and 4 = continually). Alternatively, you could **use the initial letter of the qualifier,** as in N = never. In any case, put the explanation of your coding at the bottom of the page.

5. You might want to add "Next appointment . . . " or "Symptoms" items, and add "Instructions, suggestions, directions" under "Treatments . . . " (as suggested by Muriel L. Golub, PhD, of Tustin, CA).

6. If you work in an agency setting, you might want to add such options as "Chart reviewed," "Case consultation," "Treatment team meeting attended," or "Aftercare planning meeting."

## The Problem-Oriented Record

When you are documenting the progress of a case, the challenge is to record treatment-relevant information in an accessible form. However, clinicians, because of their differing training and interests, may record such diverse topics as the process of therapy, the symptoms of a disorder, the relationship with the client, the contents of interactions and outside events, the goals of recovery or growth, or many other possibilities.

In this diversity, the word "problem" has become a label acceptable to clinicians of many disciplines and backgrounds. Lawrence Weed (1971) invented a record-keeping method when he found that the information necessary to treat a client was being recorded in medical charts in too many places to be useful. Instead of being entered under topical or discipline-based headings, all notes are keyed in Weed's method to numbered problems. This "problem-oriented record" (POR) is widely used in medicine and has been adapted to the psychotherapy setting. It may best be used in interdisciplinary settings.

As slightly modified for the psychotherapy context (see Grant & Maletzky, 1973, and Sturm, 1987), the POR format consists of four main components: (1) the problem list, which remains on top of the chart and which serves as an index to it; (2) the database of history and findings organized by topic or source; (3) the initial treatment plan; and (4) progress notes, or the continuing record of the clinician's observations and understanding of the client. Each progress note entry is recorded in the "SOAP" format (see below) and is cross-referenced to a problem on the problem list by number. Therefore, all the information in the chart is organized around problems. All evaluations and their results are thus tied to their sources and their implications for treatment. To find all of the information in the chart about a concern, the reader has only to look for its problem number on all pages.

### The Problem List

The problem list is simply a numbered listing of all problems identified by a professional or the client and used as a guide to the POR system. Once created, the list is placed at the top of the chart to serve as an index to the contents of the continuing record. Problems are defined at their current level of understanding, and are rewritten and renumbered as they become better or differently understood. Problems can be added and, when resolved, closed by making an entry and then not reusing that number. Problems could include diagnoses, difficulties with activities of daily living, and a description of all functional impairments. The column headings for a POR problem list are shown in Figure 7.1.

### The Database

The database consists of the following usual and expected psychological topics, with each entry tied to the list of problems:

- Chief complaint.

- Mental status examination results.

- Social situation—personal, familial, environmental factors.

- Personal and social history.

## Problem List for a Problem-Oriented Record (POR)

Client: _____     Page #: ____

Problems currently active: _____

_____

List reviewed and revised on this date: ____/____/____     by _____

| Problem number | Date problem recognized | Problem title/formulation | Problem status | Prob. # where problem is now included, or ... | ... Date problem resolved |
|---|---|---|---|---|---|
| 1. | | | | | |
| 2. | | | | | |
| 3. | | | | | |

FIGURE 7.1.  Column headings for a problem-oriented record (POR) problem list.

- History of other medical and psychological conditions and their treatments.

- Records obtained from other treaters.

- Results of testing, or other relevant data.

*The Paper Office for the Digital Age* does not provide separate forms for all of these, because they can be recorded in whatever format and size you may prefer. However, Chapter 6 includes forms and guides for recording most of this information.

### The Initial Treatment Plan

Psychological interventions usually require the consideration of many dimensions simultaneously, and so a treatment plan is necessary. See Section 7.1 for suggested treatment plan formats and essentials. The POR treatment plan is simply a listing of therapeutic interventions for each currently recognized and defined problem. It is the starting point for treatment, and is modified or added to through changes in the progress notes as the case progresses. The plan may include every kind of treatment by anyone (patient education, collection of more information, treatment of and by others, etc.), as well as the usual therapies.

### Progress Notes Using the SOAP Format

"SOAP" is an acronym for four kinds of information that need to be documented for each problem addressed during each client meeting. This is where the POR shines. Every note begins with the problem number for cross-reference and completeness, and continues as follows:

- S is for subjective data—the client's reports of complaints, symptoms, efforts made, changes, and difficulties. S also includes notes of the statements of others.

- O is for objective data—your observations and the observations of others; measurable signs (especially changes) of appearance and social behaviors; the results of psychological testing of the client.

- A is for assessment or analysis of the data in S and O—implications, conclusions, diagnoses, interpretations, impressions, judgments, case formulations, and analyses of the meaning of the data.

- P is for the plan of treatment (both immediate and future), as created by you and by the others concerned. Diagnostic studies, patient education, and follow-up would also be placed here.

Figure 7.2 is a completed example of a POR progress note.

You can make the SOAP format and the POR progress note "SOAPIER," and better suited for the current direction of psychotherapies. Use the SOAP format as described above, and then add the following:

- I is for intervention or implementation of the plan—what you have done to, for, or with the client relative to this problem. In this version, you would put the

**Galactic Health Care Organization**
Wellness Plaza
New Hope, PA 12345

## POR Progress Note Form

Client:  _Client, John Q._                          Page #:  _1_

| Problem number | Name | Date of note | Problem status* | Progress notes** |
|---|---|---|---|---|
| 1. | Depression | 6/9/15 | C | S: No suicidal thoughts this week<br>   More energy—started painting project<br>   Fears of being fired<br>   Spouse confirms more optimism<br><br>O: Increased facial expressions, more hand and arm gestures, faster movements<br>   BDI score = 9<br><br>A: Lessened depression<br><br>P: Maintain or add treatments as follows:<br>  • Spousal reinforcement for activities as scheduled<br>  • Cognitive therapy 1×/week<br>  • Continue meds<br>  • Consider adding new group activity—9/23/15<br>  • Reevaluate medication—10/9/15<br><br>                  Anna F. Therapist |

*Problem status codes: C = continuing focus of treatment; R = problem resolved; I = inactive problem; IT = inactive due to ongoing treatment; D = treatment deferred; N = newly identified problem; ReDf to # = problem redefined or combined with another problem whose number is indicated.

**Each entry must be related to a problem number; coded S for subjective, O for objective, A for assessment, or P for plan; and signed.

**FIGURE 7.2. Completed example of a POR progress note form.**

longer-term goals into the plan (P), and use implementation (I) for the shorter-term objectives.

- E is for evaluation or effectiveness of the intervention—that is, the outcomes of intervention, whether positive or negative. These, of course, could be recorded under S and O, but in this framework they are separated for easier revision.

- R is for revisions of the plan if it was ineffective. Again, these could be recorded under P as a new plan, but using this new heading makes the changes more salient.

## A Structured Form for Group Therapy

In keeping notes about the progress of individual clients in a therapy group, a simple check-list reduces the paperwork burden. You can add items from other forms as appropriate to the group's work and goals. Form 7.3 is a structured progress note for group therapy.

**FORM 7.3**

## Client-Generated and Co-Created Records

When clients take notes, write reflectively, or make drawings or flow charts of their problems' causes and interactions, they bring additional cognitive resources to bear on their issues. These efforts should be encouraged.

- Diaries of recollections, dreams, and relationship interactions in dynamic therapies help a client to see connections. Similar records are called "client memoranda" in social work, and "diaries," "logs," and "frequency counts" in behavioral therapies. With a smartphone (yours or the client's), it may be useful to have the client take photos (and print them out) of some of these materials, or dictate (and transcribe) ideas to review in session or add to the chart. If you take photos on your own smartphone, be careful that no identifying information is in or on the photos; delete them from your phone immediately after they have been copied or printed for the chart.

- There are many kinds of affect and behavior checklists to help identify situations for clinical interventions. In rational–emotive behavior therapy, the use of antecedent–behavior–consequence analyses will reinforce teaching in the session and build a pattern for approaching stressful situations. Lists of emotion words can help clients with alexithymia discover feelings.

- ELZ has asked some clients to keep their notes in a three-ring binder, which they may call "The Book of My [or Our] Therapy." The binder can also house handouts; notes the clients have made from assigned readings; notes taken and questions raised during reviews of their therapy sessions; observations of their family members, friends, or media characters; online searches and readings; news stories and magazine articles; self-study and journal writings; poetry and artwork; and many other items. When such materials are collected in one place, they are much more likely to be reviewed (and therefore to generate awareness and change) than if they are scattered in space and time. Other clients may prefer to keep public or private blogs, or they may wish to use apps or social media to record progress and set goals and solicit support.

- There are guides for diary writing as therapy, usually called "journal keeping" or just "journaling." Some clients may find "scrapbooking" valuable as a way to explore topics and document history.

- One of the most intriguing options is described by Albeck and Goldman (1991): The client and therapist coauthor a progress note after each session—a process these authors call "codocumentation." If each party also writes a note separately and then reviews the other's views and experiences, both parties may benefit, and to a supervisor who reads all three sets of notes they may be of great assistance.

# Group Therapy Progress Note

## Client and group information

Client's name: _____ Case #: _____

This meeting is #____ of ____ as authorized until ____/____/____

Group's name: _____ Location: _____

Date of meeting: ____/____/____ Starting time: ____ A.M./P.M. Ending time: ____ A.M./P.M. Number present: ____

Leader 1: _____ Signature: _____

Leader 2: _____ Signature: _____

## Assessment of client

1. Participation level: ❑ Active/eager ❑ Variable ❑ Withdrawn ❑ Only responsive ❑ Withdrawn ❑ Left

2. Participation quality: ❑ Attentive ❑ Minimal ❑ Preoccupied ❑ Supportive ❑ Sharing
   ❑ Intrusive ❑ Critical ❑ Monopolizing ❑ Resistant ❑ Other: _____

3. Mood: ❑ Neutral ❑ Responsive/reactive ❑ Negative ❑ Blunted ❑ Elevated
   ❑ Other: _____

4. Affect: ❑ Appropriate ❑ Anxious ❑ Depressed ❑ Irritable ❑ Angry ❑ Inappropriate ❑ Labile
   ❑ Other: _____

5. Mental status: ❑ Normal ❑ Lessened awareness ❑ Memory deficiencies ❑ Disoriented ❑ Baffled
   ❑ Disorganized/Confused ❑ Vigilant ❑ Delusional ❑ Hallucinating ❑ Other: _____

6. Change in stressors: ❑ Less severe/fewer ❑ More/more severe ❑ Same ❑ Changed stressors

7. Change in symptom severity: ❑ Same ❑ Less severe ❑ More severe ❑ Much worse

8. Coping ability/skills: ❑ No change Improved ❑ Less able ❑ Much less able

9. Suicide/violence risk: ❑ Not assessed ❑ Very unlikely ❑ Ideation only ❑ Passive death wish ❑ Threat/
   rehearsal/gesture/attempt, documented in _____

10. Other observations/assessments: _____

## Modes of interventions/treatments

❑ Support ❑ Clarification ❑ Education ❑ Exploration ❑ Problem solving ❑ Limit setting

❑ Activity plan ❑ Logistics/structure ❑ Social ❑ Socialization ❑ Reorientation ❑ Reminiscence

❑ Reality testing ❑ Confrontation

❑ Other: _____

## Topics/themes/critical incidents

❑ Relationship(s) ❑ Work issues ❑ Substance use ❑ Parenting ❑ Abuse ❑ Childhood/family of origin

❑ Homework assignments ❑ Process ❑ Other: _____

## Additional information

This is a strictly confidential patient medical record. Redisclosure or transfer is expressly prohibited by law.

---

**FORM 7.3. Structured progress note form for group therapy.** From *The Paper Office for the Digital Age, Fifth Edition.* Copyright © 2017 Edward L. Zuckerman and Keely Kolmes. Published by The Guilford Press. Permission to reproduce this material is granted to purchasers of this book for personal use or use with individual clients (see copyright page for details).

### Progress Assessment Measures

Measuring and getting feedback information on client progress has reassuring value to both therapist and client. In over 20 years of research, Michael Lambert and his collaborators have repeatedly shown that such information reduces dropout, deterioration, and the kinds or errors that rend the alliance (Lambert & Shimokawa, 2011). Feedback to therapists clearly hastens improvement and should be part of every therapist's armamentarium. The measures involved are easy to use, work in any setting, and demonstrate effectiveness for accountability. A good starting place is Lambert and Shimokawa (2011), and Goodman et al. (2013) offer a recent review of their use in substance abuse treatment. It is important to notice that some measures can assess the alliance, and thus can prevent therapy dropouts and ruptures that otherwise may get overlooked.

### Evaluating Each Therapy Session

**FORM 7.4**
When the rapport is not strong, or you suspect the client has some unarticulated reservations, or you believe that the client lacks the social skills to address these issues face to face, you can use the questions in Form 7.4 to create a form to collect immediate feedback. These questions can be offered at any point in treatment and can be used repeatedly—for example, after the 3rd, 8th, 15th, and 20th sessions. It can be distributed (perhaps mailed with a stamped, self-addressed return envelope, or downloaded and emailed back if you are using a secure channel or encryption) every 5 sessions. If you start doing this with a client, you must continue, because he or she will expect it and may hold comments for the form. See also Section 7.5 on assessing client satisfaction.

## 7.3   Case Termination

Maples and Walker (2014) introduce a new and improved conceptualization, emerging from a strengths-based model, of the final and crucial phase of therapy. They suggest the term "consolidation" for the stage involving collaboration and solidifying the gains made in therapy. While we are impressed and will adopt this term in the future, it is too unfamiliar a way to refer to this phase here.

The most important clinical issues in the termination of therapy are the maintenance of gains made and, more generally, the prevention of relapse. However, a lack of clear goals may prevent both client and therapist from knowing whether therapy is finished. Therapy should have a distinct ending even if its goals have not been accomplished. The absence of a message of closure is not only confusing to both parties, but can expose you legally (Younggren & Gottlieb, 2008). For example, if you agree to a client's decision for a premature termination or terminate a client for nonpayment of fees, doing so may be legally seen as negligent unless the client's welfare is protected. By far the most important element in termination, regardless of reason, is the client's welfare. The American Psychological Association's (APA's) code of ethics (APA, 2010, Standard 10.10) addresses the termination of professional relationships. Davis and Younggren (2009) offer much specific guidance, and Davis's book (2008) considers all aspects of termination. A list of the sections of many codes of ethics about termination can be found online (http://www.zurinstitute.com/ethicsoftermination. html).

## Session Evaluation Questionnaire

I would greatly appreciate your views and opinions about your experience in therapy with me. I will take seriously and use what you tell me to improve the care I can offer. Let me thank you in advance for your time and honesty.

Initials of client: _____   Initials of therapist: _____   Date: ____/____/____

Please describe what you got out of this session.

What was the best part?

_____
_____
_____

What did you relearn or have reinforced that you believe will aid you in dealing with your problems?

_____
_____
_____

What suggestions do you have?

_____
_____
_____

What did you want to tell me or do today that we didn't get to?

_____
_____
_____

What did I miss, or fail to focus on or ask about?

_____
_____
_____

What ideas will you take with you?

_____
_____
_____

What points do you want to have considered in our next session?

_____
_____
_____

I promise that I will consider your answers and will review these points at the start of our next meeting. Thank you.

**FORM 7.4. Session evaluation questionnaire.** From *The Paper Office for the Digital Age, Fifth Edition.* Copyright © 2017 Edward L. Zuckerman and Keely Kolmes. Published by The Guilford Press. Permission to reproduce this material is granted to purchasers of this book for personal use or use with individual clients (see copyright page for details).

## Reasons for Terminating or Transferring a Client

**You cannot terminate a client in crisis or at high risk. This is abandonment.** But you can terminate a client not in crisis for any of the reasons listed below. In these situations, terminating or continuing treatment is your professional decision, whether the MCO or anyone else agrees.

- The client has failed to pay fair and negotiated fees. Termination in such a case can be therapeutic as well.

- The client is not cooperating with treatment. You must first try to work through the client's resistance to treatment and document these efforts, but failure to follow an agreed-upon and appropriate treatment plan is essential for improvement, and nonadherence is grounds for termination. If you find yourself falling back from initially well-chosen methods because of the client's failure to carry out his or her part, you are no longer offering your best treatments and may be offering lower-quality services. Less experienced clinicians may feel pressured to continue treating nonadherent clients, thinking this is a way to build the alliance. But, unfortunately, doing so can create a liability if a client later complains and you have documented that you continued to treat a client who did not improve and who did not follow your treatment plan.

- There are conflicts of interest, disruptive romantic thoughts, countertransference, or similar issues that you have not been able to resolve.

- The APA ethics code (APA, 2010) says that you are ethically obligated to terminate when there has been little or no progress. (See "No-Improvement Terminations," below.)

- Although this is often not made explicit in the codes of ethics, you should terminate and transfer when another, incompatible therapist or therapy appears to be in the client's better interest. The client may need services you cannot offer, such as specialist methods or more intense care for safety.

- Your own needs may require you to terminate the client (e.g., you are leaving the area).

- The client has threatened you in some way. This may be a physical threat, or it may be a threat of a lawsuit, board complaint, or other action taken toward you or your family members (APA, 2010).

For clients covered by MCO payments, you must be familiar with your contracts' provisions about referral and termination, or you may create a legal liability for yourself. Read your MCO contracts and see "Continuity-of-Care Concerns," in Chapter 3 on insurance. As always, your first ethical obligation is to your client—not to an insurer, your community, or society at large.

Termination issues are best dealt with early and continually in treatment; remember that they are a major focus in the quite successful time-limited therapies. Be alert to your possible reluctance to terminate a successfully treated client who pays his or her bills reliably, is not difficult, and perhaps is pleasant to see. Nevertheless, this client may have completed her or his goals and be ready to end treatment. Being a responsible professional can be bittersweet.

## How to Terminate Treatment in Different Situations

The options offered below are designed for five kinds of termination situations. The section on dealing with premature or early terminations is based upon ideas from the Philadelphia Society of Clinical Psychologists' Committee on Ethics (1988), from Ewing (1990), and from Barnett et al. (2000). The latter two citations have discussions that are succinct and highly recommended. Shefet and Curtis (2013) offer brief guidance on making successful referrals. Kramer (1990) has written a thorough book on "bringing meaningful closure" to therapy, and Joyce et al. (2007) have addressed termination from a dynamic perspective.

### Appropriate Terminations

When the therapy is finished and the termination is mutually agreed upon, document the following:

- The reasons for termination. (Ideally, the goals of therapy have been met.)
- The client's reactions to the ending.
- Any continuity-of-care needs and plans.
- Any referrals.
- Any unfinished issues.

Although doing so is not required, you can send **a follow-up note** to each appropriately terminated client, either 1 month after the end of treatment (best because memories are fresh) or 3 or 6 months (to attend to possible relapse, continued improvement, etc.). If you do so, keep a copy. A note could include the following points. (Some explanations are provided in parentheses.)

"I hope you are doing well. Thank you for the opportunity to be helpful to you. You can always contact me in the future if I can be of help to you again."

"However, at this time I have closed your case, which means that I will not be making any appointments with you and will not be able to offer you . . . " (Specify the services you offered, to assure that the client understands what you mean by "closing your case.")

"Because I have closed your case, we will need a new intake [interim history, catch-up on developments] before we can resume treatment." (This is designed to protect you from surprise emergency calls and other kinds of unknowable involvements, without your having time to discover the changes that have happened over time or to make thoughtful decisions about your involvement.)

"If you think you can benefit from a different kind of treatment, I can refer you to other providers."

"If you were satisfied with my services, I would be happy to see anyone you choose to refer to me for help." (Sending the letter a month after the end of therapy is more likely to result in referrals, because clients seem more likely to attribute the good outcome to your efforts. This is an effective way to build your practice.)

"I will send copies of your records to any future treaters if you authorize this." (Explain how long you will keep the client's records and how they can be accessed. See Section 1.6 on record retention.)

Optional, if true: "I will be sending a questionnaire on outcomes in 6 months."

"I would be happy to receive occasional updates on how you are doing."

"My best wishes." (The generic, can't-be-misread closing.)

This note is not the place to indicate any unpaid balances due you or difficulties with insurance reimbursement. If money is owed, send the bill separately. It is always best to separate clinical and financial contents, so there is no suggestion that your clinical decisions were swayed by money concerns.

Some therapists may see such a note as purely self-promotional. You could, of course, deal with all these points in the final interview(s) instead of sending a note. It can be argued, however, that using the client's paid time is more manipulative than using your (unpaid) time to construct the note.

### Premature or Early Terminations

Premature or early terminations are ethically complex because you and your client disagree about treatment. In many cases, clients are satisfied with what they have gotten in a few sessions.

Try to handle termination therapeutically, working through the client's issues; also, document these points, your efforts, and the outcomes. Here are some suggestions for the last (or last few) therapy session(s):

- Do not argue with the client or defend yourself from any perceived attack on your abilities.

- Assert your concern for the client or family.

- Affirm the client's right to choose to terminate and to seek treatment elsewhere.

- Express your regret, respect for the client's decision, and acceptance (not agreement).

- Encourage the continuation of therapy. You can point out the "honeymoon" or "flight into health" effects and describe how they don't last. Specify the factual bases for your recommendation to continue therapy at this point. Indicate why you think it may be harmful to stop now, and describe any negative consequences you foresee. However, do not press these themes to the point that the client will feel you are doing so for your own benefit (Frick, 1999).

- Offer to resume therapy at any time in the future.

- Offer your assistance in finding another therapist. Perhaps make a referral to an agency, or provide the traditional three referral names. When you do refer or transfer a client to someone else, ethically you must make sure that the professional to whom you are sending the client is qualified (by training, credentials, experience, licensure status, etc.), or you could be vulnerable ("negligent referral"). In some underserved settings, there may be no one truly appropriate and you may have to fall back on "safety net" services.

- Unless there are extenuating circumstances, you do not have to do more than give the names of resources. You do not have to call to see whether the ex-client completed any referrals and, indeed, may not have the client's authorization to do so.

- If you think there is risk of harm, consider sending a letter by certified mail, with an even stronger recommendation to continue treatment elsewhere. You may consider asking the client sign a release of responsibility indicating that the termination is taking place against your advice. This formality may also encourage the client to reconsider. If the client refuses to sign, note this too.

- Offer your services for emergencies in the interim before the client finds a new therapist. Give him or her sufficient time (in the judgment of your peers) to find another caregiver. ELZ believes that we owe terminating clients only crisis management services.

- Offer to send your records, with the client's signed consent, to another therapist.

- Keep a copy of the letter in the client's file.

**Sometimes a client just disappears**—failing to come to an appointment and being unresponsive to a phone call or letter (at least one of which seems to be the standard of care). Adults have a right to end treatment and do not owe us any duties beyond paying for services received. In most such cases you need not do anything, but if you have some unease or concern, or just like to have closure, a letter may well be appropriate for clarification. Here is some suggested content for this type of letter, and you can borrow some wordings from the next section.

"I have not heard from you for 30 days, despite [calling you (if you did)]. I assume that this means that you have decided to end your treatment. If I do not hear from you in the next *10 business days*, I will discharge you from my practice, end our doctor–client relationship, and close your case." Optional: "I was pleased to work with you, and so I would be happy to continue our relationship if you like, at this time or in the future." In ELZ's, experience, a quarter of these clients come back for therapy; this is an easy way to build your practice.

"Continuing treatment is in your best interest, so I am referring you to these agencies." Although you don't know this because you have not seen the client recently, you should make this presumption because you cannot presume that the client does not need treatment; after all, he or she *was* in therapy.

"If an emergency arises in the next 10 business days, I am available to assist you." (This is a nonabandonment statement.)

"I will send copies of your records to any future treaters if you authorize this."

"Any money you owe to me is due immediately." (But, again, send the bill separately.)

## Necessary Terminations

In some cases, you may feel that the therapy is not finished, but you are discharging or transferring the client for one or more of the following reasons: Your own needs require it (e.g., you are leaving the area); the client requires services you are not competent to provide; financial noncooperation or insurance limitations exist; or the relationship has deteriorated into counterproductivity. Perhaps you or the client have not been able to maintain a schedule or intensity of contacts that would support significant work and change, or the client has not performed or has refused his or her responsibilities as specified in the agreed-upon treatment plan and its revisions. You should document such nonadherence and instances of "informed refusal" in your notes, to inform successor therapists and protect you from later accusations of negligence.

It is usually better to discuss the reasons for termination in person, but a call or letter may be your only option. Even when there is a face-to-face discussion, it can be a good idea to send a letter as well (and, of course, keep a copy). A **"discharged from treatment" letter** can include any of the points above, as well as the following suggestions:

- Describe what you have done (evaluated the client, discussed diagnoses and treatments, read records, initiated treatment, made referrals, etc.).

- List some of the successes and high points, if possible.

- Indicate that the purpose of the letter is to confirm your final conversations, if you had such, and to "wrap things up."

- Give the client your reasons for discharging him or her. If the client has not cooperated with your treatment recommendations, you can point to the client's apparent loss of confidence in your professional advice and methods.

- Express your regret at the ending of an important relationship.

- Recommend continuance of therapy, if clinically appropriate: "Since your condition requires treatment . . . " or "I believe you can benefit from continued treatment." Encourage the client to seek services without delay.

- Indicate that the client should now consider "our" treatment over, and that you are not, in any continuing sense, the client's therapist.

- Indicate your availability during a specific transitional period. This is not only clinically but ethically appropriate to protect you from a charge of abandonment, as noted above. You can say, "Because your condition requires treatment [or monitoring or follow-up], I will continue to be available to you only in an emergency before you find a new caregiver. You must make such arrangements immediately, because I will only provide care for a period of [1 week, 1 month, etc.]." Current opinion suggests that to be safe, you should continue to be available until the client enters another professional's relationship and care; however, ELZ's opinion differs, also as noted above.

- Remind the client that any balance due must be paid. Once again, send the bill separately, to keep the clinical and the financial aspects of treatment separate.

You can follow up with the client, to ensure that you have done all you could to make a transfer go smoothly and cause no harm to the client.

Incidentally, never accept a fee (or other payment in kind) **for making a referral.** It will appear that your choice was not made in the client's best interest, but rather for your financial benefit. Can you refer to those who rent from you or whom you supervise? Yes, but not for a per-referral fee (and you must comply with the federal anti-kickback Stark Laws).

### No-Improvement Terminations

When there has been little or no improvement despite appropriate treatment, you must terminate (see APA, 2010, Standard 10.10a). However, we seem to be poor judges of this. Stewart and Chambless (2008) found that "Overall, clinicians reported seeing clients a median of 12 sessions before concluding no progress was being made." On the basis of previous research, Knapp and Gavazzi (2012) suggest that "If a client is not making gains at the end of four sessions or does not have a good working relationship with the psychologist (in the absence of an obvious reason), the psychologist should reassess the treatment with this client." They offer a simple nine-item checklist to evaluate the situation. After you have done your best, including having reevaluated, reconsidered, and made extra efforts to get things moving forward again, you should do and document the following:

- Consult a colleague. Be sure, though, that you have honestly prepared the case, recognized and dealt with your ego involvements, and can listen openly. Modify treatment if suggested by the consultation.

- Try a different approach, with the client's permission.

- If there is still no improvement, you must terminate and refer. You must also terminate when the client is being harmed by the relationship, such as in irresolvable transference issues.

- Send a "discharged from treatment" letter as described above.

### Reluctant Terminators

When you feel that a client is ready to terminate, but the client is apprehensive or reluctant, you can encourage termination by recounting improvements and addressing resistances. You can acknowledge that it seems that the treatment's goals have been addressed, and the meetings have become "less like therapy and more like updates." Ask whether the client has noticed this, and whether this means it is time to consolidate the work or shift the focus. If you have discussed progress and options as you went along in therapy, or have labeled your treatment as "time-limited," or aimed at "getting you back on your feet" or "helping you through some bad times," then your pushing for termination will not come as a surprise.

- Depending on the length and qualities of the therapy, this type of termination may take several sessions. Consider the termination process very carefully and make a plan.

- Expect emotional reactions (relapses, development of "new problems needing immediate treatment," "wanting to be friends/business partners afterward," etc.) and process them. See Section 4.5 on dual relationships.

- Clearly indicate the reasons for termination, so that it cannot be seen as a result of the client's deficiencies. Say that termination is for the client's long-term good, that it is necessary because of managed care requirements, or whatever the truths are.

- If you believe that you (or your approach) can no longer be helpful to this person, but it's clear that she or he still needs help, offer the client the names of up to three other therapists if he or she wishes to continue therapy.

# 7.4 The Case Closing Summary

It is best to set aside time after the last session with a client, to compose a (written or dictated) summary while the case is still fresh in your mind. Just reviewing your notes and adding to them at the end, in the form of a summary, will be valuable. Writing a complete narrative on each client at the end of an episode of treatment is probably best, but this can be time-consuming unless you are doing it for personal development.

KK writes a closing note like a progress note emphasizing the pretermination sessions' content and describing plans for the future such as "Client will check back next year." ELZ recommends that you also send (with the client's permission, of course) a simple termination note to the case manager or reviewer at any MCO involved in the case, and to the referral source when appropriate. Both of these individuals have moral if not legal involvement, and everybody wants closure and likes to hear good news, even if only some of the goals were achieved.

## Outline for Dictating a Case Closing Summary

The following outline is very comprehensive and assumes that you have *not* been using the forms provided in this book.

A.  Client information.

    1. Client's name and some other basic information (e.g., date of birth, address).

    2. Referral source and reason; chief complaint.

    3. Presenting problems (e.g., problem list) and severity ratings; levels of functioning.

    4. Diagnoses.

    5. Dates of initial and final contacts, consultations, hospitalizations, referrals.

B.  Treatments, techniques, strategies.

    1.  Planned treatments.

    2.  Services actually provided. Perhaps a sentence or paragraph about each session by date, specifying:

        a.  Problems presented/addressed, targeted symptoms, homework.

     b. Relationship qualities.

     c. Process, motivations. Other statements.

C. Narrative summary of therapy, including critical incidents, unresolved problems.

D. Status of each problem at discharge/termination and severity ratings; levels of functioning.

E. Information about termination.

    1. Reasons/rationale for termination.

    2. Was treatment prematurely discontinued? (If yes, indicate why.)

    3. Originator of the decision to terminate.

    4. Recommendations and suggestions of continuing care (if any) or follow-up.

    5. Did the client accept your recommendations at discharge?

F. Optional: Lessons you have learned.

### A Termination Summary Form

**FORM 7.5**　Form 7.5 is quite different from but based on a form in Piercy et al. (1989) called Family Termination Summary, by Larry Constantine, LCSW.

## 7.5　Assessing Client Satisfaction and Outcomes

Much has been made, especially by MCOs, of the value of satisfying the consumers of health care services. Consumers' answers to simple questions about the distance from the office to a bus stop or the furniture in the office apparently have been used to remove or "disenroll" physicians from MCOs' panels of providers.

For therapists, such measures do not have great clinical import. Summarizing eight studies, Pekarik and Wolff (1996) concluded: "Research has indicated that the correlations between satisfaction and other outcome measures are low to modest, with correlations generally ranging approximately from zero to .40" (p. 202). Pekarik and Guidry (1999) again found no significant relationship for those treated by private practitioners. Examining a different group of studies, Lambert et al. (1998) came to the same conclusion.

However, "Satisfaction measures have several virtues, including ease of administration, high face validity, and appeal as indexes of treatment acceptability" (Pekarik & Wolff, 1996, p. 202), and so there may be advantages to your collecting this information. First, it can help you present your practice to MCOs as caring and well-liked by your clients; second, such data could be an alternative to having the MCOs impose their generic questionnaires on you and your clients; and, finally, a questionnaire tailored to your way of working and the kinds of problems you typically address could be part of a continual quality improvement program for your services.

### Client Satisfaction Measures

We are now living in the age of Yelp, Healthgrades, Angie's List, and other online review sites on which clients are voicing their opinions about the psychotherapy services they have

# Termination Summary

Client's name: _____  Case #: _____  Date: ____/____/____

Signature of therapist: _____  Printed name: _____

## A. Services

Referred here on: ____/____/____   Date of first contact: ____/____/____   Last session: ____/____/____

Number of sessions: Scheduled: ____   Attended: ____   Cancelled: ____   Cancelled late: ____   Did not show: ____

Type of treatment:   ❑ Individual psychotherapy, for ____ sessions   ❑ Couple/family therapy, for ____ sessions   ❑ Group therapy, for ____ sessions   ❑ Only intake/evaluation/referral   ❑ Other: _____

## B. Treatment goals and outcomes

Code outcomes as follows: N = no change, S = some or slight (about 20–35% of desired goal level), M = moderate (about 50%), V = very good (about 75–100%), E = exceeded expectations.

| # | Goal | Outcome | Code |
|---|------|---------|------|
|   |      |         |      |
|   |      |         |      |
|   |      |         |      |
|   |      |         |      |

## C. Diagnostic/functional status

Last diagnoses (ICD code #s): _____

WHODAS at end:   ❑ 12Q or   ❑ 36Q version. Totals for Cog: ____   Mobil: ____   Self-care: ____

Getting along: ____   Life acts: ____   Participation: ____   Overall total: ____

## D. Other notable aspects of treatment outcome, change, or progress

_____

_____

_____

_____

_____

_____

*(continued)*

_____
_____
_____
_____
_____
_____
_____
_____
_____
_____
_____
_____

## E. Termination decision

Decision was:   ❑ Initiated by client   ❑ Initiated by therapist   ❑ Mutually decided   ❑ MCO/insurance-affected
❑ Other: _____

## F. Reason(s) for termination

❑ Planned treatment was completed/goals achieved.   ❑ There was little or no progress in treatment.

❑ Client refused to receive or participate in services.   ❑ This is a planned pause in treatment.

❑ Client failed to attend ____ consecutive appointments without required cancellation.

❑ Client could not be reached by phone and did not respond to letters sent. Or: _____

❑ Client failed to comply with treatment recommendations.   ❑ Client moved.   ❑ Client died.

❑ Client was noncompliant with court order, probation, or other (specify): _____

❑ Client stated inability to afford continued treatment.   ❑ Client declined offer of reduced fee.

❑ Client needs services not available here, and so was referred to: _____

❑ Client engaged services elsewhere.

❑ Other: _____

## G. Date for destruction of records

____ / ____ / ____

_This is a strictly confidential patient medical record. Redisclosure or transfer is prohibited by law._

received, but psychotherapists are unable to respond due to confidentiality. In this bind, clinicians can collect their own data, using existing client satisfaction measures or developing their own measures. This data collection does not raise the ethical problems of requesting client testimonials, and it can provide meaningful information to clients. Moreover, when the data are aggregated, these summaries can be posted on one's website as a marketing tool.

The most widely used form for medical practices is the Client Satisfaction Questionnaire (CSQ-8; Larsen et al., 1979). However, based on their review of the literature, Pekarik and Wolff (1996) decided that a simpler set of four questions was sufficient:

> The client was asked, (a) "Overall, how satisfied are you with the services you received?"; (b) "Would you recommend this agency to others seeking help?"; (c) "If you were to seek help again, would you return to this agency?"; and (d) "How would you rate your therapist?" Ratings were obtained on 5-point Likert scales.

You could easily adapt or expand these questions to your practice. A 39-question version, developed for MCOs' uses, is available in Eisen et al. (1999).

If you design a client satisfaction measure of your own, make it one page long and completable in 5 minutes or less; enclose a stamped envelope addressed to you, or design an online version and use a code to make it anonymous. Ask some colleagues to review **FORM 7.6** your work and then pilot-test it. Form 7.6 contains a set of 20 questions, but these do not have any research support. The form is designed for use by groups or agencies, and so it includes space for both a letterhead and the name of the treatment provider. (If you are in solo practice, omit the blank for "Therapist's name.") Before sending out the questionnaire, enter the date of the client's last session and the therapist's name (if necessary). The use of "1   6   12   24____" is to code the number of months after the end of treatment this letter is being sent."Today's date" is to allow for the client's not completing and returning the form promptly.

There are other measures, of course. The SRS by Duncan and colleagues, which has been mentioned briefly in Section 7.1, can be read about and found at this link (https://www.researchgate.net/publication/254093433_The_Session_Rating_Scale_Preliminary_Psychometric_Properties_of_a_Working_Alliance_Measure.pdf). The SRS and similar scales are available at two other websites (http://www.easacommunity.org/PDF/p.860.2-miller_duncan_tool.pdf   and   http://www.myoutcomes.com/session-rating-scale/).   See Campbell and Hemsley (2009) for information on implementation.

KK has developed her own Getting Better measure, which blends outcomes with client satisfaction questions (see http://drkkolmes.com/product/getting-better-client-satisfaction-survey). This measure was based upon an Internet survey asking psychotherapy clients to answer questions about what they most wished they could find out about mental health providers from online review sites.

## Outcome Assessment Questionnaires

Clinicians in private practice have almost never done outcome evaluations (for a notable exception, see Clement, 1999, 2008). This is unfortunate, both because it leaves the responsibility for the improvement of clinical work to distant researchers, and because it denies clients the benefits of systematic, data-based, and tailored clinician self-improvement. To

# Follow-Up Questionnaire 1

I would greatly appreciate your views about your experience in therapy with me. I will use what you tell me to improve the care I can offer to others. What you say here will be kept completely confidential. If I use any of this data for clinical research or marketing, I will remove any names and will combine the data into groups so no one can be identified. Returning this questionnaire indicates your informed consent to participate in the survey. You can choose to withdraw from this research at any time and refuse to answer any questions. Doing this will not affect the care you might receive in the future from me. If answering any of these questions makes you uncomfortable, please skip the question. If you prefer to receive no more follow-up mailings, please check here  ❏ and return this form, or call my office and tell me.

Let me thank you in advance for your time and honesty.

Therapist's name: _____   Today's date: ___/___/___   ID #: _____

Date of last session: ___/___/___   1  6  12  24____

Your sex or gender identity: _____   Your age: ____ years

For each question, please circle a number to show how much you agree with the statement. Choose a number from 1 = "I completely **disagree**" to 7 = "I completely **agree**." If the statement doesn't apply to your experience, circle NA.

|  | Disagree | | Agree | |
|---|---|---|---|---|
| 1. I was treated with courtesy and respect by the secretary/receptionist and other staff members. | 1 2 3 4 5 6 7 | NA |
| 2. I was treated with courtesy and respect by my therapist. | 1 2 3 4 5 6 7 | NA |
| 3. I felt that the therapist was appropriately concerned about my problem. | 1 2 3 4 5 6 7 | NA |
| 4. The therapist seemed well trained and skilled in helping me with my concerns. | 1 2 3 4 5 6 7 | NA |
| 5. The therapist helped me to be comfortable enough to express what I was thinking and/or feeling most of the time. | 1 2 3 4 5 6 7 | NA |
| 6. The forms I had to fill out were not too burdensome. | 1 2 3 4 5 6 7 | NA |
| 7. It did not take too long before I got my first appointment. | 1 2 3 4 5 6 7 | NA |
| 8. I did not have to wait long between appointments. | 1 2 3 4 5 6 7 | NA |
| 9. I felt that the fees for service were affordable. | 1 2 3 4 5 6 7 | NA |
| 10. The hours for appointments were convenient. | 1 2 3 4 5 6 7 | NA |

*(continued)*

| | Disagree | | Agree | |
|---|---|---|---|---|
| 11. The location and accessibility of the office were convenient. | 1 2 3 4 5 6 7 | NA |
| 12. I received the kind of service I wanted when I came for therapy. | 1 2 3 4 5 6 7 | NA |
| 13. I received helpful information about resources in the community. | 1 2 3 4 5 6 7 | NA |
| 14. I believe that any information collected about me will be treated confidentially. | 1 2 3 4 5 6 7 | NA |
| 15. If I felt I wanted therapy again, I would return to this therapist. | 1 2 3 4 5 6 7 | NA |
| 16. I would recommend this therapist to others. | 1 2 3 4 5 6 7 | NA |
| 17. I felt that the therapy was useful. | 1 2 3 4 5 6 7 | NA |
| 18. I experienced improvement in the condition(s) or problem(s) for which I sought services. | 1 2 3 4 5 6 7 | NA |
| 19. In an overall, general sense, I was very satisfied with the services I received. | 1 2 3 4 5 6 7 | NA |

20. How many therapy/counseling sessions did you have? _____

Please add any other comments you wish about your experience with us. Use additional sheets if you wish. Thank you again for your time and efforts.

address this issue, Clement (1999) offers his own experiences and very flexible methods, which can be easily implemented by even the busiest practitioner. In addition, the books by Cone (2000) and Wiger and Solberg (2001) can be helpful, and there are computer programs to make data collection and analysis much easier. Many measures are available for assessing the outcomes of treatment; some (such as those concerning "quality of life") address overall functioning, and others are more focused on symptom change and relief. Because of **FORM 7.7** the variety available, do an Internet search to find ones tailored to your needs. Form 7.7 is a set of questions exploring your ex-client's views of the changes brought by treatment rather than the qualities of the relationship and treatment (which are explored in Form 7.6). Form 7.7 is designed to be used by a group or agency. Edit it if you are in solo practice. You might want to insert a greeting with the client's name, and you could sign the form at the bottom. It is very easy to add a simple consent question to your intake forms asking clients whether a follow-up, satisfaction, or 1-year posttreatment survey is acceptable to send to them. However, bear in mind that a consent at intake is given before treatment has unfolded. A client may feel differently after therapy, so also include clear opt-out language when your follow-up forms are sent.

# Follow-Up Questionnaire 2

I would greatly appreciate your views about your experience in therapy with me. I will use what you tell me to improve the care I can offer to others. What you say here will be kept completely confidential. If I use any of this data for clinical research or marketing, I will remove names and will combine the data into groups so no one can be identified. Returning this questionnaire indicates your informed consent to participate in the survey. You can choose to withdraw from this research at any time and refuse to answer any questions. Doing this will not affect the care you might receive in the future from me. If answering any of these questions makes you uncomfortable, please skip them. If you prefer to receive no more follow-up mailings, please check here ❑ and return this form, or call my office and tell me.

Thank you in advance for your time and honesty.

Therapist's name: _____   Today's date: ___/___/___   ID #: _____

Date of last session: ___/___/___   1   6   12   24____

Your sex or gender identity: _____   Your age: ____ years

How many therapy/counseling sessions did you have? ____

Please feel free to add further comments about each question on additional pages.

1. What was the main problem or reason that caused you to seek treatment?

2. When your treatment ended, was this problem:   ❑ Resolved, no longer a problem?   ❑ Better?
   ❑ About the same?   ❑ Worse?

3. If this problem was not completely resolved, have you gotten treatment from anyone else?   ❑ No.   ❑ Yes.
   If so, whom have you seen? _____

4. Is this problem *now*:   ❑ Resolved, no longer a problem?   ❑ Better?   ❑ About the same?   ❑ Worse?

5. Did any other problems come up during this therapist's treatment?   ❑ No or not really.   ❑ Yes.
   If so, list them below and answer the questions for each problem:
   a. New problem: _____
      Is this problem now:   ❑ Resolved, no longer a problem?   ❑ Better?   ❑ About the same?   ❑ Worse?
   b. New problem: _____
      Is this problem now:   ❑ Resolved, no longer a problem?   ❑ Better?   ❑ About the same?   ❑ Worse?

6. What parts of our therapy were most helpful to you?

_____

_____

*(continued)*

_____

_____

_____

_____

7.  What have you learned (in therapy or from anyone, anywhere) about your original problems that has been helpful to you?

_____

_____

_____

_____

_____

_____

8.  What did the therapist do that was not helpful for you?

_____

_____

_____

_____

_____

_____

9.  What could the therapist have done that he or she did not do, or did not do enough of?

_____

_____

_____

_____

_____

10. Has your therapy helped your performance at work? Or helped you deal with any family problems? Or with friends or social relationships?

_____

_____

_____

_____

_____

# CHAPTER 8

# Confidentiality
# and Releasing Records

## 8.1 Understanding Confidentiality

Over the course of Chapters 6 and 7, we have considered what client records need to be created from the first contact to the ending of therapy. We have also discussed the mandates of the Health Insurance Portability and Accountability Act (HIPAA) for protecting the privacy and security of the client health information in those records. However, HIPAA's rules are only a basic minimum, and the actual practice of securing confidentiality in psychotherapy is complex.

Our confidentiality practices require us to balance ethical principles of "nonmaleficence" (harm avoidance—"Do no harm") against "beneficence" (doing good by, in some cases, protecting others from harm—see Standard 5.05a in the American Psychological Association [APA, 2010] ethics code). This balancing must be done within the legal context of state and federal laws and regulations concerning particular clients (e.g., children, substance-abusing adults). In particular, the meaning of your actions can be very different when you are dealing with child clients rather than with adults. For reference, the sections of 10 major mental health professions' codes that concern confidentiality are available online (http://www.zurinstitute.com/ethicsofconfidentiality.html).

Unfortunately, many new clients believe that all information they give in therapy will be held in complete confidence, and many others are concerned that it will not be. Therefore, we have the responsibility to discuss confidentiality, and especially its limits, with every client. See Chapter 5 for information on discussing confidentiality with clients. Below we discuss the nature of confidentiality and its risks.

### Basic Definitions

We use many words for the status of clinical information: "sensitive," "secret," "personal," "private," "confidential," "privileged." However, only the concepts of "privacy," "confidentiality," and "privileged information" have legal standing in health care, and the meanings of these concepts are quite different. We also have to consider how "protected health information" (PHI) as defined by HIPAA interacts with these other legal definitions.

**Privacy** is frequently considered a basic right granted, by implication, mainly through the Fourth and Ninth Amendments to the U.S. Constitution. It is understood as an individual's right to decide which of his or her thoughts, beliefs, attitudes, opinions, and feelings as well as personal data will be shared with others. The individual can decide to divulge or to withhold; can decide when, how, and under what circumstances to share information; and can do so with regard to which particular others.

**Confidentiality** is a concept that exists within many professions. "Confidentiality refers to the ethical and legal obligation of a professional to maintain the private communications concerning a client, absent a specific justification for releasing the information" (Shapiro & Smith, 2011, p. 61). In all states it has legal recognition, but it is not primarily a legal concept. It is an ethic, based on respect of every client's right to privacy and on a recognition of the potentially damaging nature of some of the information we therapists collect and record.

**Privileged communication** ("testimonial privilege" or just "privilege") restricts a clinician or other person from disclosing, in an open court or in other legal proceedings, information that was given with assumed confidentiality in certain special relationships. It protects personal privacy from legal intrusions. Privilege can apply to several specific relationships and persons: spouses, attorneys, priests, and physicians, as well as to many psychotherapists. The legal bases for privileged communication are extensions of the state statutes concerning attorney–client privilege, which vary from state to state. It is granted by state rather than federal laws, and by state as well as federal court decisions (*Jaffee v. Redmond*, 518 U.S. 1, 1996; see http://www.jaffee-redmond.org).

Privileged communication is a right that belongs to a client, not to a therapist. However, it can be asserted by the therapist to protect the client (as when the therapist does not want to release the client's records) until the issues are discussed with a client, and the client then may assert or waive the privilege.

Incidentally, **nonlicensed therapists do not have a privileged relationship.** This includes intern psychologists, many "counselors," and those in training whom you may supervise. In general, students (including psychology interns, trainees, or supervisees) are not specifically covered by statutes granting privilege (Koocher & Keith-Spiegel, 2008). Also, not all healing professions have privilege. It may not have been legislatively granted to professions organized after 1965, so check your state's laws and court decisions.

**PHI** does not exactly match privilege or confidentiality or privacy. HIPAA's PHI represents the overlapping of some kinds of medical information with some ways of identifying the individual the information is about. An IQ score without any way to trace it to an individual is not PHI (as grouped data is not). A client's check to a therapist is not PHI, although it does indicate a person's having a financial relationship with a clinician, because it does not say why the person came in (which would be clinical information). The category of PHI was created by HIPAA as a preliminary federal effort to set a basic floor for privacy protection standards across the country. Recognizing that the states had already created classes of information and rules for access, HIPAA states that its rules apply ("preempt" other laws) only where other laws are less protective of (less "stringent"), or are silent, in protecting privacy. As a result, PHI includes what is privileged, as well as most information already protected.

In summary, **all privileged communications are confidential, but not all confidential communications are necessarily privileged.** A Venn diagram would show three concentric circles—the largest being privacy, the middle confidentiality, and the smallest privilege.

Gutheil (quoted in Reid, 1999, p. 91) offers this clever mnemonic: "<u>PR</u>ivilege is the <u>P</u>atient's <u>R</u>ight, while <u>CO</u>nfidentiality is the <u>C</u>linician's <u>O</u>bligation."

The rules protecting confidentiality are confused, confusing, and ambiguous, because they vary depending on at least the following circumstances:

- The topics communicated. The abuse of children, and serious threats of harm, are generally not protected; however, most of the topics discussed in therapy (sexual behaviors, family secrets, distressing feelings, etc.) are protected.

- The legal status of those present: spouse, boyfriend or girlfriend, public employee, child, employee, and cotherapist.

- Your credentials, discipline, and licensure.

- The state in which you practice. Credentialing laws, case law (court decisions), legislation, board-created regulations, and legal climate vary with jurisdiction. For example, Massachusetts law denies privilege to non-doctoral-level psychologists.

- Whether you are doing individual, couple, marital, family, or group therapy.

- A judge's discretion and personal experience.

- Whether civil or criminal actions will be involved.

- Whether the legal actions are in federal or state courts.

- Whether HIPAA regulations have preempted your state's rules because they were less protective than HIPAA's, or whether HIPAA applies because your state had no previous rules applicable to the situation.

- Other factors unknown at present.

## Common Exceptions to Confidentiality

The common exceptions to the rules of confidentiality, according to Koocher and Keith-Spiegel (2008), are as follows:

1. **When a client requests his or her own records.** HIPAA gave clients "access" to their medical records, because most states were silent on this subject. The main ethical concern is whether a client would be harmed through too full a disclosure or the client's possible misunderstanding of the record's wording or ideas. Options include (a) providing a summary rather than the full records; (b) disclosure to a third party (a mental health professional competent to understand and explain the records' contents) agreed upon by the client and the therapist; and (c) reviewing the records' contents with the client, and explaining and answering questions, before their release. Use of any one of these options should result in increased trust and prevent the misuse of the information.

   More clinically, client "requests often reflect clinical issues, such as patients wondering 'What is wrong with me?' or, 'What does my therapist think of me?' Usually it is sufficient to deal with these issues directly within psychotherapy without having to show patients their records" (Knapp et al., 1998, p. 19). With "open-access" laws, Blue Button, and similar efforts, electronic records will be much more available to clients, so consider carefully the effects your notes in electronic health records (EHRs) will have on your clients. More practically, after assuring clients that they can have the records, inquiries like "Where will you keep them?" and "Who might find them over the next 10 years?" may cause a change of mind and result in better confidentiality.

2. **When the client consents to the release of records.** To be able to give true consent, the client must have been fully informed of all aspects and likely consequences of what is to be released. This is discussed in Chapter 5, and the client's understanding can be documented by a highly specific release form, such as Form 8.2 or 8.3. Problems may arise if the client does not know all of what is in a record. If you suspect that anything you are asked for should not be released, discuss the situation with the client. If the client agrees to withholding, he or she can revoke the release or sign a revised, more limited version.

   Such a **revocation** should be fully explained in your notes and a statement developed. For example, should the client John Brown decide that no more information be shared with his primary care provider (PCP), this decision could be stated as follows: "This client has withdrawn consent for me to release any further information to his PCP after this date, and he allows me to tell the provider this."

   If the request is from a lawyer (e.g., it is a subpoena) and appears inappropriately broad, you can write a letter to both parties (the defense and the prosecution) saying that you need a more specific release or a court order, and let them decide what to do. We say more later in this chapter about coping with a subpoena.

   If you or your clients are involved in a dispute, and you are not comfortable with complying with a subpoena you receive, seek a court ruling on the limits of what to disclose. You can ask the court to decide and can discuss it with the judge. If this is not productive, the professional affairs officer of your state professional association may be very helpful (if you have joined this group). If you have purchased a "lawyer consultation" or advice plan from your state association, such contacts there would be your next step, before hiring your own counsel. More about coping with a subpoena if offered later in this chapter.

3. **When certain laws require disclosure.** Child abuse or neglect, suspected or proven, is the most common situation legally requiring disclosure. The first fact that you must know is this: Are you a "mandated" reporter of abuse? Not all providers of services are, and state rules vary. Are those you supervise, who may have different credentials or be in a different relationship with a child, mandated reporters? Does the child or the suspected perpetrator have to be your client, or the client of your employing agency? Or is a spouse's/partner's/friend's or acquaintance's report to you sufficient to trigger your required reporting? Know the difference between mandated and permissible reporting. In addition, does your state require reporting the abuse of an elderly, disabled, or vulnerable person? You must know exactly what your state laws require, because you must act immediately (usually within 24 hours).

   Besides your state association, the Child Welfare Information Gateway (https://www.childwelfare.gov) has tables of information on definitions, immunity, penalties, and procedures by state. For further guidance, you can call your state reporting agency's hotline and discuss a "hypothetical" situation for guidance.

Bear in mind, however, that a duty to report is not a release of information (ROI); the client's privilege may still hold, and you may have to assert it when the client has not, even when your client is the suspected perpetrator. Providing more than the information your state authorities legally require will require an ROI from the client.

**As you consider reporting child abuse, bear in mind the following key questions.** ELZ, a psychologist licensed in Pennsylvania, uses his own situation as an example. The Pennsylvania statutes cited here are available online (http://www.pacode.com/secure/data/049/chapter21/subchapEtoc.html).

a. **What is your relationship with the child?** In Pennsylvania, psychologists were required to have direct contact with a child who "comes before them in their professional or official capacity" (23 Pa. Cons. Stat. Ann., Section 6311) to be a mandated reporter. Recently, the requirement has been greatly extended. ELZ must now report if a person 14 years old or older reports having abused a child, even if the abuse occurred many years ago and no child is currently in danger. He also has a duty to report suspected child abuse if any patient or collateral contact discloses knowledge of a child who is currently being abused. Even where you are not legally required to report abuse (e.g., when you are an unlicensed trainee, although state laws differ), you may have the ethical or civic duty to make a report in order to protect a child or to prevent violence.

b. **Who is the perpetrator?** ELZ must report abuse by a parent, paramour, responsible person, or household resident, but need not if the perpetrator is a teacher, neighbor, or stranger, as these are criminal assaults. (He does still have a moral obligation as a citizen to protect others.)

c. **What is abuse?** It includes "a. non-accidental physical injury; b. neglect of supervision, shelter, clothes, food or medical care and not due to conditions the parent had no control over; c. sexual abuse or exploitation; d. emotional abuse" (23 Pa. Cons. Stat. Ann., Section 6303). This last must be severe, but clearly this is a somewhat ambiguous term.

d. **When did it occur?** For a physical injury, it has to have occurred within the last 2 years, but the other types of abuse do not have time limits. You generally must report even abuse that occurred some time ago, if the victim is still under 18 and thus is considered vulnerable. Some states even consider the vulnerability of other members of the household in requiring reporting.

e. **How much proof do you need to have before you report abuse?** In Pennsylvania, and most likely in your state, the answer is none. ELZ must report if he has any "reasonable cause to suspect" (23 Pa. Cons. Stat. Ann., Section 6311). This is a very low threshold, because the laws were deliberately written to protect the greatest number of children, and so they disregard professional judgment or need for evidence.

You should not try to investigate beyond the suspicion. The state agency will do the investigation. This is a sticking point for many therapists, because they do not want to serve as "police," would prefer to make a decision in what they see as the best interests of a child or family, and do not trust an agency to make good decisions. In the area of child abuse, Taube and Elwork (1990) found that disclosing the mandatory reporting issue to clients led to fewer self-reports of child neglect and punishment behaviors by caregiver clients. Similarly, Berlin et al. (1991) found that the legal obligation for psychiatrists to report child sexual abuse in Maryland was counterproductive: The number of self-referrals for child abuse and the self-disclosure rate during therapy both went to zero, and the number of children identified as abused did not increase. It appears that we mental health professionals have failed to make our need for options clear to our legislators.

Brabeck and Brabeck (2002) describe the clinical consequences of reporting or not reporting domestic violence, and nicely articulate the decisional processes:

> Reporting abuse without consent may communicate a lack of respect for the client and risks harming the therapeutic relationship, which is necessary for the client to safely explore the serious issues she [the victim] raised. Breaking confidentiality may rob the client of the opportunity to gain insight into the reasons for her silence, to name the wrong done to her and to confront others with the truth, thereby gaining control over her life. Furthermore, the client may conclude that no one is trustworthy and continue her silence regarding the abuse. . . . Finally, if the psychologist has reason to believe that the client's family will abandon her or will retaliate against her, the psychologist's disclosure might put the client at risk . . .
>
> On the other hand, by not reporting the abuse, the psychologist may collude with the client in keeping her silence and in letting the abuser maintain power and control over her, which violates her autonomy and may not be in her best welfare. . . . If the client perceives the psychologist as a person of authority, his or her participation in this system of silence may exacerbate the client's sense of powerlessness and hopelessness.
>
> The best option is for the psychologist to maintain confidentiality and use the therapeutic relationship as a vehicle to empower the client to report the abuse to appropriate authorities. . . . Such a resolution might enhance the client's sense of autonomy, maintain the trust of the therapeutic alliance, end the self-silencing that the abuse fostered and restore the power of the client's voice.

What does the client want and need from the therapist? Most likely, the client wants to process the long-concealed distress and address myriad emotions including anger, shame, sadness, guilt and a host of other issues commonly experienced by victims of sexual abuse. Sadly, the best options described above require more time than the law allows for reporting.

f. **Whom should you report to and when?** ELZ can phone 24 hours a day to a toll-free number. The Pennsylvania law does not say when, but if the danger is high, he must call immediately. If the danger is past, he may take a day or so, but he cannot put it off too long.

g. **What if you are wrong?** In Pennsylvania, ELZ has immunity for making a report in "good faith" (23 Pa. Cons. Stat. Ann., Section 6318(a–b)). ELZ believes all states grant this immunity.

h. **What if you don't make the report?** The first violation is a summary offense, and later ones are misdemeanors of the third degree (23 Pa. Cons. Stat. Ann., Section 6319).

Practically, immediately document everything you heard or saw and when the events happened and consult with one or more colleagues.

Document the actions considered and why you chose the ones you did (as usual, the watchword is "Think out loud for the record"). This is especially important if you have decided not to report.

Some states, such as Pennsylvania, require us to report impaired drivers as well. These may include drivers with epilepsy, hallucinations, disorientation, homicidal tendencies, or a history of accidents or near-misses (Knapp et al., 1998, pp. 70–73). Relatedly, in our opinion, if a client appears for a session too intoxicated to drive home, we have a moral if not a legal responsibility as citizens to intervene by negotiating safe travel or reporting the client to the police. Because there is no identified victim or certainty of an accident, our legal duty to protect will not come into play.

4. **When the client is a litigant and sues you.** Privilege cannot be used as "both a shield and a sword." That is, the client cannot waive privilege and have only some facts supportive of his or her case (the sword) opened to use against an opponent, while protecting him- or herself from the import of other facts (the shield). Once privilege is waived, it is generally waived completely. These situations are, however, negotiated between lawyers and the court, and some material often can be excluded if it is of no relevance and is potentially damaging to the client or others. If you have been formally accused of malpractice, you may generally reveal *only* the information necessary to defend yourself—not everything you were told or recorded or received in records from others.

   In regard to being the subject of lawsuits or ethics complaints, be careful about what you reveal to whom. It is natural to want to complain to or seek support from friends, colleagues, peers online, or a trusted supervisor. But these are *not* privileged conversations, and these people could be subpoenaed to testify about what you told them. If the conversations happened over email, these transcripts can also be legally discoverable. Although ethical complaints to professional organizations and licensing boards are evaluated in confidence, the information revealed is also not privileged. The amount of material revealed depends on the attorneys, the investigators, and the local procedures. (If you need support when dealing with a complaint or suit against you, get into therapy, because conversations in therapy sessions *are* privileged.)

5. **When therapy or evaluations are court-ordered.** In this situation, the results of your evaluation or records of your therapy will be sent to both sides, so you must fully inform the client of this before you perform these services. It would be a good idea to make a note that you have informed the client that anything he or she says during an evaluation may be included in your report (American Psychiatric Association, 1987). Interestingly, examinations and reports done at the request of a client's attorney may be protected by attorney–client privilege, and so may be suppressed if they are unfavorable to the client.

6. **In any legal proceeding where a client's mental status is at issue.** Lawsuits over head injuries, custody battles, adoptions, or disability claims can include allegations of emotional pain and suffering. These proceeding can bring the records you created into court and your testimony may be required by a judge. See Section 5.2 under "What to Expect from Our Relationship" for some protections, and point 3 in Section 4.4.

7. **When parents have rights to information about the diagnosis and treatment of their minor children.** See Section 8.5 and below for guidance.

8. **If your client seriously threatens an identifiable person or persons.** This is future criminal behavior, and you may have the "duty to warn or protect" (see Section 4.8 for clarification of this). Note that except in South Dakota, therapists are not required to report past criminal behavior if it is not ongoing.

9. **In any emergency**—that is, when a client's health is seriously or imminently at risk. Keep the information disclosed to a minimum—that is, what a competent client would agree would be necessary. In an emergency, HIPAA says that a client's oral consent to disclose is acceptable, but the details and rationale should be documented later. If the client is unable (not unwilling) to provide the information or to consent, break confidentiality only if withholding it would endanger the client and if the local law permits or does not forbid such disclosure.

10. **When sharing among all those involved in treatment or payment for treatment is allowed by HIPAA.** The regulations are extremely broadly worded, and apply HIPAA to all those included in the Medicare regulations (Title XI, 42 U.S.C. 1301, Section 1861(u)). As such, they seem to include just about any of the "various licensed/certified health care practitioners," as well as students and supervisees, but this breadth may conflict with your state's rules or profession's codes.

## Other Points about Confidentiality and Its Limitations

To obtain reimbursement with Medicare and Medicaid clients, providers are required to disclose more than basic identifying data. Managed care organizations' (MCOs') reviewers can ask for lots of clinical information, and a client has almost always (and without any awareness of its implications) signed a blanket ROI form to an MCO when first applying for insurance coverage. If the HIPAA regulations apply to a situation, the rule about **"minimum necessary" disclosure of PHI** (see Section 164.5029(b)) may apply. This rule requires the MCO to identify exactly what information each of its departments needs, and to seek only that information; the MCO may not request the entire medical record.

It appears that Social Security Disability Insurance offices and workers' compensation insurers routinely expect release of *all* records you create. This may be quite problematic in two ways: (1) When a client's employer is self-insured, the company's benefits staff can see records and may have few safeguards for maintaining their confidentiality; and (2) in some states workers' compensation cases are public information, and in others the press has used "open-access" laws to obtain our records. Clients need to know what will be revealed before they use their insurance, and they usually expect to use it from the beginning. Therefore, you must inform them of these risks at the start of treatment. The client information brochure (see Section 5.2 and the CD) covers this, as does Handout 5.1.

The sharing of information among members of a treatment team or care providers within an agency is generally acceptable without an ROI when the client has consented to treatment that he or she understands to involve several persons or departments within the agency (American Psychiatric Association, 1987). HIPAA is consistent with this policy, but more loosely requires only the basic consent notice obtained during notification of privacy rights (see Section 6.4). However, informed consent requires more specifics, and so completion of an ROI should be standard procedure.

Unless information is very sensitive, you do not need specific permission to share it with a consultant from whom you are seeking professional advice when this relationship was explained to and approved by the client. When you talk to a consultant about a client, omit details that might enable the consultant to identify the client (APA, 2010, Standard 4.06). This is especially important if the consultant may know the client personally or by reputation, or if a case involves sensitive disorders (e.g., child or drug abuse, sexual difficulties), or if both client and consultant are members of smaller communities. The consultant rarely needs detailed knowledge; it cannot be unlearned, and it becomes a burden to the other that he or she does not need to carry.

If you want to be more careful—perhaps because you do not know the contents of what will be revealed—you might get an authorization for consultation signed at the first meeting with the client, or document the absence of consent. This does not cover informally discussing a case with several peers, and this kind of consultation is not usually privileged, so don't do it. It is best to share clinical information only when doing so benefits the client, or else you are on thin ice.

In most states, the fact that a person is a client is itself not privileged information (although you should certainly treat it as confidential). Similarly, the dates and number of appointments, as well as billing information, are accessible to the courts (Knapp, 1994). Turning a case over to a collection agency or going to small-claims court is not a breach of confidentiality if the client is notified that it may occur and if no clinical information is shared. This notification is best included in your client information brochure. The information shared with a small-claims court should be minimal, given simply to establish the debt's legitimacy (client's identity, dates of service, fees) (APA, 2010, Standard 4.05b). Bear in mind that communications, reports, and observations made for purposes other than treatment are not covered by privilege; these include communications for employment or insurance purposes (American Psychiatric Association, 1987).

**Confidentiality survives the client's death.** The privilege usually passes to the executor or legal representative of the client, but boards have made different decisions in some states when records are to be released to coroner or police.

Finally, claims of "That's confidential" cannot be used to protect the therapist, only the client. Such claims cannot be used to conceal harmful practices, protect the autonomy of the therapist, avoid the scrutiny of peers, or defend a need to be "right" (Sweet, 1990, p. 7).

## Confidentiality and Children

With a competent adult, the person seeking services and the recipient of those services are the same; however, when the recipient of assessment or treatment services is a child, there are two "clients." In this situation, to whom does the therapist owe the duty of confidentiality? Even when the ethical duty is to the child, the legal duty will almost always be to the parents. The best resolution may be found by looking for the local answers to the following questions suggested by Morris (1993, p. 11):

1. Is a child in psychotherapy accorded legally protected privileged communication in your state?

2. If yes, what are the exceptions to privileged communications for a child in your state?

3. Is there a common-usage lower age limit for legally granting children privileged communication?

4. Is there legal precedent in your state that has tested the constitutionality of the privileged communication granted to children and adolescents?

The therapist should, of course, inform the child of all the limitations of confidentiality. For example, the child should be told that the therapist will be discussing the contents of interviews (in general ways), and if serious harm is anticipated, with his or her parents, and that ultimately nothing can be kept secret. If the therapist will be consulting with school or hospital personnel, the child should be told that as well. Obviously, the wording of both oral and written statements must suit the child's understanding and reading levels. (See Form 5.3 for a written statement suitable for an older child or an adolescent.) Parental access to information and records varies a great deal. State laws usually do not address this issue, but logic suggests that if you need parental consent to provide treatment, the parents have the right to access the records of that treatment.

In cases of silence or ambiguity in state laws, HIPAA's policy of protecting those at risk of harm may trump state laws prohibiting or mandating disclosure. If, in the determination of the professional, refusing its disclosure can diminish or prevent an imminent threatened harm to a child or another, you may do best by protecting. These are complex situations so consult fully.

## Confidentiality and HIV-Positive Clients

There are many benefits of confidentiality for HIV-positive clients (including reduced risk of discrimination), but these must be weighed against its possible social costs (such as the infection of third parties). The issues are complex because of the intersection of a legally imposed duty to protect, laws and ethics about maintaining confidentiality, and clinical case issues. Chenneville (2000) is an excellent guide to making decisions and should be consulted in these cases. Very briefly, Carey and Vanable (2013) and Dass-Brailsford (2013) address working with HIV-positive clients. Also, the APA has made efforts to enhance psychologists' ability to respond to those affected by HIV (see http://www.apa.org/pi/aids/resources/). See also Section 4.7. State laws vary widely—some states do not permit any disclosure of HIV status—and you must learn your local rules.

## An Electronic Communications Policy for Your Practice

Consider establishing an electronic communications policy for your practice. Your first step is to become informed about the current ways of communicating electronically and their risks. The next step is to develop a comprehensive policy about the use of electronic communication beyond telephones. This section describes what to consider for a basic policy if you use email. If you also actively market your practice online and use social media, you need a social media policy. This topic is addressed in Section 9.6.

If you decide to use email with clients, decide on, design, and communicate a policy for the confidential use of email. It may be reasonable to use it only for simple and routine communication of information that is not PHI, such as changes in appointment times.

If you will do more on email, consider these questions, explain them to the client, and then get written informed consent. How often you will check your email? Explain that the inevitable delay must be accepted. How can clients contact you more rapidly and assuredly than email? How might emails be made public? Might you use the contents of emails in training or supervision? Explain how the absence of contextual information in an email, normally acquired in face-to-face meetings, can lead to misunderstandings. How will you and the client address these possible misunderstandings?

KK lets clients know that email should only be used for low-risk and nonprivate information such as schedule changes, and not for clinical materials. Some clients will forget this and will use email to forward upsetting exchanges with other persons or to report clinical updates. If this occurs, KK prints up these emails and gives them to the clients, with a verbal reminder that once sent, such exchanges become a part of the legal record and may be discoverable. She deletes the originals and suggests to the clients that in the future, they should print up such materials, bring them to therapy for discussion, and then take them home to destroy.

Before using email with a client, make certain that there will not be a problem with confidentiality at the client's end. For example, family members may share the client's computer, or the client may be unable to set up a password-protected email address. Document the client's agreement to any risks at his or her end of the communications.

Unless you have fully automated backups of your emails, print out all exchanges and place them in the client's chart. Delete those left on the server. HIPAA's Security Rule requires you to have procedures for protecting the confidentiality of such messages over time.

Acquire and deploy an encryption program. There are free and simple programs available. If, during a private face-to-face meeting or even over the telephone, you and the client select a password or phrase to use to encrypt and decrypt messages, this method will provide very substantial privacy. No method is unbreakable given sufficient time and resources, but very protective programs are available at small cost that will encrypt emails, Superbills, your computer's files, portable drives, and so on. KK also has all email links on her site connect to an encrypted webform, so as to prevent the unprotected transfer of highly detailed personal information in the first contact.

Despite its risks, there are some rather safe uses for email with clients, even without encryption.

- It may be suitable for sending out intake and informational material, but not for having a client return forms with clinical information (i.e., PHI).

- As indicated above, it can be safe and convenient for administrative or logistical purposes with most clients: confirming and rescheduling appointments, sending information about resources, answering simple questions, supplying blank data-recording forms, and the like. Allowing cancellation of sessions via email may lead to its overuse when clients are under time pressure, however.

- With caution, it can be substituted for some appointments with currently active clients who cannot come to some meetings due to bad weather and other transportation limitations; for clients who have moved to another location and have not yet arranged a follow-up therapist; for clients who have disabilities or are home-bound due to illness; and the like.

- You can correspond with, educate, and refer those who find you through your writings or an Internet search about your specialties. Or you can respond to an email inquiry from a potential client with directions to your website for more information.

Moreover, email (with security measures taken) may have valuable clinical leverage. Consider the following possibilities:

1. For clients who do not do homework because of anergic depression, having them send brief daily emails about their activities can focus their thinking and increase their motivation to complete assignments. A therapist and client can decide whether the therapist will confirm receipt of the emails, or whether all communication will take place during the next session. (This suggestion comes from Dorothy Ashman, MA, of Bloomsburg, PA.)

2. For a client who makes unnecessary phone calls but takes poorly to boundary setting over these calls, allowing the client just to leave emails may meet some need, even if the client knows that the therapist may not respond and certainly won't respond immediately. The contents of the messages can be addressed in the next session. (Kathie Rudy, PsyD, of Great Neck, NY, has made this suggestion.)

3. For a client who cannot yet handle the intense intimacy of a full session or of frequent contacts, alternating face-to-face sessions with telephone or email sessions can help to maintain contact by titrating the affect and allowing different kinds of work to be done in each mode. This approach can help manage the obstacles of what would otherwise be overwhelming and disorganizing affects such as shame. (This suggestion also comes from Kathie Rudy.)

For a review of the ethical aspects of using email, an article by Drude and Lichstein (2005) is highly recommended. The discussion above concerns email with clients, but there are other related issues. For more on online case consultations, see Dvoskin (2006), and for the ethics of online therapy, see Childress (2000). The best general resource is the International Society for Mental Health Online. Its website (http://www.ismho.org) is a great starting point for information and creative ideas about online clinical services, research, and organizations.

Roy Huggins, MS, NCC, offers a very complete Communications Policy handout on this issue, as well as other valuable documents (such as a Consent to use Unencrypted Email), at his site (https://www.PersonCenteredTech.com). Just sign up for his newsletter to access them. A simple two-page Sample Electronic Communication Policy is available from the APA Insurance Trust (https://www.trustinsurance.com/download.aspx?item= SampleElectronicCommunicationPolicy.doc), and KK offers a much more comprehensive and current version (including policy about social media, not just email) at her website (http://drkkolmes.com/social-media-policy).

## A Handout on the Limits of Confidentiality

Confidentiality issues have been incorporated into the client information brochure (see Section 5.2 and the CD), because the APA ethics code (APA, 2010, Standard 4.02b) requires a discussion of confidentiality's limits before therapy begins. The same section requires discussion of new limits as new circumstances warrant it. Similarly, Handout 8.1 covers confidentiality issues in greater detail than does the brochure. It is generic enough to be applicable to most practices, and it addresses issues relevant to adult, child, and family therapy. However, it does not fully address the issue of secrets between spouses/partners in couple therapy.

We recommend offering this handout to those who raise concerns after reading the more general brochure, and to those whose referral (e.g., by the courts) or history suggests its need. The issues can then be discussed in a therapy session. Another way to use it is to make it available with other client education materials in a three-ring binder in your waiting room, as suggested in regard to various materials throughout this book.

Before using this handout, consider alterations you may need to make because of your locality, your profession or credentials, or your preferred methods of practice:

- If you treat older children, you might consider amplifying what is said here about what you have to reveal to parents or guardians.

- Weigh what you have to reveal to third-party payers with whom you have contracts. Handout 3.1 is a more specific informed consent handout for MCOs' clients.

- In section 1a of Handout 8.1, you might add that such actions are very rare for you (if this is true), and that the client would want the same notification if he or she were threatened.

- Adapt section 1c to your state's rules about the basis for reporting abuse. As noted in earlier chapters, states differ in requiring a "suspicion" standard or a "reasonable belief" standard to trigger the mandated reporting requirement. Also, states differ in their definitions of elder abuse. Usually elder abuse is defined more broadly than child abuse and includes financial exploitation (Sam Knapp, personal communication, October 2, 1996).

- Section 3b states that anyone you seek consultation from is "required by professional ethics to keep your information confidential." This is an ethical but probably not a legal requirement, because you (the person seeking consultation) are not the consultant's client, nor is your client.

- Adapt section 3c to your state's rules and preferred practices about clients' access to records. This section says, "You have a right to review these records with me." The exact means of a client's HIPAA-guaranteed "access" to his or her records varies. Releasing actual copies to the client may allow for misinterpretation, and it risks revelations to other parties. Sending them to another mental health professional for interpretation may be safest, or, as KK suggests, a summary can provide the minimum amount of information necessary for the present purpose.

   Under HIPAA's regulations on client access to your records (Section 164.524), a client does not have a right to read your psychotherapy notes (if you have created any), although you may allow such inspection. HIPAA also grants clients the right to amend their records, so you might add: "If you find errors in my records, you can ask me to correct these by adding new information to the records." Clients do not have the right to "access, inspect, and copy" information related to legal proceedings, research, or some other areas. Under HIPAA, you can limit access when you decide that access is "reasonably likely to endanger the life or physical safety" of the client

# What You Should Know about Confidentiality in Therapy

I will treat what you tell me with great care. My professional ethics (that is, my profession's rules about values and moral matters), and the laws of this state, prevent me from telling anyone else what you tell me unless you give me written permission. These rules and laws are the ways our society recognizes and supports the privacy of what we talk about—in other words, the "confidentiality" of therapy.

However, I cannot promise that *everything* you tell me will *never* be revealed to someone else. There are a few times when the law requires me to tell things to others, and there are some other limits on our confidentiality. We need to talk about these, because I want you to understand clearly what I can and cannot keep confidential. You need to know about these rules now, so that you don't tell me something thinking it will be a "secret" when I cannot keep that thing private, just between us. So please read these pages carefully, and keep this copy. At our next meeting, we can discuss any questions you have.

1. When you or other persons are in physical danger, the law requires me to tell others about it. Specifically:

   a. If I come to believe that you intend to do serious harm to another person, I am required to try to protect that person. I may have to tell the person and the police, or possibly try to have you hospitalized.

   b. If you seriously threaten or act in a way that is very likely to harm yourself, I may have to call on your family members or others who can help protect you or seek to hospitalize you. If such a situation does come up, I will try to discuss the situation with you fully before I do anything,

   c. If I believe or suspect that you are abusing a child, an elderly or disabled person, or another vulnerable person, I must file a report with a state agency. To "abuse" means to neglect or not take care of another person; to hurt that person (physically or mentally); or to sexually molest, touch, or harm that person. I do not have any legal power to investigate the situation to find out all the facts. The state agency will investigate. If this might be your situation, we should discuss the legal aspects in detail before you tell me anything about these topics. You may also want to talk to your lawyer.

   d. In an emergency where your life or health is in danger, and I cannot get your permission, I may give another professional some information to protect your life. I will try to get your permission first, and I will discuss this with you as soon as possible afterwards.

   In any of these situations, I would reveal only the information that is needed to protect you or the other person. I would not tell everything you have told me.

2. In general, **if you become involved in a court case or legal proceeding,** you can prevent me from testifying in court about what you have told me. This is called your "privilege," and it is your choice to prevent me from testifying or to allow me to testify. However, there are a few situations where a judge or court may order me to testify:

   a. In child custody or adoption proceedings, where your fitness as a parent is questioned or in doubt.

   b. In cases where your emotional or mental condition is important information for a court's decision.

*(continued)*

---

c. During a malpractice case or an investigation of me or another therapist by a professional group or licensing board.

d. In a civil commitment hearing to decide if you will be admitted to or continued in a psychiatric hospital.

e. When a court has ordered you to see me for evaluations or treatment. In this case, we need to discuss confidentiality fully, because you don't have to tell me what you don't want the court to find out through my report.

3. There are a few other things you must know about confidentiality and your treatment:

a. If you were sent to me for evaluation by workers' compensation or Social Security Disability Insurance, I will be sending my report to that agency, and it can contain anything that you tell me.

b. I may sometimes consult (talk) with other professionals about your treatment. This person is also required by professional ethics to keep your information confidential. Likewise, when I am out of town or unavailable, another therapist will be available to help my clients in an emergency. I must give this professional some minimal information about my clients, but he or she will keep it confidential, to obey his or her professional codes of ethics and our federal and state laws/regulations.

c. I am required to keep records of your treatment, such as the notes I take when we meet. You have a right to review these records with me. If something in the record might seriously upset you, I may leave it out, but I will fully explain my reasons to you.

4. Here is what you need to know about **confidentiality, health insurance, and money matters:**

a. If you use your health insurance to pay a part of my fees, the insurance company, the managed care organization (if you have one), and perhaps your employer's human resources office will require me to provide information about how well you function in many areas of your life, your social and psychological history, and your current symptoms. I will also be required to provide a treatment plan and information on how you are doing in therapy.

b. I usually give you my bill with any other forms needed, and ask you to send these to your insurance company to file a claim for your benefits. That way, you can see what the company will know about our therapy. Although I believe the insurance company will act legally, I cannot control who sees this information after it leaves my office. You cannot be required to release more information than I will provide just to get payments.

c. If you have been sent to me by your employer's employee assistance program (EAP), the program's staffers may require some information. Again, I believe that they will act legally, but I cannot control who sees this information at their offices. If this is your situation, let us fully discuss my agreement with your employer or the program before we talk further.

d. If your account with me is unpaid and we have not arranged a payment plan, I can use legal means to get paid. Generally the only information I will give to a court, a collection agency, or a lawyer will be your name and address, the dates we met for professional services, and the amount due to me.

5. **Children and families create some special confidentiality questions.**

a. When I treat children under the age of about 12, I must tell their parents or guardians whatever they ask me. As children grow more able to understand and choose, they assume legal rights. For those between the ages of 12 and 18, most of the details of things they tell me will be treated as confidential. However, parents or guardians need to be able to make well-informed decisions about therapy, and so they have the right to *general* information, including how therapy is going. I may also have to tell parents or guard-

*(continued)*

ians some information about other family members that I am told, if these others' actions put anyone in any danger.

b. In cases where I treat several members of a family (parents and children, or other relatives), the confidentiality situation can become very complicated. I may have different duties toward different family members. At the start of our treatment, we must all have a clear understanding of the purposes of our meeting and of my role. Then we can be clear about any limits on confidentiality that may exist.

c. If you tell me something your spouse or partner does not know, and not knowing this could harm him or her, I cannot promise to keep it confidential. I will work with you to decide on the best long-term way to handle situations like this.

d. If you and your spouse or partner have a custody agreement or dispute, I will need to know about it. My professional ethics prevent me from doing both therapy and custody or parental fitness evaluations.

e. If you are seeing me for marriage counseling or couple therapy, you must agree at the start of treatment that if you eventually decide to divorce, you will not request my testifying for either side. That way we can focus on what is best for your relationship. The court, however, may order me to testify.

f. At the start of family treatment, we must also specify which members of the family must sign a release form for the family record I create in the therapy or therapies. (See point 7b, below.)

6. **Confidentiality in group therapy is also a special situation.**

In group therapy, the other members of the group are not therapists. They do not have the same ethics and laws that I have to work under. You cannot be certain that they will always keep what you say in the group confidential.

7. Finally, here are a few **other points:**

a. I will not electronically record our therapy sessions without your written permission.

b. If you want me to send information about our therapy to someone else, you must sign a release-of-information or records form. I have copies of these forms that you can see, so you will know what is involved.

c. Any information that you tell me and also share outside of therapy, willingly and publicly, will not be considered protected or confidential by a court or the legal system.

   The laws and rules on confidentiality are complicated, so please raise your questions at any time. But I am not able to give you legal advice. If you have special or unusual concerns, and so need special advice, I strongly suggest that you talk to a lawyer to protect your interests legally and to act in your best interests.
   The signatures here show that we each have read, discussed, understand, and agree to abide by the points presented above.

_____     _____     ___/___/___
Signature of client (or person acting for client)                Printed name                                Date

_____     ___/___/___
          Signature of therapist                    Date

or another person, or that access might similarly harm another person identified in the record. If you do allow access, the regulations specify timely access and procedures for review of such denials of access. You should modify the wording in section 3c of Handout 8.1 to reflect how these rules apply to your practice.

- Section 4b says, "I usually give you my bill. . . . " This may not be your policy, so adapt the wording as necessary.

- For more on becoming involved in custody or divorce proceedings, see Form 5.7. Also, you could expand the policy stated in sections 5d and 5e of Handout 8.1 with these phrasings:
  - "I will not serve as a witness or provide records for such matters. If you go to court, you will have to ask another professional to do any evaluations of yourselves, your children, and your relationship."
  - "I ask you to agree that my records will not be requested in court by either party, and to keep this in mind during our therapy."
  - "I will provide a summary, but not the actual records, to the court. My charge for this summary is $N per hour of preparation time."

- Section 5f covers the question of which family members sign an ROI form. The safest method of release for a family's or couple's records is to require the consent of all adults or participants, although this is also the most complex solution.

- Because of the litigious and "paranoid" nature of our times, you might add wording like this:

- "I do not sell or in any way make available your name or any of the information you provide to me to anyone without your permission. I will not even acknowledge that you are a client of my practice without your specific permission."

The general rule is this: **Make certain that the client is informed about all the likely implications and consequences of confidentiality.** A handout like Handout 8.1, and your detailed notes, should show that you have told the client what he or she needs to know to act in his or her own best interest.

# 8.2 Maintaining Confidentiality

## Guidelines for Maintaining Confidentiality

- Encourage clients to ask questions about confidentiality concerns when they arise in therapy, and to resolve them before they make any risky revelations. When answering questions, be careful to promise very little specific protection, because you cannot know how confidential you can keep a client's specific situation until you are told it—and then it may be too late. Clients have rarely formulated their situations within the ethical or legal frameworks you are bound to live by.

- Many clinicians worry that disclosing the limits of confidentiality will inhibit the freedom of discussion necessary for effective therapy. Nowell and Spruill (1993), surveying naive college students, found that disclosing exceptions to total confidentiality did result in some inhibition of self-disclosure. However, they also found that offering a complete description of the limitations did not result in more inhibition than a brief, cursory description, which is now seen as essential.

- If in doubt, consult, as recommended throughout this book. "Never worry alone." By itself, making this effort offers you some malpractice protection, and you may learn how to protect your client. Document these consultations. ELZ recommends keeping this documentation separate from the client's records.

- Avoid giving anything like legal advice, and refer complex legal questions to the client's attorney.

- Do not gossip or otherwise talk lightly or casually about your clients. Celebrity clients, fascinating clinical phenomena, bragging, making the irresistible joke—all these are tempting conversational topics. We may try to gain points for ourselves at the expense of our clients, trusting that no one will figure out their identity or use the information, but we cannot know all the connections in peoples' lives. The best rule is *never* to discuss your clients or your work with your spouse/partner, friends, or even other therapists, but only with a formally arranged consultant or in a carefully prepared presentation. With such a rule, you won't have to keep deciding what to reveal, or feel the anxiety of uncertainty.

- Leave nothing with a client's name on it lying around anywhere—no folders, no letters, no phone notes, no trashed copies of documents. Arrange your office and office procedures to prevent the viewing of charts, appointment books, telephone messages, computer screens, and the like by clients, salespersons, cleaning or maintenance people, visitors, and other staff members. Lock your door, desk, and cabinet when you are out of the office. If you share an office, each therapist will need a locked record storage area. If you leave materials for clients to fill out, simply note, "For Dr. Doe's client" without a name.

- Be careful when you replay the answering machine, so that no one else can overhear your messages. Instruct your staff to do the same. Use password-protected "mailboxes" for your voicemail.

- Assure yourself that your answering service also understands these rules and obeys them. Ask about the staff's training, offer some hypothetical situations, and perhaps call as someone else to test the service. Since the answering service is a business associate (BA) of yours, get a BA contract for it.

- Do not use a client's name in the waiting room unless you and the client are alone. It may seem odd, but you can just make eye contact and say, "Won't you please come in?" without mentioning the client's name. If it is a first appointment, saying, "I'm Dr. Doe. Are you here to see me?" will serve the same purpose in a busy waiting area. If the office is used by professionals of other disciplines, such as dentists, they are likely to use clients' names freely; do not be swayed.

- Train all members of your staff in all aspects of the maintenance of confidentiality. For more details, see below on staff training.

- Generally, revealing information in the presence of a third party such as an uninvolved professional or a relative (but not usually a spouse, cotherapist, or clinical employee) may void the legal protection of confidentiality. When given in such a setting it is seen as public information. This also applies to your clients, so discourage them from saying private things when others (such as family or friends) are around. There is no longer privileged if a client tells other people about the session or any usually confidential information, because that means it is no longer actually held in confidence by the client.

Did the client intend a session to be confidential? The answer to this question often lies in the original reason for the session. If the client has a regular, long-term relationship with the therapist (e.g., is being treated for a disorder), then the session is solely for the client's private benefit, and clearly it is intended to be confidential. However, many people contact psychologists in connection with some legal concern. Perhaps they are in the process of or contemplating divorce, are being evaluated as parents for custody or adoption purposes, have been raped or abused and are pressing charges, are fulfilling a condition of probation, or the like. In these cases, the courts are likely to find that the client intended immediately or in the future to disclose the fact that he or she was undergoing treatment, in which case there is no evidentiary privilege. Consult legal counsel for clarification.

- *Never* discuss any kind of confidential matter on a cordless phone with a base station (as opposed to a cellphone or other wireless phone), and be sensitive to the possibility of others' listening in when a client's or your own house has multiple handsets on a line. While encryption programs for cellphones and other wireless phones are available, the nature of the signals makes listening in very difficult for all but the most well-financed organizations.

- Make sure you have sufficient sound muffling in your office. You can achieve this with white-noise generators, an air deflector in the air conditioning ductwork, double-studded and double-wallboarded walls, a radio with several speakers (set fairly loud and not under the control of the clients in the waiting room), and heavily weather-stripped or carpeted doors.

- Even if a client's spouse is in therapy with the client, it is not appropriate to discuss the client's treatment in detail with the spouse; courtesy and privacy should prevail. The law is frequently silent on the issue of the privileged status of what is said to spouses in marriage counseling, or to a therapist's assistants, staff, and employees, so you may not have protection. Court-ordered marriage counseling may be an exception to confidentiality, but check your local rules.

- Make explicit in your client information brochure how you will handle the confidentiality issues of family therapy.

- Develop a way to keep records on the individuals in group therapy in which other members are not identified and perhaps a separate record for the group as a whole. See Form 5.4, the group therapy contract.

- Develop a clear plan to dispose of your records without breaking confidentiality. See Section 1.6.

- Both ethics and HIPAA's Security Rule require you to secure the confidentiality of your **computerized client records.** (See also Section 1.5.) Your records could be read and copied by any of the following: your own staff; cleaning or building maintenance persons in your office when you are not present; anyone on your local or larger computer network (unless you have blocked access to client files); those entering through your always-on Internet connection who insert keyloggers, a "Trojan Horse" virus that sends your files to them, or other malware; a thief who steals your computer; a repair person during maintenance or upgrading; legal wiretappers; those using video-monitoring "security cameras"; and probably others.

Passwords are insufficient protection, burdensome, and likely to be misused by being changed too infrequently or used on too many accounts. Also, there are easily available programs for breaking passwords. A better solution is to encrypt all your clinical files. The liability is that you will be using a password to decrypt these files, and losing it means losing the files permanently. Use any of the free (e.g., File Locker or the built in BitLocker in Windows OS and FileVault in Mac's OS) or more convenient moderately priced encryption programs that you can download. Use and keep current a "firewall" program. You can find all these at various sites (e.g., shareware.com and download.com). For privacy tools for all kinds of electronic communication, see http://www.epic.org/privacy/tools.html, or do an Internet search for the latest tools.

## Training Employees in Privacy Practices

If your office is large enough to employ others, you have to train them in your procedures and then monitor and supervise their work. HIPAA makes formal staff training in privacy policies and practices a requirement (Section 164.530(b)), and you must "have in place appropriate administrative, technical, and physical safeguards to protect the privacy of protected health information" (Section 164.530(c)).

Training in security procedures should be included as well. Staff members *must* be trained in HIPAA, and *should* be trained in your local laws and your professional ethics to protect your clients and yourself. This training must be completed by the time your practice becomes officially HIPAA-compliant. It must be done for new employees, should be repeated at intervals, and must be documented.

Make it clear to your staff that any kind of client information must not be casually or carelessly discussed (over lunch, in rest rooms, in elevators, in restaurants, etc.), including in the office. If other staff members, employees, or even other clinicians bound by confidentiality are present when you need to communicate about a client, write the client's name down and point to it for your conversation. Similarly, do not allow your staff or office mates to refer to clients who phone or otherwise come up in conversation, except as "this client" or "he" or "she." Finally, make clear your intention to dismiss immediately anyone who breaks any of the rules of the office.

## A Checklist for Staff Training in Confidentiality

**FORM 8.1**   Form 8.1 is a checklist of the issues of greatest concern and likelihood and with references to the sections of this book where you will find some guidance on each. It is presented here as an example only; you should add items to fit your practice and revise the contents over time. It can be used to organize your training of employees (permanent or temporary, part- or

# Checklist for Staff Training in Confidentiality

When people come to this practice, they are likely to discuss some very personal information that they want to remain confidential—that is, to be known only to themselves and the clinician who is treating them. Below are this office's rules designed to protect the confidentiality of all clients' health care information and any other confidential information in this office. You should assume that *everything* is confidential in this office and treat it accordingly.

As a condition of your employment, you are required to read, understand, and agree to comply with these rules and conditions:

❑ The codes of ethics, guidelines, and state laws, as well as licensing board policies and decisions, that apply to the clinicians who work in this office and practice.

❑ The main board complaints, malpractice, and ethical issues and risks—confidentiality, dual relationships, record making and keeping, releasing records, billing, and _____.

❑ The procedures for organizing, handling, storing, and releasing of all material with clients' names or identification numbers. The rules and procedures apply to charts, forms, copies, faxes, emails/electronic messages, computer screens, appointment books/electronic schedules, answering machines/voicemail messages, message books, memos/notes, and so forth.

❑ Proper use of our computer programs that contain client information, in order to maintain its privacy.

❑ Computer security and data preservation, access, and integrity with passwords and encryption (<u>see Sections 1.5 and 8.2 of *The Paper Office for the Digital Age*</u>), backups, off-site storage, and the like.

❑ Acceptable ways of addressing clients and using clients' names on the phone, in the waiting area, or anywhere else they could be overheard by other clients and unauthorized persons.

❑ Responding to phone calls about clients (<u>see Section 8.3 of *The Paper Office for the Digital Age*</u>).

❑ Privately playing the answering machine, checking the voicemail, or calling the answering service.

❑ Casual conversations and gossip about our clients, in and out of the office.

❑ The fact that confidentiality begins with a person's first contact with our office.

❑ The fact that the confidentiality of a client's information extends after the death of the client or the professional, after you have left this employment, and into the future indefinitely.

❑ The breaking of confidentiality rules as grounds for immediate dismissal and possible legal actions.

❑ Ways to handle questions of ethics, confidentiality, access, and so forth raised by clients, by other professionals, or by situations.

*(continued)*

My signature below indicates the following:

❑ I have read and discussed:

    ❑ The Information for Clients brochure (on the CD) and/or the other routes to informed consent (Forms 5.1–5.6) used in this office.

    ❑ Other client education materials used in this practice, such as the handout on the limits of confidentiality (Handout 8.1) and the handout on managed care (Handout 3.1), as appropriate to my job functions.

    ❑ The Notice of Privacy Practices (NPP) forms (Forms 6.3 and 6.4), the form for consent to privacy practices (Form 6.5), and the various release-of-information forms (Forms 8.2, 8.3, and 8.4), as appropriate to my job functions.

❑ I have been informed about the issues and guidelines above, have had the opportunity to raise any questions, and have had my questions answered. I believe I understand the issues and concerns about confidentiality and related issues, and will ask _____ when any questions or concerns arise for me.

❑ I agree not to disclose any information about clients to parties or persons outside this practice/office/organization, other patients, or anyone else unless authorized to do so in writing by a patient (or patient's guardian or legal representative) and approved by my employing professional.

❑ If a breach of this agreement or the confidentiality of any records should occur, I agree to notify my employer immediately or, at most, within 24 hours of its discovery.

❑ I understand that any material breach of this agreement shall constitute good cause of my discharge from this employment. In addition, such a breach may subject me to financial liability and legal punishments and damages.

| | |
|---|---|
| _____ | _____ |
| Signature of employee | Printed name of employee |
| _____ | _____ |
| Signature of employee | Printed name of employee |
| _____ | _____ |
| Signature of employee | Printed name of employee |
| _____ | _____ |
| Signature of employee | Printed name of employee |

A checkmark above indicates that this topic was discussed with those present. This training was conducted by the undersigned on ___/___/___:

| | | |
|---|---|---|
| _____ | _____ | _____ |
| Signature | Printed name | Title |

full-time), answering service personnel, or anyone else with access to your records. It can also be used as an employee agreement to maintain confidentiality.

## Creating Confidential Records

Here are three methods of increasing the likelihood of confidentiality of your records:

1. **Abridge as much as possible.** This means limiting the client information collected (from the client and others), recorded, retained, and reported. Do not put information of a sensitive nature into a document if it is not *clearly* necessary to the purposes of that report or note. For example, do not repeat a client's history from earlier reports or the reports of others, unless this is essential for your present purposes. If you do incorporate others' information, you are, in effect, re-releasing information sent to you in confidence—presumably with a limited authorization—but without a current and valid ROI form from the client. Simple as this rule is, it is broken frequently. A later authorization may protect you, but why add risk to the client? You cannot control the destinies of your reports, and your primary responsibility is to your client. If the information is crucial and very sensitive , consider telling the referral source or other concerned persons orally.

2. **Ensure the client's access to his or her records.** (The rules about this access should be indicated in your client information brochure.) Access can protect clients' privacy by informing them of what information has been collected, by clarifying how it is interpreted and used, and by allowing them to make informed decisions before releasing it. All of this is empowering to clients and thus protects them in a larger sense. It is also supported by federal law and perhaps by your local laws.

3. If a client is at risk from the information, write with **discretion,** thoughtfulness, and caring.

## A Little Test

1. A physician calls to ask: "This is Dr. Jones. Did my client, Joe Smith, whom I referred to you, come in?" How should you answer?

2. Attorney Brown asks: "Did my client, Joe Smith, come in to see you?" How should you answer?

3. A caller asks: "Did my brother, Joe Smith, get to your office OK?" How should you answer?"

One or more of the following may run through your mind:

"I don't want to be rude to this source of a lot of my referrals."
"My first duty is to protect Joe's privacy, but the caller won't like my stonewalling."
"Both of us and Joe know Joe was supposed to be here, so where is the risk?"
"Is there anyone who can overhear this conversation? If not, I can bend the rules."
"Am I certain this is indeed Dr. Jones/Attorney Brown/Joe's sibling?"

However mixed your reactions may be, unless you know the caller and so are willing to take the risk of breaking confidentiality, the only acceptable answer to all three of these queries is this: "I'm sorry, but I cannot give you that information. If you will have the person [don't even use Joe Smith's name, as it could signal that he is known] sign a consent form releasing the information you want, I will check to see if he is known to us, and then I will be able to talk further with you or send you the information you want." Instruct the members of your staff today that they are never to take the risk of responding in any other way. As a way to soften the pain of refusal, you could explain the necessity of privacy; mention the professional rules (ethics); and, most convincingly, remind callers of what they would want their own therapist to say. You can offer to send a caller a copy of your release form, but don't offer to call Joe Smith, as that would demonstrate that the person is known to you.

## 8.3   Releasing Clients' Records

*Note:* See also Chapter 5 on informed consent.

The balance of this chapter offers more specific guidelines to help you answer questions such as these:

- How can you decide whether or not to honor a request for a client's records?

- How can you best protect the client's confidentiality when you do release your records?

- What legal elements must a request for the records of another professional contain?

The first of these questions is addressed in this section. Later sections include sample forms for requesting records from and releasing records to different requesters. The forms are designed to meet important legal and ethical guidelines.

### A Pretest

How sophisticated are you in weighing the relevant issues in releasing records? Pope (1988d) offers the following fictional case history.

A 17-year-old boy comes to your office and asks for a comprehensive psychological evaluation. He's been experiencing some headaches, anxiety, and depression. A high school drop-out, he's been married for a year, has a 1-year-old baby, but has left his wife and child and returned to live with his parents. He works full time as an auto mechanic, and has insurance which covers the testing procedures.

You complete the testing. During the following year you receive requests for information about the testing from:

(a) the boy's physician, an internist.
(b) the boy's parents, who are concerned about his depression.
(c) the boy's employer, in connection with a worker's compensation claim filed by the boy.
(d) the attorney for the insurance company that is contesting the worker's compensation claim.

(e) the attorney for the boy's wife, who is suing for divorce and for custody of the baby.

(f) the attorney for the boy, who is considering suing you for malpractice since he doesn't like the results of the tests.

Each of the requests asks for: (a) the full formal report, (b) the original test data, and (c) copies of each of the tests you administered (e.g., instructions and all test questions of the MMPI).

To which of these people are you legally or ethically obligated to supply all information requested? Partial information? A summary of the report? No information at all? For which requests is having written informed consent from the boy for release of information relevant? (Pope, 1988d, p. 24)

Again, this is admittedly a complex situation, and Pope does not offer answers. Before reading further, take a minute to decide which records you would send out and which you wouldn't, and to whom you would send them. ELZ's responses can be found at the end of this section (Section 8.3).

## Ethical Considerations in Releasing Records

While records must often be shared among professionals for the benefit of clients, breaches of confidentiality can destroy the trust essential for intimate work. The professions have therefore developed procedures for protecting the privacy of records. The following discussion shows how to evaluate a request for your client's records.

The basic ethical rule is that consent to release records, like all consent, must be *informed* and *voluntary*, and must be obtained from a *competent* person. These requirements are discussed in Chapter 5. Fully informed consent to release records requires that the client understand and agree to the following:

- Which specific person wants the records (name, position, affiliation, function).

- What the records sought contain, and exactly what information is sought. Knowledge can come from the client's reading the materials, or from having the materials explained to him or her.

- Why this information is sought, and exactly how it will be used. What decision(s) will be based on it? What repercussions would follow from granting or withholding permission?.This kind of understanding of implications will sometimes require discussion, sometimes extensive.

- Whether the requester can share this information with anyone else (e.g., consultants, treatment team members).

- How the information in the records can be corrected or amended.

- That the client's consent is revocable except for information already released.

- Whether the client has given permission to let the provider notify someone previously informed by an ROI if and when consent to release information is withdrawn. For example, instead of no reply when a PCP wants to check in on a client, we may get a client to give us permission to say, "Client *X* has withdrawn his or her consent for me to release any information to you." Without express permission, we cannot otherwise state this.

Do not confuse this full consenting process (becoming fully informed, acting voluntarily, having the mental capability to consent) with signing the HIPAA-required consent form acknowledging having learned about your privacy practices from your Notice of Privacy Practices (NPP) (see Form 6.5). This HIPAA consent form is not an ROI form, which you should always use.

Finally, this may seem obvious, but the client must believe that it is in his or her long-term best interest to release the records. For fuller comprehension, your ROI form should be available for the client to read. Anything the client does not understand must be explained at his or her level of comprehension, and in his or her native language if necessary.

## Legal Requirements for a Release of Information

There is no one standard term for the form documenting the request for or release of records. We have seen forms called "authorization" forms (HIPAA's term), but this seems too broad. We have seen the verbs "release," "request," "retrieve," "forward," and "obtain," and the nouns "records," "medical records," "notes," "forms," "information," and "data." For simplicity's sake, **we call every such form a "release of information" and abbreviate this term as ROI.**

Don't comply with a request to release your records if the ROI sent to you is faulty (missing some of the necessary contents listed below), because if there should be a legal, ethical, or clinical problem, responsibility cannot be assigned to the requesting party.

A release that authorizes you to "release and disclose all information, and to discuss anything pertaining to this client and the client's progress" appears to be illegally vague and broad, and may be prohibited by HIPAA regulations concerning the "minimum necessary disclosure" rules (see Section 164.502).

The minimal legal requirements for releasing records are set by the HIPAA regulations (Section 164.508) and by the Code of Federal Regulations (42 C.F.R. Part 2, Public Law 93-282, Sections 2.31(a) and 2.33, governing the confidentiality of clients' records of alcohol and drug abuse treatment). **A valid ROI must address all of the following:**

❑ Name of client. Be alert to alternative names (maiden names, shortened or nicknames, common alternative spellings, legally changed names, etc.). Date of birth is also usually sought, as is Social Security number, because many names are not unique and common ones may share birthdays. However, collecting Social Security numbers creates a risk of identity theft, so consider omitting them from your records.

❑ The name or title of the person or organization to receive the records.

❑ Either the name of the person or the organization from which records are to be released.

❑ The specific extent or nature of the information to be disclosed.

❑ The purpose of the request, the reason why these records are needed, or a description of how the PHI will be used. You may have received an ROI request by error that was created for another proceeding.

❑ The consequences of refusing to release the information, if any (e.g., loss of reimbursement for medical costs or of disability benefits).

❑ The signature of the client (or his or her representative) and the date signed. The signature must usually be given within 90 days of the time you receive the ROI. Consider also its validity.

❑ Verification that the person signing is of legal age, or documentation of his or her "emancipation."

❑ A statement that the participant has the right to revoke, in writing, this authorization; a description of the means for doing so; and the exceptions to such revocation (e.g., that it is not retroactive and thus won't apply to what has already been disclosed).

❑ When, how, or on what condition the consent will expire if it is not revoked earlier.

❑ A notice that after the PHI is disclosed, it may be redisclosed and thus is no longer protected by HIPAA regulations. Note that other federal laws may forbid this redisclosure. Redisclosure is legally complicated. HIPAA generally allows you to release others' records in your possession. Traditionally, however, we have refused to release others' records in our possession. It is also possible that the records in our possession are not the most recent and may contain errors, so sending the requester to the original source is quite rational. Know your local rules, and write your ROI to address these.

❑ If drug and alcohol information is in the records, the federal rules (42 C.F.R. Part 2) require a specific notice to be included when releasing records.

❑ An indication that you will be paid directly or indirectly for this disclosure, if that is true. This pertains to the marketing restrictions created by HIPAA and rarely if ever applies to psychotherapists. (Please don't sell a list of your depressed clients to a travel agency, even though Hippocrates apparently endorsed vacations to treat depression.)

While HIPAA allows treatment without formal consent, this was designed for emergencies and unconscious clients, so proceed with caution and obtain written consent as soon as possible. For clarification about how some of these ideas are carried out, see the ROI forms provided in Sections 8.4 and 8.5. Additional criteria may be required by your state.

## Eight Variations on the Theme of "Please Send Your Records"

Many different people may request your records in many different ways. Each request needs to be considered from ethical as well as legal perspectives. It is best to make it your policy to review all records before you release them. Look for contents that might not be in the client's best interests or might cause distress. We discuss coping with these situations under the third variation below. Consider the following discussion of eight kinds of requests.

### 1. A Routine ROI Request from a Third Party

Consider these usual bases for releasing information to a third party:

- A competent client has requested release of his or her own records. The disclosure is necessary for the client's continuing or comprehensive care by another provider or institution, for reimbursement, or for a needed consultation.

- A *surrogate* consent is received for a minor, for someone adjudicated incompetent, or for a dead person.

- A law requires disclosure (e.g., Medicare, mandatory child abuse reporting). See variation 2, below.

Now consider these possible bases against releasing information to a third party:

- The ROI request sent to you is faulty. It is missing some of the necessary contents of a proper release as listed above. As a courtesy, you could, if you are still in contact with the client, have him or her complete one of your releases (perhaps Form 8.3).

- The requester is someone you don't recognize, and you know nothing about the intended uses for this information. Because your records will often contain at least private information, you need to be careful. Call to verify who the requester is and what the requester may do with the information.

- The information in your possession is not relevant to the request (e.g., it may not pertain to the request's purposes, the decisions to be made, the time period in question, or even the client named in the request).

- Confidentiality law or privilege protects against release, and your general duty to protect confidentiality is not overcome by any recognized exception (see Section 8.1 for a list of exceptions).

- In family therapy, the "family" or "couple" cannot have legal confidentiality; only individual members have this privilege. Thus you will have to clarify and negotiate rules for release with each family member. Ideally, you have specified in your introductory materials that all members must sign the ROI or that they must choose a delegate.

- Is it completely certain that the client is fully informed about all the information in your record and the effects of passing on all this information? If not, contact the client directly to clarify the release. In one case in Pennsylvania, a client sued (successfully at first) the psychologist whom she had specifically asked to write a letter to her employer seeking a less stressful job for her, and for whom she had signed a release form. She sued for invasion of privacy and infliction of emotional distress. The psychologist probably would have received a dismissal of the case (before it went to court) if she had had the client see and authorize the release of the exact letter. It is best to have all records released be seen by the client.

- Can you withhold records if you have not been paid for your services? The APA ethics code (APA, 2010) says in Standard 6.03 that "Psychologists may not withhold records . . . that are requested and needed for a client's/patient's emergency treatment solely because payment has not been received." Notice the qualifiers "emergency" and "solely." ELZ believes the message is that you can indeed withhold records for nonpayment in nonemergency situations—for example, if the request is being made only for the convenience of the client (e.g., in support of a school transfer) and he or she is fully capable of paying you. KK makes the argument that the record belongs to the client and cannot be withheld, and that the release is much less likely to result in complaints than resisting the release is.

**Who *owns* a client's records?** This is an unsettled question. Borkosky (2014), writing about forensic evaluations, found conflicting arguments, positions, and incomplete analyses among 54 official documents from ethics codes, HIPAA, APA guidelines, and laws. He advises replacing the simple and unitary concept of "ownership" with an understanding of the "information rights" of various entities and efforts to clarify the clinician's "multiple, possibly conflicting responsibilities to multiple entities" (p. 264), using "an informed consent process." He points out that confidentiality merely keeps records secret (out of the hands of unauthorized users) and does not address the many needs and uses of records. He suggests that the primary information right belongs to the client—the "client's right to control access." The client decides who gets to use or view the records. The client must then have received detailed knowledge of the processes and consequences of release of any information to any other person, agency, or legal process in order to give fully informed consent.

- Producing reports such as testing-based assessments requires a great deal of time, and so, to assure payment, require a full payment of an estimate before the report is written. Although your raw data may be subpoenaed, you will be less likely to be taken advantage of by clients or attorneys, because the interpretations don't yet exist.

- One last point: Should you type up your notes to make them actually readable? No, just send copies of your records in whatever shape they are in. "Redacting" them is not what you were asked for, and it would tempt you to make minor revisions (for clarification or by error), which would create doubts about your veracity and integrity.

## 2. A Client's Request to See His or Her Own Records

When a client asks to see his or her own records, consider these points:

- Consider why the client wants these records, and work from there. The request may conceal other needs, which can be resolved better through different responses.

- In general, offer to review the records with the client, or offer to write an abstract of the record. This allows you to edit for emphasis or obscurity when tailoring a summary to the client's needs.

- What specific disclosures does the applicable state law require? Applicable laws will vary among workers' compensation clients; clients with disabilities, dual diagnoses, or substance use disorders; your specific discipline versus other mental health professions; and so forth.

- Consider whether there may be errors in the record, which the client has a right to see and correct by amending. The client has the right to add a statement of agreement or disagreement. These rights come from the Privacy Act of 1974 (Public Law 93-579); the HIPAA regulations; and, for clients in drug and alcohol treatment, the Drug Abuse Office and Treatment Act of 1972 (Public Law 92-255).

- The impact on the client and family of the disclosure of a diagnosis or some other information may require explanation and guidance for the client to understand productively (see variation 3, below).

*Clients' Access to Their Records under HIPAA.*

In the past, clients have had little legal or practical ability to examine their own medical records. HIPAA has given them almost unlimited ability to "access, inspect, and copy protected health information" (under Section 164.524). A client has the right to view and obtain a copy of the PHI that you created, *unless* one or more of the following applies:

- The information was collected specifically for use in a legal proceeding (civil, criminal, or administrative).

- The information is in your psychotherapy notes.

- The client is or was an inmate of a correctional institution for which you work.

- The information was generated as part of a research project that is still ongoing, and the client agreed before entering the research to delay access.

- The information was collected by a health care provider who was promised anonymity, and the information would reveal the identity of this person.

Denial of access for any of the reasons above is not a reviewable decision.

Access requests must be made in writing and must be acted on within 30 days (for records on-site) or 60 days (for those off-site). **If you want to deny the request** wholly or in part, you have to provide the denial in writing, in plain language. The denial must contain the basis for the denial; explain the rights and procedures for a review of the denial; and explain how, if he or she chooses to do so, the client can complain to you or to the Secretary of the Department of Health and Human Services (DHHS) with names and phone numbers. For more see Section 164.524 of HIPAA.

While the information would usually be in copied or printed form, it can be otherwise if the client is amenable. You can provide a summary or explanation of the information if the client agrees to this and to your fees for such a version. You can assess reasonable charges for copying and postage, but not for locating the documents.

If you don't have the information sought by the client but know who does, you must direct the client there.

*Amending a Client's Record.*

The HIPAA regulations (Section 164.526) describe how a client may seek to amend, not "correct," records with PHI. You will then simply provide a link or cross-reference, in the record, to the newer information. As noted in earlier chapters, the process of amending is as follows:

1. Never line out, white out, black out, or cut out anything in the record. Don't even write over or make more than very simple spelling corrections on the original page. This is called "altering" and is a frequent fatal vulnerability in malpractice cases. Imagine being on a jury and finding out that the professional had altered even one entry. Would you not suspect the entire record?

2. Note somewhere near the content you want to amend, by encircling it or drawing an arrow, something like "See entry of [today's date]."

3. On a page suitable for a contemporary entry, write today's date and a suitable variation of the following: "Upon reviewing my notes of [the date of the entry you wish to amend], I see I failed to mention . . . " and go on to clarify, correct, or expand the information available in the record.

This kind of cross-referencing is completely legal. Clients have the right to amend their records and should use the same procedure. You should tell clients that they may be able to amend their records if they have good reason and make a request in writing. You will use the same procedure described above. You will have to act on such a request within 60 days, and either amend the record or deny the request in whole or in part (see below for reasons for refusal). In either case, you must inform the client. If you agree to amend, you must make efforts to provide this amended record to others whom the client has identified or others who "may have relied, or could foreseeably rely, on such information to the detriment of the [client]." If you deny the request, you must explain in plain language, in writing, the basis for the denial; the client's right to and the procedure for submitting a written disagreement; a statement that you will, if the client requests it, include in future disclosures the client's request for amendment and the denial you made; and an explanation, including names and phone numbers, of how the client can complain to the covered entity (CE) or the Secretary of DHHS. The regulations allow you to limit the size of the client's request and to substitute a summary of the issues. Your records must indicate all of these exchanges and their outcome.

You can refuse to amend your records (as per HIPAA, Section 164.526(d)) if one of the following is true:

- You didn't create the record. However, you may still allow amending it if you believe that the originator of the record is no longer available.

- The record would not otherwise be available for the client to "access, inspect, and copy" (see above).

- You believe that the record is accurate and complete. It is probably best to accept the client's emendation and note that you believe the records accurate in your own emendation.

### 3. A Client's Request to See His or Her Own Records, Which Contain Potentially Harmful Information

Access can be denied if it might harm the client. If, as a licensed health care provider, you come to believe that allowing the client access to his or her PHI is likely to endanger the life, safety, or health of the client or someone else, you can deny access. This denial can be appealed and reviewed by an additional licensed health care professional (see HIPAA, Section 164.524(d)(4)).

*Distressing Information in Another's Records in Your Possession*

Here are some examples of clients who could be harmed by information in their records. One is an adult with a history of childhood sexual or physical abuse who may be unaware of or deny the abuse, but it is supported by records released to you. Another is a client for whom your records contain information that the client was adopted, but the client does not know of the adoption. In a third example, a professional's terminology that emphasizes deficits may itself cause distress or damage to the relationship.

Your plan in such a case should depend on the circumstances, your understanding of the client, and the impact of the information. Traditionally, this "re-release" of records that are in your file but created by others was forbidden, but HIPAA allows such disclosures. State laws differ, and using an authorization form will be somewhat protective. You could sidestep the issue by refusing to release to the client records generated by someone else. If you think the information will harm the client, you can withhold it; this is called "therapeutic privilege." You may not have heard of this privilege, because it is getting rarer and should be invoked only in extraordinary circumstances. However, the HIPAA regulations have revived this concept and do allow you to restrict the information a client can access (see Section 164.524(a)(3)(ii)).

In such a situation, you are asking the client to understand that some information would be upsetting, and to agree that he or she should be kept ignorant of this information (which seems to go against informed consent). You are also asking that if the information is presented to the client, he or she will not hold you responsible for any damages (which seems to ask the client to waive recourse from a harm he or she cannot anticipate—this again seems unfair). If the situation is touchy, go slowly and carefully; give full attention to maintaining the best possible relationship with the client; document the issues, rationales, and choices made; and get consultation.

### Distressing Information in Records You Created

Coping with the second type of risk draws on the discussions above and may be handled with creation of a written waiver by the client of his or her access to your records. Prepare in advance for this possibility by adding language to your client information materials. Section 5.2 includes this statement: "I may temporarily remove parts of your records before you see them. This would happen if I believe that the information will be harmful to you, but I will discuss this with you." Ideally, you have avoided using any language in the record that might exacerbate the emotional state of the client.

J. Lamar Freed, PhD, of Elkins Park, PA (personal communication, 2011), offers this guidance:

> First I would talk to the client again and be frank, i.e.: "I don't want you to see these notes because I've written them for the insurance company in a way that makes your treatment unassailable. Which means they use psychopathologizing jargon and highlight the pathological aspects of the difficulties you are having. Other psychologists will be able to read through this, but you would likely feel like you were being judged and maybe even devalued—which, as you know, is the opposite of what I do with you in our sessions. The point of notes is to have something that will jog my memory of what happened, which does not require that they be point-on accurate, and, most importantly, that they will make an insurance company reviewer, if there ever is one, pass this record over and look for some other record that they can question. I will be happy to forward this to a new psychologist, but I really don't want you to look at them without me there to explain what was meant."

What is written cannot be unwritten, and some information has distressing implications. For example, Kernisan (2013), discussing notations in Department of Veterans Affairs medical records (which are becoming more open), describes kinds of "awkwardness" that their discovery could generate: a family's being terrified by such a crushing diagnosis as "possible Alzheimer's"; suspicions raised by entries like "possible elder mistreatment" and "possible substance abuse"; indications of lessened activities of daily living needed for independence and driving and the implications of increased dependence; and information from the family that was given to the clinician in confidentiality. See also the discussion of confidentiality in Section 5.2.

### 4. A Parent or Guardian's Request for a Child's Records

Parents and guardians have a right to know about minor children's status and progress, and HIPAA gives them full access. So be careful what you write, and be diplomatic and therapeutic with the parents. (See also the forms for consent to treatment of children in Section 5.6.) Young children cannot claim confidentiality, but teens have "rights" to be respected. Be frank in advising children of their lack of legal guarantees (see Form 5.3). You may also be able to negotiate with the parents to accept less information than they desire (see Form 5.2). A full, thoughtful, and helpful guide to the confidentiality of adolescents is provided in Koocher (2008).

If parents or guardians seem to be seeking more information than you think they or others need, try educating them before releasing the data. For example, explain that by their very nature, reports tend to focus on negatives or weaknesses. You can also explore the adults' motivations for seeking the records. Take into account parents' legal obligation to know in order to protect their children, as well as their emotional concerns for their children. If there is a difference of opinion about treatment, clarifying this through discussion, or perhaps sending records to another therapist for a "second opinion," may serve the parents' needs.

In custody cases, privilege may be overridden by the "best interests of the child." Try to get permission, at intake, to prevent your notes from being subpoenaed at all or by one party if the other objects. The client information materials (under "What to Expect from Our Relationship" in Section 5.2) addresses this issue. And see Form 8.4 for a consent form for releasing information to family members.

### 5. Coping with a Subpoena

A subpoena is a request to appear for a legal proceeding, and a *subpoena duces tecum* is a request to bring one's records as well. It usually comes from a lawyer seeking information, and even if it is not signed by a judge, it requires a timely response (not necessarily compliance by sending what is requested). Court orders are signed by a judge, not a lawyer; will usually show a case or cause number; and are often stamped "Filed" with a date. Unless you succeed in efforts to quash (nullify) or modify a court order, you must comply or face contempt of court charges.

You have to *respond* to a subpoena, but you do not have to *comply* with it. Responding can be satisfied by calling the requesting attorney to tell your fees for complying (creating a summary, testimony, or a deposition, etc.) and a timeline. We suggest not even confirming that the person named in the case is your client without getting an ROI or at least verbal authorization from that client to speak with this attorney.

Subpoenas are easy to write, but alone they may be insufficient to obtain confidential medical records. Responding to a subpoena can require competent and often extensive legal consultation and advice, however, so do not depend on just this text for guidance on how to respond. The ideas offered here are illustrative, are provided only for educational purposes, and should not be considered a substitute for legal counsel. As with the rest of this book, this section contains ideas that are not legal advice. See Table 8.1 for a summary of these ideas.

If you receive a subpoena, **do not release everything** (or anything precipitously) just to be done with it, because doing that may harm the client.

- **First, review the contents of your records.** Anything you have recorded in any format can be subpoenaed. Refresh your memory for the next steps. Do not alter anything in any record. Is there material of relevance to the subpoena? Is there information that might harm the client in any way? Make some notes.

  - Some have argued that our clients are adults, and that a client should know the consequences before waiving his or her privilege with you by signing the release that accompanies a subpoena from a lawyer (We are assuming that the requested records will be available to both sides of any case and all those involved in a legal proceeding.) We believe that, at the time of signing, clients do not know the contents of our records or their implications, and so cannot give valid informed consent. Therefore, we believe that as clinicians, we have an assertive right to try to prevent harm to our clients by taking the steps below. Ultimately, however, a client controls his or her records and makes the choices.

  - If you do not find contents you think might be problematic, you can just send your records. However, if you are concerned about the effects of this material, take the next steps.

**TABLE 8.1. Coping with a Subpoena for Client Records**

- You have to respond to a subpoena, but you don't have to comply with it.

- You can involve your practice attorney at any step to help you understand your position and options.

- Make sure that the subpoena is valid (accurate about the person involved, still in force, properly signed, etc.), is properly served, and offers enough time to respond.

- Review your records. Is there material of relevance to the subpoena? Is there information that might harm the client in some way?

- If material might harm the client, explain this to the client, and discuss what is in your records.

- If the now fully informed client wants the records released, do so.

- If the client does not want the records released, or wants only some parts released, ask for permission to speak to the client's attorney.

- Ask the client's attorney for his or her understanding of your role in the legal proceedings. Are there conflicting roles? Do you have the skills and background needed? Try hard not to reveal much about the client or the case.

- If you are still uncomfortable with the release, ask the client's attorney to negotiate with the requesting attorney (if the request did not come from the client's attorney) to limit the scope of the subpoena or even excuse you from compliance. The modification of the release is done by creating a new release that replaces the older one.

- Review your records again, with your new understanding of the attorney's goals. If you do not find any risks of harms to the client, get a signed ROI from the client and send the subpoenaed information. Charge for preparing it.

- If you are still concerned, get more legal advice.

- Call the client and ask about the case. Discuss what is in your records and the level of detail. If the client does not want the records, or wants only some or parts released, ask for permission to speak to the client's attorney (which you should bill for, and the lawyer will bill the client).

- As you talk to the client's attorney, try hard to not reveal much about the client or case; you cannot unsay what you reveal, and at this point you know nothing of what is going on legally and will not be able to foresee consequences. The attorney can tell you his or her understanding of your role in the legal proceedings. What does each lawyer have in mind for you? Can you enter those roles, perform those functions, or offer those opinions? What legal and ethical roles would you assume? Advocate? Custody evaluator? Expert witness? Fact witness about your work? Are there conflicting roles? And do you have the skills and background needed?

  - You may be able to explain your involvement in the case and have the requesting attorney limit the scope of the subpoena or even excuse you from compliance. Explain your need for an ROI that meets your legal needs.

  - At any time you might (as Harry Corsover, PhD, of Castle Rock, CO, suggests) offer the lawyer choices: (1) a full mental health treatment report for the whole treatment or a part of it; (2) responses to specific questions; or (3) a detailed, session-by-session summary. The fee for each depends on the time it takes to prepare.

- With your understanding of the attorney's goals, again review your records. If you do not find any risks of harms to the client, it is still best to get an ROI from the client. Why? By authorizing the subpoena, the client has waived privilege (which is his or her legal right) but has not waived confidentiality (our legal and ethical obligation). You may then send the subpoenaed information and charge for preparing it.

- If you are still concerned with harm to the client, you should contact your own practice's attorney, or call on the legal consultation services of your professional insurance company or of your state association's professional affairs officer. Your options include challenging the relevance or validity of the subpoena by seeking to "quash" it (see APA, 2006, for more details on this option); asserting, on the client's behalf, the client's rights of privileged communication or rights under local laws, regulations, or precedents; or obtaining a protective order that would limit the information or materials to be provided to the court. You may also negotiate sending a summary, revealing only nonconfidential information that meets the request, or revealing information only in a private meeting with the judge. Sample letters are available online (http://www.centerforethicalpractice.org/motion-to-quash-a-subpoena).

- If these options prove unsatisfactory to the requesting attorney, you can seek a ruling from the court about what to disclose. Write a letter to the judge (with copies to both attorneys) explaining your desire to comply with the law, your ethical requirement to protect confidentiality absent the client's consent or a court order, and your compliance with HIPAA or other relevant statutes. You can offer suggestions such as releasing the materials only to another psychologist to prevent a wider release, narrowing what is released, or the like. APA (2006) offers additional grounds for limiting the release of records or test data.

- If you are still reluctant, an option (when exercising it is accurate) might be to tell the attorney seeking your records that, having reviewed them and understanding the role you are being asked to play, "In my professional opinion, there is nothing in the records that will help your case [or the contents will actually harm your case], and the contents will assist the other side's case." Since your records will be furnished to both sides, the attorney often will not take the risk.

- What happens if you do not comply with a subpoena? The requesting attorney will seek a court order to compel your compliance. By its very nature, a court order indicates that a judge has already authorized the request, and failure to respond to the court order may result in a contempt hearing in which you will be required to explain your behavior before the issuing judge.

    Since the lawyers are not CEs, they do not have to comply with HIPAA, but the client should know the risks involved in releasing his or her records to them. Your ROI form informs the client. **If you decide to release all or parts of the records, get your own ROI and do not depend on a subpoena, which does not parallel our ethics or the regulations that apply to us.**

- To protect yourself in the future, insert today, into your client information, statements that by signing below, "I agree never to seek my records or release them for any forensic action." Although such a statement may not hold up in a full-scale legal proceeding like a custody battle, it does put the client on notice of your unwillingness to serve in dual role—and, if the client asks about it, it can serve as an early warning of a hidden agenda for a couple nominally seeking "marriage counseling" or "couple therapy."

The APA's Committee on Legal Issues (2006) has offered guidance on understanding and coping with subpoenas and the releasing of client records and test data, and is highly recommended. A rich and far-ranging discussion by Zur (2014) is also recommended. The authoritative text for clinicians entering legal systems is Barsky (2012).

### 6. A Request or Subpoena for Test Materials, Raw Data, or Protocols of Evaluation

Psychologists have resisted allowing the public, lawyers, or anyone untrained in their interpretation to see raw test data, such as protocols of answers given to test questions and the questions themselves. There are three main rationales for maintaining such "test security":

- The data would be misunderstood by anyone not trained in their use. The same would apply to X-rays or laboratory test results; only those qualified to interpret the client's responses or the conclusions drawn from them should have access. In fact, the publishers of all high-quality tests restrict who can purchase their materials, to ensure that only those who have the training to understand the tests' appropriate clients and limitations can buy them.

- If the test questions became widely known, they would lose their discriminant validity. People seeking to present themselves as ill or incapable would learn how to "fake bad," and those wishing to conceal deficits and disorders would be able to "fake good." Disability evaluations, forensic testing, and academic assessments would lose the capability of distinguishing between people with and without psychological problem. Thus the tests' ability to provide useful information to society would be compromised.

- The test materials are copyrighted by their creators, and so they may not be given away or made public in a way that would lessen their sales.

These three reasons are incorporated into the ethical prohibition in Standards 9.04 and 9.11 of the APA's code of ethics (APA, 2010). However, these standards recognize the complexities of releases made with client approval. Such complexities are also addressed in three online papers on test security (see https://www.nanonline.org/nan/Professional_Resources/Position_Papers/NAN/_Research_Publications/Position_Papers.aspx?hkey=71602191-716a-4375-8eb8-4b4e6a071e3a). Current practice appears to compromise by distinguishing test *data* (such as scores, protocols, and interpretations, which can be released because they are about an individual) from test *materials* (which are the questions, stimuli, scoring devices, etc.). A leading publisher of psychological tests, Pearson Assessments, has responded thoughtfully to HIPAA's rules about client access to psychological tests (see http://www.pearsonassessments.com/legal-notice.html). The policy of Multi-Health Systems, another major publisher of tests, is also available online (http://www.mhs.com/info.aspx?gr=mhs&prod=service&id=TestDisclosure). Do consult these and other resources, and keep abreast of further developments in this area.

*Note:* A form for permission to test or evaluate a person is provided in Chapter 5 (Form 5.9).

### 7. A Request to Which the Client Does Not Consent

If the client has not given his or her consent to a request for records (e.g., you receive only a subpoena from opposing counsel), discuss the issues fully with him or her, to lessen any feelings of distrust and lower the risk of a HIPAA or board complaint for unauthorized disclosure. Discuss the implications of the request and your planned response with the client, and urge the client to consult his or her own attorney. Here are some other suggestions:

If you do not get consent from the client or an acceptable disposition of the request agreed to by the requester, obtain a court ruling on whether the release is proper. Let the judge be your guide.

In the absence of consent or a court order to release the records, verify that there is some other legitimate basis for the release. Perhaps the client cannot give consent. He or she may be a minor or may have been ruled incompetent because of a variety of factors (significant intellectual disability; dementia; intoxication on drugs, alcohol, or medications; etc.). The person seeking your records must seek "substitute consent" from the client's parent or guardian, or from the court of jurisdiction.

### 8. The Need to Share Records with a Consultant or Referrer

If you are operating under the HIPAA regulations, the client's initial consent allows full sharing of all relevant information among all treaters. Although doing this without an ROI would be technically correct, caution and custom urge getting a release anyway. If you have any doubts because of the kind or amount of material to be discussed or about the client's understanding, get an informed signed release. (See APA, 2010, Standard 4.06.)

## Guidelines and Considerations in Sending Records

- It bears repeating: **Never send the originals of your records anywhere.** However, courts may require the originals. For high-risk situations, keep multiple copies in different locations. And never let any lawyer's office do any copying of your records; let the lawyer employ a legal copying service or what the copies being made or check them immediately. Mistakes are messy.

- If you decide to release records, consider the extent of necessary disclosure and ways to continue to protect confidentiality as much as possible. A competently worded ROI form addresses these concerns.

- Work hard never to send your whole record, because it may contain material irrelevant to the issues at hand or involve others whose privacy should not be violated.

- Consider the likelihood that the client may read the records, reports, or materials you are sending. Ideally, you will be able to discuss the issues, costs versus benefits, and implications of releasing records with a client. Hamberger (2000) offers many specific topics and language for such a discussion, and reports that about 60% of clients who originally asked to have their entire records released changed their minds after full discussions.

- Weigh the best way to organize and present the necessary information. For example, sending written materials instead of discussing the contents of the records over the telephone will make it clearer what has and has not been disclosed. If a release must be oral, confirm in writing the contents released as soon as possible. Use fax only when you are sure of confidentiality (see Section 8.6); an encrypted fax from your computer or as part of an encrypted email may be simpler as well as more secure.

- Prepare and retain careful documentation of the following:

  - Your discussions with the client and the client's responses to the issues involved in the release, such as the contents of your records and the implications of release.

  - The information ultimately released, the release date, and the person or agency to whom or to which it is provided. Record on the ROI form before making copies (see below) which pages are included; what forms, letters, or notes are enclosed; and so on.

  - Either the ROI form signed by the client, or the explanation of why a duty to disclose without consent is present.

- ROI forms you receive and those you send to another provider (see Section 8.4) should be prepared in triplicate—an original and two copies, each separately signed in ink (preferably blue, so that it is less likely the signature has been photocopied). These should be distributed as follows: one for the client or his or her guardian; one for the party releasing the information; and one for the party receiving the information.

- Notifying the recipient that this is sensitive material is important and can be accomplished in several ways. You can use one of the more specific notices provided in Section 8.5; use your computer's printer to print this notice on peel-off labels, or have your computer put the notice in a header or footer on every page. Some therapists have had a rubber stamp made up with one of the confidentiality notices from Section 8.7, which they then stamp on each page released. But note that a stamp for each page that says simply "Do not copy" or "Confidential" or "Personal and confidential" is probably not legally sufficient notification. In addition, enclose an explanatory, cautioning, and educational cover letter with all records you send (see Form 8.5 and Section 8.3).

- If you are asked to send the record to anyone whose credentials you don't know or recognize, write or speak to him or her, and perhaps suggest that you could send the records directly to a different and more appropriately qualified professional for interpretation (with, of course, a new ROI form).

- You can certainly charge for copying your records and sending them. According to HIPAA, you cannot charge for locating and organizing your records, but only for copying, mailing, and so on. A charge of $10 to $15 seems to be common, but do charge more if your efforts justify the cost. Make certain to include and clearly mark your federal Tax Identification Number (TIN) or Social Security number on your bill, or you will waste a lot of time on the phone when requesters want to pay you. (See Section 3.2.) It seems fair to charge for records requested by non-health-care professionals who will make a profit from the record (e.g., lawyers, insurance companies). ELZ would not charge for a record sent to the client or his or her face-to-face health care provider, but would charge an organization. If a client requests that we send copies to several providers, we recommend sending a single copy to the client and letting him or her arrange things.

- In summary, "the overriding rule is *When in doubt, don't give it out!*' (The next rule, of course, is *If still in doubt, call your redoubtable lawyer*')" (Stromberg et al., 1988, p. 389; emphasis in original).

## Comments on the Pretest

At the beginning of this section, we have offered a case example from Pope (1988d) that raises many of the issues just examined. Would your answers now be different from your earlier responses? Here is ELZ's best understanding of this situation.

First, is a 17-year-old an adult in your state? If the young man in this case was not an emancipated minor, all the releases would need substitute consent.

Second, ELZ would contact the young man and tell him of the requests he had received. The issue to be dealt with would be the degree to which this man could understand the content and implications of my report. If he did not, he could not informedly release the report. ELZ would suggest that he and the young man meet (at the man's expense) to discuss the contents, and that the man consult his lawyer about the report's consequences in regard to each of the intended recipients, especially his own and the other attorneys. A revised ROI, replacing the previous one, could then be written.

Third, ELZ would not send the tests' data or copies of the tests to anyone, citing in his cover letter both the inability of nonpsychologists (all of the requesters) to interpret the tests' data accurately, and the ethical and professional need to maintain the security of the tests. ELZ would also mention in this letter that if the requesters, after reading his letter or report, believed they had a need for the raw data or results, he would consider releasing these to another sufficiently qualified psychologist who could interpret them for the requesters. ELZ would add that they should arrange this at their expense.

Fourth, ELZ would indicate to each requester that he would be willing to create a version of his report that might answer specific questions each might raise, but that since he did not know the requester's needs, he would be very reluctant to release a full report containing a great deal of material that was likely to be irrelevant to the requester's needs, might easily be misunderstood, and could embarrass the client or others. ELZ would offer to produce these revised reports at his usual per-hour fee, to be paid by the requesters in advance. The requesters would probably not initially accept this proposal. If ELZ felt the need was justified, he would telephone each one, attempt to clarify the requester's needs for information, and discuss (in a general way) whether or not his report might contain information to meet the requester's needs.

Lastly, what ELZ would charge for all of this additional correspondence, consultation, and collaboration with other parties would be another matter to be made clear to the client. KK's policy is to give clients up to 10 minutes per week of her time beyond sessions for calls or consultations. In the rare circumstances that require more time, she charges a pro-rated version of the client's usual fee.

There are, to be sure, other concerns and other possible responses.

## 8.4  Forms for Requesting and Releasing Information

Both a longer and more comprehensive ROI form (Form 8.2) and a briefer version (Form 8.3) are provided in this section. Either can be used to have a client release your records, as well as to request records from another provider.

### A Comprehensive Request/Release Form

**FORM 8.2** Form 8.2 is a very long ROI form. However, it contains everything legally and ethically necessary to protect the client's privacy and your professional practice. Everything in it is important, and everything important is in it. We recommend its use in almost all cases.

This longer form has some useful additions and advantages over typical ROIs. Specifically:

- It meets the special standards for requesting/releasing drug and alcohol treatment records, in section C.

- The last part of section C allows re-release of records created by others and in your possession (and allowed by HIPAA), but this may be against your local rules. Although this may be acceptable in an emergency or for some records whose originals cannot be obtained, it has long been standard policy to direct any requester to seek others' records from their original sources. Records in your possession may not be the latest and most accurate versions; also, you may not be able to explain all of their contents to your client so that the client can offer fully informed consent to their release. (See also the third variation on releasing records, Section 8.3.)

- Section D asks for the purposes to which the information will be put, and it offers some options. Others you might add include the following: keeping family members/significant other informed; personal use by the client; mandated treatment; and responding to a subpoena/court order from [name of source].

- Section E, permitting consultation, specifically allows telephone contacts which is both a convenience and accommodates flexibility.

- In the medical community, an immediate response to a referral is the standard—as

[FORM 8.2—Use the top of this page for your letterhead. Before using this form, revise the <u>underlined text</u> to suit your practice.]

# Authorization to Release Confidential Records and Information

❑ A previous Release of Information (ROI) dated ____/____/____ is revoked by this ROI. The recipient identified in the previous ROI may be informed that that ROI has been revoked.

**A.** Identifying information about me/the patient

Name: _____  Date of birth: ____/____/____

Other name(s) used/AKA: _____

Current address: _____

Address at time of treatment: _____

Current phone(s): _____  <u>Social Security #:</u> _____  Medical record #: _____

Name of parent/guardian (if applicable): _____  Phone #: _____

Address of parent/guardian: _____

**B.** Because I believe it is in my/our best interest, I hereby authorize the release of information described below:

<table>
<tr><td>

**FROM:  SOURCE**

Person or organization:

_____

Address: _____

_____

Phone: _____  Fax number: _____

Secure email: _____

Attention of: _____

</td><td>

**TO:  RECIPIENT**

Person or organization:

_____

Address: _____

_____

Phone: _____  Fax number: _____

Secure email: _____

Attention of: _____

</td></tr>
</table>

**C.** The records to be disclosed are marked by an × in the boxes below. The items *not* to be released have a line drawn through them. All episodes of care are to be included unless page numbers and/or dates are indicated.

❑ Inpatient or outpatient treatment records for physical/medical and/or psychological, psychiatric, or emotional illness

❑ Date(s) of inpatient admission: ____/____/____ to ____/____/____

❑ Date(s) of outpatient treatment: ____/____/____ to ____/____/____

❑ Other identifing information about the service(s) rendered: _____

   ❑ Psychological evaluation(s) or testing records, and behavioral observations or checklists completed by any staff member or by the patient

   ❑ Psychiatric evaluations, reports, or treatment notes and summaries

   ❑ Admission and discharge summaries

*(continued)*

- ❑ Treatment plans, recovery plans, aftercare plans
- ❑ Social, family, developmental histories
- ❑ Assessments with diagnoses, prognoses, and recommendations, and all similar documents
- ❑ Workshop reports and other vocational evaluations and reports
- ❑ Academic or educational records

- ❑ Information about how the patient's condition affects or has affected his or her ability to complete tasks, activities of daily living, or ability to work
- ❑ Billing records
- ❑ A letter containing dates of treatment(s) and a summary of progress

❑ Other records: _____

HIV-related information and drug and alcohol information contained in these records will be released under this consent unless indicated here:  ❑ Do not release HIV-related information.  ❑ Do not release drug and alcohol information.

❑ I authorize the re-release of any information obtained from other sources presently in the records of the person or facility indicated in section B.

**D.** I authorize the transfer of these records for the following purpose(s) or uses:

❑ Further mental health evaluation, treatment, or care  ❑ Rehabilitation program development or services

❑ Treatment planning  ❑ Research  ❑ Qualification for services or benefits

❑ Other: _____

_____

**E.** I authorize the Source named in section B above to speak by telephone and/or face to face with the Recipient in section B about the reasons for my/the patient's referral, any relevant history or diagnoses, and other similar information that can assist with my/the patient's receiving treatment or being evaluated or referred elsewhere.

**F.** I understand the consequences if I refuse to allow this release. I may not receive services by the recipient or at the recipient organization. The cost of services I may receive may not be reimbursed to any degree and so will be entirely my responsibility. I may not be eligible for programs or services that could be beneficial to me.  ❑ Other consequences have been explained to me. My consent is fully voluntary.

**G.** This request/authorization to release confidential information is being made in compliance with the terms of the Privacy Act of 1974 (Public Law 93-579) and the Freedom of Information Act of 1974 (Public Law 93-502), and pursuant to Federal Rule of Evidence 1158 (Inspection and Copying of Records upon Patient's Written Authorization). This form is to serve as both a general authorization, and a special authorization to release information under the Drug Abuse Office and Treatment Act of 1972 (Public Law 92-255), the Comprehensive Alcohol Abuse and Alcoholism Prevention, Treatment and Rehabilitation Act Amendments of 1974 (Public Law 93-282), the Veterans Omnibus Health Care Act of 1976 (Public Law 94-581), and the Veterans Benefit and Services Act of 1988 (Public Law 100-322). It is also in compliance with 42 C.F.R. Part 2 (Public Law 93-282), which prohibits further disclosure without the express written consent of the person to whom it pertains, or as otherwise permitted by such regulations. It is in compliance with the Health Insurance Portability and Accountability Act (HIPAA) of 1996, Public Law 104-191, and with the Health Information Technology for Economic and Clinical Health (HITECH) Act of 2009, Public Law 111-5.

**H.** I understand that if the person or organization that receives this information is not a health care provider or health care insurer (or other covered entity under HIPAA), the information may no longer be protected by federal privacy regulations. It may, however, be protected under other laws and regulations. I understand that the Source of the information has no control of it after it has left the Source's premises.

**I.** In consideration of this consent, I hereby release the Source of the records from any and all liability arising from the release of these records.

*(continued)*

**J.** I understand that I may cancel and revoke this ROI authorization, but that doing this will not bring back the information that was released before the ROI was revoked. I can do this at any time by writing to the person or organization named in paragraph B as the Source telling them that I want the ROI revoked.

If I do not revoke this ROI authorization, it will automatically expire ❑ 90 days from the date I signed it OR ❑ on this date: ____/____/____ OR ❑ when this event about me occurs: _____ OR ❑ when the use or purpose of this information about me is completed.

**K.** I agree that a photocopy of this form is acceptable, but it must be individually signed by me, the releaser, and a witness if necessary.

**L.** I have been informed of the risks to privacy and limitations on confidentiality of the use of facsimile machines and electronic means of information transfer, and I accept these.

**M.** I understand that I have the right to inspect and receive copies of the information to be released.

❑ I have OR ❑ I have not reviewed the records to be released.

**N.** I understand that the Source will not receive compensation for the disclosure of this information.

**O.** I will pay a reasonable fee for the copying/printing and postage or other delivery costs (if I choose these records to be sent) but will not have to pay for the retrieval of these records.

**P.** I have had the provisions of this form explained to me and believe that I fully understand this ROI, including the nature of the records, their contents, and the likely consequences and implications of their release or of my refusal to release them. I also understand that I have the right to receive a copy of this form upon my request.

**Q.** Signatures:

_____  _____  ____/____/____
Signature of patient                           Printed name                                 Date

_____  _____
Signature of parent/guardian/representative if needed            Printed name

_____  ____/____/____
Relationship                                       Date

I witnessed that the person understood the nature of this ROI and freely gave his or her consent, but was physically unable to provide a signature.

_____  _____  ____/____/____
Signature of witness                           Printed name                                 Date

(A second witness is needed if person is unable to give oral consent.)

**R.** I, a mental health professional, have discussed the issues above with the patient and/or his or her parent or guardian. My observations of behavior and responses give me no reason to believe that this person is not fully competent to give informed, competent, and willing consent.

_____  _____  ____/____/____
Signature of professional                     Printed name                                 Date

❑ Copy for patient or parent/guardian ❑ Copy for Source of records ❑ Copy for Recipient of records

are general feedback as soon as you have seen the client, and a written note in the next 2–3 business days. If you conform to this standard, you will receive more referrals. Therefore, you should clarify what you can say to the referrer as soon as possible.

The **standard message to the referring PCP** includes an expression of gratitude for her or his confidence in you; a diagnosis or diagnostic process; a preliminary treatment plan or goals; and a promise to keep the referrer informed of progress and outcome. If you are sending the person on, tell the referrer that and explain why (this is referrer education and can improve the appropriateness of the next referrals). You might also ask the referrer for any information that he or she believes would be helpful for you to have.

If you are going to have extensive discussions with the person who referred the client to you, having a completed ROI protects you more than the general "permission to consult," which is sought in Form 6.6 at intake.

Should the client decide that no information should go to the PCP, ask to be allowed simply to confirm the client's completing the referral, or perhaps just call and thank the referrer for a referral without mentioning the client's name.

- Section F asserts the voluntariness of the consent and allows the client to refuse to allow you to obtain records. This option is from HIPAA and is aimed at preventing nontreating CEs such as insurers from requiring more information than is present in routine progress notes in order for them to pay benefits (this would be "conditioning of benefits"). You might protectively refuse to treat a client who refuses to allow you to obtain past records, but when you explain the point, almost all clients will agree to let you get records.

- ELZ has used Form 8.2 when he had little confidence in the ethical sophistication of the professional to whom he was sending information. It contains, in section G, formal and legal language that may impress its recipient, and it cites all the regulations. It may thus educate (or intimidate) the recipient into following ethical practices, such as fully informing the client about what is to be released and what will be done with the information.

- Part I includes a release of liability.

- Part K adds an authorization to make copies for sending multiple records or keeping some copies for later use.

- Part L documents the client's acceptance of the inevitable and unforeseeable risks of transferring information by electronic means, such as fax, email, and other methods that are not yet common. Informed consent to this is an ethical responsibility (see APA, 2010, Standard 4.02c).

- Section N asserts that you won't be paid for providing your records. This is from HIPAA's rules on the marketing of PHI.

- In section Q, a witness is needed only when the client consents (perhaps orally) but cannot create a legitimate signature.

- Part R offers your opinion that the signer is competent.

As always, you can tailor this form to your needs in various ways.

- You may want to add any other specific records you regularly request to the list in section C.

- If you are not doing treatment, you might want to change the wording at the end of section F to indicate your need and the uses for the disclosure of the records.

- For some additional protection in section H, you might include a statement like this: "I understand and agree that in no event shall [the releaser] be liable to me, or my heirs, executors, or assigns, for any reason arising from [the releaser's] disclosure or release of my records by acting in good faith and depending on this authorization."

- Releases must have time limits. In section J of Form 8.2 it says "90 days," but if that is insufficient, you can replace it with this sentence: "It shall be valid no longer than is reasonably necessary to meet the purposes stated above, and not to exceed 1 year."

- You can add this sentence to section M: "This therapist and I have explored the likely consequences of waiving the privilege of confidentiality."

- In regard to the signatures (section Q), you might want to consider that the older a child is, the more his or her wishes should be considered and honored. So even if your state does not legally give power to an adolescent, you might want to make the adolescent a participant by having him or her sign the form to indicate "assent."

- Another point concerns who has the authority to release a child's records. In any contentious situation, you might add another signature line and require both parents' signatures.

Many ROI forms can be found on the Internet by searching for "HIPAA-compliant authorization for the release of patient information pursuant to 45 C.F.R. 164.508."

### A Briefer Request/Release Form

**FORM 8.3**  Form 8.3 is a simple, multipurpose, one-page ROI document and should meet some of your needs. It may be best used when you simply need permission to talk to a client's referrer or to request a completely routine form or two. It supports talking to a referral source after termination of treatment. It can be used for a child or an adult, to obtain or to release records. It leaves spaces to write in some specifics. It does not support the release of drug and alcohol information or HIV-related records.

## 8.5  More Specific Releases of Information

### Releasing Information to an Attorney

Health care professionals and lawyers are often in conflict, and HIPAA has made these struggles even more complicated. We often receive subpoenas with invalid generic "releases" such as "Send me all your records." The safest and usually simplest response is to write back asking the lawyer to have the client complete the ROI form you enclose. Form 8.3 contains all of the elements required for a valid authorization (see HIPAA, Section 164.508(c)(1–3)) and information to prevent its being defective (HIPAA's Privacy Rule and Section 164.508(b)(2)).

# Authorization to Release Confidential Records and Information

**A.** Identifying information about me/the patient

Name: _____  Date of birth: ____/____/____

Current phone(s): _____  Social Security #: _____  Medical record #: _____

Name of parent/guardian (if applicable): _____  Phone #: _____

**B.** Because I believe it is in my/our best interest, I authorize the release of information described below:

| **FROM:** SOURCE | **TO:** RECIPIENT |
|---|---|
| Person or organization: <br><br> _____ | Person or organization: <br><br> _____ |
| Address: _____ <br><br> _____ | Address: _____ <br><br> _____ |
| Phone: _____ Fax number: _____ | Phone: _____ Fax number: _____ |
| Secure email: _____ | Secure email: _____ |

**C.** The records to be disclosed are marked by an × in the boxes below. The items *not* to be released have a line ~~drawn~~ through them. All episodes of care are to be included unless page numbers and/or dates are indicated.

❑ Inpatient or outpatient treatment records for physical/medical and/or psychological, psychiatric, or emotional illness

❑ Date(s) of inpatient admission: ____/____/____ to ____/____/____

❑ Date(s) of outpatient treatment: ____/____/____ to ____/____/____

❑ Other identifying information about the service(s) rendered: _____

  ❑ Social, family, developmental histories

  ❑ Assessments with diagnoses, prognoses, and recommendations, and all similar documents

  ❑ Academic or educational records

  ❑ Information about how the patient's condition affects or has affected his or her ability to complete tasks, activities of daily living, or ability to work

  ❑ Billing records

❑ Other records: _____

**D.** I authorize the transfer of these records for the following purpose(s) or uses:

❑ Further mental health evaluation, treatment, or care

❑ Treatment planning  ❑ Qualification for services or benefits

❑ Other: _____

*(continued)*

**FORM 8.3. Briefer form for requesting or releasing confidential records and information (p. 1 of 2).**

**E.** I authorize the Source named in section B above to share by telephone and/or face to face with the Recipient professional in section B any information that can assist with my/the patient's receiving treatment.

**F.** I understand the consequences if I refuse to allow this release. My consent is fully voluntary.

**G.** I understand that the Source of the information has no control of it after it has left the Source's premises.

**H.** I understand that I may revoke this ROI authorization, but that doing this will not bring back the information that was released before the date of the revocation. I can do this at any time by writing to the Source named in section B. If I do not void or cancel this ROI authorization, it will automatically expire 90 days from the date I signed it.

**I.** I have had the provisions of this form explained to me and believe that I fully understand this ROI.

**J.** Signatures:

_____     _____     ____/____/____

            Signature of patient                           Printed name                   Date

_____     _____

Signature of parent/guardian/representative if needed                   Printed name

_____     ____/____/____

            Relationship                   Date

❑ Copy for patient or parent/guardian   ❑ Copy for Source of records   ❑ Copy for Recipient of records

429

Other complications include the following:

- Clients have privilege with their lawyers, and this is the highest degree of confidentiality. However, lawyers are not CEs and do not have to comply with HIPAA's expectations.

- The lawyer must provide to the CE "satisfactory assurances" of confidentiality, as described in Sections 164.512(e)(1)(ii)(A) and 164.512(e)(1)(ii)(B) of HIPAA, and you can ask for proof of what the lawyer is doing to secure the records to be safest.

- Attorneys who work with CEs may be their BAs; if so, they will need to complete BA contracts and protect the PHI. HIPAA requires that the PHI be returned to the individual or destroyed after litigation, but this may conflict with a lawyer's ethical rules and the need to maintain records to address future litigation or administration risks. BAs should assure that retained PHI is kept confidential and privileged after the relationship ends. To maintain the privacy of the PHI, both sides might sign a qualified protective order so that the information will only be used for the litigation.

- Under HIPAA, individuals do not have a right to access their PHI if it is created in anticipation of litigation. Parts of the record might not have been created for these legal purposes and so might be accessed.

- For situations when lawyers seek test materials and protocols, see the Section 8.3 discussion of the sixth variation on sending records.

Incidentally, if you are providing testing or testimony for a client, you should not agree to receive payment only if the client wins a judgment. Contingency fee arrangements could prejudice your professional opinion, make it appear distorted (and therefore worthless), and compromise your reputation. You can be certain that opposing counsel will ask you about your fee arrangement. If your fee is contingent, this will be used as a means of disparaging your findings. The number of similar evaluations and testimonies you have done can also be used to present you either as inexperienced or as a possible "hired gun" if you do a lot of testifying. You should insist on being paid in full before submitting a final version of a report or a retainer before providing any kind of testimony.

When we enter the forensic arena, we clinicians may believe that our knowledge is transferable; it is not, and we become very vulnerable there. Words have different meaning in the forensic context. Every case is different, and so the general ideas provided above are educational and not legal advice. You should always consult with your lawyer and defer to the lawyer's advice on these matters.

Bruce Borkosky, PsyD, PA, of Sebring, FL, has posted an extremely educational form, Informed Consent to Disclose Records to the Legal System (see also Borkosky & Smith, 2015), on his website to educate clients before such a release (http://www.fl-forensic.com/forms). A related form is his Informed Consent for Civil Cases.

## Releasing Information to the Client's Family

What should a therapist tell the client's family about the client? There is always the potential for conflict between a family's legitimate right to information about its members and the therapist's obligation to keep some information confidential. For example, the spouse of a client may ask a question, or the adult child of an older client may inquire. Unless the issue of who has a right to know what is clarified, staff members may refuse to provide simple and nondisruptive information about a client to an appropriate family member, because "We do not reveal client information." This response has apparently become more widespread with common misunderstandings of the HIPAA regulations.

However, Section 164.510(b)(1)(i) of HIPAA does allow release of PHI that is "directly relevant to . . . the individual's care or payment . . . [or] to the individual's health care" to a "family member, other relative, or close personal friend . . . or any other person identified by the individual" without an authorization and based solely on the consent form signed with the NPP. Getting a form such as Form 8.4 signed early in treatment can lessen problems. If you intend to release significantly different information to different persons or relatives, use several versions of this form. HIPAA has been interpreted to include same-sex marriage partners under this kind of release (see http://www.hhs.gov/ocr/privacy/hipaa/understanding/special/samesexmarriage/index.html).

**FORM 8.4**   Form 8.4, adapted from Marsh (1995), can empower both the client and family by making the process and content of family communications more explicit and informed. It sets boundaries, specifies contact persons, and then allows you to negotiate the exact information to be supplied with all parties.

### A Release-of-Records Cover Letter

It is standard practice to provide a cover letter to accompany any records you send to another professional or organization; this informs the recipient of his or her legal and ethical responsibilities. Form 8.5 combines several functions: It explains the privacy issues, addresses many of the possible defects in the ROI you received, and offers many reasons for refusing to send records. Its thoroughness can save you effort and impress medical record sophisticates (such as registered record librarians, some physicians, and defense lawyers). However, you may have to modify it to suit your setting, local laws, and practice.

**FORM 8.5**

The information in records can become outdated, inaccurate, and misleading, and releasing it can be harmful to the client's interests. The APA's record-keeping guidelines (APA, Committee on Professional Practice and Standards, 2007) and ethics code (APA, 2010, Standard 9.08) require that when this is the case, you clearly indicate their limited utility or invalidity. This is incorporated into the form. You may want to change the "I/we" format to just "I" or just "we." You may charge a "reasonable" amount for copying and mailing records, but not for locating or organizing them.

## 8.6   Confidentiality When Faxing Records or Sending Email

If you send clinical information by fax machine, you risk compromising its confidentiality—not so much in its transmission, but before it is sent and after it is received. It could be mistakenly sent to the wrong person or department by misdialing, or could be read by those at your end who should not have access, such as untrained workers. If you use online fax services, check to see that they are HIPAA-compliant (e.g., http://www.efax.com will sign BA contracts). Make sure that at least the parts of your computer containing PHI are encrypted. Also, you should make certain that the rules of confidentiality (see Section 8.1) are part of the orientation of *all* new staff members in your practice, and some

## Authorization to Release Confidential Information to Family Members

**A.** I, _____, Date of birth: ___/___/___, <u>Social Security #</u>: _____, understand that the purpose of this release is to assist with my/this patient's treatment by improving communication between professional service providers or agencies and the important individual(s) in my/the patient's life.

**B.** To further this goal, I authorize _____ to release the below-specified information regarding me/the patient to the individual(s) listed below, and to receive information from them in any format including by telephone. I have been informed of the risks to privacy of the use of electronic means of information transfer, and I accept these.

**C.** The information to be disclosed is marked by an × in the boxes below, and any items not to be released have a line ~~drawn~~ through them:

❑ Name of my therapist(s)   ❑ Name of case manager   ❑ Name(s) of treatment program(s)

❑ Diagnoses   ❑ Prognoses   ❑ Treatment plan   ❑ Scheduled appointments and attendance

❑ Progress notes   ❑ Compliance with treatment   ❑ Discharge plans   ❑ Treatment summary

❑ Psychological or other evaluations   ❑ Medications   ❑ Other: _____

**D.** This information is to be disclosed to these persons, who have the indicated relationship to me/the patient:

_____          _____
Name of person                                            Relationship

_____          _____
Name of person                                            Relationship

_____          _____
Name of person                                            Relationship

**E.** I understand that I may revoke this release at any time, except to the extent that it has already been acted upon. This release will expire  ❑ 1 year from this date OR  ❑ upon my discharge from treatment by this agency or by the person specified above OR  ❑ under these circumstances: _____

**F.** Signatures:

_____          _____          ___/___/___
Signature of patient                                   Printed name                                          Date

*(continued)*

_____    _____
Signature of parent/guardian/representative if needed                Printed name

_____    ____/____/____
                    Relationship                              Date

I witnessed that the person understood the nature of this request/authorization and freely gave his or her consent, but was physically unable to provide a signature.

_____    _____    ____/____/____
            Signature of witness                        Printed name                      Date

_____    ____/____/____
                    Relationship                              Date

❑ Copy for patient or parent/guardian   ❑ Copy for provider/therapist/case manager

❑ Copy for family member

To: _____

Date: ____/____/____

Re: the following patient: _____ Date of birth: ____/___/___

Regarding the information you requested in a letter or release of information (ROI) or consent or authorization to release information or records form dated ____/____/___:

❑ **Please find attached the records or information you requested** on the above-named patient. The charge for preparing these records is $____. Please forward this amount with the same courtesy and dispatch as I/we have used in providing this information to you. Thank you.

Also, please note the following points:

1. *Protected-information disclosure notice: Drug and alcohol disclosure.* This information has been disclosed to you from records whose confidentiality is protected by state and federal law. Federal regulations (42 C.F.R. Part 2, Sections 2.31(a) and 2.33) and state regulations prohibit you from making any further disclosure of it without the specific written consent of the person to whom it pertains, or as otherwise permitted by such regulations. A general authorization for the release of medical or other information is not sufficient for this purpose. These regulations provide for a fine of up to $500 for the first offense and up to $5,000 for each subsequent offense.

2. This is strictly confidential material and is for the information of only the person to whom it is addressed. I/we cannot accept any responsibility if it is made available to any other person, *including the patient.* Redisclosure or retransfer of these records may be prohibited, and such redisclosure may subject you to civil and criminal liability.

3. Federal and state rules restrict use of this information to criminally investigate or prosecute any patient receiving services for alcohol or drug use or for a substance use disorder.

4. Because assessments it might contain were made in the past, they may no longer be valid. The information may be outdated, inaccurate, and misleading, and so may be against the client's interests.

❑ I/we have completed the form or forms you sent and have enclosed them.

❑ You have sent a form for me/us to complete, which will take some of my professional time. If you wish this done, please forward, in the next 10 days, the sum of $____ to pay for the additional service.

❑ **I/we am unable to comply with your request for these records, because:**

　❑ Enclosed is the only available information.

　❑ No authorization or release was enclosed with your request. I/we cannot release records without such an authorization or release.

　❑ The authorization enclosed was deficient because it is or was:

　　❑ Not dated, or not dated after treatment ended.

　　❑ Dated more than 90 days prior to the receipt of your request, and so has expired.

*(continued)*

❑ Not sufficiently specific. Please indicate more specifically what information is requested.

❑ Not legally adequate.

❑ For a minor patient, but had no signed authorization by one or both parents or a guardian. (If the latter is the case, proof of guardianship is also required.)

❑ For an emancipated minor, and so a parent's or guardian's signature is not acceptable.

❑ Signed by someone other than the patient. Such authorizations must be signed by the patient unless the patient is physically or mentally unable to do so.

❑ Signed illegibly, and so we are unable to verify that it is the signature of the patient.

❑ Your request/authorization/release of records/information form does not conform to the requirements of state and federal regulations covering the release of confidential records. Because of the nature of the information contained in this record, a general medical consent form cannot be accepted. Specifically, it _____ or ❑ we have enclosed a release form for you to execute.

❑ The records you have asked for no longer exist. All records are destroyed ____ years following the date of the last clinical contact. Records of minor patients (14 years and younger) are retained for ____ years after they are no longer minors, and are then destroyed.

❑ According to our records, this information was sent to you on ____/____/____. If you have not received it, please investigate your reception methods, as there may have been an unauthorized release of protected health information. You may send another copy of your ROI form if it is still valid.

❑ Enclosed are the remaining records you requested. The other records were sent to you on ____/____/____.

❑ The records you are seeking are not complete at this time. We will send the records as soon as they are completed.

❑ After a thorough search of our files, I/we are unable to locate any record on this person with the information you provided. Perhaps he or she may have used another name, or a different spelling. If you can provide additional identifying information, we will search our records again. I certify by my signature below that, to the best of my knowledge, no records with the present information exist in our files.

❑ I/we have not provided service to this person during the time period covered by the release.

❑ I/we did not originate the records you requested, and so cannot release them.

❑ The information you requested is not available here. You might try contacting _____.

❑ The patient is deceased, so an authorization must be signed by the administrator of the estate or court officer and appropriate documentation is required (i.e., death certificate/short form, proof of being the executor of the patient's estate, letters of administration, or power of attorney, etc.).

❑ It is our policy that this information is not released directly to patients or families because of the potential for its misinterpretation, misuse, or misunderstanding. Because it may have been generated to address psychological distress and psychopathology, there may be only slight or no attention paid to strengths and positive characteristics of the client. Because evaluations it might contain were made some time ago they may no longer be valid. Statements in it require interpretation and explanation by an appropriately trained and licensed professional. If you want this information released, please send the name and address of a professional who would understand this information and a suitable ROI form or consent-to-release-records form.

❑ Other reason: _____

If you have any questions, please do not hesitate to contact me/us. If you need additional information, please return this letter with your second request for information or records.

| _____ | _____ |
| :---: | :---: |
| Signature | Printed name |

| _____ | ____/____/____ |
| :---: | :---: |
| Title | Date |

refresher training should be provided. You, the professional, are the only one who will be held responsible for violations.

Barton Bernstein, an attorney in Dallas, TX, has suggested adding a paragraph to your intake forms to let clients know that you may be faxing clinical data to their MCOs ("Legal Issues," 1992). A warning like this has been included in the client information brochure in this book (see Section 5.2 and the CD) and is part of the APA code of ethics (APA, 2010, Standard 4.02c).

A "HIPAA warning" has become a standard fixture at the end of all faxes and emails. It can be easily added to the automatic "cover sheet" used with faxes or inserted into your email's "signatures" to make it routine. Below are two versions, the first more conversational.

---

**Confidentiality Warning!!**

This communication may be **confidential and legally privileged.** If you are not the person to whom it is addressed, do not read it, copy it, or let anyone else besides the addressee see it. Please respect the confidentiality of this personal information, and respect the federal and state laws that protect its confidentiality. If this has been transmitted to you by mistake, we ask you to extend the courtesy of calling us back at the voice number listed above and telling us what went wrong. Thank you very much.

---

The following more legalistic version is based on the article cited above ("Legal Issues," 1992).

---

**Confidentiality Warning!!**

The information contained in this fax message is intended only for the personal and confidential use of the designated recipient or entity named above. As such, this communication is **legally privileged, confidential, and exempt from disclosure under applicable law.** If the reader or actual recipient is not the intended recipient or an agent or employee responsible for delivering it to the intended recipient, you are hereby notified that you have received this document in error, and that any review, dissemination, distribution, or copying of this message is strictly prohibited by federal and state laws with civil penalties. If you have received this communication in error, we apologize for any inconvenience. We would appreciate your notifying us immediately by phone and then returning the original to us by the U.S. Postal Service at the address listed above. Thank you.

---

## 8.7   Confidentiality Notifications

The sample notices follow. As indicated below, many are from Zuckerman (2010). Note that your state may have additional requirements for the release of HIV-related information or drug and alcohol information, as Pennsylvania does. If so, you may need to add the exact phrasing or citation of the appropriate laws to your releases.

**Confidential patient/client information**

**Warning:** This report may contain sensitive client information. You must protect this document as confidential medical information. Not to be duplicated. Please handle, store, and dispose of properly.

This information has been disclosed to you from records protected by federal confidentiality rules (42 C.F.R. Part 2, Public Law 93-282) and state law [e.g., Pennsylvania Law 7100-111-4]. These regulations prohibit you from making any further disclosure of this information unless further disclosure is expressly permitted by the written consent of the person to whom it pertains or as otherwise permitted by 42 C.F.R. Part 2. A general authorization for the release of information is not sufficient for this purpose. The federal rules restrict any use of the information to criminally investigate or prosecute any alcohol or drug abuse client. [Zuckerman, 2010, p. 90]

This report may contain client information. Release it only to professionals capable of ethically and professionally interpreting and understanding the information it contains. [Zuckerman, 2010, p. 90]

It is inappropriate to release the information contained herein directly to the client or other parties. If this information is released to interested individuals before they are afforded an opportunity to discuss its meaning with a trained mental health professional, it is likely that the content of the report may be misunderstood, leading to emotional distress on the part of the uninformed reader. [Zuckerman, 2010, p. 90]

This information is not to be used against the interests of the subject of this report. [Zuckerman, 2010, p. 90]

Persons or entities granted access to this record may discuss this information with the client only insofar as necessary to represent the client in legal proceedings or other matters for which this record has been legally released. [Zuckerman, 2010, p. 90]

**For a Child**

The contents of this report have/have not been shared with the child's parent(s)/guardian. She/he/they may review this report with the evaluator or his/her specific designee. Copies of this report may be released only by the evaluator or his/her departmental administrator, or in accord with the school district's policy. [Zuckerman, 2010, p. 90]

The information contained in this report is private, privileged, and confidential. It cannot be released outside the school system except by the examining psychologist/evaluator/creator of this report, upon receipt of written consent by the parent or guardian. Not to be duplicated or transmitted. [Zuckerman, 2010, p. 91]

# 8.8   **Business Associates and Privacy**

HIPAA specifies "safeguards" that we CEs must develop to prevent "unauthorized disclosures" of PHI in our possession. Of course, we must train (see Form 1.2) and supervise our employees ("W-2 employees") and independent contractors ("1099 employees")—but we also contract with others, our BAs, to perform such services for us as sending out our bills, answering our phones, updating and repairing our computers and networks, and the like. To do these things, they must "acquire," "access," "use," and perhaps "disclose" (to their subcontractors) client PHI, and so HIPAA requires that we enter into "BA contracts" in which they promise to protect our PHI to the same degree as we do with methods adapted to their functions. You should know that most of the breaches of privacy found and prosecuted by under HIPAA are due to failures on the part of BAs. Breach statistics are reported monthly (see http://www.Melamedia.com).

We do not include in this book any sample BA contracts, because they should be tailored to each kind of BA. Since most type of businesses that could be BAs have developed these contracts, just ask your BAs for theirs, or do an Internet search.

## 8.9   Privacy Violations

### Unauthorized Disclosures and Breaches

HIPAA's Omnibus Final Rule of 2013 has enlarged the original term "unauthorized disclosures" to include "breaches," defined as follows: "Breach means the acquisition, access, use, or disclosure of protected health information in a manner not permitted . . . which compromises the security or privacy of the protected health information" (45 C.F.R. Section 164.402).

We have to read this legal language carefully. It expands "unauthorized disclosure" to include "acquisition" (even without viewing the PHI or opening it on a computer) and "access" (viewing the PHI even if no use was made of it), as well as the previous "use" (basing actions on the PHI); all of these are "breaches." Furthermore, no evidence of harm or of potential harm is required to demonstrate a breach, as was previously the case.

The majority of breaches are due to burglary, theft, or misplacing of computers or drives. The DHHS requires that in a breach involving fewer than 500 persons, clinicians must notify the DHHS within 60 calendar days of discovering the breach and send a first-class letter (or email) to each individual whose privacy was compromised. The notification letter must include a brief description of what happened; the type of information disclosed; any steps individuals should take to protect themselves; a description of what is being done to investigate the breach and to mitigate its impact (such as providing credit protection); and contact information so individuals can find out more information. If 10 or more persons cannot be notified, a conspicuous notice must be placed in a local print or broadcast medium in the geographical area where the breach occurred. These burdensome consequences of a breach—the notification procedures—are preventable with encryption of the PHI. Although breaches of encrypted data have to be investigated, documented, and reported to the DHHS (http://www.hhs.gov/ocr/privacy/hipaa/administrative/breachnotificationrule/brinstruction.html), the costs and embarrassment of broad public notification are avoided.

### Complaints and Reports of Privacy Violations

**Take any and all complaints or reports of problems seriously. They can be the harbingers of ethics complaints, licensing board actions, or worse. Act immediately.**

As part of your NPP (see Section 6.4), you must offer a complaint procedure for clients to report violations of their own or others' privacy. Although general complaints are not the same as reports of privacy violations, it is simpler and more convenient to combine the two types and have them both addressed by your practice's compliance officer. Also, having a functioning complaint mechanism is part of good client relations and a valuable means of heading off more serious problems.

## A Sample Complaint Form

**FORM 8.6**   In the sample complaint form provided here (Form 8.6), we have combined a variety of problems that might arise, and have deliberately avoided the use of the word "complaint." One can have a felt "problem" long before articulating a "complaint," and so this form may detect difficulties long before they turn into actions like HIPAA complaints.

- Although HIPAA does not require anonymity to be offered, reports may be more forthcoming with it, and so Form 8.6 incorporates it.

- The form assumes that you work in a multitherapist office. Revise it for solo or small practices.

## Online Complaint Filing

A further step in resolving a complaint of a privacy violation is having the client file a complaint with the Office of Civil Rights, which is responsible for investigating complaints of HIPAA privacy violations. The forms and procedures are available online in several languages (http://www.hhs.gov/ocr/privacy/hipaa/complaints/index.html).

[FORM 8.6—Use the top of this page for your letterhead. Before using this form, review the blanks and alter it for a single clinician's office]

# Is There a Problem?

If you are not satisfied with your experiences in our office, we really want to hear from you. Please tell us. If you have a problem with anything about our practice, first speak with one of our staff.

- If the problem is with your insurance, bills, or payment, talk to _____, who is our _____.

- If the problem is with your therapy, talk to your therapist first. Most often it can be resolved, but if not, he or she will explain what to do next and what your options are.

- If you believe there has been a violation of the confidentiality or the privacy of your records, speak to our compliance officer, _____, to help us clarify and fix the situation. You can reach this person at _____.

- If you don't know whom to talk to about a problem, talk to our compliance officer for assistance.

If you would prefer to write about the situation, please fill out this simple form so we can investigate it. We will try our best to fix it, and to repair any damage that may have happened. Bringing a problem to our attention will not in any way limit your care here or cause us to take any actions against you.

If you wish to remain anonymous, you do not have to fill in the lines marked with an asterisk (*). But if you want a response from us, please do complete those items. Thank you.

*Client's name: _____  *Date of birth: ___/___/___  *Phone: _____

What is or was the problem? _____

_____

_____

_____

What would you like to see done about the problem? _____

_____

_____

_____  ___/___/___
　　　　　*Signature of client or his or her personal representative　　　　　　　　　　Date

_____　　_____　　_____
*Printed name of client or personal representative　　*Relationship to the client　　*Description of personal representative's authority

**Note: If a name is given on the form, a response must be made to that person within 30 days from when you, the compliance officer, receive this form: ___/___/___. Indicate action(s) taken on a separate page.**

**FORM 8.6. A sample complaint form.** From *The Paper Office for the Digital Age, Fifth Edition*. Copyright © 2017 Edward L. Zuckerman and Keely Kolmes. Published by The Guilford Press. Permission to reproduce this material is granted to purchasers of this book for personal use or use with individual clients (see copyright page for details).

# CHAPTER 9

# Marketing Your Practice in the Digital Age

## 9.1 Marketing Your Practice Ethically

Marketing is required for the independent practice of psychotherapy. Clients will not just walk in off the street. We are specialists, and so we must attract clients' attention through advertising; giving presentations; writing about ourselves and our work for general audiences; or having clients referred to us by other professionals, insurers, ex-clients, and agencies. There are many ways to get your practice known to others, but one of the best is word of mouth, and so this chapter begins with a focus on reaching ex-clients and the professionals ("gatekeepers") who might refer clients to you. Your fellow clinicians will be excellent sources of referrals if they are simply (and repeatedly) informed of your availability and specialties. Below we describe several means for making your services better known. All such marketing must be done in line with the ethics of your professional discipline.

### Ethics and Traditional Marketing

As required by Standards 5.01 through 5.04 of the American Psychological Association (APA) ethics code (APA, 2010), you must be accurate in representations of your credentials, qualifications, and promises in advertisements, in all forms of publicity, and when offering workshops for the public.

Traditionally, therapists do not recruit active clients of other therapists. Some view this injunction as both overly "parental" (after all, these are adult and experienced consumers who can make informed choices) and perhaps not in the best interest of the clients (who you believe may receive better services from you than from their current therapists). The APA ethics code (APA, 2010) offers guidance that emphasizes consideration of the client's welfare, full discussion of these issues to minimize confusion and conflict, and proceeding with caution and sensitivity (Standards 5.06 and 10.04).

Asking for testimonials from *ex-clients* is not explicitly prohibited by the current ethics codes, except for the American Counseling Association's (ACA's) code (ACA, 2014), but psychologists have generally frowned on such testimonials because they are so easily slanted. It is likely that only those who liked your services would be asked to testify, and few testifiers have had comparable experience with competing services to give valid reports. Some might argue that ex-clients are susceptible to a therapist's "undue influence," especially if they consider returning to you in the future.

As noted in Section 2.1, beware of fee-splitting arrangements. Paying for referrals is common and ethical in many businesses, but psychologists' practices are not purely businesses. The APA ethics code (APA, 2010) specifically forbids this (in Standard 6.07), because being paid for making referrals to one service provider and not to another is likely to distort the referrer's views of what is best for clients. Although collegial friendships are acceptable, beware of any arrangement that looks like a *quid pro quo* exchange. You may have to assert this point with some potential referrers.

As the "gatekeeping" function becomes more professionalized by managed care organizations (MCOs) and the like, fewer people will use traditional ads and brochures, and referrals will be almost exclusively made through networks and websites. Coping with this trend is discussed at length below.

## Digital Ethics: Things That Seem Like Good Ideas but Aren't

Clinicians can get carried away with the possibilities of online marketing, but remember that we cannot violate professional ethics in pursuing these possibilities. Beware of the temptation to ask current clients to leave you a Yelp.com review. If you happen to have positive Yelp reviews, do *not* copy and paste them to your website. If you wish to direct people to your Yelp reviews, simply tell your site visitors to check out your Yelp reviews, and provide a link to these.

**Do not create groups for clients on sites that compromise client confidentiality** (Facebook.com, Meetup.com, etc.). This is inviting outsiders to peruse the list of members of (what should be) a confidential group. Also, these sites do not offer business associate (BA) contracts and thus are not appropriate places to store confidential information, such as who attends your therapy groups and what each group's purpose is.

Don't post tweets on Twitter or status updates on Facebook about your sessions as a way of "bragging" about your competence to work with particular issues and your clients' improvement. These may seem like obvious bad ideas, but one need only peek at what practitioners are doing online to see that it's easy to make these mistakes. Remember that confidentiality is our primary duty to those who use our services, and it can be all too easy to slip up in online environments. Most ethics codes note that we must only share what happens in psychotherapy with those who are directly involved in treatment, and that we should share the minimum amount of information necessary when we do so. The most recent revision of the ACA code of ethics (ACA, 2014) prohibits "friending" clients on social media sites, and this rule may be adopted by other disciplines in the near future.

Some clinicians have used online coupon companies to sell discounted services. We consider this a bad idea, for several reasons: (1) Such companies will acquire the names of people who wish to contact you for psychotherapy; (2) since they collect a percentage of your earnings from the number of coupons sold, you may be engaging in "fee splitting" (which, as noted above, is a violation of the APA ethics code); (3) this method of obtaining referrals does not allow us to screen for someone's suitability to receive our services; and

(4) the company may sell more appointments than we can accommodate in our practice, leaving people to wait months for an appointment that they may urgently need.

Here are some of the ethical ways to market online:

- Create a social media presence in which you share information related to your professional areas of interest and network with other providers. You can provide psychoeducation to consumers, but don't use these sites to interact with your current clients.

- Get involved in national and local online discussion groups. Be active on them. Be helpful. Be polite. Don't engage in "flame wars" (escalating arguments). If someone is looking for a referral and you know a good clinician, share the information. If you have book suggestions or articles that may help someone, share freely. If you can recommend someone to consult on a particular issue, do so. Become known for your helpfulness and your expertise in your unique areas of interest. In fact, it can be a boon if you have an area of interest that is less common. For example, KK works with kink-identified and polyamorous clients. She is one of just a few people who are identified as serving these specialty populations on a national email discussion group of over 1,000 clinicians. This has led to referrals and consultation requests from professionals across the country who are less familiar with alternative sexual practices and lifestyles.

- If you accidentally get into a kerfuffle in an online discussion exchange, be humble. Apologize. Take responsibility. Communications through email and postings are vulnerable to misinterpretation. Remember, you are attempting to create a professional impression here, and if you do not recognize when you've misspoken or been wrong, people may remember you for that. Keep in mind that some of your own clients may have access to these postings.

## 9.2   Traditional Forms of Marketing

Ex-clients are the best sources for referrals, especially soon after a successful episode of treatment, because they have already been persuaded of the value of your work. However, if you are just starting out in private practice, you will not yet have enough ex-clients to promote your good work. It can take years to build up enough satisfied customers (depending upon whether you do brief or long-term work and whether you are being sent referrals from insurance companies), so we offer other mechanisms in this section for getting your name out there in the interim.

### Talking about What You Love as a Marketing Method

If you are an extraverted person who finds it easy to talk to others, simply talking about what you love to do and offering your business card can be an effective way to let people know about your services and how you can help. A conversation in a cafe or a chat at a party may lead to a referral. Others who may pass along your information include teachers, neighbors, police officers, nurses, clinicians in other settings, and attorneys, as well as some of the less obvious possibilities noted below. But if you're introverted or are less comfortable talking about your work, then the tips below will also help you.

## Looking for Potential Referrers

A letter is a simple and effective way to tell potential referrers that you are available. However, be strategic about the recipients. KK made the rookie mistake of sending them to other psychotherapists, who were unlikely to be in need of her services and were often in direct competition for her clients.

Cast a wide net for potential referrers: any professionals with clients who present psychological issues they do not have the skills to address, and whom you can effectively treat. You may think first of physicians, but it can also be wise to introduce yourself to complementary healers in the area surrounding your office, such as chiropractors, massage therapists, acupuncturists, and others who may hear stories of people experiencing distress. They may be eager to direct their clients to someone who is trained to deal with these issues. If you wish to be more experimental, consider contacting bartenders and hairdressers. Or you might consider developing special services for the clients of financial planners, funeral directors, family law attorneys, and civil court judges.

When ELZ joined a local hospital's adjunct staff some years ago, he was not invited to meetings, and so he mainly met physicians in the medical library and at open Christmas parties. Other practice-building efforts led him to learn that the medical librarians were very helpful, as was the secretary of the medical staff. He also gave presentations to nurses on the units at shift changes (which may be inconvenient times in some cases) and had conversations with billing staff and others. These efforts allowed ELZ to build a full-time practice in a few months.

## A Letter for Seeking Referrals from Physicians and Other Medical Staff

Below is a letter ELZ sent to the hospital's medical staff (not just physicians, but occupational therapists, physical therapists, dentists, and podiatrists) to introduce himself to other providers. It will need to be tailored to your orientation, professional situation, methods, audience, and comparative advantages, but it is a useful model. Some physicians are more eager and accepting of psychological services (pediatricians, internal medicine), and some have no need for them (radiologists, pathologists). Keep the letter undated, as you should not send this announcement to many staff members at one time. If you do, you may be inundated with referrals to which you cannot respond. Try a few practices per month. Start with the small ones to learn the "local rules," and learn from your mistakes. Indicate what you *don't* do (e.g., testing or child therapy), as well as what you do, or you will get inappropriate referrals and annoy your referral sources. It will be advantageous to identify one or two specialties, so that the referrer has a hook on which to hang your name. Without these, you will blend into the undifferentiated mass of "service providers" and be ignored. Use "collaboration" or "consultation" to describe your practice model to more readily find acceptance. Additions to this letter might address costs indirectly by indicating which insurance panels you are on; whether you offer a sliding fee scale or do *pro bono* work; and whether you have a waiting list, and that you will refer any who cannot afford to see you to appropriate community resources. Being a Medicare provider is usually advantageous.

For some settings, if you are a psychologist, you may have to explain the APA ethics code's opposition to fee splitting.

[Letterhead]

[No date]

Dear Dr. _____:

May I take a moment of your time to briefly introduce myself? I've just joined you on the staff here at _____ Hospital, and I've opened an office for the general practice of clinical psychology in the Medical Arts Building.

I treat adults (but not children) for depression, anxieties, phobias, and similar emotional disorders, using behavioral and cognitive methods that have clear scientific support of their effectiveness and efficiency. They do not involve extensive exploration of a client's childhood or unconscious mind. Instead, my methods are active, directive, and educative; I aim at solving the problems the client faces here and now.

I am keenly interested in treating conditions such as _____, _____, and _____ in close cooperation with physicians, who would of course retain the overall medical responsibility for their patients.[1]

My background includes a PhD in clinical psychology from the University of Pittsburgh and a year-long full-time internship, both of which were approved by the American Psychological Association for training specifically in *clinical* psychology. I have worked for more than a dozen years in psychiatric hospitals, community mental health centers, and centers for the treatment of intellectual disability, as well as in consultation/liaison and independent practice. Because I am a fully licensed psychologist, my fees are often partly covered by a client's health insurance.

The research on the psychological needs of medical patients has uniformly indicated a high level of benefit from psychotherapeutic services. If I can be of any assistance to you or your patients, please do not hesitate to call on me.

I have been warmly welcomed here and eagerly anticipate productive years of providing effective services to clients. Since my office is close by, I would be happy to come to meet with you, even briefly, at your convenience.

Sincerely,

_____

[Signature]

P.S. I have been very active in the local psychotherapy community, and so if a patient of yours needs a specialized service, I may be able to refer him or her to someone who can meet this need. I would be happy to answer your questions or your patient's questions at any time, and I will respond to all referrals and calls very promptly.

Practice marketers advise that it is even better to call or visit a PCP's office and to set up a brief meeting with the PCP and relevant staff members. This can be done by speaking with the office manager. One of the office manager's tasks is to protect the PCP's time, so do not push hard to spend time with the PCP. Use this meeting to introduce yourself, learn about the PCP's practice, explain your services, and ask whether the PCP could use the support of

---

[1]This statement was included as a distinction from psychiatrists, who may take over cases, to the consternation of the primary care providers (PCPs).

a psychologist to refer clients to for these issues. When you visit, ask whether you can leave educational brochures in a rack in the waiting room. Although you might bring some cookies, be careful not to be seen as an equivalent to drug company representatives, who are a major source of food and annoyance to staff. ELZ has found that senior office staff members are better sources of referrals than PCPs, who often depend on their staffs for names and resources. After a visit, follow up with your letter (made more personal), thank the PCP and staff for their time, and include your cards.

It has been repeatedly established that physicians often do not spontaneously refer their medical patients for the psychotherapy their patients need. To change this, physicians must learn to recognize the patients' needs beyond the purely medical ones, and then need to have readily accessible clinician resources (you). A way to overcome the first obstacle is to educate physicians about the criteria for appropriate referral and effective treatment. This could be done by means of a checklist or a brief screening questionnaire that a physician can use with a patient. There are many such questionnaires available to assess depression or anxiety, but tailoring one to your methods is likely best. As for being easily available, you could provide to the PCP's office copies of a single-page, faxable Behavioral Health Referral form. It should include the identifying information of the patient and PCP's office; reasons for the referral; the patient's preferences about treatment; a limited release-of-information (ROI) section; and space to tell the PCP about your follow-up.

## Seeking Referrals for Group Therapy

We all know that group therapy can be very productive, time- and cost-efficient, and can address and resolve unique issues. Why don't mental health clinicians make better use of groups? The main reason is that they don't have a sufficient flow of clients to form groups on a timely basis. How then can you increase the flow of suitable referrals? By "publicizing" your groups to all potential referrers. A letter or notice that explains what the group is about and for whom it is appropriate can be circulated often and widely. Using a consistent format and graphics will make a cumulative impression. It should provide enough information so that the professional can make intelligent referrals. We suggest the following types of information:

- Group's name, consistent with the points below.

- Group's general purpose: Therapy? Support? Supervision? Education? Training?

- Group's focus: A psychiatric diagnosis? A medical condition? A common problem in living? A shared cultural identity or orientation? Other?

- Group's status: Is it a potential group or in existence? Is it newly forming or ongoing? Is it time-limited or open-ended?

- Criteria for both inclusion and exclusion: Age? Sex? Individuals or couples? Other?

- Group leaders' credentials: Highest degree, license information, relevant special training/experience.

- Leadership style or orientation: Cognitive? Behavioral? Psychoeducational? Psychodynamic? Other?

- Meeting logistics, if set: Meeting start date, location, day of the week, time, session length, frequency.

- Contact information for referrer questions: Name, street address, phone numbers (with best times to call), email address.

- Contact information for group leader(s), if different from above.

## "Thanks for the Referral" Notes

Thank-you notes for referrals are sent as a professional courtesy, to document continuity and comprehensiveness of care, and to encourage more referrals. As such, they can also be controversial for those clinicians who believe that the sole purpose for thanking a referral source is to benefit themselves, and that thanking the source is therefore not a reason to break confidentiality, even with permission. Thus you may wish to carefully consider your own views about this before proceeding.

Any referrer wants to know, at a minimum, whether a client contacted you and entered into treatment. Medicare requires that you inform the client's physician of your providing treatment (see Section 5.2), and doing this is standard professional courtesy. If the client refuses to allow even this communication, document that. The APA ethics code (APA, 2010) no longer specifically requires you to coordinate your treatment with the client's physician, but does strongly suggest it.

During the first session with a referred client, discuss and decide with the client how much he or she wants the referrer to know about the client's entering treatment. An important question to ask is whether the referring party is a treating provider or a personal contact of the client. It can be easy to assume that Dr. Jones has sent one of his or her own patients, when the doctor really recommended you to a neighbor, a student, or a parishioner, in which case following up with the referrer may not be appropriate. A "Yes" response to the appropriate question in section C of Form 6.6 (the client demographic information form) is a sufficient release to inform the referrer that the client showed up and is being evaluated. When it would benefit the client to send a report of your findings, diagnosis, duration/ nature of treatment, progress notes, and the like, then get a signed ROI form (Form 8.2) before calling or writing to the referrer.

ELZ believes that if a referred client does not show up, you should inform the referring professional, because this is important information about the client's adherence to the referrer's treatment recommendations. However, you won't have the client's permission to release any information. Since the referrer knew of the referral (having made it), the client knew of it (having agreed to the appointment), and you knew of it (having set up the appointment), there is no breach-of-confidentiality risk. KK holds a different belief: She maintains that any information about whether an individual did or did not attend psychotherapy that is released without the individual's explicit consent is a breach of confidentiality.

You do not need to give any notification to former or current clients who refer others, because of general reasons of privacy. Also, a nonprofessional's recommendation to a friend or associate is only personal advice, and the recipient is free to ignore it.

A common and professional format is to send a note like this:

[Letterhead]

[Date]

Dear Dr. _____,

Please accept my thanks for referring _____ to me for professional services.

With a signed release-of-information form from the client, I will provide you with a written or telephone summary of my clinical impressions and recommendations soon after our meeting. If for some reason the appointments are not completed, I will let you know.

If you have any questions or other concerns that you would like me to respond to in this client's case, please contact me.

I sincerely appreciate your confidence in my services, and again thank you for this referral.

Very truly yours,

_____

[Signature]

The contents of your letter should be tailored to the referrer's involvement in treating the client and the client's needs for privacy. If the referrer is no longer involved in the client's care, or if you wish to maintain privacy, a simple thank-you note for "the recent referral" without mentioning a name can be sent. If you are actively collaborating with the referrer and sharing interventions (e.g., having a physician write the client's psychiatric medications), more details about changes in symptomatic behaviors, side effects of medications, failure to adhere to regimens, changes to treatment plans, concerns about management, and the like will be appropriate, as will more frequent correspondence. Since you are sending information to another professional, you need your client's written permission. It is better to get a current ROI form (Form 8.2) signed near the time you send this information than to rely on an older one from the intake, when the client did not know what you might send or say. For convenience, permission to make telephone consultations with the referrer or collaborator is included on the ROI form.

## Business Cards

The use of business cards in general is discussed in Section 1.2, but since they are inexpensive and easy to create on the Internet, consider developing several even for temporary uses. Cards specific to particular speaking engagements can be a strategic way to have audiences remember you. Such cards can include the title of your talk with the date, time, and room listed. These can help people remember you better, provide context, and also (if you're an introvert) allow you to invite people directly to your talk. KK has had clients contact her because they saw a photo of a presentation-specific business card that someone else posted on an online photo-sharing site. So it is true that you never know where your cards may wind up and whether they might invite a referral.

## Free Initial Meetings

**There is a risk to offering "free initial consultations,"** because a client who comes for such a consultation can become therapeutically involved with you unless you have successfully structured it as a purely evaluation session. It may be best to avoid the word "consultation," because lawyers may see this as "enticement." If one engages in "therapy" during what was presented as a free initial session, this raises the risk of being seen as exploiting the client's neediness and trust to develop a relationship that the client can no longer easily and freely leave. In other words, it may be perceived as a kind of "bait and switch." We believe that this is true even if you keep the meeting short to focus only on your compatibility, listen without offering advice (or recommendations), and try to avoid the assumption by the client that a professional relationship has been created ("If you decide you want to work with me . . . " or "At your first therapy appointment you can expect . . . "). MCOs' contracts may forbid you from seeing their clients at no fee, and you won't be certain about coverage until you meet. Charging from the beginning of therapy sets a positive and equitable expectation that the client will indeed get and has a right to "what he or she paid for."

Some clinicians do offer a "free introductory meeting" to see "how well we may work together." Harry Corsover, PhD, of Castle Rock, CO, offers an ethical and convenient option he terms "Intro+." This is "the free intro discussion and then time in our schedule to move right into a session if that is what [potential clients] choose. We say on the phone that most people choose the latter, since if they come here and decide to work with us, they would rather get started right away than have to go home and come back another day" (H. Corsover, personal communication, September 22, 2007). Other clinicians do similar things with a 15-minute "free consultation" and the ability to "continue" into a paid full 45- or 50-minute session if the client chooses.

An option would be not to charge the client and to refer him or her if it turns out to be a poor therapy match, and to charge if it is essentially the first session of therapy. Regardless of charges, all such sessions have to be performed at the highest clinical level, and all laws and regulations apply to them.

## Giving Presentations

Teaching and providing presentations are ways for many clinicians to "get the word out" about the value of their services. They are also additional sources of income and help to our colleagues and community. When you are negotiating your fees for making presentations, consider the following points:

- What are you seeking? Getting experience in presenting? Getting exposure for your practice or services? Positioning yourself as an authority? Demonstrating your expertise or uniqueness?

- The audience's finances must be considered. Is your sponsor or audience a nonprofit or for-profit organization? Consider that if you have charged one organization a low fee or no fee, others may expect the same, although you can certainly put it in your speaking contract that fee arrangements must be kept confidential.

- Because it is rarely possible to charge for preparation time, teaching and lecturing tend to be underbilled. You can try to reduce these costs by specializing in only a few topics at a time and by selling these preparations to several audiences.

- Time away from paid practice, travel time, and other incidentals can be costly, so factor these into your fee.

- You can always tell people your full fee and then decide whether you are willing to accept less or to negotiate. Remember that speaking is work, and that it should not cost you money to travel, take time off, and teach. An exception would be if you are already planning to attend a conference and the networking opportunities make it worth your while.

- If you are speaking on issues that are not directly related to clinical treatment, make sure your audience is informed during the presentation of your practice interests, so that they will think of you for potential referrals. For example, speakers presenting on treating anxiety disorders may be more likely to get referrals of anxious clients than those who are presenting on the DSM or on law and ethics. But you can change this by incorporating a bit about your own practice niches into the presentation.

- When planning a presentation, incorporate contract provisions to allow you to record it and own the recording. You can do this simply and easily on a smartphone, although hiring a professional videographer will be worthwhile for some of your work. Make sure that all attendees consent to being recorded (via circulating a sign-in sheet and posting signs that note a recording is in progress), or arrange for privacy for those who refuse consent. If your presentation allows attendees to share clinical examples, inform them that if they would like any part of what they shared deleted, they should write down the time and what they said so you can delete it. With this editing, you can offer your presentations to the public or to other professionals from your website. Becoming a continuing education sponsor is time-consuming and expensive, so working with an agency to be able to repurpose your presentation for continuing education credits may work well for you. You can also use short clips of your speaking on your website to market yourself without selling the whole talk.

- If people are pleased with your presentations, you may want to showcase your speaking evaluations on your website as a way to do further marketing. Use a spreadsheet to create graphs of your feedback and add a page to your website. When you're trying to market your talks, refer organizations to this page. For an example, see a page on KK's website (http://drkkolmes.com/speaking-ratings).

### Patient Education Handouts as Practice Marketing

At presentations and when you visit any potential referrers, provide information on disorders and treatments with easy-to-read handouts. APA offers about a dozen (http://www.apa.org/helpcenter/brochure-request.aspx), and the Canadian Psychological Association has about 50 "Fact Sheets" (http://www.cpa.ca/psychologyfactsheets). Print them yourself and add your contact information. Attend to copyright and ask permission where needed for all materials.

# 9.3  Tracking Your Referral Sources

The value of collecting information on the sources of your referrals can be expressed as the old "80/20 rule": 80% of your clients come from 20% of your referrers. (The rule is usually attributed to Wilfredo Pareto, 1848–1923, an Italian economist.) The problem is that you may not know who those 20% are, and so you may not be able to work better with them to increase those referrals. Creating a client log or form with the general headings provided in Figure 9.1 will help you to clarify the situation and understand which referral networks include you. It will also give you a clearer and more objective picture of your practice's perceived value and visibility, so that you can decide whether you wish to change to meet your goals.

When you create your own log, please adapt the headings in Figure 9.1 to the categories that best suit your practice. The kinds of data the form collects (such as your response time from initial client call to first meeting) can be used for your edification or for dealings with MCOs. Experiment with collecting other kinds of data.

If you keep this client log with your billing forms, you can fill it out monthly for all new clients. Alternatively, you can complete it at intervals, perhaps when you file your quarterly estimated taxes. Using a spreadsheet to create the log will allow more sophisticated analyses using several variables at the same time.

The referral sources can be described as follows (devise your own codes for these): Google search for "therapist" (and other terms), Facebook, LinkedIn, Yellow Pages, newspaper ad, physician [name], attorney [name], other mental health professional [name, discipline, or organization], ex-client, agency, ex-training setting, public speaking engagement, and so on. Other headings can include age (categories or numbers), sex/gender/orientation as relevant, and ideas based on what you new clients tell you as the reason they choose to see you. These categories should be modified to suit the goals of your practice. Note that ZIP codes can inform you of the geographic range of your client base, can indicate how far people will travel, and can guide your placement of advertisements or other marketing efforts. KK includes statistics as well on how many sessions a client attended (to assess the profitability of the cases), how termination occurred, and whether the client returned to treatment later. You may discover other characteristics you wish to track, such as whether the client left therapy with a paid-in-full account or with a balance owed. If you come up with others, let us know!

| Client's initials | Date client called | Date of initial meeting | Referred by (code) | Age (code) | Sex/ gender/ orientation | ZIP code or neighbor-hood | Problem/diagnosis/chief complaint (code) |
|---|---|---|---|---|---|---|---|
|  |  |  |  |  |  |  |  |
|  |  |  |  |  |  |  |  |
|  |  |  |  |  |  |  |  |
|  |  |  |  |  |  |  |  |

FIGURE 9.1. Characteristics of new clients.

*Analyzing and Using the Data on Referral Sources*

At intervals, you should examine your log of new client characteristics and collect some simple totals and percentages. Entering these numbers into a database will allow you to pose interesting questions such as these:

- Does the referrer who sends me the most cases with *X* diagnosis also have a lot of clients with *Y* diagnosis whom he or she is not sending to *me* (but might with some education)?
- Has referrer *R* begun to send me lots more clients or ones with different diagnoses than he or she did a year ago because of my marketing efforts with him or her?
- Am I getting a lot of new clients who live or work in a particular area, and so might I consider opening an office for their convenience?
- Am I getting a lot of new clients with diagnosis *D*, and so might I get more training in this, or advertise or teach this specialty?
- Which of my advertisements and other marketing efforts are most and least productive?

Examining the patterns will allow you to answer questions about your practice that will help you achieve your personal and professional long-term aims. For example:

- What is the volume of new referrals I need to meet my practice and income goals?
- Compared with last month and with last year, am I meeting my goals?
- What are my new goals for next quarter?
- What are some new methods to meet these goals?

Clement (1999) is an excellent resource for more ideas on the practical value of such information.

## 9.4   Collecting Feedback on Your Psychological Reports

The essential purpose of assessment services—whether they involve testing, interviewing, or observations—is to collect information that shapes the decisions to be made about the treatment of individuals. If you do any kinds of evaluative reports, the most valuable information for doing your best evaluations is feedback on the value of your reports from their consumers.

The list of questions below can be used to structure a simple letter, which will demonstrate that you care about satisfying the needs of your reports' recipients. Answers to these questions will provide you with information to improve your reports. You should send the questions at least yearly to school personnel, therapists, the courts, or other colleagues and professionals who make referrals to you. Modify the words if you evaluate children or are sending this to parents or other consumers.

1. Did the report give you information beyond what you already knew?
2. How helpful and realistic were . . . [here offer a list of sections and contents of your

reports, such as recommendations for therapy or training, coping with symptomatic behaviors, etc.]?

3. Did the report fail to address areas of concern to you? If so, which?

4. Do you have any suggestions or comments so that I can better meet your needs now or in the future?

Conclude the letter by expressing gratitude for the recipient's time and concern.

## 9.5   Online Marketing, or "Hanging Out Your Shingle in Cyberspace"

The Pew Foundation's Internet and American Life surveys (Fox, 2006, 2013) have found that between 72% (2013) and 80% (2006) of U.S. adults searched the Internet to obtain general health-care-related information. A high percentage of KK's clients tell her that they found her "on the Internet." Even when given your name by a referral source, many potential clients will search for information about you and your practice on the Internet. There are at least three ways of creating the essential Web presence: membership in an online directory of therapists, writing guest blog posts on other sites, and having your own website (which may or may not include a blog).

When KK started her practice in 2008, she had no intention of doing *any* traditional offline marketing. Her plan was to create the best website possible and to network by joining relevant professional groups, participating in them through email to ask questions and share information. This had been an effective way for her to make connections *before* starting practice, and so it felt natural to do the same for her business. She discovered that these online skills worked as well for her professionally as they had personally. She has been able to market her practice effectively by writing and participating in online discussions. She has also created an online professional presence on other social media sites. This is another form of marketing and networking and creates multiple professional opportunities.

### Online Directories of Therapists

If you're not quite sure that you want or need to create a website, there are other ways to have a Web presence and get your information onto the Web. Joining an online directory of therapists is simple, not too costly (perhaps $30 a month, so one new client will pay for several months of this service), and does not involve a lot of work.

When anyone enters terms like "psychotherapy" into a search engine, ads for directories pop up next to the results (see the discussion of Google AdWords, below). A click will open a search page of that directory to enter words for location or specialized services. One of the most common online directories for psychotherapists is sponsored by *Psychology Today*, and others include GoodTherapy.org (http://www.goodtherapy.org) and the APA's Psychologist Locator (http://locator.apa.org). Search engines evaluate the quality and popularity of websites and will display these in rank order, so you should try to join the directories that appear on the first page of the search's results. When you join each directory provides a template for you to enter information about you and your practice, a photo or two, and narratives describing your work.

Your local professional group may offer an online listing as part of membership. These listings can be very helpful to someone who is looking for a clinician and doesn't have any names yet. Make sure your office information is accessible from online search engines! The content you create for an online directory can be repurposed for the next step up—a blog.

## Your Blog

Blogging is another simple way to achieve a Web presence for little or no cost and without many new skills. Blog hosts offer simple free templates into which you can place text and photos by typing or using copy and paste functions. Various websites are host platforms for commonly used free or low-fee blogs (e.g., http://www.weebly.com, http://www.squarespace.com, https://blogger.com, and https://wordpress.com/website). Each has online instructions, and there are hundreds of videos and other guides on how to create and tailor blogs.

You could start out by writing a guest post on another person's popular blog. Consider joining other clinicians to create group blogs, so multiple partners share the work of updating and expanding its content. If you have your own blog, inviting a trusted colleague to write a guest post can get your site more visibility and can also provide diverse content on topics of interest to your readers.

An important consideration for bloggers is whether to allow comments. If you do, we recommend moderating comments (having them held in a queue so you can review them before they are posted to the site). You can then choose whether to publish the content and whether you want to reply to comments. Note that current clients may comment on your blog posts; people seeking help may post revealing comments to your blog; and you will also want to delete the posts of spammers and trolls. A number of psychotherapy clients of other clinicians post questions on KK's blog, so she has to be thoughtful in how she responds. She needs to be supportive and provide education without speaking negatively about other clinicians, or giving the impression that a new psychotherapy relationship is what she is offering. Some people include "common-sense disclaimers" making clear that the content they post does not constitute a clinical relationship or professional advice, and that it is provided only for entertainment or educational purposes. It should go without mention that blogging about your cases risks violating confidentiality. It is far better to discuss general issues and how you go about treating them than to tell stories about your life as a psychotherapist.

## Your Newsletter

If you are actually going to build a whole website (see below), an electronic newsletter is another wonderful way to attract people to your content and develop a valuable list of subscribers who want to know about the services you are offering. Many savvy clinicians have different newsletters for different purposes. For example, KK has one newsletter for clinicians and people who care about digital ethics. She posts an issue of this newsletter about four times a year. In it, she notes when she has new continuing education products available, posts blog entries that speak to ethical issues, and mentions when she'll be traveling to other cities to speak and teach. A good way to entice subscribers is to offer a "freebie." For example, KK's website encourages people to click on a link to get her top five tips to staying ethical as a psychotherapist on the Internet. The link brings people to a subscription form, and when they sign up for the newsletter, they are sent the tips. Some of these people contact her for paid consultation.

KK's second newsletter is targeted for people who might be interested in a psychoeducational workshop about building a healthier relationship. She offers free short video tips and announces updates for workshops, including Web-based international workshops. She has a signup widget on her website for those who want to be notified of these particular updates.

Constant Contact (http://www.constantcontact.com/index.jsp) and MailChimp (http://mailchimp.com/) are two of the most common platforms for hosting a newsletter. Depending upon your level of technical competence, you may be able to set a newsletter up on one of these platforms on your own; or you may need a bit of technical help to install the signup widget on your site, or to design the newsletter to match the theme of your site. But you can do some nice things, such as offering special VIP videos only to those who subscribe to your newsletter. The newsletter can give you a way to send out short "blasts" during the year that summarize new offerings, or to share important information that you might not typically put in a blog post. Other people also use newsletters to summarize recent blog posts and ongoing practice offerings.

## Your Own Website

A website can convey so much about you and your practice that it can save your own and your potential clients' time, reduce no-shows and inappropriate referrals, and educate clients for better work. Almost every clinician can benefit from having a website. Developing one can be creative and fun.

### Step 1. Collect, Write, and Organize What Will Be on the Site

Your website must meet ethical and legal guidelines, as well as convey in plain English what you want to say about your work to possible clients. Here are some examples of important information to include:

- Demographics: Name, degree(s), professional memberships, awards, certifications, credentials, your curriculum vitae (CV), and so on. If you have a logo, include it next to your name.

- Contact information: Street addresses of all offices, all phone numbers, all email addresses, emergency procedures. (We recommend having the contact information on each page of the website, so people don't have to look for it when they go to another page.)

- A map and directions to your office (using Google Maps, MapQuest, etc.). These are especially important if you are in a difficult area to locate. Registering with Google (http://www.google.com/business) will also literally "get you on the map" and make it easy to find you when people search for your business.

- A photo or two of you, and perhaps of your office or building. Some people like to choose soothing imagery. Make sure that if you show people receiving therapy, you make it clear that these are not actual clients. Eschew generic stock photographs of happy people, sad people, or other graphics. Make sure that you obtain permission from copyright holders for any images you want to use. It is unacceptable simply to take an image you like from another website. You can use a site such as Flickr (https://www.flickr.com) to search for Creative Commons photos that have permissions for commercial use. For more on understanding different Creative Commons licenses, look at their website (https://creativecommons.org/licenses).

### What Should the Website Content Be? How Many Pages?

Consider placing information onto different "pages" which will be reached and displayed by clicking on links. Typical contents include a Welcome page and an About page (which says a bit about your training, your style, and your areas of focus or the types of issues you most like to work with). Some people have a page for My Services or just Psychotherapy, which can list the hours you have available, your fees (if you're comfortable posting them), and what MCO or other insurance panels you are on. A photo and your contact information can be useful on each page in a sidebar or along the top. As her website developed, KK made sure that it provided answers to questions that callers tended to ask during the phone intake.

A Contact page can make sure that readers know how to set up an initial intake appointment (or, if you have a phone screening, what it entails). Many clinicians include their forms on the website, so clients can read your policies and have ready access to them without having to contact you (see Section 6.4). Your Notice of Privacy Practices (NPP) should also be uploaded here.

Some clinicians like to include a page of publications and media appearances. If you are comfortable doing so, adding a brief video for introducing visitors to your practice can serve several purposes: It helps to show your personality, lets people see whether they might feel comfortable with you, and can boost search engine visibility (especially if the video is also posted on YouTube or another popular video-sharing site). Consider including materials suitable for referrers, peers, the news media, or other audiences that suit your work.

How many pages will all this take, and how should they be organized? Start with lots of paper and create visual blocks of the information. Then move them around to logical and topical pages (note that "a page" on a website can be any length). For example, areas of clinical focus and fee or insurance information for the Psychotherapy or My Services page can be very useful to a visitor. ELZ recommends buying the larger site options (such as "99 pages") from your website host, which typically cost about $120 a year and include functions to be implemented over the years. Of course, this depends on to whom you are marketing your services: psychotherapy clients, other clinicians, or agencies? Or do you plan to create and market other products, such as books, presentations, and online workshops? For many people who simply provide psychotherapy, and wish simply to have a presence on the web, a site with a few essential pages is just fine.

### Step 2. Select a Website Hosting Service and Get the Site Up on the Internet

Be aware that the domain hosting service you choose may indicate your values to Web-savvy clients, so do some research on the reputation of your hosting service. There are very mainstream and popular ones, but there are also small companies that do a great job at hosting and that may strongly communicate your business values to others. For example, note the differences between a big host (such as https://www.godaddy.com) and a smaller one (such as http://asmallorange.com or https://www.gaiahost.coop).

If you don't want to do the work yourself, services like TherapySites (http://www.therapysites.com) will create a very complete site aimed at therapists. For a monthly fee, it will include (among other things) hosting, a domain name rental, audio and video, search engine optimization (SEO) support, forms, appointment requests, and therapy forms. All support is provided by phone, and its description of its website development process is detailed and reassuring.

### Step 3. Decide What Your Website Domain Will Be Called

The URL for KK's site is http://drkkolmes.com, and ELZ owns but does not presently use http://www.edward.zuckerman.com and uses http://www.theclinicianstoolbox.com for his business. Other savvy marketers have staked out URLs like http://bayareapsychotherapy.com, which is likely to rank high in search engine results for people looking for help with depression in the Bay Area (see the discussion of SEO below). You can also buy multiple domain names and have them redirected to your main site, if you want to get strategic. This is also a good idea if you have an unusual name. For example, KK bought http://drkolmes.com (with one "k"), and it redirects to her site.

### Step 4. Select a Website Design or a Web Designer

Most hosting services have templates for multiple-page websites, either free with the hosting or at low cost. Weebly, Squarespace, WordPress, and Blogger (see the URLs above under "Your Blog") are all sites that you may be able to easily navigate yourself, filling in prefabricated templates and designing your own site. The site-building programs may take a dozen hours to learn and more to use well, so you might prefer to invest in a designer or developer. Some beginning website developers may be interested in working on your site for a low price, so that they can use it to showcase their skills. Or ask those fellow professionals whose websites you admire who did their work for them. Hiring a designer can cost anywhere from $1,000 to $5,000, depending upon the designer's experience and what it is you want to do, so shop around. Before plunging in, consider which bells and whistles you want to include on your site, such as free downloads, signup areas for mailing lists, online scheduling software, or encrypted forms.

### Step 5. Put Your License Number on Each Page

**KK suggests having your license number up at the top of each page with your name and office information, rather than buried at the bottom of your site.** If you are not yet licensed, check with your discipline's state board to make sure you are not violating any laws regulating how and whether assistants or interns can advertise. For example, some states may not allow people who are not yet licensed to have a website; others will want the differences between licensed and unlicensed clinicians to be clear to the public and have clear information about who is supervising the work.

### Step 6. Do You Want an Auto-Scheduler?

Auto-schedulers are handy little programs that can either make your life either very happy or much more complicated. If you are OK with reviewing your schedule each week for openings, if you want people to be able to book themselves for appointments, and if you will hold the time, this can be a useful utility for you. Or if you regularly hold certain times for activities such as consultation, an auto-scheduler can let people book and purchase time online without days of email back-and-forth. You still get to respond and confirm whether the time works. KK does not let people book therapy time this way, since she does not want to release PHI to the company that manages her auto-scheduling. Her company is not compliant with the Health Insurance Portability and Accountability Act (HIPAA). She also prefers to be selective about how she schedules clients. However, she loves auto-scheduling for people who are seeking 15, 30, 45, or 60 minutes of consultation, since these sessions do not require the same level of protections as psychotherapy sessions, and since it's quite convenient to wake up in the morning with money in the inbox and a session scheduled. Some clinicians with an auto-scheduler that allows clients to book therapy appointments do not advertise this service on their sites; they only offer the link to ongoing clients after a few assessment sessions, when they are comfortable with having these clients book open times. The more expensive auto-schedulers can offer advanced features, such as showing only certain blocks of times to registered users or offering group sessions.

There are several auto-scheduler services worth considering (e.g., fullslate.com, check-appointments.com, appointlet.com, and ScheduleOnce.com). You will want to check out pricing and to determine whether any offer HIPAA compliance, Google Calendar integration, reminders, and the like. Look for the one that best serves the functions you need.

## Google AdWords

Google AdWords is advertising in which you pay a little to display your small ad. You pay more only when someone clicks on your ad to go to your website. You set a maximum you will pay for the week or month (a budget), and each click is deducted from it. You will get detailed feedback from Google regarding who clicked, which page they went to, and how productive your different wordings were. You try to make your short ad attractive but not too general, so that only those who will need you click on it, or else you waste money on unproductive page views. You can advertise locally or globally, depending on your services. Some people put a lot of effort into finding the most productive short ads, whereas others work on getting higher search rankings by improving their SEO.

## Search Engine Optimization

If you want to reach potential clients, it is worth learning about SEO or hiring someone to consult with you about whether your site is reaching the people you want it to reach. SEO improvements can make your website show up higher in search engine results ("page rank"), so that your site is on the first page or two of results when someone is looking for a service. Obviously, this is a good thing!

Try doing your own search now for your competitors' sites. Enter your city and a term like "anxiety," "depression," or "couple counseling," to see what comes up. Do you know any of these people? If you already have a site, does yours come up?

If you know nothing about SEO, you can always post to your local psychotherapy group and ask the members for referrals to the professionals who helped boost their SEO. A tutorial in SEO is beyond the scope of this book, but taking a class, buying a book, or consulting with someone can be well worth the investment if you expect your Web presence to be your primary calling card.

## 9.6   Social Media and Online Networking

Social media constitute a growing way to connect, market, and spread information. Marketing consultants will tell you that you must have a social media presence, and KK has used social media to network and market her practice for years. However, maintaining a social media presence requires continual work being responsive, writing new material, and exploring and linking ideas and people. Also, it can feel like a lot of exposure and so it is not the right approach for all personalities. You may be a clinician who is more conservative and who does not want to be so visible online. If that's the case, it's fine to skip social media. Be true to yourself!

If you use social media only for personal reasons, note that our ethics codes apply only to our professional activities. However, the Internet has a way of blending personal with professional matters. If you start using your personal email or Facebook profile to announce psychotherapy offerings (hoping that your friends might refer people), or if you post a personal ad and "bump into" your clients' dating ads on social media, note that you now have some clinical and ethical issues to manage, because your personal life has intersected with your professional life.

If you *do* decide to use social media either personally or professionally, we recommend that you use completely different email addresses from your regular one(s) to manage your separate social media accounts. Just make up several addresses on Gmail or Hotmail and use them to open your new social media accounts. You can set up these addresses to forward alerts and messages to your regular email address, so that you won't miss anything. By using a unique address for each social media account, you will prevent popping up as a "recommended friend" or "contact" to those you correspond with socially or as part of your practice. It will also keep your account from being hacked into by someone who knows your regular email address. KK learned the hard way that sites like LinkedIn and Facebook still store the old email addresses even after they've been deleted; she still shows up in searches linked to the old addresses. Starting with a "clean slate" of addresses can save you privacy headaches later. For more on protecting your online privacy, Violet Blue's book *The Smart Girl's Guide to Privacy* (available through http://smartprivacy.tumblr.com) is full of information useful to psychotherapists who want to get off "people finder" sites or just generally want to keep their Web presence clean. It is also a great resource for psychotherapy clients who have experienced harassment.

Here are some places to start if you want to be on social media. LinkedIn (https://www.LinkedIn.com) is the standard professional site, where you may wish to connect with other professionals you know, join groups related to your interests or affiliations, or even post your CV. You can post status updates and participate in discussion groups. Be aware, however, that it's very easy for anyone to create a fake profile on LinkedIn to gain access to your profile, groups, or networks. Although we suspect that very few clients might do such a thing, we have heard stories of clinicians who got LinkedIn requests from a colleague (with a profile bearing her photo and CV), only to find out later, from that colleague, that she doesn't use LinkedIn. Since impersonation is so easy, and people so rarely verify the identity of those who make contact with them on social media sites, **be *absolutely* sure that you never post *anything* online you would not want a client to see.** Also bear in mind that it is possible for your clients to be friends or colleagues with some of your online friends and contacts. The digital universe is turning even big cities into small communities. A client could happen to view your profile when your shared contact is looking at it.

Some clinicians use Facebook to create Facebook business pages, which people may "like." Others create professional Twitter accounts to tweet updates. Some have YouTube channels. Others use Pinterest to share links to psychological content. You can set up your blog to update your social media profiles automatically when you've added new content. You can share articles you have read and discuss them with professional and consumer audiences. Or you may create short educational videos and update them on your YouTube channel; embed them on your website; and share them on Twitter, LinkedIn, and Facebook.

Whatever you do, be aware that some risks come with social media. Clients may want to "follow" or "friend" you, and this can create potential clinical and ethical issues. You may inadvertently follow clients who are using pseudonyms. Clients may write to you on these sites, which are not at all confidential or secure; others may contact you, wishing to start a clinical relationship. You may be asked for a professional opinion about the diagnoses of celebrities, or about issues outside your clinical expertise. Remember that if you are using these sites as a professional, your professional ethics code standards will apply. You may want to review the sections of your ethics code on confidentiality, multiple relationships, advertising, public statements, and testimonials. Brushing up on media ethics is essential once you are on social media. And you may want to develop a social media policy.

## 9.7   Do I Need a Social Media Policy, and If So, What Should Be in It?

If you are not on social media, but still use email to correspond with clients, then you could benefit from a basic electronic communications policy. Section 8.1 discusses what this might entail. If you are actively marketing your services online and using social media sites, then you absolutely need a social media policy. KK has written a policy for psychotherapists that is often referenced and used by other clinicians, and you are free to adapt or modify it to suit the needs of your practice. This policy and the copyright permissions can be found on a page of her website (http://drkkolmes.com/social-media-policy).

An important element of a policy includes whether or not you accept "friend" or contact requests from current or former clients on social media. Some ethics codes (ACA, 2014) explicitly prohibit adding current clients as friends or contacts, whereas psychologists, social workers, and marriage and family therapists are encouraged to evaluate whether a multiple role could be damaging or exploitative to a client. Explicit prohibitions may be added in the future to other ethics codes besides the ACA's. If you have a business page or profile on Facebook or Twitter, specify whether you wish for clients to "like" or "follow" these accounts, and indicate more private ways they may view your content. You may also mention whether you will follow them back. (We recommend that you don't.)

State whether you plan to reply to messages on social media sites, which are not secure.

Be aware that all electronic exchanges with clients are legally discoverable, even if they happen on Facebook.

Anyone whose practice or office is listed on Places (within Facebook), Foursquare, or a similar location-based service may also wish to notify clients that they may be signaling to unwanted viewers that they are at a therapy appointment if their phone has GPS or location services enabled.

## Should You Search for Your Clients on Google or Social Media?

Should clinicians use search engines such as Google, or social media, to collect information about clients that will be used as part of intake, assessment, or diagnosis? Although forensic psychologists may do this as part of their investigatory role, clinicians who are seeking to develop relationships of trust and integrity should state in their policies whether or not they do such searches—and if so, under what circumstances, and whether clients will be informed when this occurs. Some clients may be too timid to ask, but they may be very relieved to read and understand your policies on this. KK suggests that if you want to differentiate between a clinically indicated search and one done for the sake of mere curiosity, consider before such a search whether you will feel comfortable documenting it in the client's chart, along with your rationale for doing it. If you wouldn't put it in the chart, it may not be clinically warranted. Remember, we have to document all professional activities that relate to client care.

## Online Client Reviews

Business review sites constitute another area of concern. Your policy may indicate that your presence on such a site is not a request for a testimonial, which is a violation of all ethics codes. KK's policy includes a statement about this, but another approach may also be posting such a notice on various sites. The following text is posted on KK's Yelp page (http://www.yelp.com/biz/keely-kolmes-psyd-san-francisco), and you are welcome to copy or adapt it. Note that the Specialties section on Yelp's business page and the History section limit the number of characters allowed in each field on Yelp's site.

> Posting a review of my services is your right as a client, and it is entirely up to you to decide whether you wish to write a review. But I gently discourage clients from posting reviews of my practice for the reasons below.
>
> 1. The American Psychological Association's Ethics Code says this about testimonials (in Principle 5.05): "Psychologists do not solicit testimonials from current therapy clients/patients or other persons who because of their particular circumstances are vulnerable to undue influence."
>
> Since you may decide to return to therapy with me at a later date, I do not request testimonials from people who have ended therapy with me.
>
> 2. Unlike other business owners who may respond to their Yelp reviews, as a psychologist, I must provide confidentiality to my clients. This means I am prevented from responding in any way that acknowledges whether someone has been in my care.
> 3. If we work together, I hope we can discuss your feelings about our work directly and

in person. This may not always feel comfortable, but discussion of your positive and negative reactions to our work can be an important part of your therapy. If we are not a good match, I'm always happy to help you find a therapist who better suits you.

4. If you do write something about my practice on Yelp, note that this is a public forum. To preserve your privacy, consider using a pseudonym that is not linked to your regular email address or friend networks.

5. If you believe that I (or any licensed mental health professional) have done something harmful, consider contacting your state licensing board to make a formal complaint. This may protect other consumers of therapy services. Be aware that details of your therapy may come up if there is a formal investigation.

In regard to the effectiveness of her therapy KK has posted her outcome data as both a marketing gesture and for general transparency. Aggregate data from those who have ended work with her is at http://drkkolmes.com/product/getting-better-client-satisfaction-survey/.

# 9.8   Teletherapy

Some clinicians are making themselves more competitive in the marketplace and filling a much-needed gap by offering remote services to clients in areas with few clinicians, clients in areas where few clinicians have certain special skills, or clients who cannot get to their offices. If your site uses keywords such as "teletherapy," it may increase your SEO for those searching for these services. Some refer to this as "Skype therapy," but we prefer terms such as "telehealth," "telemental health," or "teletherapy." We do not use regular Skype, which is not a HIPAA-compliant service.

Issues to bear in mind if you want to offer such services include the following:

- Are you licensed to provide these services? For the most part, a clinician must be licensed in the state in which a client resides. If one of your in-state clients is temporarily in another state, teletherapy is likely to be acceptable in the short term. Some states allow for temporary teletherapy practice for a limited number of days per year. An APA Practice Organization document should help clarify the laws in your situation (http://www.apapracticecentral.org/advocacy/state/telehealth-slides.pdf). The APA is also now exploring "Compacts." Several states could join a Compact, which would allow psychologists in those states to practice across state lines. You may also be contacted for your expertise by clients in your own state who live too far away for regular face-to-face sessions.

- Is a particular client appropriate for online services? Best practices include assessing the client in person for his or her suitability for this type of service during at least a few face-to-face sessions, and building an alliance. Make sure that the client is not in crisis, and that the issues for which the client is seeking care are appropriate to this type of service. Are you able to feel connected to this client in person? If not, how will you "connect" when doing so via teletherapy?

- Are you aware of the crisis resources available in the client's location? You don't want to wait for a crisis to occur to begin looking.

- What are the security and privacy mechanisms of the technology you are using? Use

HIPAA-compliant services (such as VSee.com, Zoom.us, and Regrouptherapy.com), or other video-conferencing sites that will provide a BA contract.

- Can privacy at the client's end be assured? Will others be in the room or overhear you?

- Will insurance pay for these services? Some insurers will pay for video services and not for phone sessions.

- Will your professional liability insurance cover you, or does the company consider teletherapy risky? You can always consult your insurance provider if you are unsure whether a particular scenario or case will be covered for remote therapy.

- Is this method within your areas of competence? Some argue that teletherapy is a new type of service, which requires training to develop competence. You will want to be aware of the clinical implications of using this technology for psychotherapy. If a client suggests teletherapy and you do not have relevant experience, you must disclose your lack of experience before the client can provide fully informed consent to what is for you an experimental method. You also need to indicate that if you find yourself uncomfortable with this method, you may discontinue working in this manner.

- Do you have consent forms for clients to indicate their awareness of the privacy, confidentiality, and technology risks (such as loss of connection or other technical difficulties) of engaging in such services? Provision of teletherapy requires its own separate consent form.

*Resources*

The TeleMental Health Institute has for years been a leader and offers training and much valuable guidance (http://www.telehealth.org).

*Considerations for the Provision of E-Therapy*, a 50-page book published in 2009 by the Substance Abuse and Mental Health Services Administration (SAMHSA), is available for download (http://store.samhsa.gov/shin/content/SMA09-4450/SMA09-4450.pdf).

A 25-page booklet on standards and expectations is available from the National Association of Social Workers (http://www.socialworkers.org/practice/standards/naswtechnologystandards.pdf).

An online course, *Telehealth, The New Standard: Ethical, Legal, Clinical, Technological and Practice Considerations*, is available from the Zur Institute (http://www.zurinstitute.com/telehealthresources.html). It includes a great number of relevant links.

APA's Telepsychology Guidelines are available from the APA Practice Organization (http://www.apapracticecentral.org/ce/guidelines/telepsychology-guidelines.pdf).

## 9.9  Additional Resources

The age of the Internet certainly offers new opportunities and resources for marketing one's practice. But traditional and digital methods both work. Psychologists (and others) can find more resources on practice marketing at an APA Practice Organization page (http://www.

apapracticecentral.org/business/marketing/index.aspx). Some people may also benefit from business or marketing coaching or from other forms of individualized consultation.

Books on practice development and marketing can also offer encouragement, information, and guidance on various marketing activities, such as surveying community needs and resources; writing and placing advertisements; creating newsletters; and designing and presenting workshops to the community, peers, and businesses. A list of such resources can be found in Appendix C.

# APPENDICES

# Resources

## Appendix A. Resources for Closing a Practice and Making a Professional Will

*Note*: At the time of this book's publication, only British Columbia, Oklahoma, Florida, and Oregon require psychologists to write a professional will or to notify their licensing board of their will's executor. However, these requirements are likely to become more widespread, and these practices are otherwise prudent and highly recommended. In this appendix, we present a list of resources for closing your practice and creating your own professional will.

Alban, A. (2011, January 19). *Professional wills for psychiatrists.* Retrieved from http://clinicallawyer. com/2011/01/professional-wills-for-psychiatrists

    This blog post incorporates a 2010 article from *The California Psychiatrist* by A. S. Frankel and A. Alban, "Professional Wills: Protecting Patients, Family Members and Colleagues." Alban and Frankel are both psychologist/lawyers, and their articles provide a great deal of clear information and guidance. See also Alban's March 18, 2007, blog post (http://clinicallawyer. com/2007/03/professional-wills).

College of Psychologists of British Columbia, Quality Assurance Committee. (2008, Spring). *Professional will materials.* Retrieved from http://www.collegeofpsychologists.bc.ca/docs/ ProfessionalWillMaterials-Updated.pdf

    This is an 11-page guide and template for writing a professional will.

Frankel, A. S. (2010, January 20). *Professional wills: Some concrete steps to take.* Retrieved from http:// clinicallawyer.com/2010/01/professional-wills-some-concrete-steps-to-take

    This blog post incorporates a 2010 article from the *California Psychologist* by A. Alban and A. S. Frankel (see above), "So How's It Feel to Be in Breach of the APA Ethics Code and California Law? Professional Wills: The Ethics Requirement You Haven't (Yet) Met."

Legal & Regulatory Affairs Staff. (2014, June 26). Sample professional will and additional resources for practitioners. *Practice Update.* Retrieved from http://www.apapracticecentral.org/ update/2014/06-26/professional-will.aspx

    This resource from the American Psychological Association (APA) Practice Central service of the APA Practice Organization contains links to four valuable articles: "Your Professional Will: Why and How to Create"; "Sample Professional Will"; "Further Instructions and Considerations in Preparing a Professional Will"; and "Information for Professional Executor: Files, Passwords and Contacts List."

Legal & Regulatory Affairs and APA Ethics Office Staff. (2013, January 17). Ask our attorney: Handling records of a deceased psychologist. *Practice Update*. Retrieved from http://www. apapracticecentral.org/update/2013/01-17/deceased-psychologist.aspx

About two pages from the APA Practice Central. Some problems that can arise without a professional will after a therapist dies are answered.

Luepker, E. T. (2012). *Record keeping in psychotherapy and counseling: Protecting confidentiality and the professional relationship* (2nd ed.). New York: Routledge.

Different approaches to the professional will included in this book are a Sample Checklist for Letter or Advance Directive to Designated Agent: In Case of Emergency, and a Sample Letter or Advance Directive for Designated Agent: In Case of Emergency.

National Association of Social Workers. (2012). *Retiring? Tips for closing your private practice*. Retrieved from http://careers.socialworkers.org/documents/RetiringaPrivatePractice.pdf

A brief document, but with lots of concentrated information.

Nordmarken, N., & Zur, O. *The professional will: What it is and how to write it*. Retrieved from http://www.zurinstitute.com/professionalwillcourse.html

A one-credit continuing education course based on two short articles. References for the course are listed at http://www.zurinstitute.com/professional_will_resources.html

Oregon.gov. (n.d.) *Guidelines for preparing your professional will*. Retrieved from http://www.oregon.gov/obpe/docs/guidelines_for_preparing_your_professional_will.pdf

Five pages with sample will.

Pope, K. S., & Vasquez, M. J. T. (2016). Therapist's guide for preparing a professional will. Retrieved from http://www.kspope.com/therapistas/will.php

This is Chapter 8 of the most recent edition of Pope and Vasquez's book *Ethics in Psychotherapy and Counseling: A Practical Guide*.

Reinhardt, R., & Wheeler, A. M. (2014). *Private practice preparedness: The health care professional's guide to closing a practice due to retirement, death, or disability*.

An ebook published by Smashwords (https://www.smashwords.com/books/view/419230). Thorough and current coverage of all the issues and exactly how to handle them.

Spayd, C. S., & Wiley, M. O. (2010). Closing a professional practice: Clinical and practical considerations. *Pennsylvania Psychologist*. Retrieved from http://c.ymcdn.com/sites/www.papsy.org/resource/collection/7E915DDB-4EFF-4EDF-95FD-6B087278EC3E/closing_practice.pdf

An excellent overview and introduction to the issues.

Steiner, A. (2002). *The empty chair: Making our absence less traumatic for everyone*. Retrieved from http://www.psychotherapy.net/article/psychotherapist-retirement

For many years Ann Steiner, PhD, of San Diego, CA, has offered workshops and guidance on developing professional wills. In this long article, she guides us to set up an emergency response team for when we suddenly become unable to practice. She includes forms and letters as well as advice and guidance. Her current continuing education program can be found at http://www.psychotherapytools.com/orderfrm.html#profwill_course

# Appendix B. Professional Liability Insurance Resources

## Information Resources

The Trust. https://www.trustinsurance.com

> This was the American Psychological Association Insurance Trust (APAIT) The Resources section of the website includes several articles and sample forms. Be aware that some are very dated and simplistic, and others are more informative. The site's Risk Management menu includes a book and continuing education course, *Assessing and Managing Risk in Psychological Practice: An Individualized Approach,* in a second edition for 2013 free for Trust-insured psychologists. There are about two dozen webinars on ethics and risk management and on practice issues. There is an online course about the Health Insurance Portability and Accountability Act (HIPAA)—on the Privacy Rule. There are also several current articles and the somewhat dated *HIPAA Primer,* which can be downloaded by anyone.

Meyeroff, W. J. (2010). *Buying medical malpractice insurance: A physician's guide to selecting a policy and evaluating a carrier.* Retrieved from http://www.physicianspractice.com/print/article/1462168/168 5979?printable=true

> Almost everything you need to know, with guidelines, checklists, and advice, all in seven pages.

Last but not least, **read your policy carefully.** Know and understand it. Pay special attention to the many important exclusions. You can ask the licensed agent at the agency any questions.

## Sellers of Insurance

Each seller offers different benefits and options, so do compare several.

American Professional Agency, 95 Broadway, Amityville, NY 11701; 516-691-6400 or 800-421-6694; http://www.americanprofessional.com

> Coverage is available for students and for members of all the mental health professions.

The Trust, 111 Rockville Pike, Suite 700, Rockville, MD 20850; 800-477-1200; https://www.trustinsurance.com/

> The Trust offers many kinds of insurance besides professional liability, and it no longer requires APA membership (and dues). It stands as an intermediate and marketing organization.

CPH and Associates, 727 S. Dearborn, Suite 312, Chicago, IL 60605; 800-875-1911; http://www.cphins.com

> This agency offers occurrence-based policies, a "loss assistance hotline," and coverage to all disciplines and healing professions.

Healthcare Providers Service Organization (HPSO), 159 E. County Line Road, Hatboro, PA 19040-1248; 800-982-9491; http://www.hpso.com

> HPSO offers occurrence-based for all kinds of mental health professionals. Some policies have unique features. The American Counseling Association Insurance Trust has now partnered with HPSO.

Hiscox Insurance Company, Inc., 104 South Michigan Avenue, Suite 600, Chicago, IL 60603;

866-283-7545;                http://www.hiscox.com/small-business-insurance/professional-liability-insurance/pl-coverage

This agency offers policies for psychologists and others.

National Association of Social Workers (NASW) Assurance Services, 50 Citizens Way, Suite 304, Frederick, MD 21701; 855-385-2160; http://www.naswassurance.org

This is the program manager (marketing arm) of NASW, and so it is just for social workers, but policies are detailed and comprehensive. Its agency is CPH and Associates (see above).

J. J. Negley Associates, 103 Eisenhower Parkway, Suite 101, Roseland, NJ 07068; 800-845-1209; http://www.jjnegley.com

This is a plan administrator representing several insurers.

# Appendix C.  Books on Practice Development and Marketing

Ackley, D. C. (1997). *Breaking free of managed care.* New York: Guilford Press.

Although Ackley explains the poisonous consequences of managed care with precision, the best parts of the book are those identifying and challenging the thoughts and assumptions of therapists that keep them from leaving managed care dependence. He demonstrates the value of psychology to clients and to businesses, and inspires us to follow him.

Cole, P. H., & Reese, D. (2004). *Mastering the financial dimension of your practice: The definitive resource for private practice development and financial planning.* New York: Brunner-Routledge.

Written by two therapists, this book educates readers about financial thinking and planning. It also addresses the dynamic meanings of money and of independent practice, as well as the customary and mistaken money strategies of therapists. It guides readers through creating a financial plan and carrying it out.

Grodzki, L. (2003). *Twelve months to your ideal private practice: New skill sets, essential exercises, and tools for success.* New York: Norton.

A great coach offers monthly guidance about balancing life with work and handling other real-world issues. For each month, she provides exercises, skills sets, and action plans to keep you moving. Do the work and you will succeed.

Grodzki, L. (2015). *Building your ideal private practice: A guide for therapists and other healing professionals* (2nd ed.). New York: Norton.

In this new edition of a book first published in 2000, Grodzki guides you to a blueprint for practice and a business vision. She emphasizes getting support and maintaining optimism, attracting clients with your own message, expanding your services, avoiding pitfalls, and staying successful over time.

Harris, S. M., Ivey, D. C., & Bean, R. A. (Eds.). (2005). *A practice that works: Strategies to complement your stand alone therapy practice.* New York: Routledge.

Descriptions of 23 specializations, written by professionals in each niche practice. Innovative and enthusiastic, but short on the size of the market, scientific bases, and moving from where you are to where you want to be.

Hunt, H. A. (2005). *Essentials of private practice: Streamlining costs, procedures, and policies for less stress.* New York: Norton.

Utterly practical guidance on "how to do it better" after the basic functions are working. Advice on reducing overhead, dealing with insurance, creating more efficient telephone procedures, and establishing collection policies.

Kase, L. (2005). *The successful therapist: Your guide to building the career you've always wanted.* Hoboken, NJ: Wiley.

> If you have always wanted to think like an MBA, the first 200 pages will teach you leadership, marketing, financial planning, and operational planning. The last 120 pages cover five practice areas: coaching, forensics, teaching, administration, and other fields.

Kolt, L. (1999). *How to build a thriving fee-for-service practice: Integrating the healing side with the business side of psychotherapy.* San Diego, CA: Academic Press.

> Kolt combines exercises in awareness and attitude change with tools for surveying community needs, developing specialty practices, marketing ideas, selecting an office, presenting public seminars, and using practice data for decision making. Excellent, though now slightly dated.

Lazarus, J. A. (Ed.). (2005). *Entering private practice: A handbook for psychiatrists.* Washington, DC: American Psychiatric Publishing.

> Nuts-and-bolts advice on insurance, marketing, offices, and legal and ethical problems.

Mart, E. G. (2006). *Getting started in forensic psychology practice: How to create a forensic specialty in your mental health practice.* Hoboken, NJ: Wiley.

> Just what the title says. This book tells you how to go about it, comprehensively.

Morgan, W. D. (2006). *Today's private practice: Strategies for building a thriving managed-care free psychotherapy practice.* Havertown, PA: Golden Hill.

> How to find, explore, and exploit a niche market for psychotherapy and many related functions (e.g., coaching). The author describes how he left managed care, redeploying his therapy skills from a medical illness approach to one of skill building and problem solving.

Pope, K. S., & Vasquez, M. J. T. (2005). *How to survive and thrive as a therapist: Information, ideas, and resources for psychologists in practice.* Washington, DC: American Psychological Association.

> A quarter of this book contains excellent questions and advice; the rest presents and discusses American Psychological Association (APA) guidelines. The book covers topics like finding an office, insurance, clients, and an attorney; using computers; writing a professional will; and responding to a complaint. Some checklists are provided.

Stout, C. E., & Grand, L. C. (2005). *Getting started in private practice: The complete guide to building your mental health practice.* Hoboken, NJ: Wiley.

> Comprehensive coverage of financing, startup, fee setting, risk minimization, marketing, niching, self-care, presentations, customer service skills, and many other topics. Solid information, excellently presented. Superb.

Verhaagen, D., & Gaskill, F. (2014). *How we built our dream practice.* Atlanta, GA: Practice Institute Press.

> The authors built a group practice and share how they got there in an anecdotal and humorous style in 140 pages. Highly optimistic and inspiring, but without forms or guidance on records or the nuts and bolts.

Walfish, S., & Barnett, J. E. (2009). *Financial success in mental health practice.* Washington, DC: American Psychological Association.

> An excellent survey of the financial underpinnings of practice, with advice on finding and using business consultants (accountants, lawyers), startup costs and plans, taxes, fees, and insurance billing.

Zur, O. (2006). *The complete fee-for-service private practice handbook.* Sonoma, CA: Zur Institute.

> This book addresses 57 topics, albeit too briefly.

# References

Ackley, D. C. (1997). *Breaking free of managed care: A step-by-step guide to regaining control of your practice.* New York: Guilford Press.

Adams, S., & Orgel, M. (1975). *Through the mental health maze.* Washington, DC: Health Research Group.

Aimes, M. (2011). Psychotherapy: What can go wrong. Retrieved from http://www.jamhi.org/poc/view_index.php?idx=119&d=1&w=1&e=43065

Alabama Psychological Association. (n.d.). *Client–therapist intimacy: Appropriate and inappropriate conduct.* Montgomery: Author.

Alban, A. (2010a). Can clinicians use a collection agency? Retrieved from http://clinicallawyer.com/2010/08/can-clinicians-use-a-collection-agency

Alban, A. (2010b). What is the standard of care, and why should you want to know about it? Retrieved from http://clinicallawyer.com/2010/09/what-is-the-standard-of-care

Albeck, J. H., & Goldman, C. (1991). Patient–therapist co-documentation: Implications of jointly authored progress notes for psychotherapy practice, research, training, supervision, and risk management. *American Journal of Psychotherapy, 3*(3), 317–334.

American Counseling Association (ACA). (2005). *Code of ethics.* Alexandria, VA: Author. Retrieved from http://ethics.iit.edu/ecodes/node/4192

American Counseling Association (ACA). (2014). *Code of ethics.* Alexandria, VA: Author. Retrieved from http://www.counseling.org/resources/aca-code-of-ethics.pdf

American Professional Agency. (1992). *Important information concerning your professional liability claim.* Amityville, NY: Author.

American Professional Agency. (2015). Claims made psychologist's professional and office liability policy. Retrieved from http://www.americanprofessional.com/wp-content/uploads/PSY_Contract.pdf

American Psychiatric Association. (1987). APA guidelines on confidentiality. *American Journal of Psychiatry, 144,* 1522–1526.

American Psychiatric Association. (2006). *The principles of medical ethics with annotations especially applicable to psychiatry.* Washington, DC: Author. Retrieved from http://www.psychiatry.org/psychiatrists/practice/ethics

American Psychiatric Association. (2013). *Diagnostic and statistical manual of mental disorders* (5th ed.). Arlington, VA: Author.

American Psychological Association (APA). (2003). Guidelines on multicultural education, training, research, practice, and organizational change for psychologists. *American Psychologist, 58,* 377–402. Retrieved from http://www.apa.org/pi/multiculturalguidelines.pdf

American Psychological Association (APA). (2006). *Advancing colleague assistance in professional psychology.* Retrieved from http://www.apapracticecentral.org/ce/self-care/colleague-assist-download.pdf

American Psychological Association (APA). (2010). *Ethical principles of psychologists and code of conduct.* Retrieved from http://www.apa.org/ethics/code/index.aspx

American Psychological Association (APA), Committee on Legal Issues. (2006). Strategies for private practitioners coping with subpoenas or compelled testimony for client/patient records or test data or test materials. *Professional Psychology: Research and Practice, 47*(1), 1–11.

American Psychological Association (APA), Committee on Professional Practice and Standards. (2007). *Record keeping guidelines.* Retrieved from https://www.apa.org/practice/guidelines/record-keeping.pdf

American Psychological Association (APA), Committee on Professional Practice and Standards. (2010). *Guidelines for child custody evaluations in family law proceedings.* Retrieved from https://www.apa.org/practice/guidelines/child-custody.pdf

American Psychological Association (APA), Committee on Women in Psychology. (1989). If sex enters the psychotherapy relationship. *Professional Psychology: Research and Practice, 20,* 112–115.

American Psychological Association (APA) Practice Organization. (2006). *Advancing colleague assistance in professional psychology.* Retrieved from http://www.apapracticecentral.org/ce/self-care/colleague-assist-download.pdf

Anderson, A., & West, S. G. (2011). Violence against mental health professionals: When the treater becomes the victim. *Innovations in Clinical Neuroscience, 8*(3), 34–39. Retrieved from http://www.ncbi.nlm.nih.gov/pmc/articles/PMC3074201

Anupam, B., Jena, A. B., Seabury, S., Lakdawalla, D., & Chandra, A. (2011). Malpractice risk according to physician specialty. *New England Journal of Medicine, 365,* 629–636.

Appelbaum, P. S. (1996). Suits against clinicians for warning of patients' violence. *Psychiatric Services, 47*(7), 683–684.

Appelbaum, P. S. (2000). Patients' responsibility for their suicidal behavior. *Psychiatric Services, 51,* 15–16.

Appelbaum, P. S. (2007). Assessment of patients' competence to consent to treatment. *New England Journal of Medicine, 357,* 1834–1840. Retrieved from http://www.nejm.org/doi/full/10.1056/nejmcp074045

Artman, L. K., & Daniels, J. A. (2010). Disability and psychotherapy practice: Cultural competence and practical tips. *Professional Psychology: Research and Practice, 41*(5), 442–448.

Babor, T. F., de la Fuente, J. R., Saunders, J., & Grant, M. (1992). *AUDIT. The Alcohol Use Disorders Identification Test: Guidelines for use in primary health care.* Geneva, Switzerland: World Health Organization.

Barge, B. N., & Fenalason, K. J. (1989). *Dealing effectively with malpractice litigation.* St. Paul Fire and Marine Insurance Company: St. Paul, MN.

Barlow, D. H. (2010). Negative effects from psychological treatments. *American Psychologist, 65,* 13–19.

Barnett, J. E. (2011). Utilizing technological innovations to enhance psychotherapy supervision, training, and outcomes. *Psychotherapy, 48*(2), 103–108.

Barnett, J. E., Cornish, J. A. E., Goodyear, R. K., & Lichtenberg, J. W. (2007a). Commentaries on the ethical and effective practice of clinical supervision. *Professional Psychology: Research and Practice, 38*(3), 268–275.

Barnett, J. E., Hillard, D., & Lowery, K. (2001). Ethical and legal issues in the treatment of minors. In L. VandeCreek & T. L. Jackson (Eds.), *Innovations in clinical practice: A source book* (Vol. 19, pp. 257–272). Sarasota, FL: Professional Resource Press.

Barnett, J. E., Lazarus, A. A., Vasquez, M. J. T., Moorehead-Slaughter, O., & Johnson, W. B. (2007b). Boundary issues and multiple relationships: Fantasy and reality. *Professional Psychology: Research and Practice, 38*(4), 401–410. Retrieved from http://dx.doi.org/10.1037/0735-7028.38.4.401

Barnett, J. E., MacGlashan, S. G., & Clarke, A. J. (2000). Risk management and ethical issues regarding termination and abandonment. In L. VandeCreek & T. L. Jackson (Eds.), *Innovations in clinical practice: A source book* (Vol. 18, pp. 231–245). Sarasota, FL: Professional Resource Exchange.

Barnett, J. E., & Molzon, C. H. (2014). Clinical supervision of psychotherapy: Essential ethics issues for supervisors and supervisees. *Journal of Clinical Psychology, 70*(11), 1051–1061.

Barnett, J. E., & Walfish, S. (2011). *Billing and collecting for your mental health practice: Effective strategies and ethical practice*. Washington, DC: American Psychological Association.

Barsky, A. E. (2012). *Clinicians in court: A guide to subpoenas, depositions, testifying, and everything else you need to know* (2nd ed.). New York: Guilford Press.

Beahrs, J. O., & Gutheil, T. G. (2001). Informed consent in psychotherapy. *American Journal of Psychiatry, 158*(1), 4–10.

Beck, I. C. (1990). The potentially violent patient: Clinical, legal, and ethical implications. In E. A. Margenau (Ed.), *The encyclopedic handbook of private practice* (pp. 697–709). New York: Gardner Press.

Becker-Blease, K. A., & Freyd, J. J. (2006). Research participants telling the truth about their lives: The ethics of asking and not asking about abuse. *American Psychologist, 61*(3), 218–226. Retrieved from http://dx.doi.org/10.1037/0003-066X.61.3.218

Bennett, B. E., Bricklin, P. M., Harris, E., Knapp, S., VandeCreek, L., & Younggren, J. N. (2006). *Assessing and managing risk in psychological practice: An individualized approach*. Rockville, MD: American Psychological Association Insurance Trust.

Bennett, B. E., Bryant, B., VandenBos, G. R., & Greenwood, A. (1990). *Professional liability and risk management*. Washington, DC: American Psychological Association.

Berk, M., Rubin, R., & Peck, S. (1994). *Super-pak practice builders: Forty forms for psychotherapists*. Island Park, NY: Private Practitioners Group.

Berlin, F. S., Malin, H. M., & Dean, S. (1991). Effects of statutes requiring psychiatrists to report suspected sexual abuse of children. *American Journal of Psychiatry, 148*(4), 449–453.

Berman, A. L. (2006). Risk management with suicidal patients. *Journal of Clinical Psychology: In Session, 62*(2), 171–184. Retrieved from http://ruralccp.org/lyra-data/storage/asset/berman-27c8.pdf

Bindrim, P. (1980, July). Group therapy: Protecting privacy. *Psychology Today*, pp. 24–28.

Boedecker, A. L. (1995). Practicing with integrity: Responding to a malpractice suit. *Networker: Newsletter of the New Hampshire Psychological Association, 7*(7), 2–3.

Bogie, M. (2002). *Shopping tips*. Retrieved from http://americanprofessional.com/shopping.htm

Bongar, B. (2013). *The suicidal patient: Clinical and legal standards of care* (3rd ed.). Washington, DC: American Psychological Association.

Bongar, B., Berman, A. L., Maris, R. W., Silverman, M. M., Packman, W., & Harris, E. A. (Eds.). (1999). *Risk management with suicidal patients*. New York: Guilford Press.

Borkosky, B. G. (2014). Who is the client and who controls release of records in a forensic evaluation?: A review of ethics codes and practice guidelines. *Psychological Injury and Law, 7*(3), 264–289.

Borkosky, B. G., & Smith, D. M. (2015). The risks and benefits of disclosing psychotherapy records to the legal system: What psychologists and patients need to know for informed consent. *International Journal of Law and Psychiatry, 42–43*, 19–30.

Bouhoutsos, J., Holroyd, J., Lerman, H., Forer, B. R., & Greenberg, M. (1983). Sexual intimacy between psychotherapists and patients. *Professional Psychology: Research and Practice, 14*, 185–196.

Braaten, E. (2007). *The child clinician's report-writing handbook*. New York: Guilford Press.

Brabeck, M., & Brabeck, K. (2002). Ethics rounds: Reporting past abuse, Part II. *Monitor on Psychology, 33*(7). Retrieved from http://www.apa.org/monitor/julaug02/ethics.aspx

Branscomb, L. (1996, Winter). Clinical advantages of the extended psychotherapy disclosure form: A feminist ethical perspective. *Georgia Psychologist*, pp. 46–49.

Brief for the American Psychological Association (APA) and the Pennsylvania Psychological Association as Amici Curiae Supporting Respondents, Emerich v. Philadelphia Center for Human Development, Inc., et al. (E.D. Allocatur Docket 1996 No. 145) (1996). Retrieved from http://www.apa.org/about/offices/ogc/amicus/emerich.aspx

Brodsky, S. L., & McKinzey, R. K. (2002). The ethical confrontation of the unethical forensic colleague. *Professional Psychology: Research and Practice, 33*(3), 307–309.

Bryan, C. J., Stone, S. L., & Rudd, M. D. (2011). A practical, evidence-based approach for means-restriction counseling with suicidal patients. *Professional Psychology: Research and Practice, 42*(5), 339–346.

Campbell, A., & Hemsley, S. (2009). Outcome rating scale and session rating scale in psychological practice: Clinical utility of ultra-brief measures. *Clinical Psychologist, 13*(1), 1–9.

Carey, M. P., & Vanable, P. A. (2013). Working with patients at risk for HIV and other sexually transmitted diseases. In G. P. Koocher, J. C. Norcross, & B. A. Greene (Eds.), *Psychologists' desk reference* (3rd ed., pp. 225–229). New York: Oxford University Press.

Centers for Disease Control and Prevention (CDC). (2014). Suicide and self-inflicted injury: Data for 2010. Retrieved from http://www.cdc.gov/nchs/fastats/suicide.htm

Cervantes, N. (1992). Ethical responsibility of therapists: Spousal abuse cases. *Psychotherapy Bulletin, 26*(4), 12–15.

Charles, S. C., & Frisch, P. R. (2005). *Adverse events, stress, and litigation: A physician's guide*. New York: Oxford University Press.

Chenneville, T. (2000). HIV, confidentiality, and duty to protect: A decision-making model. *Professional Psychology: Research and Practice, 31*(6), 661–670.

Childress, C. (2000). Ethical issues in providing online psychotherapeutic interventions. *Journal of Medical Internet Research, 2*(1), e5. Retrieved from http://www.jmir.org/2000/1/e5

Clement, P. W. (1999). *Outcomes and incomes: How to evaluate, improve, and market your psychotherapy practice by measuring outcomes*. New York: Guilford Press.

Clement, P. W. (2008). Outcomes from 40 years of psychotherapy in a private practice. *American Journal of Psychotherapy, 62*(3), 215–239.

Cohen, R. J. (1979). *Malpractice: A guide for mental health professionals*. New York: Free Press.

Cohen, R. J. (1990). The professional liability of behavioral scientists. In E. A. Margenau (Ed.), *The encyclopedic handbook of private practice* (pp. 651–663). New York: Gardner Press. (Original work published 1983)

Cone, J. (2000). *Evaluating outcomes: Empirical tools for effective practice*. Washington, DC: American Psychological Association.

Corcoran, K. J., & Fischer, J. (2013). *Measures for clinical practice and research: A sourcebook* (5th ed.). New York: Oxford University Press.

Coverdale, J. H., Roberts, L. W., & Louie, A. K. (2007). Encountering patient suicide: Emotional responses, ethics, and implications for training programs. *Academic Psychiatry, 31*(5). Retrieved from http://psychiatry.utoronto.ca/wp-content/uploads/2011/01/EncounteringSuicide-Academic_Psychiatry.pdf

Curlin, F. A., Odell, S. V., Lawrence, R. E., Chin, M. H., Lantos, J. D., Meador, K. G., et al. (2007). The relationship between psychiatry and religion among U.S. physicians. *Psychiatric Services, 58*, 1193–1198.

Dana, R. H. (2005). *Multicultural assessment: Principles, applications and examples*. Mahwah, NJ: Erlbaum.

Dass-Brailsford, P. (2013). Counseling people living with HIV. In G. P. Koocher, J. C. Norcross, & B. A. Greene (Eds.), *Psychologists' desk reference* (3rd ed., pp. 299–304). New York: Oxford University Press.

Dattilio, F. M. (2002). Board certification in psychology: Is it really necessary? *Professional Psychology: Research and Practice, 33*(1), 54–57.

D'Avanzo, C. E., & Geissler, E. (2003). *A pocket guide to cultural health assessment* (3rd ed.). St. Louis, MO: Mosby.

Davis, D. D. (2008). *Terminating therapy: A professional guide to ending on a positive note*. Hoboken, NJ: Wiley.

Davis, D. D., & Younggren, J. N. (2009). Ethical competence in psychotherapy termination. *Professional Psychology: Research and Practice, 40*(6), 572–578.

de Becker, G. (1999). *The gift of fear and other survival signals that protect us from violence*. New York: Dell.

DeBell, C., & Jones, R. D. (1997). Privileged communication at last?: An overview of *Jaffee v. Redmond*. *Professional Psychology: Research and Practice, 28*(6), 559–566.

DeLeon, P. H., Bock, P. S., Richmond, M. S., Mays, M., & Cullen, E. A. (2006). A perspective on the nation's antitrust policies: Implications for psychologists. *Professional Psychology: Research and Practice, 37*(4), 374–383.

Dimidjian, S., & Hollon S. D. (2010). How would we know if psychotherapy were harmful? *American Psychologist, 65*(1), 21–33.

Drude, K., & Lichstein, M. (2005, August). Psychologists' use of e-mail with clients: Some ethical considerations. *The Ohio Psychologist*, pp. 13–17. Retrieved from http://www.kspope.com/ethics/email.php#copy

Dvoskin, J. A. (2006). Internet consultation. *Newsletter of the American Psychology–Law Society, 26*(2). Retrieved from http://www.apadivisions.org/division-41/publications/newsletters/news/2006/07-issue.pdf

Dwyer, J., & Shih, A. (1998). The ethics of tailoring the patient's chart. *Psychiatric Services, 49*(10), 1309–1312.

Edwards, G. (2014). Doing their duty: An empirical analysis of the unintended effect of *Tarasoff v. Regents* on homicidal activity. *Journal of Law and Economics, 57*(2), 321–348.

Eisen, S. V., Shaul, J. A., Claridge, B., Nelson, D., Spink, J., & Cleary, P. D. (1999). Development of a consumer survey for behavioral health services. *Psychiatric Services, 50*(6), 793–798.

Ellis, M. V., Berger, L., Hanus, A. E., Ayala, E. E., Swords, R. A., & Siembor, M. (2014). Inadequate and harmful clinical supervision: Testing a revised framework and assessing occurrence. *The Counseling Psychologist, 42*(4), 434–472. Retrieved from

Emerich v. Philadelphia Center for Human Development, 720 A.2d 1032 (Pa. 1998).

Epstein, R. S., & Simon, R. I. (1990). The Exploitation Index: An early warning indicator of boundary violations in psychotherapy. *Bulletin of the Menninger Clinic, 54*(4), 450–465.

Ewing, C. P. (1990). Legal issues in terminating treatment. In E. A. Margenau (Ed.), *The encyclopedic handbook of private practice* (pp. 720–726). New York: Gardner Press.

Ewing, J. A. (1984). Detecting alcoholism: The CAGE questionnaire. *Journal of the American Medical Association, 252*, 1905–1907.

Ewing v. Goldstein, 15 Cal. Rptr. 3d 864 (Cal. Ct. App. 2004).

Falender, C. A., & Shafranske, E. (2004). *Clinical supervision: A competency-based approach.* Washington, DC: American Psychological Association.

Falender, C. A., & Shafranske, E. (2011). *Getting the most out of clinical training and supervision: A guide to practicum students and interns.* Washington, DC: American Psychological Association.

Falvey, J. E., & Cohen, C. R. (2003). The buck stops here: Documenting clinical supervision. *Clinical Supervisor, 22*(2), 63–80.

Figley, C. R. (2002). *Treating compassion fatigue.* New York: Routledge.

Folman, R. (1990). *Legislative action on therapist misconduct: Implications for clinical training and treatment.* Address presented at the annual convention of the American Psychological Association, Boston, MA.

Foster, S. (1996, January). The consequences of violating the "forbidden zone." *Counseling Today*, pp. 25–53.

Fox, S. (2006, October 29). Online health search 2006. Pew Internet and American Life Project. Retrieved from http://www.pewinternet.org/

Fox, S. (2013, July 1). Pew internet: Health. Pew Internet and American Life Project. Retrieved from: http://www.pewinternet.org/2011/05/12/social-media-in-context/

Frick, W. B. (1999). Flight into health: A new interpretation. *Journal of Humanistic Psychology, 39*(4), 58–81.

The FTC consent order text is published in its entirety. (1993, March). *APA Monitor*, p. 8.

Garber, B. D. (1994). Practical limitations in considering psychotherapy with children of separation and divorce. *Psychotherapy, 31*(2), 254–261.

Garber, B. D. (2015). *Ten child-centered forensic family evaluation tools: An empirically annotated user's guide.* Scottsdale, AZ: Unhooked Books.

Glassman, J. B. (1998). Preventing and managing board complaints: The downside of custody evaluation. *Professional Psychology: Research and Practice, 29*(2), 121–124.

Goldman, M. J., & Gutheil, T. G. (1994). The misperceived duty to report patients' past crimes. *Bulletin of the American Academy of Psychiatry and the Law, 22*(3), 407–410.

Goode, T. D. (2000). *Promoting cultural diversity and cultural competency: Self-assessment checklist for personnel providing services and supports to children with special health needs and their families.* Retrieved from http://nccc.georgetown.edu/documents/ChecklistBehavioralHealth.pdf

Goodman, J. D., McKay, J. R., & DePhilippis, D. (2013). Progress monitoring in mental health and addiction treatment: A means of improving care. *Professional Psychology: Research and Practice, 44*(4), 231–246.

Goodman, M., Brown, J., & Deitz, P. (1992). *Managing managed care: A mental health practitioner's survival guide.* Washington, DC: American Psychiatric Press.

Gottlieb, M. C. (1993). Avoiding exploitative dual relationships: A decision-making model. *Psychotherapy, 30*(1), 41–48.

Gottlieb, M. C., Robinson, K., & Younggren, J. N. (2007). Multiple relations in supervision: Guidance for administrators, supervisors, and students. *Professional Psychology: Research and Practice, 38,* 241–247.

Grant, R. L., & Maletzky, B. M. (1973). Application of the Weed system to psychiatric records. *Psychiatry in Medicine, 3,* 119–129.

Greenberg, S. A., & Shuman, D. W. (1997). Irreconcilable conflict between therapeutic and forensic roles. *Professional Psychology: Research and Practice, 28*(1), 50–57. Retrieved from http://www.drbevsmallwood.com/Forensic_vs_Therapeutic.pdf

Grisso, T., & Appelbaum, P. S. (1998). *Assessing competence to consent to treatment: A guide for physicians and other health professionals.* New York: Oxford University Press.

Grisso, T., Appelbaum, P. S., & Hill-Fotouhi, C. (1997) The MacCAT-T: A clinical tool to assess patients' capacities to make treatment decisions. *Psychiatric Services, 48,* 1416–1419. Retrieved from http://ps.psychiatryonline.org/doi/abs/10.1176/ps.48.11.1415

Group for the Advancement of Psychiatry (GAP). (1990). *Casebook in psychiatric ethics.* New York: Brunner/Mazel.

Grunder, T. M. (1980). On the readability of surgical consent forms. *New England Journal of Medicine, 302,* 900–902.

Gutheil, T. G. (1980). Paranoia and progress notes: A guide to forensically informed psychiatric record keeping. *Hospital and Community Psychiatry, 31,* 479–482.

Gutheil, T. G. (1992). Approaches to forensic assessment of false claims of sexual misconduct by therapist. *Bulletin of the American Academy of Psychiatry and the Law, 20,* 289–296.

Gutheil, T. G. (1993). Letter to the editor. *Hospital and Community Psychiatry, 44*(10), 1005.

Gutheil, T. G. (2007). Boundary issues. In J. M. Oldham, A. E. Skodol, & D. S. Bender (Eds.), *The American Psychiatric Publishing textbook of personality disorders* (pp. 421–448). Washington, DC: American Psychiatric Publishing.

Gutheil, T. G., & Appelbaum, P. S. (2000). *Clinical handbook of psychiatry and the law* (3rd ed.). Philadelphia: Lippincott Williams & Wilkins.

Gutheil, T. G., & Brodsky, A. (2008). *Preventing boundary violations in clinical practice.* New York: Guilford Press

Gutheil, T. G., & Gabbard, G. O. (1993). The concept of boundaries in clinical practice. *American Journal of Psychiatry, 150*(2), 188–196.

Gutheil, T. G., & Gabbard, G. O. (1998). Misuses and misunderstandings of boundary theory in clinical and regulatory settings. *American Journal of Psychiatry, 155,* 409–414.

Guy, J. K., Brown, C. K., & Poelstra, P. L. (1992). Safety concerns and protective measures used by psychotherapists. *Professional Psychology: Research and Practice, 23*(5), 421–423.

Haas, L. J., & Cummings, N. A. (1991). Managed outpatient mental health plans: Clinical, ethical, and practical guidelines for participation. *Professional Psychology: Research and Practice, 22*(1), 45–51.

Haas, L. J., & Malouf, J. L. (2005). *Keeping up the good work: A practitioner's guide to mental health ethics* (4th ed.). Sarasota, FL: Professional Resource Exchange.

Haas, L. J., Malouf, J. L., & Mayerson, N. H. (1986). Ethical dilemmas in psychological practice: Results of a national survey. *Professional Psychology: Research and Practice, 17,* 317–321.

Hall, R. C. W., & Hall, R. C. W. (2001). False allegations: The role of the forensic psychiatrist. *Journal of Psychiatric Practice, 7*(5), 343–346.

Hall, R. C. W., Platt, D. E., & Hall, R. C. W. (1999). Suicide risk assessment: A review of risk factors for suicide in 100 patients who made severe suicide attempts: Evaluation of suicide risk in a time of managed care. *Psychosomatics, 40,* 18–27.

Hamberger, L. K. (2000). Requests for complete record release: A three-step response protocol. *Psychotherapy, 37*(10), 89–97.

Handelsman, M. M., & Galvin, M. D. (1988). Facilitating informed consent for outpatient psychotherapy: A suggested written format. *Professional Psychology: Research and Practice, 19*(2), 223–225.

Hansen, I. C., Green, S., & Kutner, K. B. (1989). Ethical issues facing school psychologists working with families. *Professional School Psychology, 4,* 245–255.

Hansen, N. D., Randazzo, K. V., Schwardz, A., Marshall, M., Kalis, D., Frazier, R., et al. (2006). Do we practice what we preach?: An exploratory survey of multicultural psychotherapy competencies. *Professional Psychology: Research and Practice, 37*(1), 66–74.

Hare-Mustin, R. T., Marecek, I., Kaplan, A. G., & Liss-Levinson, N. (1979). Rights of clients, responsibilities of therapists. *American Psychologist, 34,* 3–16.

Harris, E. A. (n.d.) Issues with reimbursement under Medicare. https://www.trustinsurance.com/Portals/0/documents/medicare.pdf

Harris, E. A. (2013). Risk management issues of fee adjustments and sliding fee scales. *American Psychological Association Insurance Trust.* Retrieved January 16, 2014, from https://www.trustinsurance.com/Portals/0/documents/SlidingFees.pdf

Harris, S. (1993). *Ten steps to create a successful treatment plan.* Ridgewood, NJ: Ridgewood Financial Institute.

Haspel, K. C., Jorgenson, L. M., Wincze, J. P., & Parsons, J. P. (1997). Legislative intervention regarding therapist sexual misconduct: An overview. *Professional Psychology: Research and Practice, 28*(1), 63–72.

Health Information Technology for Economic and Clinical Health (HITECH) Act, enacted under Title XIII of the American Recovery and Reinvestment Act of 2009, Pub. Law No. 111-5, 123 Stat. 115 (2009).

Health Insurance Portability and Accountability Act (HIPAA) of 1996, Pub. Law No. 104-191, 110 Stat. 1936 (1996).

Health Insurance Portability and Accountability Act (HIPAA) Omnibus Final Rule, 78 Fed. Reg. 5565 (January 25, 2013). Retrieved from http://www.gpo.gov/fdsys/pkg/FR-2013-01-25/pdf/2013-01073.pdf

Heilbron, N., Compton, J. S., Daniel, S. S., & Goldston, D. B. (2010). The problematic label of suicide gesture: Alternatives for clinical research and practice. *Professional Psychology: Research and Practice, 41*(3), 221–227.

Higuchi, S. A. (1994). Recent managed care legislative and legal issues. In R. L. Lowman & R. I. Resnick (Eds.), *The mental health professional's guide to managed care* (pp. 83–118). Washington, DC: American Psychological Association.

Indest, G. F. (2013, November 12). Don't resign your professional license in the midst of an investigation. Retrieved from http://www.kevinmd.com/blog/2013/11/resign-professional-license-midst-investigation.html

Jaffee v. Redmond, 518 U.S. 1 (1996).

Jobes, D. A. (2016). *Managing suicidal risk: A collaborative approach* (2nd ed.). New York: Guilford Press.

Joyce, A. S., Piper, W. E., Ogrodniczuk, J. S., & Klein, R. H. (2007). *Termination in psychotherapy: A psychodynamic model of processes and outcomes.* Washington, DC: American Psychological Association.

Jureidini, J. (2007). The black box warning: Decreased prescriptions and increased youth suicide? *American Journal of Psychiatry, 164,* 1907. Retrieved from http://ajp.psychiatryonline.org/doi/full/10.1176/appi.ajp.2007.07091463

Kachorek, J. (1990). Record keeping. In E. A. Margenau (Ed.), *The encyclopedic handbook of private practice* (pp. 96–112). New York: Gardner Press.

Kane, L. (2013, July 24). Medscape malpractice report: The experience of getting sued. Retrieved from http://www.medscape.com/features/slideshow/malpractice-report/public#25

Keith-Spiegel, P. (1977, September). *Sex with clients: Ten reasons why it is a very stupid thing to do.* Paper presented at the annual convention of the American Psychological Association, Washington, DC.

Keith-Spiegel, P. (2013a). *Red flags in psychotherapy: Stories of ethics complaints and resolutions.* New York: Routledge.

Keith-Spiegel, P. (2013b). Confronting an unethical colleague. In G. P. Koocher, J. C. Norcross, & B. A. Greene (Eds.), *Psychologists' desk reference* (3rd ed., pp. 567–572). New York: Oxford University Press.

Kernisan, L. (2013). Six awkward concerns in my Open Notes. Retrieved from http://thehealthcareblog. com/blog/2013/01/23/six-awkward-concerns-in-my-opennotes

Kiresuk, T., Smith, A., & Cardillo, J. E. (Eds.). (1994). *Goal attainment scaling: Applications, theory, and measurement.* Hillsdale, NJ: Erlbaum.

Kirsch, I. (2011). *The emperor's new drugs: Exploding the antidepressant myth.* New York: Basic Books.

Klein, J., Macbeth, J., & Onek, J. (1984). *Legal issues in the private practice of psychiatry.* Washington, DC: American Psychiatric Press.

Knapp, S. (1992a, April 16). *Record keeping.* Handout presented at workshop, Practicing Safely and Ethically in the 1990s, Pittsburgh, PA.

Knapp, S. (1992b, April). Medicare update. *Pennsylvania Psychologist Update,* p. 7.

Knapp, S. (1994). *Pennsylvania law and psychology.* Harrisburg: Pennsylvania Psychological Association.

Knapp, S., & Gavazzi, J. (2012). Can checklists help reduce treatment failures? *The Pennsylvania Psychologist.* Retrieved from http://www.ethicalpsychology.com/2012/04/can-checklists-help-reduce-treatment.html

Knapp, S., Gottlieb, M., Berman, J., & Handelsman, M. M. (2007). When laws and ethics collide: What should psychologists do? *Professional Psychology: Research and Practice, 38,* 54–59.

Knapp, S., & VandeCreek, L. (1983). Malpractice risks with suicidal patients. *Psychotherapy: Theory, Research, and Practice, 20,* 274–280.

Knapp, S., & VandeCreek, L. (2001). Psychotherapists's legal responsibility to third parties: Does it extend to alleged perpetrators of childhood abuse? *Professional Psychology: Research and Practice, 32*(5), 479–783.

Knapp, S., VandeCreek, L., & Tepper, A. (1998). *Pennsylvania law and psychology* (3rd ed.). Harrisburg: Pennsylvania Psychological Association.

Knapp, S., Younggren, J. N., VandeCreek, L., Harris, E., & Martin, J. N. (2013). *Assessing and managing risk in psychological practice: An individualized approach* (2nd ed.). Washington, DC: American Psychological Association Insurance Trust.

Kobayashi, M., Smith, T. P., & Norcross, J. C. (1998). Enhancing adherence. In G. P. Koocher, J. C. Norcross, & S. S. Hill III (Eds.), *Psychologists' desk reference* (pp. 23–60). New York: Oxford University Press.

*Keely Kolmes, Psy.D. Business Information* Retrieved July 1, 2015, from http://www.yelp.com/biz/keely-kolmes-psyd-san-francisco

Kolmes, K. (2010). *My private practice social media policy.* Retrieved September 29, 2012, from http://www.drkkolmes.com/docs/socmed.pdf

Koocher, G. (2008). Ethical challenges in mental health services to children and families. *Journal of Clinical Psychology, 64,* 601–612.

Koocher, G., & Keith-Spiegel, P. (2008). *Ethics in psychology: Professional standards and cases* (3rd ed.). New York: Oxford University Press.

Kramer, S. A. (1990). *Positive endings in psychotherapy: Bringing meaningful closure to therapeutic relationships.* San Francisco: Jossey-Bass.

Kremer, T. G., & Gesten, E. L. (1998). Confidentiality limits of managed care and clients' willingness to self-disclose. *Professional Psychology: Research and Practice, 29*(6), 553–558.

Kruger, J., & Dunning, D. (2002). Unskilled and unaware—but why?: A reply to Krueger and Mueller (2002). *Journal of Personality and Social Psychology, 82*(2), 189–192.

Lamb, D. H., Catanzaro, S. J., & Moorman, A. S. (2003). Psychologists reflect on their sexual relationships with clients, supervisees, and students: Occurrence, impact, rationales, and collegial intervention. *Professional Psychology:Research and Practice, 23*(1), 102–107.

Lambert, M. J., & Shimokawa, K. (2011). Collecting client feedback. *Psychotherapy, 48*(1), 72–79.

Lambert, W., Salzer, M. S., & Bickman, L. (1998). Clinical outcome, consumer satisfaction, and ad hoc ratings of improvement in children's mental health. *Journal of Consulting and Clinical Psychology, 66*(2), 270–279.

Larsen, D. L., Attkisson, C. C., Hargreaves, W. A., & Nguyen, T. D. (1979). Assessment of client/patient satisfaction: Development of the general scale. *Evaluation and Program Planning, 2*, 197–207.

Legal issues: How to avoid problems with cellular phones and fax machines. (1992). *Psychotherapy Finances, 18*(2), 3.

Letter in Support of Petition for Review, Ewing et al. v. Goldstein (Court of Appeal, Second Appellate District, Division Eight), 2nd Gr. No. B1633112 (2004). Retrieved from http://www.apa.org/about/offices/ogc/amicus/ewing.aspx

Lewis, L. M. (2007). No-harm contracts: A review of what we know. *Suicide and Life-Threatening Behavior, 37*(1), 50–57.

Ley, P. (1982). Studies in recall in medical settings. *Human Learning, 1*, 223–233.

Liberman, B. (1990). Letter to the editor. *Independent Psychologist, 10*(4), 5.

Lillenfeld, S. (2007). Psychological treatments that cause harm. *Perspectives on Psychological Science, 2*(1), 53–70.

Littrell, J., & Ashford, J. B. (1995). Is it proper for psychologists to discuss medications with clients? *Professional Psychology: Research and Practice, 26*(3), 238–244.

Maden, A. (2007). *Treating violence: A guide to risk management in mental health.* New York: Oxford University Press.

Maples, J. L., & Walker, R. L. (2014). Consolidation rather than termination: Rethinking how psychologists label and conceptualize the final phase of psychological treatment. *Professional Psychology: Research and Practice, 45*(2), 104–110.

Maris, R. W., Berman, A. L., & Silverman, M. M. (2000). *Comprehensive textbook of suicidology.* New York: Guilford Press.

Marsh, D. T. (1995, January). Confidentiality and the rights of families: Resolving possible conflicts. *Pennsylvania Psychologist Update*, pp. 1–3.

Maslach, C., & Zimbardo, P. G. (2003). *Burnout: The cost of caring.* Dallas, TX: Major Books.

McArdle, E. (2003, August 18). Small firm specializes in patient abuse by therapists: Far more common than many suspect. *Lawyers Weekly USA.* Retrieved from http://www.advocateweb.org/publications/articles-2/general/small-firm-specializes-patient-abuse-therapists-far-common-many-suspect

McGee, T. F. (2003). Observations on the retirement of professional psychologists. *Professional Psychology: Research and Practice, 34*(1), 388–395.

McGoldrick, M., Giordano, J., & Garcia-Preto, N. (Eds.). (2005). *Ethnicity and family therapy* (3rd ed.). New York: Guilford Press.

McMinn, R. R., Staley, R. C., Webb, K. C., & Seegobin, W. (2010). Just what is Christian counseling anyway? *Professional Psychology: Research and Practice, 41*(5), 391–397.

Meehl, P. E. (1973). Why I do not attend case conferences. In P. E. Meehl (Ed.), *Psychodiagnosis: Selected papers.* Minneapolis: University of Minnesota Press. Retrieved from http://meehl.umn.edu/sites/g/files/pua1696/f/099caseconferences.pdf

Miller, I. J. (1998). *Eleven unethical managed care practices every patient should know about (with emphasis on mental health care).* Retrieved from http://www.oregoncounseling.org/Consumer/ElevenDeceptivePrinciples.htm

Miller, I. J. (2001). Protecting privacy with the absence of records. *Independent Practitioner, 21*(2), 78–79.

Monahan, J. (1993). Limiting therapist exposure to *Tarasoff* liability: Guidelines for risk containment. *American Psychologist, 48*(3), 242–250.

Montgomery, L. M., Cupit, B. E., & Wimberley, T. K. (1999). Complaints, malpractice, and risk management: Professional issues and personal experiences. *Professional Psychology: Research and Practice, 30*(4), 402–410.

Morris, R. J. (1993). Ethical issues in the assessment and treatment of children and adolescents. *Register Report, 19*(1), 4–12.

Morrison, J. (2015). *When psychological problems mask medical disorders* (2nd ed.). New York: Guilford Press.

Morrison, J. K., Fredrico, M., & Rosenthal, H. J. (1975). Contracting confidentiality in group psychotherapy. *Journal of Forensic Psychology, 7,* 1–6.

National Association of Social Workers (NASW). (2008). *Code of ethics of the NASW.* Washington, DC: Author. Retrieved from http://www.socialworkers.org/pubs/code/code.asp

National Center for Health Statistics. (1988). *Vital statistics mortality data: Multiple cause-of-death detail.* Hyattsville, MD: U.S. Department of Health and Human Services.

Neimeyer, G. J, Taylor, J. M., Rosensky, R., & Cox, D. (2014). The diminishing durability of knowledge in professional psychology: A second look at specializations. *Professional Psychology: Research and Practice, 45,* 92–98.

New Jersey Courts. (n.d.). *Attorney discipline.* Retrieved from https://www.judiciary.state.nj.us/oae/atty_disc/atty_disc.htm

Norris, M. P., Molinari, V., & Rosowsky, E. (1998). Providing mental health care to older adults: Unraveling the maze of Medicare and managed care. *Psychotherapy, 35*(4), 490–497.

Nowell, D., & Spruill, J. (1993). If it's not absolutely confidential, will information be disclosed? *Professional Psychology: Research and Practice, 24*(3), 367–369.

Odeh, M. S., Zeiss, R. A., & Huss, M. T. (2006). Cues they use: Clinicians' endorsement of risk cues in predictions of dangerousness. *Behavioral Science and the Law, 24*(2), 147–156.

O'Neill, P. (1998). *Negotiating consent in psychotherapy.* New York: New York University Press.

Paniagua, F. A. (2005). *Assessing and treating culturally diverse clients: A practical guide* (3rd ed.). Thousand Oaks, CA: Sage.

Papatola, K. J., & Lustig, S. L. (2015). Managing managed care's outpatient review process: Insights and recommendations from peer reviewers at a health services company. *Professional Psychology: Research and Practice, 46*(3), 161–167.

Parsons, I. P., & Wincze, I. P. (1995). A survey of client–therapist sexual involvement in Rhode Island as reported by subsequent treating therapists. *Professional Psychology: Research and Practice, 26*(2), 171–175.

Patient Protection and Affordable Care Act (PPACA) of 2010, Pub. Law No. 111-148, 124 Stat. 119 (2010).

Patten, C., Barnett, T., & Houlihan, D. (1991). Ethics in marital and family therapy: A review of the literature. *Professional Psychology: Research and Practice, 22,* 171–175.

Pekarik, G. (1985). Coping with dropouts. *Professional Psychology: Research and Practice, 16*(1), 114–123.

Pekarik, G., & Guidry, L. L. (1999). Relationship of satisfaction to symptom change, follow-up adjustment, and clinical significance in private practice. *Professional Psychology: Research and Practice, 30*(5), 474–478.

Pekarik, G., & Wolff, C. B. (1996). Relationship of satisfaction to symptom change, follow-up adjustment, and clinical significance. *Professional Psychology: Research and Practice, 27*(2), 202–208.

Peterson, C., & Seligman, M. E. P. (2004). The *Values in Action (VIA) classification of strengths.* Washington, DC: American Psychological Association.

Petry, S. S., & McGoldrick, M. (2013). Using genograms in assessment and therapy. In G. P. Koocher, J. C. Norcross, & B. A. Greene (Eds.), *Psychologists' desk reference* (3rd ed., pp. 384–390). New York: Oxford University Press.

Philadelphia Society of Clinical Psychologists, Committee on Ethics. (1988, January–February). Ethical issues in psychotherapy termination. *Pennsylvania Psychologist,* p. 10.

Piercy, F., Lasswell, M., & Brock, G. (1989). *AAMFT forms book.* Washington, DC: American Association for Marriage and Family Therapy.

Pomerantz, A. M. (2000). What if prospective clients knew how managed care impacts psychologists' practice and ethics?: An exploratory study. *Ethics and Behavior, 10*(2), 159–171.

Pomerantz, A. M., & Handelsman, M. A. (2004). Informed consent revisited: An updated written question format. *Professional Psychology: Research and Practice, 35*(2), 201–205.

Pope, K. S. (1988a). Dual relationships: A source of ethical, legal and clinical problems. *Independent Practitioner, 8*(4), 17–25.

Pope, K. S. (1988b). How clients are harmed by sexual contact with mental health professionals: The syndrome and its prevalence. *Journal of Counseling and Development, 67,* 222–226.

Pope, K. S. (1988c). Fee policies and procedures: Causes of malpractice suits and ethics complaints. *Independent Practitioner, 8*(4), 24–29.

Pope, K. S. (1988d). More on avoiding malpractice in the area of diagnosis, assessment, and testing. *Independent Practitioner, 8*(4), 23–24.

Pope, K. S. (1989). Malpractice suits, licensing disciplinary actions and ethics cases: Frequencies, causes, and costs. *Independent Practitioner, 9*(1), 22–26.

Pope, K. S. (2000). Therapists' sexual feelings and behaviors: Research, trends, and quandaries. In L. Szuchman & F. Muscarella (Eds.), *Psychological perspectives on human sexuality* (pp. 603–658). New York: Wiley.

Pope, K. S. (2014). Dual relationships, multiple relationships, and boundary decisions. Retrieved from http://www.kspope.com/dual/index.php

Pope, K. S. (n.d.). *Informed consent in psychotherapy and counseling: Forms, standards and guidelines.* Retrieved from http://www.kspope.com/consent/index.php

Pope, K. S., & Vasquez, M. J. T. (2005). *How to survive and thrive as a therapist: Information, ideas, and resources for psychologists in practice.* Washington, DC: American Psychological Association.

Pope, K. S., & Vazquez, M. J. T. (2007). *Ethics in psychotherapy and counseling: A practical guide* (3rd ed.). San Francisco: Jossey-Bass.

Pope, K. S., & Vasquez, M. J. T. (2011). *Ethics in psychotherapy and counseling: A practical guide* (4th ed.). Hoboken, NJ: Wiley.

Pope, K. S., & Vasquez, M. J. T. (2016). *Ethics in psychotherapy and counseling: A practical guide* (5th ed.). Hoboken, NJ: Wiley.

Potter, W. (2010). *Deadly spin: An insurance company insider speaks out on how corporate PR is killing health care and deceiving Americans.* New York: Bloomsbury Press.

Pressman, R. M., & Siegler, R. (1983). *The independent practitioner: Practice management for the allied health professional.* Homewood, IL: Dow Jones-Irwin.

Proskauer. (2009). HHS and FTC announce new breach notification rules for unsecured protected health information. Retrieved from http://www.proskauer.com/publications/client-alerts/hhs-and-ftc-announce-new-breach-notification-rules

Pukay-Martin, N. D. (no date). Ethical considerations in working with couples: Confidentiality within the couple. Retrieved from: http://www.e-psychologist.org/index.iml?mdl=exam/show_article.mdl&Material_ID=92

Purcell, R., Powell, M. B., & Mullen, P. E. (2005). Clients who stalk psychologists: Prevalence, methods and motives. *Professional Psychology: Research and Practice, 36*(5), 537–543.

Raoof, M. (2013, February 12). What are the suicide rates for the most common mental disorders? Retrieved from https://www.researchgate.net/post/What_are_the_suicide_rates_for_the_most_common_mental_disorders

Rashid, T. (2013). Assessing strengths in clinical practice. In G. P. Koocher, J. C. Norcross, & B. A. Greene (Eds.), *Psychologists' desk reference* (3rd ed., pp. 64–67). New York: Oxford University Press.

Reid, W. H. (1999). *A clinician's guide to legal issues in psychotherapy or proceed with caution.* Phoenix, AZ: Zeig, Tucker.

Reid, W. H. (2005). Contracting for safety redux. *Journal of Psychiatric Practice, 11*(1), 54–57. Retrieved from http://www.reidpsychiatry.com/columns/15%20Reid%2001-05%20pp%2054-57.pdf

Reed, W. J. (2013). Medical conditions that may present as psychological disorders. In G. P. Koocher, J. C. Norcross, & B. A. Greene (Eds.), *Psychologists' desk reference* (3rd ed., pp. 481–486). New York: Oxford University Press.

Rosenthal, M. B. (2000). Risk sharing and the supply of mental health services. *Journal of Health Economics, 19*, 1047–1065.

Rothschild, B., & Rand, M. (2006). *Help for the helper: The psychophysiology of compassion fatigue and vicarious trauma.* New York: Norton.

Rubenstein, A. K. (2013). Engaging the reluctant adolescent. In G. P. Koocher, J. C. Norcross, & B. A. Greene (Eds.), *Psychologists' desk reference* (3rd ed., pp. 420–424). New York: Oxford University Press.

Rudd, M. D., Joiner, T. E., Jobes, D. A., & King, C. A. (1999). The outpatient treatment of suicidality: An integration of science and recognition of its limitations. *Professional Psychology: Research and Practice, 30*(5), 437–446. Retrieved from http://dx.doi.org/10.1037/0735-7028.30.5.437

Rudd, M. D., Joiner, T. E., & Rajab, M. H. (2001). *Treating suicidal behavior: An effective, time-limited approach.* New York: Guilford Press.

Rueve, M. E., & Welton, R. S. (2008). Violence and mental illness. *Psychiatry (Edgemont), 5*(5), 34–48.

Russell, S. T., & Joyner K. (2001). Adolescent sexual orientation and suicide risk: Evidence from a national study. *American Journal of Public Health, 91*(8), 1276–1281.

Saccuzzo, D. P. (n.d.-a). *Liability for failure to supervise adequately: Let the master beware.* Retrieved from https://www.nationalregister.org/pub/educational-publications-and-resources-pub/educational-publications/liability-for-failure-to-supervise-adequately-let-the-master-beware/

Saccuzzo, D. P. (n.d.-b). *Legal update part 2: Ethical basis for standard of care in supervision.* Retrieved from https://www.nationalregister.org/pub/educational-publications-and-resources-pub/educational-publications/legal-update-part-2-ethical-basis-for-standard-of-care-in-supervision/

Sanbar, S. S., & Firestone, M. H. (2007). Medical malpractice stress syndrome. In S. S. Sanbar (Ed.), *Medical malpractice survival handbook of the American College of Legal Medicine* (pp. 9–15). Philadelphia: Mosby/Elsevier. Retrieved from http://www.panama-publishing.com/support/content/Torts-Medical-Malpractice-Stress-Syndrome.pdf

Sanchez, H. G. (2001). Risk factor model for suicide assessment and intervention. *Professional Psychology: Research and Practice, 32*(4), 351–358.

Saunders, T. R. (1993). Some ethical and legal features of child custody disputes: A case illustration and applications. *Psychotherapy, 30*(1), 49–58.

Schank, J. A., & Skovholt, T. M. (2005). *Ethical practice in small communities: Challenges and rewards for psychologists.* Washington, DC: American Psychological Association.

Schinka, J. (1984). *Personal Problems Checklist.* Odessa, FL: Psychological Assessment Resources.

Sederer, L. I., & Libby, M. (1995). False allegations of sexual misconduct: Clinical and institutional considerations. *Psychiatric Services, 46*(2), 160–163.

Seligman, M. E. P. (1995, November). The effectiveness of psychotherapy: The *Consumer Reports* study. *Consumer Reports,* pp. 734–739. Retrieved from http://www.dearshrink.com/psychotherapy_consumer_report1995_seligman.pdf

Selzer, M. L. (1971). The Michigan Alcoholism Screening Test: The quest for a new diagnostic instrument. *American Journal of Psychiatry, 127*, 1653–1658.

Shapiro, D. L., & Smith, S. R. (2011). *Malpractice in psychology.* Washington, DC: American Psychological Association.

Shea, S. C. (2011). *The practical art of suicide assessment: A guide for mental health professionals and substance abuse counselors* (2nd ed.). Berlin: Mental Health Presses. (Original work published 1999)

Shefet, O. M., & Curtis, R. C. (2013). Terminating psychotherapy. In G. P. Koocher, J. C. Norcross, & B. A. Greene (Eds.), *Psychologists' desk reference* (3rd ed., pp. 263–266). New York: Oxford University Press.

Shuman, D. W., & Foote, W. (1999). *Jaffee v. Redmond*'s impact: Life after the Supreme Court's recognition of a psychotherapist–patient privilege. *Professional Psychology: Research and Practice, 30*(5), 479–487.

Sieck, B. (2012). Obtaining clinical writing informed consent versus using client disguise and recommendations for practice. *Psychotherapy, 49*(1), 3–11.

Simon, R. I. (1992). *Clinical psychiatry and the law* (2nd ed.). Washington, DC: American Psychiatric Press.

Simon, R. I. (2008, February 1). Is it a "true" emergency?: Suicidal patients' access to their?psychiatrists. *Psychiatric Times, 25*(2), 21–24.

Simon, R. I. (2009). Suicide risk assessment forms: Form over substance. *Journal of the American Academy of Psychiatry and the Law, 3*(3), 290–293. Retrieved from http://www.jaapl.org/content/37/3/290.full

Simon, R. I. (2011, March 3). Patient violence against health care professionals: Safety assessment and management. *Psychiatric Times, 28*(2), 16.

Simon R. I. (2012). Screening for suicide risk in a brief medication management appointment. *Psychiatric Times, 29*(5). Retrieved from http://www.psychiatrictimes.com/major-depressive-disorder/screening-suicide-risk-brief-medication-management-appointment

Simon, R. I., & Shuman, D. W. (2007). *Clinical manual of psychiatry and the law.* Washington, DC: American Psychiatric Publishing.

Simpson, S., & Stacy, M. (2004). Avoiding the malpractice snare: Documenting suicide risk assessment. *Journal of Psychiatric Practice, 10*(3), 1–5. Retrieved from http://www.reidpsychiatry.com/columns/Stacy%2005-04.pdf

Skinner, H. A. (1982). The Drug Abuse Screening Test. *Journal on Addictive Behaviors, 7*(4), 363–371.

Soisson, E., VandeCreek, L., & Knapp, S. (1987). Thorough record keeping: A good defense in a litigious era. *Professional Psychology: Research and Practice, 18,* 498–502.

Sonne, J. L. (2006, Fall). Nonsexual multiple relationships: A practical decision-making model for clinicians. *Independent Practitioner,* pp. 187–192.

Sonne, J. L., & Jochai, D. (2014). The "vicissitudes of love" between therapist and patient: A review of the research on romantic and sexual feelings, thoughts, and behaviors in psychotherapy. *Journal of Clinical Psychology: In Session, 70*(2), 182–195.

Soreff, S. M., & McDuffee, M. A. (1993). *Documentation survival handbook for psychiatrists and other mental health professionals: A clinician's guide to charting for better care, certification, reimbursement, and risk management.* Seattle, WA: Hogrefe & Huber.

Spayd, C. S., & Wiley, M. O. (2001, April). Closing a professional practice: Clinical and practical considerations. *Pennsylvania Psychologist Update,* p. 8.

Staal, M. A., & King, R. E. (2000). Managing a multiple relationship environment: The ethics of military psychology. *Professional Psychology: Research and Practice, 31*(6), 698–705.

Standards for privacy of individually identifiable health information, 65 Fed. Reg. 82462 (December 28, 2000). Retrieved from https://www.federalregister.gov/articles/2000/12/28/00-32678/standards-for-privacy-of-individually-identifiable-health-information

Stanley, B., & Brown, G. K. (2008). *Safety plan treatment manual to reduce suicide risk: Veteran version.* Washington, DC: U.S. Department of Veterans Affairs. Retrieved from http://www.mental-health.va.gov/docs/va_safety_planning_manual.pdf

Stout, C. E., Levant, R. F., Reed, G. M., & Murphy, M. J. (2001). Contracts: A primer for psychologists. *Professional Psychology: Research and Practice, 32*(1), 88–91.

Stewart, R. E., & Chambless, D. L. (2008). Treatment failures in private practice: How do psychologists proceed? *Professional Psychology: Research and Practice, 39*(2), 176–181.

Straussner, S. L. A. (Ed.). (2001). *Ethnocultural factors in substance abuse treatment.* New York: Guilford Press.

Stretch, L. S., Nagel, D., & Anthony, K. (2013, Winter). Ethical framework for the use of technology in supervision. *Therapeutic Innovations in Light of Technology, 3*(2), 37–45. Retrieved from http://onlinetherapyinstitute.com/wp-content/uploads/2013/08/EthicalFramework_FEATURE_Vol3_Issue213_FINAL3-4.pdf

Stromberg, C. D., & Dellinger, A. (1993, December). Malpractice and other professional liability. In *The psychologist's legal update, 3*. Washington, DC: National Register of Health Service Providers in Psychology.

Stromberg, C. D., Haggarty, D. I., Mishkin, B., Liebenluft, R. F., McMillan, M. H., Rubin, B. L., et al. (1988). *The psychologist's legal handbook*. Washington, DC: National Register of Health Service Providers in Psychology.

Stuart, R. B. (1975). *Treatment contract*. Champaign, IL: Research Press.

Sturm, I. E. (1987). The psychologist and the problem-oriented record (POR). *Professional Psychology: Research and Practice, 18*, 155–158.

Substance Abuse and Mental Health Services Administration (SAMHSA). (2005). *Substance abuse treatment for persons with co-occurring disorders* (Treatment Improvement Protocol [TIP] Series No. 42, Report No. [SMA] 05-3922). Rockville, MD: Center for Substance Abuse Treatment. Retrieved from http://www.ncbi.nlm.nih.gov/books/NBK64197

Sue, D. W. (2003). *Overcoming our racism: The journey to liberation*. San Francisco: Jossey-Bass.

Sue, D. W. (2010). *Microaggressions in everyday life: Race, gender, and sexual orientation*. Hoboken, NJ: Wiley.

Sue, D. W., & Sue, D. (2008). *Counseling the culturally different: Theory and practice* (5th ed.). Hoboken, NJ: Wiley.

Sullivan, C. M., & Cain, D. (2004). Ethical and safety considerations when obtaining information from or about battered women for research purposes. *Journal of Interpersonal Violence, 19*, 603–616.

Sutter, E., McPherson, R. H., & Geeseman, R. (2002). Contracting for supervision. *Professional Psychology: Research and Practice, 33*(5), 495–498.

Sweet, J. J. (1990). Further considerations of ethics in psychological testing: A broader perspective on releasing records. *Illinois Psychologist, 28*(4), 5–9.

Swift, J. K., Greenberg, R. P., Whipple, J. L., & Kominiak, N. (2012). Practice recommendations for reducing premature termination in therapy. *Professional Psychology: Research and Practice, 43*(4), 379–387.

Tarasoff v. Regents of the University of California, 131 Cal. Rptr. 14, 551 P.2d 334 (1976).

Taube, D. O., & Elwork, A. (1990). Researching the effects of confidentiality law on patients' self-disclosures. *Professional Psychology: Research and Practice, 22*(1), 72–75.

Taylor, R. L. (2007). *Psychological masquerade: Distinguishing psychological from organic disorders* (3rd ed.). New York: Springer.

Thomas, J. T. (2005). Licensing board complaints: Minimizing the impact on the psychologist's defense and clinical practice. *Professional Psychology: Research and Practice, 36*(4), 426–433.

Thomas, J. T. (2007). Informed consent through contracting for supervision: Minimizing risks, enhancing benefits. *Professional Psychology: Research and Practice, 38*(3), 221–231. Retrieved from http://janettthomas.com/wpjtt/wp-content/uploads/2012/10/InformedConsentArticleJanetTThomas.pdf

Thomas, J. T. (2010). *The ethics of supervision and consultation: Practical guidance for mental health professionals*. Washington, DC: American Psychological Association.

Thompson, B. F. (2007). *The impact of false complaints in ethics and licensing board actions on the clinical practice of psychology: A critical analysis of the literature*. Proquest. Unpublished doctoral dissertation, Pacific Graduate School of Psychology–Stanford Consortium of Palo Alto, CA.

Thorn, B. E., Rubin, N. J., Holderby, A. J., & Shealy, R. C. (1996). Client–therapist intimacy: Responses of psychotherapy clients to a consumer-oriented brochure. *Ethics and Behavior, 6*(1), 17–28.

Thorn, B. E., Shealy, R. C., & Briggs, S. D. (1993). Sexual misconduct in psychotherapy: Reactions to a consumer-oriented brochure. *Professional Psychology: Research and Practice, 24*(1), 75–82.

Tracy, M. (n.d.). An ounce of prevention will pay off later for psychiatrists, their practices. Retrieved from http://www.nyspsych.org/assets/docs/prms%20tip%20-%20contingency%20planning.pdf

Ullman, S. E. (1999). Social support and recovery from sexual assault: A review. *Aggression and Violent Behavior: A Review Journal, 4*, 343–358.

Vaccarino, J. M. (1978). Consent, informed consent, and consent forms. *New England Journal of Medicine, 298,* 455.

Van Horne, R. A. (2004). Psychology licensing board disciplinary actions: The realities. *Professional Psychology: Research and Practice, 35*(2), 170–178.

Veldhuis, C. B., & Freyd, J. J. (1999). Groomed for silence; groomed for betrayal. In M. Rivera (Ed.), *Fragment by fragment: Feminist perspectives on memory and child sexual abuse* (pp. 253–282). Charlottetown, Prince Edward Island, Canada: Gynergy Books.

Vespia, K. M., Heckman-Stone, C., & Delworth, U. (2002). Describing and facilitating supervision behaviors in counseling trainees. *Psychotherapy: Theory, Research, Practice, Training, 39*(1), 56–65.

Vinson, J. S. (1987). Use of complaint procedures in cases of therapist–patient sexual contact. *Professional Psychology: Research and Practice, 18*(2), 159–164.

Volk, M. L., Lieber, S. R., Kim, S. Y., Ubel, P. A., & Schneider, C. E. (2012). Contracts with patients in clinical practice. *Lancet, 379*(9810), 7–9. Retrieved from http://europepmc.org/articles/pmc3232314

Walfish, S., & Barnett, J. E. (2009). *Financial success in mental health practice: Essential tools and strategies for practitioners.* Washington, DC: American Psychological Association. Retrieved from http://dx.doi.org/10.1037/11851-000

Walfish, S., & Ducey, B. B. (2007). Readability level of Health Insurance Portability and Accountability Act notices of privacy practices used by psychologists in clinical practice. *Professional Psychology: Research and Practice, 38*(2), 203–207.

Webster, C. D., Bloom, H., & Augimeri, L. (2009). Violence risk assessment in everyday psychiatric practice: Twelve principles help guide clinicians. *Psychiatric Times, 26*(12), 1–4.

Webster, C. D., Haque, Q., & Hucker, S. J. (2014). *Violence risk—Assessment and management: Advances through structured professional judgement and sequential redirections* (2nd ed.). Chichester, UK: Wiley-Blackwell.

Weed, L. L. (1971). *Medical records, medical education and patient care: The problem-oriented record as a basic tool.* Chicago: Year Book Medical.

Weiner, B. A., & Wettstein, R. M. (1993). *Legal issues in mental health care.* New York: Plenum Press.

Werth, J. L., Felfel, E. R., & Benjamin, A. H. (Eds.). (2009). The duty to protect: Ethical, legal, and professional considerations for mental health professionals. Washington, DC: American Psychological Association.

Whitaker, R. (2010a). *Anatomy of an epidemic: Magic bullets, psychiatric drugs, and the astonishing rise of mental illness in America.* New York: Crown.

Whitaker, R. (2010b). *Mad in America: Bad science, bad medicine, and the enduring mistreatment of the mentally ill.* New York: Basic Books.

Wiger, D. E., & Solberg, K. B. (2001). *Tracking mental health outcomes: A therapist's guide to measuring client progress, analyzing data, and improving your practice.* New York: Wiley.

Wilkinson, A. P. (1982). Psychiatric malpractice: Identifying areas of liability. *Trial, 18*(10), 73–77, 89–90.

Williams, M. H. (2000). Victimized by "victims": A taxonomy of antecedents of false complaints against psychotherapists. *Professional Psychology: Research and Practice, 31*(1), 75–81.

Williams, M. H. (2001). The question of psychologists' maltreatment by state licensing boards: Overcoming denial and seeking remedies. *Professional Psychology: Research and Practice, 32*(4), 341–344.

Wilson, S. J. (1980). *Recording guidelines for social workers.* New York: Free Press.

Winer, J. D. (n.d). An overview of handling therapist malpractice cases: Sex, drugs, suicide and bad therapy. Retrieved from http://www.wmlawyers.com/Firm-Highlights/Publications/An-Overview-of-Handling-Therapist-Malpractice-Cases-Sex-Drugs-Suicide-and-Bad-Therapy.shtml

Woody, R. H. (1988). *Fifty ways to avoid malpractice: A guidebook for mental health professionals.* Sarasota, FL: Professional Resource Exchange.

Woody, R. H. (2000). *Child custody: Practice standards, ethical issues, and legal safeguards for mental health professionals.* Sarasota, FL: Professional Resource Press.

Wright, R. H. (1981a). Psychologists and professional liability (malpractice) insurance. *American Psychologist, 36,* 1485–1493.

Wright, R. H. (1981b). What to do until the malpractice lawyer comes: A survivor's manual. *American Psychologist, 36,* 1535–1541.

Yip, P. S. F., Caine, E., Yousuf, S., Chang, S.-S., Wu, K. C.-C., & Chen, Y.-Y. (2012). Means restriction for suicide prevention. *Lancet, 379*(9834), 2393–2399. Retrieved from http://www.thelancet.com/journals/lancet/article/PIIS0140-6736%2812%2960521-2/fulltext

Younggren, J. N. (2002, May). *Ethical decision-making and dual relationships.* Retrieved from http://www.kspope.com/dual/younggren.php

Younggren, J. N., & Gottlieb, M. C. (2004). Managing risk when contemplating multiple relationships. *Professional Psychology: Research and Practice, 35*(3), 255–260.

Younggren, J. N., & Gottlieb, M.C. (2008). Termination and abandonment: History, risk, and risk management. *Professional Psychology: Research and Practice, 39*(5), 498–504.

Zhu, S., & Pierce, J. P. (1995). A new scheduling method for time-limited counseling. *Professional Psychology: Research and Practice, 26*(6), 624–625.

Zuckerman, E. L. (2010). *Clinician's thesaurus: The guide to conducting interviews and writing psychological reports* (7th ed.). New York: Guilford Press.

Zur, O. (2010). *The standard of care in psychotherapy and counseling: Bringing clarity to an illusive standard.* Retrieved from http://www.zurinstitute.com/standardofcaretherapy.html

Zur, O. (2012). Subsequent therapist syndrome: Are we our worst enemy? *Independent Practitioner, 32*(1), 10–12. Retrieved from http://www.zurinstitute.com/subsequent_therapist_syndrome.pdf

Zur, O. (2014) *Subpoenas and how to handle them: Guidelines for psychotherapists and counselors.* Retrieved from http://www.zurinstitute.com/subpoena.html

# Index

Note: *f* or *t* following a page number indicates a figure or a table.

# Feedback Form

Dear Fellow Clinician,

This book is the result of many therapists' efforts to assist their peers in coping with the rapid and complex ethical and legal developments in the independent practice of psychotherapy. Continuing changes will make parts of *The Paper Office for the Digital Age* obsolete in a few years, and so we intend to revise it to meet the evolving needs of therapists for efficient and legitimate forms, guidelines, and procedures. Please help us keep it useful and relevant by sharing your suggestions and modifications. Please send any suggestions or modifications to:

> Keely Kolmes, PsyD
> 220 Montgomery Street, Suite 400
> San Francisco, CA 94104
> drkkolmes@gmail.com

**First,** would you please tell us about your professional life?

Name: _____

Your professional title: _____ Degree(s): _____

Mailing address: _____

_____

Highest relevant credential(s): ❑ Licensed ❑ Registered ❑ Certified ❑ National Register

❑ ABPP ❑ ACSW ❑ LCSW ❑ NBCC ❑ MFT ❑ Others: _____

Member of these national association(s): ❑ AAMFT/MSCC ❑ ACSW ❑ ANA ❑ APsychologicalA

❑ APsychiatricA ❑ APsychNurseA ❑ NASW ❑ ACA ❑ Others: _____

Member of your state's professional association? ❑ Yes ❑ No ❑ No state association

Areas of practice in which you specialize: _____

Years in private practice when you bought this book: Full-time: ____ years. Part-time: ____ years.

What were the biggest obstacles to your entering private practice? _____

_____

What have been your biggest problems in private practice? _____

_____

Which ethical or legal problems or questions seem most pressing to *you* right now? _____

_____

**Now,** please tell us about *The Paper Office for the Digital Age:*

What is your overall evaluation of the book? _____

_____

What would you like to see more of? _____

_____

What could be decreased or eliminated? _____

_____

What forms or materials do you still need? _____

_____

Do you have any other comments or preferences for the next revision of *The Paper Office for the Digital Age*?

_____

_____

Thank you for your honest feedback and for purchasing our book.

Edward L. Zuckerman and Keely Kolmes

# Instructions for Installing and Using
## *The Paper Office's* Forms on Your Computer

### the Forms

e forms and handouts in this book are offered in two formats on the CD, .pdf (Portable Document Format) and .docx (Word format). Most of them are in .pdf format so you can print them out to look just as they do in the book. Almost all have been included in the .docx format as well so that you can tailor them to your practice. They retain the formatting seen in the printed versions (such as bold and italic, tabs, check boxes, etc.), although they do not always appear exactly as they do in the book. The .docx files should be easily opened by all current word-processing programs including those in various "Works," "Office," or "Suite" collections. The .pdf versions can't be modified but will print just like the forms in the book. To use a form, simply double-click on its name and the appropriate application (your word processor or Adobe Acrobat Reader) should open the file. You are then ready to work.

Because of copyright restrictions, you may not modify some forms without permission of their authors (as indicated at the bottom of the printed form in the book), so these appear only in .pdf form.

### For Windows Computers

Insert the CD, open Windows Explorer, and in the list of folders on the left side of the directory select your CD drive by clicking on the drive letter once. The contents of the CD will be shown on the right side of the directory, under "Name". You will see two folders, one called "PDF" and one called "DOCX". Copy the folders from the CD by highlighting them and hitting Ctrl + C or by using Edit, Copy from the drop down menu. Paste them into a folder where you can find easily find them, perhaps by creating a new folder on your hard drive called "PaperOffice". You may want to put the .docx versions in a folder where you keep your word-processing files.

### For Apple Computers

Insert the CD, and when the icon for the CD, labeled "PaperOffice5", appears on the desktop, double-click to open its directory. Copy the whole folder entitled "PDF" and the one called "DOCX" to your desktop by clicking on it once to highlight it, dragging the folder's icon to the desktop (or another location if you prefer), and releasing the mouse button. The computer will tell you which files it is copying. You now have two new folders, "DOCX" and "PDF", on your machine, which are the forms in two versions. You should be able to modify the forms in .docx (Word), and the forms in .pdf (Portable Document Format) are for viewing and printing in Adobe's Reader program.

### Installing Adobe Acrobat Reader

If you do not have Adobe Acrobat Reader or have an earlier version and would like to upgrade it, go to https://get.adobe.com/reader/. Older and different versions can be downloaded from http://get.adobe.com/reader/otherversions/.